Global Ecologies and Environmental Huma

MW00352179

"*Global Ecologies and the Environmental Humanities* is a must-read for anyone interested in the roots of today's environmental crisis and possible solutions to it. This book brings an important international perspective to the emerging field of the environmental humanities and reenergizes familiar concepts such as the Anthropocene, resilience, and terraforming by placing them within imperial and postcolonial contexts. It also introduces new concepts to the environmental humanities conversation, such as postcolonial disaster studies and environmental theology. Surveying a broad range of cultural aesthetics, literary genres, and geographies, and deftly moving between global and local scales of inquiry, *Global Ecologies and the Environmental Humanities* offers up a variety of exciting new methods for addressing the past, current, and future state of the world's environment."

—*Erin James, University of Idaho, USA*

"This may well be the decade that environmental humanities move to the front and centre of critical theory. This expertly assembled volume by a trio of vibrant scholars shows why. Bringing together diverse issues of disaster management, commodity frontiers and economies of scale with those of literary genres, styles, and forms the contributors show once again that our world and our texts remain indispensible to one another."

—*Upamanyu Pablo Mukherjee, Warwick University, UK*

This book examines current trends in scholarly thinking about the new field of the Environmental Humanities, focusing in particular on how the history of globalization and imperialism represents a special challenge to the representation of environmental issues. Essays in this path-breaking collection examine the role that narrative, visual, and aesthetic forms can play in drawing attention to and shaping our ideas about long-term and catastrophic environmental challenges such as climate change, militarism, deforestation, the pollution and management of the global commons, petrocapitalism, and the commodification of nature.

The volume presents a postcolonial approach to the environmental humanities, especially in conjunction with current thinking in areas such as political ecology and environmental justice. Spanning regions such as Africa, Asia, Eastern Europe, Latin America and the Caribbean, Australasia and the Pacific, as well as North America, the volume includes essays by founding figures in the field as well as new scholars, providing vital new interdisciplinary perspectives on: the politics of the earth; disaster, vulnerability, and resilience; political ecologies and environmental justice; world ecologies; and the Anthropocene. In engaging critical ecologies, the volume poses a postcolonial environmental humanities for the twenty-first century. At the heart of this is a conviction that a thoroughly global, postcolonial, and comparative approach is essential to defining the emergent field of the environmental humanities, and that this field has much to offer in understanding critical issues surrounding the creation of alternative ecological futures.

Elizabeth DeLoughrey is an Associate Professor in English and at the Institute for the Environment and Sustainability at the University of California, Los Angeles. She is coeditor of *Caribbean Literature and the Environment* (2005), and *Postcolonial Ecologies: Literatures of the Environment* (2011). She is the author of *Routes and Roots: Navigating Caribbean and Pacific Island Literatures* (2007) and completing a book about climate change, empire, and the literary and visual arts.

Jill Didur is an Associate Professor in English at Concordia University, Montreal. She is the author of *Unsettling Partition: Literature, Gender, Memory* (2006), co-editor of special issues of *Cultural Critique* on Critical Posthumanism (2003) and *Cultural Studies* on Revisiting the Subaltern in the New Empire (2003), and completing a book about imperialism, gardening, and the environment in postcolonial literature.

Anthony Carrigan was formerly Lecturer in Postcolonial Literatures and Cultures at the University of Leeds. His publications included *Postcolonial Tourism: Literature, Culture, and Environment* (Routledge, 2011), and he was a Fellow of the Rachel Carson Center for Environment and Society, Ludwig-Maximilians-Universität.

Routledge Interdisciplinary Perspectives on Literature

Global Ecologies and the Environmental Humanities

Postcolonial Approaches

Edited by Elizabeth DeLoughrey,
Jill Didur, and Anthony Carrigan

Routledge
Taylor & Francis Group

NEW YORK AND LONDON

First published 2015
by Routledge
711 Third Avenue, New York, NY 10017

and by Routledge
2 Park Square, Milton Park, Abingdon, Oxfordshire OX14 4RN

First issued in paperback 2016

Routledge is an imprint of the Taylor & Francis Group, an informa business

Copyright © 2015 Taylor & Francis

Library of Congress Cataloging-in-Publication Data

Global ecologies and the environmental humanities : postcolonial approaches / edited by Elizabeth DeLoughrey, Jill Didur, and Anthony Carrigan.
pages cm. — (Routledge interdisciplinary perspectives on literature ; 41)
Includes bibliographical references and index.
1. Ecocriticism. 2. Environmentalism in literature. 3. Postcolonialism in literature.
4. Human ecology in literature. I. DeLoughrey, Elizabeth M., 1967- editor.
II. Didur, Jill, 1965- editor. III. Carrigan, Anthony, 1980- editor.
PN98.E36G57 2015
809'.9336—dc23   2014038773

ISBN 13: 978-1-138-23581-6 (pbk)
ISBN 13: 978-1-138-82772-1 (hbk)

Typeset in Sabon
by codeMantra

Contents

List of Figures

This book is dedicated to the memory of Anthony Carrigan, our friend and collaborator. We continue to be guided by the generous spirit you brought to all of our work.

Foreword

The idea that we may be living through the beginnings of a series of overlapping and major environmental crises for humans all over the planet gains ground every day. The climate of the planet is changing with global warming, the rising seas are getting more acidic, the rate of species extinction is approaching a danger mark, the incidence of extreme weather events appears to be on the rise, and there are discussions—serious and alarming—of water and food security. Scientists are at work diagnosing problems and prescribing solutions; economists calculate the costs of market-based transition to a "green" economy; business, scientists, and engineers work together to invent technologies that will facilitate growth in a postcarbon world. What about the role of scholars who belong to interpretive disciplines that do not necessarily work with numbers and that are sometimes clubbed together under the rubric "the Humanities"? What contributions can they make as we all try to develop strategies for negotiating this multidimensional environmental crisis? Answering this question is the task that this pioneering and significant volume has set itself. It has brought together an extensive body of scholarship, representing a variety of disciplines ranging from literary criticism and film studies to history and anthropology. Their shared objective is to help define the vital and emerging field of "environmental humanities."

True to the nature of the knowledge that is produced in the humanities, the essays in this volume do not all speak with the same voice. They have shared concerns, even shared questions, but not the same answers. One reason, of course, is that the authors come from different disciplines and work on different research-objects in different parts of the world. The second reason is that by their very nature the interpretive disciplines produce observations that always make room for creative ambiguities and uncertainties. But, taken together, the essays included here allow us to see at least three areas where the insights of scholars in the humanities and the interpretive social sciences would be of critical importance in discussing the mix of strategies that might adequately address human concerns in the face of a gathering crisis of the environment.

The first is the question of narrative. Readers of this book will emerge convinced that an essential ingredient of the process by which humans make sense of crises in public life—or feel inspired to work towards solutions—is stories: narratives we tell ourselves in order to find our bearings in a new situation. In the end, scientists, engineers, technologists, economists, policy-makers, politicians, all tell different kinds of stories about the environment to various constituencies: their peers, the public, the media, funding bodies, governments. Our success in developing a globally concerted response to the climate crisis, for instance, will depend on the degree to which we can tell stories that we can all agree on.

Uniting diverse points of view is difficult to achieve, however, and at least two important reasons for such difficulty are emphasized by the various contributions to this volume. The first is what some authors and the editors here call the "unevenness of development;" that is the fact that the world so far has not only benefited from the growth of a world-capitalist economy, it is also marked, both between and inside nations, by some profoundly divisive inequities and injustices that, sadly, have accompanied that process of growth and have often resulted from it. How do we come together in a way that addresses both the need for global action and the very injustices that make such united action difficult? There is no obvious solution to this problem but it is clear that narratives that sideline complaints of injustice across a range of issues will have little purchase in public life. They are not likely to be effective in getting humans together behind any particular strategy, however rational that strategy may look to those proposing it.

There is yet another difficult issue that the authors collected here underline, and that is the question of power that inheres in narratives. This is related to but different from issues of distributive justice mentioned above. Both poststructuralist and postcolonial analyses have left a legacy that makes scholars in the interpretive disciplines suspicious of narratives that presume to speak for all of humanity without any attention to the problems that divide and differentiate people along certain axes of power, leaving some groups with much less capacity for self-representation than some powerful minorities. Any "universalist" narrative that presumes to speak for all will be subject to a hermeneutic of suspicion that postcolonial scholarship has justifiably developed. Universal narratives often act as ruses of power, the power of agentive forces and institutions (such as the World Bank or certain bodies of the United Nations or even the IPCC) that—precisely because of uneven development—have a relatively greater capacity to project themselves as acting on behalf of all while many of their actions end up privileging nations, groups, and classes that are already powerful. Here, again, the recommendation is not that we should not try to narrate in the interest of "all" but rather that such narration must not be blind to issues of power and should therefore incorporate a certain degree of self-reflexivity or self-vigilance on matters relating to those very issues.

The contours of a possible field of "environmental humanities" become visible in the essays assembled here. This is an emerging, exciting, and inter-disciplinary field of study. There is already a new journal, *Environmental*

Humanities, published from Sydney under the able editorship of Deborah Bird Rose and Thom van Dooren. This book will do much to define further the intellectual outlines of this field. Its most important contribution, however, lies in the way it rightly claims a place for the humanities in discussions of the various environmental crises that are assuming planetary proportions. For, after all, a crisis that concerns humanity as a whole cannot ever be adequately addressed if the issues of justice, power, and inequality that divide and fragment the same humanity are overlooked in the narratives we tell ourselves. Concerted global action demands that we—scientists, policymakers, politicians, activists, and academics—pay scrupulous attention to the issues that this book highlights.

Dipesh Chakrabarty
Canberra, August 22, 2014

Acknowledgments

We would like to thank the Rachel Carson Center for Environment and Society, Ludwig-Maximilians-Universität and the Deutsches Museum, and in particular the Center's directors, Christof Mauch and Helmuth Trischler, for generously supporting our workshop on Imperialism, Narrative, and the Environment in October 2012. We would also like to thank the University of California Humanities Research Institute (UCHRI) for the initial funds for the international conference Global Ecologies: Nature/Narrative/Neoliberalism, which took place in March 2013, as well as the Division of Humanities at UCLA. We are grateful to Liz Levine at Routledge for her editorial support in preparing this volume.

Introduction

A Postcolonial Environmental Humanities

Elizabeth DeLoughrey, Jill Didur, and Anthony Carrigan

The cover of our collection features two photographs by the Cuban artists Atelier Morales (Teresa Ayuso and Juan Luis Morales), prints from their series Patrimonio a la Deriva, Los Ingenios, or Adrift Patrimony: Sugar Refineries. The left-side image, entitled "Vereda" (2004), captures the ruins of the Cuban sugar plantation system, representing a verdant tropical landscape dominated by coconut palms, and visually overwhelming the small, almost toy-like, colorful steam train in the lower left corner. The Spanish word *vereda* translates as path; in establishing the first railway system of the Spanish empire, Cuba certainly was "pathbreaking" in terms of colonial modernity, monoculture, and enslaved African labor. Yet with the collapse of the Cuban sugar trade at the turn of the twenty-first century, Atelier Morales sought to document the ruins of the industry in a series of powerful images in homage to French-born Cuban lithographer Eduardo LaPlante, whose nineteenth-century representations of rural Caribbean life signify as the artists' lost "patrimony."[1] While the photograph initially may elicit a kind of tropical nostalgia—a melancholic view of an agricultural industry in ruins, an oxidizing locomotive overtaken by the fecund powers of nature—a closer examination of "nature" in the photograph reveals an always and already social landscape. This is in keeping with work in postcolonial studies which foregrounds how the history of colonialism necessitates the imbrication of humans in nature. In this case the coconut palm, that icon of ahistorical tropical islands, is better recognized as a nineteenth-century import to the Caribbean from the Pacific, a new crop replacing that infamous fifteenth-century import from across the Atlantic, the sugar cane. Moreover, the photograph has captured the specter of what resembles a cell phone tower in the alignment of the palms, anticipating an industry of new transnational pathways and networks. *Vereda* is our "pathway" into the photograph and its layers of human and nonhuman history, leading from the lower left of the image into the center of the old railway and plantation system. This suggests a new direction for tropical aesthetics that builds upon and complicates historical images of colonial landscapes and anticipates new futures. A pathway, according to the *Oxford English Dictionary*, can also be understood as a sequence of events, a course of a life, a line of thought, an argument and, we would argue, a *narrative*. This evocation of narrative is vital to engaging the history of ecological imperialism and its representational aesthetics, which inform global ecologies and the environmental humanities.

Global Ecologies and the Environmental Humanities: Postcolonial Approaches is a volume committed to extending critical conversations about nature, globalization, and culture in the context of twenty-first century environmental debates and their historical antecedents. The essays collected here are all informed by what is increasingly called the "environmental humanities," and focus in particular on how the history of globalization and imperialism is integral to understanding contemporary environmental issues. In the last decade, the field of postcolonial ecocriticism has offered important new perspectives on how environmental change is entwined with the narratives, histories, and material practices of colonialism and globalization. Postcolonial approaches emphasize how experiences of environmental violence, rupture, and displacement are central ecological challenges across the Global South, while at the same time identifying possibilities for imaginative recuperation that are compatible with anticolonial politics.[2] The aim of this collection is to build on this groundbreaking work by making a case for the foundational importance of postcolonial methods to the environmental humanities—a relatively new but rapidly expanding interdisciplinary field that seeks to bring together cultural, historical, social, and scientific dimensions of ecological thought.

Our volume focuses in particular on two themes that have major bearings on the development of the environmental humanities. First, the role that narrative, visual, and aesthetic forms play in drawing attention to and shaping our ideas about catastrophic and long-term environmental challenges such as climate change, militarism, resource extraction, the pollution and management of the global commons, petrocapitalism, and the commodification and capitalization of nature. Second, we explore how an interdisciplinary and comparative field like postcolonial studies can contribute to the scope and methodologies of the environmental humanities, especially in conjunction with the foundational work already established in areas such as political ecology and environmental justice.[3] As humanities scholars, we understand the formation of the environmental humanities to be a necessary challenge to the limitations of our own disciplinary departmentalization, and an invitation to bring the humanities into a conversation with the political, social, and environmental sciences. We support David Nye et al.'s claim that "scholars working in the environmental humanities are posing fundamentally different questions, questions of value and meaning informed by nuanced historical understanding of the cultures that frame environmental problems" (2013, 28). While we make no claim that this will result in a simple synthesis (or even "consilience," in E. O. Wilson's terms) of these different areas of inquiry, our aim is to foreground how interdisciplinary discussions of narrative, visual, and creative works from different regions can advance understanding of the specificity of ecological concerns as well as anticipatory visions for the future.

In an era of tremendous risk and uncertainty that seems to be increasingly managed by a "global ecocracy" (Sachs 1999, 67), we cannot afford to rely on the knowledge of one discipline or method alone. As anthropologist Arturo Escobar declared nearly two decades ago, "we need new narratives of life and culture" (1996, 65). These narratives, he suggests, are likely "hybrid," and "arise from the mediations that local cultures are able to effect on the discourses and practices of nature, capital, and modernity" (65). They are also clearly inspired by and reflected in literary and artistic works, which makes their analysis essential for understanding the social, cultural, and political experiences of global ecological change in specific locations and across different timeframes. We see the collection as helping to situate the—as yet rather nebulous—concept of the environmental humanities with a firm grounding in the significance of the ongoing histories of imperialism for environmental research. The conviction shared by our contributors is that a postcolonial dialogue is indispensable for establishing an effective base for the environmental humanities in the twenty-first century, and that this field has much to offer in elucidating critical issues surrounding the narration and visualization of alternative ecological futures.

In recent decades, literary scholars have expanded the geographical and historical contours of ecocriticism by exploring how writers from postcolonial, settler colonial, and decolonizing regions have imagined and inscribed the environment, providing vital perspectives on how ecological transformation is entangled with colonial expansion, capitalist industry, and globalization. In so doing, the field of postcolonial ecocriticism has always understood itself to be "interdisciplinary, transnational, and comparative" (Cilano and DeLoughrey 2007, 80), and has long engaged with the complexities of interdisciplinary dialogue as well as problematizing facile claims to the global. In using the term "global ecologies" for our title, we are cognizant of the debates in the fields of postcolonial studies, development studies, and political ecology that have critiqued "globalizing impulses" in which methods of thought are exported to postcolonial regions, and where the global and local are reduced to "simple synecdoche," so instead we advocate for a method in which "each interrupts and distorts the other" (O'Brien 2001, 143). This is in keeping with a powerful discourse in globalization and development studies that has been critical of a "neoliberal environmentalism reasserting cultural difference in the terms of making the world environmentally secure for unrestrained capitalist accumulation" (Di Chiro 2003, 206). This has implications for both the circulation of material and cultural capital, and is a key disciplinary critique about the accumulation of transnational difference as cultural value. Thus a postcolonial approach to the environmental humanities is self-reflexive in its engagement with histories and knowledges of ecological difference, particularly at an institutional level, where universities are implicated.[4]

In this collection's framing of global ecologies, we seek to avoid the "over-worlding" of postcolonial texts and contexts whereby social and ecological desires are projected onto the indigenous and/or Global South. We critique othering practices that outsource the labor of knowledge systems to an "eco-Indian," fabricate idyllic "primitive" harmonies with nature, and project the desire for mass resistance onto the Global South. We seek to avoid facile binaries that locate "green orientalism" (Lohmann 1993) in the past (a primitivism projected onto the Global South and the indigenous subject) as well as the reification of a place all too easily depicted "as a locus of anti-imperialist resistance" and critique (Huggan 2004, 704). While we engage a comparative global scope, we do so dialectically and with attention to the complexity, contradictions, and complicities of the figure of the Global South. This is why attention to narrative is so central to our project. The turn to critically situated aesthetics, narratives, and visual forms is crucial to localizing and theorizing historical texts and contexts, and helps to disrupt and situate a universalizing impulse. It is also why we are keen to establish points of dialogue with the everyday narratives of environmental negotiation and exploitation analyzed in certain strands of anthropological research, which likewise pay close attention to the contradictory interface of global and local concerns in specific communities and locations. In an epoch increasingly described as the "Anthropocene," in which a planetary humanity is rendered as a geological agent, it is all the more critical to examine the ways in which narratives situate and embed cultural and ontological experiences of ecology.

Examining how narrative, stylistic, and visual forms anticipate their circulation, and in fact may disrupt, parody, and complicate their global consumption (Huggan 2001; Mukherjee 2010, 9), can be instructive, suggesting an "aesthetics committed to politics" (Cilano and DeLoughrey 2007, 84). Postcolonial approaches to environmental texts have elucidated how writers and artists complicate canonical and colonial legacies as well as develop new forms and media. A growing body of postcolonial scholarship has examined and identified narrative tropes like the pastoral, counterpastoral, New World baroque, forest fictions, progressive realism, mimesis, counter landscaping, petrofiction, and prelapsarian visual aesthetics.[5] For example, Rob Nixon's *Slow Violence and the Environmentalism of the Poor* (2011a) turns to politically engaged nonfiction, "transnational meldings" (36), the "environmental picaresque" (45), and the strategic adoption of the "rhetoric of environmental justice" (37) by the dispossessed. We believe that focusing on how to narrate both ecological crisis and utopian visions is vital to the environmental humanities,[6] and we support Nixon's observation that, "in a world permeated by insidious, yet unseen and imperceptible violence, imaginative writing can help make the unapparent appear" (15).

Nonfiction writing often shares this imaginative vision and, whether through journalism, *testimonio*, or even scholarly work, can also elucidate what a homogenizing globalization seeks to render invisible, raising pressing questions about ethics and accountability. Nonfiction narrative forms may adopt the pastoral, as Ken Saro-Wiwa does in *Genocide in Nigeria* (1992), to strategically draw out an indigenous fall from nature created by oil companies in the Niger Delta, or to help render visible an "aesthetics of rupture and connection" (DeLoughrey and Handley 2011, 28) described by Édouard Glissant (1989) as characteristic of post-plantation narratives of the Caribbean. Due to the ways in which the histories of colonialism have displaced and alienated people from the land, the imaginative and material act of ecological recuperation is often deeply fraught. Consequently, far from any idealized notions of harmony and balance, postcolonial environmental representations often engage with the legacies of violent material, environmental, and cultural transformation. In an effort to recuperate histories that colonial narratives sought to suppress, they might take on the authoritative voices of historians or, as we see in recent novels by Helon Habila (2011) and Indra Sinha (2007), the adaptation of an "official" journalistic voice (and its parody).[7] We see such generic negotiations as offering incisive critiques of how mainstream environmental narratives are framed, drawing attention to the power relations and structural inequalities they all too frequently occlude, and contributing to the creation of alternative modes of articulation and analysis in line with the tradition of postcolonial thought and writing. As Edward Said famously remarked, "because of the presence of the colonizing outsider, the land is recoverable at first only through the imagination" (1993, 77), an observation that retains relevance as communities continue to assert ecological sovereignty in the context of changing national and global power structures. Language and narrative, including the narrative work of the visual, are integral to conceptualizing both the legacies of rupture and the possibilities of imaginative recuperation and transformation.[8]

A postcolonial environmental humanities advocates for the power of the imagination as expressed collectively across the full range of cultural practices. It draws comparatively on cultural resources to delineate a more equitable and ecologically restorative vision of the world. To that end, *Global Ecologies and the Environmental Humanities* is divided into five thematic sections that address multiscalar topics ranging from soil and plants to the planetary climate: (1) The Politics of Earth: Forests, Gardens, Plantations; (2) Disaster, Vulnerability, and Resilience; (3) Political Ecologies and Environmental Justice; (4) Mapping World Ecologies; and (5) Terraforming, Climate Change, and the Anthropocene. Together, these sections provide culturally and historically differentiated perspectives on environmental concerns across a wide variety of geographical locations— including Africa, Asia, Latin America and the Caribbean, Australasia and the Pacific, Eastern Europe, and North America—and approach ecology and globalization in ways that are centrally responsive to the specific experiences of colonialism, militarism, and/or capitalist resource extraction in these regions. Our contributions also engage with a wide range of disciplines and academic, activist, and theoretical interests that demonstrate the relevance of postcolonial and humanities-based approaches to the environment for broader audiences. Rather than being prescriptive, the essays in this volume suggest methods and ways of thinking to address large-scale challenges such as climate change and disaster vulnerability that resist the tendency toward a universalizing globalism. Moving between systemic analyses and specificities, the dialogue established throughout this collection provides comparative grounding for thinking through the conflicting scales that a global approach to the environment must address—from plants to planetarity, and commodity frontiers to the capitalist world-system. This multiscalar format allows us to bring into view the contested forms of power and agency that have led to the planet's entry into a geological epoch called by Paul Crutzen and Eugene Stoermer (2000) the Anthropocene, while paying close attention to the narratives and lived realities of ecological violence, crisis, and transformation that are intimately tied to imperialist practices.

Our volume is a collective and transnational endeavor, emerging from a series of workshops, panels, and conferences hosted by the Rachel Carson Center for Environment and Society (Ludwig-Maximilians-Universität and the Deutsches Museum), the Association for the Study of Literature and the Environment (ASLE), and by the University of California, Los Angeles. We organized these events because although we feel that the resurgence of environmental concern in the humanities has produced many inspiring exchanges between disciplines and methodologies, there is still an uncritical tendency toward "superpower parochialism" (Nixon 2011a, 34) in the framing of environmental concerns that often reflects the perceptions and preoccupations of the privileged and the Global North. As DeLoughrey and Handley have argued, "the discourse of nature is a universalizing one," and this means that scholarship "is particularly vulnerable to naturalizing dominant forms of environmental discourse, particularly those that do not fundamentally engage with questions of difference, power, and privilege" (2011, 14). There is certainly a need to address modes of universalism in light of how the global nature of environmental crises requires collective response, but it is also crucial that we consider the positionality of such claims carefully given the radically different concepts of ecology that are being employed across academic disciplines (hence the plural "ecologies" in our title). This is producing debates about political agency and responsibility in the Anthropocene, and raises the concern that certain environmental philosophies are being privileged over others in ways that reinforce the long-standing marginalization of dispossessed voices.[9]

The essays in this collection illustrate that such differences in environmental conception can be productively understood by approaching ecological research in conjunction with histories of empire and globalization. Now, more than ever, postcolonial approaches to the environmental humanities help complicate and clarify the historical power relations that underpin global ecologies. Conservative dismissals of the relevance of postcolonial approaches in the humanities are better understood as anxious responses to the field's ongoing work in disrupting Eurocentric norms and American exceptionalism in and outside the academy. Such dismissals often involve mischaracterizations of postcolonialism as a temporal marker or as an uncritical celebration of anti-colonial narratives, rather than a critical method that supports the ongoing task of decolonization on a global scale. As Robert JC Young points out, postcolonialism cannot be limited to a field, theory, or time period because its goals have always been broadly defined, including efforts to reconfigure the dominant knowledge formations of the Global North and its ethical norms; to destabilize hierarchical power structures; and to reposition knowledge from below, interrogating "the interrelated histories of violence, domination, inequality and injustice" (2012, 20). The relevance of these historical experiences is not diminishing in the twenty-first century but rather is becoming reconfigured and, in some cases, amplified as environmental conflicts deepen. Our definition of postcolonialism is therefore necessarily broad, and essays from this collection expand beyond the British/Anglophone model to considerations of colonial and ecological regimes in Russia, new extractivism in Latin America, and the material and discursive fallout of nuclear militarism in the US and the Pacific Islands. Like Rob Nixon and many others, we affirm the vitality of postcolonial methods in "an era of rampant neoliberalism and empire" (2011a, 36). The following sections of this introduction elaborate on these claims by addressing the environmental humanities as a developing field and its relevance for the ongoing legacies of empire.

DEFINING THE ENVIRONMENTAL (AND ECOLOGICAL) HUMANITIES

The environmental humanities is a new field that has—so far—only been loosely defined.[10] While the term privileges the conceptual rubric of the humanities, its disciplinary engagements necessarily extend to the arts as well as the social and environmental sciences. There has been a remarkable production in this emergent field over the last few years, including newly minted undergraduate and graduate programs, conferences, and a number of book series and open-access journals. This reflects the substantial expansion of environmental humanities research, which for many years was conducted within specific departments, and which has now been drawn into environmental studies programs and research centers that call for sustained and innovative *multi*disciplinary research.[11] Two of the main challenges as we see them now involve (1) establishing a clear definition of what environmental humanities

research entails and how it can respond effectively to global ecological challenges; and (2) devising appropriately *inter*disciplinary methodologies that
not only bring different disciplines into transformative dialogue but also constitute new forms of environmental knowledge that can be communicated
across the arts and sciences and to public audiences.

We see a postcolonial environmental humanities as what Gayatri
Chakravorty Spivak has described as "a Humanities to come" (2004, 526).
By this phrase, Spivak means a critical pedagogy that seeks an "uncoercive
arrangement of desires" between self and other including, we would add,
nonhuman others (526). This ethical claim she defines as less of a sense of
being "responsible *for*" than being "responsible *to*" (537; original emphasis),
a calling for engagement to "learn from below" (548) even as we recognize
our own limitations in doing so. To learn from below "the dominant must
first redefine herself," and this gesture requires that geography—the Global
North and Global South—"stop being read in evolutionary terms as a teleo-
logical narrative of pre-modern to modern" (Didur and Heffernan 2003, 10).
By understanding global development as complex and uneven rather than
subject to outmoded narratives of "progress," we can ensure a foundation for
the environmental humanities that is consonant with the alter-globalization
perspectives that are allied with environmental justice movements and which
foreground questions of ethics and responsibility (see also Taylor 1995;
Escobar 1995).

While the term "environmental humanities" (also known as "ecological
humanities") is relatively new, research in this area has well-established
genealogies in disciplines such as anthropology, geography, literature, history, philosophy, and science and technology studies, all of which have
contributed to the shaping of the discourses of ecofeminism, political ecology, indigenous studies, and environmental justice in the last few decades.
Some of the most significant work in bringing these perspectives together
has come from Australia, where environmental humanities research has
drawn attention to postcolonial issues even if empire has not always been
prominent in how the field has been conceived elsewhere. In issuing an
invitation for researchers to join their "ecological humanities" initiative
in 2004, Deborah Bird Rose and Libby Robin outlined a vision of the
field that is not only rooted in a combination of social and environmental
justice perspectives but is also alert to the histories of colonial settlement
and displacement, foregrounding the "ethical imperative" for "settler
society scholars [...] to be responsive to indigenous people's knowledges
and aspirations for justice" (2004, para. 1).[12] This statement retains
foundational importance for the environmental humanities at large, not
just in settler societies (including the US) but more broadly in accounting
for the global histories of dominance, displacement, and marginalization
that have accompanied imperial practices over time, along with the
integration of much of the world into the system of capitalist globalization.
It also holds resonance for unsettling instrumentalist approaches to

environmental knowledge that tend to underplay the moral and ethical dimensions of environmental crisis rather than thinking critically about how these are essential for envisioning sustainable and equitable ecological relations on a global basis.[13]

Like Rose and Robin, the editors of the inaugural issue of the journal *Environmental Humanities* (including Rose) drew upon Val Plumwood's concept of "ecohumanities perspectives" as articulated in her 2002 book, *Environmental Culture: The Ecological Crisis of Reason*, in identifying the contours of the field.[14] This is a text worth examining in terms of its commitment to ethics, an often unstated but constitutive element of both postcolonial and environmental scholarship that is foregrounded, as we have seen, in Spivak's sense of a "Humanities to come." Plumwood has argued that "two historic tasks […] arise from the rationalist hyper-separation of human identity from nature: they can be summed up as the tasks of (re) situating humans in ecological terms and non-humans in ethical terms" (8). She reminds us that these fields of knowledge are gendered, stating: "One of the problems in standard ways of thinking about the crisis is precisely this rationalist divorce between male-coded rational prudence and female-coded ethics, as if they were separate and non-interacting spheres" (9). This is perhaps no more obvious than in the disciplinary formulations around climate change, in which one sees the reentrenchment of "hard" and "soft" sciences where positivist formulations of knowledge, privileged by the IPCC (Intergovernmental Panel on Climate Change), contribute to a discourse of masculinized technocracy managing a chaotic, ever-changing feminized earth.[15] This we suggest is a cautionary tale that should be a focus of environmental humanities critique in an era in which university funding shifts to the STEM (Science, Technology, Engineering and Math) models of knowledge and labor production, and increasingly eschews the invaluable contributions of the humanities and social sciences. As we seek to build a critical body of work around the postcolonial environmental humanities, we must be attentive to the ways in which the field itself may reiterate the gendered, racial, and class privileges that have constituted the history of the "hard" sciences as well as environmental movements in the Global North.

Drawing from the methods of postcolonial and feminist scholarship, environmental humanities researchers treat knowledge as always culturally situated. Moreover, as Rose and Robin argue, a truly "ecological" humanities needs to be relational and interconnected, deconstructing hierarchies between the arts and the sciences and encouraging modes of thinking that move across cultural as well as human and nonhuman boundaries. This is consonant with how we would define the environmental humanities as a field whose core role is to offer a culturally differentiated, historically nuanced understanding of human–environmental relations, and which is self-reflexive about the limitations of any single methodological approach or philosophical standpoint. Our work here foregrounds the complex histories of empire while recognizing that current forms of globalization cannot be reduced to a simple extension of earlier practices of imperialism. A postcolonial approach to the environmental humanities therefore means relating cultural and historical analyses to cross-disciplinary ecological concerns in ways that emphasize tensions between different forms of knowledge, and that focus attention on how power relations affect environmental decision making and practices at multiple scales, from the domestic to the global.

The contributors to this volume also call attention to the necessity of expanding the geographical, political, and historical contours of the environmental humanities in relation to what could be called "critical ecologies" for the twenty-first century.[16] While the environmental humanities invokes an interdisciplinary field, critical ecologies suggests a method of reading that derives from engagements with subaltern studies, critical race, gender and sexuality studies, and an ongoing scrutiny of empire including its historical and contemporary genres and forms. It is a critical reading practice aimed at recognizing and "reducing domination" (Biro 2011, 3), and is connected to bioregionalism, ecofeminism, social ecology, and environmental justice (6). As a radical critique, it requires that we "rethink some of our fundamental socio-political institutions," most especially capitalism (6). Building on the foundational work of Marx and the Frankfurt school, critical ecologies is concerned with questions of domination, alienation, ethics, and aesthetics. Not surprisingly, political theorist Robyn Eckersley pinpoints Carolyn Merchant's *The Death of Nature* (1980)—a text that historicized how the rise of Enlightenment science feminized and therefore sought to dominate nature—as a foundational work for critical ecologies and the environmental humanities. Importantly, Merchant's work elucidated how our *narratives* of nature matter; how attitudes, policy, and actions necessarily shift when, for instance, a culture determines that the earth is no longer a figure of alterity like the planetary maternal but rather a virgin, waiting for the 'penetration' of empire, capital, and globalization (Merchant 1980, 2). This point remains of fundamental importance as cross-disciplinary work takes up the challenge of theorizing the human and experiences of embodiment in the Anthropocene.

THE ANTHROPOCENE: LOCATING THE HUMAN IN ENVIRONMENTAL HUMANITIES

In the introduction to the inaugural issue of the journal *Environmental Humanities*, the editors wrote that:

> the need for a more *integrated and conceptually sensitive* approach to environmental issues is being increasingly recognised across the humanities and the social and environmental sciences. The development of the environmental humanities might therefore be understood as a response to this need; an effort to enrich environmental research

with a more extensive conceptual vocabulary, whilst at the same time vitalising the humanities by rethinking the ontological exceptionality of the human.

(Rose et al. 2012, 2)

Certainly the *human*ities and social sciences have been charged with anthropocentrism; recent work in animal studies, posthumanism, multispecies ethnographies, and new materialism have done much to correct that history.[17] Yet a postcolonial environmental humanities would foreground how a deep understanding of historical and contemporary power relations is essential for effectively "rethinking the ontological exceptionality of the human." The history of European empire constructed a gendered and racial hierarchy of embodied and disembodied subjects along the lines of nature/culture that relegated women, the indigenous, non-Europeans, and the poor to an objectified figure of nature as much as the white propertied heterosexual male was tied to rationality, subjectivity, and culture.[18] Therefore, postcolonial approaches position the nature/human binary as political, and do not necessarily see the dismantling of this divide as the foremost intellectual priority due to the already historical imbrication of the human with nonhuman nature and place.[19] In other words, many cultures do not have a separate notion (or even term for) "the environment" (Strathern 1980), and their ethical and philosophical codes are not simply assimilable to the binaries of western knowledge configurations. Our collection is committed to accounting for the more-than-human and multispecies world, while at the same time identifying the hierarchical processes that led certain humans to be reduced to "nature" (or other species) and examining the significance of this for present-day experiences of environmental racism. We therefore raise questions as to the relevance of the shift to the "posthuman" by subjects that are not seen to be determined by race, gender, sexuality, and empire. Humanism, as Neil Badmington has argued elsewhere, "cannot escape its 'post'" (2004, 9), and there is a colonial legacy of figuring a racialized and embodied subaltern whose constructed relationship to nature and the nonhuman animal have ongoing social and political effects. Consequently, a postcolonial approach to the environmental humanities involves analyzing how empire has constructed the human and how this affects the multiplicity of subjects in humanities research.

The point raised by Rose et al. about the larger question of the "ontological exceptionality of the human" brings us to recent conversations about the Anthropocene and environmental humanities research. Dipesh Chakrabarty has recently turned his attention away from "provincializing" the universalist assumptions of Enlightenment thought in order to explore how the science of climate change, and an identification of the agency of the human species in bringing about a new geological epoch, "challenges not only the ideas about the human that usually sustain the discipline of history but also the analytic strategies that postcolonial and postimperial historians have deployed in the last two decades in response to the post-war scenario of decolonization and globalization" (2009, 198). For Chakrabarty, the attention to relations of power and exploitation raised by postcolonial scholars remains indispensible for assessing issues of environmental justice at a time when the widespread but unevenly distributed effects of anthropogenic climate change are becoming perilously manifest. However, the challenge he sets out involves approaching this by thinking across three disjunctive concepts of the human that operate in relation to life in the Anthropocene: the human as universal, rights-bearing subject (as positioned in much liberal humanist thought); the human as endowed with "anthropological difference;" and the human as a geological force, which has wreaked environmental havoc due to fossil fuel dependence and, unlike the first two conceptions, is not ontological (Chakrabarty 2012, 1–2, 13). As some of the contributions to this volume make clear, it is no doubt essential that environmental humanities research engages the new historical and ontological questions raised by climate change, and evaluates the practical and philosophical implications of thinking politically beyond intrahuman concerns. At the same time, this volume emphasizes the need for such critique to be equally attentive to intrahuman power relations and different cultural understandings of history and the environment. We believe such understandings are imperative for assessing the pervasive effects of historical exploitation and inequality on present-day environmental issues, and for producing a nuanced and emancipatory foundation for approaching global ecologies—one that avowedly addresses the complex ethical and ontological terrain on which environmental governance is based.

Understanding climate change as a geological shift created by humans leads to new conceptions of history, deep time, and of the notion of humanity, which in turn raise important questions in considering different *scales* of ontology. The planetary scale invoked by Chakrabarty is quite different from an ontological relationship to place in a context in which colonial powers render the landscape into resources to be owned, cultivated, or simply extracted. As evidenced in this volume, a central aim of a globally responsive environmental humanities is to examine the specificities of these different scales of ontology, with attention to the imperialist assumptions and practices that underpin such things as the extraction of botanical specimens in the colonies, settler appropriation of indigenous grasslands for livestock and agricultural purposes, and the importation of agricultural crops and indentured and slave labor into a worldwide network of plantations. The varying scales of ontology and ecologies involved in each of these historically specific examples require rigorous attention to the economic, material, linguistic, and epistemological assumptions that inform a sense of belonging.

While the scope of this volume is large, we make no claim that what we call postcolonial approaches to the environmental humanities—or what Donna Haraway calls "naturecultures" (2006)—need be fully commensurable. Following postcolonial methodologies that emphasize difference, alterity, and the multiplicity of narrative constructions, the perspectives in this collection offer diverse and culturally responsive modes of theorizing place, resilience, vulnerability, environmental transformation, reclamation, disaster, and violence. This concentration on the historical and cultural specificities that constitute different forms of environmental knowledge is central to the volume's contribution to the field, along with its focus on how differential power relations condition both the conceptual understandings and material transformations of global ecologies.

NARRATIVE AND THE LIMITS TO VISION

While this volume seeks to open up an interdisciplinary conversation about issues from neoliberalism and militarism to food, land, and water sovereignty, one of our shared concerns is how narrative practices have differently inflected the representation of nonhuman nature and environmental justice, and how attention to narrative and aesthetic form is fundamental to understanding environmental crisis. This is why the humanities are integral to our environmental futures. We are invested in how we tell stories about ecology that contribute to what Vandana Shiva (2005) calls "earth democracy," which is not necessarily derived from moments of crisis but rather from the everyday. Refuting institutional structures that segregate humanities-based research from empirical and scientific concerns, our collection emphasizes the profound ways in which understandings of the environment are embedded in language, narrative, history, and the cultural imagination, and how some of the most creative and urgent perspectives on ecological change are generated through postcolonial contexts and critique. "To reconfigure the environmental humanities," argues Rob Nixon, "involves acknowledging, among other things, how writer-activists in the Southern Hemisphere are giving imaginative definition to catastrophes [...] rendering [them] tangible by humanizing drawn-out calamities inaccessible to the immediate senses" (2011b).[20]

Literary scholars working in the environmental humanities such as Ursula Heise and Allison Carruth have emphasized the importance of narrative, suggesting that it is vital to imagining and articulating our future. There is a struggle, they contend, "against the concepts and stories that have enabled environmental degradation in the past and against impartial (and imperfect) ideas about nature in environmentalist thought and writing itself" (2010, 3). They ask the following "crucial question" for the field as a whole:

> which concepts and narratives from the environmentalist inventory will move environmentally oriented thought into the future, and which ones shackle environmentalism to outdated templates? (3)

Their question arises from the US debate created by Michael Shellenberger and Ted Nordhaus about whether apocalyptic renderings of climate change contribute to "feelings of helplessness" rather than incite North Americans toward political action (2004, 30). Yet apocalypse, as some of our contributors argue, is a particularly Judeo-Christian narrative tied to the Cold War, and can become a useful and familiar rhetoric to inspire political action in that particular context.[21] Other "outdated templates" for environmental storytelling would include the narrative that ecologies are constituted by natural harmony and balance rather than chaos and rupture, as historian Donald Worster (1989) and biologist Daniel Botkin (1990) have shown. Yet the pastoral and harmony of nature narratives, while themselves fictions (historically and scientifically speaking), can be effective mobilizers, raising the possibility of using rhetorical fictions that reflect accepted cultural idioms, but may not be in step with the latest scientific norms. As such, the attention to narrative in the environmental humanities might be concerned not only with the "truths" of scientific ecology but also with the strategic use of *fiction* as a mobilizing idiom.

The linguist George Lakoff has lamented that when it comes to environmental narratives, we are afflicted with "hypocognition," which is to say a "lack of ideas we need" (2010, 77). Importantly he points out that the concept, inherited from the Enlightenment, that reason is "unemotional, logical, abstract, [and] universal" has been proven false by cognitive and brain science. Instead, "real reason" is "mostly unconscious (98%); requires emotion;" and is situationally variable (73). Thus narrative and rhetoric, if they are to make any impact, need to "make sense in terms of their systems of frames" (73). This does not mean that we are limited by pre-existing cultural frames, rather it brings up the imperative to invent them in order to create new circuits of thought. Lakoff uses the example of Michael Pollan's invention of the terms of "oil-based" versus "sun-based" food systems to call attention to the politics of consumption evident in a system of petroleum-based transportation, fertilizers, and pesticides (77) that destabilize the agricultural sovereignty of small farmers and developing nations, and contribute excessively to global carbon emissions. Literary figures, scholars, journalists, and activists all contribute to the making of new terms, narratives, and therefore new frameworks of thinking and affect; notable recent examples include Crutzen and Stoermer's "Anthropocene" (2000), Martínez-Alier's "environmentalism of the poor"(2002), and Nixon's "slow violence" (2011).

While narrative has the capacity to expand our understandings, postcolonial approaches, building on feminism and deconstruction, have also emphasized its necessary limits and disjunctures. The radical critique of positivism emerging from the humanities and social sciences foregrounds a resistance, via Foucault and others, to a will to knowledge, questioning the production of epistemology itself. Accordingly, our collection builds upon the work of Plumwood and other postcolonial and feminist perspectives in recognizing the limitations of any claims to the global. As Plumwood explains, "our capacity to gain insight from understanding our social context, to learn from self-critical perspectives on the past and to allow for our *own limitations of vision*, is still one of our best hopes for creative change and survival" (2002, 10; emphasis added). Acknowledging this both critically and in the stories we choose to focus on is crucial for identifying how histories of imperialism have shaped ways of seeing "the environment," and point to alternative modes of understanding that resist what Haraway calls the masculine "god-trick," or claiming "to see everything from nowhere" (1989, 581). Just as the field of postcolonial studies argued for the *provincializing* of Enlightenment epistemologies, a move against universalism in the service of empire, postcolonial approaches to the environmental humanities are equally concerned with the gendered tension between a claim to the global and its necessary parochialization. To be self-critical is to be self-reflexive, suggesting the need for humility in recognizing our limitations of vision. This applies across disciplinary boundaries as well as local, national, and international institutions. An environmental humanities that is grounded in postcolonial methodologies might elucidate gaps between ecological knowledge systems and managerial practices—which, at their worst, can have disastrous consequences—and help critique and reframe the questions asked by environmental researchers in light of historical insights, cultural differences, and unjust power relations.

DECOLONIZING ECOLOGY

Our collection title evokes and builds on Wolfgang Sachs's groundbreaking 1993 volume *Global Ecology: A New Arena of Political Conflict*, particularly its articulation of geopolitical concerns. We see Sachs's collection, which was published in the wake of the UN Conference on Environment and Development (UNCED) held in Rio de Janeiro in 1992, as a forerunner to our own in that it emphasizes how ahistorical attention to the environment on a local or global scale fails to capture the complex social relations that have shaped and defined what we mean by ecology. Moreover, its concern with development foregrounds a topic that is all the more prescient in an era of geopolitical tension—and colonial critique from nations like India—over the relationship between development and future carbon emissions. Our collection, coming just over twenty years after Sachs's, seeks to anchor an awareness of how the science of ecology needs to be situated in history, particularly the history of imperialism; in narrative practices, especially those that defamiliarize the environment; and in the recognition that it is a contested field of enquiry, even as it is used as a resource for environmental activists.

The concept of ecology is barely one hundred years old, and has been mobilized in multiple ways over time to serve the shifting needs of colonial authority. Furthermore, as scholars such as Peder Anker (2001) note, "[t]he formative period of ecological reasoning coincides with the last years of the British Empire" (1), and the modern science of ecology was seen by imperial agencies as one of the "urgently needed tools for understanding human relations to nature and society in order to set administrative economic policies for landscapes, population settlement and social control" (2). As DeLoughrey argues (2013), ecology as an academic field was institutionalized through radiation research that arose from US nuclear testing in the Pacific Islands, connecting its formation directly to militarism and empire.[22] Our pluralization of Sachs's title seeks not only to "provincialize" ecology but also to highlight how it has been mobilized to serve the needs of different political constituencies, and to engage the work of "critical ecologies" set in motion by key contributions to imperial environmental history, development studies, critical geography, and political ecology.[23]

Sachs's collection also provides a provocative example for postcolonial and environmental humanities research due to its emphasis on confronting technocratic, "solution"-driven approaches to environmental problems that refuse to acknowledge the richness of local ecological knowledge and adaptation strategies, along with historical and cultural specificities or the systemic need to confront unequal distributions of wealth. Such managerial strategies tend to be discussed in relatively "closed" spaces, as disaster studies specialists Adolfo Mascarenhas and Ben Wisner point out, "reserved for bureaucrats, elected officials and experts," and are "often where 'acceptable risk' is determined—without consultation with those affected" (2012, 56). The need to counter such techniques is familiar to much postdevelopment and feminist thinking, and is evident in the frustration of impoverished communities in the Global South and in the North who bear the brunt of deleterious environmental change.

This uneven relationship to institutions of power presents an important challenge to environmental humanities research that seeks to support politically progressive decision-making, while deconstructing and resisting the undemocratic and frequently exploitative ecological management regimes dictated by institutions based in the Global North (from Washington, DC to the World Economic Forum at Davos). These regimes are weighted heavily toward neoliberal doctrine, and are often adopted in the Global South by corrupt political actors and networks of complicit elites. It is clearly a significant step to move from interdisciplinary reconfiguration (i.e. constructing an inclusive vision of the environmental humanities) to asserting its relevance to the many real-world practices it addresses. Yet this remains an important challenge if we are to respond meaningfully to the "mission statement" set down by another newly established online journal in the field, *Green Humanities*, to develop a collaborative research base that has "the overarching goal of coaxing our global society toward a more sustainable future" (2013). Such "coaxing" surely involves constructing a strong ethical as well as environmental response to the tendency identified by Sachs over a decade ago in *Planet Dialectics* (1999) for the post-war era of development to be replaced by a globalizing neoliberalism characterized by increasing "instability," "failure," ecological exhaustion, and security "risks" (20–22). At the same time, it may necessitate new methodologies and approaches for humanities researchers, not only to what we study and how we study it, but also to who we speak to and ask to listen. This means thinking carefully about creating or even *conjuring* new audiences, as well as redefining intellectual and institutional parameters that allow us to engage more directly with political, scientific, and economic discourse—something we hope our collection contributes toward.

GLOBAL ECOLOGIES AND THE ENVIRONMENTAL HUMANITIES: POSTCOLONIAL APPROACHES

Together, the volume's essays negotiate what we see as a productive tension between provincializing environmental research and addressing large-scale concerns such as the struggle for the global commons and shared access to resources such as soil, water, air, and the ocean. As befits a collection oriented toward the global and the postcolonial, the work represented here grapples with terms and concepts that have caused contestation across various fields: epistemologies of climate change; the Anthropocene; worlding and world ecology; globalization and globality; the planetary and planetarity. These essays draw from environmental justice and the "environmentalisms of the poor" as well as the fields of geography and political ecology, which we would like to see increasingly integrated into environmental humanities conversations. Such perspectives are crucial to helping us think through the spatial as well as temporal interrelations between capitalism, colonialism, and climate change, and uneven development on a variety of interlocking scales. They also support us in emphasizing the urgency of understanding disaster, vulnerability, and resilience in relation to differential forms of agency (human and nonhuman). The rising tide of environmental catastrophes— both slow and abrupt—is increasingly attuning global attention to issues of environmental relocation and resistance even as the historical and economic roots of these crises often remain obscured. The organization of our collection aims to help develop and even transform environmental perceptions in this light by focusing on creative and narrative works that negotiate the tensions between diasporic affiliation, forced migration, habitation conflicts, and cultural conceptions of place-attachment, which are essential to any meaningful understanding of global ecologies.

The first section examines the historical and imperial politics of forests, gardens, plantations, and "urban jungles." Entitled "The Politics of Earth: Forests, Gardens, Plantations," the contributions in this section draw attention to how postcolonial readings of particular environments can unsettle colonial and nationalist framings of ecology. They also explore the tensions and overlaps between imaginative texts and state, industrial, and scientific discourses. The essays establish a comparative dialogue between different forms of cultivation, contamination, and "ruination," to borrow a Jamaican term, which have significant implications for understanding the historical contours of global ecologies in the present. These include issues of inter-dependence and North/South relations; internal colonialism and the discourse of "nativism" in national cultures and horticultures; the relationship between environmental pollution and poverty; and the memorialization of plantation histories and destructive environmental practices.

David Arnold's "Narrativizing Nature: India, Empire, and Environment" opens our collection by using two contrasting narratives to provide a post-colonial reading of Indian environmental history. The first is that presented in the Bengali novel *Aranyak* (1939), which depicts how a city-bred outsider becomes absorbed into the world of the Indian forest, revelling in its rich vegetation while painfully aware of its impeding destruction and the poverty of its human inhabitants. For Arnold, *Aranyak* shows the difficulty of trying to "provincialize Europe" in the narrativization of nature. The second set of sources consists of environmental health narratives about Calcutta. These inscribe nature within the modern city and its urban "jungle," while ascribing many urban environmental problems, including pollution, to the poor. The chapter demonstrates that these texts invoke discursive continuities between city and countryside and between colonial and postcolonial readings of "nature."

Jill Didur's "'The Perverse Little People of the Hills:' Unearthing Ecology and Transculturation in Reginald Farrer's Alpine Plant Hunting" is also concerned with colonial era ideas about the environment and nature that circulated in the first half of the twentieth century. This essay, however, turns our attention to colonial accounts of travel and botanical exploration in South and Central Asia, and examines how colonial figures wrestled with challenges to their taken-for-granted ideas about self and other, prompted by their travels in unfamiliar landscapes in the colonial peripheries, and horticultural experiments with exotic plants in the gardens of the imperial center. Didur argues that Farrer's views on how to establish a rock garden that would best support the ecological needs of the exotic plants he collected during his travels in Asia involved a complicated renegotiation of colonial ways of seeing foreign people, cultures, and landscapes within the imperial center. With attention to discussions of ecology and transculturation in Farrer's narratives of plant collecting and rock and alpine gardening, Didur traces a practice of accommodating for difference (rather than taming the influence of the foreign) that could serve as a model for structuring countercolonial global ecologies in the present.

Lizabeth Paravisini-Gebert's "Bagasse: Caribbean Art and the Debris of the Sugar Plantation" explores the relationship between colonial cultivation, ruination, and representation in the region. The essay examines projects by Caribbean artists Atelier Morales (Cuba), Hervé Beuze (Martinique), Charles Campbell (Jamaica), and María Magdalena Campos-Pons (Cuba), reflecting on the history of sugar production through its human and environmental costs. Her analysis of these works (many of which incorporate *bagasse*, the debris left after cane is crushed, as artistic material) explores the rich expressive possibilities open to twenty-first-century environmental artists. These "ephemeral installations"—bagasse rots, reeks, decays—metaphorically illustrate how nations and peoples have been marked by the crushing and discarding of waste. By addressing the history of sugar production through bagasse, contemporary artists have entered into a complex dialogue with the specificities of past representations of sugar production and its exploitation of workers and the land, and provide a means of theorizing regional history through recourse to earth, plants, and plantations.

The section ends with Susan K. Martin's essay, "Writing a Native Garden? Environmental Language and Post-*Mabo* Literature in Australia," which augments the section's focus on the politics of the earth, turning in this case to native plant use and the idea of the Australian garden in writing of the 1990s following the *Mabo* and *Wik* decision on indigenous land rights. The term "native garden" in Australia refers not to gardens grown by Aboriginal and Torres Strait Islander (ATSI) people, although it may include these, but to the variety of gardens using plants indigenous to the Australian landmass. Native gardens in Australia, Martin points out, have complicated origins in discrete environmental, horticultural, and nationalist movements, with sometimes incongruent values. Because the *Mabo* decision used the history of Murray Islanders' gardening and cultivation in establishing indigenous land rights it potentially shifted the place of gardening and cultivation in the national consciousness. With this in mind, Martin examines how Murray Bail's novel *Eucalyptus* (1998) and the writing of Alexis Wright help us think through the idea of the garden, the "native" garden, and the circulation of the terms "indigenous" and "native" in Australian culture and horticulture, along with the possibility of reconciling understandings of space in modern Australia. One could say that of all the tropes of ecological study, place is perhaps the most profound in terms of history, knowledge, ontology, and experience. Our opening section foregrounds the complex ways in which attention to the "politics of earth" is constitutive of the environmental humanities.

Our second section, "Disaster, Vulnerability, and Resilience," engages what a postcolonial and humanities-based approach might bring to the study of disasters and of resilience in different cultural contexts, and establishes a cross-disciplinary dialogue across the humanities and social sciences. It questions how ecological vulnerability is produced in relation to specific experiences of colonialism and militarism, and examines the implications of this for how concepts of disaster risk reduction and resilience are constructed and acted upon. Rather than dismissing the sociological and scientific bases for these theories, the essays in this section discuss how they might be recalibrated in relation to postcolonial readings that draw on the rich resources of testimonials, and political, ethnographic, and fictional narratives, which combine different epistemologies and forms of witness to histories of disaster and militarism.

Anthony Carrigan's "Towards a Postcolonial Disaster Studies" makes a case for a sustained critical exchange between two interdisciplinary fields that have significant bearings on the development of the environmental humanities: postcolonial studies and disaster studies. It does this first by exploring points of overlap and disjuncture between disaster studies and postcolonial studies, connecting these to the volume's core concern with how global environmental problems are mediated creatively in different cultural locations. It then turns to the work of Barbadian poet and historian, Kamau Brathwaite, as a means of demonstrating how a postcolonial and humanities-based approach can help reframe the question of "what is a disaster" in ways that are historically sensitive and culturally nuanced. This involves addressing how postcolonial perspectives might challenge, reject, or reconfigure key disaster studies concepts such as resilience, risk, adaption, and vulnerability, while at the same time asking how disaster studies insights can help frame and inform interpretations of postcolonial disasters.

Barbara Rose Johnston's "Nuclear Disaster: The Marshall Islands Experience and Lessons for a Post-Fukushima World" examines the US history of nuclear weapons testing in the Marshall Islands (RMI), which raised both the region's and the planet's atmospheric radioactivity to critical levels, and contemporary struggles by people in the RMI and their allies to ameliorate the nation's environmental health. US military testing in the Marshall Islands involved ecological baseline studies, biological effects of radiation, the nature and behavior of radioactive fallout in the atmosphere, marine, and terrestrial environment, and the bioaccumulation of radioisotopes in the environment, food chain, and human body. A wide array of degenerative health effects resulted, including cancers and reproductive abnormalities. Using a "critical global ecologies" approach, Johnston demonstrates that the Marshallese experience with nuclear disaster and their continuing efforts to restore human and environmental health offer important lessons in this post-Fukushima world.

These questions about disaster mitigation and response are a shared concern in the third contribution to this section. Focusing on indigenous considerations of climate change and disaster, Ilan Kelman, JC Gaillard, Jessica Mercer, James Lewis, and Anthony Carrigan's co-authored essay "Island Vulnerability and Resilience: Combining Knowledges for Disaster Risk Reduction, Including Climate Change Adaptation" reminds us that no single knowledge form can be a panacea for addressing climate change and other disaster risk reduction (DRR) or long-term environmental concerns. However, indigenous knowledge in all its varied and diverse forms has the potential for contributing far more than is usually permitted in mainstream scientific literature. The authors explore the relationship between indigenous knowledge and DRR based on literature covering small island communities, where questions of vulnerability and resilience are frequently magnified. They also identify points where the primarily development-oriented, fieldwork-based examples on which the chapter is based might intersect with environmental humanities research, particularly in terms of how cultural and political insights can enhance DRR strategies. The chapter engages with one of the dominant philosophical and narrative forms with respect to global ecologies—scientific rationalism—and highlights points of departure for an increasingly holistic approach to disaster research.

In the third section, "Political Ecologies and Environmental Justice," we bring environmental humanities perspectives to bear on two areas of vital importance for conceiving new ecologies in the twenty-first century. The essays are sensitive to the tendency to romanticize oppressed communities in resisting environmental violence and extractive industries (a point that echoes Kelman et al.'s conclusions about community heterogeneity in the previous section), while emphasizing how narrative forms of literature and film intersect with regionally specific resilience and environmental justice debates. The contributors explore how a postcolonial environmental humanities speaks to political ecology's concern with questions of scale (temporal and geographic), and build a dialogue about what the "environmentalism of the poor" means in the different contexts of Africa, India, and Latin America. They also bring to the fore the challenges of claiming sustainability in relation to shifting political regimes, culturally localized forms of activism, and indigenous negotiations of capitalist modernity, neoliberalism, and state violence.

In "The Edgework of the Clerk: Resilience in Arundhati Roy's *Walking with the Comrades*," Susie O'Brien reads Roy's work as a site of critical engagement with the concept of resilience and considers the different ways this term circulates in a variety of contemporary discourses concerned with the environment. Describing the capacity to survive through turbulence, resilience has come to play a central organizing role in environmental management, and, increasingly, in discourses of development that emphasize the interdependence of culture, environment, and capitalism. Roy's recent nonfiction challenges this conception of resilience, highlighting the deployment by mining companies of the rhetoric of sustainability and creativity to provide cover for their role in environmental despoliation and the displacement of tribal peoples. Focusing on her 2011 collection, *Walking with the Comrades*, which has been widely criticized for what some see as its negativity and militancy (in contrast to Roy's 1997 Booker-Prize winning novel, *The God of Small Things*), O'Brien argues that Roy's political nonfiction reworks the concept of resilience to emphasize postcolonial environmental justice, and the vital role of the critical imagination in that ongoing project.

This focus on the aesthetics of activism is continued in "Filming the Emergence of Popular Environmentalism in Latin America: Postcolonialism and Buen Vivir," where Jorge Marcone moves the conversation beyond literature by focusing on a number of Latin American documentaries, released within the last decade, that represent recent popular environmental struggles. In contrast to the mainstream media, these documentaries focus on popular movements reacting to environmental changes brought by extractivist policies. Far from being mere cases of local resistance against transnational capitalism, the films reveal to different degrees the influence of a transnational and interethnic environmental movement, while at the same time functioning in counterpoint to one of the most influential popular environmental movements of the last fifteen years in Latin America: *Buen Vivir.* The essay examines Buen Vivir as a possible interlocutor for postcolonialism, which has introduced indigenous political ontologies at the national level. The essay concludes by offering a few suggestions regarding the potential conflicts between popular environmentalism and the current pursuit in the "First World" of the institutionalization of the environmental humanities.

In the final essay of this section, "Witnessing the Nature of Violence: Resource Extraction and Political Ecologies in the Contemporary African Novel," Byron Caminero-Santangelo addresses how two contemporary African novels provide important material for getting beyond stereotypes of violence in African culture and society that circulate in popular media. Challenging what James Ferguson calls "Africa Talk," Caminero-Santangelo reads Somalian author Nuruddin Farah's *Crossbones* (2011) and Nigerian author Helon Habila's *Oil on Water* (2010) as undermining narratives of conflict and anarchy on the continent with attention to practices of witnessing, theories of political ecology, and multiscalar narrative approaches to representing (neo)colonial history. In addressing the results of internationally financed resource extraction, his reading of both novels suggests that postcolonial histories of ecological degeneration and discursive transformation stymie precise causal analysis, dislocate oppositional identities, and complicate clear solutions.

In the fourth section, "Mapping World Ecologies," our contributors move between regional and global scales as they engage different perspectives on the historical constitution of "world ecology" and its diverse narrative and scalar claims. The essays here look at how "globatarian" approaches to ecological management facilitated a shift from interstate affiliations to neoliberal globalization; at how the capitalist world-system can be considered in terms of world-ecology; and at the generic and tropological shifts these historical processes have occasioned across a variety of narrative forms. One thread that connects with the first section of essays involves considering how particular capitalist and colonial industries imprint themselves on the way people understand, relate, and narrate experiences of environmental exploitation in postcolonial locations. The essays demonstrate the implications of systemic analysis in relation to conceptualizing alternative ecological as well as economic futures, emphasizing the importance of this approach for the environmental humanities.

Cheryl Lousley's chapter discusses how the 1983–87 World Commission on Environment and Development, which made sustainable development a global policy framework, imagined and constructed a world community through its report, *Our Common Future,* and through the public hearings it held in eleven cities on five continents. Building on early postcolonial critiques of the unequal power relations and illusory universalism of the sustainable development paradigm, the chapter examines how the world-making project of the Brundtland Commission involved an array of disjunct and heterogeneous narratives. The commission constructed its world vision by way of an aspirational narrative of global futurity, concretized in *Our Common Future* through the vernacular voices of quoted public hearing participants. However, Lousley shows how the report's aspiring sense of commonality is undercut by the public hearing transcripts, which reveal different conceptions of an imagined common world. A postcolonial narrative analysis, Lousley argues, shows how worlds, like nations, remain always in the process of being made; hence, they might be made and narrated differently.

Michael Niblett's "Oil on Sugar: Commodity Frontiers and Peripheral Aesthetics" also draws on a comparative world-ecological framework to consider issues of monocultural production, arguing in this case that literary forms are the abstract of specific socio-ecological relationships. In particular, the essay analyzes the ways in which the political ecologies of sugar and oil have impacted upon fiction from the economic peripheries of the world-system. The chapter examines the distinctive literary idioms and forms generated by this history, paying particular attention to the irrealist aesthetics through which the lived experience of the ecological dynamics common to both oil and sugar frontiers (most notably a pattern of boom-and-bust) finds expression. Exploring the ways in which petroleum and sucrose can seep into the texture of everyday life, patterning behaviors and habitus, Niblett suggests that exposing and critiquing this process of naturalization is one task that scholarship in the environmental humanities might take up. The study of literature has a key role to play here insofar as literary works provide access to affective modes corresponding to socio-ecological formations and to the transformations in human and extra-human natures through which they develop.

The final essay of this section, Sharae Deckard's "Ghost Mountains and Stone Maidens: Ecological Imperialism, Compound Catastrophe, and the Post-Soviet Ecogothic," brings Russia into the ambit of global environmental humanities, developing a theory of the ecogothic to illuminate how contemporary post-Soviet literary aesthetics register the *longue durée* of compound environmental catastrophe. The chapter examines how Olga Slavnikova's novel *2017* (2006) portrays supernatural apparitions in figuring the slow violence of Soviet-era nuclear irradiation and chemical pollution in the Urals, intimating the region's prehistory of resource colonization and industrialization during tsarist empire, and prognosticating future crises. Deckard argues that the post-Soviet uncanny of the novel crystallizes a post-catastrophic structure of feeling expressed in ecogothic motifs of nature's revenge, fears of toxification, and a sense of repetitive temporality. Nevertheless, the novel's "green spectres," Deckard shows, resist the logic of phantom objectivity which has characterized the history of ecological imperialism and resource extraction in the Urals by gesturing to an alternative ecological consciousness.

The final section, "Terraforming, Climate Change, and the Anthropocene," approaches global ecologies by exploring some of the characteristic practices and effects associated with environmental transformation in the Anthropocene. This section addresses both the deliberate terraforming of the earth by nuclear superpowers, and the consequences of humans acting as a geological force. Drawing attention to issues of ethics, politics, indigenous knowledge, and creative adaptation, the section is guided by the characteristic postcolonial commitment to increasing local autonomy while also considering obligations to planetary concerns beyond the human. The essays consider how long histories of colonial oppression, including nuclear militarism, indigenous dispossession, and slavery, heighten ecological vulnerabilities in the Anthropocene. They also examine how particular narrative forms and aesthetics highlight the potential for collaborative affiliations that resist the exploitative operations of biocapital, and the ongoing territorialization of land and sea. Addressing these new shapes of empire is one of the most important tasks of the environmental humanities in the twenty-first century.

Joseph Masco's "Terraforming Planet Earth" examines the ways in which US militarism has reconfigured the earth, bringing attention to forms of nuclear empire that are often overlooked in postcolonial (and American) studies. Engaging the US nuclear program as an instrument of ecological change, the essay examines how the global biosphere has been remade as a post-nuclear formation since 1945 and considers the implications of nuclear geoengineering for a contemporary anthropology of nature. The paper takes up the valences of the term "fallout," suggesting that it is a form of history made visible by negative outcomes. It also examines the legacies of environmental toxins, particularly those created by the nuclear age, turning to address the US Project Plowshare of the 1960–70s, a program intended to use nuclear explosives for construction purposes. Masco acknowledges that nuclear tests are not alone in changing the biosphere, yet the cumulative scale and scope of the effects of industry in the twentieth century reflects an important legacy of geoengineering in the Anthropocene.

George B. Handley's essay, "Climate Change, Cosmology, and Poetry: The Case of Derek Walcott's *Omeros*," places Walcott's work within the context of contemporary debates about the ethical and theological implications of climate change. While critical ecologies has remained by and large a secular field of scholarship, Handley turns to the ways in which poetry and its claims on the reader's faith may be relevant to the environmental humanities. The chapter seeks to help us understand the common genealogy of colonialism and the crisis of climate change, and to identify how Walcott's poetry reads the physical world against the grain of instrumental value and portrays it as a site of perpetual flux due to death, change, emergence, and creation. In light of recent calls by ecotheologians for new cosmologies that will assist us in seeing our place and our ethics in the world in new ways, Handley's interdisciplinary reading suggests poetry as one site of such reenvisioning.

In "Ordinary Futures: Interspecies Worldings in the Anthropocene," Elizabeth DeLoughrey shifts from land-based concerns to trace out the ocean's potential for a dynamic rendering of queer kinship with nonhuman others. The chapter turns to Maori author Keri Hulme's collection, *Stonefish* (2004), which inscribes the ways in which rising sea levels generate adaptive mutations in plants, mushrooms, and even humans. Hulme poses a fluid waterworld of queer kinship, an ontology of what Jane Bennett calls "vibrant matter," inscribing an intimate relationship to the seascape of Aotearoa New Zealand. Through experiments in form, the collection renders the sea, climate change, mutation, and the submarine as profoundly ordinary rather than apocalyptic. The emergence of what Hulme calls an "unseen neural network" inscribes new morphologies for an increasingly maritime world, posing an ontological and genealogical challenge to the state's territorialism of the foreshore and seabed, and deconstructing the human/nature divide found in much discourse of the Anthropocene. Posing an alternative to the discourse of apocalypse generated by anthropogenic climate change, DeLoughrey shows how Hulme positions nonhuman others as ordinary and integral to challenging the neoliberal territorialism of the settler state.

Taken as a whole, this volume asserts that a critical study of narrative—and a critical demand that the concept of ecology engage the vectors of social history—is essential to determining how we interpret and mitigate environmental crisis. Thus the work of *Global Ecologies and the Environmental Humanities* is to foreground how narrative and representational forms encode particular epistemologies and assumptions. As the authors of *The Emergence of the Environmental Humanities* suggest, this knowledge of human behavior, expression, and aesthetics is vital to shaping and developing the knowledge produced by the environmental sciences (Nye et al. 2013). Our collection, which examines narratives from documentary film, journalism, and the visual arts to history, poetry, and fantastic fiction, argues that these conversations are integral to the interdisciplinary groundwork of the environmental humanities, a field that has the radical potential to change our ecological futures.

NOTES

1. This is explored in detail by Lizabeth Paravisini-Gebert in this volume.
2. This is a point argued in DeLoughrey and Handley's (2011) introduction to *Postcolonial Ecologies* through the work of Frantz Fanon and Edward Said. See also Huggan (2004), Nixon (2005; 2011a), Vital and Erney (2006–2007), Cilano and DeLoughrey (2007), Huggan and Tiffin (2007; 2010), Wright (2010), Roos and Hunt (2010), Carrigan (2011b), and Deckard (2012). While these works sought to bring the two fields in dialogue, other authors have turned to literature with a more regional approach. See DeLoughrey, Gosson, and

Handley (2005) and Paravisini-Gebert (2005, 2008, 2009) on the Caribbean; O'Brien (2001), Mukherjee (2010), and Didur (2011a: 2011b; 2013) on South Asia; Vital (2008) and Caminero-Santangelo and Myers (2011) on Anglophone Africa; Crane (2012) and Mason et al. (2013) on settler colonies (particularly Australia, Canada, and South Africa).

3. There is tremendous work being done in North American literary scholarship on environmental justice—see for instance Adamson et al. (2002) and Stein (2004). For an introduction to relevant current issues in political ecology, see Peet et al. (2011), and Johnston (2011).

4. This extends right up to the level of global governance, including what Giovanna Di Chiro calls "Worldwatchers" (2003, 205). These include transnational institutions—from the World Bank and NAFTA to the UN and the WTO—whose approach to "saving nature" involves "whitewash[ing] the differential social and environmental impacts of globalization," and enjoining all global citizens to "put our differences aside" and "stop creating havoc, such as overbreeding, or slashing and burning the rainforests," which disrupts their vision for sustained economic growth coupled with neoliberal environmental management (205).

5. See Casid (2005); Casteel (2007); DeLoughrey and Handley (2011).

6. We share the sentiment of Huggan and Tiffin (2010) who write that "in reaching out across languages and cultures, postcolonial ecocriticism is paradoxically driven—as is this book—by the impossibility of its own utopian ambitions: to make exploitation and discrimination of all kinds, both human and nonhuman, visible in the world; and, in so doing, to help make them obsolete" (16).

7. See, for example, Nixon (2009), Mukherjee (2011), and Carrigan (2012) for examinations of Sinha's formal and narrative strategies, and Caminero-Santangelo (this volume) on Habila.

8. See Huggan and Tiffin (2007, 10); Carrigan (2011b, 24–30); DeLoughrey and Handley (2011, 5–7); Didur (2011a, 44–48).

9. See, for example, Dawson (2011), Baucom (2013), and Moore (2014), with the latter offering a sharp indictment while introducing the "Capitalocene" as a materialist alternative.

10. Important sources where the term environmental humanities is being debated and defined include the special issue of the *Australian Humanities Review* (2004), the Australian journal *Environmental Humanities*, the US-based journal *Resilience*, the report by Nye et al. (2013), and the Australian Environmental Humanities Hub (http://www.aehhub.org).

11. This has been boosted by collaborative and regional organizations such as the Nordic Network for Interdisciplinary Environmental Studies (NIES), the European Environmental Humanities Alliance (http://europeanenvironmental-humanities.org/), Environmental Humanities Now (http://environmentalhu-manitiesnow.org/), and the Environmental Humanities Transatlantic Research Network (http://environmental-humanities-network.org/).

12. For another precursor of this article, also written from an Australian perspective, see Eckersley (1998). See also Griffiths and Robin's (1997) edited collection on settler societies and environmental history.

13. There is a need for researchers across *all* disciplines to explore the points of tension and disjunction between different cultural understandings of the environment, and to highlight the extent to which these respond to and are conditioned by current and historical power relations. Another key consideration for environmental

humanities research centers on how the global drive for sustainability, with its founding emphasis on "intergenerational equity" (as inscribed from the Brundt-land Report onward), only makes sense if this includes a parallel commitment to intrahuman *equitability* across cultures and classes and across the human-nonhuman divide (see also Carrigan 2011b, 6–8).

14. Questions of ethics have long been examined in the field of history, particularly with the journal *Environmental Ethics* (founded in 1979), but outside of post-colonial studies have been less visible in literary ecocriticism.

15. See also Hulme and Mahony (2010); Yusoff and Gabrys (2011); and Kelman et al. in this volume.

16. This term was suggested by Barbara Rose Johnston at the 2013 Global Ecologies: Nature/Narrative/Neoliberalism conference at UCLA.

17. While the essays in this volume do not deal substantively with animal studies, we see this as an important growth area for a postcolonial environmental humanities that helps to figure global environmental justice issues through multispecies frameworks. See, for example, Tiffin (2001), Armstrong (2002), Ahuja (2009), Huggan and Tiffin (2010), Miller (2012), and DeLoughrey, this volume.

18. See Stepan (1982), Arnold (1996), and Moore et al. (2003).

19. See Guha (1989, 2000a, 2000b), Guha and Martínez-Alier (1997), Huggan (2004), Huggan and Tiffin (2010), Mukherjee (2010), DeLoughrey and Handley (2011), and Nixon (2011a).

20. On the need to address the different representations and temporalities of rapid onset disasters alongside long-term calamities, see Carrigan (2011a; 2011b, ch. 6; 2014; and this volume).

21. See also Skrimshire (2010).

22. On ecology and nuclearism see Masco (2012); on Pacific Island nuclearization see Johnston (2007) and Johnston and Barker (2008).

23. On European imperial environmental history see Gerbi (1985), Grove (1995), Arnold (1996), Drayton (2000), Anker (2001), and Crosby (2003; 2004).

REFERENCES

Adamson, Joni, Mei Mei Evans, and Rachel Stein, eds. 2002. *The Environmental Justice Reader: Politics, Poetics, and Pedagogy.* Tucson: University of Arizona Press.

Ahuja, Neel. 2009. "Postcolonial Critique in a Multispecies World." *PMLA* 124 (2): 556–563.

Anker, Peder. 2001. *Imperial Ecology: Environmental Order in the British Empire, 1895–1945.* Cambridge: Harvard University Press.

Armstrong, Philip. 2002. "The Postcolonial Animal." *Society and Animals* 10 (4): 413–419.

Arnold, David. 1988. *Famine: Social Crisis and Historical Change.* Oxford: Oxford University Press.

———. 1996. *The Problem of Nature: Environment, Culture, European Expansion.* Oxford: Blackwell.

Arnold, David, and Ramachandra Guha. 1995. "Introduction: Themes and Issues in the Environmental History of South Asia." In *Nature, Culture, Imperialism: Essays on the Environmental History of South Asia*, edited by David Arnold and Ramachandra Guha, 1–20. Delhi: Oxford University Press.

Badmington, Neil. 2000. *Posthumanism*. London: Palgrave Macmillan.

Baucom, Ian. 2014. "History 4°: Postcolonial Method and Anthropocene Time." *Cambridge Journal of Postcolonial Literary Inquiry* 1 (1): 123–142.

Beinart, William, and Lotte Hughes. 2007. *Environment and Empire*. Oxford: Oxford University Press.

Biro, Andrew, ed. 2011. *Critical Ecologies: The Frankfurt School and Contemporary Environmental Crisis*. Toronto: University of Toronto Press.

Botkin, Daniel. 1990. *Discordant Harmonies: A New Ecology for the Twenty-First Century*. Oxford: Oxford University Press.

Brockaway, Lucille. 1979. *Science and Colonial Expansion: The Role of the British Royal Botanical Gardens*. New York: Academic Press.

Browne, Janet. 1983. *The Secular Ark*. New Haven: Yale University Press.

Caminero-Santangelo, Byron, and Garth Myers, eds. 2011. *Environment at the Margins: Literary and Environmental Studies in Africa*. Athens: Ohio University Press.

Carrigan, Anthony. 2011a. "(Eco)Catastrophe, Reconstruction, and Representation: Montserrat and the Limits of Sustainability." *New Literatures Review* 47–48: 111–128.

———. 2011b. *Postcolonial Tourism: Literature, Culture, and Environment*. London and New York: Routledge.

———. 2012. "'Justice is on our side'? *Animal's People*, Generic Hybridity, and Eco-Crime." *Journal of Commonwealth Literature* 47 (2): 159–174.

———, ed. 2014. "Catastrophe and Environment." Special issue of *Moving Worlds: A Journal of Transcultural Writings* 14 (2).

Casid, Jill. 2005. *Sowing Empire: Landscape and Colonization*. Minneapolis: University of Minnesota Press.

Casteel, Sarah Phillips. 2007. *Second Arrivals: Landscape and Belonging in Contemporary Writing of the Americas*. Charlottesville: University of Virginia Press.

Chakrabarty, Dipesh. 2000. *Provincializing Europe: Postcolonial Thought and Historical Difference*. Princeton: Princeton University Press.

———. 2009. "The Climate of History: Four Theses." *Critical Inquiry* 35 (2): 197–222.

———. 2012. "Postcolonial Studies and the Challenge of Climate Change." *New Literary History* 43 (1): 1–18.

Cilano, Cara, and Elizabeth DeLoughrey. 2007. "Against Authenticity: Global Knowledges and Postcolonial Ecocriticism." *Interdisciplinary Studies in Literature and Environment (ISLE)* 14 (1): 71–87.

Crane, Kylie. 2012. *Myths of Wilderness in Contemporary Narratives: Environmental Postcolonialism in Australia and Canada*. Basingstoke: Palgrave Macmillan.

Crosby, Alfred W. Jr. 2004. *Ecological Imperialism: The Biological Expansion of Europe 900–1900*. 2nd ed. Cambridge: Cambridge University Press.

———. 2003. *The Columbian Exchange: Biological and Cultural Consequences of 1492, 30th Anniversary Edition*. Westport: Praeger.

Crutzen, Paul J., and Eugene F. Stoermer. 2000. "The Anthropocene." *IGBP Newsletter* 41 (17): 17–18.

Dawson, Ashley. 2011. "Slow Violence and the Environmentalism of the Poor: An Interview with Rob Nixon." *Social Text Interviews*. Accessed August 28, 2014. http://socialtextjournal.org/slow_violence_and_the_environmentalism_of_the_poor_an_interview_with_rob_nixon/.

Deckard, Sharae, ed. 2012. "Global and Postcolonial Ecologies." Special issue of *Green Letters: Studies in Ecocriticism* 16 (1).

DeLoughrey, Elizabeth. 2013. "The Myth of Isolates: Ecosystem Ecologies in the Nuclear Pacific." *Cultural Geographies* 20 (2): 167–194.

DeLoughrey, Elizabeth, Renée Gosson, and George B. Handley, eds. 2005. *Caribbean Literature and the Environment: Between Nature and Culture.* Charlottesville: University of Virginia Press.

DeLoughrey, Elizabeth, and George B. Handley, eds. 2011. *Postcolonial Ecologies: Literatures of the Environment.* New York: Oxford University Press.

Di Chiro, Giovanna. 2003. "Beyond Ecoliberal 'Common Futures:' Environmental Justice, Toxic Touring, and a Transcommunal Politics of Place." In *Race, Nature and the Politics of Difference,* edited by Donald S. Moore, Jake Kosek, and Anand Pandian, 204–232. Durham: Duke University Press.

Didur, Jill. 2011a. "Cultivating Community: Counter Landscaping in Kiran Desai's *The Inheritance of Loss.*" In *Postcolonial Ecologies: Literatures of the Environment,* edited by Elizabeth DeLoughrey and George B. Handley, 43–61. New York: Oxford University.

———. 2011b. "Strange Joy: Plant-hunting and Responsibility in Jamaica Kincaid's (Post)colonial Travel Writing." *Interventions: International Journal of Postcolonial Studies.* 13 (2): 236–255.

———. 2013. "Guns and Roses: Reading the Picturesque Archive in Anita Desai's *Fire on the Mountain.*" *Textual Practice* 27 (3): 499–522.

Didur, Jill, and Teresa Heffernan. 2003. "Revisiting the Subaltern in the New Empire." *Cultural Studies* 17 (1): 1–15.

Drayton, Richard. 2000. *Nature's Government: Science, Imperial Britain and the "Improvement of the World."* New Haven: Yale University Press.

Eckersley, Robyn. 1998. "The Death of Nature and the Birth of Ecological Humanities." *Organization* and *Environment* 11 (2): 183–185.

Escobar, Arturo. 1995. *Encountering Development: The Making and Unmaking of the Third World.* Princeton: Princeton University Press.

———. 1996. "Constructing Nature: Elements for a Poststructuralist Political Ecology." In *Liberation Ecologies: Environment, Development, Social Movements,* edited by Richard Peet and Michael Watts, 46–68. London: Routledge.

Gerbi, Antonello. 1985. *Nature in the New World from Christopher Columbus to Gonzalo Fernández de Oviedo.* Translated by Jeremy Moyle. Pittsburgh: University of Pittsburgh Press.

Glissant, Édouard. 1989. *Caribbean Discourse: Selected Essays.* Translated by J. Michael Dash. Charlottesville: University of Virginia Press.

Griffiths, Tom, and Libby Robin, eds. 1997. *Ecology and Empire: Environmental History and Settler Societies.* Seattle: University of Washington Press.

Grove, Richard H. 1995. *Green Imperialism: Colonial Expansion, Tropical Island Edens and the Origins of Environmentalism, 1600–1860.* Cambridge: Cambridge University Press.

Guha, Ramachandra. 1989. "Radical American Environmentalism: A Third World Critique." *Ethical Perspectives on Environmental Issues in India* 11: 71–83.

———. 2000a. *Environmentalism: A Global History.* New York: Longman.

———. 2000b. "The Paradox of Global Environmentalism." *Current History* 99 (640): 367–370.

Guha, Ramachandra, and Joan Martínez-Alier. 1997. *Varieties of Environmentalism: Essays North and South*. Delhi and New York: Oxford University Press.

Habila, Helon. 2011. *Oil on Water*. London: Penguin.

Haraway, Donna J. 1989. *Primate Visions: Gender, Race and Nature in the World of Modern Science*. London: Routledge.

———. 2006. "Crittercam: Compounding Eyes in NatureCultures." In *Postphenomenology*, edited by Evan Selinger, 119–24. Albany: State University of New York Press.

Heise, Ursula K., and Allison Carruth. 2010. "Introduction to Focus: Environmental Humanities." *American Book Review*, 32 (1): 3.

Huggan, Graham. 2001. *The Postcolonial Exotic: Marketing the Margins*. New York: Routledge.

———. 2004. "'Greening' Postcolonialism: Ecocritical Perspectives." *Modern Fiction Studies* 50 (3): 701–733.

Huggan, Graham, and Helen Tiffin. 2007. "Green Postcolonialism." *Interventions* 9 (1): 1–11.

———. 2010. *Postcolonial Ecocriticism: Literature, Animals, Environment*. New York: Routledge.

Hulme, Mike, and Martin Mahony. 2010. "Climate Change: What Do We Know about the IPCC?" *Progress in Physical Geography* 34 (5): 705–718.

Johnston, Barbara Rose, ed. 2007. *Half-Lives and Half-Truths: Confronting the Radioactive Legacies of the Cold War*. Santa Fe: A School for Advanced Research Resident Scholar Book.

———, ed. 2011. *Life and Death Matters: Human Rights, Environment, and Social Justice*. Walnut Creek: Left Coast Press.

Johnston, Barbara Rose, and Barker, Holly. 2008. *Consequential Damages of Nuclear War: The Rongelap Report*. Walnut Creek: Left Coast Press.

Lohmann, Larry. 1993. "Green Orientalism." *Ecologist* 23 (6): 202.

Martínez-Alier, Joan. 2002. *The Environmentalism of the Poor: A Study of Ecological Conflicts and Valuation*. Cheltenham: Edward Elgar.

Mascarenhas, Adolfo, and Wisner, Ben. 2012. "Politics: Power and Disasters." In *Handbook of Hazards and Disaster Risk Reduction*, edited by Ben Wisner, JC Gaillard, and Ilan Kelman, 48–60. London and New York: Routledge.

Masco, Joseph. 2012. "The End of Ends." *Anthropological Quarterly* 85 (4): 1107–1124.

Mason, Travis, Lisa Szabo-Jones, and Elzette Steenkamp, eds. 2013. "Postcolonial Ecocriticism among Settler-Colonial Nations." Special Issue of *ARIEL: A Review of International English Literature* 44 (4).

Merchant, Carolyn. 1980. *The Death of Nature: Women, Ecology, and the Scientific Revolution*. San Francisco: Harper and Row.

———. 2008. *Ecology: Key Concepts in Critical Theory*. 2nd ed. Amherst, NY: Prometheus (Humanity) Books.

Miller, John. 2012. *Empire and the Animal Body: Violence, Identity and Ecology in Victorian Adventure Fiction*. London: Anthem Press.

Moore, Donald S., Jake Kosek, and Anand Pandian, eds. 2003. *Race, Nature and the Politics of Difference*. Durham: Duke University Press.

Moore, Jason W. 2014. "The Capitalocene, Part I: On the Nature and Origins of our Ecological Crisis." http://www.jasonwmoore.com/Essays.html.

Mukherjee, Upamanyu Pablo. 2010. *Postcolonial Environments: Nature, Culture and the Contemporary Indian Novel in English*. Basingstoke: Palgrave Macmillan.

————. 2011. "'Tomorrow there will be more of us:' Toxic Postcoloniality in *Animal's People.*" In *Postcolonial Ecologies: Literatures of the Environment*, edited by Elizabeth DeLoughrey and George B. Handley, 216–231. Oxford: Oxford University Press.

Nixon, Rob. 2005. "Environmentalism and Postcolonialism." *Postcolonial Studies and Beyond*, edited by Ania Loomba et al., 233–251. Durham: Duke University Press.

————. 2009. "Neoliberalism, Slow Violence, and the Environmental Picaresque." *Modern Fiction Studies* 55 (3): 443–467.

————. 2011a. *Slow Violence and the Environmentalism of the Poor.* Cambridge, MA: Harvard University Press.

————. 2011b. "Slow Violence." *Chronicle of Higher Education.* June 26. http://chronicle.com/article/Slow-Violence/127968/.

Nye, David, Linda Rugg, James Fleming, and Robert Emmett. 2013. *The Emergence of the Environmental Humanities.* Stockholm, Sweden: MISTRA, The Swedish Foundation for Strategic Environmental Research. http://mistra.org/download/18.7331038f13e40191ba5a23/1378682257195/Mistra_Environmental_Humanities_May2013.pdf.

O'Brien Susie. 2001. "Articulating a World of Difference: Ecocriticism, Postcolonialism and Globalization." *Canadian Literature* 170–171: 140–158.

Paravisini-Gebert, Lizabeth. 2005. "'He of the Trees': Nature, the Environment, and Creole Religiosities in Caribbean Literature." In *Caribbean Literature and the Environment*, edited by Elizabeth DeLoughrey, Renée Gosson, and George B. Handley, 182–196. Charlottesville: University of Virginia Press.

————. 2008. "Endangered Species: Ecology and the Discourse of the Nation." In *Displacements and Transformations in Caribbean Literature and Culture*, edited by Lizabeth Paravisini-Gebert and Ivette Romero-Cesareo, 8–23. Gainesville: University Press of Florida.

————. 2009. "Caribbean Utopias and Dystopias: The Emergence of the Environmental Writer and Artist." In *The Natural World in Latin American Literatures: Ecocritical Essays on Twentieth Century Writings*, edited by Adrian Kane, 113–35. Jefferson: McFarland & Co.

Peet, Richard, Paul Robbins, and Michael Watts, eds. 2011. *Global Political Ecology.* London and New York: Routledge.

Plumwood, Val. 1993. *Feminism and the Mastery of Nature.* London and New York: Routledge.

————. 2002. *Environmental Culture: The Ecological Crisis of Reason.* London and New York: Routledge.

Roos, Bonnie, and Alex Hunt, eds. 2010. *Postcolonial Green: Environmental Politics and World Narratives.* Charlottesville: University of Virginia Press.

Rose, Deborah Bird, and Libby Robin. 2004. "The Ecological Humanities in Action: An Invitation." *Australian Humanities Review*, no. 31–32. http://www.australianhumanitiesreview.org/archive/Issue-April-2004/rose.html.

Rose, Deborah Bird, Thom van Dooren, Matthew Chrulew, Stuart Cooke, Matthew Kearnes, and Emily O'Gorman. 2012. "Thinking Through the Environment, Unsettling the Humanities." *Environmental Humanities* 1: 1–5.

Sachs, Wolfgang. 1992. *The Development Dictionary.* London: Zed Books.

————. 1993. *Global Ecology: A New Arena of Political Conflict.* London: Zed Books.

———. 1999. *Planet Dialectics: Explorations in Environment and Development*. London: Zed Books.

Said, Edward. 1993. *Culture and Imperialism*. New York: Knopf

Saro-Wiwa, Ken. 1992. *Genocide in Nigeria: The Ogoni Tragedy*. Port Harcourt: Saros International.

Shellenberger, Michael, and Ted Nordhaus. 2004. *The Death of Environmentalism: Global Warming Politics in a Post-Environmental World*. http://www.thebreakthrough.org/images/Death_of_Environmentalism.pdf.

Shiva, Vandana. 2005. *Earth Democracy*. Boston: South End Press.

Sinha, Indra. 2007. *Animal's People*. London: Simon & Schuster.

Skrimshire, Stefan, ed. 2010. *Future Ethics: Climate Change and Apocalyptic Imagination*. London and New York: Continuum.

Spivak, Gayatri Chakravorty. 2004. "Righting Wrongs." *The South Atlantic Quarterly* 103 (2–3): 523–581.

Stein, Rachel, ed. 2004. *New Perspectives on Environmental Justice: Gender, Sexuality, and Activism*. New Brunswick: Rutgers University Press.

Stepan, Nancy. 1982. *The Idea of Race in Science*. London: MacMillan.

Strathern, Marilyn. 1980. "No Nature, No Culture: The Hagen Case." In *Nature, Culture, and Gender*, edited by Carol MacCormack and Marilyn Strathern, 174–222. Cambridge: Cambridge University Press.

Taylor, Bron, ed. 1995. *Ecological Resistance Movements: The Global Emergence of Radical and Popular Environmentalism*. New York: State University of New York Press.

Tiffin, Helen. 2001. "Unjust Relations: Animals, the Species Boundary and Postcolonialism." In *Compr(om)ising Postcolonialisms: Narratives and Practices*, edited by Greg Ratcliffe and Gerry Turcotte, 30–44. Wollongong: University of Wollongong Press.

Vital, Anthony. 2008. "Toward an African Ecocriticism: Postcolonialism, Ecology and *Life & Times of Michael K*." *Research in African Literatures* 39 (1): 87–106.

Vital, Anthony, and Hans-Georg Erney. 2006–2007. "Introduction: Postcolonial Studies and Ecocriticism." *Journal of Commonwealth and Postcolonial Studies* 13 (2)–14 (1): 3–12.

Wilson, E. O. 1998. *Consilience: The Unity of Knowledge*. New York: Alfred A. Knopf.

Worster, Donald. 1989. "The Ecology of Order and Chaos." *Forest History Society and American Society for Environmental History* 14 (1–2): 1–18.

Wright, Laura. 2010. *Wilderness into Civilized Shapes: Reading the Postcolonial Environment*. Athens: University of Georgia Press.

Yusoff, Kathryn, and Jennifer Gabrys. 2011. "Climate Change and the Imagination." *WIREs Climate Change* 2 (4): 516–534.

Young, Robert JC. 2012. "Postcolonial Remains." *New Literary History* 43 (1): 19–42.

Part I

The Politics of Earth
Forests, Gardens, Plantations

1   Narrativizing Nature
India, Empire, and Environment

David Arnold

Over the past thirty years, "empire" and "environment" have become closely entangled concepts. This connectivity can be traced back at least as far as Alfred Crosby's *Ecological Imperialism* (1986), but it is a conjunction evident in many other books since then, including John MacKenzie's *Empire of Nature* (1988), Richard Grove's *Green Imperialism* (1995), Peder Anker's *Imperial Ecology* (2001), and William Beinart and Lotte Hughes's *Environment and Empire* (2007).[1] This confluence of environment and empire studies marks a significant shift away from imperial historians' earlier neglect of nature and is indicative of the wider move to the "greening of the humanities" (Nixon 2005, 233). While many historical studies remain doggedly attached to one particular empire (usually the British), the scope of eco-imperial analysis often ranges much wider, embracing entire continents or examining a long sequence of imperial interventions.[2] There is, though, no clear consensus as to what in essence characterizes the eco-imperial relationship. Approaches vary enormously—from the aggressive pathogen- and species-driven expansionism that energizes and naturalizes empire in Crosby's (1986) seminal tale of biotic conquest, to understandings of empire as a site of constructive Western engagement with indigenous environments and epistemologies, to scientific savants as ecological pioneers in Grove's rendition of what was "green" in imperialism. As opportunity and resource, the environment is mobilized to explain the political logistics of empire and the expanding of commodity frontiers. It is equally used to critique the inherent violence of empire, its territorial appropriation, and its subordination, marginalization, or elimination of nonwhite populations. If empire gave privileged access to an expanding world of nature knowledge, the imperialization of the environment provided the means to build scientific careers, creating new professional roles and institutional domains. Beyond establishing that empire's entanglement with the environment was complex, multistranded, and place-, time-, and culture-specific, it is not always clear whether empire gives retrospective valorization to precolonial states of nature or is a surrogate for, and agency of, emergent global capitalism, or even both simultaneously. All that can be said with confidence is that for most environmental historians there is a dynamic, even symbiotic, relationship between modern empires and the global phenomenon of environmental change.

If empire serves as a historical approximation for the global, then conceptually and methodologically postcolonialism brings an added sensitivity to the sources employed and to the positionality of author and text. There are various ways in which historians construct their environmental narrative or see that narrative as constructed for them by the sources on which they depend. There is, thus, a contrast between those accounts that represent nature as place-specific, fixed, and sited within a single biogeographical locale: Gilbert White's classic study, the *Natural History of Selborne*, published in 1789, is one example of this narrative genre. In works of this kind, nature comes to the author as he or she potters in the garden or goes on local walks, in the process observing changing seasons, the arrival and departure of swallows, the onset of autumn rain and winter frost. They have their counterparts in more scholarly bioregional studies of environment and history that at times stray into a kind of "romantic primordialism" or "eco-parochialism" (Nixon 2005, 236–38).[3] In this place-sited narrative, the environment is not, however, without a sense of historical sequence or even catastrophic intervention: Rachel Carson's *Silent Spring* (1962) shares something of this place-specific quality in which a much-loved environment (North America) undergoes calamitous disruption from industrial pesticides and toxic pollution.

Such an approach contrasts with those narratives in which nature is represented primarily through a process of observer itineration or through the experience of spatial and social displacement, and this second type of narrativization lies closer to most postcolonial concerns. It has at least two dimensions—the imperial and the diasporic. The former is represented by what Mary Louise Pratt identifies as the mode of perception produced by "imperial eyes" and which I have discussed similarly as "the traveling gaze" (Pratt 1992; Arnold 2006). Such narrativizations can be found in most European or North America travel accounts from the mid-eighteenth century onwards. The author goes to nature and makes comparisons and contrasts with what he or she already knows (or imagines as knowing). In these itinerant narratives, where the narrator is almost constantly on the move, there is scant possibility of developing an awareness of any cyclical pattern in nature or of registering periodic shifts in the landscape, as between drought and abundance. It is only possible to gain an immediate, often highly subjective, impression of what appears at that moment to be "picturesque" or repellent. Often enough, the standard by which such judgments are made is that of the society from which the traveler originates and regards as normality. Despite recourse to the apparent impartiality of science, such narratives project the self-importance of the traveler. Travel feeds the imperial self, and even if the experience of travel educates and transforms him or her, and opens up spaces for "transculturation," it tends to confirm many of the observers' environmental preconceptions. Not unrelated to this are narratives of diasporic replacement. In these the observer is conscious of having moved between different places of nature and the cultural and social worlds that enclose or inform them. Individuals carry with them mementos and impressions from some previous, perhaps natal, environment, but that primordial engagement is overlaid by, or in conflict with, the experiences and associations a new locale creates. The observer's gaze is that of the exiled and dispossessed rather than that of the footloose and imperious traveler, and yet a sense of disjuncture, of being out of place, is arguably common to both.

This dichotomy between the fixed and the itinerant allows me to explore two different narrative genres that pertain to the environment of British India. There is a clear distinction between the sources I use—one is a novel, the other a collection of administrative reports. My concern, however, is less with fiction versus factuality than what these sources reveal about the material character of the environments they describe (one rural, the other urban), with the narrative strategies they employ, the positionality of their authors, and the connectedness through empire of their separate approaches to "nature." The first text is a novel by a well-known Bengali writer; the other is not a single-authored work but a selection of reports and articles on environmental health in colonial Calcutta. My aim is to consider the implications of these apparently contrasting narrative forms for a postcolonial rereading of the imperial environment.

ARANYAK: OF THE FOREST

Aranyak: Of the Forest by the Bengali writer Bibhutibhushan Bandyopadhyay ([1939] 2002) was first published in the 1930s. He was born in Bengal in 1894: his father was a Sanskrit scholar, a music teacher and storywriter. The young Bibhutibhushan mainly earned his living as a teacher but between 1924 and 1930 he worked as assistant manager on an up-country estate in the Bhagalpur division of Bihar. He wrote short stories and novels in Bengali, including two volumes on the life of Apu, *Pather Panchali* (1929) and *Aparajito* (1931), which were adapted as films by the acclaimed Bengali director Satyajit Ray.[4] Nature, seen from the perspective of the Bengali village and in contrast to urban life in Calcutta, features intermittently in the Apu books and the films derived from them, but it receives the greatest attention in *Aranyak*, written between 1937 and 1939 and based on the author's experience of rural Bihar.

In a purely temporal sense, *Aranyak* cannot be described as postcolonial: it was written a decade before India's independence, and its author died in 1950, only three years after British rule ended. Written in the first person, the story tells how a young ex-college student and teacher, Satyacharan (or "Satya") lands a job as the manager of a *zamindari* estate (one of the many created by the British under the Permanent Settlement of 1793) in the forests of Bhagalpur. He lives there for six years before returning to Calcutta. *Aranyak*, which might reasonably be regarded as one of the first environmentalist novels written by an Indian, suggests certain parallels with Amitav Ghosh's *The Hungry Tide*. Written seventy years later, Ghosh's novel has a more complex storyline and a more refined environmental consciousness (of reader, author, and characters) to work with. But, like the American-born Piya in *Hungry Tide*, Satya is an educated outsider, who through experience and empathy becomes an "anxious witness" to rapid environmental change, and whose outlook and identity is transformed by contact with the local way of life and the nature that informs and surrounds it (Bandyopadhyay 2002).

For what purports to be a novel, there is not much of a story to *Aranyak*, apart from the narrator's growing love affair with the forest. *Aranyak* appears in part inspired by *Green Mansions*, W. H. Hudson's 1904 novel, in which the itinerant author's fascination with the South American jungle is articulated through his hero's love for Rima, a mysterious and alluring forest girl (Reeve 1998, 134–145). Beginning from the perspective of the footloose cosmopolitan, *Aranyak* similarly traces the unfolding encounter between the city-bred stranger and the people, plants, and animals that inhabit a remote rural environment. There are several, sometimes contradictory, strands to this encounter. Large parts of the estate are uninhabited, causing the narrator, lost in rural solitude, to suffer loneliness and homesickness for Calcutta at first. However, parts of the forest are inhabited and Satya gradually meets estate workers, local officials, and villagers (both low-caste Hindus and tribal Santhals) whose way of life he comes to respect and value without ever losing his middle-class sense of superiority. As his fascination with the forest and its inhabitants grows, immobility overtakes Satya—to the extent that it becomes hard for him to muster the enthusiasm to visit even nearby towns. In this narrative, it is the observer who becomes fixed while the poor, landless denizens of the forest are kept mobile by their constant search for subsistence. "I had come to love the open spaces and the thick green forests so much," Satya remarks, "that if I went to Mungher or Purnea for work— even for a day—I grew restless with longing to come back to the jungle and plunge myself once more into its deep silence, the exquisite moonlight, the sunset, the rain-bearing dark clouds, and its unsullied starry nights ..." (47). He eventually regards the "civilization of the forest world" as superior to that of Calcutta, the city from which he at first felt himself an unfortunate exile (182). Such is his personal transformation that when he encounters a group of city-bred Bengalis picnicking in the forest he is outraged by their crassness, their inability to appreciate the nature around them, and by the discarded tin-cans they leave behind. It is they, not Satya, who now appear "completely out of place" (189).

The novel is enlivened by its descriptions of nature: the hero is not so much Satya as the forest and its inhabitants, and long passages are devoted to this. As part of his local sensitivity, the author is particularly concerned with the names—of people as well as plants—and the identities they convey. The forest dwellers he encounters are duly named and their characters carefully delineated: these are figures who, in many imperial texts, would have remained nameless or been taken as simply representative of a racial or communal "type." Satya attaches great importance to local plant names, though he often falls back on Bengali, rather than tribal, nomenclature. In a characteristic passage, he writes:

> when I had walked on a little further and the *katcheri* [office] huts were hidden by the wild *jhau* and the jungle of *kash*, I felt that I was all alone in the world. As far as the eye could see there were dense forests flanking the expansive fields and it was all jungle and shrub—acacias, wild bamboos, cane saplings and *gajari* trees. The setting sun splashed the tops of trees and bushes with a fiery orange and the evening breeze carried the fragrance of wild flowers and grass and creepers. Every bush was alive with the cry of birds. (15)

The word "jungle," used repeatedly here and throughout in *Aranyak*, is, I will suggest shortly, highly significant.

We can take Satya as a representative of his class, the high-caste, educated Bengali elite, the *bhadralok* or "respectable people." He is at first disdainful of the "god-forsaken" environment in which he finds himself and its "barbaric" inhabitants; but he rapidly comes to develop a strong attachment to the "freedom" life in the forest provides (Bandyopadhyay 2002, 12–13, 62). This personal sense of freedom could be interpreted as an articulation of India's political quest for freedom in the 1920s and 1930s; but the implied contrast appears, more mundanely, to be with the constraints and burdens of middle-class domesticity. Nature, Satya remarks in a passage that seems to echo the sentiments of Hudson's *Green Mansions*, "makes men abandon their homes [and] fills them with wanderlust ... He who has heard the call of the wild and has once glimpsed the unveiled face of nature will find it impossible to settle down to playing the householder" (97). This individual sense of liberation (or capture) is matched by a growing appreciation of the "riches," "bounty," "wealth," and "treasures" to be found in nature (95, 196, 208, 213). It is as instinctive for Satya, as for earlier European naturalists and travelers, to represent nature through a language of material acquisition and capitalist resource, though he goes further than most of them in attempting to evoke, too, a sense of the magical and mystical in nature. "I felt within myself a sense of liberation, of being supremely detached, untrammeled. ... As I stood beneath the moonlit skies on that still silent night, I felt I had chanced upon an unknown fairy kingdom" (23). But Satya is also struck by the poverty of the people he observes (and we can note here, as in *The Hungry Tide*, how destructive the untamed environment can be). The forest might be romantic to Satya's eyes, but it remains, for the inhabitants, a "cruel land" (33, 81). Shockingly for a high-caste Bengali, they do not even eat rice but subsist on millets and crude grains. Despite the apparent beneficence of nature, the forest dwellers suffer hunger and thirst. They are afflicted by diseases they cannot cure, wounds and injuries from which they cannot recover. Ignorant of hygiene, they drink polluted water and are poisoned by contaminated food. Exploited by moneylenders, traders, and tricksters, they are further oppressed by landlords and officials. Nature is not all kind.

Despite its romantic engagement with nature, *Aranyak* is also an ecocritique—critical of the destruction caused by capitalism (albeit spear-headed by the subsistence needs of the poor) and the principle of "prog-ress" it purports to represent. Moreover, as the *zamindar*'s agent, charged with leasing out land for cultivation and increasing the estate's revenues, Satya is personally implicated in this process of exploitation and destruc-tion. He remarks: "My distant employers do not care for the landscape: all they understand are taxes and revenue money" (213). This becomes a personal dilemma. He declares himself "loth to settle people and destroy the peace of the forests," but is forced to ask himself: "was the forest going to be destroyed by my hands?" (113–14).

Toward the end of *Aranyak*, Satya is convinced that the enchanted for-est will not survive much longer: it is already endangered. Within a short time, "the exquisite forests and the distant winding open spaces would be completely erased. And in their place, what would one be gaining? Thatched houses, unbelievably ugly, fields of maize, gowal and janar, rope-cots, ban-ners flying above temples to Hanuman, an abundance of phanimansa scrub, snuff and tobacco, epidemics of cholera and smallpox." To which he can only respond by pleading: "Forests, primeval and ancient, forgive me" (196). He imagines still more traumatic changes to the once "pristine" landscape as mines and shanty towns take over, with the "chimneys of the copper factories, trolley lines, rows of *bustees* [slums] for the coolies, drains overflowing with dirty water, discarded heaps of ash spewed from engines, clusters of shops, tea-joints, cheap films …" (244). Like many a nature narrative, but strikingly for a work written in India eighty years ago, *Aranyak* too ends with a vision of the environmental apocalypse (Killingsworth and Palmer 1996).

For all his empathy with those who labor in the forest for a bare subsis-tence, Satya seems ultimately to be on the side of "deep ecology" and wil-derness preservation. He wishes that this "rich national resource" could be preserved for the nation like Yosemite or Krüger National Park, prefiguring the conservationist issues that inform *The Hungry Tide* and recent environ-mentalist debate (Bandyopadhyay 2002, 114, 213). He observes: "Human beings are only too greedy; I know that nothing would stand in the way of destroying an exquisite grove—all for a handful of cheena-grains and a couple of maize cobs. The settlers did not care much for the majesty of trees, they did not have eyes to see the grandeur of the land; their only concern was to fill their stomachs and to survive" (213). There is much in *Aranyak* that reflects (albeit from an Indian perspective) what Maria Mies (1993) has called "the white man's dilemma," an urban nostalgia for the aesthetics of an untouched nature, one in which the "natives" appear closer to nature than the city dwellers, but in which, too, the poor are blamed for not doing enough to honor and protect the wilderness they inhabit (Bandyopadhyay 2002, 213).

Satya occupies a seemingly uncolonized world, one in which nation usurps the place of empire. There is no allusion in the novel to such nationalist heroes as Gandhi, Nehru, or Bose, but Satya represents his time in the forest as a personal "discovery" of India, a phrase and a sentiment that anticipates Nehru's *Discovery of India* (1946) a decade later. The forest reveals a side of the country hitherto unknown to the author (and most middle-class Indians). "Only since coming to foreign lands," Satya remarks of the Bhagalpur forest, "had I come to know my own" (96). His nationalist self is shocked when the "innocent forest maid" with whom he is half in love has not even heard of "Bharatvarsha" (a nationalist name for India). At the same time, too, Satya's nationalist self is also half feudal: he makes no demur when villagers address him as "huzoor" ("your honor") and is pleased by his own acts of paternalistic benevolence. At one point he even refers to the forest as if it were his own personal kingdom. *Aranyak* is not explicitly a work of empire: in some ways it seems to deny its very existence and to posit instead an unmediated Indian engagement with the Indian environment. Colonialism appears very distant from the jungles of Bhagalpur. No white men intrude; the Raj receives no explicit mention. The rulers and the exploiters in this story are all Indian (though ultimately it is to the British that the landlords pay their dues just as it is the British who have set up and maintain the *zamindari* system). Almost the only point of reference to Europeans is a banyan tree, dubbed "Grant Saheb's tree" after the white man who used it as the base for survey operations thirty years earlier. The Santhal revolt against the East India Company in 1855 is mentioned only in passing; still less is said about the conflict generated by colonial forest laws since the 1870s. The collision, now familiar to historians, caused by colonial health policies and sanitary intervention, gets no coverage (a villager bribes a vaccinator not to immunize his son, who then dies of smallpox). Instead, it is Satya with his slight knowledge of hygiene and homoeopathy who tries to quell a cholera outbreak. Bibhutibhushan is silent on the forest protest movements and Gandhi-inspired *satyagrahas* of the period, just as he omits any reference to the *kisan* or peasant movements that had become widespread by the 1930s. The colonial appears exorcised rather than truly absent.

This is not a colonial text and yet one can repeatedly find in it colonial borrowings and inversions. The outsider's encounter with the jungle and its tribal inhabitants was a familiar trope in nineteenth-century European travel writing on India (Ball 1880; Arnold 2006). But where Europeans tended to present a negative view of the jungle as dark, dangerous, and unproductive, the haunt of wild beasts and bandits, Satya consciously revels in its beauty and variety as if taking delight in overturning colonialism's hostile aesthetic. *Aranyak* might almost have been subtitled *In Defense of Jungle*.

There is, though, a paradoxical episode in which in order to further beautify the wilderness, Satya sends to Calcutta for packets of Sutton's seeds containing English wildflowers: "Amongst these," he records, "the white beam, red campion and the stitchwort showed exceptional progress; the foxgloves and the wood anemones did not do badly either; but, despite our best efforts, the dog-roses and the honeysuckle could not be saved" (Bandyopadhyay 2002, 111). This is nature domesticated and Anglicized, perversely out of place, a vision of Surrey rather than life among the Santhals. One almost anticipates a postcolonial gardening-like-the-white man irony here, but Satya explains this bizarre act as arising from a "passionate desire to adorn the forest with flowers, creepers, plants and trees of all kinds" (111). He does, though, baulk at planting a bougainvillea: it is "so much a part of urban parks and gardens" that it would detract from "the special character of the forest" (112).

What also makes the environmentalism of *Aranyak* of postcolonial interest is the ultimate inability to escape imperial influence and capitalist infiltration. As already indicated, the novel offers few explicitly imperial points of reference. Strikingly, when Satya seeks to express the depth of his spiritual and emotional feeling for nature he draws on Hindu literary tradition—the Sanskrit dramatist Kalidasa, the *bhakti* poet Chaitanya. Bengalis are not beholden to the West for a language with which to glorify and spiritualize nature. However, it is otherwise when Satya turns to idioms of travel. Here he invokes European travel writing in order to convey his personal sense of venturing into the unknown: Marco Polo, Christopher Columbus, W. H. Hudson, Ernest Shackleton, and Sven Herdin all find mention. At one point Satya remarks, "I was lost in this mysterious and lonely beauty. Until this time, I had not known that there were such places to be found in India. It was like the deserts of Arizona and Navajo in the south of America that one sees in films or like the Gila River Basin described in Hudson's books" (57). There is here both a gesturing to the pre-eminence of European texts and (perhaps) a patriotic questioning of their authority, for one can find in India scenes and wonders that are "in no way inferior to the rocky deserts of Arizona or the veldts of Rhodesia" (62). But, overall, *Aranyak* suggests the difficulty—in landscape as in history—of "provincializing Europe" (Chakrabarty 2000, 3–23). To travel, above all to represent the experience of travel, it is necessary to inhabit the European imagination, even if it is then still possible to tweak it.

NARRATIVIZING URBAN NATURE

It would be easy enough to set *Aranyak* alongside a nineteenth-century British travel narrative and to make comparisons and contrasts between the two. However, I want to attempt a rather more hazardous connection, one that retains the imperial voice but transposes nature from the countryside to the city. I seek to do this in part because (for the colonial period at least) urban India has been relatively ignored in environmental histories and yet, from a present-day perspective, as urban populations continue to rise, it is surely the city environment rather than the idealized or execrated countryside that demands investigation. For this purpose, there are, so far as I am aware, few fictional representations available; but there are, in abundance, environmental narratives of another kind to be found in public health reports and commentaries from the 1860s to the late 1930s. Of course, sanitary narratives were not intended to perform the same task as novels, but works of fiction (remembering Dickens' *Hard Times* [1854]) could as well promote the cause of public health reform as any Chadwickian enquiry, just as many of the sanitary reports of the colonial period, some the length of a respectable novella, deployed well-honed narrative themes of loss and redemption and consciously deployed an elaborate, self-consciously literary, language to exhort their readers and to characterize, castigate, and lament the fate of misguided sanitary subjects. Sanitary texts speak through a number of different, often contradictory, voices, but so do many works of fiction. And although produced by individuals who were not usually native to the place they describe, sanitary narratives have a spatial specificity and locational fixity that contrast with the itinerant form of imperial gaze. Here I focus on Calcutta (Kolkata), by 1914 a city of over a million people, but the themes discussed apply equally to most Indian cities.

Although we may think of cities as unnatural places, the antithesis of the pastoral idyll or the "howling wilderness," it is striking how often in British India they were characterized by reference to precisely those elements used to identify nature in the wild. This might be universally true but, without embarking on an extensive comparative exercise, my point can only be that the apparently inappropriate transposition of nature into the urban life was seen in colonial health narratives to demonstrate the deficiencies of the Indian city and hence of the society of which it formed an indicative part. Here the idea of "jungle," already referred to in relation to *Aranyak*, has a striking salience. "Jungle" is a term which, perhaps following Upton Sinclair's 1906 novel about the Chicago slaughterhouses, has come to be widely used to describe the urban warfare "of each against all," in which the oppressed and exploited poor struggle (often vainly) to survive (1906, 91, 262).[5] It has been eloquently used to describe one's inner being—"the dark, luxuriant jungle of the self," in John Williams' apt phrase (McGahern 2003, xi). But "jungle" was also used, less metaphorically, in relation to nineteenth-century Calcutta to describe how patches of the city had subsided from civil respectability into a virtual state of nature. The report of a commission appointed to investigate the city's sanitary condition in 1885 remarked on the way in which many *bustees* (slums) were surrounded by "filth and jungle," or, through neglect, had become "swampy and jungly" (*Report of the Commission* 1885, app. 1, xxii, xxv). In this instance, and others like it, the appearance of jungle, and not its mere analogy, was used to capture the established negativity associated with rural jungles—as dangerous, unhealthy, untamed, and chaotic places. The jungles of which Bibhutibhushan wrote with such enthusiasm were considered by the British to be "noxious" places where tigers lurked and malarial fever was rife[6] ("Jungle and Malaria in Bengal" 1930, 639–40). For many of India's early environmentalists, removing jungle vegetation was essential to improving health, especially when it encroached on urban living. Jungle stood in contrast, too, to the contained and orderly spaces formally assigned to nature in the city, notably the botanic garden at Sibpur, across the Hooghly from Calcutta, which in the nineteenth century was a favored place of European resort (Stocqueler 1854, 20, 111–12, 171). However, one could, in contrary vein, interpret jungle's urban return as sign and symbol of environmental (and human) resilience. It is suggestive of this alternative reading that in his novel *Animal's People*, about the legacy of the Bhopal gas disaster of 1984, Indra Sinha welcomes the reappearance of jungle at the abandoned Union Carbide plant (Sinha 2007, 338). "Animal," his principal character, observes a "silent war" being waged at the devastated site, remarking "Mother Nature's trying to take back the land" (31).

However, urban jungle was just one of several environmental tropes used colonially to demonstrate nature's continuing hold over the Indian city, denying it the civilized modernity colonial sanitarians aspired to. It is thus argued that the Indian monsoon and a tropical climate and vegetation impeded sanitary progress and presented problems beyond those faced by public-health workers in the West. In a lecture titled "The Sanitation of Calcutta" published in the *Indian Medical Gazette* in 1884, Dr. Kenneth McLeod attributed the city's fundamental problems to being located "in the centre of a tropical delta" (1884, 201). This was in his view "a condition of profound sanitary importance," for it implied "swamp, luxuriant vegetation, high temperature, great humidity, and active decay of organic matter, vegetable and animal. Conditions more unfavourable than these for the accommodation of animal life—human and otherwise—could hardly be conceived" (201). This environmentalist logic persisted well into the twentieth century and was even used to question the increasingly dominant germ theory of disease causation.

The determining power of a "tropical" location, climate, and vegetation was not the only way in which nature threatened the city. In the late nineteenth century, a series of cyclones devastated Calcutta, exemplifying the continuing power of tropical nature over India's leading metropolis (Massey 1918, 28–42). As Colin McFarlane has remarked with respect to colonial sanitarians in nineteenth-century Bombay, "addressing sanitation meant dealing with nature ... sanitation brought city and nature together" (McFarlane 2009, 418). This encompassed discussion of climate, soil, tides, air and water quality, but also the city's many animal inhabitants. Calcutta and Bombay were animal cities, places into which animals inappropriately intruded or flourished to excess. Pigs and dogs scavenged in the streets; kites, vultures, and adjutant birds plundered from the air. Cows, protected by their sanctity, wandered the streets or were housed in insanitary hovels.[7] Markets, slaughterhouses and a host of industrial activities (like bone crushing and leather tanning) relied on the continuing presence of animals in, or on the margins of, the city. Municipal regulations sought, in the interests of human health, to control the animal population, to confine urban beasts to approved and regulated sites or eliminate them altogether. The need to control animal nature was of wider colonial concern—hence the bounties offered for the killing of tigers, snakes, and, when plague struck, rats. In the city, however, the problem of containing and regulating animal life proved particularly troublesome, especially when Indians' religious beliefs and social practices were—or were represented to be—at variance with sanitarian ideals.

Then, too, there was the problem of poison. As Pablo Mukherjee has indicated, poisoning has come to be a central motif in India's postcolonial ecocriticism, from the Union Carbide gas leak at Bhopal to the self-poisoning by pesticides of indebted Indian farmers, and, one might add, the widespread presence of arsenic in groundwater in Bangladesh and West Bengal (Mukherjee 2010; Meharg 2005). However, poisoning and pollution were common environmental tropes in the colonial period, too, not least in relation to cities. Calcutta and Bombay seemed to ooze poison. According to miasmatic medical discourse, it emanated from swamps and jungles, from *bustees* and burial-grounds, from factory chimneys and industrial effluvia.[8] Accounts of homicidal or suicidal poisoning by arsenic, opium, and *datura* figured repeatedly in police records and the annual reports of the chemical examiner—these in turn furnishing the raw material for newspaper stories and sensationalist novels. Poisoning captured a collective sense of urban environmental unease. Fear of toxic food, water, even betel nuts and medicaments, circulated in the city, fostering rumor and nurturing alarm.[9] Leakage of methane gas from city sewers was one such concern. A European witness to Calcutta's 1885 sanitary commission claimed that residents were being poisoned by gas leaking from municipal sewers and seeping into their homes. He added that, as the inhabitants of Calcutta slept with their windows wide open at night because of the heat, this "very dangerous poison" was ten times more lethal in "tropical" Calcutta than it would have been in a temperate climate (*Report of the Commission* 1885, app. 2, lxii). Decades before Bhopal, poisoning fueled fears of an urban apocalypse. In 1882, the city was rife with reports about the stench emanating from municipal sewers. The *Englishman* newspaper declared that: "Unless immediate and heroic measures are adopted to grapple with the calamity that has overtaken Calcutta, the Town will soon become uninhabitable … [t]his smell is lethal" (lxvii). Somehow Calcutta survived, but the underlying fear of environmental poisoning persisted.

In sanitary discourse, nature was also brought into troubling proximity to the civilized city by the attitudes and behavior of its Indian inhabitants. Thus, on the foreshore at Calcutta proper "sanitary observances" were being "disregarded" by "large gangs of coolies" from an adjacent mill who "foul[ed] the bank" (*Annual Report of the Sanitary Commissioner for Bengal* 1881, 67–68). It was especially the poor, with their insanitary habits and unhygienic ignorance, who were held responsible for the fecal contamination of wells and water courses, for answering "the call of nature" by sullying waste ground around factories and railroad yards. As in the jungles of Bhagalpur, this censorious literature reflects on the *environment* of the poor: it has little to say about what Ramachandra Guha and Joan Martínez-Alier have termed the environmental*ism* of the poor. In 1877, Calcutta's health officer observed:

> It is impossible to conceive of a more perfect combination of all the evils of crowded city life with primitive filthiness and disorder than is present in the native population of Calcutta. Dirt, in the most intense and noxious forms that a dense population can produce, covers the ground, saturates the water, infects the air and finds, in the habits and incidents of the people's lives, every possible facility for re-entering their bodies; while ventilation could not be more shunned in their houses than it is if the climate were arctic instead of tropical.
>
> (*Administration Report of the Calcutta Municipality* 1877, app. 1, 4)

Indian society in general, and Hindu society in particular, was seen to sanction religious beliefs and social practices that, by Western standards, were not only primitive and unhygienic, but also assumed a benevolence in nature—in fresh air, sunlight, running water, and untreated milk—which modern science repeatedly showed to be misplaced. Typical of this was colonial characterization of the Ganges, understood by devout Hindus as inherently pure and immune to contamination, as a "vast sewer" ("Notes from India" 1911, 731). At issue here were conflicting notions of how purity was constituted—whether through religious faith or by scientific endeavor—and contrasting (but not always contradictory) ideas of what "pollution," which in India held both a ritual and an environmental meaning, actually signified.[10] For Hindus, bathing in a sacred tank (reservoir) could be a means of ensuring ritual purification, but for the sanitarian it could have precisely the opposite meaning. In calling for tank-bathing to be banned, the 1885 Calcutta commission declared: "Bathing by immersion must soon pollute the purest water, and it is impossible to renew the water of tanks with sufficient frequency to keep them free from pollution" (*Report of the Commission*, 29). Here "pollution" could have only one conceivable meaning.

CONCLUSION

How do these different narrative visions—the Bengali novel, the colonial sanitary texts—enlarge our postcolonial understanding of the Indian environment? First, they suggest ways in which the discourse of rural and urban environments in India between the 1860s and 1930s can be subjected to a common process of environmental humanities analysis, even though the sources are ostensibly only about one (the forest) or the other (the city). These environments are linked materially—through urban consumption of rural products, such as timber, grain, jute, and medicinal plants sent to the city, or the wealth that absentee *zamindars*, resident in Calcutta, extracted from their rural estates.[11] But the relationship is as much perceptual as material, as the shared idiom of "the jungle" suggests. Conceptually, town and country might remain environmentally distinct, but in the texts they repeatedly intersect, becoming discursive vehicles for contrast and connectivity, for the idyllic or the apocalyptic. If Satya's grim vision of the future of the Bhagalpur forests were to be accepted, ultimately countryside and city were destined for the same environmental catastrophe. For India, where city and countryside have too often been separated, there is much to be gained by returning them to the same paradigm of environmental change and (mis)management.

Second, just as there is value in appraising representations of city and countryside alongside each other, so is there in measuring an environmental novel like *Aranyak*, written in Bengali by an Indian author, alongside the English-language, nonfiction texts of colonial sanitarians. Each has its own subjectivity, its own presumed audience, its own narrator-centered narrative. Environmental idioms and attitudes flit, often unconsciously, between one textual form and another. Satya can never entirely free himself from the colonial travel-writing genre or from the desire to plant English seeds in an Indian jungle. In both novel and sanitary text, the relationship of the poor to the environment is particularly problematic: are they the guardians of the landscape or its destroyers? Are they hapless victims or the cause of pollution, epidemics, and resurgent jungle? In both textual forms idioms of health and disease provide critical points of entry into broader issues of the benevolence or insalubrity of nature and the cultural values and scientific attitudes that inform environment use. The city is no less a "moral landscape" than the countryside, whether represented through a novel or a sanitary text.

Finally, just as there are linkages between town and countryside, between novel "fiction" and sanitary "fact," so are there between the colonial and postcolonial. The environmental situations that the forest in *Aranyak* and the sanitary cityscape of the Calcutta reports describe are not far removed from present-day scenarios. Moreover, although this essay has used "colonial" and "European" as largely synonymous, in actuality by the 1900s the voice of sanitarian discourse and environmental authority was already in part Indian. One of the most influential figures in environmental and public health debates in Calcutta between the 1890s and 1914 was that of Chunilal Bose, the Bengal government's chemical examiner and an active publicist for environmental and social reform. In this sense, among others, what for convenience we may designate as "colonial" policy and opinion increasingly incorporated Indian agency just as *Aranyak* both reflected a Bengali cultural and social consciousness and carried forward some of the legacies of imperialism into a postcolonial age.

NOTES

1. Further examples include Jim Endersby's *Imperial Nature* (2008) and edited collections such as John Mackenzie's *Imperialism and the Natural World* (1997) and Tom Griffiths and Libby Robin's *Ecology and Empire* (1990).
2. For example, J. R. McNeill, *Mosquito Empires: Ecology and War in the Greater Caribbean, 1620–1914* (2010).
3. Another instance is Clare Leighton's *Four Hedges* (1935).
4. I must confess to having a particular attachment to Ray's *Pather Panchali* (1955). It is the first Indian film I ever saw—at school in London around 1960—and it undoubtedly shaped my own expectations of India and its rural environment.
5. Apart from this rather Darwinian allusion (91, and another on 262), Sinclair gives no indication of where his idea of the jungle came from. Kipling's *Jungle Book* (1894) is a possible source, but well before that the word *jangala*, of Sanskrit and north Indian vernacular origin, had become naturalized in English and other European languages.
6. Bibhutibhushan's appreciation of the jungle coincided with medical research questioning the established view that malaria was particularly prevalent in jungle environments; see "Jungle and Malaria in Bengal" (1930).
7. For city cowsheds, see *Report of the Commission Appointed to Enquire into Certain Matters Connected with the Sanitation of the Town of Calcutta* (1885), p. 43.
8. For some of these "poisons," see *First Annual Report of the Sanitary Commission for Bengal, 1864–65* (1865), pp. 80–83.
9. On the betel nut scare, see Bengal Municipal (Medical) Proceedings (1910).
10. On this issue, see Sharma (2007).
11. Calcutta's material reliance on its vast rural hinterland has never been adequately explored: one model for such an analysis would be William Cronon's *Nature's Metropolis: Chicago and the Great West* (1991).

REFERENCES

Administration Report of the Calcutta Municipality for 1876. 1877. Calcutta: Printing Office of the Commissioners.
Anker, Peder. 2001. *Imperial Ecology: Environmental Order in the British Empire, 1895–1945.* Cambridge: Harvard University Press.
Annual Report of the Sanitary Commissioner for Bengal, 1881. 1882. Calcutta: Bengal Secretariat Press.
Arnold, David. 2006. *The Tropics and the Traveling Gaze: India, Landscape, and Science, 1800–1856.* Seattle: Washington University Press.
———. 2013. "Pollution, Toxicity and Public Health in Metropolitan India, 1850–1939." *Journal of Historical Geography* 42: 124–133.
Ball, Valentine. 1880. *Jungle Life in India: Or the Journeys and Journals of an Indian Geologist.* London: De La Rue.

Bandyopadhyay, Bibhutibhushan. (1929) 1968. *Pather Panchali (Song of the Road)* Translated by T. W. Clark and Tarapada Mukherji. Bloomington: Indiana University Press.

———. (1931) 1999. *Aparajito (The Unvanquished)*. Translated by Gopa Majumdar. Delhi, HaperCollins.

———. (1939) 2002. *Aranyak: Of the Forest*. Translated by R. Bhattacharya. Calcutta: Seagull Books.

Beinart, William, and Lotte Hughes. 2007. *Environment and Empire*. Oxford: Oxford University Press.

Carson, Rachel. (1962) 2002. *Silent Spring*. Boston: Houghton Mifflin.

Chakrabarty, Dipesh. 2000. *Provincializing Europe: Postcolonial Thought and Historical Difference*. Princeton: Princeton University Press.

Cronon, William. 1991. *Nature's Metropolis: Chicago and the Great West*. New York: W. W. Norton.

Crosby, Alfred W. 1986. *Ecological Imperialism: The Biological Expansion of Europe, 900–1900*. Cambridge: Cambridge University Press.

Dickens, Charles. (1854) 1907. *Hard Times*. London: Dent.

Endersby, Jim. 2008. *Imperial Nature: Joseph Hooker and the Practices of Victorian Science*. Chicago: Chicago University Press.

Ghosh, Amitav. 2004. *The Hungry Tide*. London: HarperCollins.

Griffiths, Tom, and Libby Robin, eds. 1997. *Ecology and Empire: Environmental History of Settler* Societies. Edinburgh: Keele University Press.

Grove, Richard H. 1995. *Green Imperialism: Colonial Expansion, Tropical Island Edens and the Origins of Environmentalism, 1600–1860*. Cambridge: Cambridge University Press.

Guha, Ramachandra, and Joan Martínez-Alier. 1997. *Varieties of Environmentalism: Essays North and South*. London: Earthscan.

Hudson, William Henry. (1904) 1931. *Green Mansions*. New York: Grosset and Dunlap.

"Jungle and Malaria in Bengal." 1930. *Indian Medical Gazette* 65: 639–640.

Killingsworth, M. J., and J. S. Palmer. 1996. "Millennial Ecology: The Apocalyptic Narrative from *Silent Spring* to Global Warming." In *Green Culture: Environmental Rhetoric in Contemporary America*, edited by Carl G. Herndl and Stuart C. Brown, 21–45. Madison: University of Wisconsin Press.

Kipling, Rudyard. 1894. *The Jungle Book*. London: Macmillian.

Leighton, Clare. 1935. *Four Hedges: a Gardener's Chronicle*. New York: Macmillian.

MacKenzie, John M. 1988. *The Empire of Nature: Hunting, Conservation and British Imperialism*. Manchester: Manchester University Press.

———, ed. 1990. *Imperialism and the Natural World*. Manchester: Manchester University Press.

Martínez-Alier, Joan. 2002. *The Environmentalism of the Poor: A Study of Ecological Conflicts and Valuation*. Cheltenham: Edward Elgar.

Massey, Montague. 1918. *Recollections of Calcutta for Over Half a Century*. Calcutta: Thacker, Spink.

McGahern, John. 2003. "Preface." In *Augustus*, written by John Williams, vii–xiii. London: Vintage Books.

McLeod, Kenneth. "The Sanitation of Calcutta." 1884. *Indian Medical Gazette* 119: 201–203.

McNeill, J. R., 2010. *Mosquito Empires: Ecology and War in the Greater Caribbean, 1620–1914*. Cambridge: Cambridge University Press.

Meharg, Andrew A. 2005. *Venomous Earth: How Arsenic Caused the World's Worst Mass Poisoning*. Basingstoke: Macmillan, 2005.

Mies, Maria. 1993. "White Man's Dilemma: His Search for What He Has Destroyed." In *Ecofeminism*, edited by Maria Mies and Vandana Shiva, 132–163. London: Zed Books.

Mukherjee, Upamanyu Pablo. 2010. *Postcolonial Environments: Nature, Culture and the Contemporary Indian Novel in English*. Basingstoke: Palgrave Macmillan.

Nehru, Jawaharlal. 1946. *The Discovery of India*. New York: The John Day Co.

Nixon, Rob. 2005. "Environmentalism and Postcolonialism." In *Postcolonial Studies and Beyond*, edited by Ania Looma, Suvir Kaul, Matti Bunzil, Antoinette Burton, and Jed Esty, 233–251. Durham: Duke University Press.

"Notes from India." 1911. *Lancet*, 178: 731–732.

Pather Panchali. 1955. Directed by Satyajit Ray. West Bengal: Government of West Bengal.

Pratt, Mary Louise. 1992. *Imperial Eyes: Travel Writing and Transcultural*. London: Routledge.

Reeve, N. H.1998. "Feathered Women: W. H. Hudson's *Green Mansions*." In *Writing the Environment: Ecocritcism and Literature*, edited by Richard Kerridge and Neil Sammells, 134–145. London: Zed Books.

Report of the Commission Appointed to Enquire into Certain Matters Connected with the Sanitation of the Town of Calcutta. 1885. Calcutta: Bengal Secretariat Press.

Sharma, Meenakshi. 2007. "Polluted River or Goddess and Saviour? The Ganga in the Discourses of Modernity and Hinduism." In *Five Emus to the King of Siam: Environment and Empire*, edited by Helen Tiffin, 31–50. Amsterdam: Rodopi.

Sinclair, Upton. 1986. *The Jungle*. New York: Penguin.

Sinha, Indra. 2007. *Animal's People*. London: Simon & Schuster.

Stocqueler, J. H. 1854. *The Hand-Book of British India*. 2nd ed. London: W. H. Allen.

United Kingdom, India Office Records. 1910. Bengal Municipal (Medical) Proceedings. Sept. 25–26. British Library, London.

White, Gilbert. (1789) 1949. *The Natural History of Selborne*. London: Dent.

2 "The Perverse Little People of the Hills"

Unearthing Ecology and Transculturation in Reginald Farrer's Alpine Plant Hunting

Jill Didur

> To be a great gardener a man must be close to Mother Earth in spirit, able to work with his hands as well as with his brain; a man who loves the growing plant and will sacrifice material things to understand it. It was such men as these who in the twentieth century made English gardens and gardeners the envy and pride of the world, who put the hardy rock plant in the van of horticulture, designed the rock garden, and the landscape garden, discovered the alpine, and showed the world how gardening might bring peace and contentment to a ravaged generation.
>
> (Kingdon-Ward 1948, 20)

On the surface, it is laughable how Frank Kingdon-Ward's 1948 *Commonsense Rock Gardening* characterizes British horticultural practice as ushering in an era of "peace and contentment," even while Britain was in the midst of the sometimes violent dismantlement of its empire. One of the most prolific plant hunters of his generation, Kingdon-Ward is the author of over two dozen books that recount the details of his botanical expeditions, provide descriptions of the exotic plants he collected, and offer advice on how to grow those foreign plants back in the gardens of Britain. Despite the irony of Ward crediting plant hunting and British gardening with setting an example for the world given the role botanical exploration has played in furthering empire, I want to suggest that narratives about botanical exploration and rock and alpine gardening can be a resource for countercolonial thought in the environmental humanities.

This chapter focuses on rock and alpine garden culture in the first half of the twentieth-century and its relation to colonial accounts of travel and botanical exploration in South and Central Asia. I examine how colonial plant hunters and garden writers like Frank Kingdon-Ward, William Robinson, and Reginald Farrer, came to question their taken-for-granted ideas about alterity through travels in unfamiliar landscapes in the colonial peripheries, and horticultural experiments with exotic alpine plants in the gardens of the Britain. Taking the work of Farrer as my central example, I argue that plant hunters' advice to amateur gardeners on how to create the necessary ecological conditions for exotic alpines to thrive in the gardens of Britain, relied on a renegotiation of colonial ways of seeing foreign people, cultures, landscapes, and environments within the imperial center. Plant hunters' discussions of the ecological and aesthetic conditions most suited to the needs of foreign rock and alpine plants hinge on a practice of accommo- dating, rather than taming, the influence of the foreign, and encourage gar- deners to consider how this might extend to the communities and landscapes from where the plants were extracted.

Transculturation—a concept first used in 1947 by anthropologist Fernando Ortiz to describe the transformation of Cuban culture in the wake of Spanish colonialism—is central to this discussion. Ortiz uses the concept to describe how the impact of the slave trade, plantation culture, and colonialism continue to reverberate in Cuban culture since the time of European contact; relying heavily on botanical metaphors, he defines transculturation as a violent experience of being "torn from" one's place of origin, and "suffering the shock of this first uprooting and a harsh transplanting" (1995, 100). Though Ortiz's definition of transculturation emerges out of a discussion about the transformation of culture in the aftermath of plantation colonialism, its use of botanical metaphors and ideas of uprooting and transplanting underscore its relevance to a discus- sion of the history of botanical colonialism. However, rather than focusing on this process in the colonial periphery, I will instead follow Mary Louis Pratt in asking the "heretical" question: "[W]ith respect to representation, how does one speak of transculturation from the colonies to the metropo- lis?" (1992, 6). "Transculturation," as Pratt points out, "is a phenomenon of the contact zone" (6). "While the imperial metropolis tends to under- stand itself as determining the periphery [...] it habitually blinds itself to the ways in which the periphery determines the metropolis—beginning, perhaps, with the obsessive need to present and re-represent it peripheries and its others continually to itself" (6). "Borders and all," Pratt reminds us, "the entity called Europe was constructed from the outside in as much as from the inside out" (6). Transculturation in relation to the history of botanical exploration, expresses itself indirectly in a variety of ways at the British imperial center in the first half of the twentieth century— from a fascination with accounts of botanical expeditions in colonial regions, to the popularity of rock and alpine gardening and advice books on how to design a garden best suited to the needs transplanted exotics. Examining both garden and travel writing, I argue that twentieth-century alpine plant hunters like Farrer, Robinson, and Kingdon-Ward, "present and re-present" the periphery to themselves and the imperial metropolis in ways that signal a transformation of their habitus through travel in South and Central Asia that reverberates in their views on imperial gar- dening culture back in Britain. With attention to transculturation in dis- cussions of ecology and garden aesthetics in Farrer's narratives of plant collecting and rock and alpine gardening, I consider how British rock and alpine garden culture might provide a model for structuring counter- colonial global ecologies in the present.

"THE TRUE ALPINE GARDEN SPIRIT?"

Judging by the conference proceedings for a 1936 meeting and exhibition on "rock gardens and rock plants," jointly organized by the Royal Horticultural Society and Alpine Garden Society, British gardeners in the first half of the twentieth century saw the task of domesticating foreign plants to their rock and alpine gardens as an extension of colonialism's civilizing mission. In his opening address to the conference, the President of the RHS, Lord Aberconway, relates an anecdote about a gardener who encouraged him to purchase a particular alpine plant for his garden "because [he] had always heard that it is a very difficult plant to grow" (1935, 8). Aberconway uses this anecdote to illustrate how he sees the fledgling Alpine Garden Society as engaged in a "cause" that is "just and good," and goes on to describe "the true alpine garden spirit" as guiding the British public's desire "to grow difficult plants for the same reason we prefer to climb difficult mountains" (8). Of course, Aberconway's coupling of the history of mountaineering with rock and alpine gardening unwittingly draws attention to how imperial discourse underpins the history of *both* leisure activities; as Stephen Slemon (2008) has argued, "mountaineering has consistently been narrativized as playing a socially symbolic role in the advancement of European imperialism" (240). Victorian mountaineer and Oxford don, H. B. George, for example, describes "the climbing spirit," as "a form of restless energy, that love of action for its own sake, of exploring the earth and subduing it, which has made England the colonizer of the world" (George in Hansan 1995, 320). "Mountaineers themselves," explains Peter Hansan, "employed the language of empire to justify their climbing" (1995, 320).

Lord Aberconway's remarks also suggest, however, that the conditions required for "difficult" alpine plants to flourish in the imperial center depended on the transculturation of English garden culture. In contrast to Aberconway's view of British plant hunters and gardeners as engaged in an exercise of "exploring and subduing the earth," attention to the relationship between colonial plant-hunting memoirs and garden writing makes it possible to see the practice of imagining, hunting, growing, and writing about alpine plants as governed by a logic of accommodation, and recognition of the earth's agency. The plant-hunting memoirs and garden writing of Reginald Farrer, for instance, can be read as an example of a colonial subject who came away from his experience of foreign plants and people with a view that questioned the idea that they were in need of a civilizing influence or domestication. Where, for example, Farrer's travel accounts acknowledge how his access to "difficult to grow" alpine plants from South and Central Asia is mediated by unfamiliar ecologies and climates, he also registers his dependence on the local communities and guides who assisted him in his plant collecting. Farrer's garden manuals go on to provide detailed and sometimes cheeky reminders to

British gardeners on how to design their gardens to best reproduce the natural aesthetics of exotic alpine plants' original environments, as well as and the ecological conditions required for them to flourish once they are transplanted into the gardens of Britain. Views such as Farrer's that "spanned the colonial divide between the West and its others" (Mueggler 2008, 136) represented a significant departure from the logic of extraction characteristic of colonial botanical science; in that mode, the identity of a plant was isolated from the people and places it originated from, a practice reflected in the use of the Linnaean classification system. As Pratt has argued, "[n]atural history extracted specimens not only from their organic or ecological relations with each other, but also from their places in other peoples economies, histories, social and symbolic systems" (1992, 31). The ecological demands of rock and alpine plants reversed this trend in the first half of the twentieth century, putting pressure on gardening culture in a Britain to adapt itself to the needs of "exotics." Farrer's accounts of travel and gardening advice, therefore, reveal a man who saw the need for plant hunters and gardeners to enter into relations of interdependence not only with the plants they collected, but also with the people, landscapes, and ecological conditions from which they had been extracted.

The early twentieth-century rock and alpine garden in Britain was often ill designed and frequently failed to provide the conditions for alpine plants to thrive. In the opening pages of Farrer's 1912 garden manual, *The Rock-Garden*, for instance, he reviews this early tendency in British gardening practice in prose saturated with biting condescension:

> Times have wholly changed for the rock-garden. Fifty years ago it was merely the appanage of the large pleasure ground. In some odd corner, or in some dank tree-haunted hollow, you rigged up a dump of broken cement blocks, and added bits of stone and fragments of statuary. You called this "the Rockery," and proudly led your friends to see it, and planted it all over with Periwinkle to hide the hollows in which your Alpines had promptly died. In other words, you considered only the stones, and not the plants that were to live among them. (1–2)

Farrer's tendency to mock and dismiss expensive, ill-conceived rock gardens that were unable to sustain the plants they contained was well known by this time, and was a consistent theme in all of his garden writing throughout his life. More than just representing an occasional reference to the horticultural community's ignorance of the specific ecological conditions foreign alpine plants required to thrive in the English garden, Farrer's writing is symptomatic of a complicated renegotiation of colonial responses to alterity during the first half of the twentieth century. In an interesting reversal of cultural superiority associated with colonial endeavors, horticultural practice transformed the cultural and material character of the imperial center through its links to botanical exploration.

EXOTICS IN THE GARDEN

The relationship between gardens in the imperial center and the colonial periphery is one that Rebecca Preston has described as offering "a very private form of imperial display which quietly expanded the horizons of its audience and allowed for a form of imaginative travel beyond, yet framed by the realm of home" (2003, 195). The making of these "Other landscapes suggested by exotics and their arrangement within the garden," Preston notes, "were arguably as important in shaping the imaginative geographies of British imperialism as exploration and travel abroad" (195). The presence of exotics in the imperial garden at home, therefore, was always in tension with the activities and accounts of botanical exploration in the colonies and their border regions. Like other forms of what Said calls "domestic imperial culture" (1993, 95), writing about botanical exploration and British garden culture in the late nineteenth and early twentieth century was a phenomenon fraught with the contradictory discourses that both legitimated, but also threatened, and occasionally undermined the project of empire.

The use of the term "exotic" as a noun to refer to a plant that one cultivates in a foreign environment dates back to the mid-sixteenth century. Earlier uses of the term as an adjective connote something that is introduced from abroad. From the Greek *exotikos*, meaning literally "from the outside," exotics introduced in Britain during the colonial era "helped frame the unknown world in a familiar context, and their culture in the home landscape allowed a personal as well as national understanding of far-away place" (Preston 2003, 195). "The exotic" as Graham Huggan suggests in a more general sense, "is the perfect term to describe the domesticating process through which commodities are taken from the margins and reabsorbed into mainstream culture" (2001, 22). In the context of this discussion of rock and alpine gardening, however, it is important to note the unfinished or multidirectional quality of this absorption process. "This process," Huggan explains, "is to some extent reciprocal; mainstream culture is always altered by its contact with the margins, even if it finds ingenious ways of looking, or of pretending to look, the same" (22). Exoticism is a discourse that sustains the pretense that the cultural transaction taking place can be regulated in a manner that leaves the mainstream intact even while this is not actually the case. "To keep the margins exotic," writes Huggan, "—at once threateningly strange and reassuringly familiar—is the objective of the mainstream; it is an objective which it can never fail to pose, but which it can never reach" (22).

It follows, therefore, that the process of exotic plant domestication is never fully resolved. "Domestication," as Anna Tsing argues,

> is ordinarily understood as human control over other species. That such relations might also change humans is generally ignored. Moreover, domestication tends to be imagined as a hard line: You are either in the human fold or you are out in the wild. Because this dichotomisation stems from an ideological commitment to human mastery, it supports the most outrageous fantasies of domestic control, on the one hand and wild species self-making on the other. (2012, 144)

Nowhere does the success of integrating the exotic into the mainstream through mutual transformation become more obvious in horticultural practice than in the history of the rock and alpine gardening; the failure to adapt the ecological conditions of the garden to the needs of the alpine plant will result in its death after transplantation. It is the tension between the domestication and circulation of otherness in relation to exotic plants, and their singular status as living objects, that makes the aesthetic and material practices associated with rock and alpine gardening so visibly ambiguous. In fact, Reginald Farrer's interest in cultivating alpine plants from Asia in Britain is a good example of how some forms of globalization resist the collage and eclecticism characteristic of mainstream contemporary postmodern global culture.[1] During the period of the rock and alpine gardening "craze" (1900–1950), Farrer's oeuvre stresses the conditions required for alpine plants to flourish in the gardens of Britain, and urges gardeners to adapt the condition of their gardens to the soil and climatic needs of their exotics. This particular period of horticultural history and the writing and gardening practices associated with it, therefore, serve as an important reminder of how popular culture concerned with exoticism is a potential source of transculturation in the imperial metropolis—a starting point for questioning taken for granted assumptions about domestication, difference, and alterity.

PLANT HUNTING AND THE RISE OF ECOLOGY

Before examining the move toward transculturation and rethinking exoticism in Farrer's work, it is useful to review the history of rock and alpine gardening and its ties to the emergence of ecological discourse. The emergence of rock and alpine gardening culture is embedded in the history of alpine exploration, tourism, and mountaineering, all activities that began in Europe and later expanded to the Asian Himalayan region. Rock and alpine gardening is a movement that gained momentum in the late nineteenth century, prompted by a shift away from relying on Victorian glass houses with a large staff to cultivate exotic species, toward the idea of maintaining a more self-sufficient "rockery," where hardy or "gardenworthy" plants could be "naturalized," or expected to be maintained outdoors on a year-round basis. Early interest in alpine plants in Europe, however, was initially generated by their medicinal uses in the eighteenth century. As Lambin points out, early eighteenth-century accounts of travel and exploration in the Swiss Alps rarely referred to alpine flora in any significant way, focusing instead on the geological characteristics of different mountainous regions (1994, 241). Interest in alpines' horticultural value only came with increased access to the mountainous regions of Europe during the nineteenth century as a result of newly built roads and trains, a modern phenomenon that made holidaying in alpine regions more common. As British tourism in Swiss alpine landscapes surged, plants from the region were brought home by amateur botanists and serious horticulturists as mementos of their experiences abroad, adding to the desire to cultivate them in British gardens (242).

Despite this almost two hundred year trajectory of cultural and historical interest in alpine landscapes, the popular practice of building alpine gardens as we would recognize them today did not really gain momentum until the late nineteenth century. One of the most well-known rock gardens in Britain at this time was designed in 1871 by James McNab at the Royal Botanic Garden, Edinburgh. McNab's effort is especially significant to my discussion, as his design placed much emphasis on providing the ideal soil and drainage conditions for growing the alpine plants, a distinguishing feature of the rock garden movement. As McNab explained in a December 1871 issue of *The Garden*, the success he achieved in maintaining alpines in the small compartments with soil tailored to the needs of individual plants encouraged him to transfer plants previously maintained in pots into the main outdoor rockery (Thomas 1989, 67). While garden historians note that there was no real consensus on what a rock garden should look like at this time, a strong emphasis came to be placed on creating miniaturized versions of mountainous landscapes. For example, Frank Crisp's alpine garden (built in 1880), was made up of "moraines and marble glaciers at the foot of a model Matterhorn, a reduced version of the famous Swiss peak that Ruskin had so minutely studied" (Lambin 1994, 244). William Robinson's *Alpine Flowers for English Gardens*, first published in 1870, sought to capitalize on the growing interest in alpine plants in English gardens, and emphasized what was described as a "wild" aesthetic for rock garden design.[2] In Robinson's book, he personifies alpine plants as "mother of earth['s] … loveliest children" possessing a hardiness and exceptional beauty that enables them to thrive in high altitude conditions, or what he calls, "Nature's ruined battleground" (1870a, x). Robinson emphasized a horticultural style that came to be associated with the idea of the "natural garden," with alpine plants characterized as innocent children of Nature, in need of protection by a benevolent figure.[3]

The idea of the garden as a 'nature preserve' which emerged at this time has been linked to reactions against the visible effects of the industrial revolution on the environment in Britain, and the influence of Darwin's theory of evolution (Wolschke-Bulmahn 1992, 195). While horticulturists may not have known the extent of the effects of human agricultural and industrial activity on the climate, air, water, and soil conditions, there was a shared sense that a new period in environmental history had begun. For example, Sheail notes that naturalists began to draw past and present comparisons between the status of plants observed in Floras and Fauna compiled in the mid-eighteenth century, with changes in the same context a hundred years later found in publications such as Babington's 1860 *Flora of Cambridgeshire* (1982, 131). Furthermore, links between horticultural practice and Darwinian thought can also be attributed to the close intellectual relationship between Robinson and Darwin. When, for example, William Robinson became a Fellow of the Linnaean Society in 1866, his nomination was sponsored in part by Charles Darwin. As Wolschke-Bulmahn notes, Darwin's theory of evolution "pushed man from his pedestal as the pride of the Creator and integrated him as the last link into a chain of animal ancestors. The biblical world view was criticized as anthropocentric, and plants were judged to have the same rights as human beings" (1992, 196).[4] Naturalists and horticulturists, therefore, simultaneously questioned anthropocentric understandings of the environment, and became increasingly aware of the dramatic environmental changes produced by human activities.

The foundations of modern ecology are also connected to this same period in British environmental history, and an iteration of this can be seen in rock and alpine gardening practice at the time. The *OED* explains that the term *ecology*, derived from the Greek *oikos* for "house," was first coined in 1876 by E.R Lankester in the "Preface" to the English translation of Ernest Haeckel's *The History of Creation,* a text intended to popularize the theories of Charles Darwin. In Robinson's writing about the "wild garden" in particular, "the garden as a place for the protection of plants as living beings of divine origin gained priority" (Wolschke-Bulmahn 1992, 195).[5] By the beginning of the twentieth century, plant studies began to regularly take into account "the close relationship between natural vegetation, and its component organisms, and its habitat" (Sheail 1982, 135). Publications such as Tansley's "The Problems of Ecology" (1904) and *Types of British vegetation* (1911), and Clements' *Research Methods in Ecology* (1905), were evidence of the shift in natural science from the study of individual plants "to acquiring knowledge of the associations or combinations in which plants occur" (Sheail 1992, 135).[6] Rather than focusing on human impact on the environment, British ecologists were more preoccupied with edaphic factors, or the influence of soil and climate on plant species (Sheail 1992, 136). While Darwin is credited with being the first to draw attention to the effects of soil on plant life (edaphology), the importance of soil composition to the success of horticultural practice was first showcased in alpine and rock gardening, a factor that would make or break a British gardener's ability to maintain exotic plants from Asia. Thus, though Preston argues that "naturalization of exotics was not a rejection of botanical imperialism; it was its logical culmination" (2008, 208), this brief history of the emergence of the rock and alpine gardening movement suggests such a definitive conclusion is unfounded; on the contrary, horticulturists attention to the environmental conditions required to "naturalize" rock and alpine plants in the gardens of Britain involved a sophisticated understanding of alpine ecologies, thus producing a gardening practice that was entangled in the transculturation rather than reassertion of domestic imperial attitudes and assumptions during this time.

THE ROCK GARDEN AND TRANSCULTURATION

The survival of exotic alpines depended on the special instructions and insights from plant hunters—figures who could be said to be operating with a growing awareness of the complicated relationship between people, plants, and ecology. Reginald Farrer's accounts of plant hunting in Asia and gardening in Britain recall Tsing's criticism of "wild species self-making" (2012, 144), and emphasize a practice of domestication that could serve as a broadly applicable model for understanding the transcultural complexity of global ecologies in the present. The alpine plants figured in Farrer's garden writing are caught up in a matrix of affect, capitalism, fantasies of human domination, and unacknowledged collaboration with local communities—a matrix that defies the assumed "hard line" (Tsing 2012, 144) between the West and its others. The dream of seamlessly domesticating exotic plants in British gardens could, therefore, be said to have been productively derailed by the actual experience of finding and collecting these plants at the colonial peripheries, and transplanting them into the gardens of England. In order to successfully cultivate exotic alpines, gardeners in the imperial center were confronted with a new set of horticultural practices that unsettled the taken for granted "divides between social and natural, or subject and object," and contributed to a transculturation of the supposedly settled identity of "the West" (Mueggler 2008, 136). In other words, the plant hunting and garden writing of figures like Farrer, Kingdon-Ward, and Williams, relied—at least partially—on alternative ways of knowing the Other, on accommodating cultural difference, and on acknowledging the mutual re-shaping of Northern and Southern ecologies.

An early example of this transcultural orientation in rock and alpine gardening can be found in the "opening pages of a "Preface" to William Robinson's 1893 edition of his by then well-known book, *The Wild Garden*. Anxious to avoid misunderstandings about his appropriation of the term "wild" in relation to the garden, Robinson explains that the term "is applied essentially to the placing of perfectly hardy *exotic* plants under conditions where they will thrive year round" (xxiv–xxv; original emphasis). "It has nothing," emphasizes Robinson, "to do with the old idea of the 'Wilderness'" (xxiv–xxv).[7] Furthermore, Robinson's *The English Flower Garden*, despite its title, can be seen as a reaction against the kind of nationalism Preston characterizes as influencing British garden practices in this period; citing nationalist attitudes in the garden writing of one of his contemporaries, Robinson laments that "[s]ome new writers have no heart for the many beautiful [foreign] things in the shape of trees and shrubs which we have known during the past generation or two" (1883, 17). "Now if any fact is clear," continues Robinson,

> the garden's charm often arises from variety. [...] This writer and others like him, need to be taught that it is absolutely impossible to make a beautiful garden without the variety which he says is useless. They have not, of course, any idea of the dignity and beauty of the trees of Japan, the Rocky Mountains, and Northern Asia or America. (18)

While some British garden writers attempted to translate the concept of the "wild garden" into a narrower notion of an English garden, the popularity of rock and alpine gardening (which emerged in concert with the "wild garden") surpassed this nationalism and pulled the movement in new directions from the early to mid-twentieth century.[8]

REGINALD FARRER'S "PERVERSE LITTLE PEOPLE OF THE HILLS"

When Reginald Farrer embarked on his 1914–16 plant-hunting expedition in Gansu province of the Tibet–China border region (chronicled in his memoir, *On the Eaves of the World* [1917]), he was very much a participant in an imperial project to construct what was imagined as a unified and coherent archive of its colonial territories and peripheries. Like other plant hunters of his generation (such as Frank Kingdon-Ward, Joseph Rock, and George Forrest), Farrer's career as a nurseryman, commercial plant hunter, travel writer, and horticulturist could also be said to have been shaped by this regime of knowledge production. Farrer, however, demonstrated a more tenuous relation to British colonial interests than his celebrated contemporaries; in fact, throughout his life, Farrer's personal papers suggest he struggled with a fear of being socially marginalized by his elite Oxbridge contemporaries (Shulman 2002).

Born into a family of landed gentry, Farrer was homeschooled by his mother, a woman of deep Christian religious convictions, and taught himself botany as a young child growing up in the hills of Clapham, England (see Figure 2.1). Despite this privileged upbringing, Farrer found himself in an exilic relation to the British establishment; a closeted gay man, described by his contemporaries as possessing an unbearably high-pitched and screechy voice (the result of a cleft palate that was never successfully remedied by a series of painful surgeries as a young boy), he nevertheless aspired to enter into the elite circles of his Oxbridge peers (Shulman 2002). Upon arrival at Oxford, for example, in correspondence with his mother, he repeatedly reminded his parents to address his letters to "Esquire Reginald Farrer,"

Figure 2.1 Reginald Farrer, c. 1894–1902. Courtesy of Farrer Estate/RHS Lindley Library.

send carefully selected fresh-cut flowers from their estate every week to demonstrate his family's wealth, and provide him with a living allowance that would allow him to holiday with his elite classmates (Farrer Family Collection 1880–2004, RJF/2/1/1 & 2). The majority of his time at Oxford was occupied with his failed effort to achieve recognition as a novelist, idolizing the work of Jane Austen, and constantly advising his parents by mail on how to properly maintain his gardens and short-lived commercial nursery.

However, Farrer's writing about plant hunting and rock gardening (a career that was initially secondary to his ambition to be a novelist), suggests a rethinking of his desire for acceptance into elite circles, and his emerging critical views on colonial authority and cultural superiority. Where contemporaries such as Rock, Forrest, and Kingdon-Ward worked to establish what Mueggler calls a "mode of presence" (2005, 447) that emphasized an attitude of authority and colonial superiority in relation to the people and landscapes they visited, Farrer's accounts of his travel in Japan, and later the Tibet–China border region, accommodate for a more flexible subject position, influenced by an ironic and sometimes exilic relation of European culture, and place plants at the center of attention. Where the accounts of his contemporaries' expeditions emphasize a performance of masculinity that was defined by an idea of "individual integrity and freedom from subjugation," class superiority, and "the ability to establish, protect, provide for and control a home" (Mueggler 2005, 4), Farrer, on the other hand, often eschews these roles in his accounts of his plant-hunting activities. Joseph Rock, for example, is described by Mueggler as "carry[ing] his sociality about with him, like a snail carrying its shell—or rather a hermit crab which, at each resting place, finds another shell and collects objects to arrange about it" (2011a, 169).[9] Farrer, alternatively, seemed more open to having his sociality orchestrated for him by others, including those he encountered in Ceylon, Japan, and later, the Tibet–China border region. "Far from the strong silent and stoic ideal of the imperial male traveler," argues Jeff Mather in an article that examines the influence of Austen's work on Farrer's writing (2009), "Farrer is loquacious, articulate, and constantly ironic" (55). More generally, the kind of sociality engineered by Farrer versus his contemporaries tended toward an openness to otherness and a recognition of transculturation.

Farrer's 1904 travel account, *The Garden of Asia*, offers some of the first indications that he will not resort to Orientalist discourse in his assessment of the foreign people and strange landscapes he encounters during his visit to Japan. Farrer's book pays special attention to plants and horticultural practices he observes during his nine-month trip and is characterized by comments about the beauty of the unfamiliar landscape, respect for the specificity of Japanese gardening practices, and the integrity of Japanese garden design. Farrer decries evidence of Western influence in Japan, describing it as degrading an otherwise distinct and valuable cultural heritage. In Tokyo for example, Farrer laments how the neighborhood of Shimbashi "has suffered more disastrously than almost any other from the official passion for Western methods" (1904, 8). This is evidenced for him by the presence of bowler hats and phonographs in the market (9), and telegraph wires overhead in the streets (11). With a backhanded reference to the contemporary craze for *japonisme* in England, Farrer describes how he encounters an ideal Japanese garden while searching for lodgings in Tokyo:

> Attached to one house, there was a little garden, perhaps three yards square. It was not ambitious. It did not aspire to rivulets and bridges and paraphernalia. But it was perfect. [...] That garden built up in its mossy court, was a pure joy to the eye. (15)

Here Farrer's observations suggest that even the smallest and simplest garden in Japan outstrips the more elaborate examples of *japonisme* he has encountered in England, a trend he associates with excess and gaudiness.

Farrer's reflections on Japanese culture and gardening, and his criticism of English attempts to mimic Japanese gardening through cliché or stereotypical ideas of an Asian garden design, set his relationship apart from uninformed practices of cultural appropriation. When discussing a visit to a Japanese garden nursery, for example, Farrer notes how "the untutored savage eye of the West entirely fails to see any difference between a perfect specimen ten inches high, three centuries of age, and thirty pounds in price, and its neighbour of equal height, of five years' growth, and five shillings value" (18). Reversing the primitive versus civilized binary common to descriptions of East and West relations, Farrer's comments attribute Japanese horticultural practice with a refined attention to form that the ignorant Westerner would miss. Of course, as Tachibana et al. point out (2004), such a positive view of Japanese culture was not uncommon at the time. "Respect for Japan," they note, "increased with its rise as the major imperial power in the East, after victorious wars with China (1895) and Russia (1905) and the establishment of colonies on the Asian mainland and Pacific islands" (367).[10] However, while Farrer's reflections on Japanese culture and gardening might simply be seen as an extension of this mood, his insistence on recognizing where English attempts to adapt Japanese gardening aesthetics departed from local practices, and criticism of those who engaged in cliché or stereotypical ideas of an Asian garden design, sets his relationship apart from more uninformed practices of cultural appropriation.

These and other descriptions of his experiences in Japan are notable for their emphasis on the highly specialized aesthetic practices governing Japanese gardening culture, the need for the cultural outsider to educate him- or herself about a different horticultural tradition, and the absence of any qualification of the praise he affords the Japanese approach, an otherwise common quality of other English views of non-European garden design. In his later book, *My Rock-Garden* (1908a), Farrer muses that his own preference might be for

> a Japanese garden stocked with European alpines; and when I say Japanese garden, I don't mean a silly jungle of bamboos, with Tori, and a sham tea-house, and Irises, and a trellis—I mean a rocky glen, a pinnacle flank of mountain such as every other cottage in Kioto possesses, and has possessed, for half a dozen generations. (10)

Farrer's remarks suggest a desire to adapt his rock garden *to* the Japanese garden principles in ways that would become central to the practice of rock gardening he encouraged—a form of transculturation (or what might be called "transcultivation") that does not imagine the European influence as an improvement of but rather an innovation on another well-established foreign practice; something that could be called call a counter-colonial horticultural aesthetics.

Not only did Farrer lack the kind of formal scientific training of his contemporary plant hunters, he seemed to shy away from it, rejecting the role of the natural scientist in the accumulation of knowledge about the colonial territory. Where plant hunters like Forrest and Rock relied primarily on photography to document their botanical specimens, Farrer, on the other hand, reportedly preferred to paint his specimens rather than use his camera. Ann Farrer (1991) has documented that in Farrer's private diaries "[h]e complains about the chemicals necessary in producing a photograph and he does not speak of his camera and its pictures with the love he shows for his paintbox and paintings" (64). Even after the era, when the practice of including botanical drawings as part of an expedition record had been supplanted by photography (such as in his book, *On the Eaves of the World*), he continued to paint watercolors of these same flowers. The painted "doubles" of these plants (not included in the book but subsequently exhibited in 1918), might be read as a secondary or even closeted record of Farrer's Gansu trip. When, for example, earlier in the trip Farrer encounters a new variety of alpine poppy, *Meconopsis pratti* (see Figure 2.2), he paints it and adds a hand written caption on the paper mount:

> Note: No my dear Lady, it is no good saying your Aunt Matilda grows this in her garden at Balham. She doesn't. It is a new species introduced for the first time into cultivation by me in 1914. Siku 30.6.14. (An inscription on *Meconopsis pratti*, 1914, Farrer Estate/ RHS Lindley Library. Lindley Library image collection.)

Figure 2.2 **Meconopsis pratti**, Siku, June 30/14, painted by Reginald Farrer in China, 1915. Courtesy of Farrer Estate/RHS Lindley Library.

Farrer's cheeky inscription on the painting reminds a British gardener of the *Meconopsis pratti's* far-flung and unfamiliar origins and taunts a potential viewer who might seek to domesticate its transplantation in England too seamlessly. There is a similar visual narrative rehearsed in several of the watercolors Farrer painted during the same trip, which unlike most botanical drawings, emphasize the context in which plants were found. For example in his painting of *Trollius pumilis* (Farrer Estate, RHS Lindley Library), Farrer inserts a statue of the Buddha carved in a nearby rock, a detail he playfully claims has turned the flowers white (Reginald J Farrer Collection, RBGE). Buddhism, it should be noted, played a significant role in Farrer's life; much to his family's dismay, during a 1908 trip to colonial Ceylon, he converted to Buddhism. This was no small gesture of rebellion given the strict Anglican upbringing he received in his family. In a letter from Colombo, Ceylon, dated February 8, 1908, under a heading "Received into Buddhism," Farrer reports how he has "taken refuge in the Buddha." "I therefore coldly realized," writes Farrer,

> that I was doing the right inevitable thing: but at this point your "little yellow people" surged up in my gorge and I found myself influenced emotionally by all that damned "dominant race" rubbish—which however true & valuable politically, is such utter balls in the higher sphere of ethics. It was quite a second before I realized that, in morals, there can never be any dominance but goodness & wisdom—quite a second before I could honestly stick out my bottom & plumb down my head on the floor before two ancient men, probably of fifty time my pedigree, certainly of a hundred times my wisdom, knowledge and virtue. However, realizing that in them I was adoring the virtue not the yellow skin. I duly knelt without reproach, and so the ceremony ended, and we scattered, bumbling about the Library.
>
> (Farrer Family Collection 1880–2004, RJF/2/1/2)

Farrer's detailed account of his emotional state during the conversion ceremony confirms his growing skepticism about the racial discourse that underpinned British colonial policy during this period, and the act of conversion itself signals a radical break with this mindset. "The indeterminacy of conversion," writes Gauri Viswanathan "poses a radical threat to the trajectory of nationhood." (1998, 16). In *Outside the Fold* (1998), Viswanathan argues that conversion to a minority religion was one of the most powerful forms of dissent during the colonial era. "By undoing the concept of fixed, unalterable identities," she explains,

> conversion unsettles the boundaries by which selfhood, citizenship, nationhood, and community are defined, exposing them as permeable borders. Shifts in religious consciousness traverse the contained order of culture and subtly dislodge its measured alignments, belying the

false assurance that only change from the outside has the power to disrupt. (1998, 16)

Farrer's conversion, a decision he never recanted during his lifetime, was greeted by his family with what his cousin Osbert Sitwell described as "a subdued polar shivering" (Shulman 2002, 36). Furthermore, though his observance of Buddhist practices throughout his life was "highly selective" (to say the least), he often referenced his ideas on Buddhism in his published books (for example in his travel account, *In Old Ceylon* [1908]), and gained "considerable notoriety" back in Britain for wearing what were described as "Buddhist" robes (see Figure 2.3), (though Shulman suggests these were likely only "Japanese court robes he bought in Tokyo") (36).

Farrer's open praise for both the plants and unique natural settings in which he first encountered them was also extended at times to the local people who worked as part of his expedition team. For example, his watercolor

Figure 2.3 Reginald Farrer in robes. Image from the collection of the Royal Botanic Garden Edinburgh.

painting of the *Iris tenuifolia* (Farrer Estate, RHS Lindley Library), unlike more scientific botanical drawings, includes a sketch of a small town of in the lower left-hand corner, reminding his viewers of the local communities and people he encountered and relied on for labor during the two year span of the trip. Farrer's writing also acknowledges the skill and sometimes superior abilities of his Chinese servants in helping him collect and preserve his plant seeds and specimens. For example, shortly after describing how he had encountered some wild *Viburnum fragrans* and stopped in a village to press the specimens he had collected, Farrer writes:

> I had imagined that here I might make myself useful by arranging our flowers for the press, but was soon shown [...] by the Mafu, who took them from me with a calm firm hand, and dealt with them himself in such a way as cured me forever of the fancy that I could dry flowers, an art on which in former days, I had rather piqued myself. But nothing can compare with the untiring expert neatness of the Chinese; and after I had once seen the Mafu at his task I left the business wholly in his hands from that time forth. ([1917] 1926, 99–100)

Though there are many examples of Farrer exhibiting the standard racist attitudes toward the non-European crew members who performed invaluable services for him during his expedition, this thoughtful reflection on the Mafu's skill in pressing flowers represents a departure from the attitudes other British colonial plant hunters during this same period.

Farrer's growing transcultural outlook is also underpinned, I argue, by his increasing awareness of alpine plants as nonhuman entities that required the adaptation of the ecology and aesthetic design of their newfound homes in the Britain in order to thrive. Farrer's recognition of alpine plants in this way, I argue, required what could be called an alternative "mode of presence" from that adopted by figures like Ward and Rock—a "learning to pay attention" to the "technologies, commerce, organisms, landscapes, peoples, practices" that Donna Haraway associates with "companion species" (2006, 19). In his earlier 1908 book, *My Rock-Garden,* written between the trips to Japan and China, Farrer stresses that that the rock gardener must acquaint himself with the specific needs of the plants he wants to grow and be prepared for "the huge uncertainties of gardening" (1), especially when "dealing with the perverse little people of the hills" (2). As suggested at the outset of this chapter, the perception of alpine plants as difficult to grow is one that has been associated with rock gardening since its inception. Significantly, however, Farrer casts aside Robinson's patronizing vision of alpines as "mother of earth['s] [...] loveliest children"(1870a, x), in favor or a vision of them as unruly, disruptive, foreign, and (delightfully) "perverse" additions to the British garden that demand accommodation. In *My Rock-Garden,* Farrer emphasizes that his gardening advice is derived from experience growing alpine plants in his own garden, and the particular conditions of the soil, climate, and light that prevail in that location. "[T]he gardener," Farrer warns, "is sternly confronted by the truth that what suits in Surrey is death in Westmorland; that what serves in Yorkshire loam is fatal in Suffolk sand; that what sunny Sussex favours, Cumberland's rainfall makes deadly" (1). The advice Farrer gives British gardeners in *My Rock-Garden* makes it clear that horticultural knowledge was beginning to accommodate for the complexity of what made certain plants gardenworthy in one location but not in another, and the necessity of matching or adapting the ecology of the English garden to the needs of the foreign plant. In the example above, as in other stories of his encounters with valued plants during his travels in South and East Asia, Farrer's description is informed by an explicit tension between the plant's origin and its newfound home in the English rock garden.

CULTIVATING EDGES IN THE ENVIRONMENTAL HUMANITIES

If descriptions of the incorporation of exotic plants into Caribbean plantation culture in the eighteenth and nineteenth century served, as Jill Casid argues, as "a kind of displacement whereby anxieties about racial mixing are registered on a different field, soil rather than bodies" (2004, 9), Farrer's description of the plants he collects and transplants into his English rock garden seem to reverse this practice in the early years of the twentieth century.[11] "The perverse little people of the hills" are given priority, personalities, and treated as valued additions to the so-called "wild garden" aesthetic that came to dominate British gardening practice at the turn of the century. As Anna Tsing argues, if we are to reinsert "love" into the relations between people, plants, and places (2012, 148), "we might undertake to know something of the point of view from disordered but productive edges—the seams of empire" (151). My attention to the status of ecology, transculturation, and plants as companion species in early twentieth-century travel writing concerned with plant hunting in Asia, and rock and alpine garden manuals in the imperial center, seeks to investigate these kinds of "disordered but productive edges." As Susie O'Brien argues elsewhere in this collection, "an interest in what happens at edges, meeting places and contact zones as sites of uncertainty, collaboration and—sometimes (but not always)—productive surprise" (2015, 192), has the potential to yield new ways of imagining global ecologies. Attention to the "edgework" (1) in plant-hunting and garden writing of figures like Reginald Farrer draws our vision "away from the middle ground (in more than one sense) towards macro and micro fields of action" (7), and toward the zones of contact where transculturation unfolds in potentially transformative ways. The transculturation of the aesthetic and ecological conditions needed for alpine plants to thrive in English rock gardens in the first half of the twentieth century forced horticultural enthusiasts and experts to confront orientalist assumptions about the superiority of British horticultural practice, and expressed a general unsettling of the edges of colonial and national attitudes toward alterity. Farrer's garden and travel writing expresses a "love" (Tzing 148) for adapting the soil of the English garden to the peripheral needs of his treasured foreign alpines, and he chides imperial gardeners who fail to rethink their rock garden's material, ecological, and aesthetic qualities from the ground up.

NOTES

1. David Harvey describes this as a scenario where "a strong sense of 'the Other' is replaced [...] by a weak sense of 'the others'" (Harvey 1990, 301).
2. While Robinson's alpine gardening book may not represent the most rigorous guide to alpine horticulture (Lambin [1994] notes, for example, that it is relatively thin on actual knowledge of alpine environments), it draws on many of the same themes and assumptions about nature and the environment that came to inspire popular rock and alpine gardening at the turn of the century.
3. As many garden historians point out, Robinson was not the first to advance these ideas about the garden, though he was the one best known for popularizing the idea of the natural garden through his writing. Garden designer Shirley Hibberd and botanist Forbes Watson are seen as some of the first to argue for "the treatment of flowers as individual living beings" (Ottewill 1989, 53).
4. The plot of Nayantara Sahgal's novel, *Plans for Departure*, set at an Indian hill station in 1914, includes a Bengali scientist who is conducting research on the idea "that plants have animal (or human) traits" (1986, 116).
5. Issues of economics also came into play in Robinson's conception of the wild garden. Not only does Robinson see this form of gardening as more natural because it is more suited to the English climate, he also emphasizes that it was more economical than the formal style of the English garden, which relied on glass houses to maintain the plants in the winter and additional labor "bed them out" in the summer. In the forward to the third edition of his *Alpine Flowers for the English Garden* (1879), for example, he criticizes "[a]mateurs who cultivate numerous hot-house plants, and who generally have not a dozen of the equally beautiful flowers and northern and temperate regions in their gardens, might grow an abundance of them at a tithe of the expense required to fill a glasshouse with costly Mexican or Indian Orchids" (1879, xii).
6. See Susie O'Brien (2007) for a discussion of ecocriticism's sometimes uncritical mobilization of the science of ecology in representations of the environment as a universal, cybernetic, and fully interconnected global ecosystem. In this essay, I am working to establish an understanding of the relationship between the ecological needs of alpine plants that have evolved in the South and Central Asia and the ecological conditions of the rock and alpine gardens where they were transplanted in Britain.
7. *The Wild Garden* (1870) has been reprinted ten times, most recently in 2010, a testament to the enduring influence of Robinson's ideas in garden culture.
8. Writing about the more nationalist tendencies associated with German horticulturist Willy Lange (a figure heavily influenced by Robinson), Wolschke-Bulmahn

observes, "[o]ne thing is certain [...] as national, as truly German or English, and as wild or natural as they wanted their gardens to be, neither Lange nor Robinson let slip the chance to realize impressions they had gained on their travels" (1992, 202).

9. Mueggler has relatively little to say about Farrer's plant hunting and garden writing except to briefly discuss his final expedition to the Yunnan border with Burma where Farrer spent some time in the village of Hpimaw. Significantly, however, this account of the expedition is not written by Farrer, but by Cox in *Farrer's Last Journey* (1926); Farrer died in Burma in 1920 and did not publish an account of this trip. Based on Cox's account of the trip, Mueggler characterizes Farrer's writing about plant hunting as "about vision; how to see the essence of alpine peaks, screes, and meadows and how to concentrate that essence in the jewel-like microcosm of a rock garden" (2011b, 26). Mueggler suggests that Farrer "found he could not see" (26) in Hpimaw, a gesture understood as Farrer being unable to assimilate the Asian landscape to European expectations for the Alps. As I hope my analysis here suggests, this view does not take into account Farrer's depiction of foreign landscapes, plants, people, and cultures in his oeuvre as a whole.

10. This period of mutual admiration was highlighted at the 1910 Japan–British exhibition in White City, London where the official circular for the exhibition announced the intentions of the two countries to "cement and make greater and more lasting friendship between two great 'Island Empires'" (Tachibana et al. 2004, 368).

11. Promotional material for the hundreth-anniversary edition of the Chelsea Flower Show in 2013 emphasized that predominance of rock garden displays during the first forty years of the event.

REFERENCES

Aberconway. 1935. "Conference Opening Address. By the Lord Aberconway, President, Royal Horticultural Society." *Rock Gardens and Rock Plants: Conference Proceedings for the Royal Horticultural Society and the Committee of the Alpine Garden Society*: 8–10.

Allen, D.E. 1980. "The Early History of Plant Conservation in Britain." *Transactions of the Leicester Literary & Philosophical Society* 72: 35–50.

Casid, Jill H. 2004. *Sowing Empire: Landscape and Colonization*. Minneapolis: University of Minnesota Press.

Chelsea Centenary: 100 years of the RHS Chelsea Flower Show. 2013. Royal Horticultural Society.

Clements, Frederic E. 1905. *Research Methods in Ecology*. Lincoln: Nebraska

Cox, E. H. M. 1926. *Farrer's Last Journey*. London: Dulau and Co Ltd.

Farrer, Anne. 1991. "Farrer as Illustrator: The Diaries of Reginald Farrer." In *Reginald Farrer: Dalesman, Planthunter, Gardener*, edited by John Illingworth and Jane Routh, 64–72. Lancaster: Centre for North-West Regional Studies, University of Lancaster.

Farrer, Reginald J. 1904. *The Garden of Asia*. London: Methuen.

———. 1908a. *My Rock-Garden*. London: Edward Arnold.

———. 1908b. *In Old Ceylon*. London: Edward Arnold.

———. 1912. *The Rock-Garden*. London T.C. & E.C. Jack.

———. [1917] 1926. *On the Eaves of the World*. London: Edward Arnold.

Ernst Haeckel.1868. *The History of Creation*, 3rd ed. Vol. 1. Translated by E. Ray Lankester. London.

Hansen, Peter, H. 1995. "Albert Smith, the Alpine Club, and the Invention of Mountaineering in Mid-Victorian Britain." *Journal of British Studies* 34 (2): 300–324.

Haraway, Donna J. 2007. *When Species Meet*. Minneapolis: University of Minnesota Press.

Harvey, David. 1990. *The Condition of Postmodernity*. London: Blackwell.

Huggan, Graham. 2001. *The Postcolonial Exotic: Marketing the Margins*. New York: Routledge.

Lambin, Denis A. 1994. "From Grottoes to the Alps—A Contribution to a History of Rock and Alpine Gardens." *The Journal of Garden History* 14 (4): 236–256.

Mather, Jeff. 2009. "Camping in China with the Divine Jane: The Travel Writing of Reginald Farrer." *Journeys* 10 (2): 45–64.

Mueggler, Erik. 2005. "'The Lapponicum Sea': Matter, Sense, and Affect in the Botanical Exploration of Southwest China and Tibet." *Comparative Studies in Society and History* 47 (3): 442–479.

———. 2008. "George Forrest's Rhododendron Pardise." In *Timely Assests: The Politics of Resources and Their Temporalities* by Elizabeth Emma Ferry and Mandana E. Limber eds. 129–167. Santa Fe: School for Advanced Research Press.

———. 2011a. *The Paper Road: Archive and Experience in the Botanical Exploration of West China and Tibet*. Berkeley: University of California Press.

———. 2011b. "The Eyes of Others: Race, 'Gaping' and Companionship in the Scientific Exploration of Southwest China." In *Explorers and Scientists in China's Borderlands, 1880–1950*, edited by Denis M. Glover et al., 26–56. Seattle: University of Washington Press.

O'Brien, Susie. 2007. "'Back to the World': Reading Ecocriticism in a Postcolonial Context." In *Five Emus to the King of Siam: Environment and Empire*, edited by Helen Tiffin. 177–199. Amsterdam: Rodopi.

Ortiz, Fernando. 1995. *Cuban Counterpoint: Tobacco and Sugar*. Translated by Harriet De Onís. Durham: Duke University Press.

Ottewill, David. 1989. *The Edwardian Garden*. New Haven: Yale University Press.

Pratt, Mary Louise. 1992. *Imperial Eyes: Travel Writing and Transculturation*. New York: Routledge.

Preston, Rebecca. 2003. "'The Scenery of the Torrid Zone': Imagined Travels and the Culture of Exotics in Nineteenth-Century British Gardens." In *Imperial Cities: Landscape, Display and Identity*, edited by Felix Driver and David Gilbert. 194–201. Manchester: Manchester University Press.

Reginald J. Farrer Collection at the Royal Botanic Garden Edinburgh: Farrer Family Collection. 1804–2004. RJF 2/1/1 (written materials) and RJF2/1/1 (photographic materials). Edinburgh: Royal Botanic Garden, Edinburgh.

Robbins, David.1987. "Hegemony and the Middle Class: The Victorian Mountaineers." *Theory, Culture, and Society* 4: 579–601.

Robinson, William. 1870a. *Alpine Flowers for English Gardens*. London: John Murray.

———. 1870b. *The Wild Garden; or, Our Groves & Shrubberies Made Beautiful by the Naturalization of Hardy Exotic Plants: With a Chapter on the Garden of British Wild Flowers*. London: J. Murray.

Robinson, William. [1870] 1879. *Alpine Flowers for English Gardens*, 3rd ed. London: John Murray.

———. 1883. *The English Flower Garden: Style Position and Arrangement*. London: J. Murray.

Sahgal, Nayantara. 1986. *Plans For Departure*. New Delhi: HarperCollins.

Said, Edward. 1993. *Culture and Imperialism*. New York: Knopf.

Sheail, John. 1982. "Wild Plants and the Perception of Land-use Change in Britain: An Historical Perspective." *Biological Conservation* 24 (2): 129–146.

Shulman, Nicola. 2002. *A Rage for Rock Gardening: The Story of Reginald Farrer, Gardener, Writer and Plant Collector*. Surrey: Bookmarque Ltd.

Slemon, Stephen. 2008. "The Brotherhood of the Rope: Commodification and Contradiction in the 'Mountaineering Community'." In *Renegotiating Community: Interdisciplinary Perspectives, Global Contexts*, edited by Dianna Brydon and Willam D. Coleman, 234–245. Vancouver: University of British Columbia Press.

Tachibana, Setsu, Stephen Daniels, and Chris Watkins. 2004. "Japanese Gardens in Edwardian Britain: Landscape and Transculturation." *Journal of Historical Geography* 30 (2): 364–395.

Tansley, Arthur George. 1904. "The Problems of Ecology." *The New Phytologist*. 3: 191–200.

———. 1911. *Types of British vegetation*. Cambridge: Cambridge University Press.

Thomas, Graham Stuart. 1989. *The Rock Garden and its Plants: From Grotto to Alpine House*. J. M. London: Dent and Sons Ltd.

Tsing, Anna. 2012. "Unruly Edges: Mushrooms as Companion Species." *Environmental Humanities* 1: 141–154.

Viswanathan, Gauri. 1998. *Outside the Fold: Conversion, Modernity, and Belief*. Princeton: Princeton University Press.

Wolschke-Bulmahn, Joachim. 1992. "The 'Wild Garden' and the 'Nature Garden'—Aspects of the Garden Ideology of William Robinson and Willy Lange." *The Journal of Garden History* 12 (3): 183–206.

Wolschke-Bulmahn, Joachim, and Gert Groening. 1992. "The Ideology of the Nature Garden. Nationalistic Trends in Garden Design in Germany During the Early Twentieth Century." *The Journal of Garden History* 12 (1): 73–80.

3 Bagasse

Caribbean Art and the Debris of the Sugar Plantation

Lizabeth Paravisini-Gebert

The recent emergence of *bagasse*—the fibrous mass left after sugar cane is crushed—as an important source of biofuel may seem to those who have experienced the realities of plantation life like the ultimate cosmic irony. Its newly assessed value—one producer of bagasse pellets argues that the "symbol of what once was waste, now could be farming gold" ("Harvesting" 2014)—promises to increase sugar producers' profits while pushing into deeper oblivion the plight of the workers worldwide who continue to produce sugar cane in deplorable conditions and ruined environments. Its newly acquired status as a "renewable" and carbon-neutral source of energy also obscures the damage that cane production continues to inflict on the land and the workers that produce it. The concomitant deforestation, soil erosion and use of poisonous chemical fertilizers and pesticides on land and water continue to degrade the environment of those fated to live and work amid its waste. It obscures, moreover, the role of sugar cane cultivation as the most salient form of power and environmental violence through which empires manifested their hegemony over colonized territories throughout the Caribbean and beyond.[1]

In the discussion that follows, I explore the legacy of the environmental violence of the sugar plantation through the analysis of the work of a group of contemporary Caribbean artists whose focus is the ruins and debris of the plantation and who often use bagasse as either artistic material or symbol of colonial ruination. I argue—through the analysis of recent work by Atelier Morales (Cuba), Hervé Beuze (Martinique), María Magdalena Campos-Pons (Cuba), and Charles Campbell (Jamaica)—that artistic representation in the Caribbean addresses the landscape of the plantation as inseparable from the history of colonialism and empire in the region. Embedded in these representations of the ruins and debris of the sugar plantation "landscape" are a number of colonial and neocolonial relationships to the environment that engage central themes in artistic and literary production in the region: land tenure, diaspora, slavery and indentured servitude, family networks, community, and modernity, among others. In their multifaceted representations through photographs, paintings and installations, these artists insist on the eloquent capacity of the engagement with ruins and debris—chief among this debris, bagasse—to address the continuing impact of colonial and imperial power on the landscapes and peoples of the region. This visual engagement, moreover, also insists on its political nature, as it seeks to denounce the ruination brought to the Caribbean islands by the plantation and to display for viewers perhaps unfamiliar with the history of the plantation the despoiled environments that local populations continue to inhabit. My analysis of this work owes much to the critical and methodological tools developed under the aegis of the environmental humanities for the study of narrative and post-colonial ecologies in the Caribbean region.[2] It seeks to push the boundaries of our definitions of the environmental humanities to encompass the work of visual artists engaging with postcolonial ecologies and addressing the ruination that empire left in its wake. Their works offer highly nuanced *visual* narratives, versions of a history of imperial ruination that draw upon a broad range of traditions of visual representation and whose importance in narrating the story of empire has received scant attention to date.

My interest in the ecological impact of the plantation stems from a deep personal connection to the history of sugar production in my home island. For decades, my father worked for the Aguirre Sugar Cane Mill, the last operational sugar refinery in Puerto Rico, which closed its doors in 1993. As a result, my childhood and adolescence were dominated by the rhythm of the cane planting and harvesting seasons and by the absorbing narratives of the day-to-day struggles of the cane workers—some of them my relatives— who represented the largest segment of the population in our small town and whose children were my classmates. The history of my maternal family is intricately bound with relentless efforts to escape and then stay away from the cane fields.

The landscapes of my hometown were dominated by cane; its cyclical evolution from green stalk crowned with flowery spumes to pungent bagasse served as backdrop to our yearly routines. As children, we anxiously awaited the burning of the fields before harvest and pretended to ice skate on the pavement made slippery by the falling ashes while our mothers rushed to get the clothes off the line before they were covered in soot. We played among the rows of canes, careful to avoid the razor-sharp leaves of the stalks, and begged for rides on the narrow-gauge trains bringing the canes to the mill in Aguirre. We were also keenly familiar with the troubles of the *tiempo muerto*, with the unemployment and penuries of the fallow season when there was no employment and therefore no income.

When the cane industry began its slow decline in the 1960s, we followed closely the fate of the land—and of the local economy—as cane ceased to be what we saw everywhere we turned. The collapse of the sugar industry developed across several decades and impacted the landscape and our townspeople in myriad ways: fallow fields were reclaimed by bush; new crops were tried in order to provide a new economic base; ostrich farms came and went; short-lived oil refineries polluted the air, the soil and the water, leaving rusty carcasses and unexplained maladies in their wake; a plan to build a lab monkey–breeding facility split the community; housing developments named after former plantations sprung on former cane land; solar panel farms replaced failed pineapple farms; genetically modified seed–processing plants experimented without regulation on the land—while the ruins of the sugar *central* rusted away as a much photographed "romantic" ghostly *revenant*. The deforested hills, nonetheless, remained denuded; without the trees, the rains have not returned. What is not irrigated remains parched, arid land. At school we read our writers' attempts to come to terms with our problematic history as cultivators of sugar, responding viscerally against nineteenth-century exalted celebrations of landscapes dominated by the swaying flower of the sugar cane plant—the *guajana*—to be found in works like José Gautier Benítez's 1846 poem "A Puerto Rico." We also discovered the complexities of tales of individual struggle between financial security and ethical treatment of both workers and the environment, as in Enrique Laguerre's 1935 novel *La Llamarada*, with its sad lament for the loss of the mighty and once abundant *ausubo* trees to the spread of the canelands. It was a story that reverberated across the islands through other poems, novels, and short stories.

Rooted in the culture of sugar cultivation, our readings of its representation in literature and art were guided by our understanding of its economic, social, and environmental realities. Even then, albeit in the most unsophisticated ways, the question of how to adequately represent this most disturbing development in the history of the Caribbean region loomed large before us. The issues have grown more complex, more nuanced, but the question of how best to represent this historical trauma ethically while creating art whose aesthetic quality engages us with its vexed and vexing history of human and environmental exploitation remains a central one. This is the basic question I would like to address through the analysis of a number of examples drawn from the work of artists equally familiar with the nuances of the region's history of cane cultivation.

A central aspect of my query addresses these artists' environmental premises. United States' artist Lynne Hull has developed a list of principles— listed on the Green Museum's website under "What is Environmental Art?—that can guide us towards an understanding of the qualities we seek in art that addresses ecological concerns. Environmental artists seek to create art that "informs and interprets nature and its processes, educates us about environmental problems," and "is concerned or incorporates environmental forces and materials." It should help us "re-envision our relationship to nature, proposing new ways for us to co-exist with our environment" while it "reclaims and remediates damaged environments, restoring ecosystems in artistic and often aesthetic ways." Such art can be ephemeral, and is often produced in collaboration with others in order to underscore community goals or the cooperative nature of environmental remediation efforts."[3] This definition, however, broad as it is, needs to be expanded if it is to include artists whose work explores the specificities of imperial practices that have resulted in despoiled landscapes and the obstacles to reclamation and remediation in small postcolonial nations whose economies are unable to support complex land rehabilitation schemes. The fate of the landscape, for the artists whose work I discuss here, is fundamentally tied to questions of power and empire. Echoing Ann Laura Stoler, their goal is not simply "to mount a charge that every injustice in the contemporary world has imperial roots, but rather to delineate the specific ways in which peoples and places are laid to waste, where debris falls, around whose lives it accumulates, and what constitutes [in the words of Derek Walcott] 'the rot that remains'" (Stoler 2013, 29).

The representation of the Caribbean plantation in art is rooted in the landscape-with-sugar-plantation tradition that dominated the development of Caribbean artistic expression from the seventeenth to the nineteenth century—produced mostly by amateur artists or traveling professional painters. Artists like Frans Post (1612–1680), Agostino Brunias (1730–1796), Michel-Jean Cazabon (1813–1888), Víctor Patricio Landaluze (1828–1889), and Eduardo Laplante (1818–1860), or amateurs such as the diplomat and traveler Pierre Eugene du Simitiere (1737–1784) produced reassuring images that captured the landscape, architecture, and economic potential of the plantation without addressing the harshness of its labor conditions or the system's immersion in global patterns of exchange dependent on slavery and the slave trade. These consumable images of picturesque otherness, like the American plantation paintings that John Michael Vlack examines in *The Planter's Prospect: Privilege and Slavery in Plantation Paintings*, fulfilled "an important social function: they made a positive visual argument on behalf of plantation society" and "constituted a pleasant propaganda that covered plantation life with a sweet veneer of tranquility" (Vlack 2002, 89, 109).[4]

New approaches to the depiction of the plantation through art emerged following emancipation in the British colonies in the mid-1830s among Creole painters sympathetic to the abolitionist movement. Influenced by new social theories ranging from Jean-Jacques Rousseau's *Of the Social Contract* (1762) to Karl Marx's *Capital* (1867) this new work challenged previous images of the plantation and slavery as benign institutions. Moving from the romanticized views of the plantation house to depictions of the boiling houses or of laborers struggling in the fields, these new images offered a critique of the plantation system that reflected emerging labor and prodemocracy movements in the Caribbean. Perhaps best known among them is turn-of-the-twentieth-century Puerto Rican painter Francisco Oller (1833–1917), whose series of paintings of Puerto Rican plantations remain as a challenge to the power of an established Creole plantocracy. Oller sought, as Katherine Manthorne (2001) has argued, to problematize the familiar bucolic presentations of the plantation, seeking instead to depict them "as sites of interaction between races—between white Creole elite and slaves of African descent—[his] plantation images represent an attempted synthesis of the overlapping narratives of land control/reform and race that engulfed Puerto Rico during his lifetime" (2001, 321). These plantation images—*Hacienda La Fortuna* (1885, Brooklyn Museum) most particularly—show fields covered in debris during the cane harvest, from the debris left on the field as oxen carts move the cane to the mill to growing piles of bagasse outside the mill building after processing. Workers mill about this debris, signaling an identification between labor and plantation waste that disrupts the viewer's expectations from earlier plantation paintings.

Oller was not alone in his critique of the plantation through art. Its negative legacy is powerfully addressed by Cuban painter Wifredo Lam in his most famous work, *The Jungle* (1943), where he sought to capture "the drama of my country" and "disturb the dreams of the exploiters" through the creation of phantasmagoric African warriors adrift in a forest of cane (Fouchet 1976, 188–189). As sugar production in Cuban and Puerto Rico moved from medium-sized family-owned concerns to huge corporation-owned *centrales* (US-owned "factories in the fields") after the Spanish-American War (1898), Oller's careful deconstruction of the plantation order was echoed in the work of photographers such as Jack Delano (1914–1997), who arrived in Puerto Rico in the early 1940s as part of the New Deal's Farm Security Administration to chronicle the lives of cane workers (see Figure 3.1).

Figure 3.1 Jack Delano, *TFSA Borrower and Participant in the Sugar Cane Cooperative, Río Piedras, Puerto Rico* (December 1941), photographic slide. Courtesy of the Library of Congress.

Delano's work challenged the confident image of prosperity and bounty that emerged out of official depictions of the industrialized sugar production featured in newspapers, government reports and tourist postcards.[5] It refocused attention away from these images of the industrial plantation as "modern" landscape and toward the plight of workers in the fields and the dignified poverty of their homes and families. His portraits of Puerto Rican cane workers underscored their individuality and inscribed them into the history of labor exploitation and institutionalized poverty that was the legacy of the "bucolic" plantation of earlier representations. In many of his portraits of cane workers in the field, as we see above, Delano used cane and bagasse as background, immersing his subjects in the fields of cane production and its debris. He was particularly interested in chronicling the experience of workers—like the ones pictured above—who had joined a cooperative to plant cane to sell to the American mills, one of the many ventures through which cane workers sought to better their economic circumstances through gaining some measure of control over the land. His aesthetic and ideological approach to the depiction of the plantation is echoed in the work of other prominent artist of the mid-twentieth century, perhaps chief among them Cuba's Mario Carreño and Jamaica's Albert Huie, whose iconic plantation paintings captured the collective and unifying nature of hard labor in the cane fields at a crucial moment in the history of labor organization in the twentieth century and who, as Oller and Delano before them, depict the cane workers as embedded literally and metaphorically in the canes and bagasse. Delano's photographs, like the work of Carreño and Huie in Cuba and Jamaica, were crucial documents in the development of a nationalist critique of the industrialized plantation in Puerto Rico. Circulated freely through newspaper articles, history textbooks, postcards, and pro-independence political posters—and generously contextualized by Delano himself through multiple press interviews and presentations in a wide variety of venues—the ubiquitous images became instantly recognizable markers of nationalist goals, embraced particularly during the resurgence of the pro-independence movement in the 1970s and 1980s.

Contemporary Caribbean artists have sought to engage the vexed history of the visual representation of the plantation in the region through *dialogues* with earlier iconic images. That is the case of a photographic series by Atelier Morales (Cuban architect Juan Luis Morales and his wife and artistic partner Teresa Ayuso) who in *Los Ingenios: Patrimonio a la deriva* (*Adrift Patrimony: Sugar Refineries* 2004) seek to capture "with a bitterly beautiful technique of digital photography and gouache the ruined remnants" of the once thriving sugar industry in Cuba (Santiago 2005). The series uses as a point of departure the work of French painter and lithographer Eduardo Laplante, whose thirty-eight lithographs of Cuba's principal sugar plantations illustrated Justo Cantero's excellent study of the history and condition of the island's principal mills in 1857, *Los Ingenios: Colección de vistas de los principales ingenios de azúcar de la isla de Cuba*. Laplante's "colorful landscapes of smokestacks towering higher than royal palms and his romanticized view of life on the plantations" (Santiago 2005) served as the inspiration for Atelier Morales' reimagining of the Cuban plantation landscape (see Figure 3.2).

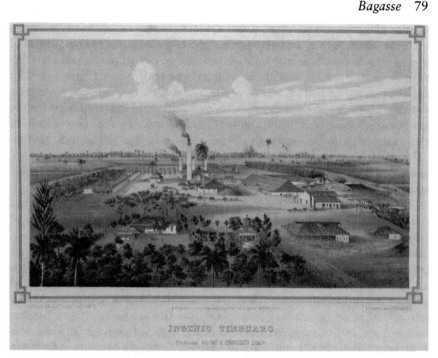

Figure 3.2 Eduardo Laplante, *Ingenio Tinguaro*, from Justo G. Cantero's *Los Ingenios: Colección de vistas de los principales ingenios de azúcar de la isla de Cuba* (1857).

Atelier Morales' *Los Ingenios/The Sugar Mills* consists of twenty-five images, in editions of ten each (with the exception of two images in editions of fifteen), signed and painted with gouache. The project was envisioned in 2002, shortly after the Cuban mills closed, as an attempt to "reflect on heritage and loss caused by abandonment, negligence and corruption, all consequences of inefficient and unilateral political systems" (Menocal 2004). The photographs capture the sugar mills of Laplante's iconic lithographs as they are today—the old machinery rusted, the wood buildings crumpled, the sites abandoned, some half-submerged in water, others covered by bush. They also, perhaps unintentionally, leave ample evidence of the myriad ways in which land was misused. The photographs of the ruin mills, with their brooding, poignant depiction of the collapsed buildings and rusted machinery, can be linked to the recent interest in ruins photography, with their aestheticization of the abandonment and decline of architectural and natural spaces that were once central to Cuba's national iconography (see Leary 2011 and Mullins 2012). Their ghost-like appearance recalls figures associated with sugar production and slavery, like zombies or *revenants* from a forgotten past—they also emerge from the bush or disrupt the landscape as unfathomable, unnatural debris. Their dialogue with the nineteenth-century images that precede them, however, allows Atelier Morales to transcend the simply maudlin and to transmute Laplante's romanticized view of life in the plantation, which already negated a history of forced labor and land abuse, into a contemporary "tale of loss and an ode to poetic memory." As Morales and Ayuso described in an interview with Fabiola Santiago: "An entire industry destroyed, a way of life lost and no one thought to at least preserve some of these historical relics and turn them into museums for the generations" (Santiago 2005). Stoler (2013) speaks of the trauma behind the treatment afforded to "sites of decomposition that fall outside historical interest and preservation" (13), a sentiment echoed in Atelier Morales' project to bring to the spaces photographed the honor due to them "as ruins of empire proper."

The photograph of the Tinguaro plantation reproduced here (see below) captures the evocative quality of Atelier Morales' sense of patrimonial and historical loss. The corroded machinery emerging from the luscious vegetation, its reddish rust in glaring contrast to the vivid green, forces us to confront the poignancy of the decaying infrastructure of an abandoned and superseded industry. The image, on the other hand, can also be read as an illustration of another kind of decline and obsolescence—that of nature trying to regain its ascendance over the formerly abused plantation terrain and the infrastructure through which this mistreatment was achieved. The ambivalent quality of this nostalgia—as Morales asserts—is clearly imprinted in the composition of images like that of the abandoned boats before the sweep of what remains of the old palm-lined plantation driveway in the photograph *Unión* (2004) or the harmonious sequence of palm trees and rusted building posts seen in *Constancia* (2004). It points to loss and romantic regret, while also functioning politically as a not-too-subtle critique of the Castro government for allowing this part of Cuba's historical legacy to go to ignominious (rather than properly honored) ruin. The critique, as Morales argues, is not centered on ideological concerns, but on a preoccupation with erasure and, concomitantly, with rescue (see Figure 3.3).

This concern with erasure encapsulates the environmental component of Atelier Morales' project, as the representation of the ruins amidst encroaching bush (*Tinguaro, Vereda, Cimarrones*), the partly submerged plantation structures of *Narciso*, or the fallow grasslands of *La Angosta* brings to striking visual light what Jamaicans so poetically call "ruinate"—the type of useless bush that is left after formerly cultivated cane land has been abandoned, illustrating the toll of the plantation on formerly fertile lands. As a photograph, *Tinguaro* works both as a beautiful image of the *recovery* of the rusted machinery through art or as an equally beautiful nostalgic image of the process of erasure of a historical marker about to disappeared into ruinate. As Michelle Cliff describes it:

> *Ruinate*, the adjective, and *ruination*, the noun, are Jamaican inventions. Each word signified the reclamation of land, the disruption of

TINGUARO

Figure 3.3 Atelier Morales, **Tinguaro** (2004), from the **Adrift Patrimony: Sugar Refineries** series, photograph and gouache. Courtesy of Atelier Morales.

cultivation, civilization, by the uncontrolled, uncontrollable forest. When a landscape becomes ruinate, carefully designed aisles of cane are envined, strangled, the order of empire is replaced by the chaotic forest. The word ruination (especially) signifies this immediately; it contains both the word *ruin*, and *nation*. A landscape in ruination means one in which the imposed nation is overcome by the natural-ness of ruin.

(Cliff 2003, 157)

At the center of Atelier Morales' concerns with Cuba's disappearing patri-mony, we find a preoccupation with the integrity of the island nation that echoes Michelle Cliff's concerns with ruinate. They share the same unease about how to address creatively the problematic legacy of the plantation system in Jamaica and Cuba from their exile. As environmental photog-raphers and artists and exiled Cubans, Morales and Ayuso have created an art stemming from a space of nostalgia, a space of in-betweeness from which they address their perception of the Cuban regime's neglect of the island's historical and architectural patrimony while simultaneously cap-turing the environmental manifestations of the systemic misuse of the land. This in-betweeness is conveyed through what I would call, for lack of a better term, their work's *intervisuality*, to borrow from Julia Kristeva's *Desire in Language* (1980)—their insistence on creating visual materials that shape their meaning through clearly articulated dialogues with other images, working against codes imparted to the viewer through earlier iconic representations. Their images of plantation ruins are metaphorically super-imposed on earlier, *whole*, depictions of the spaces and architecture now ruined—a superimposition conveyed in more recent work through lenticu-lar photographs that allow for the image to move or change when viewed from different angles. (Exhibits of *Adrift Patrimony: Sugar Plantations* dis-play the photographs by Atelier Morales alongside Laplante's prints of the same spaces). The juxtaposition—whether through side-by-side displays of the before-and-after of the spaces represented or achieved through lenticu-lar technologies—articulates wholeness and ruin simultaneously, thereby capturing loss as a concrete and specific wrenching from a historical past. The nostalgia is embedded in the interstices between the two images. What is lost is captured as much through the representations of the rusted metal debris left behind as through the disappearance of what has been carted away and is no longer visible in the new image: cane, slaves, bagasse, for-ests, provision grounds—the human and vegetable debris most vulnerable to time and the elements.

These concerns are shared by Martinican artist Hervé Beuze, who has built an impressive body of work focused on a sustained critique of Martinique's history of sugar production, which he addresses through installations that use fermenting and pungently smelling bagasse as prime material. His most important project of the last decade, presented in a number of different iterations, is titled *Machinique*, an amalgam of the words *Machine*, *Inique* (iniquitous), and *Martinique*. The project's design is a simple one—sculptures in the shape of the island of Marti-nique are generally filled with bagasse, cane leaves, or trash and then set in place (i.e. placed on the floor of a former sugar mill, suspended in the air or floating on a pond), deriving their particular meaning from the installation's context. His goal is that of establishing an "archeology of the territory" of Martinique's sugar cultivation through what he has called his "Matrice-Cartes" or Master (matrix/womb) Maps (Ravion-d'Ingianni 2007, 5). The project stems from Beuze's understanding of mapping as "the point of departure of the geographic, military and human conquest of the world"; his maps, he has explained "are linked to notions of borders and peripheries" (Ravion-d'Ingianni 2007, 5). All the map installation and sculptures he has produced are, in his words, "one single series of islands [...] different facets of one entity" (Ravion-d'Ingianni 2007, 9).

In the project's first iteration in 2001, installed in a Martinican park, the form was at its simplest—merely a metal outline of the island filled with a pile of bagasse. His 2003 installation at Martinique's superb Sugar Cane Museum (with the outline of the island filled with cane leaves) added nuance to the basic premise through its mirroring a map of Martinique owned by the Museum (a map of the *Terres de l'Isle de la Martinique concédées par la Compagnie des Iles, les seigneurs propriétaires et la Com-pagnie des Indes Occidentales),* which showed the lands given to planers for cane cultivation in 1671, the foundations of Martinique's plantation society—and by its setting (the Museum is located in a former sugar mill and displays machinery, implements, documents, and photographs pertaining to sugar cultivation on the island). The work was placed on polystyrene floating in the middle of a pond and on panels set on the ground Beuze identified the location of the island's first sugar plantations, making of his installation a "spatial inventory" that anchored the production of sugar and rum on the island. The installation was meant to highlight how these ancient divisions of the land continue to hold sway over island land tenures (Brébion 2011, 85). Beuze has described the series as "an attempt 'to perceive the marrow of our being in the world,' through forms and materials associated with sugar production" and plantation debris (Walmsley 2011, 82). Beuze's privileging of the island's silhouette as a container for plantation debris invites us to read his art installations as meditations on Martinique's history as a dumping ground for capitalism's refuse, as a geographical spaced crushed altogether by the forces of empire. The use of the silhouette allows him to effectively link the protocapitalistic enterprise that gave birth to the would-be nation to the crushing of landscapes and lives. His reflection on the series as aiming to grasp "the marrow of our being in the world," moreover, speaks to the depth of this colonial exploitation as having reached the marrow—the very source of the blood—of the nation, crushing it to the bone.

Beuze's most memorable *Machinique* (2007) installation (see Figure 3.4) was mounted at the old distillery buildings of Habitation Clément, one of Martinique's best-known producers of artisanal rums. The Clément Distillery was founded in 1887 by Homère Clément, the son of a tailor who studied medicine in France and rose to become a *grand mulâtre* after purchasing a bankrupt plantation, the Domaine d'Acajou, where he developed the techniques of rum production that would in time make him "the father of rhum agricole." His *domain*, now known as Habitation Clément (Clément Plantation) is a popular heritage tourism site in Martinique; its historical buildings frequently house art exhibits sponsored by the Fondation Clément. Like the Maison de la Canne (The Sugar Cane Museum), the Clément Distillery provided an ideal "context" for the display of Beuze's installation. Both have been praised for the excellence of the historical research guiding their restoration and curatorial efforts. Beuze's work both benefitted from their reputation for high curatorial quality while providing "authentic" special contexts that both validated his critique of the system and allowed his work to enter into a dialogue with the objects and portraits of cane workers displayed in the venues alongside his installation. In the *Machinique* installation at the Habitation Clément, the "map" was suspended over the grinding machinery of the former sugar factory by thin plastic threads. The juxtaposition of the bagasse-filled map, the plantation implements, and the life-size portraits of the cane workers in a room from whose large open windows one could see the still active cane fields gave

Figure 3.4 Hervé Beuze, *Machinique* (2007), bagasse, plastic wire and metal
structure, 5 × 2.5m. Fondation Clément. Photograph by Dino
Feigespan.

this installation a poignant cumulative quality, highlighting the specificity
of Beuze's concerns with landscape, history, and debris.

Anne Walmsley and Stanley Greaves, commenting on the piece in their
book *Art in the Caribbean*, underscore the multiple resonances of the installation's venue: the use of bagasse "as a powerful symbol of the crushed
spirit" of the formerly enslaved; the map's suspension as a "gigantic spider
in the middle of its web" as a reference to the Anansi trickster/god figure

of Caribbean folklore, who often takes the shape of a spider; and its suspension as a reference to the island's existence in limbo, "surrounded by free nations, yet still attached to the colonial power as a formal part of it, a puppet controlled by outside strings" (Walmsley and Greaves 2011, 82). For Beuze, the importance of the venue rested on its forcing the viewer to "confront the vastness of the architectural space and the reality of the elements that composed it: the grooved wheels oozing grease, the geometry of the modern metallic framework" (Ravion-d'Ingianni 2007, 7). He also calls attention to what he describes as the "quasi artisanal" nature of the process of installation: "the patient work of collection and assemblage, the repetitive gestures that allowed him to line up the cane leaves, the delicate piling up of the bagasse, all confer on the installation the airy and fragile appearance of a weaving loom" (Ravion-d'Ingianni 2007, 9). Beuze is not alone in seeking to equate the intense labor involved in the preparation of his installations to the labor of workers in the cane fields, seeing in this labor equity a symbolic identification with the crushing enterprise of empire through slavery and postslavery exploitation.

These "ephemeral installations," as Beuze describes them, have been inspired—as the artists has repeatedly asserted—by Glissant's assessment in his *Caribbean Discourse*, that "because the collective memory was too often wiped out, the Caribbean writer [or artist], must 'dig deep' into this memory, following the latent signs that he has picked up in the everyday world" (Glissant 1989, 64). It is a preoccupation that links his work with that of Atelier Morales, placing them in a creative continuum. Moreover, the ephemeral quality of Beuze's work—bagasse rots, smells, decays and transforms into compost—underscores an element of central importance to Beuze—the ways in which Caribbean nations and peoples have been marked by the crushing and discarding of cane turned into bagasse and of the bodies whose very blood marrow has joined this imperial debris. Beuze has frequently described his work as a metaphor for the impact of colonization on the people of the Caribbean, left crushed and drained like bagasse, a metaphor reinforced by the pungent smell of the fermenting bagasse of his installations—the sweetly rotting smell that signals both decomposition and transformation. Hence the poignancy of his installation at the Habitation Clément, fermenting canes that signal both the crushing exploitation of sugar cane production and the redefinition on an industry that has turned rum production into Martinique's quintessentially artisanal product.

In more recent work, Beuze, who has used his signature Matrice-Carte concept to address a multiplicity of themes, has devoted his installations to other environmental concerns facing Martinique. His silhouettes of Martinique have been filled in with garbage (disposing of refuse is a rising problem in Martinique) and also with canned food to highlight Martinique's acute levels of food insecurity. The island produces only 2 percent of what it consumes and even minor problems with shipments of basic foodstuffs can lead to severe and immediate food shortages. In installations like the 2009 reiteration of Machinique, you see the silhouette of Martinique placed under looming pieces of sugar mill equipment, a juxtaposition that negates the nostalgia of the images by Atelier Morals we saw earlier. Gleaming and menacing—as if to express the possibility of their eternal return, as possible *revenants* or returning ghosts—the machinery hovers over the island, ready to crunch cane again at any moment.

The sugar mill as *revenant* also haunts María Magdalena Campos-Pons' *Sugar/Bittersweet*, a site-specific installation commissioned by the Smith College Museum of Art in Northampton, Massachusetts, for exhibition in November 2010. Born in 1959 in the Matanzas province of Cuba, Campos-Pons (who has lived in Boston since 1989) has spoken frequently about her personal connection to Cuba's history of sugar production with which her family's history is intermingled. She grew up near one of the now-defunct sugar factories in the town of La Vega, and lived in the former slave barracks of a plantation of the kind featured both in Eduardo Laplante's prints and Atelier Morales' photographs, sharing with the latter a deeply felt and historically complex relationship to sugar. Matanzas was a center of Cuban sugar production from the late eighteenth into the twentieth century as well as at one time a port of entry for African slaves. Her own great-grandfather was brought from Nigeria to Cuba as a slave, while her great-grandmother, a Chinese woman said to be from Canton, came to Cuba as an indentured servant to work in the sugar fields. "Sugar is the reason the town was built as a plantation [...], sugar is what my ancestors worked in, sugar was the main product of La Vega, sugar is Cuba," Campos-Pons has explained, adding that the exhibit "has a lot to do with home, place and territory" (Bell 1998, 35). Like Beuze, Campos-Pons' preoccupation with place and territory has led her to recreate the space of the plantation in installations that seek to immerse the museum goer in the visual and olfactory experience of being amidst the debris of the sugar field. Campos-Pons does not work with bagasse—a material not readily available in the northeast region of the US, where she works and teaches—but seeks instead to recreate the olfactory quality so striking in Beuze's work through the inclusion of fermenting sugary confections (see Figure 3.5).

Given her interest in the recreation of the plantation space in the museum space, *Sugar/Bittersweet* is conceived as a sugar cane field represented by "a gridded layout of wooden carved stools, each containing a spear positioned upright from the stools," which reference the slaves who worked in the sugar fields (Smee 2013). Its initial impact is described by Sebastian Smee in a review for *The Boston Globe* as "weirdly thrilling" (2013). The spears pierce columns of actual raw sugar disks and cast-glass forms, becoming "visual metaphors for the tall, graceful stalks of the sugar cane plant;" roped-together Chinese weights allude to the weighing of the crop after harvest and to the Chinese indentured servants that included her grandmother (McQuaid 2010). In all, the installation, which is accompanied by a video

Figure 3.5 María Magdalena Campos-Pons, *Sugar/Bittersweet* (2010), mixed-media installation, including wood, glass, raw sugar, metal, video, and stereo sound; dimensions variable. Courtesy of the Smith College Museum of Art. Photograph by Stephen Petegorsky.

of interviews with Afro-Cuban subjects, shows how Cuba's deep involvement in the production of a major commodity impacted millions of Creoles, Africans, and Chinese. As a result the work, "rather than envisioning sugar as a crystallized and easily melted confection," conjures through the use of squares and discs of white and brown sugar respectively, not sugar's syrupiness—to which the exhibit constantly alludes, but to the less appealing human and environmental exploitation that accompanies it (Buttenwieser 2011). The installation included actual sugary cakes, the smell of which was "contagious, pervasive" (Buttenwieser 2011).[6] Set against sterile white floor and walls, the work conjures the barrenness of the soil to which such labor led. The sterility marks the physical transformation of the land that created the plantation's landscape. Where Beuze used bagasse and debris to conjure the ecological devastation the sugar plantation left in its wake, Campos-Pons trusts emptiness to speak of the lives and landscapes sacrificed to the advance of sugar production on her home island. This is an element underscored both through the references to forced migration throughout the installation and through the videos, which capture the narratives of subjects whose lives were significantly impacted by cane—particularly those of Campos-Pons' own family.

Like Beuze, Campos-Pons also invokes the exploitation implicit in the production of sugar by engaging in the laborious task of handmaking many of the objects included in the installation. Cuba's sugar fields, Campos-Pons has explained, loomed large for her as places of familial and historical import. "When I tried to figure out how to construct the field, I could see in my mind, in my dreams, that green field, the sugar field. I wanted to express mobility and flexibility and sturdiness. I wanted to show what sugar production means to Africans" (Buttenwieser 2011). She designed and crafted the spears herself and made the glass discs that appear in her installation. Throughout the production of the exhibit, she explained, she remained constantly aware of the labor she was doing being somehow akin to how much labor goes into producing sugar. Her self-described task, in part, was to translate the extremely hard work entailed in this substance, to offer a sense of the intense effort involved—the relentless labor associated with sugar production (Buttenwieser 2011). There is in this recreation of the intensity and relentlessness of plantation labor, both in Campos-Pons and Beuze, an element of penance—an understanding that as artists they have been spared the life of their ancestors but must remain committed to speaking to the history of a colonial enterprise that claimed millions of lives and decimated hundreds of thousands of acres of land in the name of capitalist profit. Like Beuze, Campos-Pons trusts to the importance of immersion in the cane field (visual, olfactory, spatial) to bring the museum audience into contact with the realities of sugar production.

In 2009, the same year Beuze opened his most recent iteration of *Machinique*—its bright yellow island with the menacing machines over it—and just months before Campos-Pons *Sugar/Bittersweet* installation opened, Jamaican artist Charles Campbell unveiled the first iteration of his monumental *Bagasse* cycle, later featured in *Wrestling with the Image: Caribbean Interventions*, a 2011 exhibit at the Museum of the Americas in Washington DC (see Figure 3.6).

Figure 3.6 Charles Campbell, *Transporter* 2 (2011), screen print on card, metal clips, 101 × 101cm; *Bagasse* (2009) acrylic on canvas, 550 × 220cm. Courtesy of the artist.

Campbell, now the head curator of Jamaica's National Gallery of Art, shares Beuze's commitment to creating spaces for reflection by immersing the viewer in the materiality of the historical and ecological realities of Caribbean islands that share the same trajectory of imperial ruin. This Campbell accomplishes primarily through "a graphic codification" that seeks to transform daily experience "into patterns and signs": in his work, miniature Dutch slave ships transform into DNA sequences, and atom-like forms become flocks of migrating birds (Cozier 2011, 11). I want to focus here on two of his recent installations. *Actor Boy/Bagasse* (2009–2010) features large-scale paintings of forms suggesting atoms and mandalas filled with *trompe l'oeil* detail that references a multiplicity of historical, cultural and environmental themes: slavery, the slave trade, bird migration/forced migration, slave ships, the sea, conflict and violence—all presented through repeated patterns in the service of the creation of the larger images. The second series, *The Transformer Project* (2011), translates the motifs and forms he developed in the first *Bagasse* series into large but remarkably light three-dimensional objects (primarily painted or laser-cut round sculptures, see above) on whose surface the earlier motifs are applied with a variety of techniques to produce "a play between heavily loaded political narratives and utopian ideals, image and object" (see Campbell's website at http:// charlescampbellart.com).

Both installations share the same backdrop: a large-scale black-and-white painting that reproduces the visual disorder of milled cane and "speaks to the island's economic lifeblood that was once tended by slaves" (Tischler 2011). The painting, *Bagasse*, represents a bed of crushed canes as if seen from above, offering a vertical view of what is normally a horizontal landscape. In the painting, Campbell uses the same *trompe-l'oeil* of the accompanying paintings and sculptures to incorporate "embedded in the frenzied and telling lines"—hidden in the bagasse itself, that debris of the history and environmental devastation of the plantation—repeated images of the Dutch slave ships that brought their human cargo to the Caribbean. Tamara Flores writes that the painting "negates the traditional association of a painting as a window onto the world and as a beautiful object to offer instead a bleak vision of an anti-landscape. In a stark palette of black and white, the artist portrays a bird's-eye view of crushed stalks of sugar cane on the ground," suggesting "chaos and destruction" and forcing us, through a life-size representation of plantation debris covering the land, to "witness the traces of suffering that remain, stark reminders of the legacy of slavery" (Flores 2011, 21). In a review of the *Wrestling with the Image* exhibit, Marta Fernández Campa speaks of an "ironic resemblance between [Jackson] Pollock's abstract work and the literal image of the bagasse in Campbell's painting," whose significance is enmeshed in the privileging of abstract over conceptual art in the west (Fernández Campa 2012, 12). Campbell has explained his use of bagasse as "a metaphor for an economic system that views society and human relationships as by-products," as part of a project that "attempts to re-image the past in a way that liberates the future" (Cozier and Flores 2011, 42). This point in underscored by Michaeline Crichlow, when she writes:

> Here, Campbell seems to ask us to imagine history approached from the angle of its recyclable elements. But to experience the full impact of such imagining consider the way in which this crop was introduced into the so-called New World, the bitter sweetness of its production, its global reach sweetening the diets of so many, linking diverse geographies and fates, and the way in which it facilitated the crushing of so many humans, disposable bodies, and like bagasse considered detritus but not quite. Bagasse is now recycled as the ultimate product of sustainability and resilience as a form of energy. Its black and white appearance, captured here, is rendered stunning, abstract, a large triptych sanitized and objectified for a different presence and imagination.
> (2013, 131)

Bagasse shares with Campbell's earlier work, *Transformations and Meditations* (2004), a deeply ecological foundation. In *Bagasse*, the crushing of the natural world (what Campbells calls "the unnatural") creeps out from the interstices of the crushed cane, neither hidden nor forgotten. This unnaturalness, however, is balanced by a complex interplay of motifs that link the possibility of transcending the experience of slavery through the cyclical processes of the natural world. The installations show the natural order (the migrating bird and the metamorphosing insect, for example) as *healing* the wounds and violence of history. Migrating birds stand for slaves in the ship's hold before breaking into a flock in flight; butterflies interrupt patterns of "meditations" on slavery and violence. Campbell sees these transformative paintings and sculptures as means of suggesting "possibilities that exist outside of the deterministic view that may be implied by work that points to the past," of pointing to "the necessity of halting the trajectory that propels them from past events to future actions." On his website, he cites the work of Buckminster Fuller, the early environmental activist and designer of the geodesic dome, as a major influence on the development of his art, giving Fuller credit for inspiring his "playful use of pattern and symmetry" to counterbalance the "gravity of the underlying issues" he seeks to address. The sculptural forms of his sculptures, Campbell has argued, "point to Fuller's idea of a rational utopia" and allow him to navigate "between heavily loaded political narratives and utopian ideals, object and image, public and private spaces" (see Campbell's website at http://charlescampbellart.com).

Campbell's work seems to encapsulate the concerns of this subset of contemporary Caribbean artists whose "ephemeral installations," often so dependent on their evanescent material, underscore a shared preoccupation with the ways in which Caribbean nations, peoples and environments have been marked by the crushing and discarding of cane turned into molasses, bagasse, ruined environments and impoverished exploited lives. His work shares with that of the other artists discussed here an insistence on the representation of the Caribbean region's legacy of colonial violence as constitutive to environmental representation. Together, their depictions of ruined landscapes and the crushing of cane through which this ruination is articulated, points to a violence that equally affects humans and nonhumans in an unbroken continuum. From Atelier Morales' sugar mill ruins, through Beuze and Campbell's insistence on the power of bagasse to capture the exploitation inherent to the plantation, to Campos-Pons incorporation of the sweet smell of decay in her symbol-laden reconstruction of a sugar field, these works demonstrate that the landscape of the plantation becomes a canvas for the reconstitution of the violent history of the Caribbean environment and the people who inhabit them.

In "There is a Country in the World," Dominican poet Pedro Mir spoke of the Caribbean as "an implausible archipelago/of sugar and alcohol" in which land and men "belong[ed] to the mill," exhorting his readers to "tell the wind the surnames/of the thieves and the caverns/and open your eyes on a disaster/the peasants have no land" (Mir 1949, 12, my translation). The works discussed above channel the spirit of Mir's passionate poem of dispossession as articulated through the landscape, bringing to museum audiences (local and international) powerful visual invitations to reconsider the legacy of the plantation as still holding sway over the islands' ecologies and peoples. I value in them, above all, their commitment to the recreation of the experience of the cane field—its heat, intense labor and crushing fatigue in return for impoverished lives—in ways that turn personal histories into emblematic visual narratives of the specificities of imperial ruination. Following Glissant's exhortation to "dig deep" in order to recover traces of ancestral memories, they have found in their close familial connections to the plantation a point of departure for the recreation of conflicted and vexed historical landscapes.

NOTES

1. The environmental impact of the sugar plantation can be measured primarily through deforestation and the resulting soil erosion, loss of fertility and desertification (See Paravisini-Gebert 2011). A secondary impact has been that of species extinctions and loss of biodiversity (see Paravisini-Gebert 2014).
2. This includes, most particularly, *Caribbean Literatures and the Environment* (2005), edited by Elizabeth DeLoughrey, Renée Gosson and George Handley, and *Postcolonial Ecologies* (2011), edited by DeLoughrey and Handley.
3. This definition is drawn from guidelines for environmental art on the website of Greenmuseum (http://greenmuseum.org), an online museum for the global environmental art movement. Their list is based, according to the website, on guidelines suggested by the artist Lynne Hull. See http://greenmuseum.org/what_is_ea.php).
4. See also Thompson (2006) and Mitchell (1994).

5. For more on the impact of Delano's photographs see Rivera (1997), Benítez (1988), Goldman (1988), and Jack Delano (1997).
6. See Buttenwieser, "Sweet Sugar." This olfactory element, also true of Beuze's bagasse-filled island silhouettes, is one of the most salient features of Tania Bruguera's work on sugar production for the 2000 Havana Biennial. The work was installed in a tunnel at la Fortaleza, a small colonial Havana fortress formerly used as a penitentiary cell and visitors entered the exhibit at one end of a guarded, cave-like space whose floor was covered by a thick bed of bagasse that kept fermenting in the heat at an increasing pace as the exhibit unfolded and which made walking through the exhibit somewhat hazardous. The first impression, as a result, was of the powerful and pervasive odor of fermentation. Disoriented by the darkness, the smell, and the effort required for walking over the bagasse, the viewer was drawn toward a blue light emanating from the distance that turned out to be a television screen silently projecting looped video images of Fidel Castro in his best "líder máximo" stance. A number of naked men were to be met during the trajectory. They made a series of repetitive gestures: one bowed rhythmically, another rubbed himself as if trying frantically to remove a stain, and so on. It was, in the opinion of one critic, "as though Bruguera were presenting a philosophy of (national) history, in which people journey through a collective experience that can only be comprehended once they've reached its end, whereupon 'the past' reveals itself as having consisted of repeated rituals and empty gestures" (Israel 2001,148).

REFERENCES

Bell, Lynne. 1998. "History of People Who Were Not Heroes: A Conversation with Maria Magdalena Campos-Pons." *Third Text* 43: 33–42.

Benítez, Marimar. 1988. "El caso especial de Puerto Rico." In *El espíritu latinoamericano: arte y artistas en los Estados Unidos*, edited by Luis Cancel et al., 79–80. New York: Harry N. Abrams.

Brébion, Dominique. 2011. "Les Departements Français des Ameriques à l'heure du Post-tropicalisme." *UGR* 736. http://www.ugr.es/~hum736/revista%20electronica/numero14/07/deptos%20franceses.pdf.

Buttenwieser, Sarah. 2011. "Sweet Sugar, Salty Tears: The Introspective Art of Magdalena Campos-Pons." *HandEye Magazine.* March 17. http://handeyemagazine.com/content/sweet-sugar-salty-tears-0.

Cantero, Justo G. 1857. *Los ingenios: Colección de vistas de los principales ingenios de azúcar de la isla de Cuba.* Illustrations by Eduardo Laplante. Havana: Luis Marquier. [Project Gutenberg EBook #39312].

Cliff, Michelle. 2003. "Caliban's Daughter." *Journal of Caribbean Literatures* 3 (3): 157–160.

Cozier, Christopher. 2011. "Notes on Wrestling with the Image." In *Wrestling with the Image: Caribbean Interventions*, edited by Christopher Cozier and Tatiana Flores, 1–15. Washington: Art Museum of the Americas/Organization of American States.

Cozier, Christopher, and Tatiana Flores, eds. 2011. *Wrestling with the Image: Caribbean Interventions.* Washington: Art Museum of the Americas/Organization of American States.

Crichlow, Michaeline A. 2013. "Human Traffic—Past and Present." *Cultural Dynamics* 25: 123–140.

Christopher, Matthew. 2012. "Confessions of a Ruin Photographer Part III: On Dealing with the Dead." *Abandoned America.* http://www.abandonedamerica.us/confessions-of-a-ruin-pornographer.

Delano, Jack. (1997). *Photographic Memories.* Washington: Smithsonian Institution Press.

DeLoughrey, Elizabeth, and George Handley, eds. 2011. *Postcolonial Ecologies: Literatures of the Environment.* New York: Oxford University Press.

DeLoughrey, Elizabeth, Renée K. Gosson, and George Handley, eds. 2005. *Caribbean Literature and the Environment: Between Nature and Culture.* Charlottesville: University Press of Virginia.

Gautier Benítez, José. 1906. "A Puerto Rico." *Poemas de José Gautier Benítez.* San Juan: Tipografía Heraldo Español.

Fernández Campa, Marta. 2012. "Caribbean Art in Dialogue: Connecting Narratives in *Wrestling with the Image.*" *Anthurium* 9: 1–14.

Flores, Tatiana. 2011. "In Defense of Palm Trees." In *Wrestling with the Image: Caribbean Interventions*, edited by Christopher Cozier and Tatiana Flores, 16–25. Washington: Art Museum of the Americas/Organization of American States.

Fouchet, Max-Pol. 1976. *Wifredo Lam.* New York: Rizzoli.

Glissant, Édouard. 1989. *Caribbean Discourse: Selected Essays.* Ed. Michael Dash. Charlottesville: University Press of Virginia.

Goldman, Shifra. 1994. "Under the Sign of the Pavas: Puerto Rican Art and Populism in International Context." In Shifra Goldman, *Dimensions of the Americas: Art and Social Change in Latin America and the United States*, 416–432. Chicago: University of Chicago Press.

"Harvesting Sweet Energy." 2009. *The Hand that Feeds U.S.* http://www.the-handthatfeedsus.org/farm2fuel_Harvesting-Sweet-Energy.cfm.

Israel, Nico. 2001. "VII Bienal de la Habana." *Art Forum International* (February): 147–148.

Kristeva, Julia. *Desire in Language: A Semiotic Approach to Literature and Art.* New York: Columbia University Press, 1980.

Laguerre, Enrique. 1981. *La llamarada.* Río Piedras, PR: Editorial Cultural.

Leary, John Patrick. 2011. "Detroitism." *Guernica*, January 15. http://www.guernicamag.com/features/leary_1_15_11/.

Manthorne, Katherine. 2001. "Plantation Pictures in the Americas, circa 1880: Land, Power and Resistance." *Neplanta: Views from South* 2: 317–353.

McQuaid, Cate. 2010. "'Sugar' Is a Bittersweet Autobiography: Cuban-born Artist Puts Her History on Display." *Boston Globe.* November 9. http://www.boston.com/ae/theater_arts/articles/2010/11/09/maria_magdalena_campos_ponss_sugar_is_a_bittersweet_autobiography/.

Menocal, Nina. 2004. "The Sugar Mills/Los Ingenios." http://www.ateliermorales.com/LOS%20INGENIOS.html.

Mir, Pedro. 1962. *Hay un país en el mundo y 6 momentos de esperanza.* Santo Domingo: Claridad.

Mitchell, W. J. T., ed. 1994. *Landscape and Power.* Chicago: The University of Chicago Press.

Mullins, Paul. 2012. "The Politics and Archaeology of 'Ruin Porn.'" *Archeology and Material Culture.* August 19. http://paulmullins.wordpress.com/2012/08/19/the-politics-and-archaeology-of-ruin-porn/.

Paravisini-Gebert, Lizabeth. 2011. "Deforestation and the Yearning for Lost Landscapes in Caribbean Literatures." In *Postcolonial Ecologies: Literatures of the Environment*, edited by Elizabeth DeLoughrey and George B. Handley, 99–116. New York: Oxford University Press.

———. 2014. "Extinctions: Chronicles of Vanishing Fauna in the Colonial and Post-Colonial Caribbean. In *The Oxford Handbook of Ecocriticism*, edited by Greg Garrard, 340–357. London and New York: Oxford University Press.

Ravion-d'Ingianni, Sophie. 2007. "Les Cartes d'Hervé Beuze, matrices d'anthropométries identitaires." In *Hervé Beuze: Matrices* [exhibition catalog]. Martinique: Fondation Clément.

Rivera, Nelson. 1997. *Visual Arts and the Puerto Rican Performing Arts, 1950–1990*. New York: Peter Lang.

Santiago, Fabiola. 2005. "The Art of the Americas Is Hot." *Hispanic* 18: 52–53.

Smee, Sebastian. 2013. "Campos-Pons Ambitious 'My Mother Told Me' Wanders." *Boston Globe*, September 12. http://www.bostonglobe.com/arts/theater-art/2013/09/12/art-review-maria-magdalena-campos-pons-mother-told-tufts-university/4dPf3H72RBEK5lmhz9nm7N/story.html.

Thompson, Krista. 2006. *En Eye for the Tropics: Tourism, Photography and Framing the Caribbean Picturesque*. Durham: Duke University Press.

Tischler, Gary. 2011. "Beautiful Complexity Makes Up Contemporary Jamaica." *The Washington Diplomat*. July.http://www.washdiplomat.com/index.php?option=com_content&view=article&id=7905:beautiful-complexity-makes-up-contemporary-jamaica&catid=1475:july-2011&Itemid=482.

Vlach, John Michael. 2002. *The Planter's Prospect: Privilege and Slavery in Plantation Paintings*. Chapel Hill: University of North Carolina Press.

Walmsley, Anne and Stanley Greaves. 2011. *Art in the Caribbean: An Introduction*. London: New Beacon Books.

"What is Environmental Art?" 2010. *Greenmuseum*. http://greenmuseum.org/what_is_ea.php.

4   Writing a Native Garden?

Environmental Language and Post-*Mabo* Literature in Australia

Susan K. Martin

In Murray Bail's award winning 1998 Australian novel *Eucalyptus* the protagonists, Holland and his daughter Ellen, live in a "garden" which consists
of every variety of Australian Eucalypt, painstakingly planted by the father.
The Eucalypts become the object of a rather odd fairy-tale quest set up by
Holland. Any man seeking his daughter's hand in marriage must first correctly identify every Eucalypt.[1] This garden is both the ultimate Australian
garden—consisting entirely of eucalypts, the archetypal Australian tree—
and very close to not being a garden at all ("the bewildering facts of so many
eucalypts in one spot, so many obscure species" [58]). It is an expanse that is
all trees, disorganized, all native, perhaps too much like a forest.

Landscape and environment have dominated Australian understandings
of national identity and belonging, particularly in the postcolonial context.
Narratives of self and place, including fictional narratives, have remained very
important in the negotiations of postsettlement culture with a fragile environment. This chapter considers Post-*Mabo* fiction about forms of gardening and
cultivation. The 1992 Australian High Court Mabo v the State of Queensland
(hereafter *Mabo*) decision was a national watershed for Indigenous land rights,
but also for thinking about the land. The discussion also draws on the work
of the environmental humanities, or "ecohumanities," whose stated aim in the
Australian context is to "situate humans within ecological systems, and to re-
situate non-humans in ethical terms" (Ecological Humanities n.d.). Australia
has been at the vanguard of the theorizing of Ecological Humanities. As has
been the case in other settler cultures such as Canada, the environment in Australia has been central to the formation of the national imaginary. Strands of
ecological theory in the humanities have arisen from contestation of conservative national investments in "bush" culture and opposing ideas of empty wilderness. This might be seen coming together usefully in Deborah Bird Rose's
Reports from a Wild Country (2004), where she outlines the non-Indigenous
investment in a bush ethos and bush lifestyle which appropriates Indigenous
belonging, and also touches on environmental movements which assume
that authentic and protected environments are empty of human populations, even the human population which has existed fruitfully, if not stati-
cally, in Australia for at least sixty thousand years. Cognate work being done
by influential figures including philosopher Val Plumwood, and workers in
the fields of landscape history, geography and archaeology including Libby

Robin, Tim Bonyhady, Lesley Head, Bill Gammage, and George Seddon all contributed to the early formation of a body of Australian work interrogating human-environmental relations within frameworks informed and enriched by humanities research, and inflected by specific Australian contexts.

Australian ecological humanities has been inflected by the lateness of the colonial enterprise on the continent, which pushed environmental and human impact into a different modern era and raised the possibility of addressing or stemming the extent of colonial impacts witnessed elsewhere. The specificity of the dryest continent (which yet stretches across temperate and tropical zones) has also influenced a prevailing national narrative of war against the environment ("fighting" fires; "battling" droughts and floods, etc.). This particularly virulent construction of human identity "*against* nature" (Tiffin and Huggan 2010, 6) has spurred a strong counter narrative of "connectivity" (Rose and Robin 2004). As in other settler colonial societies, Indigenous knowledge—Aboriginal history, theory, science and ways of knowing—was first unrecognized or discounted and has more recently been acknowledged, incorporated, and also misappropriated in attempts to come to terms with and repair non-Indigenous Australian records of dispossession of people and destruction of place, as various commentators note (Tiffin and Huggan 2010; Head 2000; Read 2000).

Rose and Robin comment on the perceived need for new "stories of our place in the biosphere, stories of the human organism as a living moment in connection with environment." While they warn, rightly, that "the world already has its own stories" this chapter does look at the extent to which Australian fiction after *Mabo*, particularly immediately after *Mabo*, drew on existing stories and created new ones in order to engage with a newly configured relationship between peoples and place.

Here I examine the way in which specific legal redefinitions of place have inflected the ways that fictional narratives write or rewrite, the environment and human and plant relationships with it in metaphorical and concrete terms. The importance of the "native garden" in this formulation is that it posits the paradox of coexistence and almost impossible balance at the heart of Australian political and environmental life: native belonging with artificial garden, reconciliation between Indigenous and non-Indigenous people, extant environment and invaders, pristine and mongrel culture. Arguably one of the first ways to make this balance conceivable is to imagine it—to narrate it, to tell it to ourselves as a story.

In *Eucalyptus* the idea of the "native garden" is established early in the novel. The fact that what is around the house is not a forest, or just a paddock planted with trees, comes when Holland starts to consider the habit he has fallen into of planting different eucalypt species. When he looks at his plantings, he considers the issue in terms of design:

> After a dozen or so plantings Holland stood back and saw he would have to plant others here and there, to avoid giving an odd, lopsided look.

In this he followed the great painters and English Landscape gardeners who struggled with the difficulty of reproducing the randomness of true harmony, demonstrated so casually in nature.

(Bail 1998, 38)

The introduction of aesthetics pushes the planting into the realm of gardening. The planting of single, featured, species has already removed the property and Holland's planting from being a simple case of revegetation and regeneration. Such revegetation projects in Australia, as Allaine Cerwonka points out, often slide into a fantasy of complete restoration and reparation of land post invasion, an abnegation of guilt and responsibility (Cerwonka 2004, 121–45).

After the wind break, the "rubber plantation" and the ornamental avenue, [all eucalypt] Holland turned his back on mass formations. From now on he concentrated on individual species, planted singly [...]. Many years were spent culling, reducing most species to a single healthy specimen.

(Bail 1998, 42–43)

This "gardenesque" manner of planting—featuring single species, and the culling, is combined with that most traditional and indicative of gardening practices, weeding: "only the acacia has more species than the eucalyptus—but look at the acacia, a series of pathetic little bushes. Whenever on his property Holland saw clumps of wattle, as the acacia is called, he lost no time pulling them out by the roots" (36).

It is one specific statement, when the plantings are identified as producing a particular kind of transformation on the land, that ultimately moves Holland's garden and the book into a different context.

Holland set up a swing for Ellen on [a Blue Gum's] lower branches. Here the land fell away and rose again in gentle waves. It was as bare and as dusty as shorn sheep, until rendered park-like by Holland's hand.

(40)

"Park-like" is a familiar and potent term in Australian colonial history. It recurs like a mantra in the descriptions of the earliest white arrivals—for instance in George Worgan's description of Sydney Cove, Port Jackson, in 1788, the year of the arrival of the "first fleet" of white settlers:

[I]n our Excursions Inland, which I believe have not exceeded 30 or 40 Miles in any Direction, we have met with a great Extent of Park-like Country, and the Trees of a moderate Size & at a moderate distance from each other, the Soil, apparently, fitted to produce any kind of Grain and clothed with extra-ordinarily luxuriant Grass.

(1978, 6)

The same kind of descriptions, and the term, occur in the official journals of early white explorers including John Oxley, Charles Sturt, Thomas Mitchell, and early settlers, men and women, such as Elizabeth Macarthur.[2] Perhaps one of the very first to evoke the comparison was Sidney Parkinson, the draftsman employed by Joseph Banks, viewing the shoreline from Captain Cook's *Endeavour*, who observed, like his companions, that "the trees, quite free from underwood, appeared like plantations in a gentleman's park" (Gammage 2011, 5).

Holland's plantation garden is moved, through the use of this term, into the realm of the English Garden movement, and the Enclosure Acts, enhanced by Ellen's Romantic swing, and already invoked in the reference to English landscape gardeners. But the specific term "park-like" makes a direct connection between this narrative and its garden and the colonial appropriation of Aboriginal cultivation practices.

What rendered the landscape "park-like" for early settlers and explorers, as Bill Gammage has most recently outlined, was the extensive environmental cultivation, mostly by selective burning, practiced by the Indigenous people. Whether or not you call this detailed management "gardening," it rendered the landscape parklike to European eyes, and thereby made the place visually and physically accessible for colonial appropriation. Something which already resembled a "gentleman's park" appeared destined to become exactly that, particularly when, as Gammage points out, even the closest observers recognized the puzzling lack of undergrowth, existence of meadows where there should be trees, and other signs of management, as "natural," and therefore as available land (2011, 5–15). Thus this phenomenon was widely seen but not recognized. This was fortuitous, as it would have stood in the way of the doctrine of *terra nullius* (that Australia was "waste" uncultivated ground, and therefore unused and available for settlement).

The novel *Eucalyptus* (which does not use its terms unselfconsciously) raises a number of questions that lurk within Australian fiction and culture about place, cultivation and identification, particularly after the 1992 Australian High Court *Mabo* decision and the overturn of *terra nullius,* and the subsequent 1996 Wik Peoples v Queensland (hereafter *Wik*) ruling that pastoral leases did not automatically extinguish Native Title—that, importantly, "it was possible for two types of land title to apply to the one piece of land" (Stevenson 1996, 6; see also Wik Peoples v Queensland 1996; Collins 2004, 2–3). The *Wik* decision was going through the courts during the writing and publication of *Eucalyptus.* The narrator comments on the nature of the story of *Eucalyptus* as yet another Australian fiction concerned with environment and landscape: "Yes, yes: there's nothing more dispiriting, *déjà vu*, than to come across another story of disappointment set in the Australian backblocks" (1998, 24), although this, like much of the novel, is either calling for a "new mythology for Australian literature" (McNeer 2002, 171) or is just parodic and resistant, as Amanda Johnson argues (2011, 14). At the same time Bail likens

Holland's planting to an act of writing: "A paragraph is not so different from a paddock—similar shape, similar function." The discussion continues, "[t]he rectangle is a sign of civilisation: Europe from the air. Civilisation? A paragraph begins as a rectangle and by chance may finish up a square. [...] A paddock has an alteration in the ending for the point of entry, just as a paragraph has an indentation to encourage entry" (1998, 32, 33). The book is like gardening, and farming, a colonial tool of appropriation and reshaping, and a possible tool of reparation and reconciliation.

Bail is self-reflexively aware of the associations of his topic, and extends them. The name of the protagonist, Holland, invokes New Holland, an early colonial name for Australia before its specific invaders had been finalized. The narrator comments also on the colonizing nature of the eucalypt which has been "exported to different countries in the world [and ...] infected the purity of these landscapes" (23).[3] The stories which the suitor goes on to tell track the paths of the eucalypt, nationally and internationally, a set of tales which can be seen as either bridging the parochial with the cosmopolitan, or, as Paul Sharrad argues, shoring up its "nationalist core" with a "secondary array of dispersed and unelaborated references to other lands" (2007, 35).

Eucalyptus is the ultimate taxonomic book: the challenge is for the prospective suitor to apply the proper Latin botanic name to each of the trees in the garden, and although it must not be forgotten that the novel constantly plays, through this quest, on language and the impossibility of classification, it also works with and uses the imperial and empirical systems of classification that underlay European colonialism, as many commentators have pointed out.[4]

In the novel, it is the lover with stories rather than just names (although they are stories which illustrate the names—mnemonic stories, perhaps) who wins the heart of the girl in the garden. The garden with a history is the one that inspires her. That the storyteller rather than the classifier wins her may seem a win for the reader desiring an anti-colonial ending. The landscape (and garden) without history has been identified throughout settler Australian history as the problem with non-Aboriginal Australian national identification.

In the Aboriginal writer Alexis Wright's narrative, "A Family Document" (2001), the grandmother makes a garden in Cloncurry that is full of story and memory for the narrator. It is not a particularly traditional garden, it is full of "Chinese cabbage, parsnips, carrots and other Asian vegetables as well as grapevines [...] flowers such as petunias, zinnias, and everlasting daisies"(2001, 236). In addition, "[h]er yard contained an assortment of trees, all of which she grew, such as cedars, fig, oleander, chinky apple tree, banana and poinciana trees. Not one weed grew in her yard because she would wake up early every morning to rake the yard" (236). Unlike Holland's plantings, these are all introduced trees. The grandmother's garden is different for other reasons. It is an inclusive space, a place for family and connection whereas Holland uses the trees to exclude and winnow and demarcate his property. Finally the story makes clear that it doesn't matter what the grandmother grows because she is of the country. "Grandma attached no importance to being Waanyi other than it being a state of being"; "Grandma's way of transmitting knowledge was to tell the stories about the country. These were the stories that arise from nature" (238, 239).

In *Eucalyptus*, the stories tied to each planted tree are sometimes about displacement, sometimes about emplacement, but whatever they are they cannot be the same sort of tree story as the one at the heart of "A Family Document" in which Grandma's mother was "'found' [with] another little Waanyi girl sitting up a tree in the bush somewhere between Brunette Downs and Lawn Hills." Wright asks, "why two frightened little Waanyi girls were found up a tree alone in the bush. Where were their families? Why were they hiding in the tree? Were they the survivors of one of Hann's [the man who "found" them] murderous attacks on their people?" (227–29). That the narrator's great grandmother belongs in and to the tree, and not to Hann, is quite clear. This is part of a quite different sort of cultivation and planting going on in this story: the "vision still firmly planted" in the minds of Grandma's descendants. It is the seeding and growth of story and remembering in those who follow. The narrator's youngest daughter, named "Lily, Alice, Anna, Badjawa, is named after her grandmothers and her great, great, great grandmother [...] a senior Waanyi traditional owner [...] told [her] that Badjawa means the Wild Plum tree"(240).[5] The European names and imposition of the gardenlike "Lawn Hill" are re-sited by this survival, and the identification of the child with a sequence of names which incorporates both the introduced lily *and* the native plum tree.

Alexis Wright has talked about her fiction as truth telling—as a way of conveying truth with less pain to the community. This story is a family history, not apparently fictionalized, and using a number of oral techniques—repetition, questions, blocks of unexplained events approached from an oblique angle. The story, like Wright's fiction, is absolutely mapped onto country—so that the narrative is like travelling across the land, events are traced onto place, onto plants and trees, and they derive meaning from each other. In Wright's writing, meaning must be attached to place. She has commented to one interviewer: "I develop my novels on ideas of seeing how the land might respond to different stories" (Vernay 2004, 171). Wright in this story, as elsewhere, warns against taking people from their country, and her happy ending is in the Grandmother's visit back to country.

Wright's 1997 novel, *Plains of Promise*, which appeared the year before *Eucalyptus*, is less optimistic than "A Family Document" (and Bail's novel) in its vision of cultivation. *Plains of Promise* opens with a tree, a poinciana—not here a symbol of life, growth or development, but a symbol of destruction and parasitism. "The biggest tree on St Dominic's mission for Aborigines grew next to the girls' dormitory. It was the only tree that had survived from the twenty-one seeds contained in a seed pod brought by the first missionary on the long and arduous trek to the claypans expanding across the northern Gulf country" (3). The pod is a gift of the missionary's niece. It comes from and represents European culture and appropriation. The pod was used as a weapon on the journey (for whacking the mule) and the seed finally planted:

> God's celebrated poinciana tree came into being surviving the claypans, the droughts and the Wets to grow large and graceful in the presence of three generations of black girls laughing in their innocence as if nothing mattered at all. Its roots clung tighter to the earth when the girls cried out for their mothers or wept into its branches when they were lonely or hurt, enduring the frustration and cruelty of their times. The tree grew in spite of all this. Healthy and unexploited, unaffected when illness fell on all sides, witnessing the frequent occurrence of premature deaths, none of which affected the growth of God's tree. (3)

This tree of invasion is now a weed in Australia. In the novel it serves as a perch for the crows of death. It clearly represents the life-sucking properties of colonialism, and perhaps its irreversibility as well—how colonizing culture changes everything, permanently, how it flourishes at the expense of the indigenous how it changes the landscape, shifts the shape of understanding, like the form of a paragraph does in Bail. Another example is the banana plantation that the missionary, Jipp, starts in the cemetery:

> Whenever someone was buried a young banana plant was planted at the head of the grave: "where there is death, there will always be life," Jipp would proclaim to his grieving flock. And in his diary he wrote: "the fruit is visual evidence that there will always be life everlasting in the whiteman's faith." A practical point to show the virtues of acquiring Christian faith: that here at St Dominic's, all could feel secure in the knowledge that no one would die of hunger. (32)

In fact only the captive dormitory children, who have no choice, will eat this tainted fruit: "the bananas recalled those who were no more; buried and mangled up in the roots of the plantation. When eaten the fruit caused a head-to-toe rash that spread throughout the dormitories" (32). Again the crop of colonialism is misery and death and disease. Disrespect for Indigenous customs and beliefs bears fruit, destroys the land down to the roots, and even marks the body. The plantation goes to ruin and disrepair, and is infested with snakes. It becomes the venue for Jipp to rape the child Ivy, repeatedly; an action described as "A personal expression of his power over the Mission" (33).

Throughout the novel, damage to the land is inseparable from damage to the people—and the people are badly damaged. At one point the central character, seeking some connection to her people and her country, is described as "like a wasted spore, inconsequential, [who] floated about unconnected" (283). Of course, in my reading—a non-Indigenous woman's reading—the true meaning of that remains elusive. At best, stories coexist, and are cultivated side by side in space, but they are not, yet, mutually fully accessible. "Within Australian Indigenous conceptions of country, country is bound with story itself: 'stories are told to and by this ancestral land.'"[6]

Plains of Promise shows a land that is unhealthy because the people who belong to it are disconnected from it. This is an issue of care, including cultivation. Cultivation as gardening is more obviously central to *Eucalyptus*; even if it is not the most crucial in either novel. A circulating question in this, and other fiction, and certainly in Australian culture is: what is a garden? It becomes a fundamental problem for Australia partly because the occupation of the continent is based on the false principle noted earlier, that the land was not cultivated—*terra nullius*—unused, waste land.

This premise was overturned by the 1992 *Mabo* ruling, and then *Wik*, which discredited the *terra nullius* premise at the foundation of Australian settlement, and recognized Indigenous Australian property rights. The *Mabo* ruling was, itself, partly based on an interpretation of gardens—and the long-term ownership (and concept of ownership) and cultivation of food gardens by Torres Strait Islander [TSI] people (*Mabo v State of Queensland* (No. 2)). This was a triumph for Indigenous people, and also in a paradoxical way a reinforcement (from one side) of a Eurocentric understanding of gardening and cultivation, of ownership, and land usage—that is, in terms of the European, or Eurocentric law, quite different understandings of ownership and cultivation were translated into a Western model of cultivation which for once worked somewhat in the favor of indigenous colonized people.[7]

Part of the judgment by Moynihan, J. acknowledges the importance of the garden in Murray Island life in the *Mabo* case in these terms:

> Gardening was important not only from the point of view of subsistence but to provide produce for consumption or exchange during the various rituals associated with different aspects of community life. Marriage and adoption involved the provision or exchange of considerable quantity of produce. Surplus produce was also required for the rituals associated with the various cults at least to sustain those who engaged in them and in connection with the various activities associated with death. Prestige depended on gardening prowess both in terms of the production of a sufficient surplus for the social purposes such as those to which I have referred and to be manifest in the show gardens and the cultivation of yams to a huge size. Considerable ritual was associated with gardening and gardening techniques were passed on and preserved by these rituals. Boys in particular worked with their

fathers and by observations and imitations reinforced by the rituals and other aspects of the social fabric gardening practices were passed on.
(*Mabo v Queensland* 1992)

Discussions of the *Mabo* judgment did not particularly focus on gardening except to the extent that under white law gardening constituted a recognized form of cultivation and ownership which enabled the overthrow of a doctrine of right to colonization based on the assertion that the Indigenous inhabitants did not cultivate the land or assert recognizable property rights in it. New Zealand is an obvious comparison, where recognizable gardening and cultivation practices, although they did not prevent colonization, altered the understanding of prior occupation of the land (Dawson 2010).

I do not want to argue that *Eucalyptus* is a direct response to *Mabo* or *Wik*, but it is part of the complex sequence of ideas about how non-Indigenous Australians might cultivate belonging and write themselves into a land even more problematically "theirs" than it was before.[8] Internationally the 1990s was a decade which saw some symbolic shifts in the profile and understanding of Indigenous people, most notably in the controversial UN declared "International Year of Indigenous people," 1993. Former British colonies—Anglo-settler colonies—saw distinct shifts in treaty and land right acknowledgments across the decade. In New Zealand the 1990s was a major period for the lodgement and processing of claims under the Treaty of Waitangi Tribunal, after the 1985 law change which covered claims back to 1840. In Canada the Oka crisis—a confrontation about the misuse of a sacred site—raised public awareness at the beginning of the decade, and which also saw the creation of Nunavut Territory and the Nisaga'a Treaty (Editors 1996).

Australia's Native Title processes and the *Mabo* decision need to be seen in the context of these international movements and their accompanying narratives. Ken Gelder and Paul Salzman in their study of contemporary Australian fiction see the 1990s as invested in a concept of home, which moved from hopes of reconciliation to conservative anxiety, or even xenophobia (2009, 19). Another central disruptive text about ownership and settlement in Australia which came out even closer to the moment of *Eucalyptus*, and seems to resonate equally with its narrative, is *Bringing them Home: the "Stolen Children" Report* (Australian Human Rights Commission 1997). The fragmented, coded stories, which the unnamed, undescribed suitor tells to Ellen Holland, linked to every eucalypt on the property, echo oddly the fragmented, freighted stories of the stolen children which punctuate the *Report*, and which are similarly—but so differently—matched to geographical location, and are equally, but completely differently, about lost love, separation, misunderstanding. This uncanny resonance, by no means intentional, occupies the same discursive space in time, and about place.[9] This brings us back, in a roundabout way, to [new] Holland's native garden of eucalypts.

WHAT IS A GARDEN?

What is a garden? What elements contribute toward making a space of ground a garden? This is a complex enough question in itself (see Cooper 2006, 2; M. Miller 1993; Ross 1999), but becomes even more complex in Australia when the word "native" is added. The general understanding of a garden is that it is a cultivated space, an artificial space, a space of introduced and ordered planting which unambiguously shows difference from what was there before and from its current surroundings, a human phenomenon (Whittaker 1999). In all these ways, Holland's plantings fit the definition of garden.

This is more clearly true of a number of garden styles common to Australia, as elsewhere; formal gardens of all sorts, the cottage garden, the gardenesque which separates and displays individual species. By contrast some native gardens, wild gardens, "natural gardens" or "natural landscapes" follow an imperative to recreate what was there before, or to blend seamlessly into indigenous surroundings, or to "match" those surroundings, to conceal or deny human intervention. Even more formal native gardens may be informed by the desire and the intention to plant things which "belong", which thrive in native conditions, which, by definition, do not stand out, and do not declare their own cultivated status.

The term "native garden" is used widely in Australia. It refers not to gardens grown by Aboriginal and Torres Strait Islander (ATSI) people, although it may include these, but to the variety of Australian gardens using plants indigenous to the Australian landmass. Native gardens in Australia have complicated origins in discrete environmental, horticultural, and nationalist movements, with sometimes incongruent values. Where gardens and belonging are obviously connected, gardens and reconciliation are a less obvious fit, but in Australia these movements are harnessed. In a place where race riots can include prominent display of the slogan "We grew here, you flew here" and the language of invasives, and environmental endangerment passes between native garden movements, environmental movements, and anti-immigration movements, "planting" and nativeness has a very specific circulation (Mirmohamadi 2003; 2006).

More formal, European, English, and exotic gardens have been described as nature in culture and culture in nature and as a third space—"an attempt at the reconciliation of opposites which constrain our existence" (Miller 2003, 25), a mediating point between culture (Pollan 1996), and nature a "mixture of culture and nature" (Hunt 2000, 34). The native garden is generally in contrast to this particular notion of balance. At one end of the spectrum of native gardens is the purely indigenous garden, a garden consisting entirely of plants indigenous to the area in which it is planted. The planting of what "belongs" in some cases attempts to erase culture from that equation, and assert origin rather than originality—to return to untouched nature (notably an idea of untouched nature without people)

(Head 2000). They may even be informed by a philosophy that eschews the "mastery of nature" some theorists identify as intrinsic to Western epistemological understandings of the world, and as damaging to it (Rigby 2009, 165; Plumwood 1993). They are gardens which in some contexts might be classified as revegetation, or something other than a garden. However even gardeners of native gardens using plants which are not exclusively endemic, or even exclusively Australian, frequently comment that some visitors do not recognize their garden as a garden. Conversely an indigenous garden can still be, and be seen to be, a highly controlled space, whose arrangements, trimmings and design declare themselves as the product of culture despite the naturalization of the plants.

In one of a sequence of interviews with "native gardeners" on their gardens, gardener JH commented on the fate of a five-acre garden by Australian garden designer Bruce Mackenzie which was entirely removed by the new owners:

> it's not seen as a garden because it's native plants, and that's not a garden, that's bush and [the new owner] said oh, those sticks and grass. So it's interesting to see what people see as a garden.
>
> (JH 2007)

Garden commentator Jo Hambrett describes this as the "'native gardens are a jumble of dry sticks' school of thought" (2004, 6).[10]

For some, then, the native garden is a negative space—the space where a garden might be. A successful bush garden becomes so like the bush, that for a "standard" gardener the garden part of the equation is invisible—it is seen *as* bush, not garden, as wilderness not cultivation. It is seen as a space requiring gardening. In the novel *Eucalyptus*, the garden/property is a space located somewhere between garden and bush. Eucalypts are indigenous to the property, as they are to practically every place in Australia, but Holland's careful cultivation of his eucalypts, weeding them down to single specimens, and adding a great many varieties not native to the area or even the state, render it an artificial space, and make particular claims about place, control, and ownership of the "native."

In a discussion of gardens as works of art, the philosopher Tom Leddy raises the importance of human involvement in understanding a garden as a garden: "Think about the following situation (which is actually imagined in Kant's *Critique of Pure Judgment*). You are wandering through the woods and you run across a clearing, a little meadow, and you ask yourself, 'Is this a garden, or is this a natural phenomenon?'" (Whittaker 1999). Leddy goes on to ponder the difference the possible involvement of Native American gardeners makes.

One can extrapolate the Australian context from this, where similarly, as noted, the site being looked at may have been extensively or partially planned and shaped by Indigenous people, and over a much longer period, "managing a continental estate" as Gammage describes (2009, 20).

The possibility of a "purely natural phenomenon" is thus brought into question in ways Leddy doesn't really engage with. Leddy is talking about human intervention in the making of a site into a garden, and the expectation that meaning will be embedded in such a site—that it has an author (a single author), in fact, and that the presence of this author makes the garden a potentially readable text.

In *A Philosophy of Gardens*, David E. Cooper argues that gardens cannot be appreciated simply as nature because "gardens, unlike mountains, are human artifacts imbued with purpose" (2006, 39). He also argues, against such commentators as M. Miller, Ross and Leddy, that gardens are not equivalent to works of art. Unlike an artwork, even "environmental art," gardens are mutable, subject to the natural world, not so constrained by generic expectations. They "are 'impermanent' in various respects, eschew privileged viewpoints, are not 'framed', and lend themselves to the practical purposes" (2006, 32–33).

John Dixon Hunt's somewhat more pragmatic position on the relationship between gardens and art is that garden making is "an art of a special sort in that [...] it involves the inclusion of 'natural materials' which are to some extent beyond the control of the designer" (2000, 15). Hunt, in his definition, raises a point important to the identification of many Australian native gardens as gardens rather than bush; that gardens occupy "*a relatively small space of ground (relative, usually, to accompanying buildings or topographical surroundings)*" (14). That is, the constraint of boundaries, and the presence of buildings at least implies that the associated space of ground is cultivated, is a garden, although, as in the Hambrett discussion above, some native gardens are perceived as simply an identifiable space that should be a garden, or could be gardened (a little like that first settler view of Australia as "naturally" parklike, perhaps). In the same description, Hunt suggests a garden is identified by its relation to place, including "invocation of indigenous plant materials," a description that implies that indigenous plant materials are not intrinsically part of a garden, but external to it, something with which the garden must negotiate, but also be differentiated from: "*[t]he garden will thus be distinguished in various ways from the adjacent territories in which it is set*" (14, 15).

In a discussion of a garden form generally seen to be at the other end of the spectrum from the native garden, topiary, Isis Brook and Emily Brady comment, "these gardens were created in part to tell us about who we are and the position of the human being in the order of nature" (2003, 132). The same might be said of native gardens, although obviously their statement is a different one. This is another paradox of the native garden—*if* we take as its apotheosis, the ideal toward which all native gardens tend, the entirely indigenous garden which successfully recreates the plant life endemic to the area presettlement, in a formation natural to that vegetation (and this is assuming a lot) then the garden with the most overt message about the position of human beings in the order of nature (that humans are external to it, that human intervention can erase itself, can achieve restoration/reparation) would also be the garden most in danger of obscuring or losing that message through its nearness to an "ungarden," to the abnegation of all things man-made or constructed in the way it is presented.[11]

CONCLUSIONS

A number of post-*Mabo* texts narrativize cultivation of space as part of the quest for belonging—including *Eucalyptus,* Andrew McGahan's *The White Earth* (2004) and some of Alex Miller's novels.[12] The idea of the native garden in *Eucalyptus* is a long way from such an idea. The taxonomic impulse, and the nature of the "collection," belies this, as does the fairy-tale quest around the hand of the daughter, who is identified by some commentators as representing the landscape (Grbich 2001, 145).

A decade or so later, Indigenous writers might be seen to have developed a very different commentary to that being posited in the first few years after *Mabo* and *Wik.* At one point in Alexis Wright's epic *Carpentaria* (2006), Norm Phantom is rescued from the sea and from white men by a community of bush people, the "ghostly tribe" who are themselves like gardens: "Norm watched in stunned silence as he saw that they were dressed in what looked like sodden, inflorescent compost heaps where the rain ran through the crumpled leaves, bush blossoms, tangled strands of grasses and twigs before splashing down onto the muddy ground" (303). These people assist Norm to rescue his grandson, Bala, from the storm flood—Bala is clinging to a eucalypt he thinks is his mother. Later, the corrupt and compromised white policeman in the novel, Truthful, dreams that he answers the door of the Police Station to find its rose garden full of "deep red roses" blooming and the station itself full of ghostly Aboriginal people, gray and sea shiny, just before he discovers the bodies of three Aboriginal boys, dead in custody (357–58). The chasm between the white population and the environment, and their alien forms of cultivation, are mapped even more clearly in this later novel. When Norm's son, Will Phantom, returns to Uptown looking for his family, the populace are cutting down all the trees in their attempt to get rid of bats. The pointlessness of this activity, and its marker of alienation is made clear by Will's noting that a cyclone is coming which will strip the trees (and indeed when it comes it erases the town), but they don't notice because they are too busy with their "ceremony of belonging" (the tree cutting) (465).

By contrast when Will is washed out to sea he winds up on a floating island of compacted debris, which sprouts a garden and rapidly becomes covered with flowers and food plants: tomatoes, peanuts, fertilizing bees, "peach, apricot, almonds" (495). This floating island seems idyllic, but it is a torment to Will, and it is too fragile and fragmented to last, partly because it is largely made up of the detritus and wreckage, including bodies, of the town. Its existence might suggest the possibility of a future made out of remains, but only for those still meaningfully connected to the land and able to read it. The novel's radically "irresolvable text" is part of its accomplishment.[13] In Kim Scott's 2010 novel, *That Deadman Dance*, about the opening up and loss of possibilities of cooperation in early Western Australian settlement, the gardens are in the charge of the carefully named Sergeant Killam. The white settler Governor and the Aboriginal population share in planting a tree on the grave of the man, Doctor Cross, who was the mediator of cross-communication and possibility between the invaders and the invaded, but it is a tree which marks an end of cooperation (177).

As noted earlier, Murray Bail's garden in *Eucalyptus*, his planted paddocks, is explicitly likened to writing. That novel naturalizes, or at least plants, a set of narrative forms in the landscape at a distinct historical moment when the narrative about the landscape and its recognition became imperative—in particular the recognition of what the eucalypts in the landscape meant to the first settlers, and how they might have to be read again by the existing non-Indigenous population.

Bail's and Wright's writings from the 1990s can be seen as responses to the new narrative of *Mabo*, *Wik*, and the *Stolen Children* report. Bail's story is so determinedly postmodern, self-reflexive, ironic, and knowing, that there is a question as to whether it can be seen as moving toward some idea of replenishing the landscape with better stories. *Eucalyptus* disavows taxonomy—the unsuccessful suitor, Cave, who is able to name every tree, is involved in a quest shown to be meaningless by the more mysterious, unnamed, never fully seen, not necessarily white, suitor whose stories show that the name is not the important detail of a thing, and that things and names can just be coincidence. The narrator, or "Bail," also indicates that the classification of the eucalypt is open-ended—the finite task is actually impossible—the narratives of *terra nullius* and gentlemen's parks are undone.

However this same detail of the open-ended nature of the taxonomic project can equally suggest that these, and other "gardening" stories are doomed to reiterate their originary narrative, to appropriate or cover existing stories. Bail's turning of gardening into writing might just be scratching a place on the surface, or worse, another imperial taxonomic narrative.

Alexis Wright's stories, even before her 2006 novel *Carpentaria*, and the most recent *The Swan Book* (2013), revealed both embeddedness and damage at such profound levels, as to suggest that cultivation of this garden may be almost impossible, and there may be no meeting place or coexistence for such narratives. The uncanny conjunction of Bail's narratives of the eucalypt garden with Wright's poisoned garden might, or should, also remind us of Alison Ravenscroft's warning about *Plains of Promise* and Indigenous narratives in general: "there are countries onto which this text opens that as a white woman (with all the limitations of that position) I am unable to enter, worlds of meaning that I am unable to read" (2010, 71).

The native garden embodies various aspirations of many non-Indigenous Australians for postcolonial reconciliation of the Australian population, and

Australian stories—to restore the "native," or assert belonging, or live in harmony with indigeneity and yet to acknowledge difference, to align native and cultivation without opposition. It may also contain the impossibility (tragic and fruitful) of such a dream. The documents around Native title constantly refer to the legal "fiction" of *terra nullius* and its redundancy (*Wik Peoples v Queensland*). Perhaps "real" fiction can write the way forward. What non-Indigenous and Indigenous Australians *hope* for is embodied in that most vexed and provisional narrative from the *Wik* judgment, which argues that pastoral leases and native title can coexist, and continues: "The extent to which the two interests could operate together is a matter for further evidence and legal analysis".[14] The next sentence in *Wik* suggests that in any conflict of interest, the pastoral lease must dominate. The challenge is to change that sentence.

NOTES

1. Murray Bail's *Eucalyptus* won the 1999 Miles Franklin Award, and the 1999 Commonwealth Writers' Prize (Bail 1998).
2. Oxley describes, "the timber standing at wide intervals, without any brush or undergrowth, gave the country a fine park-like appearance. I never saw a country better adapted for the grazing of all kinds of stock than that we passed" (1820, 5); Sturt's journals contain comments about "those open grassy and park-like tracts, of which so much has been said, characterise the secondary ranges of granite and porphyry" (1833, xxxi). Thomas Mitchell similarly describes, "masses of casuarinae enclosed open spaces covered with rich grass; and, being in some directions extensive, afforded park-like vistas, which had a pleasing effect, from the rich combination of verdure and shade, in a season of excessive heat" (1839, 94) and land which is, "fine, open, park-like, and with much anthistiria, and other grass" (1848, 251).
3. See Martin 2004 for a discussion of the colonizing eucalypt.
4. From Foucault (1973) to more explicit treatments in, for example, Crosby (1986), Pratt (1992), Ritvo (1997), Miller and Reill (1996), and Carruthers and Robin (2010).
5. Oddly one article on "hermeneutic tourism" suggests using the novel *Eucalyptus* to enrich heritage interpretation of Western New South Wales, without referencing any Indigenous literary texts such as Leane (2011), Wright (1997–2012), or Scott (1999) as likely guides to regional Australia, perhaps because of the mixed heritage interpretation they offer, although they do suggest Rachel Perkins' film, *One Night the Moon* (2003). See Ablett and Dyer (2009, 223).
6. Alison Ravenscroft (2012, 31) quoting Alexis Wright.
7. This is despite a claim in the judgment that: "The majority argued that it was not necessary to superimpose a regime of property rights that were approximate to those known to English common law and that to do so defeated the purpose of protection and recognition" (Strelein 2009, 11).
8. This is not a situation unique to or in Australia, but perhaps held in common by settler cultures, as Jill Didur has pointed out, rightly commenting: "The dilemma of David Lurie and Lucy in Coetzee's *Disgrace* (1999) as well as Rayment in *Slow Man* (2005)."

9. See Ken Gelder and Jane Jacobs *Uncanny Australia* (1998), for discussions of the uncanny in relation to Indigenous and non-Indigenous narratives of place.
10. Although Hambrett also comments, "A garden is Nature Controlled after all. It is the amount of maintenance that will dictate the look of the garden far more than the plant choice" (2004, 6).
11. "ungarden" is from Turner (1925).
12. See Miller (2002; 2008). See also Dolin (2013).
13. Ravenscroft (2012, 60).
14. The full extract is: "Such an interest could, in law, be exercised and enjoyed to the full without necessarily extinguishing native title interests. The extent to which the two interests could operate together is a matter for further evidence and legal analysis. Only if there is inconsistency between the legal interests of the lessee (as defined by the instrument of lease and the legislation under which it was granted) and the native title (as established by evidence), will such native title, to the extent of the inconsistency, be extinguished" (Wik Peoples v Queensland 1996).

REFERENCES

Ablett, Phillip Gordon, and Pamela Kay Dyer. 2009. "Heritage and Hermeneutics: Towards a Broader Interpretation of Interpretation." *Current Issues in Tourism*. 12 (3): 209–233.

Aitken, Richard. 2010. *The Garden of Ideas: Four Centuries of Australian Style*. Carlton: Miegunyah Press with State Library of Victoria.

Australian Human Rights Commission. 1997. *Bringing them Home: the 'Stolen Children" Report*. http://www.hreoc.gov.au/social_justice/bth_report/index.html.

Bail, Murray. 1998. *Eucalyptus*. Melbourne: Text.

Brook, Isis, and Emily Brady. 2003. "Topiary: Ethics and Aesthetics." *Ethics & the Environment* 8 (1): 126–142.

Carruthers, Jane, and Libby Robin. 2010. "Taxonomic Imperialism in the Battles for Acacia: Identity and Science in South Africa and Australia." *Transactions of the Royal Society of South Africa* 65 (1): 48–64.

Cerwonka, Allaine. 2004. *Native to the Nation: Disciplining Landscapes and Bodies in Australia*. Minneapolis: University of Minnesota Press.

Coetzee, J.M. 2000. *Disgrace*. London: Vintage.

———. 2005. *Slow Man*. Milson's Point: Knopf.

Collins, Felicity, and Therese Davis. 2004. *Australian Cinema after Mabo*. Cambridge and Port Melbourne: Cambridge University Press.

Cooper, David E. 2006. *A Philosophy of Gardens*. Oxford: Clarendon Press.

Crosby, Alfred. 1986. *Ecological Imperialism*. Cambridge: Cambridge University Press.

Dawson, Bee. 2010. *A History of Gardening in New Zealand*. Auckland: Godwit.

Dolin, Kieran. "Post-*Mabo* Fiction." 2013. Paper presented at the Conference of the Association for the Study of Australian Literature, Wagga, July 2–5.

Ecological Humanities. N.d. "About us." *Ecological Humanities*. http://www.ecologicalhumanities.org/about.html.

Editors. 1996. "Crown Proposals for the Settlement of Treaty of Waitangi Claims: Summary—Digest." *Australian Indigenous Law Reporter* 91 (708): 1–4.

Foucault, Michel. 1973. *The Order of Things*. New York: Vintage.

Fox, Paul. 2004. *Clearings: Six Colonial Gardeners and their Landscapes*. Carlton: Miegunyah.

Gammage, Bill. 2011. *The Biggest Estate on Earth: How Aborigines Made Australia*. Crows Nest: Allen & Unwin.

Gelder, Ken, and Jane Jacobs. 1998. *Uncanny Australia: Sacredness and Identity in a Postcolonial Nation*. Carlton: Melbourne University Press.

Gelder, Ken, and Paul Salzman. 2009. *After the Celebration: Australian Fiction 1989–2007*. Carlton: Melbourne University Press.

Grbich, Judith. 2001. "The Scent of Colonialism: *Mabo, Eucalyptus* and Excursions within Legal Racism." *The Australian Feminist Law Journal* 15: 121–148.

Grossman, Michele. 1998. "Reach on Out to the Other Side: *Grog Wars* and *Plains of Promise*." *Meridian* 17 (1): 81–87.

Hambrett, Jo. 2004. Rise of the Australian Plant Garden. Paper read at the Friends of the Royal Botanic Gardens, July 28, Sydney. http://www.aila.org.au/canber-ragarden/creating/history.pdf.

Head, Lesley. 2000. *Second Nature: The History and Implications of Australia as Aboriginal Landscape*. Syracuse: Syracuse University Press.

Hunt, John Dixon. 2000. *Greater Perfections: The Practice of Garden Theory*. London: Thames & Hudson.

"JH", interview by Susan K Martin, July 1, 2007, unpublished interview, Tape 13 Growing Australian Project, transcript.

Johnson, Amanda. 2011. "Archival Salvage: History's Reef and the Wreck of the Historical Novel." *Journal of the Association for the Study of Australian Literature* 11 (1): 1–21.

Leane, Jeanine. 2011. *Purple Threads*. St. Lucia: University of Queensland Press.

[Mabo v the State of Queensland]. 1992. Mabo v the State of Queensland (No. 2) [1992] HCA 23; (1992) 175 CLR 1 (3 June 1992). *High Court of Australia*. http://www.austlii.edu.au/cgi-bin/sinodisp/au/cases/cth/high_ct/175clr1.html?stem=0&synonyms=0&query=~mabo ().

Martin, Susan K. 2004. "The Wood from the Trees: Taxonomy and the Eucalypt as the New National Hero in Recent Australian Writing." *Journal of the Association for the Study of Australian Literature* 3: 81–94.

McGahan, Andrew. 2004. *The White Earth*. Crows News: Allen & Unwin.

McNeer, Rebecca. 2002. "Happily Ever After: William Shakespeare's *The Tempest* and Murray Bail's *Eucalyptus*." *Antipodes* 16 (2): 171–176.

Miller, Alex. 2008. *Landscape of Farewell*. Crows Nest: Allen & Unwin.

———. 2002. *Journey to the Stone Country*. Crows Nest: Allen & Unwin.

Miller, David Philip, and Peter Hanns Reill. 1996. eds. *Visions of Empire: Voyages, Botany, and Representations of Nature*. Cambridge: Cambridge University Press.

Miller, Mara. 1993. *The Garden as an Art*. Albany: State University of New York Press.

Mitchell, Thomas Livingstone. [1839] 1965. *Three Expeditions into the Interior of Eastern Australia, With Description of the Recently Explored Region of Australia Felix, and the Present Colony of New South Wales*. 2nd ed. London: T. and W. Boone. Reprint, Adelaide: Libraries Board of South Australia.

———. [1848] 1969. *Journal of an Expedition into the Interior of Tropical Australia, in Search of a Route from Sydney to the Gulf of Carpentaria*. Reprint, New York: Greenwood Press.

Mirmohamadi, Kylie. 2006. "Talking about Native Plants." *Colloquy* 12: 91–102.

———. 2003. "'Wog plants go home': Race, Ethnicity and Horticulture in Australia." *Studies in Australian Garden History* 1: 91–108.

Museum of Australian Democracy. N.d. "Mabo v Queensland No. 2 1992 (Cth)." *Documenting a Democracy: Australia's Story.* http://foundingdocs.gov.au/item-did-33.html.

Oxley, John. (1820) 2003. *Journals of Two Expeditions into the Interior of New South Wales: Undertaken by Order of the British Government in the Years 1817–18.* London: John Murray, London.

Perkins, Rachel. 2003. *One Night the Moon.* Film. Directed by Rachel Perkins.

Plumwood, Val. 1993. *Feminism and the Mastery of Nature.* London: Routledge.

———. 2002. "Decolonising Relationships with Nature." *Pan* 2: 7–30.

Pollan, Michael. 1994. "Against Nativism." *New York Times*, May 15.

———. 1996. Second Nature: A Gardener's Education. London: Bloomsbury.

Pratt, Mary Louise. 1992. *Imperial Eyes: Travel Writing and Transculturation.* London and New York: Routledge.

Ravenscroft, Alison. 1998a. "Politics of Exposure: An Interview with Alexis Wright." *Meridian* 17 (1): 75–80.

———. 1998b. "What Falls from View?: On Re-reading Alexis Wright's *Plains of Promise*." *Australian Literary Studies* 25 (4): 70–84.

———. 2012. *The Postcolonial Eye: White Australian Desire and the Visual Field of Race.* Farnham: Ashgate.

Read, Peter. 2000. *Belonging: Australians, Place and Aboriginal Ownership.* Cambridge: Cambridge University Press.

Rigby, Kate. 2009. "Dancing with Disaster." *AHR Ecological Humanities* 46: 131–144.

Ritvo, Harriet. 1997. "Zoological Nomenclature and the Empire of Victorian Science." In *Victorian Science in Context*, edited by Bernard Lightman, 334–353. Chicago: University of Chicago Press.

Rose, Deborah Bird. 2004. *Reports from a Wild Country: Ethics for Decolonisation.* Sydney: University of New South Wales Press.

Rose, Deborah Bird, and Libby Robin. 2004. "The Ecological Humanities in Action: An Invitation." *Australian Humanities Review*, nos. 31–32. http://www.australian humanitiesreview.org/archive/Issue-April-2004/rose.html.

Ross, Stephanie. 1999. "Gardens' Powers." *Journal of Aesthetic Education* 33 (3): 4–17.

Scott, Kim. 1999. *Benang.* Fremantle: Fremantle Arts Centre Press.

———. 2010. *That Deadman Dance.* Sydney: Picador PanMacmillan,

Sharrad, Paul. 2007. "Estranging an Icon." *Interventions: International Journal of Postcolonial Studies* 9 (1): 31–48.

Shepherd, Thomas. 1836. *Lectures on Landscape Gardening in Australia.* Sydney: William McGarvie.

Stevenson, Brian. 1996. *The Wik Decision and After: Research Bulletin 4/97* Brisbane: Queensland Parliamentary Library. http://www.parliament.qld.gov.au/docu ments/explore/ResearchPublications/researchBulletins/rb0497bs.pdf.

Strelein, Lisa. 2009. "Recognising Native Title in Australian Law: Mabo v Queensland [No. 2]" In: Strelein, Lisa. *Compromised Jurisprudence: Native Title Cases since Mabo.* Canberra: Aboriginal Studies Press: 9–21.

Sturt, Charles. 1833. *Two Expeditions into the Interior of Southern Australia During the years 1828, 1829, 1830, and 1831: with Observations on the Soil, Climate,* and General Resources of the Colony of New South Wales. 2 vols. London: Smith, Elder and Co. http://adc.library.usyd.edu.au/view?docId=ozlit/xml-main-texts/p00096.xml.

Tiffin, Helen, and Graham Huggan. 2010. *Postcolonial Ecocriticism: Literature, Animals, Environment.* London: Routledge.

Turner, Ethel. 1925. *The Ungardeners.* London and Melbourne: Ward, Lock.

Vernay, Jean-Francois. 2004. "An Interview with Alexis Wright." *Antipodes* 18 (2): 119–122.

"Waitangi Tribunal." N.d. *Waitangi Tribunal.* http://www.justice.govt.nz/tribunals/waitangi-tribunal#1.

Whittaker, Richard. 1999. "A Conversation with Tom Leddy: Is This a Garden?" *Works & Conversations.* November 21. http://www.conversations.org/story.php?sid=41.

[Wik Peoples v Queensland]. 1996. Mabo v the State of Queensland. ("Pastoral Leases case") [1996] High Court of Australia 40; (1996) 187 CLR 1; (1996) 141 ALR 129; (1996) 71 ALJR 173 (23 December 1996). *High Court of Australia.* http://www.concernedhistorians.org/content_files/file/LE/172.pdf.

Worgan, George B. (1788) 1978. *Journal of a First Fleet Surgeon.* Sydney: Library Council of New South Wales; Library of Australian History. http://purl.library.usyd.edu.au/setis/id/worjour.

Wright, Alexis. 1997. *Plains of Promise.* St. Lucia, QLD: University of Queensland Press.

———. 2001. "A Family Document." In *Storykeepers,* edited by Marion Halligan, 223–240. Potts Point: Duffy & Snellgrove.

———. 2006. *Carpentaria.* Sydney: Artamon: Giramondo.

———. 2013. *The Swan Book.* Sydney: Artamon: Giramondo.

Part II

Disaster, Vulnerability, and Resilience

5 Towards a Postcolonial Disaster Studies

Anthony Carrigan

Since its inception in the 1950s, disaster studies as an interdisciplinary field has been concerned with managing crisis situations, seeking to reduce vulnerability and assist post-disaster recovery. This has become increasingly important over the last few decades as the various risks that inhere in human–environmental relationships have been amplified not only by anthropogenic climate change but also by the capitalist exploitation of natural resources. Both these processes have accelerated in the period of expansive globalization following World War II (see Figure 5.1), resulting in natural hazards' frequent conversion into large-scale catastrophes. It is no surprise that these take a disproportionate toll on the world's poorest communities, many of which are still grappling with the legacies of western colonialism and neocolonial practices. The World Bank is more than aware that developing countries suffer the most from disasters (World Bank 2014), and as Naomi Klein's work on "disaster capitalism" highlights (2007), these regions have been subjected to systematic dispossession through the spread of free-market doctrine. In addition to increased environmental vulnerabilities, the social crises that have shadowed political decolonization—including war, genocide, and systemic poverty—have been catastrophic for large numbers of people, radically transforming natural and built environments in ways that coincide with current forms of ecological imperialism. All this makes disaster response and management central to postcolonial concerns, with postcolonial studies emerging over the last three decades in the context of global problems such as accelerating economic disparities, resource scarcity, climate change, and US-led wars. In particular, disaster analysis can shed light on how specific colonial practices produce differential forms of vulnerability, raising the question of what happens if we treat postcolonial studies *as* a form of disaster studies and vice versa. The aim of this chapter is to open up some perspectives on this relationship through consideration of what a postcolonial disaster studies might entail. Its core conviction is that postcolonial studies has much to contribute both in recalibrating applied fields such as disaster studies, and in advancing the environmental humanities' commitment to imagining alternatives to ecological destruction. This involves analyzing the cultural politics that accompany narratives of disaster mitigation and recovery, and foregrounding the conceptual changes that are required to decrease vulnerability.

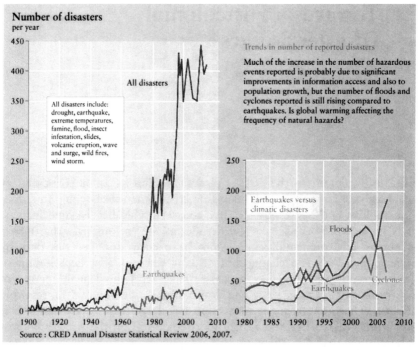

Figure 5.1 Number of reported disasters per year since 1900. Credit: Riccardo
Pravettoni, UNEP/GRID-Arendal (http://www.grida.no/graphicslib/
detail/number-of-disasters-per-year_1408).

My contribution begins by tracing a genealogy of disaster studies, arguing
for the need to bring it into productive exchange with postcolonial methodologies and connecting this to our volume's core concern with how global
ecologies are mediated creatively in different cultural locations. The development of disaster studies is compelling for postcolonial and environmental
researchers partly because of how it embeds empirical findings in policy-
oriented frameworks, and partly for its role in situating disaster response as
key to what Andrew Ross calls "planetary management"—a process whose
"centralized rationalization" tends to obscure the social causes of global
crises (1991, 207–08; see also Sachs 1993, 19–20). It is precisely this occlu-
sion that a postcolonial approach to disaster must confront, and at the most
fundamental level this involves reframing the question of "what is a disaster?" in postcolonial contexts. At the same time, it is important to think
through how postcolonial studies can benefit from confronting disaster
head on, not least as the concept is enmeshed with many of the field's abiding concerns—from forced migration and displacement to trauma, memory,
and forgetting—which in turn must be seen as central to developing a properly global approach to the environmental humanities. To illustrate how
this might operate conceptually, I turn in the second part of the chapter

to the work of Barbadian poet and historian, Kamau Brathwaite, and in particular his genre-defying epic, *MR* (2002). Brathwaite's work is particularly intriguing because of his long-standing engagement with sudden and prolonged experiences of catastrophe, and because of how it emphasizes the power of language, imaginative writing, literary criticism, and narrative form in helping us to understand the relationship between very different types of disaster. I find the blend of creative and critical insights in *MR* to be highly suggestive in establishing connections between cultural experiences of catastrophe and global concerns, and I read it as a framework through which postcolonial studies and disaster studies can be seen as mutually constitutive. I conclude by considering how Brathwaite's work—and the observations I make here—might be integrated with disaster research, not least through highlighting how language affects our approach to disasters.

DECOLONIZING DISASTER STUDIES

I will begin by tracing a genealogy of academic disaster studies following World War II, as I see this as not only symptomatic of but deeply entwined with the historical processes that ushered in the "age of ecology" (Worster 1994, ix) and the "development era" (Sachs 1993, 4). There are obvious continuities between inter-empire disaster management practices in the nineteenth and early twentieth century and their post-1945 successors (see e.g. Davis 2001; Mukherjee 2013). However, I am primarily concerned here with how disaster studies was institutionalized at the same time as the postwar geopolitical shifts that are central both to postcolonial studies and to the global cultural–economic transitions that accompany the formation of the UN and the International Bank for Reconstruction and Development (to evoke the World Bank's original disaster-responsive title). I am also interested in how the field has interpreted the exponential rise in catastrophes—both social and "natural"—since the mid-twentieth century, which has accompanied rapid economic globalization and continues to be magnified by accelerating gaps between rich and poor. There is a stark contradiction between the institutionalization of disaster risk reduction—signaled by the UN Office of that name—and the rising tide of global catastrophes, compounded by the sense that "never again" has become "wherever again," as Rwandan President Paul Kagame put it bluntly in 2000 (cited in Mirzoeff 2005, 36).[1] Considering disaster studies' post-1945 genealogy is therefore helpful for articulating how postcolonial research can critique and extend the field's commitment to vulnerability reduction through a reframing of the disaster concept.

Disaster studies began to emerge as a coherent field in the United States in conjunction with the "Strategic Bombing Surveys" conducted during World War II, which were devised to assess civilian "morale" in the context of "sustained military attacks" (Bolin 2007, 119). Its growth as a sociological research area came in the context of Cold War militarization, with the US government sponsoring the formation of a Disaster Research Group under the aegis of the National Academy of Sciences in 1952 (Perry 2007, 5). In subsequent decades, the initial "reactive [...] command-and-control civil defense approach" has given way to more methodologically diverse perspectives, organized mainly "around the twin concepts of risk management and sustainable hazard mitigation" (Britton 2005, 66). This has been partly due to the rise of the risk paradigm in sociological research, and partly due to critiques dating back to the 1970s from a number of materialist-inspired geographers, anthropologists, and historians such as Kenneth Hewitt, Anthony Oliver-Smith, and Ben Wisner. Their work helped reconfigure mainstream disaster studies approaches, emphasizing the need to address not just the *agents* of "natural" disasters (e.g. environmental phenomena such as hurricanes, earthquakes, and droughts), but also the social, political, and economic *processes* that put particular groups at risk and underpin the scale of disasters. Nevertheless, the durability of technocratic management strategies (focusing on the four "stages" of disaster management: mitigation, preparedness, response, and recovery) coupled with a largely US-centric approach continues to perpetuate critical blindspots that limit the field's global applicability even as its findings are adopted by multinational actors like the UN and the World Bank.

Tellingly, it took until 1998—the end of the UN-designated International Decade for Natural Disaster Reduction—for the landmark collection of essays *What Is a Disaster?* to be published, with its stated intention being to bring sociological disaster studies into sustained dialogue with other disciplinary perspectives. The need for this is dramatized by the volume's title question, which registers an abiding tension between researchers who "assume physical happenings, independent from human actions, are necessary for disaster," and those who see disaster more as a "social construction," as the volume's editor puts it (Quarantelli 1998a, 3). Given that social and political debates over the causes of disasters go back at least as far as the nineteenth century, as Mike Davis (2001) and others have shown in relation to British imperial policy and famine, what the prolonged nature of this debate attests to is partly the tendency for disaster researchers to favor *inductive* approaches (i.e. responding empirically to experiential observations) over *deductive* methods (working from theoretically informed standpoints). Such prioritization has resulted in a number of prominent ellipses or, as Hewitt puts it more critically, "excluded perspectives" (1995), with scant attention paid to the relationship between history, identity politics, and vulnerability—including categories like race, gender, class, religion, disability, and a whole raft of non-human concerns—or to how economic processes like structural adjustment have increased hazard vulnerability and "magnified losses from disasters" (Bolin 2007, 118).

This leads to a number of observations that will no doubt perplex postcolonial researchers: the fact that in editing *What is a Disaster?*, Quarantelli admitted to failing to "find anyone [...] who used primarily a non-Western frame" (1998b, 271); the assertion by Bob Bolin, in the single chapter dedicated to "Race, Class, Ethnicity and Disaster Vulnerability" in the 2007 *Handbook of Disaster Research*, that disaster specialists tend to "rely on *commonsensical* treatments of racial and ethnic categories rather than using in-depth sociohistorical and ethnographic analyses" (2007, 117; my emphasis); and the predilection for separating out or "typologizing" disasters rather than considering the much messier ramifications of what the UN calls "*complex emergencies* (or sometimes *compound disasters*)," which can involve "mixtures of civil strife, famines, genocidal activities, epidemics, and large-scale displacement and movement of refugees" (Quarantelli 1998b, 263; original emphasis).[2] As several critics have observed, approaches to disaster that fail to engage with the social, economic, and political dimensions of hazard production can ultimately sustain rather than mitigate catastrophes (see e.g. Hewitt 1995). This point is given a darker edge in Klein's work, which situates the manufacture of "sustainable disasters" as a deliberate neoliberal strategy. Indeed, if we accept the force of Klein's argument (2007)—that free market hegemony has been attained on a global level through the exploitation of disasters—then the exponential rise in post-1945 disasters illustrated in Figure 5.1 suggests such events are in fact *products* of neoliberal policies that both feed from and create entrenched vulnerability.

Certainly any approach that prioritizes returning post-disaster communities to a pre-disaster "norm" has serious flaws given the forms of disenfranchisement that precede and are exploited by reconstruction processes (as the aftermath of Hurricane Katrina horrifically exposed). The inappropriateness of such models is even more pronounced in the many contexts where catastrophic events are consistently entwined with "ordinary," "chronic," or "slow onset" disasters (including poverty, debt, ecological degradation, underdevelopment, and militarism), or where the state itself constitutes a "hazard."[3] Yet the close affiliations disaster studies has shared with normative politics (especially, though not exclusively, in the US) has rendered it slow to reformulate itself in ways that might be responsive to these structural conditions. Put more polemically, the field has yet to disentangle itself fully from the epistemic violence associated with its institutional birth—forged during the Cold War and entwined with military–industrialism's global spread. It is therefore necessary to consider how disaster studies might be actively reconstituted in relation to this genealogy and to its more contemporary entanglement with technocratic decision-making at the level of global environmental governance—a point which is essential to the work of the environmental humanities more broadly.

There has, encouragingly, been something of a transformation in disaster research over the last decade or so—catalyzed partly by considerations of 9/11 (Scanlon 2005, 13)—with increasing attention now being paid to the relationship between disasters, development, and globalization;

to indigenous knowledge and disaster risk reduction; and to the cultural dimensions of catastrophes.[4] The field has also been boosted through perspectives from political ecology and progressive humanitarian studies, with Anthony Oliver-Smith in particular emphasizing the need to address how disasters are manifestations of historical vulnerabilities that are produced at the intersection of environment and society, and which cannot be disentangled from systemic power structures (1998, 189). Yet there is virtually no sustained analysis of the relationship between colonialism and disaster. It is in this context, then, that I want to expand the sense of paradigm change captured in progressive disaster research by asserting the importance for the field a) to find points of critical exchange with postcolonial studies, with a particular focus on the connections between vulnerability production, imperialist practice, and cultural response; and b) not to treat this simply as another "dimension" to be appended in future handbooks, but as necessarily *constitutive* of the field's future transformation and relevance.

In making this argument, I am aware of the usual barriers it presents for establishing meaningful synergies between postcolonial studies and disciplines outside—and sometimes within—the humanities. I am more optimistic in this case, though, about the possibilities for sustained and substantive exchange precisely because the sheer scale of contemporary disasters is prompting serious methodological shifts in disaster research itself. In fact, the recent Routledge *Handbook of Hazards and Disaster Risk Reduction* (2012) opens with a plea for more "critical thinking, along with departure from disciplinary norms and expectations, and the euphemisms and politeness of diplomatic language used by United Nations organisations" (Wisner et al. 2012, 3). The unbridled effects of climate change coupled with the yawning wealth disparities that underpin global economic crises are two high profile challenges to conventional vulnerability analysis, and disaster research must also respond to the many "resurgent" resistance movements across the Global South that highlight how "ecological and human disposability" have been catastrophically "conjoined" (Nixon 2011, 4). Turning to the cultural, historical, and economic implications of postcolonial critique is in this sense crucial if the field is to achieve genuine and sustained disaster mitigation in global contexts. The corollary is that such a transformation requires not only significant input and exchange from postcolonialists, but that postcolonial studies itself must engage in similarly transformative modes of *praxis* that take it beyond its humanities-based comfort zone. Indeed, I would suggest that one thing postcolonial studies should avowedly stand *for* is progressive disaster mitigation, and this form of collaboration—uneasy and volatile as it may be—represents one way of achieving the real-world changes the field theoretically demands. Such collaboration will be all the stronger for being situated at the heart of an emergent vision of the environmental humanities. This requires postcolonial and environmental humanities researchers to move from "interdiscursive" techniques of knowledge combination (i.e. borrowing ideas and methods from other disciplines in order to pursue conventional forms of critique; Huggan 2008, 5–6) to what Ato Quayson identifies as a more "instrumental" approach to interdisciplinarity (2000, 24–25). This involves actively embedding conceptual insights derived from cultural and historical analyses into broader, collaborative research projects that are oriented towards achieving change in real-world practices.[5]

There is much to be learned in this sense from how disaster researchers work together to communicate beyond academic contexts. In particular, those of us working within the humanities can look to build on disaster studies' success as an *applied* research formation that can speak to—and potentially challenge—political perspectives on crisis management and reconstruction. This does not mean foregoing the humanities-based strengths of our research, or what Quayson (2000, 25) calls the "synoptic" approach to postcolonial interdisciplinarity (i.e. bringing ideas from different disciplines together for the purpose of anti-imperial critique). Rather it is an opportunity to channel this approach towards a self-conscious reformulation of disaster studies methods, which from an environmental humanities perspective must include a more rigorous understanding of how narratives shape our perception and understanding of what constitutes a disaster. It is especially interesting in this light that, along with the lack of attention to identity categories, there has been scant consideration of disaster narratives and imaginative depictions more broadly in mainstream disaster research. This is something that literary and cultural critics can redress directly in conjunction with related disciplines like history by exploring how postcolonial texts challenge, reject, or reconfigure key disaster studies concepts such as resilience, risk, adaption, and vulnerability.[6] At the same time, postcolonial and environmental humanities researchers should ask how disaster research can frame and inform textual readings of specific disasters, and use this as a basis for establishing new methodologies that engage different audiences.

There is certainly a willingness in disaster studies to embrace literary and cultural findings, with a number of researchers emphasizing that disasters are less "accident[s]" than "representation[s] of reality" (Gilbert 1998, 9), and that "perception[s] of risk and vulnerability" are "clearly mediated through linguistic and cultural grids, accounting for great variability in assessments and understandings of disasters" (Oliver-Smith 2004, 17). Some, such as Hewitt, anticipate Rob Nixon's influential arguments in *Slow Violence and the Environmentalism of the Poor* (2011) by highlighting the need to listen to "the plight and *stories* of distinctly more vulnerable members of society," and create a discourse that speaks "of missing persons or unheard voices; of 'hidden damage' and 'shadow risks' and, more severely, of 'silent' or 'quiet violence'" (1995, 120; my emphasis). Postcolonial and environmental humanities research can obviously foreground these concerns by exploring how writers, intellectuals, and artists working in non-western contexts theorize and represent specific experiences of disaster in relation to distributions of power. This involves attending to the resilience of what Ann Stoler calls "imperial formations"—a term she uses to "register the ongoing quality of processes of decimation, displacement, and reclamation" that remain active outside of formal imperialism, and create *"repositories of vulnerabilities* that [...] last longer than the political structures that produced them" (2008, 193, 203; my emphasis). It also requires a methodologically inclusive approach to how these narratives can help reconstruct the disaster field itself—attending to the "long emergencies of slow violence" (Nixon 2011, 3) and "dialectics of ordinary disaster" (Davis 1995) that are bound up with different forms of colonialism and which present fundamental challenges to the technocratic applicability of event-based disaster modeling.

The rest of this chapter puts these ideas into practice by using Kamau Brathwaite's recent literary-historical work as a platform from which to begin reframing the question of "what is a disaster" in light of postcolonial concerns. Brathwaite is an interesting figure to consider because he has always adopted an interdiscursive approach in his work, theorizing catastrophe in particular through a combination of historical and literary insights that place colonialism at the heart of the story. He was also a member for many years of the board of UNESCO, the experience of which informs *MR*'s frustrations with how the history of empire is often excised from international discussions (2002, 58–62). The language and histories of catastrophe that saturate *MR* provide a direct contrast to the more managerial approaches to disaster that characterized the UN's International Decade for Natural Disaster Reduction in the 1990s, during which Brathwaite continued his involvement with UNESCO and composed most of the manuscript. Brathwaite's work in *MR* represents a great example of what a postcolonial disaster studies might look like precisely because it rejects technocratic dictats in favor of comparative inquiry, and seeks to act as a "witness/crossroad from world to word to self & from self to other selves w/what i can only call humility" (2002, 68). In this sense, it can help us to create a self-reflexive theory of how interdisciplinarity might operate through combining environmental humanities and disaster studies insights. Moreover, given that the text is hard to get hold of and arguably inaccessible to the uninitiated, I want to highlight the importance of critical interpretation in mediating between Brathwaite's poetic approach to colonialism and catastrophe and the conceptual adaptations needed for a postcolonial disaster studies to emerge.

MR, RADIANCE, AND RECONSTRUCTION

Throughout his distinguished career, Kamau Brathwaite has been alive to the intersections of history, aesthetics, and catastrophe in colonial and postcolonial contexts, and the Caribbean in particular. He famously describes the need for Caribbean writers to reforge English in ways that "approximate [...] the *natural* experience, the *environmental* experience," asserting that "[t]he hurricane does not roar in pentameters" (1984, 10; original emphasis). This statement foregrounds the constitutive presence of natural hazards in the region, and elsewhere he observes how "[t]he beauty of the Caribbean is (re)born out of the catastrophic origins of the Yucatan-Atlantis cordillera and the volcanoes & earthQuake flues & flows that rim & ruim the Caribbean sea" (2006, 7; see also Carrigan 2011, 111).[7] Since the 1990s, Brathwaite's interest in the double-valence of disasters—both generative and destructive—has become increasingly manifest, and his recent work has led to a comparative and increasingly epic cosmology of catastrophe that situates it at the heart of postcolonial concerns.

One powerful example comes in a 2005 interview conducted by Joyelle McSweeney shortly after Hurricane Katrina hit New Orleans and the Gulf Coast. McSweeney opens the interview by asking how Brathwaite interprets this and other recent disasters given his long-standing interest in the subject, to which he responds:

> My position on catastrophe [...] is, I'm so conscious of the enormity of slavery and the Middle Passage and I see that as an ongoing catastrophe. So whatever happens in the world after that, like tsunamis in the Far East and India and Indonesia, and 9/11, and now New Orleans, to me these are all aspects of that same original explosion, which I constantly try to understand. What is it that causes nature to lunge in this cataclysmic way, and what kind of message, as I suspect it is, what message is Nature [sic] trying to send to us? And how are they connected, these violent forces that hit the world so very often—manmade or nature-made or spirit-made—they hit us increasingly violently.
>
> (McSweeney 2005)

Brathwaite's eloquent response foregrounds a number of concerns that can be considered central to an emergent notion of postcolonial disaster. These include (1) the "ongoing" effects of colonialism *as catastrophe*—or "worldquake," as Brathwaite calls it elsewhere (2002, 127)—in relation to a series of seemingly disparate social and natural catastrophes; (2) the intimate relationship between power, exploitation, violence, and disaster; and (3) a multivalent concept of "nature" as material and metaphysical entity (alluded to in the switch to capitalized form, "Nature"), which emphasizes its historical agency and corresponds with how Brathwaite uses "catastrophe" to evoke the cultural, psychological, and metaphysical dimensions of "disaster" as a physical process. The significance of these points is partly that they speak to Stoler's historicized vision of imperial formations, which also involves "[m]aking connections where they are hard to trace" between psychological suffering and physical destruction of landscapes, homes, and infrastructure (2008, 195). But whereas Stoler's interest resides in what she calls "imperial debris"—that is, material remnants of accretive disasters or various forms of "ruination" (193–194)—Brathwaite focuses more on the dialectic between destructive processes and disastrous events or, as disaster specialist Ilan Kelman puts it, the "fuzzy clusters" of experiences that elide "[c]atastrophic and chronic disasters" in global societies (2003, 118). Importantly, Brathwaite's comments indicate how the designation "postcolonial disaster" can help negotiate the dichotomy between event and process. This is because it *always implies* the kind of "complex emergencies" or "compound disasters" evoked in humanitarian and disaster relief discourse, which are conditioned by the "ruinous" (Stoler 2008, 195) consequences of specific imperial formations.

Where Brathwaite's work becomes even more compelling from the perspective of reconfiguring and extending the *forms* through which disasters are analyzed is in his insistence on the significance of conceptual transformation and imaginative response. Asserting that "Art must come out of catastrophe" (McSweeney 2005), Brathwaite sets out a provocative counterpoint to Theodor Adorno's famous 1951 assertion that "to write poetry after Auschwitz is barbaric" (1981, 34), reflecting elsewhere in his work on how "[t]here has been a vast river of postHiroshima catastrophe & suffering [...] yet creativity & hope" that calls for a "whole new *reconstruction* of history and possibility" (2005; 1990, 33; my emphasis). Such conceptual reconstruction crucially accompanies the more familiar forms of post-disaster reconstruction relating to flattened infrastructure and transfigured environments. It also underlines the importance of attuning post-disaster reconstruction policies to historical and imaginative insights, and identifying how artistic works and intellectual critique are *implicated* in recovery processes.

Brathwaite elaborates on this by commenting that: "One thing about catastrophe, for me, is that it always seems to lead to *a kind of* magical realism. That moment of utter disaster, the very moment when it seems almost hopeless, too difficult to proceed, you begin to glimpse a kind of radiance on the other end of the maelstrom" (McSweeney 2005; my emphasis).[8] The "glimpse [...] of radiance" Brathwaite evokes is enticing as it promises to shed light not only on literary representations of disaster (as the reference to magical realism seemingly implies) but on the way in which the concept is framed and understood in (largely western) academic discourse. This is not because it somehow redeems the tarnished notion of a "radiant tomorrow" captured in mid-twentieth-century development discourse (Sachs 1999, 21); rather, the image conjures a sense of epiphanic transformation associated with epistemological change. This correlates with Val Plumwood's still arresting opening to *Feminism and the Mastery of Nature* (1993, 1), which also draws on disaster discourse as a metaphor for conceptual transformation, and retains epiphanic relevance for establishing a progressive framework for the environmental humanities. Such reframing is essential to Brathwaite's most extended engagement with catastrophe, conceptual reconstruction, and aesthetic response: his epic, 700-page mediation on magical realism, *MR*.

Winner of the Casa de las Americas Prize for literary criticism in 1998, and published in full in 2002, *MR* is a formally dazzling inquiry into magical realism's emergence, concentrating on the Caribbean and Latin America in particular. While this single-genre focus might seem incompatible with a broader analysis of the many narrative and artistic forms used to represent disasters, Brathwaite's characterization of the term through multiple, often elusive definitions presents it more as an *alternative epistemology* or *mode of understanding* than a conventional literary genre as such, which emerges in contradistinction to the catastrophic epistemologies embedded in western colonialism. Or as he puts it:

this new work of the Caribbean Améric
–as which collapses time & space
& integrates them into new maps w / a new
vocab, opt ic & METAPHOR – another
way therefore of hearing & VOICING
the vision – seems to me a real

promethean
response to catastrophe (natural + social
like slavery & colon ialism & the ru le
of the cau dillo Plan tation)

an **orphean**
response to NATURE (m kissi of landscape),
& the people – the FOLK CULTURE

– the **NATION**
LANGUAGE CULTURE of that landscape

a **sycoraxian**
nurturing of all this as a response
to downpression
[...]
& an

ogotemmellean
response to the need to restore
COSMOLOGY
(*problematic unmiracle of fragmentation*)
& when/wherever i find this
(these) breaking the scarface
of our culture i call out

MR
– magic/al eben **miracle** realism –

(2002, 382–384)

This visionary passage exemplifies how Brathwaite positions magical realism as "a form of post-catastrophe art istic cosmology [...] engaging prismatically [...] all [...] the elements of one's culture towards a moment of *transformation.* healing" (649–50). On one level, this involves a distinctly Caribbean response to compound disaster, which builds on Édouard Glissant's and Wilson Harris's sustained engagements in their oeuvres with crisis, catastrophe, and regeneration (Harris is especially prominent in *MR*). The passage is representative of how *MR* itself disrupts conventional academic formats—along with any imagined boundary between the critical and the creative—in line with what Brathwaite elsewhere describes as a regional "geo-psyche" (1990, 26). This is shaped by experiences of fragmentation, which result partly from negotiating the transformations caused by recurring environmental hazards and partly from the abuses and transfigurations of "colon ialism & the ru le of the cau dillo Plan tation." The "mkissi" or spirits of local landscapes are necessarily responsive to the various ways in which the Caribbean was "*inaugurated* in catastrophe" (Small Axe Project 2011, 134; original emphasis; cf. Anderson 2011, 7), with the plantation system underpinning the region's location as a crucible of colonial modernity and globalization. This has been instrumental in creating a sense of alienation between nature and society (DeLoughrey et al. 2005, 1, 4)—along with the "cosmological" rupture Brathwaite describes—while at the same time shaping the many identifiable "cultures of disaster" across the region (to adapt Greg Bankoff's term for creative adaptation to environmental hazards in the Philippines; 2003).

On another level, it is precisely these features that underpin how "MR's critical ideas/theory cross-reference other transcultural IIIW concerns" (Brathwaite 2002, 347), making the artistic innovations Brathwaite describes relevant to the *global* forms of disaster evoked throughout his study, and which are brought together in creative works such as his elegiac post-9/11 poem "Ark." This references a litany of postcolonial examples—Bhuj, Grenada, Jenin, Bhopal, Rwanda—before reaching the pregnant conclusion "Manhattan in Afghanistan" (2010, 82–86). The poem follows *MR*'s logic by foregrounding the conjuncture between imperialism, environmental exploitation, and compound disaster in ways that unsettle assumptions that globalization's relationship with catastrophe is "inherently unpredictable" because the processes involved are supposedly "discontinuous in [...] space and time" (Oliver-Smith 1998, 193). By focusing on conditions that render certain disasters chillingly calculable, Brathwaite instead offers a globally oriented correlative to Derek Gregory's account of "the colonial present" in the Middle East, which likewise favours "recovering [...] spatial stories," "connecting different places and combining different time-scales" (2004, 19–20). The parallel is accentuated by Gregory's interest in humanities-based (contra "humanitarian") approaches to complex emergencies, drawing on postcolonial methodologies and quoting numerous literary and artistic intertexts, albeit without ever quite clarifying their implications for geopolitical exegesis.

While *MR* is more allusive than comprehensive in its examples, the text complements Gregory's work in resisting the tendency for disasters to be "treated as [...] archipelagos of extreme [...] random events" that are "cordoned off as areas of spatial disorganization or national security crisis" (Hewitt 1995, 117) or even "conceived of as existing beyond history and, therefore, politics" (Anderson 2011, 21). Resisting this is key for disaster studies in order to refute the tendency for many economically disadvantaged states to be portrayed as crisis-ridden "risk zones," situated less as sites of progressive reconstruction (or what Brathwaite calls "healing") than as "security" threats for western states, ever-threatening to be "engulfed by disaster" (Sachs 1999, 21–22). Such rhetorics often determine approaches to disaster response and management, instituting exceptionality in place of comparative discussion of how vulnerability is produced.[9] Brathwaite's alternative cartography helps reframe understandings of disastrous history in this respect as it is not only temporally and geographically expansive, but also asserts *continuities* between "natural + social" catastrophes that remain subdued in disaster studies but should be the subject of postcolonial critique.[10]

Brathwaite uses a literary method to approach this issue by looking at how creative works encode both what he calls "the literature of negative catastrophe," which is associated (somewhat problematically) with social realism, and "the literature [...] of optimistic catastrophe," which is aligned more with magical realism (2002, 347). This is relevant to environmental humanities research and disaster studies more generally because the ambivalence between destructive and generative responses captured in artistic representations reflects the complex social and psychological conflicts that are experienced during the reconstruction process. Throughout *MR*, Brathwaite urges the need to strike a balance between how postcolonial representations of disaster on one hand hold "a broken mirror up to broeken nature," and on the other hand reconfigure these "broken parts [...] to go [...] beyond the crisis/disruption" and reveal "the [...] [**HINTERLAND**] of wholeness & restoration, re/vision, healing" (2002, 323). The tentative—even slightly distorted—wording here captures the sense of fragmentation that accompanies catastrophes (cf. Blanchot 1995), while at the same time responding to the violent dialectics of fracture and reconstruction that underpin the production of disaster in many postcolonial locations. This anticipates both a reading strategy for critics looking at postcolonial disaster texts, and a platform for articulating how humanities-based work can advance comprehension of what disaster researchers readily admit is "the least understood aspect of emergency management": recovery (Smith and Wenger 2007, 234).

I have discussed elsewhere the need to alter mainstream "recovery" paradigms in relation to the many disabilities and disabling environments produced by disasters (Carrigan 2010). This seems crucial in developing what, according to hazard mitigation specialists Gavin Smith and Dennis Wenger, "does not exist": a "comprehensive theory of sustainable community disaster

recovery" (2007, 245). Brathwaite's approach in *MR* takes this thinking
further by seeing one core element of MR epistemology as involving "the
making/discovery/improvisationary recovery of new/ancient necessary sur-
vival/transcendent concept(s)/forms [. . .] thru habilitation/rememory/adap-
tation/improvization [. . .] into forms of maronage/possession/resistances
into the emancipation/liberation of space/time/anima" (2002, 370). The key
terms in this passage chime provocatively with—even riff directly off—
progressive disaster commentaries that see vulnerability reduction as dependent on replacing technocratic "attempts to control the environment" with
"approaches that [...] stress flexibility, adaptability, resilience and capacity"
(Hilhorst and Bankoff 2004, 4). Such resonances seem more than coincidental
given Brathwaite's ongoing involvement in UNESCO during the UN's International Decade for Natural Disaster Reduction. Importantly, Brathwaite
tempers uncritical celebration of qualities such as adaptation by emphasizing
"emancipation/liberation" as part of long-term (and never linear) recovery
processes, which can be politicized, augmented, or set back in the aftermath
of specific disasters. One of the benefits of comparing and historicizing postcolonial disaster representations in this light is that they provide culturally
responsive insights into post-disaster adaptation and community solidarity, while at the same time dramatizing the stresses and frictions that are
exacerbated by differential experiences of colonialism. This reading strategy
again involves examining dialectics of negative and optimistic catastrophe,
and accounting for how adaptation and recovery are figured in the language
of those who have survived disasters. The poetic form of Brathwaite's work
draws attention to the importance of listening to these voices and ideas
as they are expressed through multiple modes of representation alongside
everyday narratives, and outside of the conventional forms of academic or
technocratic discourse. Considering how these experiences are represented in
the long-term is also important as we know that terms like "resilience" and
"capacity" can operate as western discourses that are all too willingly appro-
priated in neoliberal ideology as a smokescreen for inaction (when there is
no economic motivation for intervention) or continued exploitation (often
under the banner of "aid;" see also O'Brien in this volume).

The "glimpse of radiance" (McSweeney 2005) that Brathwaite associates with many creative responses to postcolonial catastrophes parallels
academic convictions that disasters are always "opportunities" for change
by situating anticolonialism at the heart of effective disaster response and
mitigation. This in turn requires critical engagement with the challenges
historical exploitation poses for conceptualizing sustainable community
recovery. What does recovery mean, for instance, in a context like Haiti,
where the predisaster paradigm was characterized by enforced poverty, ecological exhaustion, and political abuse?[11] How does recovery differ from
its cognate, reconstruction, and do both work as thresholds between negative and optimistic catastrophe? Is recovery an appropriate term in contexts of collective trauma and long-term injustice? And how do postcolonial

commentators activate the legal and pecuniary connotations of recovery (as in recovering losses) *alongside* the need to "recover" occluded narratives and voices? As *MR* demonstrates, the kind of epistemological reframings these questions demand rely on nuanced conversations between postcolonialists and disaster researchers working from various scientific, sociological, and humanitarian backgrounds. However—and crucially for my argument here—such exchange can only be emancipatory in substance if the principles that emerge from *MR* are also applied to the institutional treatment of disasters and the language used to describe them, and I would like to close with a few further reflections on the challenges of facilitating conceptual reconstruction in this light.

CONCLUSION: FROM CLOSURE TO COLLABORATION

Part of the brilliance of *MR* is that it functions as a performative example of what it claims magical realist or post-catastrophe art provides: a "promethean" response to compound disaster that offers "another way [...] of hearing & VOICING the vision" (2002, 382). Brathwaite's own comparative vision of catastrophic history emphasizes the importance of pushing back at the dominant strains of risk-based analysis, which tend to focus more on *future* apocalyptic scenarios, and to look instead at how postcolonial texts depict *past and present* experiences of real-world catastrophes along with their deep-lying causes. This is a change that needs to be effected still within literary and cultural studies, particularly as critics interested in issues of catastrophe, apocalypse, and climate change have been much more willing to turn to the American and Hollywood apocalyptic imaginings like Cormac McCarthy's novel *The Road* (2006) or Roland Emmerich's film *The Day After Tomorrow* (2004) than to representations of lived disasters in contexts outside the Global North.[12] Such transformation is vital both in terms of maximizing literary studies' contribution to "humanizing" disaster studies—placing identity politics and social stories at the core of understanding disaster—and in seeing vulnerability reduction as predicated on culturally and historically nuanced understandings of human–environmental relations. This includes how differential experiences of trauma, environmental devastation, and post-disaster aid are inflected by histories of oppression that continue to evolve in the present, and attending to what Mark Anderson calls the "cultural politics of catastrophe"—a term he uses to elucidate how certain narratives compete to "hold sway over the collective imagination and [...] political establishment" in the wake of disasters (2011, 2).

Instituting such an approach requires creative thinking if we are to negotiate the various and often catastrophic communication barriers that emerge between different stakeholders and constituencies. This is an issue that Brathwaite again identifies in *MR* by focusing on the distinction between what he calls "closed" and "open" systems of thought, with the former associated partly with the impetus for colonial conquest and the latter focusing on responses to fragmentation and reconstruction. As he puts it:

> - CLOSE(D) ≈ 'critical', argumentative often nit-pickin (in defence of the invariant STATUS QUO even STATUS CROW), 'Aristotelian' rather than 'Platonic', MISSILIC ATTACK/COUNTERATTACK as crucial strategy in defence of their CADEUS/CITADEL/ESTABLISHMENT
>
> - in 'contrast' to the OPEN/CONSTITUATIVE (collecting/accumulation of parts or fragments, trying to see/evoke/create a PATTERN - this pattern is usually (but not necessarily) diff from the CLOSED/ESTAB in that for one thing it will be DYNAMIC/IN MOTION/xhibiting features of FISSION & KINESIS - xplosive or xploding in contrast to CLOSE(D) Systems which tend towards implosion on the way not to BLACK HOLES & MR but to ENTROPY

(2002, 36)

While the contrast between open and closed systems sets up a seeming binary, along with the predictable political affiliations this entails, Brathwaite complicates this by suggesting that his work, and magical realism, and, I would argue, most forms of postcolonial critique emerge from the tensions and contradictions *between* these systems. In so doing, they all represent ways of negotiating the conflicts produced in what Brathwaite calls "westem" society (with the pun troubling the distinction between geography, historical development, and epistemology), and shed light on more "open" forms of practice. This contradiction needs to be positioned methodologically at the heart of a self-conscious decolonization of disaster studies, which does not simply involve labelling the various strands of the field as "open" or "closed," but considers how they might be brought together in a process of transformation towards a more "open" research formation as a whole.

Perhaps the most pertinent example here is the need to adapt the conceptual "system" that generated the "What is a Disaster?" debate so as not only to accommodate alternative concepts of disaster (incorporating non-empirical perspectives and prioritizing culturally localized definitions), but also to be more *deductive* about the political links between vulnerability production, environmental exploitation, and post-disaster reconstruction. The category of "postcolonial disaster" represents a further point of synthesis here because it clearly counters the segregated approach to historical and cultural processes that haunts mainstream disaster studies, hinting instead at a productive response to what Brathwaite calls "the lack of truly consistent collective interdiscipline," and the "'problematic' of conversation between academics & between academics & 'Other(s)'" (2002, 89). It also implies a research formation whose most obvious contribution to "policy and practice" involves a direct critique of "closed system" disaster management that fails to contribute to the work of decolonization, and this is precisely where I see a form of postcolonial studies that situates itself *as* disaster studies making a productive intervention.

There is no doubt that "closed spaces abound" in the disaster management field, which tend to consolidate power rather than reduce risk (Mascarenhas and Wisner 2012, 56–57). It is also evident that a postcolonial disaster studies must confront the many exploitative, normalizing, and deeply exclusionary practices that accompany managerial approaches to reconstruction. In fact, Brathwaite says as much when he complains in a 2006 interview that Caribbean aid gets "automatically contaminated [...] by donors *and* menagement-receivers," who represent organizations like "the IMF the WTO NAFTA the EPA" and are more "interested in imposing a solution— not soulution!—that has been already agreed-on somewhere on Madison Avenue or Wall Street or Paris or the G8 at Davos or Geneva or in the Br Museum" than in listening to the concerns of "*local people*" (Brathwaite and Sajé 2009, 247; original emphases). However, *MR* makes a case for negotiating these power structures in ways that are more strategically nuanced than belligerently oppositional. As the puns that characterize Brathwaite's work suggest, this involves emphasizing the power of *language* in revising key disaster studies tenets and risk reduction practices—an issue that postcolonial and humanities-based research is especially well placed to address.

Throughout this chapter, I have highlighted how creative texts such as *MR* offer epistemological alternatives to the dominant rhetorics through which disasters are framed, providing new vocabularies for talking about the relationship between catastrophic events, histories, and—perhaps most significantly— processes of recovery and reconstruction. The last quotation from Brathwaite builds on this directly through its use of language: the term "menagement-receivers" highlights patriarchy's inscription in managerial logics, while the distinction between "solutions" and "soulutions" intimates a vital recalibration of "menagement-speak." The technocratic language of "solutions" is rife in disaster studies, and is often complicit with exclusionary approaches to recovery and with retrenchment of the very processes that exacerbate pre-disaster vulnerability through structural ignorance. This is because it is bound up in a logic of top-down, quick-fix intervention, disregarding the need for an ongoing and sustainable commitment to reconstruction that guards against the tendency for catastrophes to be exploited in ways that produce further disenfranchisement. Postcolonial disasters are not simply "problems" to be "solved;" rather, they are compound processes that demand attention to systemic factors, colonial histories, and—no less importantly—forms of creative response. The significance of this is apparent from how Brathwaite refuses to reject entirely the discourse of "solutions" but reconstitutes it so as to place cultural and endogenous perspectives at its core. His work suggests that meaningful reconstruction is not just participatory but must be attuned to the metaphysical and psychosocial needs of affected communities and environments, and should be understood as inscribed in the language used by affected peoples themselves. Transposing the term "solution"—with its dark historical resonances—to "soulution" is much more than a semantic sleight; it is an invitation to orient disaster studies away from its complicities with militarism, neocolonialism, and capitalist exploitation, and towards the emancipatory vision of recovery and "healing" that Brathwaite avows. It is also a way of anticipating a shift towards more "open" systems of analysis and response that are consonant with postcolonial and ecological critique. Such transformation—at once linguistic and conceptual—is essential for strengthening the claims of postcolonialism, disaster studies, and the environmental humanities to progressive mitigation, and is part of the work of decolonization on which the reduction of global vulnerability depends.

ACKNOWLEDGMENTS

This research for this chapter was supported by a Fellowship at the Rachel Carson Center for Environment and Society, Ludwig-Maximilians-Universität, and by the Arts and Humanities Research Council (UK). I would like to thank the participants at the workshop on Imperialism, Narrative, and the Environment at the Rachel Carson Center in 2012 for their feedback, including my co-editors, and thanks also to the editors of *What Postcolonial Theory Doesn't Say* (Routledge, 2015), which features a version of this chapter.

NOTES

1. This sentiment continues to be reiterated in relation to contemporary social catastrophes, with one recent example coming in a special report by Christine Jennings for *The Guardian* in November 2013, focusing on victims of genocide from Bosnia to Syria (Jennings 2013).
2. The latent implications of this for postcolonial studies are laid bare when Quarantelli lists Rwanda, Cambodia, Mozambique, and Afghanistan as examples of complex emergencies in *What is a Disaster?* (1998b, 263) but fails to identify—much less comment on—the historical connections between such cases. See, for example, O'Dempsey and Munslow (2006) for a more progressive humanitarian account of the connections between colonialism and complex emergencies in Africa.
3. For further discussion of these ideas, see especially Davis (1995), Hewitt (1995, 1998), Lewis (1988), Lewis and Kelman (2012), Mileti (1999), Pelling (2001), and Wisner et al. (2004).
4. See, for example, Bankoff et al. (2004), Collins (2009), Lewis (1999), O'Dempsey and Munslow (2006), Pelling (2003), and Wisner et al. (2004) on disasters, development, and globalization; Kelman et al. (2012) and Shaw et al. (2009) on indigenous knowledge and disaster risk reduction; Bankoff (2003), Oliver-Smith and Hoffman (1998), and Hoffman and Oliver-Smith (2002) on cultural dimensions of catastrophes. See also Boano and Garcia (2013) for an example of one of the few essays that thinks through post-disaster reconstruction with a postcolonial framework in mind.

5. See Kelman et al. in this volume for an example of collaborative disaster risk reduction work that embeds postcolonial and environmental humanities perspectives in its format.
6. See Carrigan (2014) for a collection of essays dealing with representations of catastrophe and environment that covers a range of postcolonial island examples.
7. Brathwaite's poetic style involves an idiosyncratic use of English that involves building gaps, fissures, and apparent "misspellings" into his work. This disrupts the authority of ideas and concepts associated with repressive and/or colonial ideologies, while also representing the fragmentation and reconstruction of language and culture in the Caribbean. All deviations from Standard English in this and subsequent quotations from Brathwaite are reproduced exactly.
8. "Magical realism" is used to describe a literary genre in which prosaic and everyday occurrences are blended with those that appear (to many western readers at least) to be marvelous or magic. Brathwaite's use of the term in *MR* relates less, however, to the usual generic description than to a method of representing and interpreting a world marked by the ravages of European colonialism and historical oppression.
9. See Franks (2013) for a media-oriented perspective on this in relation to famine and aid.
10. See, for example, Kelman (2012) and Hilhorst (2013) for disaster research that is helping to close this gap.
11. This question reflects Brathwaite's more general attention in *MR* to how communities and artists go about "reconstruct[ing] a reality that is [...] inhabitable" in the context of long-term experiences of "neglect decay disease invasion interposition violence [...] trauma of SLAVERY culture SHOCK of colonialism dictatorship anarchy betrayal abandonment environmental collapse [...] natural disasters catastrophes & changelings" (2002, 390, 71). See also McRuer (2010) for a short but suggestive post-earthquake commentary on Haiti, which identifies potential for embodied and collective resistance in what appear to be highly disabling contexts.
12. Popular and sensationalist disaster narratives also tend to make up the focus of the few chapters in disaster studies textbooks on disaster representation (e.g. Berger and Wisner 2013; Webb 2007).

REFERENCES

Adorno, Theodor. 1981. *Prisms*. Translated by Samuel Weber and Sherry Weber. Cambridge: MIT Press.

Anderson, Mark. 2011. *Disaster Writing: The Cultural Politics of Catastrophe in Latin America*. Charlottesville: University of Virginia Press.

Bankoff, Greg. 2003. *Cultures of Disaster: Society and Natural Hazards in the Philippines*. London and New York: Routledge.

Berger, Gregory, and Ben Wisner. 2012. "Hazards and Disasters Represented in Film." In *Handbook of Hazards and Disaster Risk Reduction*, edited by Ben Wisner, JC Gaillard, and Ilan Kelman, 121–130. London and New York: Routledge.

Blanchot, Maurice. 1995. *The Writing of the Disaster*. Translated by Ann Smock. Lincoln: University of Nebraska Press.

Boano, Camillo, and Marisol Garcia. 2013. "Lost in Translation? The Challenges of an Equitable Post-Disaster Reconstruction Process: Lessons from Chile." In *Beyond Shelter after Disaster: Practice, Process and Possibilities*, edited by David Sanderson and Jeni Burnell, 75–91. London and New York: Routledge.

Bolin, Bob. 2007. "Race, Class, Ethnicity and Disaster Vulnerability." In *Handbook of Disaster Research*, edited by Havidán Rodríguez, Enrico Quarantelli, and Russell Dynes, 113–129. New York: Springer.

Brathwaite, Kamau. 1984. *History of the Voice: The Development of Nation Language in Anglophone Caribbean Poetry*. London: New Beacon.

———. 1990. "History, the Caribbean Writer, and *X/Self*." In *Crisis and Creativity in the New Literatures in English*, edited by Geoffrey Davis and Hena Maes-Jelinek, 23–45. Amsterdam: Rodopi.

———. 2002. *MR*. 2 vols. New York: Savacou North.

———. 2005. "CP No News is Not Good Newes." *Save CowPastor*. http://tomraworth.com/augupdate.html.

———. 2006. "Preface." In *Volcano: A Memoir*, by Yvonne Weekes, 7. Leeds: Peepal Tree.

———. 2010. *Elegguas*. Middletown, CT: Wesleyan University Press.

Brathwaite, Kamau, and Natasha Sajé. 2010. "KB in Utah." *Ariel* 40 (2–3): 203–274.

Britton, Neil. 2005. "What's A Word? Opening Up The Debate." In *What is a Disaster? New Answers to Old Questions*, edited by Ronald Perry and Enrico Quarantelli, 113–21. Philadelphia: Xlibris.

Carrigan, Anthony. 2010. "Postcolonial Disaster, Pacific Nuclearization, and Disabling Environments." *Journal of Literary and Cultural Disability Studies* 4 (3): 255–272.

———. 2011. "(Eco)Catastrophe, Reconstruction, and Representation: Montserrat and the Limits of Sustainability." *New Literatures Review* 47–48: 111–128.

———, ed. 2014. "Catastrophe and Environment." Special issue of *Moving Worlds: A Journal of Transcultural Writings* 14 (2).

Collins, Andrew. 2009. *Disaster and Development*. London and New York: Routledge.

Davis, Mike. 1995. "Los Angeles After the Storm: The Dialectic of Ordinary Disaster." *Antipode* 27 (3): 221–241.

———. 2001. *Late Victorian Holocausts: El Niño Famines and the Making of the Third World*. London: Verso.

The Day after Tomorrow. 2004. Directed by Roland Emmerich. Los Angeles: 20th Century Fox.

DeLoughrey, Elizabeth, Renée Gosson, and George Handley. 2005. "Introduction." In *Caribbean Literature and the Environment: Between Nature and Culture*, edited by Elizabeth DeLoughrey, Renée Gosson, and George Handley, 1–30. Charlottesville: University of Virginia Press.

Franks, Suzanne. 2013. *Reporting Disasters: Famine, Aid, Politics and the Media*. London: Hurst.

Gilbert, Claude. 1998. "Studying Disaster: Changes in the Main Conceptual Tools." In *What Is a Disaster?: Perspectives on the Question*, edited by Enrico Quarantelli, 11–18. London and New York: Routledge.

Gregory, Derek. 2004. *The Colonial Present*. Oxford: Blackwell.

Hewitt, Kenneth. 1995. "Sustainable Disasters? Perspectives and Powers in the Discourse of Calamity." In *Power of Development*, edited by Jonathan Crush, 115–128. London and New York: Routledge.

————. 1998. "Excluded Perspectives in the Social Construction of Disaster." In *What Is a Disaster?: Perspectives on the Question*, edited by Enrico Quarantelli, 71–88. London and New York: Routledge.

Hilhorst, Dorothea, ed. 2013. *Disaster, Conflict and Society in Crises: Everyday Politics of Crisis Response*. London and New York: Routledge.

Hilhorst, Dorothea, and Greg Bankoff. 2004. "Introduction: Mapping Vulnerability." In *Mapping Vulnerability: Disasters, Development and People*, edited by Greg Bankoff, Georg Frerks, and Dorothea Hilhorst, 1–9. London: Earthscan.

Hoffman, Susanna, and Anthony Oliver-Smith, eds. 2002. *Culture and Catastrophe: The Anthropology of Disaster*. Sante Fe: School of American Research Press.

Huggan, Graham. 2008. *Interdisciplinary Measures: Literature and the Future of Postcolonial Studies*. Liverpool: Liverpool University Press.

Jennings, Christine. 2013. "From Bosnia to Syria: The Investigators Identifying Victims of Genocide." *The Guardian*. November 13. Accessed March 13, 2014. http://www.theguardian.com/law/2013/nov/10/bosnia-syria-victims-of-genocide-dna.

Kelman, Ilan. 2003. "Beyond Disaster, Beyond Diplomacy." In *Natural Disaster and Development in a Globalizing World*, edited by Mark Pelling, 110–123. London and New York: Routledge.

————. 2012. *Disaster Diplomacy: How Disasters Affect Peace and Conflict*. London and New York: Routledge.

Kelman, Ilan, Jessica Mercer, and JC Gaillard. 2012. "Indigenous Knowledge and Disaster Risk Reduction." *Geography* 97 (1): 12–21.

Klein, Naomi. 2007. *The Shock Doctrine: The Rise of Disaster Capitalism*. London: Allen Lane.

Lewis, James. 1988. "On the Line: An Open Letter in Response to 'Confronting Natural Disasters, An International Decade for Natural Hazard Reduction.'" *Natural Hazards Observer* 12 (4): 4.

————. 1999. *Development in Disaster-prone Places: Studies of Vulnerability*. London: Intermediate Technology Publications.

Lewis, James, and Ilan Kelman. 2012. "The Good, The Bad and The Ugly: Disaster Risk Reduction (DRR) Versus Disaster Risk Creation (DRC)." *PLOS Currents Disasters* 1 (1): 1–24.

Mascarenhas, Adolfo, and Ben Wisner. 2012. "Politics: Power and Disasters." In *Handbook of Hazards and Disaster Risk Reduction*, edited by Ben Wisner, JC Gaillard, and Ilan Kelman, 48–60. London and New York: Routledge.

McCarthy, Cormac. 2006. *The Road*. London: Picador.

McRuer, Robert. 2010. "Reflections on Disability in Haiti." *Journal of Literary and Cultural Disability Studies* 4 (3): 327–332.

McSweeney, Joyelle. 2005. "Poetics, Revelations, and Catastrophes: An Interview with Kamau Brathwaite." *Rain Taxi Review of Books*. December 10. http://www.raintaxi.com/poetics-revelations-and-catastrophes-an-interview-with-kamau-brathwaite/.

Mileti, Dennis. 1999. *Disasters by Design: A Reassessment of Natural Hazards in the United States*. Washington: John Henry.

Mirzoeff, Nicholas. 2005. "Invisible Again: Rwanda and Representation after Genocide." *African Arts* 38 (3): 36–39; 86–95.

Mukherjee, Upamanyu Pablo. 2013. *Natural Disasters and Victorian Empire: Famines, Fevers and the Literary Cultures of South Asia*. Basingstoke: Palgrave MacMillan.

Nixon, Rob. 2011. *Slow Violence and the Environmentalism of the Poor.* Cambridge: Harvard University Press.

O'Dempsey, Tim, and Barry Munslow. 2006. "Globalisation, Complex Emergencies and Health." *Annals of Tropical Medicine and Parasitology* 100 (5–6): 501–515.

Oliver-Smith, Anthony. 1994. "Peru's Five Hundred Year Earthquake: Vulnerability in Historical Context." In *Disasters, Development and Environment*, edited by Ann Varley, 31–48. Chichester: Wiley.

Oliver-Smith, Anthony. 1998. "Global Changes and the Definition of Disaster." In *What Is a Disaster?: Perspectives on the Question*, edited by Enrico Quarantelli, 177–194. London and New York: Routledge.

———. 2004. "Theorizing Vulnerability in a Globalized World: A Political Ecological Perspective." In *Mapping Vulnerability: Disasters, Development and People*, edited by Greg Bankoff, Georg Frerks, and Dorothea Hilhorst, 10–24. London: Earthscan.

Oliver-Smith, Anthony, and Susanna Hoffman, eds. 1998. *The Angry Earth: Disasters in Anthropological Perspective.* London and New York: Routledge.

Quarantelli, Enrico. 1998a. "Introduction: The Basic Question, Its Importance, and How it is Addressed in this Volume." In *What Is a Disaster?: Perspectives on the Question*, edited by Enrico Quarantelli, xii–xviii. London and New York: Routledge.

———. 1998b. "Epilogue: Where We Have Been and Where We Might Go." In *What Is a Disaster?: Perspectives on the Question*, edited by Enrico Quarantelli, 234–273. London and New York: Routledge.

Quayson, Ato. 2000. *Postcolonialism: Theory, Practice or Process?* Cambridge: Polity.

Pelling, Mark. 2001. "Natural Disasters?" In *Social Nature: Theory, Practice and Politcs*, edited by Noel Castree and Bruce Braun, 170–188. Oxford: Blackwell.

———, ed. 2003. *Natural Disaster and Development in a Globalizing World.* London and New York: Routledge.

Perry, Ronald. 2007. "What is a Disaster?" In *Handbook of Disaster Research*, edited by Havidán Rodríguez, Enrico Quarantelli, and Russell Dynes, 1–15. New York: Springer.

Plumwood, Val. 1993. *Feminism and the Mastery of Nature.* New York and London: Routledge.

Ross, Andrew. 1991. *Strange Weather: Culture, Science and Technology in an Age of Limits.* London: Verso.

Sachs, Wolfgang. 1993. "Global Ecology and the Shadow of 'Development.'" In *Global Ecology: A New Arena of Political Conflict*, edited by Wolfgang Sachs, 3–21. London: Zed.

———. 1999. *Planet Dialectics: Explorations in Environment and Development.* London: Zed.

Scanlon, T. Joseph. 2005. "Foreword." In *What is a Disaster? New Answers to Old Questions*, edited by Ronald Perry and Enrico Quarantelli, 13–18. Philadelphia: Xlibris.

Shaw, Rajib, Anshu Sharma, and Yukio Takeuchi, eds. 2009. *Indigenous Knowledge and Disaster Risk Reduction: From Practice to Policy.* New York: Nova.

Smith, Gavin, and Dennis Wenger. 2007. "Sustainable Disaster Recovery: Operationalizing an Existing Agenda." In *Handbook of Disaster Research*, edited by Havidán Rodríguez, Enrico Quarantelli, and Russell Dynes, 234–247. New York: Springer.

Stallings, Robert. 2005. "Disaster, Crisis, Collective Stress, and Mass Deprivation." In *What is a Disaster? New Answers to Old Questions*, edited by Ronald Perry and Enrico Quarantelli, 237–274. Philadelphia: Xlibris.

Stoler, Ann. 2008. "Imperial Debris: Reflections on Ruins and Ruination." *Cultural Anthropology* 23 (2): 191–219.

Small Axe Project. 2011. "The Visual Life of Catastrophic History: A Small Axe Project Statement." *Small Axe* 15 (1): 133–136.

Webb, Gary R. 2007. "The Popular Culture of Disaster: Exploring a New Dimension of Disaster Research." In *Handbook of Disaster Research*, edited by Havidán Rodríguez, Enrico Quarantelli, and Russell Dynes, 430–440. New York: Springer.

Wisner, Ben, Piers Blaikie, Terry Cannon, and Ian Davis, eds. 2004. *At Risk: Natural Hazards, People's Vulnerability and Disasters*. 2nd ed. London and New York: Routledge.

Wisner, Ben, JC Gaillard, and Ilan Kelman. 2012. "Challenging Risk." In *Handbook of Hazards and Disaster Risk Reduction*, edited by BenWisner, JC Gaillard, and Ilan Kelman, 1–8. London and New York: Routledge.

World Bank. 2014. "Disaster Risk Management Overview." *The World Bank: IRBD IDA*. March 25. http://www.worldbank.org/en/topic/disasterriskmanagement/overview#1.

Worster, Donald. 1994. *Nature's Economy: A History of Ecological Ideas*. 2nd ed. Cambridge: Cambridge University Press.

6 Nuclear Disaster

The Marshall Islands Experience and Lessons for a Post-Fukushima World

Barbara Rose Johnston

From 1946 to 1958, the United States detonated sixty-seven atomic and thermonuclear bombs in the Marshall Islands United Nations Trust Territory: atomizing entire islands, blanketing the twenty-two populated atolls with dangerous levels of radioactive fallout, creating a nation that has been forever changed by the toxic and mutagenic nature of nuclear militarism.[1] This chapter considers the varied meanings and legacies of this nuclear colonialism from a critical global ecologies perspective. A critical global ecologies perspective considers the ways that human notions, values, and actions both shape and contort biophysical ecosystems with anthropogenic consequence on local and global scales; consequences that can lead to or fuel ecocide, ethnocide, and genocide; consequences that place front and center the ethical imperative for greater social and environmental justice.

Atomic science and nuclear militarism gave birth to an absolutely unique ecology, artificially creating elements that, through their radiogenic and mutagenic behavior, have the potential to fundamentally alter the physical nature of local and planetary systems and the varied life that these systems support. As I have discussed elsewhere (Johnston 2007a), in an effort to understand and exploit the immense power of the atom, a nuclear colonialism emerged based upon naive notions that geographic and temporal distance buffers and protects the colonizing power from the mutagenic and potentially deadly forces birthed and unleashed upon host communities. For communities colonized by nuclear militarism—an ecosystem of radiogenic communities located near uranium mines, mills, and enrichment plants, weapons production facilities, military "proving" grounds, battlefields, and nuclear waste dumps—decolonization not only involves coming to terms with the ulcerating consequences of human environmental rights abuse, it necessarily demands recognition of ethnocentrism and its role in shaping and legitimizing inequitable relationships; in defining the goals and loci of power in governance; and, in defining and imposing contorted understandings of reality.

Even in the contexts of immense inequity, the power of lived experience can make visible hidden truths and encourage transformative change. Thus, this examination of the human-environmental legacies of nuclear colonialism appropriately begins with the voice of Lijon Eknilang, a Marshallese nuclear survivor:

On the morning of 1 March 1954, the day of the "Bravo" shot, there was a huge, brilliant light that consumed the sky. We all ran outside our homes to see it. The elders said another world war had begun. I remember crying. I did not realize at the time that it was the people of Rongelap who had begun a lifelong battle for their health and a safe environment. Not long after the light from Bravo, it began to snow in Rongelap. We had heard about snow from the missionaries and other westerners who had come to our islands, but this was the first time we saw white particles fall from the sky and cover our village. Of course, in 1954, Marshallese children and their parents did not know that the snow was radioactive fall-out from the Bravo shot. The fall-out that our bodies were exposed to caused the blisters and other sores we experienced over the weeks that followed. Many of us lost our hair, too. The fall-out was in the air we breathed, in the fresh water we drank, and in the food we ate during the days after Bravo. This caused internal exposure and sickness. We remained on Rongelap for two and one-half days after the fall-out came. The serious internal and external exposure we received caused long-term health problems that affected my parents' generation, my generation, and the generation of my children. Then we were told that we had to leave Rongelap. Some of us left by airplane, but most of us on a large ship. We did not take our belongings or our animals. We did not know, when we left on 3 March 1954 that we would be leaving our homes for almost three years.

In June 1957, when we did return, we saw changes on our island. Some of our food crops, such as arrowroot, completely disappeared. Makmok, or tapioca plants, stopped bearing fruit. What we did eat gave us blisters on our lips and in our mouths and we suffered terrible stomach problems and nausea. Some of the fish we caught caused the same problems. These were things that had not happened before 1954. Our staple foods had never made us ill. We brought these problems to the attention of the doctors and officials who visited us. They said we were preparing the foods incorrectly, or that we had fish poisoning. We knew that was impossible because we had been preparing and surviving from these foods for centuries without suffering from the problems that appeared after 1954. Although our blisters, burns and hair loss eventually cleared up, we later experienced other, even more serious problems.

It has always been interesting to me that even the people who were not on Rongelap in 1954, but who went there with us in 1957, began to experience the same illnesses we did in later years. Foreign doctors and other officials called those people the "control group," and we were told the sickness of that group proved our illnesses were common to all Marshallese. We did not believe that, and we learned only recently that the "control group" had come from areas that had also been contaminated by radioactivity from the weapons tests.

Our illnesses got worse, and many of us died. We had to believe that our island was radioactive, and we evacuated ourselves from Rongelap in 1985. The Rongelapese have been living in exile ever since. My own health has suffered very much, as a result of radiation poisoning. I cannot have children. I have had miscarriages on seven occasions. On one of those occasions, I miscarried after four months. The child I miscarried was severely deformed; it had only one eye. I have also had thyroid surgery to remove nodules. I am taking thyroid medication which I need every day for the rest of my life. Doctors recently found more nodules in my thyroid, which have to be removed in the near future. I have lumps in my breasts, as well as kidney and stomach problems, for which I am receiving treatment. My eyesight is blurred, and everything looks foggy to me. Others in my community suffered, as well. Many children and seemingly healthy adults died unexpectedly in the years following Bravo—the reasons for which none of us fully understood at the time. [...]

We began to learn about leukemia for the first time when the body of Lekoj Anjain, a 15-year old boy who had been strong and healthy, was return to Rongelap in a coffin. We did not understand his illness or the illnesses for which we were sent to the United States to be treated. Many of us were sent from our islands for the first time in our lives to hospital in the United States and Guam. We had surgeries and treatments which we knew little about because we did not speak English and, in most cases, there were no translators. Some of us had brain tumors and other cancers removed. In more recent years, we have come to learn that some of us had our entire thyroids removed [...]

Women have experienced many reproductive cancers and abnormal births. Marshallese women suffer silently and differently from the men who were exposed to radiation. Our culture and religion teaches us that reproductive abnormalities are a sign that women have been unfaithful to their husbands. For this reason, many of my friends keep quiet about the strange births they had. In privacy, they give birth, not to children as we like to think of them, but to things we could only describe as "octopuses," "apples," "turtles," and other things in our experience. We do not have Marshallese words for these kinds of babies because they were never born before the radiation came. [...] Many of these women are from atolls which foreign officials have told us were not affected by radiation. We know otherwise, because the health problems are similar to ours. One woman on Likiep gave birth to a child with two heads. Her cat also gave birth to a kitten with two heads. There is a young girl on Ailuk today with no knees, three toes on each foot and a missing arm. Her mother had not been born by 1954, but she was raised on a contaminated atoll. The most common birth defects on Rongelap and nearby islands have been "jellyfish" babies. These babies are born with no bones in their bodies and with transparent skin. We can see their brains and hearts beating. The babies usually live for a day or two before they stop breathing. Many women die from abnormal pregnancies and those who survive give birth to what looks like purple grapes which we quickly hide away and bury.

My purpose for travelling such a great distance to appear before the Court today, is to plead with you to do what you can [...] not to allow the suffering that we Marshallese have experienced to be repeated in any other community in the world. While no government or other organization can fully restore the health of the Marshallese people or our environment, steps can be taken which will make it less likely that the same kinds of horrors will be experienced again. I know first-hand what the devastating effects of nuclear weapons are over time and over long distances, and what those effects mean to innocent human beings over several generations. The story of the Marshallese people since the nuclear weapons tests has been sad and painful. Allow our experience, now, to save others such sadness and pain. I ask the Court to consider the experience of the Marshallese and to give the people of our world what security you can for their health and for the safety of the environment upon which their survival depends [...].

(ICJ 1995, 25–28)[2]

For years Lijon Ekilang traveled the world sharing her lived experience in various political arenas, giving voice to the human suffering resulting from nuclear militarism in the Marshall Islands. She spoke at the first World Uranium Hearing in Salzburg in 1992, and her testimony was so memorable that more than twenty years later her story of the Marshallese plight was recounted in a speech by Navajo Nation President Joe Shirley, Jr. at the opening of the second Indigenous World Uranium Summit.[3] In the break following President Shirley's speech, a number of indigenous leaders spoke to me about the importance of the Marshallese presence at the 1992 World Uranium Hearing. They repeatedly emphasized that it was her testimony that helped indigenous delegates from diverse communities understand that their experiences with radiation and other toxic poisons in the air, food, soil, water, plants, and human bodies was not unique; their suffering is a form of nuclear colonialism shared by the indigenous peoples around the world who disproportionately host nuclear militarism. Lijon Eknilang's advocacy work in Salzburg and in other international arenas inspired and continues to shape a global native, aboriginal, first nations, and indigenous environmental justice movement. Moreover, her 1995 testimony to the International Court of Justice was part of the body of evidence that moved that court to declare that the threat or use of nuclear weapons was a violation of international humanitarian law, a ruling that continues to influence and encourage the movement for a total ban on nuclear militarism.

Despite such powerful outcomes, the remedial actions sought by Lijon Eknilang and other Marshall Islanders have yet to generate meaningful remedy. Nuclear proliferation continues, Marshallese environment and health continues to degenerate, and the world continues to experience new nuclear disasters, as the earthquake, tsunami, and Fukushima nuclear meltdown in Japan illustrates.[4] Below, I review some of the consequences of exposure to a radioactive and toxic environment and the varied scientific and political efforts to shape, control, and deny human environmental outcomes in the Marshall Islands. The underlying intent here is to make visible the controlling processes that structure and sustain nuclear colonialism; to consider "the mechanisms by which ideas take hold and become institutional in relation to power" (Nader 1997, 711). It is argued that control over science and the related information that supports government policy—be it public health, military dominance, or an ever expanding economy—represents a core element in the architecture of power of both the colonial and so-called postcolonial state, and a primary means by which embedded ethnocentric notions come to dominate human understanding of reality. This argument is very much situated in an environmental humanities and global critical ecologies perspective; historicizing ecological abuse, social activism, and evasions of responsibility to demonstrate the dynamic forces at play. Contorted conclusions resulting from the controlled and heavily censored production and dissemination of scientific knowledge can be countered via the obvious truths evident in lived experience.

NUCLEAR COLONIALISM IN THE MARSHALL ISLANDS

Between 1946 and 1958, the United States detonated twenty-three nuclear bombs on or above Bikini, forty-three more devices on or above Enewetak, and another device approximately eighty-five miles from Enewetak, atomizing entire islands and blanketing the entire Marshallese nation with measurable levels of radioactive fallout from twenty of these tests.[5] The total explosive yield of nuclear militarism in the Marshall Islands was equivalent to more than seven thousand Hiroshima bombs. Iodine-131 comprised an estimated two percent of the resulting radioactive fallout; all told some 8 billion curies of I-131 were released into the atmosphere above the Marshall Islands: forty-two times greater than the 150 million curies released as a result of the testing in Nevada, 150 times greater than the 40 million curies released as a result of the Chernobyl nuclear disaster.[6]

Hydrogen bomb tests, especially the March 1, 1954 Bravo Test, were immensely destructive (cf. Breslin and Cassidy 1955).[7] The Castle Bravo explosion was visible from 250 miles with a mushroom cloud stretching

60 miles across; it vaporized several small islands and left a mile-wide crater on the atoll and generated heavy radioactive fallout across a 50,000 square mile area. It remains, to this day, the largest and "dirtiest" nuclear weapon the US ever tested. Communities living immediately downwind suffered near fatal exposures,[8] and people on Rongelap, Ailinginae, and Utrik atolls were evacuated.[9] One consequence of these tests is that the entire nation was exposed to dangerous levels of fallout, a fact documented in the 1950s but kept classified until after a Compact of Free Association had been negotiated and adopted by US Congress.

US military testing in the Marshall Islands was a scientific enterprise involving the detonation of nuclear bombs, the testing of biochemical[10] and ballistic missile weapons, and radiation ecology studies. This militarized scientific agenda established an ecological baseline in the marine and terrestrial environment; subsequent studies chronicled the nature and behavior of radioactive fallout in the atmosphere, marine, and terrestrial environment, and the bioaccumulation of radioisotopes in the environment, food chain, and human body.[11]

Collectively, this radioecology research documented the presence and movement of radioisotopes in the environment and food chain. For example, radioiron (Fe-55) in fallout from the 1958 nuclear tests was documented in terrestrial and marine environments, including lagoon sediments, coral reefs, and reef fish, with alarming levels in goat fish liver. This knowledge was not shared with the scientific world until 1972, nor shared with Marshallese until the declassification order supporting an Advisory Commission on Human Radiation investigation forced bilateral disclosure to the Marshall Islands Government in the 1990s. The movement of cesium through the soils, and bioaccumulation in coconut crabs, trees, and fruit—a primary source of food and liquid in the Marshallese diet—was also documented, with restrictions on the consumption of coconut crab periodically issued without explanation.

To understand the human health effects of acute exposure to high levels of radiation, under the guise of humanitarian aid in 1954 the people of Rongelap, Ailinginae, and Utrik, were enrolled as human subjects in a classified medical research program known as "Project 4.1." Merril Eisenbud's comments in a classified 1956 scientific research planning conference are insightful:

> We think that one very intriguing study can be made and plans are on the way to implement this—"Uterik" Atoll is the atoll furthest from the March 1 shot where people were exposed got initially about 15 roentgens and then they were evacuated and they returned.
>
> They had been living on that Island; now that Island is safe to live on but is by far the most contaminated place in the world and it will be very interesting to go back and get good environmental data, how many per square mile; what isotopes are involved and a sample of food changes in many humans through their urines, so as to get a measure of the human uptake when people live in a contaminated environment.

Now, data of this type has never been available. While it is true that these people do not live, I would say, the way Westerners do, civilized people, it is nevertheless also true that these people are more like us than mice. So that is something which will be done this winter.

(ACBM 1956:232–33)[12]

In 1957, the goal of establishing a living laboratory to study the movement of radiation through the environment, food chain, and human body and the related human health effects of low-level exposure to radiation in a controlled setting was achieved when the Rongelap community was repatriated to their contaminated atoll.[13] Over the next four decades, US medical teams traveled to the Marshall Islands to document radiogenic health on select islands and conduct human subject experiments without informed consent. All told, some 539 men, women, and children from Rongelap, Utrik, Likiep, Enewetak, and Majuro atolls served as human subjects in studies documenting the varied late effects of radiation.[14]

This classified research generated an array of findings. Acute exposures to radiation stimulate short-term effects. Late effects can emerge many years following initial exposure. Radioiodine-131 adheres to and accumulates in the thyroid stimulating the production of benign and cancerous nodules and interfering with the production of hormones, leaving pregnant women and children especially vulnerable. And people who were not exposed to an acute level of ionizing radiation but were exposed to low-levels on a daily basis because they lived in an area contaminated by fallout also developed thyroid and other radiogenic health problems.

The classified nature of this research also meant that the relationships between nuclear weapons testing, fallout, contamination of the environment, human subsistence in that environment, and degenerative health were not explained to the Marshallese until decades had passed. Human radiation experimentation records declassified in the 1990s demonstrate degenerative health outcomes from radiation exposure, including changes in red blood cell production and subsequent anemia; metabolic and related disorders; immune system vulnerabilities; musculoskeletal degeneration; cataracts; cancers and leukemia; miscarriages, congenital defects, and infertility. Declassified documents also demonstrate that US scientists fully expected adverse health effects to not only occur in the first generation of people exposed to fallout, but in the subsequent generations of people who live in a contaminated setting. Marshallese health records bear out these expectations.

LONGTERM EXPERIENCES WITH NUCLEAR DISASTER

In 1995, the United States released a previously classified document indicating that fallout from the 1954 Bravo test occurred at hazardous levels on twenty-eight atolls throughout the Marshall Islands. The entire nation, not simply the four atolls identified by the US in 1954, is downwind and the whole country has been adversely affected by nuclear weapons (Breslin and Cassidy 1955, discussed in Johnston and Barker 2008, 28). In 2002, research was commissioned by the RMI Nuclear Claims Tribunal to examine environmental conditions in areas that prior US surveys ignored, demonstrated the continuing presence of dangerous levels of radiation on six atolls in the southern part of the nation (Behling et al. 2002). Given the bioaccumulative nature of the contamination caused by the nuclear testing, population-wide low-level exposure continues via food and water consumption, and inhalation of dust and cooking fire smoke. Chronic exposure generates cumulative and synergistic effects, especially cancer.

Medical records and testimony of experts led the RMI Islands Nuclear Claims Tribunal to recognize some thirty-six forms of radiogenic cancers and disease as resulting from nuclear weapons test exposures. A review of Tribunal awards in 2007 found that most awards were for thyroid cancers and disease, pulmonary and lung cancer, cancers of the blood, bone marrow, and lymph nodes, breast cancer, and cancers of the ovary (Johnston and Barker 2008, 242).

Chronic and acute radiogenic exposure also impacts immune system response, creating a population-wide vulnerability to infectious and noncommunicable disease.[15] And, noncommunicable disease and degenerative health conditions, especially conditions associated with radiation-exposure and life in a heavily contaminated environment, are crippling an already overtaxed health infrastructure.

Comparing the relative health of US residents with that of its former territorial citizens, the Marshallese, is insightful: First, in the US, the diabetes prevalence rate is 9.35 percent. In the Marshall Islands the rate is 27.06 percent, the third highest rate in the world, and diabetes is the number one cause of death.[16] Second, infant mortality in the US is about six deaths per thousand; in the Marshall Islands the 2012 rate is about twenty-three per thousand, a rate comparable to Kazakhstan, another nation victim to nuclear testing.[17] Finally, on average, Americans live for some 77.5 years; in the Marshall Islands the end of life comes considerably sooner, 15 years sooner, as overall longevity is 62 years.[18]

With the adoption of a Compact of Free Association with the United States in 1986, the Republic of the Marshall Islands inherited a grossly inadequate health care system, one that historically relied on US funding and infrastructure to transport and treat. There is no oncologist resident in the Marshall Islands, no means to treat cancers and other radiogenic disease, and few means to treat noncommunicable disease. Lacking internal technical capacity, medical infrastructure, and the economic means to address healthcare needs at home, for the Marshallese, medical migration has become a societal norm. Today the majority of nuclear survivors live in exile, largely on borrowed or rented Marshallese land on Kwajalein, Majuro, Kili, or in Hawai'i and the continental US.

Bilateral agreements between the US and the RMI have resulted in modest levels of assistance in attending to some of the nation's radiogenic environment and health issues in the Rongelap, Utrik, Enewetak, and Bikini Atoll communities.[19] Attempts to remediate radiation hotspots on areas of some islands and to rebuild homes on the island of Rongelap, for example, suggest that someday refugees from Rongelap may have the choice of returning home.[20] However, given the degree of contamination and remediation limitations, return to a traditional self-sufficient way of life in heavily contaminated atolls like Rongelap is impossible. Remediation has occurred under the guidance and with scientific assistance from the US Department of Energy whose definition of "safe" levels of exposure assumes that people will avoid known hotspots on Rongelap island, will restrict their dietary consumption of local foods to below 30 percent, the nation's interisland transportation system will be able to regularly deliver imported foods, residents will be able to garner the income to pay for food imports, and residents will avoid visiting or collecting food and water from many of the sixty other islands in Rongelap atoll. These islands, and many, many others in the heavily contaminated northern atolls, have been declared off-limits to human life for the next 24,000 years.

SEEKING REMEDY

As an indigenous island nation, the Marshallese enjoyed a self-sufficient sustainable way of life before nuclear weapons testing. Nuclear weapons fallout and bioaccumulation in the environment and human body compromised the health of the individuals, communities, and an entire nation. The Marshallese have experienced the loss of traditionally held land and marine resources without negotiation or just compensation; a human subject experimentation program that arguably violated the Nuremburg code; and, when negotiating the terms of independence in free association with the United States, were severely hampered by the US refusal to fully disclose the full extent of military activities, including the scientific documentation of the environmental and health impacts of serving as the Pacific Proving Ground for weapons of mass destruction.

In 1986, in exchange for dropping a series of damage claims pending in the US Courts and securing limited independence for the United Nation's Strategic Trust Territory, a Compact of Free Agreement was established. Under the terms of Section 177 in that agreement, the United States agreed to establish a $150 million reparations fund and the Marshall Islands Government agreed to the US request that it establish a reparation mechanism to receive and adjudicate personal injury and property damage claims. Due to the classified nature of US military activity and related radiation ecology and health research, negotiations occurred under a grossly inequitable context. Specifically, Marshall Islands representatives were unaware of the full extent of documented damage, injury, and harm associated with US military testing and related human radiation research in the Pacific Grounds. In 1988, the RMI Nuclear Claims Tribunal began its work, functioning with its limited pool of resources and the right to return to US Congress to expand that pool should conditions change or new information come to light.

The Marshall Islands Nuclear Claims Tribunal brought in independent experts to evaluate the extent of damage and to develop remedial recommendations. After a decade of investigation and hearings involving some seven thousand personal injury claims, 2,127 Marshallese were found to be eligible for medical compensation from some thirty-six different forms of cancer and other radiogenic disease, and some were awarded compensation for their experiences in human radiation experiments. Hundreds of claimants and deceased individuals who suffered from cancer of "unknown primary" origin were deemed ineligible for compensation, as were the many whose medical records were destroyed by hospital fire, inadequate storage and other reasons. Many more personal injury awards would have been made by the Tribunal had adequate medical diagnostic services been available in the Marshall Islands. In fact, the absence of any diagnosis was the norm for most people throughout the period of nuclear testing in the Marshall Islands.[21]

Despite decades of remedial attention from the US, the fundamental conditions of life in the Marshall Islands remain tenuous and, given climate change and associated rising sea levels, are expected to further deteriorate (c.f. Ahlgren, Yamada, and Wong 2014). The Marshallese have, however, identified proactive strategies that might be taken to reduce risk, to grow healthy and safe food, to enhance individual, family and community health; strategies detailed in the Nuclear Claims Tribunal's awards to repair and compensate Bikini, Enewetak, Utrik, and Rongelap atoll communities. These include proposals to decontaminate soils, reduce the presence of radioisotopes in the food chain, educate and train a new generation of Marshallese radiation health experts, provide holistic health care and other measures that seek to rebuild a sustainable and healthy way of life. However, given that the United States government rejects the notion that they have an obligation to fully fund the Nuclear Claims Tribunal, the Marshall Islands Government is severely challenged to meet their societal obligations to uphold fundamental rights to life, health, a healthy environment, and a culturally viable way of life.[22]

Recognizing these continuing issues, in his September 12, 2012 mission report on the Marshall Islands and the US, Mr. Călin Georgescu, United Nations Special Rapporteur on the implications for human rights of the environmentally sound management and disposal of hazardous substances and waste, observed that the human rights consequences of nuclear contamination involve, at the most fundamental levels, the loss of a healthy environment that sustains a viable, culturally distinct, Pacific Island way of life. Acknowledging the many constraints and impossibilities in this heavily polluted context—atomized islands, high-level nuclear waste dumps, chronic and acute health effects to individuals in the past, present, and in the generations to come—the

UN Special Rapporteur called for the US, with additional support from members of the United Nations and other interested parties, to engage in meaningful actions that seek to restore a culturally vibrant, healthy, sustainable way of life for the Marshallese people. In concrete terms, this requires full disclosure, cooperation, and assistance from the US in addressing the environmental contamination and human health ramifications of past and current military use of the Marshall Islands; full access to data associated with environmental surveys, medical records, and related scientific research involving Marshallese subjects (including the collection and use of biological samples); full funding by the US of the Nuclear Claims Tribunal awards to compensate and address the personal health and environmental impacts. Bilateral and international partnerships are also needed to develop the educational capacity, technical expertise and related infrastructure; as are actions that demonstrate a guarantee of non-repetition in the violations of bioethical norms and humanitarian law suggested by human subject experimentation, and in the violations of humanitarian law resulting from the development, testing and use of weapons of mass destruction. (United Nations Human Rights Commission, A/HRC/21/48/Add.1).[23]

The US rejected the validity of a human rights review of nuclear weapon testing, arguing "that nuclear testing is not, fundamentally, an issue of 'management and disposal of hazardous substances and wastes'." Citing the adoption of a Compact of Free Association and expenditures of $600 million to date for various technical problems, the US assured the United Nations that "Experts and scientists from across the US Government will continue their decades long engagement in the Marshall Islands to address the issues that arose from our nuclear testing" (The Legacy of US Nuclear Testing and Radiation Exposure in the Marshall Islands). The US disagreed with a number of assertions of human rights law within the report, and rejected the finding that there is a continuing obligation for the United States or the international community to encourage a "final and just resolution" of the issue.

Lacking the necessary infrastructure and resources to remediate the environment and treat the noncommunicable disease and related degenerative health conditions resulting from nuclear colonialism, in October 2012, Marshall Islands President Christopher Loeak declared a state of health emergency (Loeak 2012). As of this writing, while other nations and international agencies have provided modest assistance, the US has expressed no interest in discussing a reparation plan, providing full funding for personal injury, property damage, and consequential damage awards made by the Nuclear Claims Tribunal, or address in any significant and meaningful fashion the recommendations of the UN Special Rapporteur.

FROM RADIATION ECOLOGY TO NUCLEAR ECOLOGIES

What are the means by which the US is able to deny a continuing obligation to effectively attend to the consequences of its nuclear war games?

Throughout the Cold War period, the US government was able to control the shape and content of scientific findings on radiation ecology and human health consequences in ways that managed public fears, diffused the international movement for a comprehensive ban on nuclear weapons testing, and countered protests against the introduction and expansion of civilian nuclear power industries. Classified research coupled with the public release of select, sanitized versions of scientific research allowed widespread acceptance of the notions that exposure to low levels of radiation poses no threat to human health, and that the mutagenic nature of the forces unleashed through nuclear militarism, at any level, poses no threat to the human species (Johnston 2007b, Goldstein and Stawkowski 2014).

Classified research findings that contradicted the official narrative were typically censored, and the scientists who authored such reports suffered reprisal and blacklisting. For example, in the aftermath of Hiroshima and Nagasaki, physical anthropologist Earle Reynolds conducted Atomic Bomb Casualty Commission research demonstrating that Japanese children exposed to the radioisotopes in fallout were smaller than their counterparts, with lowered resistance to disease and a greater susceptibility to cancer, especially leukemia. His completed research demonstrated that atmospheric testing posed a global threat to human health, and his data and final report was submitted in 1953. His work was suppressed, and when he attempted to make his conclusive findings public, Reynolds saw his work discredited (Price 2007). Similarly, nuclear scientist and medical researcher John Goffman demonstrated the somatic and cancer-risk effects resulting from exposure to low-level radiation, for example, work that posed a significant threat to the expansion of civilian nuclear power. Publication of his work resulted in a blacklisting campaign waged by the Atomic Energy Commission and his former employer, Lawrence Livermore National Laboratory (Semendeferi 2008). Reviewing the documented record of government-sponsored efforts to suppress and deny these and similar scientific findings, the 1994 US Advisory Commission on Human Radiation Experiments (ACHRE) concluded that the radiation health literature of the Cold War years was a sanitized and scripted version meant to reassure and pacify public protests while achieving military and economic agendas, a finding recently reconfirmed by the President's 2008–2009 Cancer Panel Report (ACHRE 1994, Leffall and Kripke 2010).

While open access laws and formal apologies were instituted in the 1990s as one means to repair acknowledged Cold War–era abuses, the management of information to control public perception of and concern for nuclear disaster (and thus protect political and economic interests) continues to be a primary objective in governance, and has been especially evident following the March 11, 2011 earthquake, tsunami, and nuclear meltdown in Japan. The nuclear nightmare that is Fukushima has prompted the reemergence of familiar questions: Radiation is invisible, so how do you know when you are in danger? How long will this danger persist? How can you reduce the hazard to yourself and your family? What level of exposure is safe? How do you get access to vital information in time to prevent or minimize exposure? What are the potential risks of acute and chronic exposures? What are the related consequential damages of exposure? How do you rebuild a healthy way of life in the ulcerating aftermath of nuclear disaster?

Given that public information on radiation health effects largely reflects the flaws and biases deeply embedded in a classified Cold War–era research designed to serve military government and industry interests, definitive answers are difficult to find. For example, the research assumption that radiogenic health effects must be demonstrated through direct causality (one isotope, one outcome) meant that science on cumulative and synergistic effects was not pursued, and when new methodologies and techniques for identifying and assessing such effects emerged, significant barriers existed to incorporating research findings (Goldstein and Stawkoski 2014). Discounting or ignoring the toxic nature of varied radioisotopes meant health risks were assessed and regulations promulgated solely on the basis of reconstructed acute exposures and outcomes. Thus, public health attention has largely focused on radiation poisoning and deadly cancers, ignoring immune system vulnerabilities, non-communicative disease, and reproductive and congenital disorders.

The contortions generated by a classified and colonized radiation health science has allowed the repetitive vocalization of this core message: Humans have evolved in a world where radiation from the sun and naturally occur-ring elements was present, and radiation at some levels is natural and ben-eficial. Any adverse heath effect of radiation exposure is the occasional and accidental result of high levels of exposure. Any resulting adverse heath effect from radiation exposure is limited to the individual, not his or her offspring. Nuclear powered operations are safe and their periodic low-level releases represent no threat to human health. The occasional nuclear disas-ter generates localized hotspots that can be contained and remediated.[24]

Cold War classification and the continuing incestuous nature of govern-ment, military, and industry agendas has made it difficult to challenge the assumptions that underlie this "trust us" narrative. This narrative, in one form or another, has been increasingly present in government and industry press releases and media reports since March 11, 2011 (cf. Perrow 2013). Yet despite this persistent mantra, a body of knowledge has generated over the years that stands in sharp contradiction, including the declassification of US human radiation experiment records in the mid-1990s and the release of similar USSR records in the years following the break-up of the Soviet Union, the reassessment of the Atomic Bomb Casualty Commission records and new research conducted by Japanese scientists, the translation and pub-lication of long-term research on Chernobyl workers and other survivors, and the efforts to understand and repair the damages from nuclear weapons testing and related fallout in the Marshall Islands.

From this record of studied and lived experience, what do we know? We know that fallout and the movement of radionuclides through marine and terrestrial environments makes its way into the food chain and the human body. We know that the bioaccumulation of radioisotopes amplifies the relatively small "trace amounts" in the environment and, when ingested, generates larger exposures and significant adverse health outcomes. We know that ingestion of even the smallest particle of a long-lived isotope can result in degenerative health and deadly cancers. We know that acute exposures are further complicated when followed by chronic exposure, as such assaults have a cumulative and synergistic effect on health and wellbeing. We know that chronic exposure to low-level radiation does more than increase the risk of developing cancers; such exposure threatens the immune system, results in changes in fertility and increased rates of birth defect, increased rates of cancers, physical and mental retardation, metabolic disorders and premature aging. We know that the toxicity of contaminants in fallout, as well as the radioactivity, represents significant public health risks. We know that the effects of such exposures extend across the generations.[25]

Consider, for example the translation and summation of radiation health research on Chernobyl survivors published by the New York Academy of Sciences (Yablokov et al. 2009). Health effects not only include widespread occurrence of thyroid disease and cancers (for every case of Chernobyl-induced thyroid cancer, there are about a thousand other cases of thyroid gland pathology, resulting in the multiple endocrine illness of millions of people). Post-Chernobyl studies confirm increased morbidity, impairment and disability, oncological disease, accelerated aging, and increased non-malignant disease (blood, lymph, cardiovascular, metabolic, endocrine, immune, respirator, urogenital, bone and muscle, nervous system, ocular, digestive and skin). These health effects are not simply limited to the generation of people exposed to fallout. Given the long-lived nature of radioisotopes and their toxic, bioaccumulative, and mutagenic nature, nuclear ecologies take on a life of their own, morphing across space and time, with potentially profound intergenerational impacts.

CONCLUSION

Examining the consequences of exposure to a radioactive and toxic environment and the varied scientific and political efforts to shape, control, and deny human environmental outcomes in the Marshall Islands from a global critical ecologies perspective makes visible the artifice and function of postcolonial statehood. Decolonization serves as a political means to deny the degenerative and mutagenic consequences of hosting nuclear disaster and, with statehood, transfers liability from the culpable party, the US, to a victimized Marshallese nation.

The Marshall Islands experience with seven decades of life and death in the US's nuclear "Pacific Proving Grounds" offers many lessons relevant to the larger world. The humanitarian consequences of nuclear devastation are not limited in time and space. Rather, environment and health consequences and related societal burdens expand over time. Political efforts to attend to the human and environmental disaster resulting from nuclear fallout have historically served to limit economic liability by ignoring or denying the humanitarian reality of ulcerating conditions. Control over science and public access to scientific findings has been central in this effort. No single nation can attend to nuclear disaster and its ulcerating consequences. Understanding and attending to the full array of issues that result from nuclear disaster requires national, bilateral, regional, and global commitment and action. And, meaningful remedies require transparency, accountability, and effective actions that repair, restore and ensure "never again." Thus, independent, transparent, accessible science—citizen science—is essential in tackling the issues made visible via a critical global ecologies perspective.

The ideal of governance as embodied in the world's constitutions is that the state serves as the institutional mechanism that secures the fundamental rights of its citizens to life and livelihood. The Marshallese experience and continuing struggles, and the still evolving dimensions of Japan's nuclear disaster illustrate a vast distance between this ideal and the real. In the weeks, months, and years following the 3/11 Fukushima meltdown, to pacify public fear and thus reduce the economic ramifications of another "Chernobyl," statements from industry and government minimized and, at times, censored information on the extent and content of radiation emissions, fallout, and its accumulating presence in the atmosphere, water, soil, food chain, and human body in Japan, the United States, and the global community. Although the consequences of this institutionalized denial may have indeed kept nuclear industry and international trade relatively viable, it is the Japanese citizen and global downwind and down-current communities—human and otherwise—whose exposures and potential degenerative health subsidizes this economic well-being.

Every stage in the evolution of the Marshallese and the Fukushima nuclear nightmares involves struggles to control the content and flow of information to preempt panic and the related loss of trust in government, to reduce liability, and to protect powerful military and economic interests. Nuclear disaster occurs in both places for the same reason: the ability to control, restrict, and contort scientific data to achieve the immediate needs of military and economic priorities at the cost of the environment and public health. Short-term stability is prioritized over the long-term health of people and the environment on which they depend.

There are many other lessons to be learned here, not the least of which is how to respond, adjust, and adapt to the environmental hazards and health risks associated with life in this nuclear world. As the world's nations reassess their commitment to nuclear militarism and nuclear power operations, now more than ever, we need to utilize all data to inform our decisions, especially the experiences of the world's radiogenic communities. We need to recognize that science, in its funding, production, and public policy application, is the product of social desire, cultural beliefs, and political-economic aspirations—biases are inherent and must be recognized. And, in so doing, critical questions emerge: Who is doing the science that shapes nuclear regulatory and safeguard policy and disaster response? To address what questions? According to what notion of significant variables and relevant data sets? What assumptions are used in collecting, developing and assessing data, and determining significant findings? To what end does science serve?

NOTES

1. This chapter has been greatly strengthened thanks to the helpful comments and suggestions from Elizabeth DeLoughrey and Anthony Carrigan. For additional detail on Marshall Islands nuclear history, environment, and health see Barker (2012), Johnston (1994, 131–41; 2013) and Johnston and Barker (2008).
2. Lijon Eknilang died in August 2012. Her efforts to communicate what it means to be a nuclear survivor and advocate for accountability live on in publications and films, and her experiences and concerns are echoed by other Marshallese anti-nuclear activists. See, for example, Giff Johnson's biography of Darlene Keju (2013), the "Nuclear Survivor" audiofiles of the Marshall Islands Story Project (http://mistories.org/nuclear.php) and Adam Horowitz's documentary "Nuclear Savage: The Secret Islands of Project 4.1."
3. I attended the second Indigenous World Uranium Summit, in Window Rock, Arizona. President Joe Shirley's speech and reactions by other attendees are recorded in my conference notes, dated November 30, 2006.
4. The use of depleted uranium in military battlefields and training grounds is a recognized form of radiologic disaster. See, for example, United States health monitoring and compensation programs for veterans of Gulf War, Bosnia, Operation Enduring Freedom, Operation Iraqi Freedom, and Operation New Dawn "who may have been exposed to depleted uranium through their presence on, in or near vehicles hit with friendly fire; entering or near burning vehicles; near fires involving DU munitions; or salvaging damaged vehicles" (US Department of Veteran Affairs 2014).
5. The human cost of this strategic trusteeship has been assessed many times. See Congress of Micronesia Special Joint Committee Concerning Rongelap and Utirik Atolls (1973), Giff Johnson (1979), Harvard Law Student Advocates for Human Rights (2006), and Johnston and Barker (2008).
6. Comparable data for Fukushima is difficult to locate given inadequate monitoring immediately following the initial March 11, 2011 event. According to a US Nuclear Regulatory Commission presentation, approximately 13,513,513 curies of Iodine I-131 was released. See Brock and Milligan (2013, 2).
7. Breslin and Cassidy (1955) was declassified by the US in 1994 and delivered to the Republic of the Marshall Islands (RMI) in 1995. This document reports significant levels of radiation from fallout measured in 1954 at sites on twenty-eight atolls, of which twenty-two were populated during Operation Castle (March 1 through May 14, 1954). Thus, the US has been aware since 1954 that all Marshallese residents were exposed to dangerous levels of radioactive fallout

as result of the atmospheric weapons tests, a finding reconfirmed by Behling et al. (2002).

8. Evacuation occurred a full day after US military personnel were evacuated from nearby Rongerik. See Deines et al. (1991); also, National Cancer Institute (2004).

9. The USS *Renshaw* visited Likiep on March 6, 1954 and documented high levels of radioactivity. Citing the logistical problems of moving a large population, the US opted to leave residents in situ with no medical aide or assistance.

10. Project Shipboard Hazard and Defense (SHAD) tests were conducted off of Enewetak in September and October 1968, among other things testing areal dissemination of an anthrax-simulating agent, Staphylcoccal enterotoxin B, a toxin that causes incapacitating food poisoning with flulike symptoms that can be fatal to the young, elderly, and people weakened by long-term illness (see Morrison 1969). For a description of Marshall Islands experience with this fallout, including fatalities, see Johnston and Barker (2008, 231, 236); for health effects from exposure, see US Department of Defense Project SHAD Factsheet.

11. See Dunning (1957) and Conard (1975, 1991). Independent reviews of the environment and human effects research record occurred following declassification in 1995. See Johnston and Barker (2008) and Rudrud et al. (2007).

12. This quote appears in Johnston (2007b) where it is discussed in greater context.

13. Utrik community was returned to their contaminated atoll three months after the 1954 Bravo Test, and then exposed to additional fallout from fifty subsequent nuclear detonations (1956–1958). Despite this prior and repeated exposure to high levels of radiation, the Atomic Energy Commission scientists designated this community as a "control" group, with the more heavily exposed Rongelap and Ailinginae population serving as the primary 4.1 research group.

14. This human radiation experimentation was recognized as an abusive violation of fundamental rights. See Johnston and Barker (2008), ACHRE (1995), and the Marshall Islands Nuclear Claims Tribunal (2007) judgment in the Rongelap claim.

15. Brookhaven Lab medical surveys document changes in red blood cell production, bone marrow function, and chronic disease in radiation-exposed populations. Subsequent research conducted by the Radiation Effects Research Foundation demonstrated immune cell response to radiation and the finding that "persons with higher radiation exposures have lower numbers of CD4 T cells and elevated levels of various inflammatory proteins in their blood" and "a slight dose-related decrease in immunity has been observed against certain viral infections." See Radiation Effects Research Foundation (2011).

16. Comparative prevalence rate (percent of the World Health Organization standard). Sources for these comparative figures are International Diabetes Federation (2012), Perez Williams, and Hampton (2005), Yamada et al. (2004), and US Embassy, Majuro, Marshall Islands (2007).

17. World Health Organization Global Health Observatory Data Repository, MDG 4: Child Health: Infant mortality, data by country, http://apps.who.int/gho/data/node.main.526.

18. United National Development Program (2006); World Health Organization (2006). Note that all these Marshallese health indicators are influenced by population-wide exposure to ionizing radiation, and RMI inability to adequately address these health issues is one of the many legacies of nuclear colonialism.

19. Despite the 1990s release of declassified documents from 1954 demonstrating nation-wide exposure to dangerous levels of fallout, the US still argues that their obligation to provide medical assistance and repair the environment is limited to the four northern atolls.
20. Workers associated with the Marshall Islands US Department of Energy Assessment & Radioecology Program, US Department of Energy.
21. Testimony of Bill Graham Public Advocate (retired), Marshall Islands Nuclear Claims Tribunal before the House Committee on Foreign Affairs Subcommittee on Asia, the Pacific, and the Global Environment May 20, 2010.
22. Recognition that the Nuclear Claims Tribunal was grossly underfunded was acknowledged in 2010 by the President's Cancer Panel with the recommendation that the US honor and fully fund Tribunal judgments.
23. See Jacobs and Roderick (2012) for a helpful critical review of this reparation template.
24. See also the work of Hugh Gusterson (1998, 2008).
25. This summation and portions of this discussion appear in previously published online commentaries (see Johnston 2011a).

REFERENCES

Advisory Committee on Human Radiation Experimentation. 1995. *The Human Radiation Experiments: Final Report of the President's Advisory Committee.* Washington: US Government Printing Office.

Advisory Committee on Biology and Medicine. 1956. "Meeting minutes. May 26 and 27, 1956." US Atomic Energy Commission. https://www.osti.gov/opennet/servlets/purl/16106479/16106479.pdf.

Ahlgren, Ingrid, Seiji Yamada, and Allen Wong. 2014. "Rising Oceans, Climate Change, Food Aid and Human Rights in the Marshall Islands." *Health and Human Rights* 16 (1): 69–81.

Barker, Holly M. 2012. *Bravo for the Marshallese: Regaining Control in a Post-Nuclear, Post-Colonial World.* Belmont: Wadsworth.

Beatty, Mark E., Tom Jack, Sumathi Sivapalasingam, Sandra S. Yao, Irene Paul, Bill Bibb, Kathy D. Greene, Kristy Kubota, Eric D. Mintz, and John T. Brooks. 2004. "An Outbreak of Vibrio cholerae 01 Infections on Ebeye Island." *Clinical Infectious Diseases* 38: 1–9.

Behling, H. J. Mauro, and K. Behling. 2002. *Final Report: Radiation Exposures Associated with the U.S. Nuclear Testing Program for Twenty-one Atolls/Islands in the Republic of the Marshall Islands.* McLean: S. Cohen and Associates.

Breslin, Alfred, and Melvin E. Cassidy. 1955. *Radioactive Debris from Operation Castle, Islands of the Mid-Pacific, United States Atomic Energy Commission, New York: New York Operations Office.* United States Atomic Energy Commission. January 18. http://www.yokwe.net/ydownloads/RadioactiveDebrisCastle.pdf.

Brock, Terry, and Patricia A. Milligan. 2013. "Fukushima Health Effects" Power point Presentation. United States Nuclear Regulatory Commission. http://homer.ornl.gov/nrc/conf/fukushima_health_effects_nov_2013.pdf.

Center for Disease Control and Prevention. 2005. Tuberculosis in the U.S.-affiliated Pacific Island Jurisdictions (USAPI), 2005. http://www.cdc.gov/tb/statistics/reports/surv2005/PDF/pacificisalands_summary.pdf.

———. 2006. Trends in Tuberculosis—United States, 2005. http://www.cdc.gov/mmwr/preview/mmwrhtml/mm5511a3.htm.

———. 2007. "World TB Day 2007." *Morbidity and Mortality Weekly Report Weekly*, March 24. http://www.cdc.gov/mmwr/preview/mmwrhtml/mm5611a1.htm.

Conard, Robert A. 1975. *A Twenty-year review of medical findings in a Marshallese population accidentally exposed to radioactive fallout, BNL Technical Report 50424.* Upton: Brookhaven National Lab.

———. 1991. *Fallout: The experiences of a medical team in the care of a Marshallese population accidentally exposed to fallout radiation, BNL Technical Report 4644.* Upton: Brookhaven National Lab.

Congress of Micronesia, Special Joint Committee Concerning Rongelap and Utirik Atolls. 1973. *A Report on Rongelap and Utrik to the Congress of Micronesia Relative to Medical Aspects of the Incident of March 1, 1954—Injury, Examination and Treatment.* Fifth Congress of Micronesia, February.

Deines, Ann C., David L. Goldman, Ruth R. Harris, and Laura J. Kells. 1991. *Marshall Islands Chronology: 1944–1990.* Rockville: History Assoc. Inc. Prepared for the US Dept of Energy under contract DE-AC08–87NVI0594. https://www.osti.gov/opennet/servlets/purl/16365116-E12H1n/16365116.pdf.

Dunning, Gordon M. 1957. *Radioactive Contamination of Certain Areas in the Pacific Ocean from Nuclear Tests: A Summary of the Data from the Radiological Surveys and Medical Examinations.* Washington: US Atomic Energy Commission.

Goldstein, Donna M., and Magdalena E. Stawkowski. 2014. "James V. Neel and Yuri E. Dubrova: Cold War Debates and the Genetic Effects of Low-Dose Radiation." *Journal of the History of Biology* (2014): 1–32. doi: 10.1007/s10739–014–9385–0.

Gusterson, Hugh. 1998. *Nuclear Rites: A Weapons Laboratory at the End of the Cold War.* Berkeley: University of California Press.

———. 2004. *People of the Bomb: Portraits of America's Nuclear Complex.* Minneapolis: University of Minnesota Press.

Harvard Law Student Advocates for Human Rights. 2006. *An Evaluation of Continuing US Obligations Arising out of the US Nuclear Weapons testing Program in the Marshall Islands.* Harvard Law School. http://archives.pireport.org/archive/2006/April/MarshallIslandsReport.pdf

Hyde, Terri B., Gustavo H. Dayan, Justina R. Langidrik, Robin Nandy, Russell Edwards, Kennar Briand, Mailynn Konelios et al. 2006. "Measles Outbreak in the Republic of the Marshall Islands." *International Journal of Epidemiology* 35 (2): 299–306. doi:10.1093/ije/dyi222.

International Court of Justice. 1995. Testimony of Lijon Eknilang to the International Court of Justice, The Hague, 14 November 1995, President Bedjaoui presiding in the case in Legality of the Use by a State of Nuclear Weapons in Armed Conflict (Request for Advisory Opinion Submitted by the World Health Organization) and in Legality of the Threat or Use of Nuclear Weapons (Request for Advisory Opinion Submitted by the General Assembly of the United Nations): 25–28. http://www.icj-cij.org/docket/files/93/5968.pdf.

International Diabetes Federation. 2012. *IDF Diabetes Atlas,* 5th ed. http://www.idf.org/sites/default/files/5E_IDFAtlasPoster_2012_EN.pdf.

Jacobs, Robert, and Mick Broderick. 2012. "United Nations Report Reveals the Ongoing Legacy of Nuclear Colonialism in the Marshall Islands." *The Asia-Pacific Journal* 10 (47): 1.

Johnson, Giff. 1979. "Micronesia: America's 'Strategic' Trust." *The Bulletin of the Atomic Scientists* 35 (2): 10–15.

———. 2006. "Marshalls Top Northern Pacific in Tuberculosis" *Pacific Islands Report*, May 15. http://pidp.org/archive/2006/May/05-15-12.htm.

———. 2013. *Don't Ever Whisper: Darlene Keju. Pacific Health Pioneer, Champion for Nuclear Survivors.* Majuro, Marshall Islands: n.p.

Johnston, Barbara Rose. 1994. "Experimenting on Human Subjects: Nuclear Weapons Testing and Human Rights Abuse" in *Who Pays the Price? The Sociocultural Context of Environmental Crisis*, edited by Barbara Rose Johnston, 131–141. Washington: Island Press.

———. 2007a. "Half-lives, Half-truths and Other Radioactive Legacies of the Cold War." In *Half-Lives and Half-Truths: Confronting the Radioactive Legacies of the Cold War*, edited by Barbara Rose Johnston, 1–23. Santa Fe: School for Advanced Research Press.

———. 2007b. "more life us than mice: Radiation Experiments with Indigenous Peoples." In *Half-Lives and Half-Truths: Confronting the Radioactive Legacies of the Cold War*, edited by Barbara Rose Johnston, 25–53. Santa Fe, NM: School for Advanced Research Press.

———. 2011a. "Waking up to a Nuclear Nightmare" *Truthout*. April 4. http://www.truthout.org/waking-nuclear-nightmare.

———. 2011b. "Human Rights, Environmental Quality, and Social Justice." In *Life and Death Matters: Human Rights, Environment, and Social Justice.* 2nd ed. Edited by Barbara Rose Johnston, 9–27. Walnut Creek: Left Coast Press.

———. 2012. "Nuclear Betrayal in the Marshall Islands. UN Special Rapporteur—US Nuclear Testing Continues to Violate Human Rights in the Marshall Islands" *Counterpunch*. September 17. http://www.counterpunch.org/2012/09/17/nuclear-betrayal-in-the-marshall-islands/.

———. 2013. "Nuclear Weapons Tests, Fallout, and the Devastating Impact on Marshall Islands Environment, Health and Human Rights." In *Unspeakable Suffering: The Humanitarian Impact of Nuclear Weapons*, edited by Beatrice Fihn, 88–93. Geneva: Reaching Critical Will/Womens International League for Peace and Freedom. http://www.reachingcriticalwill.org/images/documents/Publications/Unspeakable/Unspeakable.pdf.

Johnston, Barbara Rose, and Holly M. Barker. 2008. *The Consequential Damages of Nuclear War: The Rongelap Report.* Walnut Creek: Left Coast Press.

Kuletz, Valerie. 1998. *The Tainted Desert: Environmental and Social Ruin in the American West.* New York: Routledge.

———. 2001. "Invisible Spaces, Violent Places: Cold War Nuclear and Militarized Landscapes." In *Violent Environments*, edited by Nancy Lee Peluso and Michael Watts, 237–260. Ithaca: Cornell University Press.

Lawrence Livermore National Laboratory, US Department of Energy. N.d. "Documents." *Marshall Islands DOE Assessment & Radioecology Program.* Accessed August 30, 2014. https://marshallislands.llnl.gov/documents.php.

Lefall, LeSalle D., and Margaret L. Kripke. 2010. *Reducing Environmental Cancer Risk—What We Can Do Now, President's Cancer Panel 2008-2009 Annual Report.* US Department of Health & Human Services, National Institute of

Health, National Cancer Institute. http://deainfo.nci.nih.gov/advisory/pcp/annual Reports/pcp08–09rpt/PCP_Report_08–09_508.pdf.

Loeak, Christopher J., President, Republic of the Marshall Islands. 2012. Proclamation Declaring a State (Health) of Emergency. October 2. https://docs.google.com/file/d/0BykGfxP2ZUSCNm4yNHhhX1BwOWc/edit?pli=1.

Marshall Islands Nuclear Claims Tribunal. 2007. "Before the Nuclear Claims Tribunal, Republic of the Marshall Islands: In the Matter of The Alabs of Rongelap, et al. ..." [i.e. the "Rongelap Decision"]. April 17. http://www.moruroa.org/medias/pdf/RONGELAP_DECISION%202007.pdf.

Morrison, John H. 1969. *Deseret Test Center Final Report on DTC Test 68–50, March 1969.* SECRET. Fort Douglas, UT: Department of the Army, Deseret Test Center. http://www.dod.mil/pubs/foi/operation_and_plans/Exercises_and_Projects/1017.pdf.

Nader, Laura. 1997. "Controlling Processes: Tracing the Dynamic Components of Power." *Current Anthropology* 8 (35): 711–738.

National Cancer Institute. 2004. "Estimation of the Baseline Number of Cancers Among Marshallese and the Number of Cancers Attributable to Exposure to Fallout from Nuclear Weapons Testing Conducted in the Marshall Islands." http://dceg.cancer.gov/RMIdocs/9–28Response_appendix.pdf.

Perez Williams, Deanna, and Ann Hampton. 2005. "Barriers to Health Services Perceived by Marshallese Immigrants." *Journal of Immigrant Health* 7 (4): 317–326.

Perrow, Charles. 2013. "Nuclear Denial: From Hiroshima to Fukushima." *The Bulletin of the Atomic Scientists* 69 (5): 56–67.

President's Cancer Panel. 2010. *Reducing Environmental Cancer Risk: What Can We Do Now. 2008–2009 Annual Report.* National Cancer Institute, National Institutes of Health, US Department of Health and Human Services. http://deainfo.nci.nih.gov/advisory/pcp/annualreports/pcp08–09rpt/PCP_Report_08–09_508.pdf.

Price, David. 2007. "Earle Reynolds: Scientist, Citizen and Cold War Dissident." In *Half-Lives and Half-Truths: Confronting the Radioactive Legacies of the Cold War,* edited by Barbara Rose Johnston, 55–57. Santa Fe: School of American Research Press.

Radiation Effects Research Foundation. N.d. "Effects on the Immune System." Accessed August 17, 2014, http://www.rerf.jp/radefx/late_e/immunity.html.

Rudiak-Gould, Peter, and Jessica A. Schwartz. "Insularity and Interconnection: Competing Territorial Imaginaries in the Marshall Islands." In *Negotiating Territoriality: Spatial Dialogues Between State and Tradition,* edited by Allen Charles Dawson, Laura Zanotti and Ismael Vaccaro, 216–229. New York: Routledge.

Rudred, Regina Woodrom, Julie Walsh Kroeker, Heather Young Leslie, and Suzanne Finney. 2007. "The Sea Turtle Wars: Culture, War, and Sea Turtles in the Marshall Islands." SPC *Traditional Marine Resource Management and Knowledge Information Bulletin* 21: 3–29.

Semendeferi, Ioanna. 2008. "Legitimating a Nuclear Critic: John Gofman, Radiation Safety, and Cancer Risks." *Historical Studies in the Natural Sciences,* 38 (2): 259–301. DOI: 10.1525/hsns.2008.38.2.259.

The Legacy of US Nuclear Testing and Radiation Exposure in the Marshall Islands http://majuro.usembassy.gov/legacy.html

United Nations Human Rights Commission. 2012. Report of the Special Rapporteur on the implications for human rights of the environmentally sound management and disposal of hazardous substances and wastes, Călin Georgescu;

Addendum: Mission to the Marshall Islands (27–30 March 2012) and the United States of America (24–27 April 2012). A-HRC-21–48-Add1_en. September 3. http://www.ohchr.org/Documents/HRBodies/HRCouncil/RegularSession/Session21/A-HRC-21–48-Add1_en.pdf.

United Nations Development Programme. 2006. *Human Development Report 2006.* http://hdr.undp.org/sites/default/files/reports/267/hdr06-complete.pdf.

United States Department of Defense. 2002. Project SHAD Factsheet: DTC Test 68–50. http://mcm.dhhq.health.mil/Libraries/CBexposuresDocs/dtc_68_50.sflb.ashx.

United States Department of Veterans Affairs. N.d. "Depleted Uranium." Accessed August 30, 2014. http://www.publichealth.va.gov/exposures/depleted_uranium/#sthash.emt GRvlh.dpuf.

US Embassy, Majuro, Marshall Islands. 2007. "Diabetes Wellness Center Opens in Marshall Islands' Capital." Press release. January 19.

World Health Organization. N.d. "Infant Mortality Data by Country." *Global Health Observatory Data Repository: MDG 4: Child Health.* Accessed November 11, 2012. http://apps.who.int/gho/data/node.main.526.

———. 2007. *The World Health Report 2006.* http://www.who.int/whr/2006/en/.

———. 2012. *Global Tuberculosis Report 2012.* http://apps.who.int/iris/bitstr eam/10665/75938/1/9789241564502_eng.pdf.

———. 2014. "Tuberculosis. Fact Sheet No. 104. Revised March 2014." http://www. who.int/mediacentre/factsheets/fs104/en/.

Yablokov, Alexey V., Vassily B. Nesterenko, and Alexey V. Nesterenko. "Chapter III. Consequences of the Chernobyl Catastrophe for the Environment." *Annals of the New York Academy of Sciences* 1181 (1): 221–286.

Yamada, Seiji, Anna Dodd, Tin Soe, and Tai-ho Chen. 2004. "Diabetes Mellitus Prevalence in Outpatient Marshallese Adults on Ebeye Island, Republic of the Marshall Islands." *Hawaii Medical Journal* 63 (2): 45–51.

7 Island Vulnerability and Resilience

Combining Knowledges for Disaster Risk Reduction, Including Climate Change Adaptation

Ilan Kelman, JC Gaillard, Jessica Mercer, James Lewis, and Anthony Carrigan

No single knowledge form can be a panacea for addressing climate change and other disaster risk reduction (DRR) or long-term environmental concerns. However this chapter argues that indigenous knowledge in all its varied and diverse forms has the potential for contributing far more than is usually permitted in mainstream scientific literature. Our aim here is to highlight the relationship between indigenous knowledge and DRR in small-island contexts, where questions of vulnerability and resilience are frequently magnified. We also identify points where the primarily development-oriented, fieldwork-based examples in this chapter might intersect with environmental humanities research, particularly in terms of how cultural and political insights can enhance DRR strategies. We do this in awareness of the historical power relations—not least imperialism—that have worked to segregate indigenous knowledge from empirical scientific traditions (see e.g. Whitt 2009), and aim to open up pathways toward more empowering modes of synthesis and exchange in support of DRR. The chapter engages self-consciously with one of the dominant philosophical and narrative forms with respect to global ecologies—scientific rationalism—and highlights points of departure for an increasingly holistic and methodologically variegated approach to disaster research. This involves two parallel forms of knowledge combination: between indigenous and non-indigenous perspectives on DRR, and between scientific research articulations and emerging environmental humanities concerns.

Our contribution is therefore partly an experiment in form, as it seeks to combine recommendation-oriented approaches to DRR with elements of postcolonial critique, and to reflect on the different experiences of empowerment, political strategy, and prioritization that arise from the various case studies on which the chapter is based. The guiding principle is one of openness, and we seek to build on the important injunction laid down by indigenous commentators, such as Linda Tuhiwai Smith in *Decolonizing Methodologies* (1999), to listen to and actively privilege the knowledge and worldviews of indigenous peoples and to align research practices with indigenous politics and beliefs. Given this chapter's comparative focus, the tensions raised here are concomitantly broad in scale and by no means resolvable in a single essay, but we hope the discussion will present avenues for collaboration with environmental humanities researchers that can extend the considerations raised across this section of the collection. The chapter begins with a terminological overview that outlines the theory and practice of indigenous knowledge and DRR, including climate change adaptation (CCA), with reference to resilience and vulnerability. It then considers a series of vignettes regarding real-world indigenous DRR resources, approaches to knowledge mapping, and issues regarding knowledge combination and co-production. We conclude by summarizing some emergent principles for DRR in indigenous contexts and reflecting on how environmental humanities research can help ensure indigenous knowledge is incorporated and respected as part of a progressive approach to DRR, including CCA.

INDIGENOUS KNOWLEDGE, RESILIENCE, AND VULNERABILITY

The term *indigenous knowledge* does not have a universally accepted definition. It tends to refer to a body of knowledge passed down through generations in a given locality and acquired through the accumulation of experiences, relationships with the surrounding environment, and community rituals, practices, and institutions (Brokensha et al. 1980; Fernando 2003; Sillitoe 1998). Other expressions that complement or overlap with indigenous knowledge include "traditional knowledge," "indigenous technical knowledge," "folk knowledge," "local knowledge," "vernacular knowledge," "people's knowledge," "traditional environmental knowledge," and "traditional ecological knowledge." These phrases are not directly synonymous, and are often differentiated according to the academic discipline, context, and conceptual language being used. Here, we will stay with the phrase "indigenous knowledge," understanding that its ethos applies to these other knowledge descriptions as well. Commonly accepted characteristics of indigenous knowledge include being relatively unique to and embedded within a specific community, culture, or society over a time period, while at the same time being highly dynamic in its constitution, responding to changing circumstances and cross-cultural interactions.[1]

Although indigenous knowledge is not necessarily transferable or relevant to other locations, it is too often ignored in discussions on DRR, including CCA, with the assumption that more "recent," "modern," or "technological" knowledge is superior to communities' own traditions and approaches (Shaw et al. 2008, 2009; Wisner et al. 2004). Indigenous knowledge is also often incorrectly characterized as static and ancient, rather than dynamic and modern, and imagined in opposition to "western" or "scientific" knowledge. Such suppositions are profoundly at odds both with the perspectives of indigenous islanders and most current anthropological research on island cultures,[2] so it is important that they are confronted within mainstream discussions about DRR and CCA. Over recent decades, recognition has increased among development researchers, policymakers, and practitioners that a combination of knowledges is needed for DRR, including CCA. This involves identifying and valuing the contribution indigenous knowledge can make to development work in conjunction with academic findings in this area, and working with indigenous peoples as "co-producers" of knowledge (see e.g. Berkes 2009, Maclean and Cullen 2009), especially in relation to the twin emphasis placed in DRR research on "vulnerability" and "resilience."

Vulnerability and resilience have become dominant scientific concepts when examining disasters through the lens of development.[3] The institutionalization of this paradigm can be traced to the 1970s, which witnessed the formal intersection of the long literature of disaster studies (going back to e.g. Carr 1932; Prince 1920; White 1942; 1945) with ongoing work in international development. This was spurred on by some specific disasters such as the Sahel drought (see e.g. Comité Information Sahel 1975; Copans 1975) and earthquakes in Central America. One important paper published at this time was O'Keefe et al.'s "Taking the 'naturalness' out of natural disasters" (1976), which saw human development-related behavior as the root cause of so-called "natural" disasters. The paper memorably labelled the Guatemala earthquake of February 4, 1976 a "classquake," foregrounding how poor development practices created and perpetuated poverty and vulnerability (1976, 566).[4]

There is now a consistent emphasis on how human actions, behaviors, decisions, and values produce vulnerability within disaster-related literature, and this has been accepted to varying degrees by development policymakers and practitioners.[5] At the same time, people have found creative ways of dealing with hazards; of implementing vulnerability reduction; and of coping with a disaster's aftermath—strategies that are collectively termed "resilience" in scientific literature (Gaillard 2007, 2010; Manyena 2006; Wisner et al. 2004). Resilience can be built through actions such as engineering appropriate seismic resistance and creating the social structures to maintain them, or learning to live with rather than be devastated by periodic flooding.[6] While resilience and vulnerability have some converse characteristics, they are not exact opposites since aspects of both can exist simultaneously—or they might be equally limited or equally strong with respect to different hazards. Each can be viewed as a separate process overlapping with the other and with many other development concepts, without a universal definition.

Development research, policy, and practice have a long history of analyzing vulnerability and resilience differentially across a wide range of cultural contexts. Sometimes, these words are used explicitly, and at other times the concepts are implied or discussed within other scientific or contextual framings, such as the sustainable livelihoods approach or participatory development.[7] In addition, not all languages have words for "vulnerability" and "resilience," and the very ideas can be alien to certain cultures, with examples including indigenous Pacific Islanders and indigenous Arctic peoples (Kelman et al. 2011). It is therefore important to remain wary of how these terms can function as western discourses that reinforce negative assumptions and reflect colonial power relations. The environmental historian Greg Bankoff, for instance, makes the case for vulnerability to be viewed as the latest iteration of blanket characterizations of the Global South, which have shifted from focusing on tropicality and disease in the eighteenth and nineteenth centuries (to be "cured" by western medicine), to underdevelopment and poverty in the twentieth century (to be redressed through western aid), to the current focus on hazards and vulnerability (to be mitigated by western science) (Bankoff 2001, 28). This is an area, then, where further input from the humanities could be useful in clarifying the political valences of resilience and vulnerability discourse across different contexts, and not least in relation to its adoption by global environmental governance institutions like the UN and international finance institutions.

As is often noted, risk makers are different from the risk takers, as those implicated in exacerbating hazards and vulnerabilities are different from those who have to negotiate their effects on a daily basis. Yet despite the need to explore vulnerability and resilience in relation to a complex array of intersecting risks (emergent and structural), much of the technocratic emphasis tends to be on specific hazard manifestations and not on the causes and processes that underlie their propensity to be experienced as disasters (Wisner et al. 2004, 2012). Critical perspectives on these underlying processes are both timely and necessary, given that the increasing dominance and expanding discourses of climate change—another multiscalar process severely exacerbated by human activity—has fuelled further concentration on hazards in environmental governance circles without fully considering structures of vulnerability and resilience (Kelman and Gaillard 2010).

Uncertainties around the evolution of climate conditions are used to constitute a powerful argument and narrative for considering "Nature" as the major threat (White 2004), even though this relies on a faulty separation of "Nature" from human activity. The comparatively recent injection of climate change into disaster and vulnerability research is evident in the Intergovernmental Panel on Climate Change (IPCC), where vulnerability was defined as:

> the degree to which a system is susceptible to, and unable to cope with, adverse effects of climate change, including climate variability and extremes. Vulnerability is a function of the character, magnitude, and rate of climate change and variation to which a system is exposed, its sensitivity, and its adaptive capacity.
>
> (IPCC 2007, 883)

This definition emphasizes climate characteristics, notably quantitative parameters, without examining human conditions and values that operate alongside and in relation to these. That is, the fundamental tenets from past vulnerability and resilience research are left out, along with any meaningful engagement with history and distributions of power. The latest IPCC report addresses many of these critiques by defining vulnerability as "[t]he propensity or predisposition to be adversely affected. Vulnerability encompasses a variety of concepts including sensitivity or susceptibility to harm and lack of capacity to cope and adapt" (IPCC 2014, 28). Yet the lessons from previous DRR work are still not fully incorporated.

In between these two reports, the IPCC Special Report on Managing the Risks of Extreme Events and Disasters to Advance Climate Change Adaptation (SREX) moved some way toward reengaging with broader vulnerability perspectives. But its title belies its ethos. The emphasis, by definition and by mandate, is still "to advance climate change adaptation" (IPCC 2012). The text displays a clear tension between authors who place climate change in wider contexts and those who prefer to isolate and analyze it as if it were beyond other disaster and vulnerability concerns. At present, the latter group remains in the ascendency, bolstered by the close alignment between its technocratic approach and the well-established modes of "planetary management" (Ross 1991) that characterize global environmental governance strategies.

This conceptually segregated approach to climate change—which is often unhelpfully emphasized in mainstream media narratives as well—tends to distract policymakers from the root causes of vulnerability: human behavior, decisions, and values, which must be understood historically and politically across cultures, and which frequently augment hazards and hazard drivers including climate change. As a consequence, climate change becomes a perfect scapegoat for disasters, vulnerability, and lack of resilience, as the act of evoking a phenomenon of global scale and diffuse responsibility obviates sustained analysis of root causes (Kelman and Gaillard 2010). By exploring and applying different knowledges, it might be feasible to reclaim the ground lost to this particular appropriation of "climate change" without neglecting its real-world implication in the production and mitigation of other hazards. One way of doing this is to integrate it into a DRR framework that is responsive to different knowledge claims and global power relations, in line with postcolonial methodologies.

DRR AND INDIGENOUS PEOPLES

According to the UN's International Strategy for Disaster Reduction, DRR refers to "systematic efforts to analyse and manage the causal factors of disasters, including through reduced exposure to hazards, lessened vulnerability of people and property, wise management of land and the environment, and improved preparedness for adverse events" (UNISDR 2012). By definition, this includes CCA since climate change affects hazard parameters.

It is worth noting that all actions implemented for CCA have been previously used and documented for DRR, especially those related to structural vulnerability reduction, which has positive consequences in relation to a wide range of hazards (Shaw et al. 2010a, 2010b; Wisner et al. 2004, 2012). This does not preclude instances where hazard modification can play an important role in overall risk reduction, with examples like the project to reduce carbon dioxide release from Lake Nyos in Cameroon potentially preventing thousands of future deaths (Bang 2009).

Nevertheless, hazard modification frequently increases disaster risk. For instance, relying on structural defenses to reduce flood risk, without a balance of other approaches, tends to control small floods in the short term, but leaves people more vulnerable and with higher risk to larger floods over the long term (Etkin 1999). From a progressive scientific perspective, focusing on vulnerability reduction and building resilience has the greatest potential for achieving successful DRR. Indicative examples include establishing building and planning codes—and monitoring and enforcing them—to minimize hazard-related infrastructure damage, and supporting social networks to identify and take care of marginalized and isolated people in the community—while tackling the root causes of the marginalization and isolation—so they can be integrated into and take charge of their own DRR activities.

Many indigenous peoples have generated, maintained, and applied a broad knowledge base for DRR, covering hazards, vulnerabilities, and resiliences, with island communities being particularly poignant examples.[8] For centuries—and sometimes millennia—indigenous peoples across many different environments have dealt with changes around them, caused by natural variability or by their own actions, and shaped their own "cultures of disaster" (Bankoff 2003) or ways of living with hazards. Nonetheless it is important not to romanticize indigenous knowledge resources, as certain groups display limited knowledge of the risks they face. Sometimes this occurs as a result of hazards not being frequent enough to be experienced and remembered, such as a volcanic gas release or eruption occurring for the first time since human settlement. Sometimes, ellipses in indigenous knowledge are produced by successive waves of migration, such as Pacific peoples' movement around the Pacific Ocean (Hau'ofa, 1993), or by the long-term transformations exerted by forces like western colonialism, Christianity, and capitalism, as well as the introduction of cash economies, cash cropping, and alien species, which have frequently devastated ecosystems and undermined resources for resilience. Contemporary pressures such as urbanization, climate change, deforestation, and globalization are continuing the trend of large-scale transformations that increase indigenous peoples' vulnerability to disasters (Ferris 2011; Wisner et al. 2012), not least by affecting how knowledge bases and values change, and how knowledge is either passed along or becomes discounted.

These processes and power relations are crucial to a systemic understanding of risk, but they remain marginalized in mainstream DRR conversations.

Recognition of this can be correlated with the fact that continuing advances in science and technology have not had a clearly discernible positive advantage for indigenous peoples in reducing disaster vulnerability (Weichselgartner and Obersteiner 2002; Wisner et al. 1977). Frequently, available approaches are not applied, such as providing indigenous peoples with forecasts that they can understand and use in advance of storms or floods. In other circumstances, approaches are applied insensitively and out of the cultural context, causing more problems than they solve.

One example comes from the volcanic Manam Island in Papua New Guinea (Mercer and Kelman 2010). Residents of Baliau village build traditional houses with long sloping roofs, contributing toward reducing collapse and fire potential from volcanic ash. Local materials assist in strengthening the roofs, which in turn increases wind resistance. However, such construction techniques have come under pressure from the introduction of ostensibly more "modern" roofing made from corrugated sheets, which some residents in Baliau interpret as symbols of wealth and class status, as well as appearing up-to-date. The corrugated sheeting reduces fire risk, but its shape, texture, and pitch might not let volcanic ash slide off as easily, leading to possible collapse—and low-pitch sheets tend to be blown off in high winds and can be lethal if they hit someone. Their desirability therefore increases certain short-term risks while serving to make communities more dependent on the external economic and trade resources required for purchasing corrugated sheeting, displacing indigenous knowledge as it draws communities into globalized patterns of labor and exchange.

This is a familiar sequence of events for small island communities worldwide, and has been intensified by rapid environmental change and the shifting values of younger people. It is further augmented by DRR approaches that fail to recognize or acknowledge the value and applicability of indigenous knowledge, which would entail consulting with communities to identify culturally and contextually appropriate approaches (Mackinson and Nottestad 1998), although the failure of technocratic fixes may ironically draw attention to the relevance of indigenous risk reduction strategies.[9] Yet rather than concretizing unhelpful binaries between "western" scientific DRR approaches and indigenous knowledge, disaster researchers should look to combine indigenous and non-indigenous perspectives on past strategies and possible future changes, including climate change, acknowledging that such perspectives are already the products of generations of intercultural exchange even as they capture different ideologies and worldviews (see also Whitt 2009). Such an approach can produce and institute new DRR narratives, incorporating CCA, that promote indigenous knowledge as part of a much more culturally nuanced and context-respondent series of risk reduction strategies, which are more fully cognizant of the various forces that have worked to efface indigenous perspectives previously and to deny possibilities for co-produced research.

To improve DRR, indigenous peoples must be active players in their own (possibly multicultural) communities, assessing and determining how they wish to reduce vulnerabilities and build resilience. External specialists need to learn when they might be required to assist and how—something that indigenous peoples frequently and forthrightly request when external actors try to implement DRR techniques, including for CCA. This in turn requires policymakers and practitioners to work closely and respectfully alongside indigenous populations, including communicating in local languages and recognizing the cultural and epistemological specificity of terms such as resilience, vulnerability, and environment, which are not always shared across cultures. Such work involves viewing DRR as a cooperative venture that can only be advanced if it is conducted equitably, with indigenous peoples acting as research partners in the co-production of knowledge (see e.g. Berkes 2009, Maclean and Cullen 2009). Additionally, vulnerability reduction will be most successful in the long term if DRR strategies, including for CCA, are not only constructed dialogically on the basis of islanders' changing values, politics, and beliefs, but also remain vigilant to external interests that might seek to exploit vulnerability rather than reduce risk. This involves bearing in mind how small islands have been positioned historically as sites of militarism, tourism development, and scientific exploration, all of which can bring neocolonial power dynamics into play when local interests are pushed aside by more powerful external actors.[10]

EXAMPLES IN PRACTICE: INDIGENOUS DRR AND KNOWLEDGE MAPPING

This section provides several vignettes illustrating the need for a combined approach to DRR knowledge production based on the scientific literature from mainly development-related projects. The method here involves surveying a number of examples from islands across the world, with the purpose of highlighting possibilities for further case studies that draw on the longitudinal insights generated in the environmental humanities, and accounting for how hazards, risks, resilience, and vulnerability feature in local stories and place narratives.

The people of Simeulue, an island off the west coast of Aceh, Indonesia, provide the first example. They passed down stories describing a tsunami that devastated their island on January 4, 1907 (Gaillard et al. 2008). A Simeuluean word *smong* was coined which defined three stages of the tsunami (Figure 7.1). First, the ground would shake, representing a strong earthquake. Second, the sea would recede quickly. Third, a large, powerful wave would hit the coast causing widespread flooding. Without this knowledge in response to observing the initial stages of *smong*, the people of Simeulue might not have aimed for higher ground after they felt a large earthquake on December 26, 2004.

Simeulue's experience on that day was not unique. The Moken Sea Gypsies in Thailand also survived the 2004 tsunami because of indigenous

Figure 7.1 A poster advertising the use of the Simeulue indigenous term *smong* (for
        tsunami) in Banda Aceh, Indonesia, February 2006. Photograph by
        JC Gaillard.

knowledge. Arunotai (2008) describes the people's observations and understanding of the sea's behavior, and in particular their tendency to take pre-
cautionary measures as a result of environmental signals, their village site
choice, and their boat-handling skills. All those factors combined to indicate
that something strange was happening to the sea, so they evacuated the
coast and survived the tsunami.

While it is important to recognize the knowledge that led to a positive outcome in these examples, we should be wary of framing indigenous knowledge as a failsafe mode of resilience. In the case of Simeulue, the people's successful evacuation must be tempered with the knowledge that not all tsunamis lead to the sea retreating beforehand, and that many tsunamis hit far beyond the location where the initiating earthquake can be felt. Additionally, the destruction wrought by the earthquake and tsunami meant that external assistance was still needed. In the case of the Moken Sea Gypsies, it is important to note that tsunamis can happen when people are asleep or less aware of or reactive to the sea's signals, so the strengths and limitations of indigenous cultural resources should be considered alongside the need for external monitoring, warning, and emergency support.

This leads to an exciting point of future collaboration for environmental humanities and disaster studies, which involves thinking through the ambivalent registers of resilience in relation to external intervention. Resilience provides a ready framework for communicating the resources of indigenous knowledge to mainstream research communities, but it can also be used as an excuse for *not* providing external assistance if it is taken to indicate a community's "innate" capacity for dealing with hazards. Environmental humanities research can help delineate the cultural, political, and historical factors that need to be accounted for in evaluating not just the need for combining knowledges but also the effects of how the resulting strategies are implemented over time. In some cases, this means politicizing resilience, and emphasizing the need for it to be defined (or redefined) in specific contexts through close collaboration and consultation with indigenous peoples.

Another promising example of knowledge combination for DRR involves the introduction of participatory three-dimensional maps (P3DM) that incorporate indigenous knowledge (Gaillard and Maceda 2009; Cadag and Gaillard 2012). This method was used in early 2010 in a small and marginalized community on Mindanao in the southern Philippines (Figure 7.2). It enabled local Subanon indigenous people to collaborate with dominant Cebuano migrants, local authorities, scientists, and a regional NGO's staff toward reducing risks associated with droughts, landslides, and floods.

The P3DM method proved useful in facilitating the participation of the most marginalized segments of the community—Subanon, women, the elderly, and children—and in fostering a dialogue between them and the dominant populations. P3DM also contributed to raising people's awareness of their own community by allowing the mapping of assets and dangers; by better integrating DRR with the community's day-to-day sustainability and development processes; by being comparatively low-cost to set up and run; and by emphasizing the community's indigenous knowledge without relying solely on it.

The importance of maps based on a combination of indigenous and nonindigenous interpretations for communicating DRR was shown by Haynes et al. (2007) working on Montserrat, a British Overseas Territory in the

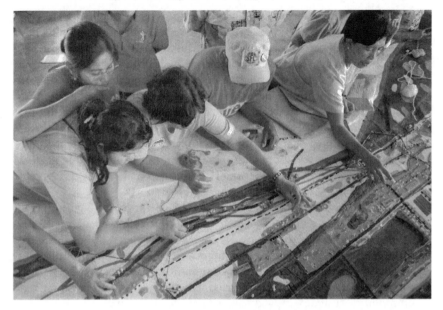

Figure 7.2 Participatory three-dimensional map (P3DM) of Josefina, Zamboanga del Sur, Philippines, in January 2010. Photograph by JC Gaillard.

Caribbean. They tested three mapping forms to determine which approach was easiest for the population to connect to their landscape: (1) Top-down, flat, plan-view maps with contour lines—which are usually used by scientists; (2) three-dimensional computer-generated maps giving oblique perspectives of the island; and (3) aerial photographs also giving an oblique perspective. Montserratians were least able to relate to plan-view maps, with slightly more recognition shown for the three-dimensional maps. In terms of orienting themselves and identifying key features of their island, the aerial photographs with an oblique perspective were more effective for Montserratians than the other two forms of mapping. This result is interesting as it highlights how visual as well as narrative modes impact on the facilitation of DRR, and how maps may be refined or co-produced through consideration of local people's visualization techniques. In this case, it is clear that cartographic and related representational forms must be seen as subject to adaptation and modification if they are to fulfill their potential as tools for empowering communities, rather than simply providing resources for external DRR management.

On Ambae Island, Vanuatu, a volcanic crisis in 1995 led to emergency managers trying to implement top-down approaches with limited community consultation, fermenting distrust between the local islanders and those from the capital, Port Vila, and outside of Vanuatu (Cronin et al. 2004). By working with the community on the community's terms, and by respecting and combining different knowledges, Cronin et al. (2004) used participatory techniques to develop guidelines and an alert system for dealing with future eruptions that were accepted by the community and external emergency managers. That work centered on asking the community to draw maps, including women's groups and men's groups. These were then compared to externally produced maps, including geological features and projected volcanic hazards during an eruption. The community was able to co-produce improved DRR resources based on its own internally variegated forms of knowledge, while respecting and accepting external knowledge. We can consider such maps as vernacular representations of space and place that should also be interpreted historically and in conjunction with the stories and mythologies that connect to local environmental understandings. These examples highlight the need to account for how different representational forms are implicated in vulnerability reduction and resilience enhancement, and should be considered as part of a more holistic approach to DRR.[11]

COMBINING KNOWLEDGES

Several of the examples in the previous section intimated the importance of combining knowledges to reduce vulnerability to a variety of hazards. Indigenous knowledge can play a vital role in context-specific DRR strategies, but the best results are likely to be achieved by creating a mutually beneficial dialogue between indigenous and non-indigenous DRR perspectives, with the aim of co-producing enhanced risk reduction strategies. One of the main challenges involves formalizing this as an action for development, a task that is now underway with respect to DRR including climate change.

In Papua New Guinea (PNG), for instance, Mercer et al. (2009, 2010) advanced a method for combining academic research with indigenous risk reduction strategies from three case study villages. A process framework for collaborative community engagement was designed to support communities in extending DRR strategies based on their own ideas, interests, stories, and experiences, but without neglecting wider contexts. That framework was applied within the communities of Kumalu, Singas, and Baliau in PNG and modified according to islanders' recommendations, providing a basis for consolidating knowledge in relation to changing experiences of vulnerability and resilience.

The experience of flooding in Singas (Mercer and Kelman 2008) parallels that of volcanic hazards in Baliau discussed earlier (Mercer and Kelman 2010). The village is sited along the banks of a river that floods annually during the rainy season. The river not only represents a potential hazard but also supports the community's livelihoods through crop irrigation. Consequently, the people of Singas are proactive in implementing DRR for flooding, but recognize that their own knowledge and community-based strategies might not be enough to negotiate climate change challenges. Indigenous knowledge is applied in five specific areas: building methods, social linkages, land use planning, food strategies, and environmental management. As the flooding regime changes, especially due to climate change, external knowledge can assist the community in considering alternative crops without losing diversity, and by indicating expectations for the future climate that could affect the flooding regime. In fact, the framework developed by Mercer et al. (2009, 2010) has been adjusted to deal with the hazards arising from climate change (Kelman et al. 2009).

While the examples so far have dealt with relatively localized evidence, their insights can orientate approaches to knowledge co-production in a range of contexts. This kind of collaborative outlook coincides with the political solidarity efforts of many indigenous coalitions and sovereignty groups—from national and regional organizations to representation on the UN Permanent Forum on Indigenous Issues—which have helped to combat global power imbalances and share ideas with respect to large-scale challenges such as climate change. The Many Strong Voices (MSV) program is a good example of this, which draws together peoples from the Arctic (many of whom live on islands, such as Baffin Island and Greenland) and Small Island Developing States (SIDS) with the aim of building on specific indigenous experiences and research findings with respect to climate change (see http://www.manystrongvoices.org).[12] MSV supports indigenous peoples at their own request in exchanging knowledge about, and devising approaches for dealing with, the climate change challenges facing their communities within wider sustainability contexts.

While mapping is one medium that can be used for knowledge co-production, websites are another that typically combine a variety of representational styles and as such are of key interest to environmental humanities research more broadly. The MSV website is an especially intriguing source of analysis for postcolonial and environmental humanities researchers as it functions both as a knowledge repository and a kind of narrative conduit, providing indigenous groups with comparative visibility and autonomy in framing the challenges they face (cultural, ecological, political, and economic). The website can be viewed in some ways as a performative response of Epeli Hau'ofa's famous injunction to reject the discourses of belittlement, disempowerment, and despair that have enshrouded small island states, and to focus instead on the vast cultural resources that islanders in the Pacific and elsewhere have for confronting environmental and development challenges (Hau'ofa 1993). This has lead to MSV receiving international approbation, being cited by *The Guardian* newspaper as one of the top ten climate change campaigns (Lytton 2013), and now boasting a headline endorsement on its website from Richard Branson (somewhat ironically, considering the aviation industry's substantial carbon footprint). There are some obvious tensions in Branson's assertion that MSV's "critical work fills the gap between those affected by adverse climate impacts and political and business leaders focused on creating big picture solutions," emanating not least from how it conflates and hierarchizes the work of political and business elites. At the same time, Branson's presence testifies to and helps enhance MSV's relative visibility to global audiences, along with the consistent and credible alternative it offers to how climate change has been addressed at many research and practice levels, including the IPCC (2007, 2012, 2014). For the MSV partners, reducing greenhouse gas emissions and improving land use practices such as preventing deforestation (termed "mitigation" in climate change glossaries) is seen in tandem with—not separated from—adjusting to the unavoidable impacts of climate change and exploiting the positive consequences (termed "adaptation" in climate change glossaries). By making this point collectively, MSV has given peoples in the two regions increased presence in international arenas such as the annual climate change negotiations, emphasizing the resources of their knowledges and claiming positions of priority in managing funds.

Dovetailing mitigation and adaptation raises key questions of responsibility, ethics, and accountability, including support for mitigation and adaptation, and compensation. The international climate change negotiations conducted through the United Nations Framework Convention on Climate Change (UNFCCC) have been addressing these issues with varying degrees of success. This has provided a foundation for postcolonial and ethically motivated critiques of global climate change politics. International discussions of climate change are often marked by historical power relations, as the richer countries have resisted significant mitigation efforts and have made it difficult for the poorer countries to obtain adequate access to resources to solve the problems they face. Although indigenous peoples from locations like the Arctic and SIDS have contributed little to greenhouse gas emissions, they generally wish to be involved in climate change mitigation, and to apply their own knowledge and expertise to dealing with problems created by others. This helps to set an example for the rest of the world, and it is strongly in their favor, for instance, to lessen their dependence on diesel fuel, which has to be flown or shipped in to island communities at great expense, and requires generators that are noisy, polluting, and need maintenance. In fact, most isolated Arctic and SIDS states would prefer to be energy self-sufficient and many are working toward this, thereby contributing to climate change mitigation while helping their own communities. This does not preclude simultaneous adaptation, since the climate is changing rapidly.

While critiques of the global governance process remain as necessary as ever, initiatives such as MSV provide forums for indigenous groups to collate and apply their own knowledge; to request assistance through and beyond international climate change frameworks; and to tackle the environmental challenges they face by combining knowledges. This creates a context through which MSV partners can continue to call for the rest of the world to take responsibility for climate change while implementing aggressive mitigation actions, combining a pragmatic outlook with political intent, and advancing a collaborative mode of negotiation and resistance—which can then apply to wider DRR contexts.

MOVING FORWARD: PRINCIPLES AND PRACTICES

Based on the different vignettes addressed in this chapter, three main principles can be adduced for combining knowledges as part of broader DRR strategies, including CCA. The first centers on contextualization and transferability. Rationalist approaches to development work, including DRR, often assume the objectivity of the work (Martin 1979). One implication of this is that techniques, knowledge, or methods developed in one case study are presumed to be transferable to other places; context is assumed not to matter. This may work in some instances but by no means in all. Indigenous knowledge is, conversely, often assumed to be non-generalizable because it is context specific, and relevant and applicable most to its current location (Brokensha et al. 1980; Fernando 2003; Sillitoe 1998). However, as many pan-indigenous movements have shown, including MSV, it is possible for these ideas to travel effectively (particularly in relation to shared pressures like climate change) without overwriting local differences, and many indigenous knowledge systems are inclusive, worldly, and pluralistic in outlook (Whitt 2009, 34). It is possible, then, to see combined approaches to indigenous DRR as comparatively applicable and transferable among different locations, as long as such strategies are always recontextualized and adapted in line both with ecological particularities and culturally specific worldviews.

Climate change, as one topic within DRR, represents a challenge both for academic researchers studying it and for communities who are attempting to adapt to it and deal with related hazards on a daily basis. This is another case in which an open approach to knowledge exchange is needed. Communicating academic research findings on climate change can be helpful in orienting communities with regard to the spatial and temporal diffuseness, origins, and scale of climate change, particularly in terms of integrating possible risks and impacts as part of their knowledge base. This requires sensitivity to how knowledge is shared across languages (particularly minority languages)— including attention to the different tensions and valences that are attached to concepts like environment, resilience, and sustainability—and a commitment to co-producing and disseminating knowledge outside of conventional academic forums such as international conferences. At the same time, it is important to establish the degree to which indigenous knowledge systems have already adapted to incorporate elements of climate change science, and to be responsive to how indigenous peoples may interpret climate change cosmologically (indigenizing it as part of a broader sequence of stories) or politically (in relation to historical power relations and struggles).

Such interpretations can inform academic DRR research as it takes indigenous knowledge and cultural specificity into account, and perhaps starts to enlarge the narrative forms and different modes of mediation used to communicate and refine ideas dialogically. Platforms such as the Island Vulnerability website and the MSV program are particularly useful for facilitating this process, as they provide different forms of data access and dissemination (including through visual modes like photography), which increase inclusivity for people who are not able to travel to or participate in academic meetings. Such plural and interactive forms of mediation can help enable interested groups to identify which knowledges may be transferable across contexts. These platforms can also demonstrate how indigenous peoples have already dealt with swift changes in climate (Nunn et al. 2007)—a process that extends the repertoires of indigenous knowledge systems on an everyday basis.

The second principle for combining knowledges involves promoting trust and self-help. It is important for external DRR researchers and collaborators to find out what specific risk reduction strategies have been used by indigenous peoples in the past, as this can provide shared entry points for addressing disaster-related concerns that have not been experienced for some time or that are comparatively new for such communities. Rather than imposing external views and approaches, building on knowledge already respected by a community helps to orientate its members, values their current knowledge base, and empowers them to recognize existing capacities and where they might want to mobilize external assistance in developing DRR strategies (Mercer et al. 2009, 2010). This co-production of knowledge can contribute to reducing dependence on external aid because it emphasizes the power and importance of knowledge and decision-making processes within communities, rather than simply turning to external sources for assistance with DRR concerns, including for CCA. It can also occasion a change in one of the master narratives of development—dependence—through a form of collaborative investment that improves self-sufficiency.

The co-production of knowledge promotes trust, both in the effectiveness of community-based resources for DRR and of outsiders, while increasing respect for indigenous people's ownership of policies and actions, and developing self-confidence in their abilities (Wisner 1995; Haynes et al. 2008). Such collaboration can consolidate broader power bases when tackling the deleterious forms of environmental transformation that affect DRR and vulnerability in SIDS, such as military territorialization and resource extraction (from industrial fishing to mining the sea bed)—and of which climate change is arguably one. Postcolonial and environmental humanities critique has a significant role to play here through highlighting the protocols needed to reduce structural vulnerabilities; identifying insidious risks and forms of violence; and increasing resilience by integrating DRR into political strategy. This mode of knowledge combination involves using insights about the historical production of vulnerability—which a postcolonial environmental humanities positions as cultural as well as political—to frame specific development-driven research agendas. Fostering trust and self-reliance can be seen from this perspective as dependent on understanding the many different scales of power relations that may undercut indigenous knowledge and community autonomy when development initiatives are imposed from without.

The third principle involves not assuming community homogeneity or uniformity of indigenous knowledge. No community, indigenous or otherwise, is homogenous or displays a single, cohesive form of knowledge that applies to everyone (Cannon 2007; Walmsley 2006). Work to promote and apply indigenous knowledge should recognize and factor in disparities within a community along with disagreements or differences in knowledge. For instance, many Pacific Islands had Christianity introduced over the last century, but it was not uniformly accepted across communities or populations. Strong tensions exist between indigenous knowledge based on endogenous values and belief systems and that which has adapted to Christian philosophies. Some Tuvaluans do not accept that sea-level rise could inundate them, for instance, because in their interpretation of the Bible, God told Noah there would never be another flood (Farbotko 2005). This attitude is not fatalism, but indicates how sea level rise has been outside of this particular culture and knowledge system until recently. DRR, including CCA, needs to account for differing views and should strive to hear and include a community's varying sets of knowledge, especially where one group dominates others.

DRR knowledge and implementation strategies, including for CCA, need to be translated so that different community sectors understand and can respond to them. That is not just about using local languages, dialects and colloquialisms, but also refers to using appropriate media and venues. Some people prefer to read scientific papers and to surf websites. Others have strong oral traditions, and develop ideas not through watching a laptop presentation in a meeting room, but by sitting in a circle, eating, gossiping, and listening to an elaborate story or legend. In other instances, art, music, and dance are used to engage community or environmental issues in specific instances and venues. Working with indigenous peoples for DRR, including CCA, means engaging all sectors of the community, rather than presuming singularity of knowledges and modes of exchange. And this is precisely where an intersection with the environmental humanities can be fruitful in helping to situate and interpret scientific findings—and academic research more broadly—as one aspect in a constellation of narrative forms that complement or compete with one another to impact on how people view and deal with disaster risks. Environmental humanities researchers can contribute to DRR, including CCA, by exploring the tensions regarding how and in what proportion knowledges are combined, and by providing a richer sense of longitudinal perspective (by addressing literary and historical narratives, for instance) than can be achieved in discrete, fieldwork-based case studies. The self-reflexive value of juxtaposing this chapter among the more humanities-based contributions to this collection, then, is to help illuminate where the principles, observations, and practical recommendations outlined here might be enhanced through future collaborations. This involves combining applied DRR strategies with cultural, historical, and political perspectives on resilience and vulnerability, and considering how ideas about DRR including CCA are translated across different global contexts.

The conclusions of the essay tally well with postcolonial studies' overarching investment in supporting self-determination and empowerment, while at the same time establishing protocols for respectful knowledge combination, co-production, and exchange. It is not always straightforward for external agents to include indigenous peoples in DRR, but this is part of the challenge of supporting people's efforts to enhance resilience on their own terms, and involves recognizing the advantages and limitations of different participatory processes (Cooke and Kothari 2001; Hickey and Mohan 2004; Pretty 1995). Self-reflexivity and evaluation must be a continual activity to ensure that attempts to incorporate indigenous knowledge into DRR initiatives, including for CCA, are not causing or exacerbating more problems than are solved. Some of the more difficult questions emerge when there is a conflict between indigenous and non-indigenous assessments of risks, such as in the case of some Tuvaluans whose religious beliefs preclude acceptance of future inundation (see e.g. Kennedy et al. 2008; Tibby et al. 2007). In such cases, a balance needs to be struck between, on one hand, ignoring or overriding indigenous knowledge and community interests that would lead to detrimental impacts, and on the other hand, accepting that detrimental impacts are one of the possible results of decisions based on indigenous knowledge and local empowerment. It must also be recognized that DRR decisions based on academic research can lead to detrimental impacts in the community or elsewhere. Effective knowledge combination and co-production can help negotiate these tensions, but ongoing trust and collaboration are needed to achieve the potential for positive exchange.

The environmental humanities can contribute to this process of collaboration and co-production by ensuring that indigenous people's ideas, thoughts, philosophies, and worldviews are included in DRR conversations, thereby broadening the scope and explanatory power of the field. Environmental humanities research can also emphasize the need to use, engage with, and analyze self-reflexively the full range of narrative and media forms through which environmental knowledge is conveyed. With exchange across knowledge bases and honesty in what people can and cannot achieve on their own, DRR and CCA researchers can draw on the best wisdom that those inside and external to communities can provide—not least for dealing with the rapidly changing ecological conditions produced by climate change.

NOTES

1. Consideration of indigenous knowledge is also essential to the broader task of developing a postcolonial environmental humanities. The way in which indigenous scholars and activists such as Laurelyn Whitt characterize "indigenous knowledge systems" draws attention to how they "typically place considerable

significance and value on [...] gaining access to the perspective of the other-than-human (2009, 34). Whitt emphasizes how "[t]his commitment to a non-anthropocentric epistemological pluralism [...] runs directly counter to the commitment to anti-pluralism typical of the dominant knowledge system," and in particular to rationalist or "neopositivist" ideologies that assert supposed "value-neutrality" and segregate a narrowly demarcated notion of "science" from discussions of power and politics (34; xiv).

2. See, for example, Clifford (2013) for a helpful overview with reference to Pacific Island cultures in particular.

3. See further background and detailed histories in Gaillard (2007, 2010), Hewitt (1983, 1997), Lewis (1999), Manyena (2006), Mileti et al. (1999), and Wisner et al. (2004, 2012).

4. O'Keefe et al.'s work also contributed to corroborating contemporaneous discussions concerning "The myth of the natural disaster" (Ball 1975) and "The Un-natural Disasters" (Tiranti 1977).

5. For academic literature that emphasizes this link see, for example, Hewitt (1997), Lewis (1999), Mileti et al. (1999), Oliver-Smith (1986), Steinberg (2000), and Wisner et al. (2004), (2012), and for policy-oriented reinforcement see Global Network of Civil Society Organisations for Disaster Reduction (2009, 2011); UNISDR (2002).

6. See Coburn and Spence (2002); Lewis (2003) on seismic resistance; Cuny (1991) on flooding.

7. See Chambers (1995) and Chambers and Conway (1992) on sustainable livelihoods; Cooke and Kothari (2001) and Pretty (1995) on participatory processes.

8. See, for example, Campbell (1984) and the Island Vulnerability website (www.islandvulnerability.org) for further context and resources.

9. See also Schmuck-Widmann's research (2001) in Bangladesh, which highlights the missed opportunities that occurred when external engineers dismissed islanders' knowledge concerning flow on the Jamuna River.

10. See Klein (2007) for a highly critical take on the relationship between neoliberal economic reforms and disasters on a global level. The case of Montserrat, following the series of volcanic eruptions beginning in 1995, also provides a vivid demonstration of conflicts between a range of external scientific, touristic, and (neo)colonial interests and the concerns of the islanders (see e.g. Carrigan 2011; Pattullo 2000; Skelton 2000).

11. This is one of the many areas where there are possibilities for synthesis between analyses of literary narratives and the construction of DRR principles, which could involve exploring how tensions between different knowledge claims and worldviews have been portrayed in particular cultural contexts over time.

12. See also Kelman and West (2009), Kelman (2010), and the comparable Climate Frontlines program (http://www.climatefrontlines.org/en-GB).

REFERENCES

Arunotai, Narumon. 2008. "Saved by an Old Legend and a Keen Observation: The Case of Moken Sea Nomads in Thailand." In *Indigenous Knowledge for Disaster Risk Reduction: Good Practices and Lessons Learnt from the Asia-Pacific Region*, edited by Rajib Shaw, Noralene Uy, and Jennifer Baumwoll, 73–78. Bangkok: UNISDR Asia and Pacific.

Ball, Nicole. 1975. "The Myth of the Natural Disaster." *The Ecologist* 5 (10): 368–371.

Bang, Henry N. 2009. "Natural Disaster Risk, Vulnerability and Resettlement: Relocation Decisions Following the Lake Nyos and Monoum Gas Disasters in Cameroon." PhD dissertation. University of East Anglia.

Bankoff, Greg. 2001. "Rendering the World Unsafe: Vulnerability as Western Discourse." *Disasters* 25 (1): 19–35.

———. 2003. *Cultures of Disaster: Society and Natural Hazards in the Philippines.* London and New York: Routledge.

Berkes, Fikret. 2009. "Indigenous Ways of Knowing and the Study of Environmental Change." *Journal of the Royal Society of New Zealand* 39 (4): 151–156.

Brokensha, David, Dennis M. Warren, and Oswald Werner. 1980. *Indigenous Knowledge Systems and Development.* Lanham: University Press of America.

Cadag, Jake R.D., and JC Gaillard. 2012. "Integrating Knowledge and Actions in Disaster Risk Reduction: The Contribution of Participatory Mapping." *Area* 44 (1): 100–109.

Campbell, John R. 1984. *Dealing with Disaster: Hurricane Response in Fiji.* Honolulu: Pacific Islands Development Program.

Cannon, Terry. 2007. "Reducing People's Vulnerability to Natural Hazards: Communities and Resilience." Paper presented at the WIDER Conference on Fragile States—Fragile Groups: Tackling Economic and Social Vulnerability, Helsinki, June 15.

Carr, Lowell Juilliard. 1932. "Disaster and the Sequence-Pattern Concept of Social Change." *The American Journal of Sociology* 38 (2): 207–218.

Carrigan, Anthony. 2011. "(Eco)Catastrophe, Reconstruction, and Representation: Montserrat and the Limits of Sustainability." *New Literatures Review* 47–48: 111–128.

Chambers, Robert. 1995. "Poverty and Livelihoods: Whose Reality Counts?" *Environment & Urbanization* 7 (1): 173–204.

Chambers, Robert, and Gordon R. Conway. 1992 [1991]. *Sustainable Rural Livelihoods: Practical Concepts for the 21st Century.* Discussion Paper 296. Brighton: Institute of Development Studies, University of Sussex.

Clifford, James. 2013. *Returns: Becoming Indigenous in the Twenty-First Century.* Cambridge: Harvard University Press.

Coburn, Andrew W., and Robin J. S. Spence. 2002. *Earthquake Protection.* London: Wiley.

Comité Information Sahel. 1975. *Qui se nourrit de la famine en Afrique?* Paris: F. Maspero.

Cooke, Bill, and Uma Kothari. 2001. *Participation: The New Tyranny.* London: Zed Books.

Copans, Jean, ed. 1975. *Sécheresses et famines du Sahel.* Paris: F. Maspero.

Cronin, Shane J., David R. Gaylord, Douglas Charley, Brent V. Alloway, Sandrine Wallez, and Job W. Esau. 2004. "Participatory Methods of Incorporating Scientific with Traditional Knowledge for Volcanic Hazard Management on Ambae Island, Vanuatu." *Bulletin of Volcanology* 66 (7): 652–668.

Cuny, Fred C. 1991. "Living with Floods: Alternatives for Riverine Flood Mitigation." *Land Use Policy* 8 (4): 331–342.

Etkin, David. 1999. "Risk Transference and Related Trends: Driving Forces Towards More Mega-Disasters." *Environmental Hazards* 1 (2): 69–75.

Farbotko, Carol. 2005. "Tuvalu and Climate Change: Constructions of Environmental Displacement in the *Sydney Morning Herald.*" *Geografiska Annaler: Series B, Human Geography* 87 (4): 279–293.

Fernando, Jude L. 2003. "NGOs and Production of Indigenous Knowledge under the Condition of Postmodernity." *The Annals of the American Academy* 590 (1): 54–72.

Ferris, Elizabeth. 2011. *The Politics of Protection.* Washington: The Brookings Institute.

Gaillard, JC. 2007. "Resilience of Traditional Societies in Facing Natural Hazards." *Disaster Prevention and Management* 16 (4): 522–544.

———. 2010. "Vulnerability, Capacity, and Resilience: Perspectives for Climate and Disaster Risk Reduction." *Journal of International Development* 22 (2): 218–232.

Gaillard, JC, Elsa Clavé, Océane Vibert, Azhari, Dedi, Jean-Charles Denain, Yusuf Efendi, Delphine Grancher, Catherine C. Liamzon, Desy Rosnita Sari, and Ryo Setiawan. 2008. "Ethnic Groups' Response to the 26 December 2004 Earthquake and Tsunami in Aceh, Indonesia." *Natural Hazards* 47 (1): 17–38.

Gaillard, JC, and Emmanuel A. Maceda. 2009. "Participatory 3-dimensional Mapping for Disaster Risk Reduction." *Participatory Learning and Action* 60: 109–118.

Gearheard, Shari, Matthew Pocernich, Ronald Stewart, Joelie Sanguya, and Henry P. Huntington. 2009. "Linking Inuit Knowledge and Meteorological Station Observations to Understand Changing Wind Patterns at Clyde River, Nunavut." *Climatic Change* 100 (2): 267–294.

Global Network of Civil Society Organizations for Disaster Reduction. 2009. *"Clouds but little rain …"—Views from the Frontline: A Local Perspective of Progress Towards Implementation of the Hyogo Framework for Action.* Teddington, UK: Global Network of Civil Society Organisations for Disaster Reduction.

———. 2011. *If We Do Not Join Hands: Views from the Frontline 2011.* Teddington, UK: Global Network of Civil Society Organisations for Disaster Reduction.

Hau'ofa, Epeli. 1993. *A New Oceania: Rediscovering our Sea of Islands.* Suva: University of the South Pacific.

Haynes, Katharine, Jenni Barclay, and Nick Pidgeon. 2007. "Volcanic Hazard Communication Using Maps: An Evaluation of their Effectiveness." *Bulletin of Volcanology* 70 (2): 123–138.

Haynes, Katharine, Jenni Barclay, and Nick Pidgeon. 2008. "The Issue of Trust and its Influence on Risk Communication during a Volcanic Crisis." *Bulletin of Volcanology* 70 (5): 605–621.

Hewitt, Kenneth, ed. 1983. *Interpretations of Calamity from the Viewpoint of Human Ecology.* London: Allen & Unwin.

———. 1997. *Regions of Risk: A Geographical Introduction to Disasters.* Essex: Addison Wesley Longman.

Hickey, Samuel, and Giles Mohan. 2004. *Participation: From Tyranny to Transformation.* London: Zed Books.

Intergovernmental Panel on Climate Change (IPCC). 2007. *Climate Change 2007: Synthesis Report.* Geneva: IPCC.

———. 2012. *Managing the Risks of Extreme Events and Disasters to Advance Climate Change Adaptation: A Special Report of Working Groups I and II of the Intergovernmental Panel on Climate Change.* Cambridge: Cambridge University Press.

———. 2014. *Fifth Assessment Report. Working Group II: Impacts, Adaptation, and Vulnerability.* Geneva: IPCC.

Kelman, Ilan. 2010. "Hearing Local Voices from Small Island Developing States for Climate Change." *Local Environment* 15 (7): 605–619.

Kelman, Ilan, and JC Gaillard. 2010. "Embedding Climate Change Adaptation within Disaster Risk Reduction." In *Climate Change Adaptation and Disaster Risk Reduction: Issues and Challenges*, edited by Rajib Shaw, Juan M. Pulhin, and Joy Jacqueline Pereira, 23–46. Bingley: Emerald.

Kelman, Ilan, James Lewis, JC Gaillard, and Jessica Mercer. 2011. "Participatory Action Research for Dealing with Disasters on Islands." *Island Studies Journal* 6 (1): 59–86.

Kelman, Ilan, Jessica Mercer, and Jennifer West. 2009. "Combining Different Knowledges: Community-based Climate Change Adaptation in Small Island Developing States." *Participatory Learning and Action Notes* 60: 41–53.

Kelman, Ilan, and Jennifer West. 2009. "Climate Change and Small Island Developing States: A Critical Review." *Ecological and Environmental Anthropology* 5 (1): 1–16.

Kennedy, Jim, Joseph Ashmore, Elizabeth Babister, and Ilan Kelman. 2008. "The Meaning of 'Build Back Better': Evidence from Post-tsunami Aceh and Sri Lanka." *Journal of Contingencies and Crisis Management* 16 (1): 24–36.

Klein, Naomi. 2007. *The Shock Doctrine: The Rise of Disaster Capitalism*. London: Allen Lane.

Lewis, James. 1999. *Development in Disaster-prone Places: Studies of Vulnerability*. London: Intermediate Technology.

———. 2003. "Housing Construction in Earthquake-Prone Places: Perspectives, Priorities and Projections for Development." *Australian Journal of Emergency Management* 18 (2): 35–44.

Lytton, Charlotte. 2013. "Top 10: Climate Change Campaigns." *The Guardian*. November 15. http://www.theguardian.com/global-development-professionals-network/2013/nov/15/top-10-climate-change-campaigns.

Mackinson, Steven, and Leif Nottestad. 1998. "Combining Local and Scientific Knowledge." *Reviews in Fish Biology and Fisheries* 8 (4): 481–490.

Maclean, Kirsten, and Leanne Cullen. 2009. "Research Methodologies for the Co-production of Knowledge for Environmental Management in Australia." *Journal of the Royal Society of New Zealand* 39 (4): 205–208.

Manyena, Siambabala Bernard. 2006. "The Concept of Resilience Revisited." *Disasters* 30 (4): 433–450.

Martin, Brian P. 1979. *The Bias of Science*. Canberra: Society for Social Responsibility in Science (ACT).

Mercer, Jessica, and Ilan Kelman. 2008. "Living with Floods in Singas, Papua New Guinea." In *Indigenous Knowledge for Disaster Risk Reduction: Good Practices and Lessons Learned from Experiences in the Asia-Pacific Region*, edited by Rajib Shaw, Noralene Uy, and Jennifer Baumwoll, 46–51. Bangkok: United Nations International Strategy for Disaster Risk Reduction.

Mercer, Jessica, and Ilan Kelman. 2010. "Living Alongside a Volcano in Baliau, Papua New Guinea." *Disaster Prevention and Management* 19 (4): 412–422.

Mercer, Jessica, Ilan Kelman, Sandie Suchet-Pearson, and Kate Lloyd. 2009. "Integrating Indigenous and Scientific Knowledge Bases for Disaster Risk Reduction in Papua New Guinea." *Geografiska Annaler: Series B, Human Geography* 91 (2): 157–183.

Mercer, Jessica, Ilan Kelman, Lorin Taranis, and Sandie Suchet-Pearson. 2010. "Framework for Integrating Indigenous and Scientific Knowledge for Disaster Risk Reduction." *Disasters* 34 (1): 214–239.

Mileti, Dennis, et al. 1999. *Disasters by Design: A Reassessment of Natural Hazards in the United States.* Washington: Joseph Henry Press.

Nunn, Patrick D., Rosalind Hunter-Anderson, Mike T. Carson, Frank Thomas, Sean Ulm, and Michael J. Rowland. 2007. "Times of Plenty, Times of Less: Last-millennium Societal Disruption in the Pacific Basin." *Human Ecology* 35 (4): 385–401.

O'Keefe, Phil, Ken Westgate, and Ben Wisner. 1976. "Taking the Naturalness out of Natural Disasters." *Nature* 260 (5552): 566–567.

Oliver-Smith, Anthony. 1986. *The Martyred City: Death and Rebirth in the Andes.* Albuquerque: University of New Mexico Press.

Pattullo, Polly. 2000. *Fire from the Mountain: The Tragedy of Montserrat and the Betrayal of its People.* London: Constable.

Pretty, Jules N. 1995. "Participatory Learning For Sustainable Agriculture." *World Development* 23 (8): 1247–1263.

Prince, Samuel H. 1920. *Catastrophe and Social Change.* PhD diss. Columbia University, New York.

Ross, Andrew. 1991. *Strange Weather: Culture, Science and Technology in an Age of Limits.* London: Verso.

Schmuck-Widmann, Hanna. 2001. *Facing the Jamuna River: Indigenous and Engineering Knowledge in Bangladesh.* Dhaka: Bangladesh Resource Centre for Indigenous Knowledge.

Shaw, Rajib, Juan M. Pulhin, and Joy Jacqueline Pereira, eds. 2010a. *Climate Change Adaptation and Disaster Risk Reduction: Issues and Challenges.* Bingley: Emerald.

———, eds. 2010b. *Climate Change Adaptation and Disaster Risk Reduction: An Asian Perspective.* Bingley: Emerald.

Shaw, Rajib, Anshu Sharma, and Yukiko Takeuchi, eds. 2009. *Indigenous Knowledge and Disaster Risk Reduction: From Practice to Policy.* Hauppauge: Nova.

Shaw, Rajib, Noralene Uy, and Jennifer Baumwoll, eds. 2008. *Indigenous Knowledge for Disaster Risk Reduction: Good Practices and Lessons Learnt from the Asia-Pacific Region.* Bangkok: UNISDR Asia and Pacific.

Sillitoe, Paul. 1998. "The Development of Indigenous Knowledge." *Current Anthropology*, 39 (2): 223–252.

Skelton, Tracey. 2000. "Political Uncertainties and Natural Disasters: Montserratian Identity and Colonial Status." *Interventions* 2 (1): 103–117.

Smith, Linda Tuhiwai. 1999. *Decolonizing Methodologies: Research and Indigenous Peoples.* London: Zed Books.

Spence, Robin, Ilan Kelman, Erica Calogero, Guillermo Toyos, Peter Baxter, and Jean-Christophe Komorowski. 2005. "Modelling Expected Physical Impacts and Human Casualties from Explosive Volcanic Eruption." *Natural Hazards and Earth Systems Sciences* 5 (6): 1003–1015.

Steinberg, Ted. 2000. *Acts of God: The Unnatural History of Natural Disaster in America.* New York: Oxford University Press.

Tibby, John, Marcus B. Lane, and Peter A. Gell. 2007. "Local Knowledge and Environmental Management: A Cautionary Tale from Lake Ainsworth, New South Wales, Australia." *Environmental Conservation* 34 (4): 334–341.

Tiranti, Dexter. 1977. "The Un-natural Disasters." *The New Internationalist* 53: 5–6.

United Nations International Strategy for Disaster Reduction (UNISDR). 2002. *Disaster Reduction for Sustainable Mountain Development: 2002 United Nations World Disaster Reduction Campaign.* Geneva: UNISDR.

———. 2012. *UNISDR Terminology on DRR.* Geneva: UNISDR. http://www. unisdr.org/we/inform/terminology.

Walmsley, Jim. 2006. "The Nature of Community: Putting Community in Place." *Dialogue* 25 (1): 5–12.

Weichselgartner, Juergen, and Michael Obersteiner. 2002. "Knowing Sufficient and Applying More: Challenges in Hazard Management." *Environmental Hazards* 4 (2): 73–77.

White, Gilbert F. 1945. *Human Adjustment to Floods: A Geographical Approach to the Flood Problem in the United States.* Research Paper No. 29. University of Chicago, Illinois.

White, Rodney R. 2004. "Managing and Interpreting Uncertainty for Climate Change Risk." *Building Research & Information* 32 (5): 438–448.

Whitt, Laurelyn. 2009. *Science, Colonialism, and Indigenous Peoples: The Cultural Politics of Law and Knowledge.* Cambridge: Cambridge University Press.

Wisner, Ben. 1995. "Bridging 'Expert' and 'Local' Knowledge for Counter-Disaster Planning in Urban South Africa." *GeoJournal* 37 (3): 335–348.

Wisner, Ben, Piers Blaikie, Terry Cannon, and Ian Davis. 2004. *At Risk: Natural Hazards, People's Vulnerability and Disasters*, 2nd ed., London and New York: Routledge.

Wisner, Ben, JC Gaillard, and Ilan Kelman, eds. 2012. *Handbook of Hazards and Disaster Risk Reduction.* London and New York: Routledge.

Wisner, Ben, Phil O'Keefe, and Ken Westgate. 1977. "Global Systems and Local Disasters: The Untapped Power of Peoples' Science." *Disasters* 1 (1): 47–57.

Part III

Political Ecologies and Environmental Justice

8   The Edgework of the Clerk

Resilience in Arundhati Roy's *Walking with the Comrades*

Susie O'Brien

In photo and video footage of the 2013 Jaipur Literature Festival, the name of the event's sponsor is impossible to miss. On banners adorning crowded entranceways, and backdrops to speaking events, the festival's 2013 motto, "Carnival of Values," appears beneath the insignia of Tata Steel, echoing the company slogan, "Values Stronger than Steel." By its own reckoning, the company's sponsorship of the festival reflects its foundational commitment to service and belief in "the interconnectivity of the enterprise, the environment and the community" (Tata Steel Ltd. 2011, 2). However, as its 2009–2010 report to shareholders also hints, Tata Steel's turn to philanthropy also comes in response to a business climate buffeted by the 2008 financial crisis and by growing demands for corporate responsibility. In a variety of ways, sponsorship of the literary festival bolsters the Tata brand by highlighting the company's expansiveness and flexibility. In a (Tata Steel-sponsored) NDTV program about the festival, company vice president, Partha Sengupta, responds to a gently lobbed question about the surprising association of the "great huge industrial giant" with an "intellectual melting pot of culture and books": "Steel is associated as being staid and boring. [...] So we thought we would make it interesting, make it more colourful, make it more approachable. The concept is fantastic, the literature fest is wonderful, and we have found our place under the sun, because we have found like-minded people" ("Jaipur Lit Fest" 2013). The message manages to be both conservative and liberal, suggesting that Tata Steel saw its own long-held values echoed in the literary festival, but also that the company recognized the need to change and update its brand in the fact of changing times. A skeptical reading might argue that Tata Steel's image needed burnishing not because of the boring reputation of steel, but because of the Tata Group's track record of violently displacing *adivasi* (tribal people) and farmers from their lands ("Orissa tribals" 2011; "Singur Land" 2013). Tata's move is part of a trend, scathingly observed by Arundhati Roy (2012), in which mining companies "have embraced the Arts—film, art installations and the rush of literary festivals that have replaced the '90s obsession with beauty contests." The rationale seems to be this: that the problems of resource depletion, pollution, and human rights abuses will fade in significance amidst the happy clamor of a "carnival of values."

This corporate strategy highlights, in an unexpected way, a key task of the environmental humanities. It is not enough simply to elaborate the connection between culture and environment, or insist on the centrality of "values" to discussions of the environment—moves that have already been adroitly made by industries heavily involved in environmental despoliation; rather, the environmental humanities needs to think critically about the historical conjunctures that have produced the values conventionally associated with culture and environment—and now, increasingly, with their exuberant conjunction. This chapter focuses on a term that has come to play a key conceptual role in the conjunction of culture and environment and the enlistment of both in the service of capitalist growth: resilience. Resilience has many specific, and often contested, definitions within different fields, some of which are elaborated below. What has come to be a key connotation—the capacity to survive through turbulence—has come to play a central organizing role in environmental management and in discourses of development that emphasize the interdependence of culture and environment. Resource industries like Tata Steel increasingly see that a critical factor in their own success in the face of uncertainty is expanding their activities to harness public discussions around culture and environment and the role of industry in sustaining both.

Arundhati Roy is a writer who has trenchantly highlighted this process; her recent work is the focus of this chapter. Roy's 1997 Booker Prize-winning novel, *The God of Small Things*, affirmed the resilience of nature and the imagination in the face of the implacable force of history. The novel earned worldwide acclaim, making Roy, for a time, the symbol of India's cultural and economic flourishing. In the decades since, Roy has turned to non-fiction, abandoning the lyrical tone and innovative form of her fiction for a critical, documentary realist style. She has also become markedly less popular, charged with militant negativity that is, her critics claim, unhelpful to India's quest to thrive in the tumultuous twenty-first century. This chapter focuses on a work that has drawn significant criticism: Roy's 2011 collection, *Walking with the Comrades*. Exploring the complex role of militant Marxists in supporting *adivasi* struggles against the expropriation of their land by mining companies, the book demands a critical interrogation of popular articulations of culture, environment, and capitalism. In doing so, it reworks the concept of resilience to emphasize postcolonial environmental justice and the vital role of the critical imagination in that ongoing project.

OUTSIDE THE "CARNIVAL OF VALUES": *WALKING WITH THE COMRADES*

The story that is the subject of the title essay in *Walking with the Comrades*, is an unlikely one for several reasons. First, it is unusual that the Maoists, whose campaign against bauxite mining in the Dandakaranya forest has made them targets of Indian military operations, would risk their security by inviting Roy to view and write about their operation. Second, it is surprising that Roy—who, in *The God of Small Things*, decried the dogmatic militarism of "big things," which included Marxism along with colonialism, Christianity, and the state—took up the invitation to walk with the unapologetically violent Maoists. But it is also unlikely for a third, more banal reason: her scheduled meeting with the contact for the comrades almost didn't happen. After waiting for months to set up the meeting, she writes, she received a typewritten note, advising her to be at the agreed on location, at any of four given times on two given days; the window was to allow for the possibility of "bad weather, punctures, blockades, transport strikes and sheer bad luck" (2011, 37). The note went on to say "Writer should have camera, tika and coconut. Meeter will have cap, Hindi *Outlook* magazine and bananas. Password: Namaskar Guruji" (38). She arrives at the first appointed time, with all the requisite items, and is approached by a young boy wearing chipped red nail polish, who asks, simply, "Are you the one who's going in?" He reaches into a Charlie Brown knapsack and pulls out a soggy note that says "'*Outlook nahi mila*' (Couldn't find *Outlook*)" (50). As for the missing bananas, he explains "'I ate them' ... 'I got hungry'" (50). A key purpose in her relation of this meeting is to highlight the absurdity of the government's routine characterization of the Maoists as "India's single biggest internal security challenge'" (39). It also highlights the contingency of things, the delicate balance of purpose and surprise through which collectivities come together and meaning coalesces. The meeting is thus a useful starting place to talk about a different model of resilience than the one promised by the merger of art and steel.

On the simplest level, resilience describes the ability to subsist through change and cope with surprise—qualities evident in Roy's meeting with Mangtu (not his real name). While the chipped red nail polish and Charlie Brown knapsack negate the media image of the Maoists as a highly disciplined and ruthless fighting machine, the apparent randomness of both the outfit and the meeting convey an amazing capacity to adapt and improvise in the face of inevitable disruption or "sheer bad luck." The remainder of Roy's account of her time with the Maoists locates the power and precarity (as well as the moral ambiguity) of their struggle in the context of the broader goal of protecting tribal sovereignty over the forest. She highlights the embeddedness of the lives of the Dongria Kondh and other *adivasi*, in local ecosystems. She also documents the complexity and brutality of the forces—industrial, military, and cultural—that threaten the life of the forest, in the name of national "resilience," and explores paths of resistance, including the violent path of the Maoists.

Among the strengths of *The God of Small Things* was its delicate illumination of a capacity for survival and adaptation amid vulnerability and brokenness. In both style and theme, the novel affirmed the values of transformation, openness and play, which it celebrated as conducive to life, in opposition to forces of convention, identity and rationality. Roy comments wryly on the shifts that mark her turn to political nonfiction:

> As a writer, a fiction writer [...] I worry that I am allowing myself to be railroaded into offering prosaic, factual precision when maybe what we need is a feral howl, or the transformative power and real precision of poetry. Something about the cunning, Brahmanical, intricate, bureaucratic, file-bound, "apply-through-proper-channels" nature of governance and subjugation in India seems to have made a clerk out of me."
>
> (2009, 4)

The figure of the clerk, consigned to the tasks of record and account keeping, is not only *not* associated with creativity but also frequently indicted, along with the symbolic figure of the bureaucrat, as the enemy of innovation, freedom and thought itself. I want to suggest, conversely, two somewhat contradictory things: first, that we think about Roy's assumption of this role in relation to resilience, that is, as an adaptive strategy, adopted in the face of new kinds of turbulence, to promote the survival of fragile life systems. And second, that we recognize the problem with overvaluing resilience and that we consider both the objects, relations, and processes it brings into focus and those it elides.

It is important to stress these elisions, in the context of the now commonplace invocation of resilience as an unquestionable value, perhaps *the* unquestionable value, to which businesses, governments, social organizations, institutions, and individuals aspire. More than simply a measure of viability in the face of change, it has come to function as a sign of the fitness, even the moral worthiness, of things in and of themselves. Without wanting to argue that the positive value attached to resilience is entirely misplaced, I support the argument, advanced by Jeremy Walker and Melinda Cooper (2011) and others,[1] that we need to critique its too-comfortable alignment with the ideals of neoliberalism and associated values of flexibility, deregulation, and social Darwinism. In analyzing Roy's writing, I aim to articulate a more critically reflexive idea of resilience, encompassing: (1) a focus on the dynamic tension between forces of change and conservation, transformation and integrity, necessary to sustaining natural-cultural webs of existence; (2) an attention to scale that requires shifting one's vision away from the middle ground (in more than one sense) toward macro- and microfields of action; and (3) an interest in what happens at edges, meeting places and contact zones as sites of uncertainty, collaboration and—sometimes (but not always)—productive surprise.

NEW KINDS OF TURBULENCE

Before turning to Roy's work, a brief discussion of the concept of resilience is necessary. Conceived in the 1970s by forest ecologist C. S. Holling, resilience ecology focuses on complex adaptive systems, which are characterized by constant movement between periods of stability and processes of transformation. This movement itself is governed by what Holling calls "panarchy," a term that describes:

> the cross-scale and dynamic character of interactions between human and natural systems. It draws on the Greek god Pan, a symbol of universal nature, to capture an image of unpredictable change, and fuses this with notions of hierarchies—cross-scale structures in natural and human systems. The term embodies notions that sustain the self-structuring capacity of systems (system integrity), allow adaptive evolution, and at times succumb to the gales of change.
>
> (Holling, Gunderson, and Peterson 2001, 89)

A crucial tension exists in these periods of change, when order is replaced by "uncertainty, novelty, and experimentation" (Walker and Salt 2006, 82), between the functions of what Holling calls "mobilization" and "retention" (1986, 307), or what Carl Folke (2006) terms "revolt" and "remember" (259). Renewal depends on "the degree to which [a system] is capable of self-organization (vs. lack of organization or organization faced by external factors) and the degree to which the system can build and increase the capacity for learning and adaptation" (Folke 2006, 260–61).

Resilience theory has particular salience at a time when all the earth's systems are being challenged by multiple, rapid and non-linear changes brought about by human industrial activity: the element of "ebullient surprise" (Holling 2009) that is a constituent part of life has assumed a larger, more unpredictable role in the order of things, and resilience theory gives us a way to describe and even to measure the capacity to work through, rather than be undone, by it. It also entails the recognition that natural systems are not infinitely self-correcting, that "resilience can be and has been eroded, and that the self-repairing capacity of eco-systems should no longer be taken for granted" (Folke et al. 2004, 558). In other words, in addition to giving us a new, and largely positive, vocabulary to understand change, it also highlights the finite capacity of organisms and systems to survive the kinds and degrees of turbulence they currently face.

Resilience is a key theme in *The God of Small Things*, which counters forces of convention and rationality—expressed in the "laws that lay down who should be loved and how. And how much" (Roy 1997, 33)—with the values of transformation, openness, and play. Love resonates symbolically with creativity in its transformational capacity and its unlawfulness; just as her characters thwart the laws against miscegenation and incest, Roy's writing jubilantly messes with conventions of literal sense, embedding the crude and lumbering referentiality of "big" ideas like History, whose cliché banalities are mockingly signposted in uppercase, in a sea of small things, drawn together in lush and unlikely metaphorical alliance. Recalling the discussion of resilience ecology from earlier: linkages are broken and new ones formed, symbolic order is replaced by "uncertainty, novelty, and experimentation" (Walker and Salt 2006, 82). In this way, even in the face of individual deaths, the possibility of life and love is preserved.

The publication of *The God of Small Things* coincided with India's emergence from prolonged economic crisis into a period of exuberant renewal that spawned the slogan "India Shining." The timing was fortuitous. As Shoma Chaudury (2012) explains, "an ebullient middle-class was looking for a mascot. Roy came tailor-made from heaven: she had an elfin beauty, a diamond flash in her nose, a mane of gorgeous hair, a romantic back-story and a manuscript that triggered an international bidding war ... it was a done deal: Arundhati Roy was India's triumphant entry on the global stage."[2] Roy's Booker-Prize win was hailed as not just a single shiny element, but an emblem of the role of culture more broadly in India's glittering global renaissance. Culture, in the form of art, literature and film, came increasingly to be seen, in India as elsewhere, as an expression of the inventiveness, tolerance, flexibility, mobility, imagination and wit that underwrite liberal, democratic society. The less publically noted part of India's global emergence is that it coincided with (was enabled by) a deepening of the gulf between rich and poor, the displacement of hundreds of thousands of *adivasis* from their lands, and the devastation of those lands by mines and megadams. This story is critical to understanding both Roy's move from artistic/creative to political/critical writing, and the response that greeted the shift.

Beginning in 1998 with *The End of Imagination*, Roy has produced a series of critical essays whose subjects include nuclear weapons, dams, the Indian occupation of Kashmir and, most recently, mining. In *Walking with the Comrades* in particular, survival is associated not with perverse beauty or stubborn acts of creation against the unimaginative, prohibitive regulations of history; rather it takes the form of a resolute, and straightforward "no" to the forces of development. It comes down to a plea with the bald and simple resonance of the political slogans she mocked in *The God of Small Things*: "Can we leave the bauxite in the mountain?" (Roy, 2011, 35; 2010) The question, which has assumed the status of a kind of refrain in Roy's recent work, is striking in its uncompromising opposition to development, as well as its—for Roy—unnuanced literalness.

Roy is not the first Indian literary writer to draw attention to the inextricably connected problems of environmental destruction and the displacement of *adivasi*; Mahasweta Devi, for example, has been documenting the politics of forestry and megadams in her fiction since the 1970s.[3] What is noteworthy about Roy is the swerve in both her perspective and her popularity that marks her recent work. No longer is she hailed as an emblem of positive change in India; rather, as Chaudury (2012) notes, Roy's "very existence—her persona and her politics—has become a sort of affront to a certain strata of Indians," who complain that: "her only creative position is opposition." Among her prominent detractors is the environmental historian Ramachandra Guha (2000a) who, though he proclaims himself to be on the same side as Roy "objectively speaking" (with respect, specifically, to the hazards of megadams), condemns Roy's "unredeemingly negative" attitude and opposition to the spirit of "innovative compromise" (2000b). Guha also decries what he sees as the absence in her writing of "intellectual probity and judgment" and "a proper sense of gravitas."[4] These—arguably contradictory—critiques of Roy are compatible with a liberal model of change, which sees India as a work in progress, an imperfect but functioning democracy, evolving in the direction of ever-expanding freedom, guided by principles of sustainable development.

REVOLT AND REMEMBER

In contrast to the conventional amalgam of conservative and liberal beliefs that animate this development narrative, Roy offers an assessment that is more attuned to the resilience principles of "revolt" and "remember." Democracy, she asserts, is not a universal ideal but a habitable concept that, in the developed world, has become a brittle shell, an alibi for the collusion, between politicians, lobbyists, media, and the legal system to concentrate the distribution of wealth in the hands of the already massively wealthy. Roy makes it clear that she is not damning democracy outright. Democracy is—and should be—"the utopia that all 'developing' societies aspire to" (2009, 1), she maintains. The problem is with the "working model," whose efficiency is represented by the fusion "of democracy and the free market ... into a single predatory organism with a thin, constricted imagination that revolves almost entirely around the idea of maximizing profit" (2). This model of democracy supports the "war" in the forest, which is being conducted to clear tribal settlements for mining—a war of which "the government is both proud and shy" (2011, 38). The shyness might be attributable to the government's anxiety about being seen to contravene the Forest Rights Act that (belatedly) in 2006 gave forest dwellers legal rights to land and the traditional use of forest produce. A vast public relations exercise provides a diversion from the stark politics of this violation, in the form, for example, of mediagenic exercises such as a 2009 "public" hearing into a new steel plant in Lohandiguda, Dantewada. Villagers were allegedly prevented from attending the meeting, where a group of government-approved participants, including contractors and real estate agents, voted overwhelmingly to support the project (Tripath 2012). Mainstream media accounts of the hearing pronounced it a success, demonstrating the critical role of the culture industry in sanctifying the "innovative compromise" between the market and the state.

This role is not confined to distorted news coverage, but encompasses a broader culture project that is flourishing under the rapidly spreading mantle of corporate philanthropy, encompassing events like the Jaipur Literary Festival, and prizes such as Vedanta Resource's "Creating Happiness

Project," a competition for youth to make videos about sustainable develop-ment.[5] In this way, resource industries secure a lock on the future, forged through an inseverable knot between capitalism and the imagination. Here is one explanation for Roy's adoption of the mantle of the clerk, one that deploys the strategy of record-keeping ("remember") in the service of resis-tance ("revolt"). As Rob Nixon (2010) notes, Roy's turn to the essay can be understood partly as a matter of "genre and scale": "the agile personal essay was set against the ponderous, strategically impersonal epic report" (76). Roy's essays, Nixon points out, "stage intimate assaults on the cal-culated opacity, the profoundly consequential tedium, of the technocratic report that camouflages violence while clearing a path for it in a language scoured of emotion" (76). But her essays are importantly written against, not only "the hydro-bureaucrat's report" (77), but also the culture project that provides a vital source of fuel for the ideology of neoliberal progress.

This function is consistent with Roy's self-described vocation as the "clerk" who provides a detailed account of things,[6] in a context in which "things" turn out to be not just more complex than they seem, but ulti-mately unassimilable within a single frame of vision. This accounts, perhaps, for what Guha condemns as "a conspicuous lack of proportion" in her writ-ing (2000a). Rob Nixon (2010) characterizes Roy's tactics more positively as "decentred" (77), comparing her to Edward Abbey and Jamaica Kincaid, who are, like Roy,

> cantankerous, rowdy, irreverent, but also tenderly specific, alternating
> between blasts of sarcasm, parody, vehemence and blunt anger, on the
> one hand, and, on the other, an evocative lyricism toward detailed life
> forms. Roy, Kincaid, and Abbey are all exponents of what Raymond
> Williams called "militant particularism," but are equally exponents of
> the calculated overgeneralisation. (77)

The juxtaposition of tender specificity and abstraction arguably works, in the sense of what Jacques Rancière (1995) has termed political aesthet-ics, unsettling the "distribution of the sensible," to make visible things that remain unseen in the general order of things (30).

AGAINST THE MIDDLE

In defending the legitimacy of traditional *adivasi* ways of life against this ideology, it is important not to confuse or conflate the aesthetic or romantic appeal of the small—which Roy was maybe guilty of in *The God of Small Things*—with the moral legitimacy of the tribals' fight to maintain sover-eignty over their lands, on which her work has increasingly focused.[7] There is also a case to be made for their position, and Roy's attempt to articulate it, with reference to scale, which is a crucial element in resilience ecology.

Resilience depends on an interplay between scales, which operate according to different temporal cycles that are calibrated within a larger system; to understand anything, then, we need to pay attention to what is going on at scales above and below observed phenomena. Part of what Roy tries to do in her writing is to illuminate those scales that are invisible in the normal view of things—i.e. mainstream media accounts of the war in the forest.

These include: the chironjee, silk cotton, and mango trees that begin to flower during her time in the forest (2011, 143); the "cowbells, snuffling, shuffling, cattle-farting" she hears as she falls asleep (53), and the list given to her by villagers "of seventy-one kinds of fruit, vegetables, pulses and insects they get from the forest and grow in their fields, along with the market price. It's just a list. But it's also a map of their world" (144). She also relates the history of state involvement in the area, solidified in the 1950 adoption of the Indian Constitution, which "ratified colonial policy and made the state custodian of tribal homelands" and "overnight [...] turned the entire tribal population into squatters on their own land" (43), thus connecting what is happening in the Dandakaranya forest with the displacement of tens of millions of people throughout the country over the last six decades to accommodate the "development" schemes of dams, mines, and irrigation projects (43). She further situates present conflicts within a temporal scale that exceeds secular history, explaining: "The low, flat-topped hills of south Orissa have been home to the Dongria Kondh long before there was a country called India or a state called Orissa. The hills watched over the Kondh. The Kondh watched over the hills and worshipped them as living deities. Now these hills have been sold for the bauxite they contain (1). Evoking the time of the gods exceeds the horizons of rational temporality, albeit in a conventional way. A more profound instance of temporal dissonance occurs in Roy's characterization of the four-lane highway "crashing through the forest" in Dantewada as "the opposite of a ghost" (39). The logic is simple: "if ghosts are the lingering spirits of someone or something that has ceased to exist," the highway is its opposite, "the harbinger of what is still to come" (39), but the formulation is unsettling in a more foundational way: the real is more and less than itself, Roy is suggesting, just as the present is not just the present, but a partial view of things, whose excision from a living network of past experience and future possibility involves a kind of violence.

It might seem like a bit of a stretch to use the ecological concept of scale to describe the range of Roy's focus. She is obviously no scientist (or historian, as Guha complains), and does not amplify the evidence available to our senses by telling us what is going on at the cellular or geological level. However her focus on the "big" and "small" scales that are normally concealed from view usefully unsettles the political perspective of the dominant middle. I mean this in more than one sense: first, Roy's account of the war in the forest upsets the legitimating narrative of India shining, based on the flourishing of the middle class. It does so by shedding light on the dynamic of state and corporate exploitation of tribals in which the economic possibilities and ideological virtue of the middle class is sandwiched. Second, her sympathy with the rebels affronts the sensibilities associated with that class, whose common sense encompasses the seemingly antithetical values of balance and radical mobility, in keeping with the imperative to keep buoyant India's fortunes in the system of global capitalism.

In describing this sensibility, I am drawing Andrew Pendakis's theorization of the emergence, over the last decades of the twentieth century, of a political position he calls the "radical middle." Thoroughly pragmatic, and immersed in the situation at hand, which it purports to see clearly, unfettered by political dogma, this perspective is characterized by its explicit rejection of the cautious conservatism traditionally hailed as the middle ground, in favor of dynamism and innovation. "One of the basic conceits of today's radical center," writes Pendakis, is its claim to have exited the dialectics of big and small for a nonconforming third option based on intelligent solutions (2010, 199). This approach to governance, characterized by boosts to industry, private-public partnerships, and a claw-back of social programs—coincident with a new emphasis on resilience (see Hoggett 2001)—has been a significant feature of India's development in the last two decades. Roy's writing destabilizes the normative view of this "middle" ground by documenting the violence that frames it.

EDGE EFFECTS

This documentary function is not just different from, but explicitly opposed to, popular texts like the film *Slumdog Millionaire* that celebrate the "amazing spirit and resilience" of the poor (Roy 2012, 13). Roy's sarcastic use of the word "resilience" to describe the made-for-export idea of India exemplified by *Slumdog* merits analysis. The "resilience" of the poor in this myth consists not just in their amazing capacity to survive—even to thrive—in the most brutal conditions but even, in some exemplary instances, to find in those conditions, cultivated by the virtues of pluck, doggedness, and entrepreneurial zeal, fertile ground from which to transform themselves into millionaires. Poverty in this narrative is not just a minor obstacle to be overcome, affirming the bourgeois value of hard work, but an essential structuring component of the story, what we might call its "catalyzing edge." The appeal of "poverty porn" is both aesthetic and moral, enabling a bracing encounter with suffering that excites the audience's sympathy while also providing an inoculatory effect: by encountering suffering (and diversity, and suffering *as* diversity) in this mediated form, we undergo a gentle transformation, contributing to our own resilience.

The practice of distilling and incorporating the survival strategies of the weak in order to enhance the strength, or, in this case, the resilience of the dominant group is familiar to scholars of colonialism. In the case of the war in the forest, Roy documents with mocking incredulity the military's establishment of a Counter-Terrorism and Jungle Warfare College (the motto: "Fight a guerilla like a guerilla"), whose goal, in Roy's words, is to "[turn] corrupt, sloppy policemen (straw) into jungle commandos (gold)" by teaching them to "run, slither, jump on and off airborne helicopters, ride horses (for some reason), eat snakes and live off the jungle" (2011, 49). The military's crude, even comical attempt to figure out how to live in the forest like indigenous people complicates a charge often leveled at Roy that she's engaged in (Guha again) a "romantic celebration of *adivasi* lifestyles" (2000a).

In support of Roy's defense of tribal peoples, Rob Nixon (2010) notes that, whether they inhabit floodplains or deserts (or in this case forests), "to live adaptively on the land through cycles of mobility makes environmental and nutritional sense" (74), to which he adds a qualification: "To say as much is not to romanticise ways of life that are often arduous, fraught with danger, and may at times result in resource mismanagement. [...] However the perils of mobile adaptation to the risky, unpredictable provisions of river, flood plain and the forest they sustain pale besides the perils of the life of the megadam refugee. (74, n. 40). Or any environmental refugee, for that matter. In defending the subsistence lifestyles of *adivasi*, Nixon, along with Roy, is describing a model of complex adaptation, which consists in constant negotiation with diverse and overlapping cycles of a changing environment, and stands in stark contrast to the crude and violent vision of innovation that has come to dominate Indian, no less than North American, society, and which legitimates the displacement of tribal people from their land as a benevolent effort to help them adjust to the "inevitable" changes of capitalist modernity.[8]

It's tempting, and to some extent legitimate, to think about subsistence and capitalism as embodying two rival versions of resilience, or two different kinds of "edgework," to borrow a term from sociology. The first, most familiar, use of the term in that discipline describes a rigorously managed confrontation with uncertainty in which the goal is to approach as closely as possible, without actually crossing, the line between life and death. Along with skills specific to particular risk activities (such as extreme sport), edgeworkers demonstrate "a form of mental toughness that is crucial for maintaining control over situations and people most people see as completely uncontrollable," along with "flexibility—the ability to 'ad hoc' a response and avoid crossing the line between form and formlessness" (Lyng 2009, 112). Edgework in this formulation mobilizes a concept of resilience that resonates with the risk-taking behavior of stock traders; indeed sociologists note a noncoincidental historical correlation over the last few decades between the burgeoning of edgework and the intensification of neoliberalism (128).[9]

In ecology, the concept of edges has a different resonance, but one that is also associated with enhanced resilience. As zones of transition between two different habitats or stages of succession, edges, or ecotones, are associated with high levels of biodiversity and interchange (Odum 2004, 517), whose benefits are seen increasingly to accrue to human societies who inhabit them. Edges are "zones of social interaction, cross-fertilization, and synergy" (Turner et al. 2003, 440), whose inhabitants have "a greater capacity for flexibility" (439). Terms such as "resources," "capacity," "synergy," and "capital" help to bridge the hyphen between "social" and "ecological" in the increasingly familiar term "social-ecological resilience."[10] Edge effects are not all benign; some species do better on edges than others, and not all edges are conducive to biodiversity. The accelerating fragmentation of ecosystems by large-scale forestry, agriculture and mining, erode rather than enhance biodiversity, and disrupt the complex feedback mechanisms on which social as well as ecological systems' resilience depends. Ecological resilience theory insists on recognizing a complexity that is frequently denied in popular adoptions of the concept.

Extracting the meaning of ecological resilience from neoliberalism isn't that simple, however. Edges in ecology are grounded in places, where distinct networks of life counter the totalizing (and individualist) opposition between being and nothingness in the sociological concept of edgework. However there is a sense in which ecology is similarly totalizing, wedded to the concept of the complex adaptive system that itself has no edges but is rather infinitely incorporative. It is this tendency among other things that Jeremy Walker and Melinda Cooper (2011) suggest informs the "intuitive ideological fit" of resilience ecology with theories of natural volatility that inform neoliberal economic policy (144).

Emerging in the 1970s, resilience theory and neoliberal economic theory each addressed, from different premises, the limits of top-down management in forestalling crisis in complex systems. While ecological resilience theory highlighted the liabilities of models of ecological management based on maximum sustainable yields, neoliberal economic theory asserted that, in the words of Friedrich Hayek, "the natural complexity of market phenomena was such that no centralized authority could hope to predict, much less control, the precise evolution of individual elements in the system" (Walker and Cooper 2011, 149). Hayek challenged the Keynesian welfare state, a variant, as he saw it, of central planning, to predict or manage economic conditions. Far from forestalling serious crises, he argued, these policies were more likely to cause it by stifling its inherent variability. The market, in this formulation, assumes the unquestioned priority of a natural ecosystem, for which volatility is not an external threat to be managed, but an inherent feature of its resilience and one that must be protected at all costs.

Thus Walker and Cooper describe the emergence of a security industry whose prime function is to increase the resilience of "critical infrastructure" to a slew of threats, including terrorism, disease, natural disasters, and financial crises (2011, 153; see also Lakoff 2007, 267). Crisis-prevention is hereby replaced by a "'culture' of resilience, and management strategies that, as they put it, "replace the short-term relief effort [...] with a call to permanent adaptability in and through crisis" (Walker and Cooper 2011, 154). Walker and Cooper cite the ironically termed "'regeneration'" of

New Orleans, post-Hurricane Katrina, with its "selective-exclusion of the African-American poor" as an example of this kind of strategy (154). The displacement of tribal people in India to accommodate development projects such as mega-dams and mines is another. In both cases, the security imperative of enhancing the "critical infrastructure" (a concept that conveniently blurs the distinction between public utilities and private enterprises) legitimates the removal of people seen as impediments to the project. This can be positively spun by appealing to the value of resilience, not only of the nation, but also of the *adivasis* themselves, whose survival the state, and many commentators on both the left and the right, maintain, depends on integration into capitalist modernity. Resilience here, as Walker and Cooper have it, "risks being the measure of one's fitness to survive in the turbulent order of things" (157).

The resilience of this model of resilience thinking is both political, in its amenability to neoliberalism, and epistemological, in its capacity for infinite expansion and reflexivity, such that the critique that characterized resilience ecology is reabsorbed into the workings of systems theory itself (Walker and Cooper 2011, 157). "'Resilience thinking'" Walker and Cooper conclude, "cannot be challenged from within the terms of complex systems theory but must be contested, if at all, on completely different terms, by a movement of thought that is truly counter-systemic" (157). To conclude, I will suggest ways in which *Walking with the Comrades* participates in such a counter-systemic movement.

What is needed is a different, a third, model of "edgework," one that is crucial to the environmental humanities, but takes its immediate inspiration from Wendy Brown's 2005 essay collection *Edgework: Critical Essays on Knowledge and Politics*. A key objective of Brown's project is to explore the limits of prevailing ways of imagining present crises, and the capacity of critique to forward the aims of justice. I think this is also Roy's project, one that speaks to the form as well as the content of *Walking With the Comrades*. The trope of walking situates the story Roy is telling in a particular time and place: in radical contrast to the extreme activity usually signaled by edgework, walking is slow and can (though does not always) facilitate an attentive engagement with physical surroundings. Most importantly, she walks *with* the comrades in a spirit of solidarity, in the recognition—however provisional—of their claim as custodians of the future of the forest.

The groundedness of this activity is essential, in the sense not just of observing at first hand the forest ecology but also of giving the Marxist politics espoused by the rebels (which represents a different kind of materialism) a local inflection. This is critical first in terms of refuting charges of anti-historical romanticism that have been leveled at her by urban Marxists. In describing the delicate coalition of soldiers and farmers that is emerging in the forest, Roy says:

> It's not an Alternative yet, this idea of Gram Swaraj with a Gun. There is too much hunger, too much sickness here. But it has certainly created

the possibilities for an alternative. Not for the whole world, not for Alaska or New Delhi, nor even perhaps for the whole of Chhasttisgarh, but for itself. For Dandakaranya [....] Against the greatest odds it has forged a blueprint for its own survival. It needs help and imagination, it needs doctors, teachers, farmers.

It does not need war.

But if war is all it gets, it will fight back. (2011, 132)

Roy concurs with the Maoists in identifying the corporate and state operations in the forest as war, under the guise of benign development. However the "blueprint for survival" she cites is based not just on the science of Marxism (as totalizing in a different way as the theory of complex adaptive systems) but primarily on the integrity and fragility of life—both cultural and ecological—in the Dandakaranya forest.

A significant wrinkle in the story arises in the figure of Roy herself, both the partiality of her perspective, as an outsider with neither indigenous nor specialist knowledge, and her status *as* a figure, whose celebrity arguably distorts the currency of her story (granting it greater or less legitimacy depending on your perspective). From the start, it is clear that she is out of her comfort zone: waiting to meet her contact, she recalls, "I wondered if someone was watching me and having a laugh" (2011, 51), and later, as she enters the forest, notes "I had no idea where we were going" (51). Her ability to engage with the beauty of her surroundings is compromised by the difficulty of navigating them: as the first day turns into night, she reports:

I long to look up at the night sky, but I dare not. I have to keep my eyes on the ground. One step at a time. Concentrate.

I hear dogs. But I can't tell how far away they are. The terrain flattens out. I steal a look at the sky. It makes me ecstatic. I hope we're going to stop soon. (53)

Her narrative is laced with doubt, conveyed in the repetition of phrases that convey lack of knowledge—"I don't know" or "I can't tell"—and with confounded expectations, not least regarding the comrades themselves, who emerge alternately as more human and more brutal than she anticipates. And when she sounds confident, it often comes across as awkward, such as when she says of one of the Maoists: "from the way she hugs me I can tell she is a reader. And that she misses having books in the jungle" (62).

An ungenerous reading, following Guha, would see this comment as a display of Roy's extreme vanity. More charitably, one could read it as debunking stereotypes of the Maoists as naïve children or ignorant thugs. There is perhaps some truth in both interpretations, but a third is also possible: the image of reading as a vector of connection between Roy and Comrade

Maase interrupts the flow of her narrative, drawing attention away from the main action of the story (the Maoists, the forest), to lodge uncomfortably in the domain of representation, and the act of interpretation that marks her encounter with the Maoists and our encounter with her story. Reading is not just a source of sustenance and connection—though it is that.[11] It is also an encounter with otherness, a friction of misapprehension and appropriation, accommodation and surprise.[12] It is a kind of edgework that takes place not between being and nothingness but between different registers of knowledge—a distinction that becomes particularly crucial in the forests of Danyakaranya.

This returns us to the meeting that inaugurates Roy's story, the meeting that almost didn't happen. In order to understand the "complex adaptive system" of the forest—one that encompasses the lived texture and history of its inhabitants along with the mining and military operations that threaten their violent displacement, it is necessary to walk with the Maoists. The walk is the most recent stage in the path Roy has taken away from the one she set out on in *The God of Small Things*—a powerful imaginative defense of the resilience of fragile human and natural ecologies. Roy is still interested in resilience here but recognizes that the "creativity" that is a much vaunted part of resilience, as it is familiarly understood and increasingly called for, has become fuel to the expansion and intensification of neoliberalism. In order to expose this process, Roy trades in her novelist's perspective for that of the clerk and aligns her narrative sympathies with the revolutionaries whose doctrines she playfully pulled apart in her fiction. What emerges is not synergy; the distance between herself and the Maoists never quite closes, and the story never quite coheres, in theme or form, around a singular meaning. It is, however, an example of the kind of critical "edgework" that is vital to discussions of resilience, inviting us to consider not just how to achieve it, but also what we mean by it, and whether it is the best value to guide us in our inquiry into possible, desirable, postcolonial, and ecological futures.

NOTES

1. See, for example, Zebrowski (2009), Joseph (2013), Evans and Reid (2014).
2. Padmini Mongria (2007) offered an early, incisive commentary on Roy's international celebrity in a paper presented at the 1997 "India: Fifty Years After" conference in Barcelona. See also Huggan (2001).
3. That Devi, the recipient of numerous literary awards, has never received the kind of attention that Roy has, is a matter of critical concern (Lal 2003). It is also worth noting that, while Devi enjoys a large and growing following among postcolonial academics, Roy's nonfiction has received comparatively little academic attention; even as her star has fallen in India, she is more likely to be taken up as a case study of postcolonial celebrity than a serious author (Rao 2008).

4. The latter refers specifically to Roy's lack of due respect for judges of the Supreme Court, whose impartiality she criticized during hearings into the progress of the dam.

5. To protest the enlistment of art in the service of propaganda, and to shame the artists who had agreed to participate as judges, a group of activists sponsored a competition for videos satirizing the project under the title "Faking Happiness."

6. In solidarity with clerkdom, Andrew Pendakis (2010) suggests: "We have to remember that the difference between *what is* and *what could be* is sublimely boring; it requires a tenacity that is quiet, persistent, determinate and sweet. Which is to say that, in the age of the manager-heretic there may be nothing more revolutionary than a bureaucrat" (216–17).

7. In the case of the Dongria Kondh, the Supreme Court of India upheld this principle, determining in 2013 that Vedanta had embarked on its bauxite mine without sufficient consultation. Following a referendum in which all twelve affected villages rejected the mine, the Ministry for Environment and Forests quashed the project (Woodman 2014).

8. In light of the fifty million people displaced by development projects, only a fraction of whom have been resettled (2011, 19), Roy notes "when the government begins to talk of tribal welfare, it's time to worry" (43).

9. John Coates's *The Hour Between Dog and Wolf* (2012) identifies neurochemical similarities between traders and extreme athletes—a compelling idea that does not address the significance that it is the present historical conjuncture that has allowed both to flourish.

10. DeLoughrey, Didur, and Carrigan note problems with this term in the Introduction to this volume.

11. The pieces of paper that arrive in daily batches communicating information from other branches of the movement are called "biscuits," the name highlighting the capacity of information to serve as sustenance—an ambiguity that interestingly inverts the situation of the banana that, intended as code, ended up becoming food.

12. I use the word "friction" here in Anna Tsing's sense of "the awkward, unequal, unstable and creative qualities of interconnection across difference" (2005, 3).

REFERENCES

Brown, Wendy. 2005. *Edgework: Critical Essays on Knowledge and Politics*. Princeton: Princeton University Press.

Chaudhury, Shoma. 2012. "The Shape of the Beast." *Tehelka* 9 (44). http://www.tehelka.com/the-shape-of-the-beast/.

Coates, John. 2012. *The Hour Between Dog and Wolf: Risk Taking, Gut Feeling and the Biology of Boom and Bust*. Toronto: Random House.

Evans, Brad, and Julian Reid. 2014. *Resilient Life: The Art of Living Dangerously*. Cambridge: Polity.

Folke, Carl. 2006. "Resilience: The Emergence of a Perspective for Social-Ecological Systems Analysis." *Global Environmental Change* 16: 253–267.

Folke, Carl, Steve Carpenter, Brian Walker, Marten Scheffer, Thomas Elmquist, Lance Gunderson, and C.S. Hollling. 2004. "Regime Shifts, Resilience, and

Biodiversity in Ecosystem Management." *Annual Review of Ecology, Evolution, and Systematics* 35: 557–581.

Guha, Ramachandra. 2000a. "The Arun Shourie of the Left" *The Hindu*, November 26. http://www.hindu.com/2000/11/26/stories/13260411.htm.

———. 2000b. "Perils of Extremism." Letters. *The Hindu*, December 17. http://www.hindu.com/2000/12/17/stories/1317061b.htm.

Hoggett, Paul. 2001. "Agency, Rationality and Social Policy." *Journal of Social Policy* 30: 37–56.

Holling, C. S. 1986. "The Resilience of Terrestrial Ecosystems: Local Surprise and Global Change." In *Sustainable Development of the Biosphere*, ed. W.C. Clarke and R. E. Munn. 292–316. Cambridge: Cambridge University Press.

———. 2009. "Interview with Buzz Holling." *Stockholm Resilience Centre*. June 2. http://www.stockholmresilience.org/21/research/research-videos/2–6–2009-interview-with-buzz-holling.html.

Holling, C. S., Lance Gunderson, and Garry D. Peterson. 2001. "Sustainability and Panarchies." In *Panarchy: Understanding Transformations in Human and Natural Systems*, ed. Lance Gunderson and C. S. Holling. 63–102. Washington: Island Press.

Huggan, Graham. 2001. *The Postcolonial Exotic: Marketing the Margins*. Abingdon: Routledge.

"Jaipur LitFest gave opportunity to display our values: Tata Steel." 2013. NDTV. February 2. http://www.ndtv.com/video/player/just-books/jaipur-lit-fest-gave-opportunity-to-convey-our-values-tata-steel/263847.

Lakoff, Andrew. 2007. "Preparing for the Next Emergency." *Public Culture* 19 (2): 257–271.

Lal, Priya. 2003. "Crossing Borders, Writing Back: The Work of Arundhati Roy and Mahasweta Devi. *Pop Matters*. July 24. http://www.popmatters.com/column/lal030724/.

Lyng, Stephen. 2009. "Edgework, Risk and Uncertainty." *Social Theories of Risk and Uncertainty: An Introduction*, edited by Jens O. Zinn. 106–37. Malden: Wiley-Blackwell.

Joseph, Jonathan. 2013. "Resilience as Embedded Neoliberalism: A Governmentality Approach." *Resilience* 1 (1): 38–52.

Mongia, Padmini. 2007. "The Making and Marketing of Arundhati Roy." In *Arundhati Roy's The God of Small Things: A Routledge Study Guide*, edited by Alex Tickle, 103–09. Abingdon: Routledge.

Nixon, Rob. 2010. "Unimagined Communities: Developmental Refugees, Megadams, and Monumental Modernity." *New Formations* 69 (3): 62–80.

Odum, Eugene, Richard Brewer, and Gary W. Bennett. (1953) 2004. *Fundamentals of Ecology*. 5th ed. Pacific Grove: Thomson Brooks Cole.

"Orissa Tribals to Continue Opposing Tata Steel Project." 2011. *The Hindu*, January 3. http://www.thehindu.com/todays-paper/tp-national/orissa-tribals-to-continue-opposing-tata-steel-project/article1026068.ece.

Pendakis, Andrew. 2010. "The Dialectics of Middleness: Towards a Political Ontology of Centrism." Dissertation. McMaster University. http://digitalcommons.mcmaster.ca/dissertations/AAINR73972/.

Rancière, Jacques. 1995. *Disagreement: Politics and Philosophy*. Translated by Julie Rose. Minneapolis: University of Minnesota Press.

Rao, Nagesh. 2008. "The Politics of Genre and the Rhetoric of Radical Cosmopolitanism; or, Who's Afraid of Arundhati Roy?" *Prose Studies* 30 (2): 159–176.

Roy, Arundhati. 1997. *The God of Small Things*. Toronto: Vintage, 1998.

———. 2009. *Field Notes on Democracy: Listening to Grasshoppers*. Chicago: Haymarket.

———. 2010. "Can We Leave the Bauxite in the Mountain? Field Notes on Democracy." Public lecture. Harvard University, Cambridge. April 1. https://www.youtube.com/watch?v=22LNT3H_YjY.

———. 2011. *Walking with the Comrades*. London: Penguin.

———. 2012. "Capitalism: A Ghost Story." *Outlook India*, March 26.

"Singur Land Should Be Returned to Farmers: Supreme Court to Tata Motors." 2013. *NDTV*. July 10. http://www.ndtv.com/article/india/singur-land-should-be-returned-to-farmers-supreme-court-to-tata-motors-390222.

Tata Steel Ltd. 2011. *Creating Value for the Community: Corporate Sustainability Report, 2009–10*. http://www.tatasteel.com/sustainability/pdf/csr-09-10.pdf.

Tripath, Purnima S. 2012. "Battle for Bastar." *Frontline* 29 (8). http://www.frontline.in/static/html/fl2908/stories/20120504290803200.htm.

Tsing, Anna. 2005. *Friction: An Ethnography of Global Connection*. Princeton: Princeton University Press.

Turner, Nancy J., Iain J. Davidson-Hunt, Michael O'Flaherty. 2003. "Living on the Edge: Ecological and Cultural Edges as Sources of Diversity for Social-Ecological Resilience." *Human Ecology* 31 (3): 439–460.

Walker, Brian, and David Salt. 2006. *Resilience Thinking: Sustaining Ecosystems and People in a Changing World*. Washington: Island Press.

Walker, Jeremy, and Melinda Cooper. 2011. "Genealogies of Resilience: From Systems Ecology to the Political Economy of Crisis Adaptation." *Security Dialogues* 42 (2): 143–161.

Woodman, Jo. 2014. "India's Rejection of Vedanta's Bauxite Mine is a Victory for Tribal Rights." *The Guardian*. January 14. http://www.theguardian.com/global-development/poverty-matters/2014/jan/14/india-rejection-vedanta-mine-victory-tribal-rights.

Zebrowski, Christopher. 2009. "Governing the Network Society: A Biopolitical Critique of Resilience." *Political Perspectives*, 3 (1). http://www.politicalperspectives.org.uk/wp-content/uploads/2010/08/Vol3–1–2009–4.pdf.

9 Filming the Emergence of Popular Environmentalism in Latin America

Postcolonialism and Buen Vivir

Jorge Marcone

On September 28, 2011, the British newspaper *The Guardian* published in its US online edition an unexpected piece of news regarding politics in South America. The day before, tens of thousands of Bolivians had taken to the streets to decry the perceived betrayal by Bolivia's first indigenous president, Evo Morales, of his prime constituencies: native groups and environmentalists. The people were responding to the violent police action of a few days earlier that broke up a march by indigenous protestors against a proposed highway that would run through a protected Amazon reserve ("Bolivians March" 2011). In 2010, recalled *The Guardian*, Morales decided to pursue a 190–200 mile (300–310 km), $420-million jungle highway funded by Brazil through the Isiboro-Secure Indigenous Territory National Park (TIPNIS), in the eastern lowlands state of Beni. About 1,000 people began a march on La Paz, Bolivia's capital, in mid-August from Beni's capital, Trinidad, to protest against a decision that they viewed as an open invitation to loggers and coca-planting settlers, and overall a threat to human and nonhuman park inhabitants. A government crisis followed this incident of violent repression. Bolivia's defense minister resigned immediately in protest, and the interior minister followed, accepting responsibility for police actions. Morales himself suspended the highway project, and promised to let voters in the affected region decide the future of the highway in a referendum.

The government's policy on the highway seemed to contradict other actions taken by Morales's regime. In 2009, Morales had championed a new constitution that granted autonomy to Bolivia's thirty-six indigenous groups. He also promised to protect indigenous people from industry and developers. Indeed, the Morales administration, recognized *The Guardian*, promotes some of the most progressive environmental policies of any government in the world. Internationally, Bolivia is heralded for these innovative policies. But since winning the election in December 2005, Morales has been forced to weigh development against environmental protection. Other Latin American countries, including those currently governed by the "new" or "progressive" Left that were raised to power as a consequence of popular discontent with neoliberal policies, are facing the same dilemma. How can nations that are dependent on natural resource extraction for income—that would be devoted to social policies against poverty—chart an environmentally conscious course towards economic development and justice?

Popular environmental struggles, in rural and urban settings, indigenous or not, have been the focus of a significant number of documentaries released within the last fifteen years. The majority of these documentaries narrate, in an epic or even melodramatic mode, the resistance of a diversity of social movements against irresponsible and corrupt practices by transnational corporations and state officials that threaten these peoples' territorial rights and access to natural resources and pollute their environments. Nevertheless, this environmental activism still remains mostly unnoticed by the general public, within and outside Latin America, even though it has played a prominent role in opposing neoliberal policies of natural resource extraction and in renewing the agenda of the political Left in Latin America. Thus, the first goal of this chapter, following Robert JC Young's defense of postcolonial studies on the basis of the visibility of the marginalized that it fosters (Young 2012, 23), is to call further attention to the kind of visibility that the films facilitate for these movements. This visibility agrees with Young's assertion that postcolonial studies need to engage more with contemporary indigenous struggles, particularly the way these collectivities may envision societal pluralism. In a way, this popular environmentalism is an attempt by its activists not to become the migrant and hybrid subaltern of the global economy that, according to Dipesh Chakrabarty, has been the main focus of postcolonial studies (Chakrabarty 2012, 7–8). On the other hand, these indigenous movements also involve building transnational and interethnic alliances with other environmentalist and indigenous or nonindigenous groups and resorting to a diversity of narratives, discourses, and media for shaping responses to environmental crisis and transformation, and conceptualizing alternatives to current practices.

Secondly, the representation in film of the emergence of popular environmentalism in Latin America posits some challenges to the postcolonial that can be phrased in the same way Chakrabarty evaluates postcolonial studies in the Anthropocene: postcolonial critiques are not irrelevant or redundant but are insufficient (Chakrabarty 2012, 9). In this case, however, the insufficiency does not concern Chakrabarty's efforts to introduce the notion of the human as geological force; rather it relates to the frequent neglect in the films of the more-than-human ontologies and temporalities associated with indigenous politics in Latin America. In a familiar postcolonial vein, the documentaries prefer to focus on critical moments of local resistance to global and state forces, and on protest against the exclusion of indigenous actors in the decision-making process regarding uses of territory by the national state. Unfortunately, the films offer only a glimpse of different ways of the human interacting with the nonhuman. Just as is happening today in the environmental humanities and postcolonial studies, indigenous movements are revisiting the relation of the human to the nonhuman particularly because of the political implications such distinctions hold for their struggles for territory and autonomy at local, national, and planetary levels. They have introduced into political debates about the nation-state different ontologies of the human, the nonhuman, and their inter-relationship, which conflict with the underlying ideologies of economic development. As anthropologist Marisol de la Cadena has argued for Andean indigeneities in twenty-first-century Latin America, these actors and their discourses "may inaugurate a different politics, plural not because they are enacted by bodies marked by gender, race, ethnicity, or sexuality demanding rights, or by environmentalists representing nature, but because they bring earth-beings to the political, and force into visibility the antagonism that proscribed their worlds" (De la Cadena 2010, 346). The struggles represented in these documentaries are just limited illustrations of larger more-than-environmental social movements whose existence and political ontologies, paradoxically, remain silenced in the films although they underlie them.

The context of conflict, illustrated in the opening anecdote, speaks of the complexity that permeates decolonial politics, which also impacts upon popular environmentalisms, indigenous and nonindigenous. Nowadays, the popular environmentalism portrayed in the documentaries is caught at a crossroads between the still influential neoliberal extractivism, on the one hand, and the rise of a "new extractivism" among leftist governments, on the other. Once again, but this time coming from "friend" and not foe, the question of whether environmentalism and ecological thinking, particularly indigenous episte-mologies and ontologies about the nonhuman, are part of the solution of social exclusion and poverty has been raised at many levels of national politics. The significant economic growth that has come out of the globalization of national economies in Latin America in the last decades has impressively reduced the quantitative indicators of extreme poverty and unemployment. In turn, this "success" is putting pressure on environmentalist and decolonial agendas, even under "progressive" and "nationalist" governments that still resort to such discourses and co-opt them for their own immediate purposes.

In the following sections, we look at how the films stage and contribute to popular environmental movements, how they fail to reference consis-tently more-than-human ontologies, and what this might mean for analyz-ing these documentaries under the rubric of a postcolonial environmental humanities. We also consider the most emblematic and maybe influential indigenous popular environmentalism currently in Latin America, the plurality of activism and discourses gathered under the umbrella term of *Buen Vivir*. Although the Buen Vivir movement is not behind every single documentary, it will serve us as an alternative frame for thinking through the politics of the human and the nonhuman that has so far remained in the background of postcolonial studies, and that is challenging neoliberal and leftist politics alike.

SLOW WARS

A corpus of documentaries released within the last fifteen years on recent popular environmental struggles would include, among others, the following Latin American countries: *The Water is Ours, Damn It!* (Sheila Franklin, Bolivia, 2000); *Choropampa: The Price of Gold* (Stephanie Boyd and Ernesto Cabellos, Peru, 2002); *Switch Off* (Manuel Mayol, Chile, 2005); *The Power of Community: How Cuba Survived Peak Oil* (Faith Morgan, Cuba, 2006); *Cartoneros* (Ernesto Livon-Grosman, Argentina, 2006); *Recycled Life* (Leslie Iwerks and Mike Glad, USA/Guatemala, 2006); *Tambogrande: Mangos, Murder, and Mining* (Ernesto Cabellos Damián and Stephanie Boyd, USA/ Peru, 2006); *A Convenient Truth: Urban Solutions from Curitiba* (Giovanni Vaz del Bello, Brazil, 2007); *Thirteen Villages Defending Water, Air and Land* (Francesco Taboada Tabone, Mexico, 2008); *When Clouds Clear* (Danielle Bernstein and Anne Slick, USA/Ecuador, 2008); *The Trees Have a Mother* (Juan Carlos Galeano and Valliere Richard Auzenne, USA/Peru, 2008); *Crude: The Real Price of Oil* (Joe Berlinger, USA/Ecuador, 2009); *La travesía de Chumpi* (Fernando Valdivia, Peru, 2009); *Waste Land* (Lucy Walker, UK/ Brazil, 2010); *Yasuní. El Buen Vivir* (Arturo Hortas, Ecuador, 2012); *Garbage or Resource? A Dominican Republic Experience* (Natasha Despotovic, Dominican Republic, 2013); and *Fighting for the Futaleufú* (Stephanie Haig, Chile, 2013). In these narratives, there is a major focus on disasters or fear of risks related to toxicity derived from new large-scale extractive industries and urban development sponsored by national governments and financed by transnational capital. The documentaries concentrate on what Rob Nixon has successfully called *slow violence*, or the plurality of overlapping consequences due to environmental degradation that extend in time and space. Environmental slow violence is the reality or risk that these communities anticipate and seek to prevent.

The concept of violence, argues Rob Nixon in *Slow Violence and the Environmentalism of the Poor* (2011), is not always a "highly visible act, event focused, time bound, body bound" (3). Rather, slow violence implies attritional catastrophes that overspill clear boundaries in time and space. It should include too, I would argue in light of these documentaries, the war of attrition carried out by transnational corporations and even national governments against the resistance by locals and their transnational allies. Slow violence is not just attritional but also exponential: "it can fuel long-term, proliferating conflicts in situations where the conditions for sustaining life become increasingly but gradually degraded" (Nixon 2011, 3). Of course, slow violence posits political and legal challenges when the consequences of such actions will not accrue to the perpetrators. In addition to the impact of pollution, the long-term consequences of displacement, either due to migration or to loss of access to the land and its resources, qualify too as slow violence. Often the threatened community capitulates and is scattered. Or, as in the case of our documentaries, the community refuses to move or is incapable of doing so, but its world is undermined, effectively making it a community of refugees in place (Nixon 2011, 19). The concept of slow violence thus interprets the environmental degradation caused by extractivism and development as a deliberate aggression against those perceived as expendable, and not as the unfortunate collateral damage of progress or of national interests. Importantly, the notion of slow violence is often prefigured in the movements themselves as the very risk they are trying to avoid by resisting the takeover of their land.

Another entry point to the resistance depicted in these documentaries is the concept of the *environmentalism of the poor* developed by Joan Martínez-Alier (2003). He also refers to these social movements as forms of "popular environmentalism," "environmental justice," "livelihood ecology," or "liberation ecology," even if these groups do not call themselves "environmentalists." Martínez-Alier's analysis starts by calling attention to the fact that, for these groups, the environment is a source and requirement for livelihood. And that more often than not the "locals" are neither the beneficiaries of Western development, nor partners on sustainable cultural and environmental projects. Furthermore, the ecological disruption, adds Martínez-Alier, is co-extensive with damage to the social fabric. One common feature, notes he, is that often these communities or alliances of communities assert their rights on the basis of indigenous and historical territorial rights, but they also resort to discourses on the sacredness of Nature and Life, or to other "discredited" philosophies of Nature, from a modern point of view, risking the taint of superstition, animism, vitalism, and anthropomorphism. Taking into consideration Martínez-Alier's observations, Nixon alerts us to how although the neoliberal era has intensified assaults on resources, resistance has intensified too, "whether through isolated site-specific struggles or through activism that has reached across national boundaries in an effort to build translocal alliances" (2011, 4). In any case, these communities have to patch together improvised alliances against "vastly superior military, corporate, and media forces" (4). These "resource rebels," therefore, cannot afford to be focused on a single issue: their environmental interests "are seamed through with other economic and cultural causes as they experience environmental threat not as a planetary abstraction but as a set of inhabited risks" (4).

In February 2011, an Ecuadorian judge ordered Chevron to pay an $8.6 billion fine and an equal amount in punitive damages to 30,000 Amazonian residents represented by the *Frente de Defensa de la Amazonía*, an alliance of Ecuadorean indigenous and nonindigenous peoples. After more than ten years of litigation, Chevron was found responsible for dumping billions of gallons of toxic oil waste into the Ecuadorean Amazon. This fine is the second-largest total assessed for environmental damages behind the $20 billion compensation fund for BP's Gulf of Mexico oil spill. Immediately, Chevron vowed to appeal, and suggested that it would not pay under any circumstance. At the time, Chevron was closing its operations in the Ecuadoran rainforest. The plaintiffs announced that they planned to appeal because, to their understanding, the fine was too low. The story of the long struggle that led to this event is related by director Joe Berlinger in *Crude: The Real Price of Oil* (2009).

The litigation started with a lawsuit initially filed in 1993 in New York, when Amazonian residents sued Texaco, which was then purchased by Chevron. The slow violence against Amazonian indigenous and nonindigenous peoples, however, started more than twenty years earlier. By 1972, Texaco had built a trans-Andean pipeline, which connected its Amazonian oil fields with a Pacific port. Over the years, Texaco left behind more than three hundred oil wells, about nine hundred open waste pits, twenty-two processing facilities, numerous pumping stations, and an oil refinery. The open waste pits consist of deposits of wastes that surface during the drilling process—sludge, water, and unusable heavy crude— along with untreated chemical muds and industrial solvents essential for drilling. Unlined and open, these pits have allowed toxic chemicals to seep and overflow into water and soil systems throughout the region, severely contaminating the environment and jeopardizing the lives of local people. In addition to the pollution, this industry impacted on the region through the network of roads linking oil wells that facilitated the homesteading of the region by more than 200,000 poor Spanish-speaking farmers or *colonos* (colonists). After a ten-year legal battle in the US federal court in New York, Texaco/Chevron won a legal motion in 2002 to have the case relocated to Ecuador.

In *Tambogrande: Mangos, Murder, Mining* (2006), Ernesto Cabellos Damián and Stephanie Boyd tell the story of an alliance of communities reunited with the main purpose of stopping the extraction of gold under the town of San Lorenzo, and surrounding agricultural land in Northern Peru by the Canadian corporation Manhattan Minerals, or Manhattan Sechura. The *Frente de Defensa*, on this occasion, was a union of peasants, urban dwellers, and other social actors willing to join in defending San Lorenzo, and the agricultural land reclaimed from the desert by landless peasants who migrated to the area several generations ago for cultivating mangos, lemons, oranges, and mandarins. At the time when the documentary was filmed, the *Frente* was claiming that the locals were running a profitable agricultural business. Initially, the *Frente* responded with some ambiguity to the acts of violence triggered by the cheap compensation offered by Manhattan Sechura to the displaced San Lorenzo residents, and to the racist overtones in their communications. An angry mob burnt some of the new houses that the company had built for those willing to move out from San Lorenzo. However, after the unresolved assassination of Godofredo García Baca, one of its legendary leaders, the *Frente* carried out a nonviolent campaign, political and cultural, that drew the attention of the national media. As much as it was battling against Manhattan Sechura, the *Frente* was also combatting the national government which the local residents found to be an accomplice of the transnational corporation, rather than a defender of the interests of the people. In 2002, the government agreed to a referendum but only 1.3 percent of the population voted in favor of the mine. In 2003, the project was officially cancelled by the government of Peru.

In *Thirteen Villages Defending Water, Air and Land* (2008), Francesco Taboada Tabone narrates the activism of an alliance of indigenous communities in the state of Morelos, south of Mexico City. The documentary focuses on two struggles in particular. The first one is the attempt by the government to privatize a local aquifer that has provided the communities with potable water for generations. Back in the 1930s, the communities built an aqueduct with the support of the then president Lázaro Cárdenas. Now the government wants to appropriate these waters for supplying a new suburban development. The second environmental conflict is a government plan for opening a garbage dump nearby the city of Cuernavaca that would pollute the land of indigenous and nonindigenous farmers. In both cases, the people are struggling mainly against the authoritarianism and corruption of the national and the state governments. The locals claim to own, or to have priority over, natural resources due to their historical connection to the land: the sustainability of their communities depends on the stewardship of the land that the communities and farmers have practiced until now based on indigenous knowledge and values. The recent conflicts, they argue, are just episodes of the same colonialism that started more than five hundred years ago. Six years after the documentary was released, the thirteen towns are still confronting governmental development plans. Today, the community of Tepoztlán is again up in arms fighting the construction of a new highway that would cut across a Protected Natural Area within its territory.

Many of the struggles portrayed in these documentaries have several features in common. The fundamental one is the communities' activism against governmental decisions with dangerous consequences, real or potential, for their welfare and future; and against a decision-making process that excludes them. In these films, a diversity of local stakeholders who are in conflict with each other regarding the access and use of the land, set differences aside and reunite in *Frentes de Defensa*. Their members are interested in securing their territorial rights and in holding to the land as a source of livelihood and community. Their control over the land and its resources is seen as an alternative to the exaggerated or even real benefits of the jobs and income that would come with the large-scale development projects, or to the inevitable migration to the city that would follow after the industry stops employing locals or when they are left with a deteriorated environment. The communities' leaders have developed a deep mistrust of corporations and of their own national governments, based on their own memory or information from other communities with negative experiences of both actors. In their discourse, these *Frentes* debate the meaning of "development," and confront the capitalist growth model for its devastating environmental costs, and for the social inequities brought about by that degradation. Often in these documentaries, popular leaders deliberately connect the past history of European colonization to the current neoliberal or "New Left" policies sanctioned by the state through which their rights to natural resources are under attack, and the health of individuals and the social fabric of communities are degraded. This tension, in turn, leads these *Frentes* to demand ways of effectively participating in the creation of policies that affect them most. Of these movements, we may say what anthropologist Suzana Sawyer argued about the Ecuadorean case in her *Crude Chronicles: Indigenous Politics, Multinational Oil, and Neoliberalism in Ecuador* (2004): that indigenous struggles over land and oil operations in Ecuador have been as much about pollution and the material use and extraction of rainforest resources as they have been about reconfiguring national and transnational inequality, such as the silence around racial injustice and rewriting narratives of national belonging.

This archive of documentaries provides coverage of local popular environmentalisms and their transnational political strategy that cannot be found in mainstream news media or their archives; in fact, overall the coverage of these movements has been negative or critical of their impact on "national progress." The documentaries' environmental justice foci, and epic modes of narrative, are crucial to how they contribute to the struggles they portray. The investigative character of the genre requires the production team spend long periods of time on location following closely the leaders of the social movements in their dealings with communities, transnational allies, the media, and of course the activists' efforts to get the attention of arrogant decision makers in government or transnational corporations. The documentaries join the movements' campaigns, and therefore producers and directors coordinate the production of their projects with the movements' needs as they unfold. However, despite the fact that these struggles extend over several years, against enemies with vastly superior resources, the narratives in the documentaries do not provide insight into any serious doubts and weaknesses in their leaders, or into major internal conflicts within these coalitions. The *Frentes de Defensa* appear as motivated and disciplined despite the toll that the wars of attrition are imposing on their members. These documentaries show the "versatile possibilities of politically engaged nonfiction" that Nixon enthusiastically endorses because of "nonfiction's robust adaptability, imaginative and political, as well as to its information-carrying capacity and its aura of the real" (2011, 25). However, from a critical point of view, this epic narrative behind the documentaries clearly raises a difficult issue regarding such political film making: has their partisan nature become an impediment to full political understanding of what is or has been going on in these popular environmentalisms?

BUEN VIVIR

These documentaries prefer to emphasize visible acts of confrontation against neoliberal governments that promote transnational investment in extractive industries, at the expense of portraying two aspects of popular environmentalism that are becoming more important in the current "post-neoliberal" scenario of the new extractivism. The first is the alternative ways through which the actors involved in these popular environmentalisms interact with the nonhuman on an everyday basis. The second is something that the documentaries, with a few exceptions, ignore: how each individual struggle relies on and contributes to the rise of popular environmentalism in Latin America. This process can be illustrated with the Buen Vivir movement. Buen Vivir is not behind every single instance of popular environmentalism, but it is the resulting product of the accumulation of struggles throughout Latin America since the mid-1990s. At this point, Buen Vivir represents the political possibilities and limitations of popular environmentalisms in Latin America, and an innovative indigenous thinking on ecology and decolonization that can be placed in dialogue with the "environmentalism of the poor" and other postcolonial approaches to environmentalism. I would like therefore to consider it in more detail to show how it complements and extends the epic but largely human-focused narratives of contestation found in the documentaries by suggesting a philosophical outlook that provides one potential way of negotiating the tensions between neoliberalism and new extractivism outlined above.

Evolving in Latin America since the early 2000s, Buen Vivir or Vivir Bien, are the Spanish words used to describe alternatives to development focused on the good life in a broad sense. Buen Vivir, explains Thomas Fatheuer (2011), is the umbrella term for an emergent network of more-than-environmentalist discourses and social movements inspired by indigenous knowledge about humans, animals, plants, landscapes, and the nurturing of life and community. It borrows heavily too from Western sources. Thus, Buen Vivir is a complex set of several rights, most of them found in the Western tradition (freedom, health, education, food, shelter), in the same hierarchical level with another set of rights that include, among others, participation, communities, protection, and also the rights of nature.

The term Buen Vivir is actively used by social movements and has even reached its way into two new Constitutions in Ecuador (approved in 2008) and Bolivia (approved in 2009). It is a plural concept with two main entry points, as Eduardo Gudynas (2011) has explained. Early formulations of Buen Vivir emerged in reaction to classical development strategies, either due to their negative social or environmental impacts, or their debatable economic effects. It refers, in contrast, to alternatives to development emerging from indigenous traditions, and in this sense the concept explores possibilities beyond the modern Eurocentric tradition. The richness of the term is difficult to translate into English. Gudynas explains that it includes the classical ideas of quality of life, but with the specific conviction that well-being is only possible within a community. Furthermore, in most approaches the concept of "community" is understood in an expanded sense that includes nature. Buen Vivir therefore embraces the broad notion of well-being and cohabitation with others and other-than-humans.

The status of Buen Vivir as an umbrella term speaks to another important characteristic of the movement. According to Gudynas (2011), there are many different interpretations of Buen Vivir depending on cultural, historical, and ecological settings. One of the most well-known approaches to Buen Vivir is the Ecuadorian concept of *sumak kawsay*, the Quechua wording for a fulfilling life in a community, together with other persons and other-than-humans. More or less at the same time that *sumak kawsay* became spoken about in Ecuador, in Bolivia the similar Aymara concept of *suma qamaña* emerged. Other examples are the Guarani ideas of "harmonious living" (*ñandereko*), "good life" (*teko kavi*), the "land without evil" (*ivi maraei*) and the "path to the noble life" (*qhapaj ñan*). The idea of the "good life" (*shiir waras*) is shared by the Shuar of Ecuador, like the "harmonious living" (*küme mongen*) of the Mapuches of Chile. All these ideas of Buen Vivir are specific to each culture, with its own language, history, social and political contexts, and placement in diverse environments. There is no sense in trying to apply the concept to other regions; other cultures will have to explore and build their own Buen Vivir. Thus, the Ecuadorian *sumak kawsay* is not identical to the Guarani *ñandereko*, and these two are different from all the others. There is no room for an essentialist position. It is not possible to identify one idea of Buen Vivir as the best for becoming the standard reference to be followed by all other indigenous groups in Latin America.

Buen Vivir should not be understood as a nostalgic and idealized return to a distant precolonial time. It is not a static concept, but an idea that is continually being created. Gudynas (2011) finds that the Bolivian idea of *suma qamaña* is an excellent example of this powerful process. Although extremely popular, both inside and outside Bolivia, there is strong evidence that *suma qamaña* is not found in the everyday life of Aymara rural communities, but that the term was a recent creation by the Aymara sociologist Simón Yampara Huarachi. Buen Vivir is not restricted to indigenous postures. Similar approaches are found in other mixed or multicultural settings. A good example is the "quiet life" of the Cambas, the inhabitants of the forest at northern Bolivia, resulting from more than 150 years of mixing and hybridization of different ethnic groupings. Their defense of well-being, security, happiness and identity in tropical forests is the result of a contemporary cultural mix.

Other approaches to the Buen Vivir, explains Gudynas (2011), came from some small, usually marginalized critical positions within modernity, which are resistant to classical development and its deviations. The first involves critical studies on development in general and postdevelopment in particular such as those stemming from the work of Colombian anthropologist Arturo Escobar. In this case, most of the relations mutually reinforce ideas like *suma qamaña* or *sumak kawsay.* The second involves radical environmental postures, particularly deep ecology and other biocentric approaches. They reject the anthropocentric perspective of modernity, and their recognition of intrinsic environmental values is analogous to positions found in several indigenous perspectives on Buen Vivir, particularly from the indigenous nations in tropical forests. The last position involves feminist perspectives, with their radical critique of gender roles and its links to societal hierarchies but also to the domination over nature. These and other examples show that Buen Vivir should not be conceived as a position limited to non-Western knowledge, but as a useful concept that can support and enhance critical traditions looking for alternatives to development.

Struggles that learn from each other; networks of information that sustain the creation of knowledge and value pulling in similar directions but avoiding reductionism, essentialization or universalism: Buen Vivir is akin to the kind of "eco-cosmopolitanism" that Ursula Heise (2008) has argued for, which is conceived as a form of attachment and belonging beyond national, ethnic, class, and species borders (55). Buen Vivir does not necessarily presuppose that tradition and order, stagnancy and immobility are self-evidently worth perpetrating. Buen Vivir, indeed, is an eco-cosmopolitanism that values human difference derived from tradition, history, and location, and yet presupposes a shared humanity that wishes to engage in the conversation about Buen Vivir, alternatives to development, and "imagined communities" of both humans and non-humans. Acknowledgement of local difference, of indigenous plurality, and of more-than-indigenous and more-than-human pluralities is crucial, along with encouragement of exchange and transformation: there is a basic but particular comparativism energizing Buen Vivir, and other popular responses to global and local environmental affairs, which explains Buen Vivir's openness to discourses of global dissemination, and to intra- and transnational alliances and exchanges.

The definition and practice of Buen Vivir's comparativism comes from a larger and widespread reflection by many social movements on how to think cultural diversity and its communication. Since the early 1990s, the model of interculturalism has become increasingly influential in indigenous cultural and educational policies, grassroots movements, and even in political theories of the state in Bolivia, Colombia, Chile, Ecuador, and Peru (Walsh 2008). Its fundamental premise is that although Anglophone multiculturalism has been a useful concept for recognizing a context of cultural plurality and tolerance, it has failed to recognize the internal plurality of each culture, and the inescapability and desirability of intercultural dialogue for mutual enrichment, for questioning our own and each other's cultures, and for building new social relationships and living conditions (Walsh 2008, 140). The goal of interculturalism among indigenous movements is not merely to achieve recognition, tolerance, or even acceptance of their differences, but to reach a negotiation where such differences can contribute to the development of new forms of coexistence, collaboration, and solidarity.

The principle of interculturalism as a mode of horizontal relations points toward the inequalities at work in society that impede this, but which can be addressed precisely by making such exchange happen. Coexistence and integration cannot occur if one of the parties is hierarchically above the other. As Buen Vivir clearly illustrates, popular environmentalism in Latin America is more than the narrative of resistance that the documentaries focus on. The discourses on nature to which they resort, ancestral or environmentalist, are more than strategic weapons for asserting their territorial rights in the media. There is a broader transformative potential—or reality—that appears as secondary or not explicitly represented in the documentaries. That potential consists of different and new proposals on the interaction of the human and the nonhuman that aspire to be part of alternative political, economic, and even scientific paradigms. This aspiration has also become a challenge to the extractivism of Latin America's "New Left."

EARTH–BEINGS IN POLITICS

In her essay "New Left = New Extractivism" (2010), Rachel Godfrey Wood points out that Venezuela, Bolivia, and Ecuador (and even Peru, I would add, under its current "nationalist" President, Ollanta Humala) are all highly dependent on exporting hydrocarbons and minerals, and their governments have shown a strong desire to perpetuate natural resource extraction in order to capture the substantial rents that lie in their nations' subsoils. "New extractivism," explains Gudynas, differs from the "old extractivism" in that the state captures a greater proportion of the surplus generated by the extractive sectors, and directs part of these resources toward financing social programs and the development of infrastructure, with which the state gains social legitimization, and which allows governments to define themselves as progressive (Gudynas 2010). The "new extractivism" retains, however, negative environmental and social impacts, as well as economic dependency on foreign demand for such resources. The New Latin American left in power, explains Gudynas, is heir to the idea of continuing progress, based on technology, and nourished by the riches of nature.

Gudynas's observation fits well with Chakrabarty's (2009) argument that Left and Right alike have been dependent on the kinds of extractive industry that have brought about the Anthropocene epoch and the current climate crisis; as he puts it, "whatever our socioeconomic and technological choices, whatever the rights we wish to celebrate as our freedom, we cannot afford to destabilize conditions (such as the temperature zone in which the planet exists) that work like boundary parameters of human existence. These parameters are independent of capitalism or socialism" (2009, 218). "New

Extractivism" would exemplify, too, what Walter Mignolo identifies, in *The Darker Side of Western Modernity: Global Futures, Decolonial Options* (2011), as the *dewesternization* of capitalism; in this case, a state capitalism of a leftist persuasion still caught within the fantasy of development and growth at the expense of life. *Decoloniality*, on the other hand, would be precisely a delinking from economic coloniality, in short, the ideology of "growth and development." The paradigm of growth and development is being confronted by the paradigm of life, to live in plenitude, in harmony among people and with nature. Rather than identifying this shift as a New Age and romantic fashion, Mignolo insists that it is a formula that has been shifting people all over the world, fighting against governments and their support of transnational corporations.

For Marisol de la Cadena, in her *Indigenous Cosmopolitics in the Andes* (2010), the emergence of indigeneities in twenty-first-century Latin America has come with an increasingly frequent presence on political stages in the Andes of "earth-beings" (animals, plants, and landscapes as sentient beings), and "earth practices," or the human interactions with the former (the respect and affect, or nurturing, necessary to maintain the condition between humans and other-than-humans that makes life in the Andes) (De la Cadena 2010, 340–41). This visibility in politics at the national level is, in fact, a challenge that conjures other-than-human entities to the political sphere, as actors or as issues. The representation of this indigenous and environmentalist intervention into political ontologies—a "political-epistemic insurgency," according to Catherine Walsh—is missing in the documentaries discussed in the first part of this essay, and would be a welcome addition to their focus on the struggle for livelihood and cultural rights. Or, alternatively, the awareness of the current political impact of these discourses of "earth beings" and "earth practices" would help the audience of these films to interpret such language in an unfamiliar way.

For de la Cadena, this excessiveness is not residual of "primitive" indigenous cultures, or simply a strategic essentialism for the interpellation of indigenous subjectivities (De la Cadena 2010, 336). Rather, it is disrupting the conceptual field of politics to the point where it is no longer just a manifestation of "indigenous culture" but a disagreement between worlds taking place in the field of political ontology. Labeling the presence of earth-beings in politics as manifestations of "ethnic difference" contains and denies once more the indigenous difference (De la Cadena 349). It is true that "ethnic politics" demanding "cultural rights" may even articulate the need to include the indigenous in politics but at the price of being honored as "beliefs" that do not have a chance of expressing an epistemic alternative to scientific and economic paradigms "working toward the production of the common good (productive efficiency, economic growth, even sustainable development) designed to satisfy a homogenous humanity benefiting from an also homogenous nature" (De la Cadena 2010, 350). The plurality does not stop at multiculturalism but it is a project for multinaturalism.

The transnational, interethnic, and multimedia political strategies, as well as political ontologies of popular environmentalisms, carry significant implications against any essentialist way of thinking the indigenous Other. De la Cadena has proposed a definition of indigeneity that in fact can be illustrated with the documentaries themselves: "Thus seen, albeit hard to our logic, indigeneity has always been part of modernity and also different, therefore never modernist" (De la Cadena 2010, 348). This clarification is very useful at a time when the exclusion of other political ontologies is justified by questioning the authenticity of the indigenous when it does not show signs that match essentialist definitions. In April 2013, for instance, the Peruvian Minister of Energy and Mining argued that Quechua communities of the Andes should not be considered as "indigenous" under the Peruvian law that mandates that extractive companies must negotiate agreements with indigenous communities before starting the exploitation of natural resources. His argument relies precisely on the notion that indigeneity lies outside of modernity: the Andean indigenous communities mixed with the Spanish colonizers in the past, conduct formal community assemblies, and are not isolated as Amazonian indigenous peoples are.

As the documentaries often show, indigenous leaders speak in modern terms in order to be recognized as legitimate adversaries and for translating their practices into politically acceptable speech (De la Cadena 2010, 349). Furthermore, argues de la Cadena, the indigenous is an *indigenous-mestizo* aggregate, not only because it is a historical formation coming out of colonization, but because it is a socionatural formation since identity is not divorced from the view of the other-than-human. Indigenous identity is not merely "ethnic:"

> Participating in more than one and less than two socionatural worlds, indigenous politicians are inevitably hybrid, usually shamelessly so. Relations with other-than-human beings take place along with activities such as participating in judiciary trials, organizing a workers union, participating in environmental NGOs, even working for a capitalist organization. (353)

The political context in the twenty-first century has been so far one in which indigenous movements have become the protagonists of unprecedented historical ruptures and innovations. This aspect of the environmental struggles portrayed in the documentaries has been overlooked or underrepresented. However, if we keep it in mind we can reread those struggles in the films as instances of more than a local fight for protecting sources of livelihood, but attempts throughout Latin America to articulate the politics of different socionatural worlds. "Indigenous movements," explains de la Cadena, "may meet those—scientists, environmentalists, feminists, egalitarians of different stripes—also committed to a different politics of nature, one that includes disagreement on the definition of nature itself" (346). Just as the extractivism of the Latin American "New Left" is challenging the politics of popular environmentalism in terms of national interests, Buen Vivir and other popular environmentalisms are challenging the anticolonial stance of these governments. They challenge "big development," from the Right and from the Left, because of the inequity brought by extractivism's environmental impact. But, more interestingly, Buen Vivir and other popular environmentalisms are testing the "New Left's" cultural relativism which, while it acknowledges different epistemologies, nevertheless presupposes or affirms the universality of the modern understanding of the interface between nature and society. This splitting between popular environmentalisms and the "New Left" in power is a scenario that raises, by analogy, important questions of ecological politics and citizenship for the institutionalization of the environmental humanities.

POPULAR ENVIRONMENTALISM AND THE RISE OF THE ENVIRONMENTAL HUMANITIES

Environmental humanities is an umbrella term for the scholarly work done by researchers focusing on cultural factors for explaining human environmental change: customs, preferences, values, identities, power relations, worldviews, epistemologies, and ontologies (Nye et al. 2013, 32). Its practitioners also seek to identify what constitutes environmentally relevant knowledge, and affirm the need to include cultural values, political and religious ideas, and other deep-seated human behaviors in understandings of the environment (Sörlin 2012, 788). In a time of rapid environmental change, "the environmental humanities engages with fundamental questions of meaning, value, responsibility and purpose" (Rose et al. 2012, 1). Undoubtedly, then, in order to introduce oneself to some of the key environmental discourses, narratives, epistemologies, ontologies, and values in Latin America, an environmental humanities agenda will have to venture outside of the written word of the lettered intellectual into films, and even the Internet, and to pay considerable attention to popular environmentalisms. These movements are redefining the policies of the nation-state through the principles of interculturalism, the request for further decentralization, and the caution against the ideology of "growth and development."

Although the history of what is covered currently under the environmental humanities goes back several decades, there seems to be a significant impulse or mandate toward its institutionalization in research centers. To a great extent the major argument for the need of this institutionalization seems to be an awareness of the complexity behind the "failure" in the implementation of public policies, and of environmental organizations for fostering the values needed for building sustainable societies and environmental citizenship (Nye et al. 2013, 4). As Sverker Sörlin puts it: "The background is the current inadequacy of the established science, policy, and economic approaches" (Sörlin 2012, 788). The current political context in which Latin American popular environmentalism takes place calls attention to a counterintuitive argument for the logic of the environmental humanities: the "failure" of environmental policies from above is related to the self-cooptation of environmental discourses and movements by governments and international developmental agencies that still cannot help but see their own environmental promises as incompatible with the urgency to remediate extreme poverty and unemployment (which would require an annual economic growth of 5 percent to 7 percent for ten to fifteen years) with the injection of foreign investment in extractive industries (30 percent or 40 percent of all foreign investment).

In Latin America the "failure" of public policies based on scientific and economic approaches is not due to the lack of attention to cultural factors arising from disciplinary prejudices; rather, it is due to the deliberate disowning of those cultural values that once were embraced. The conflict of popular environmentalisms with the "New Left" in power, giving to it the benefit of the doubt (as Unai Villalba does in "Buen Vivir vs. Development"), speaks of inevitable complex transitions (a "post-neoliberal" transition?) that would be followed by the implementation of policies that could lead, for instance, to a Buen Vivir model (Villalba 2013). An environmental humanities agenda for Latin America has no choice but to follow Young's (2012) call to postcolonial studies to give visibility, in this case, to the contradictions of the "New Left" in power, and its confrontations with popular environmentalisms and invite the interpretation of the latter's narratives and discourses within that context.

It is true that the environmental humanities are emphasizing the importance of indigenous and local knowledge as part of a radical reconfiguration of our understanding of the living world, and as a consequence of the interdisciplinary, transnational, and cross-cultural vocation of the field and the scope of the issues under study (Rose et al. 2012, 4). However, we have learned that indigenous and local knowledge are too part of a radical reconfiguration of our understanding of political ontology being played at the national and transnational scales. Environmental humanities researchers are also willing to embrace a sense of urgency that unsettles the conventional humanities regarding the tension involved in a simultaneous critique of dominant narratives and the involvement in action directed toward "helping to shape better possibilities in dark times" (Rose et. al. 2012, 3). There is an expectation that the environmental humanities will produce knowledge with a strategic value in solving environmental problems, and for achieving the larger goal of creating sustainable societies (Nye et al. 2013, 5–6). There is the expectation, too, that the environmental humanities will communicate its findings clearly, effectively, and at the appropriate level of detail (Nye et al.

2013, 8). It is this sense of urgency itself, analogous to the one we have noticed in the Latin American "New Left," which may end up undermining the environmental humanities' own goals. Will this mandate for action allow for a necessary dissonance between the solutions the environmental humanities attempts to put forward and the political ontologies of indigenous movements, including space to disagree about understandings of human and other-than-human interactions? Or will this pressure for solutions lead the environmental humanities to not be willing to engage with indigenous ontologies whose ultimate aspiration is a political-epistemic insurgency?

The question of how the environmental humanities articulates its engagement with more-than-environmental indigenous movements, and their political ontologies, is not only open but potentially conflictive. Will the imperative to deliver the production of the common good in urgent times hold us to the "ethnic politics" described earlier in regard to indigenous knowledge, or limit indigenous participation to local issues? Popular environmentalism can be an ally of the environmental humanities or it may test the latter's ultimate cultural relativism which, although it acknowledges different epistemologies, still presupposes the universality of its own conclusions about the interface between nature and society. Nevertheless, in the current scenario in Latin America, popular environmentalisms and the emergent field of environmental humanities could become allies or partners in struggles of resistance, and in developing innovative institutions, policies and discourses for addressing, for instance, adaptation to climate change. Furthermore, in principle, the environmental humanities share basic values with Buen Vivir and the popular environmentalisms to which the documentaries draw attention. Neither believes in the separation of "Nature" and "Humanity," and both ask a common ontological question with serious political ramifications: "How are human identities and responsibilities to be articulated when we understand ourselves to be members of multispecies communities that emerge through the entanglements of agential beings?" (Rose et al. 2012, 3). In Latin America, the Buen Vivir movement is leading this reflection and transformation.

REFERENCES

"Bolivians March Against Evo Morales over Jungle Highway Crackdown." 2011. *The Guardian*, September 28. http://www.guardian.co.uk/world/2011/sep/29/bolivians-march-against-evo-morales.

A Convenient Truth: Urban Solutions from Curitiba. 2006. DVD. Directed by Giovanni Vaz del Bello. USA: Mother and Son Productions.

Cartoneros. 2006. DVD. Directed by Ernesto Livon-Grosman. Watertown, MA: Documentary Educational Resources.

Chakrabarty, Dipesh. 2009. "The Climate of History: Four Thesis." *Critical Inquiry* 35 (2):197–222.

————. 2012. "Postcolonial Studies and the Challenge of Climate Change." *New Literary History* 43 (1): 1–18.

Choropampa: The Price of Gold. 2002. DVD. Directed by Stephanie Boyd and Ernesto Cabellos. Peru: Guarango.

Crude: The Real Price of Oil. 2009. DVD. Directed by Joe Berlinger. USA: First Run Features.

De la Cadena, Marisol. 2010. "Indigenous Cosmopolitics in the Andes: Conceptual Reflections beyond 'Politics.'" *Cultural Anthropology* 25 (2): 334–370.

Escobar, Arturo. 1995. *Encountering Development: The Making and Unmaking of the Third World.* Princeton, NJ: Princeton University Press.

Fatheuer, Thomas. 2011. *Buen Vivir: A Brief Introduction to Latin America's New Concepts for the Good Life and the Rights of Nature.* Berlin: Heinrich Böll Foundation.

Fighting for the Futaleufú. 2013. Film. Directed by Stephanie Haig. New York: VIMEO. http://vimeo.com/88886235.

Garbage or Resource? A Dominican Republic Experience. 2013. DVD. Directed by Natasha Despotovic. Dominican Republic: GFDD/FUNGLODE.

Gudynas, Eduardo. 2010. "The New Extractivism of the 21st Century: Ten Urgent Theses about Extractivism in Relation to Current South American Progressivism." *Infoshop News,* January 21. http://news.infoshop.org/article.php?story=20100421011214362.

————. 2011. "Buen Vivir: Today's tomorrow." *Development* 54 (4): 441–447.

Heise, Ursula K. 2008. *Sense of Place and Sense of Planet: The Environmental Imagination of the Global.* New York: Oxford University Press.

La travesía de Chumpi. 2009. Film. Directed by Fernando Valdivia. New York: Vimeo. http://vimeo.com/59512111.

Martínez-Alier, Joan. 2003. *The Environmentalism of the Poor: A Study of Ecological Conflicts and Valuation.* Cheltenham: Edward Elgar.

Mignolo, Walter D. 2011. *The Darker Side of Western Modernity: Global Futures, Decolonial Options.* Durham: Duke University Press.

Nixon, Rob. 2011. *Slow Violence and the Environmentalism of the Poor.* Cambridge, MA: Harvard University Press.

Nye, David, Linda Rugg, James Fleming, and Robert Emmett. 2013. *The Emergence of the Environmental Humanities.* Stockholm: MISTRA [Swedish Foundation for Strategic Environmental Research].

The Power of Community: How Cuba Survived Peak Oil. 2006. DVD. Directed by Faith Morgan. USA: The Community Solution.

Recycled Life. 2006. Film. Directed by Leslie Iwerks and Mike Glad. *YouTube.* http://www.youtube.com/watch?v=VEe8nmwd4iE.

Rose, Deborah Bird, Thom van Dooren, Matthew Chrulew, Stuart Cooke, Matthew Kearnes, and Emily O'Gorman. 2012. "Thinking Through the Environment, Unsettling the Humanities." *Environmental Humanities* 1: 1–5.

Sawyer, Suzana. 2004. *Crude Chronicles: Indigenous Politics, Multinational Oil, and Neoliberalism in Ecuador.* Durham: Duke University Press.

Sörlin, Sverker. 2012. "Environmental Humanities: Why Should Biologists Interested in the Environment Take the Humanities Seriously?" *BioScience* 62 (9): 788–89.

Switch Off. 2005. DVD. Directed by Manuel Mayol (Chile). Barcelona: Andoliado Producciones.

Tambogrande: Mangos, Murder, Mining. 2006. DVD. Directed by Ernesto Cabellos Damián and Stephanie Boyd. Peru: Guarango.

Thirteen Villages Defending Water, Air and Land. 2008. DVD. Directed by Francesco Taboada Tabone. Mexico: Atahualpa Caldera, Fernanda Robinson, Francesco Taboada Tabone, CRIM-UNAM, and GAIA A.C.

The Trees Have a Mother. 2008. Film. Directed by Juan Carlos Galeano and Valliere Richard Auzenne. *Films on Demand.* http://digital.films.com/play/WNHAND.

Villalba, Unai. 2013. "Buen Vivir vs. Development: A Paradigm Shift in the Andes?" *Third World Quarterly* 34 (8): 1427–1442.

Walsh, Catherine. 2008. "Interculturalidad, Plurinacionalidad y Decolonialidad: Las Insurgencias Político-Epistémicas del Refundar el Estado." *Tábula Rasa* 9 (July–December): 131–152.

Waste Land. 2010. DVD. Directed by Lucy Walker. USA: Arthouse.

The Water Is Ours, Damn It! 2000. DVD. Directed by Sheila Franklin. Amherst, MA: 1world communication.

When Clouds Clear. 2008. DVD. Directed by Danielle Bernstein and Anne Slick. USA: Clear Films.

Wood, Rachel Godfrey. 2010. "New Left = New Extractivism in Latin America." *Blog International Institute for Environment and Development,* June 29. http://www.iied.org/new-left-new-extractivism-latin-america.

Yasuní. El Buen Vivir. 2012. Directed by Arturo Hortas. New York: Vimeo. http://vimeo.com/43112933.

Young, Robert JC. 2012. "Postcolonial Remains." *New Literary History* 43 (1): 19–42.

10 Witnessing the Nature of Violence

Resource Extraction and Political Ecologies in the Contemporary African Novel

Byron Caminero-Santangelo

Since 9/11, a colonial imaginary of Africa as a space of negation has been given new energy. In a reversal of the defusionist myth, its "weak states" are represented as sources of a contagious violence against which the United States must secure itself (Sharp 2013, 238, 242–45). Somalia and the Niger Delta, in particular, have been positioned as lawless places where a primal criminality manifests itself in piracy and kidnapping and renders supposedly civilizing capitalist development impossible. Such representation relies on a (neo)colonial projection of bounded geographical identities that suppresses the violent impact of imperialism in the past and that continues to enable devastating policies of intervention and resource extraction (Gregory 2004; Morton 2013; Sharpe 2013).

Two relatively recent novels, Helon Habila's *Oil on Water* (2010) and Nuruddin Farah's *Crossbones* (2011), challenge the prominent Western narratives of violence in Somalia and the Niger Delta and the geopolitical rubric underpinning them. They offer decolonizing stories grounded in both the specificity of place and its mediation by histories of uneven economic and political relationships linking it with the world "beyond." For example, they foreground the ways that such relationships have generated violent ecological transformations that cannot be separated from exponentially degenerating social conditions. In other words, like so many scholars working in political ecology, postcolonial studies, and the environmental humanities, Farah and Habila suggest that violence needs to be understood in relation to the imbrication of the social and ecological and the political significance of geographic and temporal scale. In the process, both authors evoke a form of postcolonial witnessing that makes visible oft occluded kinds and causes of violence and that disrupts the structures of perception enabling invisibility (Morton 2013, 180, 184–85; Nixon 2011, 14–16; Young 2012, 20–23). At the same time, *Oil on Water* and *Crossbones* bring attention to the difficulty of generating explanatory narratives that can help make sense of severely damaged places. They suggest not only how deep engagement with a "place" can reveal the limitations of current imperial discourse, but also how it can frustrate efforts to imagine effective resistance to the injustices and kinds of violence enabled by such discourse.

The two novels involve searches for *relatively* innocent outsiders drawn into violent conflict. In *Oil on Water*, a young reporter, Rufus, seeks a

British woman kidnapped by militants amid the "oil wars" in the delta, while in *Crossbones* an academic, Ahl, looks for his stepson recruited by Islamic fundamentalists in the US and brought to Somalia as a soldier for El-Shabab. These searches are closely linked with quests for explanatory narratives. Like Rufus, Ahl's brother Malik is a journalist; both Rufus and Malik are willing to put themselves in greater and greater danger to get to the "truth" of the violence and destruction they witness. As the characters navigate geographies severely damaged and made increasingly unintelligible by interconnected kinds of violence—including the violence to ecological communities by processes of primitive accumulation (oil extraction and illegal industrialized fishing)—they become aware of the inadequacy of dominant discourses offered up by the media, foreign experts, and different political interests (oil companies, El-Shabab, the military, pirates, militants), and reliant on the formulation of identities generated by reductive geographical imaginaries.

Through their representations of characters' quests for the "truth" of violence, *Oil on Water* and *Crossbones* foreground not only the ways environmental transformation is a crucial component of social conflict but also how such transformation must be understood in terms of imperial relationships shaping and linking places. They emphasize that conditions in the Niger Delta and Somalia cannot be understood through the centering of a bounded scalar category (the self, family, community, nation, region, etc.) or in terms of any outside/inside rubric.

In this sense, *Oil on Water* and *Crossbones* can fruitfully be read in relation to various conundrums that are made salient by the intersection of postcolonial studies and the environmental humanities and that have long troubled political ecology. In exploring the complicated, often repressed relationships underpinning violence, political ecologists address "the politics of scale": the political significance of using a single, autonomous scale (local community, nation, region, space of transnational capital, etc.) and/ or of using a decentered multiscalar analytic in the process of characterizing crises (Watts and Peet 1996, 4). For example, political ecologists suggest that analysis focused on ecological change as primarily driven by local conditions is inadequate as it fails to take account of unequal relationships working at larger scales and, at the same time, that representing the particularities of place "as inherent properties can easily serve to mask the power relations that make them visible in the first place" (Heise 2008, 46). However, whether in the context of political ecology, postcolonial studies, or the environmental humanities, the issue of "the politics of scale" can be fraught for those striving to make visible local conditions and marginalized perspectives that have been rendered invisible by hegemonic narratives, while, at the same time, taking into account processes and structures (geopolitical relationships, the movement of global capital, transnational environmental changes) operating at wider scales. In David Harvey's terms, they must address a geographical dialectic in which narratives produced at "local scales" are not "in some way subservient to the larger story," nor is "locality (place) where the unique 'truth of being' resides." (Harvey 2009, 229).

While addressing the politics of *geographic* scale, Rob Nixon also emphasizes the importance of temporal scale as it relates to the unspectacular time of what he terms the "slow violence" of environmental catastrophe, an attritional "violence of delayed destruction [...] that is typically not viewed as violence at all" (2011, 2). As Nixon notes, slow violence poses "strategic and representational" challenges to those trying to bear witness to it; they must "plot and give figurative shape to formless threats whose fatal repercussions are dispersed across space and time" and they must work against the "perceptual habits that downplay" such violence (2011, 3, 10, 15).

This issue of slow violence connects with another challenge facing political ecology and the environmental humanities: how to address, indeed how to discuss, the imbrication of the social and the ecological in analysis of environmental transformation and its significance. How can one take into account the "causal powers" in natural processes and the importance of "actual ecosystems around the world, where people, microbes, plants and animals interact" while also acknowledging that these processes and systems are always mediated by social history? (Peluso and Watts 2005, 25; Peet, Robbins, and Watts 2011, 23) This task is not easy, since it entails acknowledging, in David Harvey terms, a "world that is actively being shaped and reshaped by a wide array of intersecting socio-ecological processes (some but not all of which are intimately expressive of human activities and desires) operating at different scales" (2009, 231).

To address the challenges posed by scale and the imbrication of the social and ecological necessitates looking closely at how they play out in specific places. Conceptualizing place as "the grounded site of local-global articulation and interaction" is an important step towards this goal (Biersack 2006, 16). According to Doreen Massey, places are "located differentially in [a] global network": "each place is the focus of a distinct mixture of wider and more local social relations," and "all these relations interact with and take a further element of specificity from the accumulated history of a place" (1997, 323). This approach can potentially help political ecology avoid a reliance on universalizing theory which subordinates the local "to a global system of power relations" while attenuating the risk of downplaying the incredible vertical power of uneven relationships working at larger scales (Biersack 2006, 9). At the same time, such an approach complicates the conceptualizing of resistant identities and resource conflicts; it foregrounds the ways that place and local communities have been shaped by colonial modernity and resists a naturalizing construction of a local community as "the natural embodiment of the 'the local'" and "as an undifferentiated entity with intrinsic powers, which speaks with a single voice" (Watts and Peet 1996, 24). In many ways, postcolonial studies encourages this kind of approach to place. As a field, it has always highlighted the challenge of balancing attention to local difference with the relational construction of place and identity through asymmetrical imperial power.

Oil on Water and *Crossbones* both share this vision of place and bring into relief the challenges it poses for those trying to bear witness to violence. As characters try to orient themselves and understand their experiences, they repeatedly find that the long-term impact of traumatic socio-ecological transformation and the subsequent disruption of boundaries and identities stymie their efforts to generate coherent narratives about the Niger Delta and Somalia. These novels emphasize the point that "the local itself is thoroughly unfamiliar to many individuals, and may be epistemologically as unfathomable in its entirety as larger entities such as the nation or the globe," in large part because of the transformation of places and "the structures of perception, cognition and social expectations associated with them" by processes operating at larger scales (Heise 2008, 41, 53–54). In this sense, *Oil on Water* and *Crossbones* both encourage humility in terms of knowledge about cycles of violence and offer bleak perspectives on the possibility for stopping or even stalling them.

However, their respective formal and thematic treatment of witness narratives also results in a difference between them in terms of the issue of knowledge production. Both novels emphasize the need for journalists to refuse to reproduce hegemonic geographic discourses and to serve as witnesses who record what such discourses suppress. Yet, Habila's postmodern sensibility implicitly denies the value of trying to bring together the story told by the individual witness together with narratives about how violent conditions have been historically produced and, more specifically, about how (neo)colonial relationships have worked over time to create the situation in the Niger Delta. The result is a decreased sense of place as shaped by imperial forms of global connectivity. In contrast, *Crossbones* comes much closer to a vision that might be associated with postcolonialism and political ecology in its focus on the value both of exploring the precise limitations of various explanatory historical narratives and of trying to understand in specific terms how neoliberal capitalism and contemporary geopolitics have shaped socio-ecological violence in places like Somalia; in the process, Farah suggests that the project of knowledge production will be most fruitful if it is approached as a collective and open process bringing into conversation the testimony of witnesses and different kinds of "expert" discourse.

The activist-writer Ken Saro-Wiwa famously characterized gas flaring and oil spills in the Niger Delta as a form of genocidal violence. His manifesto *Genocide in Nigeria* claimed that the Ogoni people were left "half-deaf and prone to respiratory diseases" and that their main livelihoods, farming and fishing, were being destroyed by the poisoning of air, water, and soil (1992, 81–82). This situation, Saro-Wiwa argued, was caused by the willful negligence of the international oil industry and the Nigerian government and evolved from Nigeria's development along (neo)colonial lines.

Since Saro-Wiwa's death in 1995, conditions have only grown worse. A UN report published in July 2011 established that the Niger Delta is one of the most polluted places on earth and would take thirty years and one billion dollars to clean up (if the industry could be held accountable) (Dixon 2011). As the report also notes, the oil companies still fail to follow even the most basic procedures for maintaining their operational infrastructure and for environmental protection. Meanwhile, the Delta has witnessed a "calamitous descent into violence" (Watts 2007, 38). Armed rebel groups have proliferated and turned to kidnapping oil workers and sabotaging installations; armed gangs and ethnic militias fight for control of the oil-bunkering trade or for protection money from oil companies; and the Nigerian government continues to protect the interests of the oil industry using all the means of coercion at its disposal (Rowell, Marriott, and Stockman 2005, 15, 99).

In *Oil on Water*, the journalist Rufus offers a firsthand account of the conditions produced by this history. As he and Zaq, an aging alcoholic journalist, search for the militants and their captive, Isabella Floode, among the creeks and in the villages, they observe a dying landscape and an ecosystem that has gone silent with "birds draped over tree branches, their outstretched wings black and slick with oil" and fish bobbing "white-bellied between tree roots" (2010, 10–11). Striving to depict the slow violence of oil through different senses, Rufus evokes its impact on place using narrative techniques such as a visual analogy based on the long term, cancerous effect of smoking and the embodiment of toxic poisoning's smell; he sees a "patch of grass suffocated by a film of oil, each blade covered with blotches like the liver spots on a smoker's hands," and when he puts his face over a well he reels back: "Something [...] lay dead and decomposing down there, its stench mixed with the unmistakable smell of oil" (10). Environmental violence is closely bound with an unfolding social catastrophe, reflected by the many deserted villages he visits. With "the dwindling stocks of fish" and "the rising toxicity of the water" (18), the people are forced to leave, the communities break up, and they end up in vast urban slums where "unemployed youth" become "full of anger" and turn to crime or armed resistance (95–96). Manipulation and, when necessary, the use of force by the oil industry and the government are also crucial components of this process. The companies buy off community leaders (153), pay protection money to militant groups (38), and are able to instrumentalize the legal system and the military to force communities that resist into consenting to their "demands" (42–44).

In his activist writing, Saro-Wiwa effectively challenged what he called "shellspeak," a form of (neo)colonial development discourse that has "imperialized the wishes and worldviews" of the wealthy and powerful (Escobar 2001, 194). Shell had historically claimed both to bring economic progress to the Delta and to follow the strictest environmental guidelines in its operations (Okonta and Douglas 2001, 63). Cataloguing the damage done to the Niger Delta's ecosystem and to the health and livelihoods of the Ogoni and drawing on the voices of other Ogoni activists from the past, Saro-Wiwa positioned himself as a witness to the injustices that make visible the ways the company's rhetoric of care and development is a lie.

Like Saro-Wiwa, Habila mocks the oil companies' (neo)colonial development discourse. James Floode, the husband of Isabella and a petroleum engineer, tells Rufus, "You people could easily become the Japan of Africa, the USA of Africa, but the corruption is incredible [...] Our pipelines are vandalized daily, losing us millions ... and millions for the country as well. The people don't understand what they do to themselves ..." (103). This representation echoes Shell's and Chevron's narrative depicting illegal oil bunkering as the main source of danger from oil spills and suggesting that the oil industry offers an opportunity for development undermined by a lack of restraint among "the people." In response and following in the footsteps of Saro-Wiwa, Rufus makes visible what the industry's rhetoric suppresses. He notes that the Delta's inhabitants are only trying to get "some benefit" from the pipelines which have "brought nothing but suffering to their lives, leaking into the rivers and wells, killing the fish and poisoning the farmlands" even as they are told "that the pipelines are there for their own good" (103). Rufus's description of Floode's house serves as an elaboration on his rejoinder. Protected by "a tall, barbed-wire-topped wall" and "about half a dozen security men," it is "one of the many colonial-style buildings on the Port Harcourt waterfront, where most of the wealthy expatriate oil workers lived" (100) and includes all the perks necessary to maintain Floode's sense of privilege and power: "his cocktail, his split-unit air-conditioning, his alluring maid, his BBC news" (108). The scene as a whole suggests that such spaces of affluence in Nigeria and in the Global North are part of a geography of injustice shaped by oil.

If Habila's role as witness entails a reiteration of Saro-Wiwa's story of catastrophe in the Niger Delta, their perspectives differ in terms of their relative emphasis on the transformations of consciousness wrought by oil extraction. Saro-Wiwa claimed that a transcendent Ogoni "genius" grounded the passive resistance Movement for the Survival of the Ogoni People (MOSOP) and would be the foundation of a semi-autonomous Ogoni state within a Nigerian federation (1995, 110). This naturalizing representation of ethnic identity elides difficult issues regarding the transformative impact of Nigeria's historical development and of colonial modernity more generally. In particular, he suggests that identification with this identity can overcome the forms of consciousness leading to corruption, oppressive relationships, divisions, and violence he associates with the Nigerian state and the colonial setup of Nigeria.

In contrast, Habila depicts the poisoning of consciousness by oil in ways that bring into question the kind of inherent collective identity posited by Saro-Wiwa. In *Oil on Water*, the people of the Delta have been deeply shaped by what the journalist Ryszard Kapuscinski called the "fairy tale of oil," a deceptive narrative in which oil wealth magically generates individual or communal progress and which undermines other stories about the meaning of development and the means of survival (1982, 34). The novel suggests that this narrative works in mutually reinforcing ways with the material impact of the oil industry. As oil becomes the only game in town, as structural pressures and desperation escalate, people must increasingly invest their hopes in petrodollars and their dreams become colonized.

Habila highlights this corruption of consciousness through his treatment of the discourse of financial compensation. Whenever the language of "reparation" or oil "rent money" is invoked, it is always in situations in which characters are convincing themselves or others to do something criminal for the sake of personal gain or in which people and/or the land are being instrumentalized (107). In other words, *Oil on Water* suggests that "compensation" and, more generally, the hope of development through petrodollars will remain a destructive force given infrastructural and discursive conditions in the Delta and Nigeria as a whole; it is part of, rather than a solution to, the problem. In this sense, the novel can be read as bringing attention to the dangers of Saro-Wiwa's and MOSOP's demands for a much higher "percentage of oil revenue" to be paid to "the minorities of the delta and its environs" from "oil royalties and mining rents" (1992, 98; 1995, 45). In fact, the increased allocation of such income to the Niger Delta in the past fifteen years has spurred a new "wave of violence" as different groups have fought over access to compensation money (Watts 2007, 46).

The novel also problematizes a narrative of resistance which depicts the "rebels" as the embodiment of a place that is intrinsically in opposition to petrocapitalism and its effects. The armed militants led by "the Professor" claim to be "the people" and "the Delta" and to "represent the very earth on which [they] stand" (163). As a result, they say, "this land belongs to" them (232). The novel questions such naturalizing rhetoric in two ways. First, "the people" and "the land" are represented as having been transformed by oil in ways that undermine straightforward projections of resistant identity based on them. Second, Habila emphasizes how such rhetoric suppresses the ways the Professor and his group are part of the destructive processes associated with oil. They remain reliant on oil wealth, instrumentalize and objectify "the people" they claim to represent, and contribute to the ecological devastation of "the land." As he concludes his story, Rufus imagines the Professor's sabotage of an oil refinery resulting in "thousands of gallons of oil floating on the water, the weight of the oil tight like a hangman's noose around the neck of whatever life-form lay underneath" (238).

Any hope in *Oil on Water* is associated not with armed resistance but with cultural narratives and practices which might enable healing and ground ways of life that challenge the fairy tale of oil. Such efforts are clearly associated with the island of Irikefe and with Chief Ibiram's community. The inhabitants of the island have promised "never to abominate" the river with violence and focus on care for ecological and human health, "to bring a healing, to restore and conserve" (128, 137); this commitment enables them to "to keep this island free from oil prospecting and other activities that contaminate the water and lead to greed and violence" (129). Similarly, the village from which Chief Ibiram comes recognized the lie of petrodevelopment and the importance of an ethic of care for the land: "though they may not be rich, the land had been good to them, they never lacked for anything.

What kind of custodians of the land would they be if they sold it off? And just look at the other villages that had taken the oil money" (43).

Even after their village is taken over by the military because they said "no" to the oil company's and government's offers to buy their land, Ibiram and ten families refuse the corrupting power of "compensation": "We didn't take their money. The money would be our curse on them, for taking our land." Always on the move, they are "looking for a place where [they] can live in peace. But it is hard" (45).

Ibiram's story becomes a means of foregrounding the incredible difficulty of maintaining or establishing alternative spaces under the conditions in the Niger Delta. Eventually he and the ten families are forced to try to find "some sort of work" in Port Harcourt; the danger, in this situation, is that the community "would be swallowed up, its people dispersed" (196). They have become a group with "nowhere to go," now that their land has been gutted of its "capacity to sustain by an externalizing, instrumental logic," whose "cohesive reliance" has been pushed to the limit by "the militarization of both commerce and development" (Nixon 2011, 4, 19). Yet, in the end, their search for a place of "peace" is closely connected to the hope and sense of "optimism" Rufus has when he thinks about his sister Boma healing in Irikefe. This ending suggests that at least some of the building blocks for survival are embedded in Ibiram's community. They reject the lie of oil money and compensation, even under the most extreme pressure; they repeat a narrative embodying the ethics of ecological interdependence and care; and they emphasize preservation of an existing community rather than a return to a condition existing in the past. Their willingness to move, to go "into uncertain waters," is particularly important (239); it signals a movement away from the geographic identities, forms of claim making, and notions of ownership (of "the land") which the novel depicts as an integral part of crisis in the Delta.

In *Oil on Water*, journalists can contribute to the process of detoxifying the Delta through a witnessing that challenges the world-making discourses of the powerful. Both "the Major" and "the Professor" try to manipulate Rufus into repeating their different narratives of conflict. The former tells the reporter "I decide who is a criminal and who is not," and attempts to get him to accept this version of identity, mostly through fear (60). Similarly, the Professor believes that he can force Rufus into spreading the militants' claim that they represent "the people": "That is why I am letting you go, so you can write the truth. And be careful, whatever you write [...] I am watching you" (232). However, Rufus refuses the role of embedded reporter. He insists he must "be a witness" (60) and show "first hand" the horrors of "how nations are built, how great men achieve their greatness" (63).

In order to serve as "a witness," the reporter must confront the complexities of a place that has been shaped by interlocking forms of toxicity and relinquish the role of authoritative truth teller. Throughout his writing, Habila treats efforts by professionals and intellectuals to assume the mantle of authority through explanatory narratives with profound suspicion (which may be why he labels the militant leader "the Professor"). In the course of *Oil on Water*, Rufus gives up his quest for "the big story" that will explain what is happening in the Delta. Instead, he settles for recording both the story of what he has experienced and the stories told by those he meets. Even these are rendered in a fragmented narrative that shifts bewilderingly in time and space and that has significant temporal gaps which frustrate the desire for a linear timeline or coherent map. As Stephanie LeMenager notes, the "jumps in Rufus's account correspond to a dissolving of spatial boundaries and identities" and are connected with his efforts to make visible the conditions in the Delta created by oil extraction; these conditions challenge "the ordering necessary to plotting, where pattern [...] assures some degree of transmissibility and potential for action" (2013, 128).

Ultimately, in its focus on the "dissolving of spatial boundaries and identities" and its rejection of attempts to plot the relationships that have created conditions in the Delta, *Oil on Water* can be described as postmodern. In this regard, the novel has clear similarities with Habila's earlier novel *Waiting for an Angel*, which Ali Erritouni argues projects a profound "postmodern suspicion of metanarrative" and rejection of "the *notion* of historical totality" (emphasis mine) (2010, 145). In terms of a sense of place, "the Niger Delta enters the reader's consciousness [...] as an atmosphere of feeling" and Habila refuses to link "'feeling' [...] to material history" (LeMenager 2013, 128, 130). In contrast with Saro-Wiwa, who includes numerous documents from other Ogoni activists in *Genocide in Nigeria*, Habila's focus is on witnessing as an individual act. If "the novel raises broad questions about the value of witnessing and writing of what is witnessed" (LeMenager 2013, 130), it also severely limits the range of possible answers to those questions by focusing primarily on the temporality and geography of the witness's experience. The result is that while *Oil on Water* brings to consciousness aspects of the crisis in the Niger Delta suppressed by various discourses, it also elides the *historical* generation of the situation by specific (neo)colonial relationships. It has few references to the history of how foreign national governments, oil companies, the Nigerian petrostate, and resistance movements have shaped that crisis. The combination of the novel's postmodern sensibility and relative lack of historical reference generates a sense of commodity determinism ("the oil curse"), and, in turn, the conception of place as shaped by global relationships that is potentially opened up by Rufus's discussion with Floode becomes attenuated.

The novel's sensibility also elides the issue of how different kinds of readers might be positioned in specific ways. For example, the American reader might be encouraged to reflect on his or her contribution to conditions in a vague way (as a consumer of oil) but is discouraged from framing responsibility in terms of a particular position (as an *American* consumer and citizen). She or he is not encouraged to think about the political relationship between the US and Nigeria—a relationship shaped by a focus on "energy security" and the war on terror since 9/11 (Rowell, Marriott, and Stockman 2005; Douglas et al. 2005; Watts 2004). If, as Rob Nixon notes, a central representational challenge is how Americans can be made to "attend more imaginatively to the outsourced conflicts inflamed [...] by [their] military adventurism [...] and the global environmental fallout over the past three decades of American-led neoliberal economic policies" (2011, 34–35), *Oil on Water* not only ignores this challenge but actually suppresses the ways that recent imperial relationships have shaped violence in the Niger Delta.

Like *Oil on Water*, Nuruddin Farah's novel *Crossbones* foregrounds the relationship between a form of spectacular violence in Africa often foregrounded in Western media and the slow violence of environmental catastrophe catalyzed by resource extraction. Specifically, Farah repeatedly references the ways that piracy off the coast of Somalia has been shaped by illegal foreign fishing and toxic dumping and that piracy has, in turn, contributed to various kinds of social violence in Somalia itself. Farah leaves little doubt that initially many of the pirates were angry, desperate fisherman suffering from the degradation of Somalia's rich ocean resources by "illegal foreign fishing in the Somali Sea." As the narrator notes, many Somalis "say that this unchecked robbery has caused joblessness among the fishermen and led them to piracy. In fact, Somali fishermen appealed to the United Nations and the international community to help rid them of the large number of foreign vessels, estimated in 2005 at about seven hundred" (2011, 73). The destruction of marine resources by such fishing is well documented. As Clive Schofield notes, fishing by foreigners "keen to exploit the absence of offshore surveillance and enforcement efforts" threatens "Somalia's enormous, resource-rich maritime domain" with the "danger of collapse" (2008, 102). The anger and desperation of coastal communities have also been fueled by the illegal dumping of toxic waste by foreign vessels. At one point, the narrator references a "country profile compiled by the United Nations' own Food and Agricultural Organization in 2005" (73) which confirmed that from the early 1980s "uranium radioactive waste, lead, cadmium, mercury, industrial, hospital, chemical, leather treatment and other toxic waste" were dumped along Somalia's beaches, causing "health and environmental problems to the surrounding local fishing communities" (Eichstaedt 2010, 38).

In foregrounding the significance of foreign fishing and toxic dumping, *Crossbones* undermines the reified notion of geographic identity apparent in much of the journalistic analysis of piracy in Somalia. Despite his description of coastal environmental degradation, Peter Eichstaedt ultimately proclaims that "the plague of piracy [...] is a symptom of a much deeper problem: Somalia itself" (2010, 4). Meanwhile, Robert Kaplan explains piracy in terms of a bounded regional history; the "whole Arabian Sea," he asserts, "has been crawling with pirates since time immemorial" (2010, 298–99). Both Kaplan and Eichstaedt base their causal analysis on a single, coherent geographic identity (nation and region, respectively). *Crossbones* undermines such analysis by persistently referencing the ways that piracy was catalyzed by slow environmental violence and by exploitative relationships linking Somalia with the world.

More generally, as Pico Iyer noted in a review, *Crossbones* is about "the limitations of journalism" and challenges "calm overviews and confident predictions we might expect from an expert" (2012, 41). The centrality of this theme is reflected in the professions of the two half-Somali brothers, Ahl and Malik, visiting Somalia for the first time. Ahl is an academic with a PhD in linguistics from SOAS who lives in Minneapolis and researches all things Somali, while Malik is a free-lance journalist with expertise in zones of conflict who hopes to write a story that will tell the truth about violence in Somalia. Like *Oil on Water*, Farah's novel depicts the transformative, toxic aspect of violence as frustrating the desire for such a story. Despite their expertise, the brothers often find themselves unable to navigate their surroundings and baffled by their experiences. In a sense, the deeper a journalist like Malik delves as he tries to understand Somalia, the more he tries to serve as a witness, the more uncertain he becomes about the frames he uses to generate narratives about it. Through its representation of his quest, *Crossbones* suggests that any one point of view or kind of discourse will necessarily fail to deliver an adequate explanation or representation of such a situation. The difference between *Oil on Water* and Farah's novel in this regard is that *Crossbones* upholds the value of discourses that are not necessarily based on the recording of individual experience and the value of *trying* to understand violence by connecting witness narratives with social history.

Farah has always focused on decentering collective identity and representations of place by emphasizing both how Mogadishu and Somalia straddle "global connections and local intimacies" and the importance of those who have been marginalized and instrumentalized by the powerful—especially women, children, animals, and the nonhuman world (Myers 2011, 145). Yet, in *Crossbones* this decentering entails a stronger focus on global economic processes and geopolitical relationships than it does in his Blood in the Sun trilogy. In *Maps* and *Secrets*, the focus on how these processes and relationships shape Mogadishu and Somalia is more muted, and the scalar scope of the novels in terms of setting is more limited. These novels deconstruct the nation in large part by decentering the family, which is often represented not only as connected to but also as standing in for (as a "micro-cosmic model" of) the Somali collective (Alden and Tremaine 2002; Hitchcock 2007; Ngaboh-Smart 2000; Sugnet 1998). This leads in the Blood in the Sun trilogy to small scale solutions, with the reconstitution of families and friendships situated as offering some hope for healing. Increasingly, these small-scale solutions have been brought into question in the recent trilogy (*Links, Knots, Crossbones*). A change in one scale—the family, a house, a place—cannot stand in for a solution to problems generated at larger scales and the structured sets of relations they entail.

The emphasis on multiscalar origins of violence in *Crossbones* may explain why the novel is even darker than Farah's previous work, even more pessimistic about reversing a toxic trajectory. The novel highlights the horrific transformations resulting from a history of extreme violence. For example, Malik notes that among Mogadiscians the memory of "trauma has cauterized people's suffering, minimizing it," and, as a result, he envisions them dancing "around the enemy dead" when the Ethiopians are expelled, "giving into the debasing pleasure in poisoning themselves with the toxins of vengeance" (224–25). In *Crossbones* the operation of violently transformative "toxins" must be understood in relation to different but interlocking temporalities and spaces. First, "nothing in Somalia makes sense until one places it in the 'before,' 'after,' and 'during' of" its "civil war context" (181). Second, the "frame of reference" of national history must be understood in relation to the history of regional and global political relationships. Malik remembers "that a UN annual situation report on Somalia [...] claimed there were twelve countries involved in the Somali conflict—Eritrea, Ethiopia, Iran, Libya, Egypt, Kenya, Iraq, China, Italy, the United States, France and Britain" (244).

Finally, *Crossbones* depicts neoliberal capitalism as a toxin creating inequalities locally and globally. In the novel, neoliberalism's crucial contribution to violence is reflected in the Bakhaaraha market at the heart of Mogadishu. "Those who manage this institution" have increasingly focused on supporting which ever political actors would most advance the market's economic interests (153). Initially, it was a site of opposition to neocolonialism under the dictator Siad Barre. Later, it supported a clan leader, and then, "during the 2006 routing of the US-supported warlords," gave the Islamic Courts "weapons and funds" that tipped the balance of power. The priority is always on maximizing financial gain; the market "offers immense profits in a country where business doesn't pay tax, as there are no state structures in place to levy or collect it," and the managers do their best to maintain these extreme free-market conditions (153–54). More generally, the economic interests of the powerful and their embrace of neoliberal discourse drive violence. As one pirate lord and supporter of the Islamic Courts, Ma-Gabadeh, proclaims, "I, too, like many others, contributed to the creation of the crisis and then profited. [...] We are enjoying the turmoil" which is "the ideal situation for growth of capital" (185–86).

If the issue of piracy brings into relief the toxicity of slow environmental violence wrought by foreign economic interests, *Crossbones* suggests that this violence cannot be understood as stemming only from the work of "foreign" agents since it has also been shaped by the pursuit of "capital" among those like Ma-Gabadeh. For example, he made his fortune when he built a business partnership with an Italian fishing firm with whom he had dealt in his capacity as an official in the Ministry of Fisheries right before the collapse of Somalia's state structures. He then "established a frozen-food company centered on the fishing business, harvesting lobster and exporting it to Italy." Eventually, he funded an armed militia unit "specializing in the highjacking of the ships" and "became a heavy-weight businessman with some fifty gun-mounted Technicals" who backed El-Shabab with funds and "his thousand-strong armed militia" (181–82).

Under such conditions, nationalist anti-colonial rhetoric becomes a way to elide the ways that some Somalis benefit from horrifically transformative violence and that they are aligned with international financial networks. As a result, it is little surprise that in *Crossbones* such characters forcefully argue that the pirates are anti-imperial warriors defending the nation's resources. Ma-Gabadeh claims that he has been motivated by the desire to help the "coastal areas in the northeast" from which he comes and which have been devastated by those who are "illegally in our seas" (186). Fidno, a man working as a mediator for the pirates, argues that the foreigners are the true "sea bandits," while the pirates are "conscientious avengers fighting to save our waters from total plunder" and constitute a kind of coastguard protecting "sea resources against continued foreign invasion" in the absence of a functioning state (210–11). In *Crossbones*, such claims are rendered problematic by the fact that some Somalis have benefited from the ecological devastation of maritime resources, from "the absence of a functioning state," and, more generally, from the perpetuation of the various kinds of violence plaguing Somalia.

Crossbones does not question Ahl's recognition of "the stark reality, the dire conditions of most Somalis, the absence of food and environmental security, the never-ending conflict" (216). Rather, the novel brings into question discourses structured by unified geographical categories generated by both imperialism and neocolonial nationalism that serve the interests of the powerful, occlude complicated relationships between the global and the local, and, as a result, contribute to socio-ecological violence and injustice. In turn, Farah's critical representation of many journalists is often grounded in the ways their frames of reference are based on such categories; for example, he explores how the geopolitical imaginary underpinning the causal analysis of a journalist like Peter Eichstaedt ("the plague of piracy" is "a symptom of a much deep problem: Somalia itself" [2010, 4]), serves to make invisible the socio-ecological violence "dispersed through capitalist relations" in an era of neoliberal globalization (Sharpe 2013, 245).

In *Crossbones*, as in *Oil on Water*, if a journalist is to resist serving the interests of the powerful and privileged, s/he must persistently strive to make the invisible visible and to bring into question the discursive mechanisms which generate invisibility. However, if Malik "seldom trusts the truth of the version he hears until he has dug deeper and deeper and gotten to the bottom of the matter" (365), getting to this "bottom" remains extremely difficult. First, those with the means of violence at their disposal can silence versions of "the truth" that challenge their own; journalists visiting or living in Somalia write under the persistent threat of assassination. Second, the "deeper" one delves to find the truth of place, the more the long-term transformations wrought by violence and the many interconnected sources of that violence expose the limitations imposed by any single form of witnessing and any single frame of reference. Malik initially displays an overweening confidence in his ability to navigate conditions in Mogadishu but he increasingly becomes aware of the need for local guides. At the same time, "local knowledge" is inadequate since an understanding of perspectives from other places and of imperial relationships is crucial. Ultimately, the search for the truth requires bringing into conversation multiple perspectives based on differing frames of reference and kinds of expertise. Malik may not "get to the bottom of the matter," but as he progressively works with local journalists, as he becomes part of a truly transnational professional collective, he increasingly makes visible invisible catalysts for violence and becomes a threat to the interests of the powerful. His near death experience by a roadside bomb and the uncertainty of his survival near the end of the novel makes clear the forces aligned against such work. However, a cause for optimism is the community of journalists who come "in droves to the hospital" some of whom "have even autographed Malik's cast, noting the dates and places where they worked with him on assignment" (381).

Even more than character development or the representation of a professional collective, the form of *Crossbones* highlights the kind of knowledge production the novel endorses. The narrative draws from numerous and various sources about piracy including media accounts, organizational reports, and academic publications from different parts of the world including, of course, Somalia and Africa more generally. The list of texts Farah "read, consulted, or borrowed from" in the acknowledgments section at the end of the novel is extensive (383–85). These sources reflect different ways of understanding piracy generated by a plethora of social, geographical, and experiential positions. Many of them offer the kind of historical and political framing absent from, even implicitly suppressed by, *Oil on Water.* Farah certainly brings into question some of these sources more than others, but he does not necessarily reject the kinds of expertise they represent. In fact, while he refuses to endorse the perspective of any one of them, he suggests that as they are all brought into dialogue with each other and with other kinds of narratives—particularly witness narratives— they become a collective means to bring into relief the complex, multiscalar (unequal) power dynamics at work, and to bring attention to the ways different kinds of discourses work to produce certain kinds of knowledge and suppress others.

After describing a far-flung global network of actors who enable and profit by piracy, Fidno proclaims "What is happening here is beyond your or anyone else's imagination" (364). Other characters repeatedly note about piracy, "something doesn't add up" (74). Ultimately, *Crossbones* refuses to fulfill the reader's desire for a clear, full understanding of "what is happening" and it does not "add up" the different points of view in order to illuminate a totalizing explanatory narrative; such closure and synthesis is impossible, given the nature of violence in the novel. However, it does draw attention to the importance of exploring the connections and tensions among as many kinds of expertise, discourses, and perspectives (from different positions) as possible, rather than relying on an individual "imagination," in order to make visible hidden "toxins" that underpin the spectacular violence of piracy and their obscured causes.

Crossbones's emphasis on the importance of understanding socioecological violence in terms of the histories of imperial processes operating in different ways at interrelated scales aligns it, more than *Oil on Water*, with political ecology, with postcolonial studies, and with an emergent postcolonial environmental humanities. At the same time, Farah's approach to the generation of knowledge about the nature of violence in places like Somalia or the Niger Delta would suggest that these fields will be most fruitful when they embrace, rather than try to resolve or reconcile, the tensions and competing perspectives they open up in relation to place, scale, and nature.

REFERENCES

Alden, Patricia, and Louis Tremaine. 2002. "How Can We Talk of Democracy? An Interview with Nuruddin Farah." In *Emerging Perspectives on Nuruddin Farah*, edited by Derek Wright, 25–46. Trenton: Africa World Press.

Biersack, Aletta. 2006. "Reimaging Political Ecology: Culture/Power/History/ Nature." In *Reimaging Political Ecology*, edited by Aletta Biersack and James Greenberg, 3–40. Durham: Duke University Press.

Dixon, Robin. 2011. "Nigerian Oil Spills Have Created Ecological Disaster." *Los Angeles Times*, August 5.

Douglas, Oronto, Dimieari Von Kemedi, Ike Okonta, and Michael Watts. 2005. "Alienation and Militancy in the Niger Delta: Petroleum, Politics, and Democracy in Nigeria." In *The Quest for Environmental Justice: Human Rights and the Politics of Pollution*, edited by Robert D. Bullard, 239–54. San Fransisco: Sierra Club.

Eichstaedt, Peter. 2010. *Pirate State*. Chicago: Lawrence Hill.

Erritouni, Ali. 2010. "Postcolonial Despotism from a Postmodern Standpoint: Helon Habila's *Waiting for an Angel*." *Research in African Literatures* 41 (4): 144–61.

Escobar, Arturo. 2001. "Place, Economy, and Culture in a Post-Development Era." In *Places and Politics in an Age of Globalization*, edited by Roxann Prazniak and Arif Dirlik, 193–217. New York: Rowman & Littlefield.

Farah, Nuruddin. 2011. *Crossbones*. New York: Penguin.

Gregory, Derek. 2004. *The Colonial Present*. Oxford: Blackwell.

Habila, Helon. 2003. *Waiting for an Angel*. New York: W.W. Norton.

———. *Oil on Water*. 2010. New York: W.W. Norton.

Harvey, David. 2009. *Cosmopolitanism and the Geographies of Freedom*. New York: Columbia University Press.

Heise, Ursula. 2008. *Sense of Place and Sense of Planet*. Oxford: Oxford University Press.

Hitchcock, Peter. 2007. "Postcolonial Failure and the Politics of Nation." *South Atlantic Quarterly* 106 (4): 727–752.

Iyer, Pico. 2012. "Somalia: Diving into the Wreck." *New York Review of Books*, November.

Kaplan, Robert D. 2010. *Monsoon: The Indian Ocean and the Future of American Power*. New York: Random House.

Kapuscinski, Ryszard. 1982. *Shah of Shahs*. New York: Harcourt.

LeMenager, Stephanie. 2013. *Living Oil: Petroleum Culture in the American Century*. Oxford: Oxford University Press.

Massey, Doreen. 1997. "A Global Sense of Place." In *Reading Human Geography*, edited by Trevor Barnes and Derek Gregory, 315–323. London: Arnold.

Morton, Stephan. 2013. "Violence, Law, and Justice in the Colonial Present." In *The Oxford Handbook of Postcolonial Studies*, edited by Graham Huggan, 179–196. Oxford: Oxford University Press.

Myers, Garth. 2011. *African Cities: Alternative Visions of Urban Theory and Practice*. London: Zed.

Ngaboh-Smart, Francis. 2000. "*Secrets* and a New Civic Consciousness." *Research in African Literatures* 31 (1): 129–136.

Nixon, Rob. 2011. *Slow Violence and the Environmentalism of the Poor*. Cambridge: Harvard University Press.

Okonta, Ike, and Oronto Douglas. 2001. *Where Vultures Feast: Shell, Human Rights, and Oil in the Niger Delta*. San Francisco: Sierra Club.

Peet, Richard, Paul Robbins, and Michael J. Watts. 2011. "Global Nature." In *Global Political Ecology*, edited by Richard Peet, Paul Robbins, and Michael J. Watts, 1–47. New York: Routledge.

Peluso, Nancy Lee, and Michael Watts. 2005. "Violent Environments." In *Violent Environments*, edited by Nancy Lee Peluso and Michael Watts, 3–38. Ithaca: Cornell University Press.

Rowell, Andrew, James Marriott, and Lorne Stockman. 2005. *The Next Gulf: London, Washington and Oil Conflict in Nigeria*. London: Constable and Robertson.

Saro-Wiwa, Ken. 1992. *Genocide in Nigeria: The Ogoni Tragedy*. London: Saros International.

———. 1995. *A Month and a Day: A Detention Diary*. Oxfordshire: Ayebia.

Schofield, Clive. 2008. "Plundered Waters: Somalia's Maritime Resource Insecurity." In *Crucible for Survival: Environmental Security and Justice in the Indian Ocean*, edited by Timothy Doyle and Melissa Risely, 102–115. New Brunswick: Rutgers University Press.

Sharpe, Joanne. 2013. "Africa's Colonial Present: Development, Violence, and Postcolonial Security." In *The Oxford Handbook of Postcolonial Studies*, edited by Graham Huggan, 235–252. Oxford: Oxford University Press.

Sugnet, Charles. 1998. "Nuruddin Farah's *Maps*: Deterritorialization and 'the Postmodern.'" *World Literature Today* 72 (4): 739–746.

Watts, Michael. 2004. "Violent Environments: Petroleum Conflict and the Political Ecology of Rule in the Niger Delta, Nigeria." In *Liberation Ecologies: Environment, Development, Social Movements*, edited by Richard Peet and Michael Watts, 273–298. New York: Routledge.

———. "Sweet and Sour." 2007. In *Curse of the Black Gold: 50 Years of Oil the Niger Delta*, edited by Michael Watts, 36–47. New York: Powerhouse.

Watts, Michael, and Richard Peet. 1996. "Liberating Political Ecology." In *Liberation Ecologies: Environment, Development, Social Movements*, edited by Richard Peet and Michael Watts, 3–47. New York: Routledge.

Young, Robert JC. 2012. "Postcolonial Remains." *New Literary History* 43 (1): 19–42.

Part IV
Mapping World Ecologies

11 Narrating a Global Future

Our Common Future and the Public Hearings of the World Commission on Environment and Development

Cheryl Lousley

> For though the common world is the common meeting ground of all, those who are present have different locations in it.
> —Hannah Arendt, *The Human Condition* (1958, 57)

Our Common Future is the report of the World Commission on Environment and Development, a United Nations commission in place from 1983–87, headed by Gro Harlem Brundtland, and commonly known as the "Brundtland Commission."[1] The commission is historically important because it made sustainable development the dominant international environmental policy paradigm, extending ecological concerns beyond pollution to also include resource and development challenges specific to the Global South, such as food insecurity, deforestation, rapid urbanization, and an inequitable international trade regime. The commission's work culminated with the 1992 Rio de Janeiro "Earth Summit" (formally known as the UN Conference on Environment and Development, or UNCED), at which a number of international environmental agreements were opened for signature, most notably the Convention on Biological Diversity and the Framework Convention on Climate Change.

As Finger notes, the commission's conception and practice of "global politics" was a significant dimension of its conceptualization of sustainable development (1993, 43). Its work was symbolic more than prescriptive, aiming to create—during the latter stages of the Cold War arms race—a new, international vision of world cooperation centered on ecological concerns. To create this shared vision, the Brundtland Commission conducted public hearings in eleven cities on five continents, inaugurating, as Carl Death (2010) has argued in relation to the subsequent UN environment and development conferences, a new practice for legitimizing an imagined global community with its own global public sphere (see also Borowy 2014, 5).[2] Narratives gathered from the Brundtland Commission's hearings are interspersed throughout the commission's widely disseminated report, showing the extent to which localized grassroots perspectives were pivotal to what it called its "trademark" global consultations (World Commission 1987, 359).

Taking a postcolonial environmental humanities approach, this chapter analyses these narratives through which ecological globalism was imagined and contested in the commission's public hearings and final report. It is important to return to the narratives of the World Commission on Environment and Development in order to appreciate how a well-intentioned, utopian project for worldly cooperation, singularly attentive to the unevenness of development, has also contributed to the perpetuation of environmental injustices. Narration involves the ordering of story through genre, tense, tropes (recurring figurative language), and voice, and is implicitly shaped by a range of inclusions and exclusions. Postcolonial studies emphasize how narration is political in both content and form. In terms of *content*, which has been to date the primary focus of postcolonial critiques of sustainable development and its global governance models, critics examine the distribution of resources and power, asking whose land will count as property or commons and whose futures are envisioned and enabled to flourish.[3] In terms of *form*, postcolonial scholars ask whose voices claim the authority to imagine a present and "fashion a future" (Scott 1999), and whose voices and forms of narration are not heard.[4] Postcolonial narrative study reads for gaps, contradictions, and fissures that expose the contingency and incompleteness of seemingly authoritative, all-inclusive narratives. Postcolonial narrative study also foregrounds *context*—the particular intersections of history, culture, science, geography, and social position that shape what is seen, said, and understood. The cultural specificity of narrative forms matters for postcolonial studies: there are points of incommensurability across cultures and contexts that cannot be assimilated into a singular, "global" set of resolutions without losing significance and meaning. Narration, finally, is also productive: it not only reflects but also actively creates the meaning-laden worlds in which we live and act. A nuanced appreciation of the narrative modes adopted in environmental politics and policy, as postcolonial environmental humanities research offers, can help us be more attentive to environmental justice when we strive to articulate collective sentiments for social change.

The Brundtland Commission's world-making project involved a range of disjunctive narratives and counternarratives. First, I outline how the commission organized its work so as to foster an imagined world community comprising heterogeneous voices, and which could come together, by way of the commission's public hearings, to engage in a democratic conversation, seemingly replicating on a world scale the practices of nation-state pluralist democracy. Second, I discuss how the commission's narrative performance of pluralism as a response to structures of economic inequality imagines the world as if outside colonial histories and postcolonial contexts. Third, I show how the Brundtland Commission constructed its imagined world by way of an aspirational narrative of global ecological futurity, concretized through the localized voices of public hearing participants, which placed Third World ecological problems in the past while deferring justice to the future. Finally, I highlight how the archival hearing transcripts reveal other narrative modes and temporalities, including recollections of historical ecological injustices that live on in memory and in socio-economic structures, and testimonial narratives about lives devastated by ecological hazards and loss that demand immediate redress and action in the "global now." The oral addresses given to the Brundtland Commission, I argue, expose the contingency of the globalism that prevailed, showing how the commission's largely *apolitical* project was made into a political site by participants who, in their very appearance at the public hearings, became "world subjects," making claims on the world as a site for collective action and identification.

GLOBAL HEARINGS, IMAGINED WORLDS

More than twenty years after the 1992 Earth Summit—with Rio+10 and Rio+20 conferences having come and gone—and more than thirty years after the first meeting of the Brundtland Commission, international justice and dialogue on world-scale ecological and economic relationships remain pressing and daunting challenges. The recent turn in resistance and occupy movements towards "the common"[5]—a key word in the evocative title of the commission's report, *Our Common Future*[6]—shows a revival of utopian projects for imagining new forms of worldly cooperation. While primarily pragmatic in its mandate and recommendations, the World Commission on Environment and Development was nevertheless a utopian endeavor (Sörlin 2013, 193), with an aim to provide the vision and inspiration for international, national, and regional-level action to "build a future that is more prosperous, more just, and more secure" (World Commission 1987, 1). And yet the Brundtland Commission's utopian ecological vision turned out to be easily accommodated within neoliberal globalization, which increased inequality, insecurity, and impoverishment.[7] The commission contributed to a shift from the interstate system of internationalism to globalization, in which state authority and territory became oriented more towards transnational than national interests and flows (Appadurai 1996; Sassen 2008). Postcolonial scholars, in particular, have criticized the commission's role in legitimizing new institutions for global-scale environmental governance and neoliberal practices of deregulation and privatization (see e.g. *The Ecologist* 1993; Escobar 1994; Sachs 1993b). The "global reach" (Shiva 1993, 149) or "vantage point" (Sachs 1993a, 17) of the sustainable development paradigm appeared as a mode of neo-imperialism when it enabled greater corporate access to nature in the Global South.[8]

Postcolonial critics have been concerned with how the "global" is often taken to be synonymous with human universality, spatially extensive economic integration, and planetary-scale Earth systems—making each, in turn, appear aligned with the others.[9] Anna Lowenhaupt Tsing (2005) argues that there is a plurality of globalisms, which should neither be dichotomously opposed to the local, nor equated with a single planet-encompassing system. Moreover, as Saskia Sassen details, globalization is made operational *within* nation-states, not only at a "global scale" (2008, 4).[10] All scales, including "the global," are *made*, not simply there; they are constructed in imagination and narrative as well as through social practices and material interactions in particular, networked locales and physical systems (Tsing 2005). Tsing's argument builds on Benedict Anderson's classic text on nationalism, *Imagined Communities* (1983), which explains how a nation is an imaginary construction: it is "*imagined* because the members [...] will never know most of their fellow-members, meet them, or even hear of them, yet in the minds of each lives the image of their communion" (2006, 6; italics in original). Recognizing the constructed nature of imagined globalisms is not to dismiss their efficacy or value, but rather to open up their authorizing narrative and rhetorical strategies to analysis (see also Robbins 1999). Tsing (2005) cautions against forgoing globalism or universalism since imagining universality—whether at local, national, world, or global scales—often underlies social and political arguments for equality, justice, freedom, autonomy, and humanitarianism.[11] Instead, she encourages a historicized analysis of globalisms and universalisms: what narratives "conjure" them to life (2005, 57), how they travel, how they work, and how they are translated culturally and linguistically.

From its first meetings, when it adopted the nomenclature of a "World Commission," the World Commission on Environment and Development sought a process by which its recommendations could become universal; neither its "world" status nor any universal relevance of environmental concerns could be taken as *a priori* principles.[12] Its efforts to create an imagined world community were especially driven by the implementation failures of the two preceding commissions on the "common world." The Palme Commission on Disarmament and Security, on which Gro Harlem Brundtland served, released its report *Our Common Security*, in 1982 (Independent 1982). The Brandt Commission on North–South relations, completed in 1980, titled its 1983 follow-up report *Common Crisis*, in order to emphasize how "development" was not only a task of so-called "developing" countries but required a "new economic order" worldwide (Independent 1983, 3). Neither received much traction among policy makers, despite the involvement of internationally recognized diplomats and scholars. To avoid a similar fate, the Brundtland Commission aimed to raise broad awareness and build support for its recommendations so that its work would have lasting effect. The international public hearings were central to this support-building strategy: they would be public events, open to media, and involve civil society participants who would both contribute their ideas to the commission's work and, most importantly, take an active role in pushing for implementation of the commission's recommendations at national and international levels.[13]

The hearings became symbolic of the commission as representative of "the world" because they were held at dispersed locales in Asia, Africa, South America, North America, and Europe. Although the people that provided input at the eleven hearings were a tiny portion of the actual world's population, participation in the hearings symbolically offered an approximate transnational equivalent to the national experience of creating an imagined community among strangers. The public hearings were framed for their audiences as if they were constitutive of a world-scale public sphere, in which citizens could speak freely among themselves on the common political questions of their time. For example, Gro Harlem Brundtland's opening address at the 1985 Oslo public hearing, delivered at a time when Brundtland represented the Official Opposition in the Norway Parliament, begins by saying, "I am speaking today in my homeland, yet I represent an international group of citizens, a World Commission whose aim is the care and future improvement of the planet which we all share."[14] Commissioner Stanovnik from Yugoslavia similarly reminds the participants at several public hearings that the Charter of the United Nations "says: we the people of the world. It does not say: we the governments of the world."[15] This insistent distinction between national-level "government" and world-scale "people" conjures an image of world community, just the kind of "horizontal comradeship" Anderson describes as the nation (2006, 7). These declarations also suggest that the commission's focus is the imagined world community, not the governments with whom all public hearing arrangements were negotiated, and who would be the agents responsible for implementation. Herein lies the commission's utopian approach to global ecology as a democratic worldwide concern. Participants in the public hearings, however, offered more varied and often antagonistic approaches to the presence of a "world commission" and its imagined world community.

Public hearings were a prominent aspect of the new environmental legislation of the 1970s enacted in many Western countries with an emphasis on a public's right to know about and provide consent for exposure to environmental hazards.[16] The Brundtland Commission's hearings, however, involved an act usually associated with *citizenship* being performed in a context without a governing authority. This absence of formal authority is underscored at the 1986 Harare, Zimbabwe, hearing when Brundtland speaks for a moment "as Prime Minister of Norway" to condemn the apartheid government of South Africa and announce Norway's imminent passage of a bill imposing economic sanctions.[17] Brundtland could switch roles, however, precisely because of the *public* nature of the hearings. And because they were public, the hearings were treated by many participating groups and individuals as political spaces in which to make accountability demands of state and non-state actors, particularly the loan agencies who support government initiatives but also the United Nations itself. Despite the commissioners' repeated statements of independence, participants often addressed the commission as "the Commission from the United Nations,"[18] and thereby responsible for dealing with Third World–debt burdens, the power of transnational corporations, and other international inequalities. The participation by high-ranking host government officials at each hearing—often making public statements and announcements that the audience was later invited to comment on—meant that the hearings were also used as an opportunity to place national citizen concerns on the public record. Questions, demands, and challenges were directed to political representatives at several hearings, some of them highly adversarial.

For example, participants refused to allow the 1985 São Paulo hearing in Brazil to end without a statement by the commission condemning government inaction on the environmental health crisis in the industrial city of Cubatão, known in the 1970s as "the Valley of Death" because of its high levels of pollution (Roberts and Thanos 2003). Describing "the high rate of children that were born without a brain," suffering from anencephaly, lawyer Fabio Feldman spoke before the commission to declare the situation in Cubatão "a violation of human rights."[19] Others challenged the compliance of the commission with state authorities, arguing that the city of Cubatão imposed a factory shut down to improve air quality for the visit of the commissioners, who travelled through by bus and did not stop to talk to any local people—an action that Gro Harlem Brundtland herself acknowledges and excuses on the basis of limited time and translation.[20] Many of the activists speaking at the São Paulo hearing use their time to present counterhistories of the Brazilian state, tracing the censorship and suppression of political activities under the military regime and their role in accelerating industrial exploitation and forest clearance. The composition of the World Commission is itself challenged for including in its ranks the Brazilian Minister of the Environment because he served with the military government. The public nature of the hearings, with both prearranged speakers and open-floor microphones and question periods, thus enabled participants to use the opportunity to make relations of capital, state, and environment visible to others both domestically and internationally, even if the hearings and commission itself would not be capable of resolving these political issues.

WORLD-MAKING AND UNEVEN DEVELOPMENT

A key postcolonial concern is how historical legacies of colonial resource extraction and underdevelopment shape contemporary inequalities of wealth, resources, and power. The Brundtland Commission focused its attention on "the world" because international inequalities and uneven development were central to its mandate, discussions, and recommendations. It was the first UN commission to have a majority Third World membership among the commissioners (the Eastern Bloc was also well represented), and the opening chapter of *Our Common Future* was titled "From One Earth to One World" to denote its shift from the monolithic spaceship Earth imagery of a generation earlier.[21] The term "uneven development," which Brundtland uses in her foreword (World Commission 1987, xii), was expanded upon by geographer Neil Smith to describe the pattern of capital accumulation that simultaneously produces "development at one pole and underdevelopment at the other" (Smith 1984, 6). This emphasis on capitalism as a single "world system" that produces economic disparities through spatial differentiation was crucial for challenging naturalized notions of development as something that Third World nations simply "lacked;" instead, it links the "developed" / "underdeveloped" difference to the politico-economic structures of European colonialism that Third World liberation movements had so recently overthrown (see Rodney 1981; Wallerstein 1974).[22] The economic reform recommendations of the Brandt Commission worked from these "dependency theory" perspectives, which highlight structural interlinkages, and they also figured prominently in Brundtland commissioner debates (Borowy 2014, 20–21).

Iris Borowy, in her recent history of the Brundtland Commission, places the debates about uneven development at the core of her account. She emphasizes how, "Above all, the central idea of global environmentalism, i.e. a common challenge in the one world shared by people, which had developed in the North, was partly rejected in the South, where daily experience indicated that neither the problems nor the wealth created by environmental destruction were in any way equitably shared" (2014, 89). "Several commissioners," Borowy notes, "pointed out that the economic development of low-income countries was being blocked by the set-up of the international economic system, which forced governments to prioritize debt repayment and export-oriented production at high environmental cost over feeding their people" (2014, 89). These concerns appear throughout the report and recommendations of the commission, which presents a clear statement that equitable international economic exchange is a foundational condition for sustainable development (World Commission 1987, 17, 67), while at the same time locating solutions in increased Northern financial investment and loans to the South (World Commission 1987, 76–78).

Economic disparities, however, appear ahistorical in the report—as if simply the state of the world, rather than the product of social relations of colonialism, capitalism, and regional alliances—and outside any political antagonisms or interests. For all that the report and its quoted hearing participants are cautious and often critical of growth-driven capitalist economic strategies, they name few adversaries or beneficiaries, and provide little historical or social context for described ecological conditions. In focusing on a systemic view, in which environment and economy are interlinked, the report flattens the world into a series of nodes in one, single network. Moreover, the commission's near-achievement of consensus was heralded as a sign of the potential for unified world action, suggesting that geopolitical divisions, as represented by its diverse commissioner membership, could be overcome to build the more just and prosperous future it envisioned. Both Brundtland's foreword and the opening chapter of *Our Common Future* conclude by emphasizing how agreement and consensus was achieved despite the differences among the commissioners

(World Commission 1987, xii–xiii, xiv–xv, 23; see also MacNeill 2007).[23] As Brundtland states in her preface, "as we worked, nationalism and the artificial divides between 'industrialized' and 'developing,' between East and West, receded. In their place emerged a common concern for the planet" (World Commission 1987, xii). She reiterates this transcendence of history and difference a few paragraphs later: "we all became wiser, learnt to look across cultural and historical barriers" (xiii).

That the hearings, too, involved common transnational participation from diverse and disparate people was highlighted in *Our Common Future* by featuring quotations from participants in text boxes, on every second or third page. The *diversity* of quotations—each associated with a particular, localized hearing because city and country is listed under each one—functions to illustrate (*regardless of what is said*) the participation of a range of differently located people, each contributing a unique opinion to this single "world" conversation. The acknowledged national and geographical dispersion of the participants is crucial to the transcendent image of global communion that was generated by their simultaneous participation. This narrative performance of transnational consensus models the commission's declarations that "increased international cooperation" and "a functioning multilateral system" are "required" and "fundamental" for sustainable development (World Commission 1987, 41).

The achievement of unity despite difference is a common sentimental and utopian trope.[24] Its emphasis in *Our Common Future* is noteworthy for several reasons. First, one might otherwise expect that environmental determinism would be the source of the universalism of *Our Common Future*: that whatever "the future" brings, it will be shared by all "in common" because of planetary scale ecological systems—an argument that sociologist Ulrich Beck makes in *World Risk Society* (1999). But the Brundtland Commission, composed of serving and former politicians, academics, and high-ranking international agency public servants, was aiming to create broad-based support for transnational action, and to avoid the doomsday fatalism associated with 1970s environmentalism, particularly the Club of Rome's *Limits to Growth* (see Borowy 2014, 13, 30–31). The commission therefore emphasized how a "common world," as political philosopher Hannah Arendt (1958) once argued, is what people *make* through public thought and conversation.[25] The significance of the commission's public hearings, too, lies precisely in this performative staging of a pluralist world engaged in the political act of building its future. For example, the first hearing participant quoted in *Our Common Future*, an Indonesian publisher, argues for greater and more meaningful participation by people in development. He speaks for the redistribution of both wealth and power in order to alleviate poverty—a radical argument, but one that is recuperated into the report's pluralism by its very presence as an active, contributing perspective.

Second, the report symbolically places the achievement of unity and consensus in the future, as the culmination of the world-scale political process the commission has set into play in the present. The commissioners and hearings serve to model on a small-scale the consensus that the world will come, in the future, to achieve on a large scale. To make this point, the first chapter of the report, titled "A Threatened Future," opens with the declaration that "The Earth is one but the world is not" (World Commission 1987, 27). The narrative leads from despair to optimism when disunity is overcome: "We also found grounds for hope: that people can cooperate to build a future" (28). This temporal trope implies that political antagonisms should be relegated to the past, and they have no place in an ecological future. The future, in this particular utopian construction, is thus imagined as a time without politics, since antagonism is foundational to political life (see Mouffe 2000). Moreover, uneven development, as a geopolitical fracture that belies any claim to a common world of political equals, appears like it will be resolved "over time" in the commission's narrative of progression from past to future. The Brundtland Commission here draws on "international development" as a progress narrative, in which the very term "development" and, especially, the adjective "developing" (as in "developing country"), implies a chronological progression towards a better state.

Two contradictory world narratives are thus implied in this utopian image of world consensus across difference. On the one hand, there is a plurality of voices that are in the process of speaking to and hearing one another at the same time. On the other hand, there is a temporal continuum from past to future through which differences are resolved. Both acknowledge and, simultaneously, *neutralize* the geopolitical implications of uneven development by way of an image of collective identity. Discussing the narratives that create authoritative images of the people unified as a nation, postcolonial literary critic Homi Bhabha names the synchronous one "performative" because it displays the present-day actions of the political body (1994, 147); in Frantz Fanon's words, "the fluctuating movement that the people are *just* giving shape to" (quoted in Bhabha 1994, 152; italics in original). Bhabha names the second narrative, which locates an origin of the nation in a past that is to be continued into the future, "pedagogical" because this imagined origin is meant to instruct the political body on what it is and will be (147); any troubling pluralisms of the present that might disrupt the image of collectivity are comfortably displaced by the continuity of tradition.

For Bhabha, what is interesting about these two ways to narrate the nation—and which we can see mirrored in the commission's efforts to narrate *the world*—is precisely the way their temporalities conflict, thereby exposing the contingency of this imagined community. The "performative" suggests the citizens of the present, fully present; the "pedagogical" indicates the citizens as inheritors of a now absent, only remembered, common past. These two temporalities—synchrony and succession—disclose the representational practices required for authorizing the nation. In their *disjuncture*, Bhabha suggests, they expose the anxieties and insecurities of a nation's claims to spatial integrity and temporal continuity—fissures through which marginal subjects may act and speak. The *redoubled* narration reveals how tenuous the collectivity is: the cultural image of the nation, the world, or the globe is never exactly co-extensive with "the people," or with its apparent past. Nations—and worlds—remain always in the process of being made, which reminds us how they might be made and narrated differently. The commission's narratives reveal how a world vision of pluralist cooperation gains coherence and legitimacy so as to appear simply universal. However, the plurality of perspectives in the present also represents historically shaped differences and structural inequalities, which was the basis for political demands for national self-determination by formerly colonized nations, and for gender equality and other social and economic justice claims by oppressed groups.

FUTURE AS ALIBI

The postcolonial anthropologist David Scott (1999, 2004) suggests that narratives of the future—and associated struggles for the authority to imagine and shape a future—are pivotal in political thought. He points out that social and political movements may remain attached to particular narratives of futurity that have since lost their salience as historical conditions change. They become "old utopian futures"—*past* futures, as Reinhart Koselleck puts it (quoted in Scott 2004, 1). For Scott, it is important to recognize that some futures are now dead-end political projects in order to develop new political projects more responsive to the present moment. But his work has broader relevance in helping to show how *futurity* can be *historicized* through the study of narratives and narrative forms, and how collective identities, such as the nation or the world, are shaped not only around historical origins and invented traditions but also in relation to particular hopes and aspirations of a future to come. Environmental narratives are often studied in relation to changing ecological conditions rather than to political subjectivities and collective identities precisely because the political project of environmentalism has seemed to be so obviously about the future.

Since the 1940s, narratives of global environmental futurity tended to be apocalyptic, drawing especially on desertification imagery to depict barren lands where resources are scarce[26] and human existence is reduced to the condition philosopher Giorgio Agamben (1998) terms "bare life," when "the species and the individual as a simple living body become what is at stake" (3). American ecologist William Vogt's 1948 international bestseller *Road to Survival*, initiator of the genre (see Sörlin 2013), threatened that unless "man readjusts his way of living [...] to the imperatives imposed by the *limited* resources of his environment, we may as well give up hope of continuing civilized life. Like Gadarene swine, we shall rush down a war-torn slope to a barbarian existence in the blackened rubble" (Vogt 2013, 190; italics in original). Vogt's animalized and satanic contrast between "civilized life" and "barbarian existence" exemplifies the role "bare life" plays as the excluded outside in conceptions of the good life. As Agamben argues, working from Aristotle, "[t]he fundamental categorical pair of Western politics is not that of friend/enemy but that of bare life/political existence, zoë/bios, exclusion/inclusion. There is politics because man is the living being who, in language, separates and opposes himself to his own bare life" (1998, 8). Vogt's "blackened rubble"—or, by analogy, "bare earth"—imagery is foundational to his depiction of bare life (2013, 190). As "bare earth," a physical place is depicted as if without sustenance and, hence, any possible bio-cultural meanings and practices; the terrain might be earth but does not count as productive, and as such the lives lived there do not appear worth living.[27]

In the development discourse that emerged in the same postwar period as Vogt's apocalyptic manifesto, the prevalence of famine imagery depicted the decolonizing world in terms of "bare life" conditions that modernization would resolve (Escobar 1994). Development as a "cultural struggle," whereby people strive to articulate and bring into being their own visions of a good life, was thereby depoliticized and decontextualized into a form of technical knowledge practiced on other people's bodies and ecologies (Escobar 1994, 16; see also Crush 1995; Ferguson 1990; Rist 2002). These popular development and environment discourses merged in the period leading up the Brundtland Commission. In an inversion of modernization discourse (see Chakrabarty 2009), Third World pasts and presents, reductively represented as forms of "bare life," function to allegorically *prefigure* First World apocalyptic *futures* in texts such as Paul Ehrlich's (1968) *Population Bomb*, which opens with an impression of the First World traveller feeling overcrowded in Delhi. The Brundtland Commission offered its report *Our Common Future* as a plan for reversing such apocalyptic expectations through worldwide cooperation rather than reentrenched development divides between affluent and impoverished peoples. Bare life and bare earth rhetoric recur in the report—the "Threatened Future" chapter repeatedly cites desertification threats and its opening paragraph refers abstractly to those who "live with the prospect of hunger, squalor, disease, and early death" (World Commission 1987, 27). But these images are invoked as a *potential past* that a sustainable future will have left behind.

An alternative futurity is constructed in *Our Common Future* by way of the quotations from the public hearings. One quoted speaker emphatically states, in a rejection of bare-life discourse, "You talk very little about life, you talk too much about survival [...] there are peoples here in Brazil, especially in the Amazon region, who still live, and these peoples that still live don't want to reach down to the level of survival" (World Commission 1987, 40). In the report, a shared "common future" is not empirically claimed or depicted; instead, it is narratively performed as a global convergence of *aspirational* narratives, which function to show there is international will to overcome current problems. That many of the quotations do not directly endorse the transnational commission, the concept of sustainable development, or its recommendations (and are, at times, even critical of it, as with the statement above) underscores how their role is to speak for the future as a common *desire*: what is universalized is the desire for something else, thereby providing legitimacy for a global project of change. "The world is unfortunately not what we would like it to be," reads one quotation from a youth representative at the Oslo hearings (quoted in World Commission 1987, 164). "We have a chance to develop a new direction," says a speaker at the Jakarta hearings (111). "We have to find a new ethic," says a speaker at the São Paulo hearing (71); a scientist at the Moscow hearings repeats this point: "What is needed today is the moulding of a new ethos" (285). "New attitudes towards the environment" is the focus of a high school student addressing the Ottawa hearings (112). "The will to dream in us all" is what must be sustained as "we approach the millennium," says an environment and peace activist at Ottawa (301); while an environmental activist at the São Paulo hearing declares that "the greatest crime" is "the death of hope […] especially that of the young of believing in a future" (299).

The diversity of statements, each associated with a particular, localized hearing, demonstrates that this future is no homogenous vision to be imposed on all. Rather, the meaning of the worldly "we" here, as Berlant has said of the nation in the symbolism of the United States, is the utopian "promise" of future salvation (1991, 32). "In the utopian mode," Berlant writes, we find "that the American people as now symbolically constituted transcend their own history, having embarked on a mission of moral and political perfection in which the problems of the past appear, when they appear, as an abyss from which the national project has liberated us" (40). The Brundtland Commission's utopian mode suggests its catalogue of localized disasters will be overcome through a global project, which, as the quotations seemingly show *by their very address to the commission*, disparate individuals and peoples identify and place their hopes with. Sutured into the report, these voices are sutured into globality. In the process, as represented in the report, their imagined futures are dislocated from their places of articulation. The hearing participants become what Roland Barthes terms an "alibi" (1973, 123), seeming at once full of concrete meaning and at the same time empty of it because they serve as a signifier of something else: a global hope for a better future. Each specified locale finds its future in this global project; in turn, the global project takes on substance through these concrete examples. The future appears *open* because dehistoricized and deterritorialized into a vague longing, while the subjects speaking this desire are differentiated and emplaced in order to give it empirical presence. Their particular voices and environments are strung together to signify *everywhere* and hence *everyone*, but the future they describe is unplaced, *nowhere*, utterly generic. For many of the hearing participants, however, such as the contingent from Cubatão, the *specific* industrial, political, ecological, and cultural context in which they are situated—a concentrated petrochemical refinery port—is pivotal to their demands.

Present-day ecological problems become distanced as if already the past—as a sign of what is to be transcended—when described in the commission's utopian mode. A key dimension of the World Commission's futurity is that the "global" is not now but will come in "the future," a construction that rests on a spatio-temporal differentiation that positions the Third World in "another Time"—the past (Fabian 1983, 27). Postcolonial historian Dipesh Chakrabarty vividly allegorizes how this seemingly neutral temporal progression is in fact geopolitical. He describes modernization discourse as "an imaginary waiting room of history," where "[w]e were all headed for the same destination [...] but some people were to arrive earlier than others" (2009, 8). The post–World War II international development paradigm in which sustainable development participates repeats this "'first in Europe, then elsewhere' structure of global historical time," in which "modernity or capitalism look not simply global but rather as something that became global *over time*, by originating in one place and then spreading outside it" (7; italics in original). Implicitly, this temporal construction, common to colonial anthropology, follows what Fabian terms the "denial of coevalness" (1983, 27), or a refusal to see different cultures as being of the same time. Chakrabarty (2009) points out how *the future* is foreclosed for "developing" nations in these narratives of historical progression: their future already exists, merely elsewhere, in the First World. World Commission Secretary-General Jim MacNeill places the Third World present into another time—the time of the First World's past—in his final comments at the 1985 São Paulo hearing. MacNeill tells the audience that "however awful some of your problems are and I am thinking of Cubatão and your tropical forest problems, however awful they are, the lessons of past experiences [are] that most, if not all of them are reversible."[28] His evidence, he claims, comes from his Canadian experience, which has shown that lakes and fisheries can come back from the dead—this a mere six years before the collapse of the Atlantic cod fishery in eastern Canada.

MacNeill's statement exhibits the developmentalist logic described by Chakrabarty, whereby the non-West is perpetually playing catch-up to a future that emerges "first in the West, and then elsewhere" (2009, 6). As Chakrabarty argues, this temporal narrative depoliticizes its Eurocentric premises, or the way that "first in Europe" is "somebody's way of saying 'not yet' to somebody else" (8): a structuring difference and inequality legitimized by way of a *universalized future promised but deferred*.[29] Throughout the commission's hearings and report, testimonial evidence and political demands to redress existing ecological loss and suffering, international inequalities, and transnational regulatory gaps are deferred by placing the global in the future: *now* is "not yet" global; the global will be something "other" than this. The "global" can remain shiny with possibility, immune to criticism *because it has not yet arrived*, while Third World demands and experiences can be symbolically jettisoned to the past, since their resolution *has already come* in the First World.

SLOW VIOLENCE, TESTIMONIAL NARRATIVES, AND THE GLOBAL NOW

Postcolonial literary critic Rob Nixon (2011) uses the term "slow violence" to extend our understanding of violence to include the *longue durée* of suffering experienced with ecological hazards, resource diminishment, and livelihood loss. It is a concept that resists the mode of deferral by showing how ecological violence takes time: to say "not yet" is to condone ongoing violence. As Nixon explains, "Violence is customarily conceived as an event or action that is immediate in time, explosive and spectacular in space, and as erupting into instant sensational violence" (2). He implores us to understand that violence is also slow, that it "occurs gradually and out of sight"; climate change, for example, is a form of "violence that is dispersed across time and space, an attritional violence that is typically not viewed as violence at all" because the affected people—*in the present*—tend to be poor, socially marginalized, and/or live in geopolitical peripheries (2). The association of violence with immediacy and spectacle suggests that other modes of representation are required to make slow violence public and visible in the places distant from its effects. Nixon highlights the role of "writer-activists" who act as *witnesses* to slow violence, especially through nonfictional forms like journalism and memoir (4). By relaying direct experiences of slow violence, they disrupt the "spatial amnesia" whereby the "unsettlement" and displacement of communities by development projects and ecological decline is forgotten and erased from national and world memory (151).

The narrative mode of witnessing is called "testimonial," because, as if in a court of law, lived experiences are provided as evidence to attest to an unjust situation. A prominent strategy for exposing human rights abuses in Latin America at the time of the Brundtland Commission, testimonial narratives (also known as *testimonio*) are presented by many speakers at the commission hearings, including the residents of Cubatão who called for *immediate*—not deferred—response from the World Commission and other authorities. At the 1985 hearings in Jakarta, Indonesia, a medical doctor formerly employed by the multinational company Union Carbide in Jakarta presents her personal experience as evidence of hazardous working conditions: "I found that the drinking water contained mercury. And then there are chemical hazards everywhere in the factory. And I asked them to do something for that chemical hazard. And I asked them to treat their wastewater before the lead flow out of that waste water. And I tried writing the salary of the workers."[30] Dr. Meizar's story ends with a list of company refusals to meet her requests and a standoff that led to her forced resignation. Her statement is made just three months after the December 1984 explosion of Union Carbide's pesticide factory in Bhopal, India, which caused thousands of deaths and hundreds of thousands of people to be injured (World Commission 1987, 3, 228–29).

Throughout the hearing records are testimonial narratives like Dr. Meizar's in which participants use life experiences to tell a story of environmental hazard or loss. At times, these stories are presented as anecdotal evidence that must suffice because no research or data exists to document the problem. Others are presented as human rights violations. Others ask for there to be an audience to hear and acknowledge the injustice. A man from the Association of the Rural Workers in the State of Acre, Brazil, representing the rubber tappers being dispossessed by the large land owners moving into the Amazon forests, stands before the commission in São Paulo, speaking through an interpreter, to say, "I have come here to register the suffering."[31] At the 1986 Quebec City hearing in Canada, with the Canadian federal minister of the environment in the audience, activist Jean-Pierre Drapeau attempts to read into the public record a federal government statement regarding low-level military flights over indigenous lands, which had claimed these lands were empty of inhabitants. Repeatedly interrupted by the Quebec provincial minister of environment, who is facilitating the meeting, Drapeau then reads out, in French, a witness statement—"un témoignage"—by Guy Belfleur, an Innu community member living in the area, that details the community's observations of a decline in caribou, the effects on beaver, and mass fish kills due to the flights and based on years of experience on the land.[32] At the 1986 Halifax, Canada, hearing, activist Charlie Musial localizes himself as a Cape Breton Island resident who knows better in response to a self-congratulatory presentation by a provincial level planning council about discontinuing large-scale pesticide spraying in the forests. Musial's speech from the floor, which at times directly addresses by name the various provincial government officials present, is authorized by his insistence on local memory: "I know because I was there," he says.[33]

None of these statements from the public hearings are quoted in *Our Common Future*, likely because testimonial narratives are difficult to accommodate in the report's chronopolitics of future deferral. The testimonial mode places these experiences in the global now: present-day suffering from past or ongoing socio-ecological hazard and loss to which any imagined world community should already be responding. The speakers name political situations and call for responsible authorities—for there to be *responsive* authorities—to hear their complaints and recognize their legitimacy. In placing these demands before the commission, at times accompanied by a list of the local- and national-level authorities that have been previously contacted without success, participants claim a place for themselves within an imagined world community. One woman at the São Paulo hearing describes a five-year fight against industrial air pollution in Baha Funda, Brazil, where she claims, "In every house there is at least one or two sick people." She goes on to say, "We have asked the Health Secretariats and this government and our Brazilian government to inquire into this [...]. We were not heard. We went to every level of government, to the mayor, to the government, to the State Assembly."[34] Many indeed ask the commission to recommend the creation of an international court that could have the authority to hear cases of transnational or state-sanctioned environmental crime.

In play during these public hearings is a working out of what collective determination and governance could and should be in relation to globalizing capital forces and colonizing national forces. Even though the Brundtland Commission lacked formal authority, its staging of itself as a global public forum—a site through which "the world" could see and talk about itself—gave it a symbolic presence as a global authority figure, a symbolic role it both claimed and disavowed, as when commissioners emphasized its weakness in relation to the "real" international power-wielders (such as the United Nations, the multinational corporations, or planetary and ecological systems). Precisely in forming a visible, present body that may be *addressed* on behalf of "the world," the commission makes globality appear coherent and responsive, subject to political demands. In addressing the commission— and being addressed by it—participants and spectators become world subjects, recognizing themselves, even when opposed, in relation to world-scale collective action. At the same time, a heteroglossic world—of cacophonous alterity, dissent, demands, and alternatives—is revealed as already in existence. The public hearing participants who chose to act as witnesses to slow violence refused to wait for some other future to arrive; instead, they name the global as *now,* give a *history* to their socio-ecological conditions, and claim the commission as a public site for "socioenvironmental memory" (Nixon 2011, 25).

CONCLUSIONS

In *After Globalization,* Eric Cazdyn and Imre Szeman suggest that the "common sense" of globalization has involved a certain foreclosure of the future: globalization seemed inevitable because it was impossible to imagine an "after" to globalization (2011, 37). Projected into the future—always in the process of arriving with the latest new technologies and shrinking nation-state—globalization is also strangely "atemporal," as if "once begun, it could never end" (37). Sustainability is a similarly atemporal concept, an imagining of the future suspended into a perpetual present.[35] To imagine an "after" to sustainability is baffling because to achieve "sustainability" would be to ensure there is no end—in the apocalyptic bare earth imaginary of the Global North. But "bare earth" is not simply a future vision— it is an imagined future based on the slow, violent despoliation of *other people's lives* in the past and present. Rather than locating bare earth in some "undeveloped" past that the Global South will leave "over time" as it "catches up" to the Global North, or in some apocalyptic future to be forestalled by a global project of sustainable development, the witnesses who made statements at the public hearings spoke of particular, historically located places and people subject to a slow violence that should be placed on the public record and for which responsible parties should be held to account.

While narratives themselves do not make or remake Earth systems, they do play a major role in making some people's livelihoods, experiences, and cultural meanings *count* in ecological and political work. The significant achievement of the World Commission on Environment and Development in conjuring an imagined world community should be appreciated in its fullness, for the heterogeneous voices and narrative modes through which *many* made a claim on the world—in the present and for their futures. The voices of participants at the public hearings of the World Commission on Environment and Development were heard and valued, as the many quoted in the final report attest—and yet the debates about the environmental responsibilities, histories, and politics of "the world" were more complex than the report's emphasis on consensus and shared aspiration makes them appear. As we continue to grapple with the challenges of cooperation and governance on transnational environmental processes such as climate change, it is important to resist narratives that construct a common world around de-historicized practices of global consensus, and that postpone demands for justice into another time that has not yet come. We should be cautious of constructing the future as an alibi for our inability to redress ecological problems in the present because of their trenchant immersion in specific economic and political configurations. The historical and political contexts in which people spoke to the commission mattered for their political demands and for the ways in which they constructed their position in relation to a "world" they participated in bringing to life. Postcolonial environmental humanities research shows how their voices and stories are very much still pertinent today, even if left only as traces in the memories of participants and the cassette tapes and transcriptions of the commission archives.

NOTES

1. This research was supported by a Social Sciences and Humanities Research Council of Canada Insight Development Grant. I thank my two research assistants, Kameela Amer and Joshua Overbeek, for their help in working with the World Commission documents.
2. The public hearing approach was continued in the lead-up to the 1992 Earth Summit as "Global Forums," also known as citizens' summits (Finger 1993, 45), where nongovernmental organizations from multiple countries and regions met concurrently with government-to-government negotiations, a practice also used at the 1972 UN Conference on the Human Environment in Stockholm and now common at UN climate change conferences.
3. On the politics of sustainable development and global environmental governance, see Kapoor (2008), Luke (1997), Martínez-Alier (2003), Mies and Bennholdt-Thomsen (1999), and Sachs (1999).

4. On narrative as authorization, discussed further in my section entitled "World-Making and Uneven Development," see Bhabha (1994); on the voices and forms "not heard" within universalist narratives, see Spivak 1986, 1988, and 1998.

5. The "common" has both political and economic meanings, as Michael Hardt and Antonio Negri recount in their anti-capitalist manifesto *Commonwealth* (2009). For political philosopher Hannah Arendt (1958), the common is the public (as opposed to private) realm around which political life takes shape. In economic terms, a "commons," as economist Elinor Ostrom (1990) outlines, is a resource shared by a group, often under communal property regimes (not the "free-loader" economics vividly popularized by Garrett Hardin in the 1960s as "The Tragedy of the Commons"). "The common" for Hardt and Negri (2009) is a form of social relations created through post-Fordist modes of production that rely on collaborative and shared knowledge, and thus could provide the basis for communal reclamation of labor, production, and wealth. For a cautionary critique, see Federici (2011).

6. The Brundtland Commission was the third in a series of international commissions that focused on imagining a "common world;" first was the Brandt Commission on North–South relations, followed by the Palme Commission on Disarmament and Security. These three commissions shared what Dirlik calls a "global neo-Keynesianism" (2007, 137)—a vision of some form of universal, redistributive welfare state—that was "stillborn" due to the coinciding ascendance of neoliberal globalization.

7. For all the later convergences of sustainable development and neoliberalism, it is nevertheless important to recognize how the Brundtland Commission's recommendations and processes were more Keynesian than neoliberal. Borowy (2014) provides an overview of how much the Brandt Commission and Brundtland Commission recommendations were at odds with neoliberalism. She notes, for example, how the Brandt Commission not only "called for major changes in the international economic order, especially for a large-scale transfer of resources from high- to low-income countries," but also "proposed an automatic form of raising international revenues by placing a levy on a long list of transactions, including international trade, international investment, on hydrocarbons and non-renewable minerals" (44). The Brundtland Commission's very emphasis on governmental and international institutions—its faith in civil service rather than markets—shows how much its discourse precedes neoliberalism.

8. For key postcolonial and political economy critiques of sustainable development as contributing to a new resource grab in the Global South, see Adams (1995), *The Ecologist* (1993), O'Connor (1993), Sachs (1993b), and Shiva (1999).

9. Insisting that "the 'global' is not planetary," Shiva (1993) explains that the particular "global" of the Earth Summit was a set of interests "local" to a particular geopolitical class, but naturalized as if coextensive with the Earth itself: "What at present exists as the global is not the democratic distillation of all local and national concerns worldwide, but the imposition of a narrow group of interests from a handful of nations on a world-scale" (154). Postcolonial critic Gayatri Spivak (2003), drawing on Shiva's analysis, similarly insists on distinguishing between the "global" and the "planetary." She writes, "The globe is on our computers. No one lives there. It allows us to think that we can aim to control it. The planet is in the species of alterity, belonging to another system; and yet

we inhabit it, on loan" (72). In particularizing the "globe" as a technology-generated image, Spivak (2003) attends to language as a form of ideology—a means by which powerful interests can appear to be acting for the common good because these images and ideas circulate as if autonomous objects, with their conditions of emergence and beneficiaries unnamed and absent.

10. Sassen uses the term "denationalizing" to indicate how globalization involves "micro-processes" within nation-states that re-orient authority away from the nation (2008, 1–2).

11. James Youngblood Henderson's (2008) account of how state-suppressed indigenous peoples won recognition of distinct status at the United Nations through their appeal to the universalist claims of international human rights is a strong example.

12. See MacNeill (2007, 248, n13) on how the commission named itself.

13. For a detailed review of the development of the commission's public relations and public hearings approach and their divergence from the earlier commissions and reports, see Borowy (2014, 39–48, 65–66, 157); see also MacNeill (2007).

14. Gro Harlem Brundtland, "Address," in *Verbatim transcripts of the Public Hearings of the World Commission on Environment and Development held in Oslo, June 24–25, 1985*, vol. 35, doc. 10, archive of the International Development Research Centre (IDRC), Ottawa (following p. 14). Subsequent citations of these archival transcripts are referred to only by place, date, document, and page number.

15. Tokyo Public Hearing, February 27, 1987, vol. 38, doc 48, p. 44; also Jakarta Public Hearing, March 26, 1985, vol. 35, doc. 7, p. 62.

16. Some of these public hearings even had strong results, such as the 1974–77 Berger Inquiry in Canada, which travelled to Dene and Inuit aboriginal communities along the MacKenzie River Valley for their opinions and successfully recommended a ten-year moratorium be placed on pipeline construction on unresolved land claims due to aboriginal opposition (see Berger 2010).

17. Harare Public Hearing, September 18, 1986, vol. 37, doc. 34, p. 20.

18. São Paulo Public Hearing, October 28–29, 1985, vol. 36, doc. 16, p. 10.

19. São Paulo Public Hearing, October 28–29, 1985, vol. 36, doc. 15, p. 19.

20. São Paulo Public Hearing, October 28–29, 1985, vol. 36, doc. 17, p. 131.

21. The phrase "one Earth" comes from the report of the 1972 Stockholm United Nations Conference on the Human Environment (Ward 1972), which was entitled *Only One Earth: The Care and Maintenance of a Small Planet.*

22. The dependency theory approach, however, became outdated with globalization and neoliberalism because it understood differentiation within national and regional terms, rather than differentiation *within* nation-states and networked global cities in response to globalized capital flows. See Dirlik (2007), Ferguson (2006), Harvey (2006), and Sassen (2008) for elaboration.

23. The commission did not achieve full consensus in that one commissioner from the Global South, Mexican Commissioner Pablo González Casanova, resigned, and others threatened to leave (see Borowy 2014, 105, 118, 124, 152).

24. See Lousley (2013) for an in-depth discussion of sentimental tropes in 1980s development representations.

25. Arendt writes, "This world [...] is not identical with the earth or with nature [...]. It is related, rather, to the human artifact, the fabrication of human hands, as well as to affairs which go on among those who inhabit the man-made world

together" (1958, 52). Further, "To be political, to live in a *polis,* meant that everything was decided through words and persuasion and not through force and violence" (26).

26. See Robin, Sörlin, and Warde's (2013) history of the concept "environment" and associated key texts, which focus on desertification, population, and pollution; also see their forthcoming volume *Environment: A History.*

27. I propose this concept of "bare earth" by analogy with Agamben's (1998) "bare life" because it has a slightly different connotation from scarcity, which retains an economic context, and from concepts of the state of nature because demarcated as a state of exception not a primitivist origin.

28. São Paulo Hearing, October 28–29, 1985, vol. 36, doc. 17, p. 125.

29. For further discussion of the rhetoric of deferral in development and globalization discourse, see Dirlik (2007) and Sarkar (2008).

30. Dr. Meizar, Jakarta Public Hearing, March 26, 1985, vol. 35, doc 7, p. 84.

31. São Paulo Public Hearing, October 28–29, 1985, vol. 36, doc. 16, p. 45.

32. Quebec Public Hearing, June 1, 1986, vol. 37, doc. 31, p. 19.

33. Halifax Public Hearing, May 31, 1986, vol. 37, doc. 29, p. 84.

34. São Paulo Public Hearing, October 28–29, 1985, vol. 36, doc. 17, p. 71.

35. The concept of sustainable development has many origins, but a significant one is Goodland and Ledec's steady-state economics paper on "economic well-being" that could be "perpetuated continually" (Borowy 2014, 98).

REFERENCES

Adams, W.M. 1995. "Green Development Theory? Environmentalism and Sustainable Development." In *Power of Development,* edited by Jonathan Crush. London and New York: Routledge.

———. 2008. *Green Development: Environment and Sustainability in a Developing World.* 3rd ed. London and New York: Routledge.

Agamben, Giorgio. 1998. *Homo Sacer: Sovereign Power and Bare Life.* Stanford: Stanford University Press.

Anderson, Benedict. 2006. *Imagined Communities: Reflections on the Origin and Spread of Nationalism.* London: Verso.

Appadurai, Arjun. 1996. *Modernity at Large: Cultural Dimensions of Globalization.* Minneapolis: University of Minnesota Press.

Arendt, Hannah. 1958. *The Human Condition.* Chicago: University of Chicago Press.

Barthes, Roland. 1973. *Mythologies.* London: Paladin.

Beck, Ulrich. 1999. *World Risk Society.* Cambridge: Polity Press.

Berger, Thomas. 2010. *Northern Frontier, Northern Homeland.* Vancouver: Douglas & McIntyre.

Berlant, Lauren Gail. 1991. *The Anatomy of National Fantasy: Hawthorne, Utopia, and Everyday Life.* Chicago: University of Chicago Press.

Bhabha, Homi K. 1994. *The Location of Culture.* London: Routledge.

Borowy, Iris. 2014. *Defining Sustainable Development for Our Common Future: A History of the World Commission on Environment and Development.* London and New York: Routledge.

Cazdyn, Eric, and Imre Szeman. 2011. *After Globalization*. London: Wiley-Blackwell.

Chakrabarty, Dipesh. 2009. *Provincializing Europe: Postcolonial Thought and Historical Difference*. New ed. Princeton: Princeton University Press.

Crush, Jonathan, ed. 1995. *Power of Development*. London and New York: Routledge.

Death, Carl. 2010. *Governing Sustainable Development : Partnerships, Protests and Power at the World Summit*. London and New York: Routledge.

Dirlik, Arif. 2007. *Global Modernity: Modernity in the Age of Global Capitalism*. Boulder: Paradigm.

The Ecologist. 1993. *Whose Common Future? Reclaiming the Commons*. Gabriola Is.: New Society.

Ehrlich, Paul R. 1971. *The Population Bomb*. New York: Ballantine.

Escobar, Arturo. 1995. *Encountering Development: The Making and Unmaking of the Third World*. Princeton: Princeton University Press.

———. 2004. "Beyond the Third World: Imperial Globality, Global Coloniality and Anti-Globalisation Social Movements." *Third World Quarterly* 25 (1): 207–230.

Fabian, Johannes. 1983. *Time and the Other: How Anthropology Makes Its Object*. New York: Columbia University Press.

Federici, Silvia. 2011. "Feminism and the Politics of the Commons." *The Commoner*. http://www.commoner.org.uk.

Ferguson, James. 1990. *The Anti-Politics Machine: "Development," Depoliticization, and Bureaucratic Power in Lesotho*. Cambridge: Cambridge University Press.

———. 2006. *Global Shadows: Africa in the Neoliberal World Order*. Durham: Duke University Press.

Finger, Mathias. 1993. "Politics of the UNCED Process." In *Global Ecology: A New Arena of Political Conflict*, edited by Wolfgang Sachs, 36–48. London: Zed Books.

Haraway, Donna J. 1991. *Simians, Cyborgs, and Women: The Reinvention of Nature*. New York: Routledge.

Hardt, Michael, and Antonio Negri. 2009. *Commonwealth*. Cambridge: Harvard University Press.

Harvey, David. 2006. *Spaces of Global Capitalism: Towards a Theory of Uneven Geographical Development*. London: Verso.

Henderson, James Youngblood. 2008. *Indigenous Diplomacy and the Rights of Peoples: Achieving UN Recognition*. Saskatoon: Purich.

Independent Commission on Disarmament and Security Issues. 1982. *Common Security: A Blueprint for Survival*. New York: Simon & Schuster.

Independent Commission on International Development Issues and Willy Brandt. 1983. *Common Crisis: North-South Cooperation for World Recovery*. London: Pan.

Kapoor, Ilan. 2008. *The Postcolonial Politics of Development*. New York: Routledge.

Lohmann, Larry. 1993. "Resisting Green Globalism." In *Global Ecology: A New Arena of Political Conflict*, edited by Wolfgang Sachs, 157–169. London: Zed Books.

Lousley, Cheryl. "Band Aid Reconsidered: Sentimental Cultures and Populist Humanitarianism." In *Popular Representations of Development: Insights from Novels, Films, Television, and Social Media*, edited by David Lewis, Dennis Rodgers, and Michael Woolcock, 174–192. London: Routledge, 2013.

Luke, Timothy W. 1997. *Ecocritique: Contesting the Politics of Nature, Economy, and Culture*. Minneapolis: University of Minnesota Press.

MacNeill, Jim. 2007. "From Controversy to Consensus – Building Global Agreement for Change." *Environmental Policy and Law* 37 (2–3): 242–248.

Martínez-Alier, Joan. 2003. *The Environmentalism of the Poor: A Study of Ecological Conflicts and Valuation.* Cheltenham: Edward Elgar.

Mies, Maria, and Veronika Bennholdt-Thomsen. 1999. *The Subsistence Perspective: Beyond the Globalised Economy.* New York: Zed Books.

Mouffe, Chantal. 2000. *The Democratic Paradox.* London: Verso.

Nixon, Rob. 2011. *Slow Violence and the Environmentalism of the Poor.* Cambridge: Harvard University Press.

O'Connor, Martin. 1993. "On the Misadventures of Capitalist Nature." *Capitalism, Nature, Socialism* 4 (3): 7–40.

Ostrom, Elinor. 1990. *Governing the Commons: The Evolution of Institutions for Collective Action.* Cambridge: Cambridge University Press.

Rist, Gilbert. 2002. *The History of Development: From Western Origins to Global Faith.* London: Zed Books.

Robbins, Bruce. 1999. *Feeling Global: Internationalism in Distress.* New York: New York University Press.

Roberts, J. Timmons, and Nikki Demetria Thanos. 2003. *Trouble in Paradise: Globalization and Environmental Crises in Latin America.* New York: Routledge.

Robin, Libby, Sverker Sörlin, and Paul Warde. 2013. "'The Environment' How Did the Idea Emerge?" In *The Future of Nature: Documents of Global Change*, edited by Libby Robin, Sverker Sörlin, and Paul Warde, 157–159. New Haven: Yale University Press.

Rodney, Walter. 1981. *How Europe Underdeveloped Africa.* Washington D.C.: Howard University Press.

Sachs, Wolfgang. 1993a. "Global Ecology and the Shadow of 'Development.'" In *Global Ecology: A New Arena of Political Conflict*, edited by Wolfgang Sachs, 3–21. London: Zed Books.

———, ed. 1993b. *Global Ecology: A New Arena of Political Conflict.* London: Zed Books.

Sachs, Wolfgang. 1999. *Planet Dialectics: Explorations in Environment and Development.* New York: Zed Books.

Said, Edward W. 1994. *Orientalism.* New York: Vintage Books.

Sarkar, Bhaskar. 2008. "The Melodramas of Globalization." *Cultural Dynamics* 20 (1): 31–51.

Sassen, Saskia. 2008. *Territory, Authority, Rights: From Medieval to Global Assemblages.* Princeton: Princeton University Press.

Scott, David. 1999. *Refashioning Futures: Criticism after Postcoloniality.* Princeton: Princeton University Press.

———. 2004. *Conscripts of Modernity: The Tragedy of Colonial Enlightenment.* Durham: Duke University Press.

Shiva, Vandana. 1993. "The Greening of the Global Reach." In *Global Ecology: A New Arena of Political Conflict*, edited by Wolfgang Sachs, 149–156. London: Zed Books.

———. 1999. *Biopiracy.* London: Zed Books.

Smith, Neil. 1984. *Uneven Development: Nature, Capital, and the Production of Space.* London: Blackwell.

Sörlin, Sverker. 2013. "Commentary: William Vogt, Road to Survival (1948)." In *The Future of Nature: Documents of Global Change*, edited by Libby Robin, Sverker Sörlin, and Paul Warde, 191–194. New Haven: Yale University Press.

Spivak, Gayatri Chakravorty. 1986. "Three Women's Texts and a Critique of Imperialism." In *"Race," Writing, and Difference*, edited by Henry Louis Gates, 262–280. Chicago: University of Chicago Press.

———. 1988. "Can the Subaltern Speak?" In *Marxism and the Interpretation of Culture*, edited by Cary Nelson and Lawrence Grossberg, 271–313. Urbana: University of Illinois Press.

———. 1998. "Cultural Talks in the Hot Peace: Revisiting the 'Global Village.'" In *Cosmopolitics: Thinking and Feeling beyond the Nation*, edited by Pheng Cheah and Bruce Robbins, 329–348. Minneapolis: University of Minnesota Press.

———. 2003. *Death of a Discipline*. New York: Columbia University Press.

Tsing, Anna Lowenhaupt. 2005. *Friction*. Princeton: Princeton University Press.

Vogt, William. 2013. "Road to Survival (1948)." In *The Future of Nature: Documents of Global Change*, edited by Libby Robin, Sverker Sörlin, and Paul Warde, 187–190. New Haven: Yale University Press.

Wallerstein, Immanuel. 1974. *The Modern World-System: Capitalist Agriculture and the Origins of the European World-Economy in the Sixteenth Century*. New York: Academic Press.

Ward, Barbara. 1972. *Only One Earth; the Care and Maintenance of a Small Planet; an Unofficial Report Commissioned by the Secretary-General of the United Nations Conference on the Human Environment*. New York: Norton.

World Commission on Environment and Development. 1987. *Our Common Future*. Oxford: Oxford University Press.

12 Oil on Sugar

Commodity Frontiers and Peripheral Aesthetics

Michael Niblett

This chapter analyses the ways in which the political ecologies of sugar and oil have impacted upon fiction from the economic peripheries of the world-system. Produced and utilized as energy sources under capitalist relations of production, oil and sugar have been deeply imbricated in histories of colonial conquest, imperial domination, and the gross exploitation of human and extra-human nature. The chapter examines the distinctive literary idioms generated by this history, paying particular attention to what I will term *irrealist* registers, such as gothic and magical realism. In so doing, it considers how petroleum and sucrose can seep into the texture of everyday life, patterning behaviors and habitus.

Oil and sugar are not just material products, but cultural phenomena too. The transition to oil as the dominant energy source powering the world-economy, for example, involved not only the development of new forms of industry, but also the emergence of a new, oil-soaked cultural apparatus and of new bodily investments and modes of affect "materialized in particular types of vehicles, homes, neighbourhoods, and cities" (Sheller 2004, 229). In this way, the "necessity of oil to our functioning social systems" was naturalized, inculcated into our habitus (MacDonald 2013, 4). Something similar might be said of sugar, which in shaping bodies, tastes, habits, and even emotional geographies (sugar "highs" and "lows") has permeated the fabric of the social world.[1]

Exposing and critiquing this process of naturalization is one task that scholarship in the environmental humanities might usefully take up. As Graeme MacDonald has argued with respect to oil: "Part of the point in theorizing energy as cultural is [...] to expose and determine reasons for our acculturation to its hierarchy of material (and, increasingly, immaterial) forms and the manner in which they dictate fundamental aspects of social life and organization" (2013, 10). In this connection, the study of literature has a key role to play insofar as literary works provide access to the structures of feeling and affective modes corresponding to specific socio-ecological formations. Drawing on the work of Louis Althusser, Michael Sprinker suggests that the specific formal work pursued by literature and art might be identified as the representation of lived experience by means of perceptions and feelings. Distinguishing between ideology and art, Sprinker argues that both "present the 'lived experience' of a particular social formation at a given moment in history, albeit in distinct ways. The mode of presentation in art is perceptual or phenomenal: in it we see and feel the lived experience of ideology. Ideology thus appears in aesthetic presentation, but at a distance" (1987, 282). Hence, not only might literature enable a sense of how, say, the domination of a society by the political ecologies of petroleum or sucrose is lived and perceived at the level of daily practice; but also, insofar as literary texts perform the "distantiation of ideological materials" (Sprinker 1987, 282), they can help us to "see" the cultural ideologies of oil or sugar, thereby contributing to the denaturalization of the hold these commodities exert over social life.[2]

Crucially, any exploration of such issues must take into account the asymmetries of power surrounding the uneven articulation of the production and consumption of oil and sugar across the modern world-system. If environmental humanities research is to analyze fully the effects had by these mass commodities on the organization of human and extra-human natures, it is necessary for it to consider how they are enmeshed in the systemic logic of the capitalist world-economy.[3] In particular, it must attend to the way in which their production has historically been bound up with processes of colonial and imperialist exploitation. In this chapter, I concentrate precisely on novels from those peripheral regions of the world-system that have been subject to imperialist intrusion and in which the production of oil or sugar dominates socio-economic life. Beginning with a comparison of general tendencies in the literary registration of oil and sugar frontiers, I move on to a more detailed consideration of petrofiction and the representational problems posed by oil. In the final section of the essay, I return to the textual encoding of the sugar frontier, examining the way in which the ecological dynamics common to both this and the oil frontier (most notably a pattern of boom-and-bust) might produce certain similarities in aesthetic responses to the lived experience of these dynamics. As indicated above, the category of the irreal will be central to the analysis that follows, since it represents one of the key stylistic mannerisms through which the cultural logics of oil and sugar find expression. I borrow the concept of irrealism from Michael Löwy, for whom it designates "the absence of realism rather than an opposition to it"; an irrealist work might include elements of the fantastic, marvelous, or dreamlike (2007, 194–95). Such elements, I will suggest, speak very directly to the feelings of strangeness and rupture engendered by petro- and saccharine-dominated economies.

KING SUGAR AND THE BLACK DEMON: REPRESENTATION AND COMMODITY FETISHISM

If, as Roberto Schwarz argues, literary forms are "the abstract of specific social relationships" (1992, 53), then are they not also the abstract of specific ecological relationships? I think this is necessarily the case. Contrary to how they appear under capitalism, nature and society are not separate entities but form a dialectical unity. Even to say this, however, is to leave open the possibility of falling back into a Cartesian dualism; for in seeking to show how nature and society "interact," we run the risk of continuing to think of them as discrete categories. Rather, "nature" and "society" must be grasped as singular abstractions and as the *results* of the dialectic of human and extra-human natures. This is the view put forward by environmental historian Jason W. Moore, for whom the term "ecological" should be understood as designating "the matrix of human and extra-human natures, and the historically-specific ways through which symbolic and material relations are interwoven and provisionally stabilized" (2011a, 5). "Relations between humans", asserts Moore, "are messy bundles of human and biophysical natures, and bound up, at every turn, with the rest of nature" (2012, 227). The differently specific ways in which these natures are woven together within and across successive eras is determined ultimately by the prevailing mode of production, itself constituted through a particular set of dialectical relations between human and extra-human natures. In this perspective, capitalism is a "world-historical matrix" that "knits together humans with the rest of nature [...] within a gravitational field of endless accumulation" (2012, 227). The modern world-economy, then, is simultaneously a world-ecology. Accordingly, the processes through which this world-economy develops, including industrialization, colonization, and imperialism, must be understood as not merely having consequences for the environment, but as ecological projects—as both producers *and* products of specific forms of life and environment making.[4] Thus, if social relations are always bundles of human and extra-human natures, then all that literary form works upon (the material conditions, cultural practices, and experiential modalities of society) is ecological—is a relation between humans and the rest of nature.

The ecological coordinates of literary forms become most obvious in situations where the production of a single commodity dominates economic life. Such situations are usually to be found in the peripheries of the world-system, where the effect of colonization and capitalist imperialism has often been to convert these areas into specialized zones for the production of primary goods to supply the global cores. The distinction between regions locked into the production and export of such commodities, and those dependent upon them but for which this dependency can be displaced or concealed precisely by the externalization of the production process, is crucial to distinguishing between the aesthetic registration of commodity regimes in different global locations. One could justifiably argue, for example, that oil dominates the economic life of *all* countries in the world-system today on account of its saturation of the infrastructure of modernity. On this basis, we might answer in the affirmative to MacDonald's question: "is not *every* modern novel to some extent an oil novel?" (2012, 7). The necessary qualifications to such an affirmation then turn on the differential articulation of the production and consumption of oil across an uneven world-system. Peter Hitchcock observes that the occluded and yet critical role of oil on the global stage has a symptomatic purchase on what states would prefer not to say about their constitutive logics, however much these exceed the reliance on a single commodity (although too many states are indeed one-commodity economies). This need not or should not deter any fictional representation, but oil is a cultural logic that dares any writer to express its real, not as some character or passing reference, but as a very mode of referentiality, a texture in the way stories get told.

(2010, 86)

I would suggest that in those peripheral locations that have indeed become reliant on the production of a single commodity, especially where this has occurred in the context of imperialist incursion and the nakedly violent reorganization of social relations and everyday practices, literary texts are more likely to rise to the challenge of (in Hitchcock's terms) expressing the real of oil, or of whatever the regnant commodity is—or at least that such works will make more visible its texturing of cultural production. In so doing, they can contribute to denaturalizing its role in structuring social life and organization.

The hold exerted by sugar over many societies in the Caribbean offers a useful starting point for considering the effects on literary production of the organization of nature around the demands of a single commodity. Commenting on the role of sugar in Saint-Domingue (Haiti), Michel-Rolph Trouillot has observed:

Sugar was not simply the major source of revenues. It had acquired a *social culture*: the socially drawn monopoly to subject to its refraction all other commodities and human beings themselves. Socially selected, socially identified, it became the principle around which human life was organized. Towns were built because of its proximity. Time was marked by its harvest. Status was linked to its possession. In Saint-Domingue there was a [...] ramified *sugar culture*.

(1982, 372)

Where a commodity so overdetermines all facets of society, its influence on aesthetic practice will be correspondingly marked. In this instance, literary forms will be the abstract of socio-ecological relations mediated through a "sugar culture." In *Cuban Counterpoint*, his seminal study of the influence of sugar and tobacco on the development of Cuban society, Fernando Ortiz provides some indication of the stylistic peculiarities likely to be engendered under such circumstances, but also demonstrates how techniques of narrativization and figuration can help make visible deeply embedded power relations. As Keith Sandiford notes, Ortiz constructs sugar "as a profoundly resonant signifying body within a universe of social, moral and political signs. [He] systematically and definitively interprets the production of sugar as a master signifier whose signs could be shown to permeate the entire body politic of producers and consumers" (2000, 32). Indeed, in seeking to show how the semiotics of sugar saturates social reality, Ortiz turns sugar into a dramatic character in its own right. The plant becomes an historical personage, a social actor "with political preferences, personal passions, philosophical orientations, and even sexual proclivities" (Coronil 1995, xxviii).

The obvious reference point here is Marx's analysis of commodity fetishism. Under capitalism, the products of labor "appear as autonomous figures endowed with a life of their own": as soon as a table, say, emerges as a commodity, it "changes into a thing which transcends consciousness. It not only stands with its feet on the ground, but, in relation to all other commodities, it stands on its head, and evolves out of its wooden brain grotesque ideas" (Marx 1976, 165, 163). In the context of a "sugar culture," something like a more intense version of this fetishism arises: sugar not only stands on its head and evolves grotesque ideas out of its sucrose brain; it wanders about the place, pontificating and indulging its passions. Hence the more than descriptive significance of the appellation "King Sugar," which not only attests to sugar's social power in the Caribbean and other sugar plantocracies, but also suggests the element of phantasmagoria surrounding the plant as it (to paraphrase Marx) rises up on its hind legs and confronts its subjects.[5]

The personification of sugar cane was a common trope in colonial celebrations of white Creole culture in the Caribbean.[6] But the same trope also features in the oral tales of the enslaved and in the fiction of later Caribbean writers, where it functions as a way to protest the devastating impact of sugar on the lives and landscapes of the region. In *Creole Folktales* (1995), for example, Patrick Chamoiseau dramatizes the hold sugar has exerted over the bodies of Martinicans, presenting characters who are simultaneously over- and underfed in illustration "of a land where crops grow in abundance but offer no sustenance" (Loichot 2013, 39). In "Nanie-Rosette et sa bouche douce," Nanie-Rosette is a glutton whose "bouche douce" ("sweet mouth" or "sweet tooth") is also, as Valérie Loichot argues, a "sugar mouth" (the word *dou* can mean "sugar" in Martinican Creole). A continuity is thereby established "between Nanie-Rosette's body and the object of her uncontrollable compulsion. Nanie-Rosette eats sugar and *is* sugar. In this way, she is also part of the machinistic extension of the sugar industry, a piece in its clockwork, which does not gain anything from it" (Loichot 2013, 40). Thus, Nanie-Rosette not only personifies sugar; in a sense, she becomes its product, her body fundamentally shaped by its political ecology. Once more we are in the "bewitched, distorted, upside-down world" of the capitalist *Erscheinungsform*, with King Sugar the progenitor of its own producers (Marx 1981, 969).

Oil, too, has known personification in literary representation. Indeed, its power to transform societies and energize global infrastructures means it has often appeared as more than an historical personage: if sugar is an "agricultural monarch" (Galeano 1973, 71), oil is frequently presented as an all-powerful demon or god. Consider Upton Sinclair's 1927 novel *Oil!*, in which crude is characterized as a "black and cruel demon," an "evil Power which roams the earth, crippling the bodies of men and women, and luring nations to destruction by visions of unearned wealth, and the opportunity to enslave and exploit labour" (2007, 548). More recently, Reza Negarestani, in his theory-fiction *Cyclonopedia* (2008), has declared:

> Petroleum's hadean formation developed a satanic sentience through the politics of in-between which inevitably "wells-up" through the God-complex deposited in the strata [...] to the surface. Envenomed by the totalitarian logic of the tetragrammaton, yet chemically and morphologically depraving and traumatizing Divine logic, petroleum's autonomous line of emergence is twisted beyond recognition. Emerged under such conditions, petroleum possesses tendencies for mass intoxication on pandemic scales (different from but corresponding to capitalism's voodoo economy and other types of global possession systems).
> (2008, 17)

As Negarestani's personification of petroleum as a telluric entity with a "satanic sentience" amply demonstrates, oil tends to push cultural expression toward a gothic register. Sugar, too, has its gothic and monstrous associations (one need only think of the Haitian zombie, the representative figure of the dehumanized worker in the cane fields). But arguably oil's phantasmagoric commodity character is of a darker hue than sugar's—appropriately enough given the dark viscosity of crude and its role as an unseen energy source capable of animating otherwise immobile objects. Negarestani's *Cyclonopedia* stands as an extreme expression of this shadowy ubiquity, not least because it attempts to figure the materiality and symbolic logic of oil in such explicit fashion. Even in literary works in which the presence and impact of the petroleum industry is otherwise clearly registered, it is rare to find the same level of direct engagement with the substance of oil itself.

Think, for instance, of Laura Restrepo's novel *The Dark Bride* (1999). Set against the backdrop of the operations of the US Tropical Oil Company in Colombia in the 1940s, the narrative centers on the city of Tora, "distinguished in the great vastness of the outside world as the city of the three p's: *putas*, *plata*, and *petróleo*, that is, whores, money, and oil" (2003, 2). The novel not only registers the effects of an oil boom on society, but also figures the process of oil extraction, with a number of scenes set on the drilling platforms of El Centro. However, the substance and semiotics of oil are never dealt with explicitly in terms of oil itself: present across the text, they are always displaced on to something else, most notably the descriptions of Tora's prostitutes, whose way of being is frequently evoked in terms that recall the cultural logic of petroleum. At one point, for example, the narrator states that she has been told that the women always sat "*con recato*": "A curious and archaic word, *recato*. [...] *Recato*: a magical term when it refers [...] to a *puta*. From the Latin *recaptare*—to hide what is visible—it seems to refer to a secret world that avoids exhibition and which is, significantly, contrasted with the Latin *prostituere*, to debase, put before the eyes, expose" (133). Of all the prostitutes, it is the beautiful and mysterious Sayonara who embodies most completely this cultural logic of the non-said. Like oil, she emerges as an enigmatic commodity, one secured on contested ground—"Her bedroom was conquered territory, the camp of any army, and her white sheet was the flag of her purchased love" (237)—and around which everything else comes to revolve: "in the splendid egoism of her beauty, [...] [she became] the very centre of that whole universe, the privileged object of all love" (163). The gendering of oil through its identification with Sayonara (underscored by the novel's title) highlights the imbrication of the commodification and exploitation of female bodies with the commodification and exploitation of extra-human nature. Like oil too, moreover, Sayonara's is a volatile identity, one whose "real" is impossible to pin down: she arrives in Tora as "the girl," her past shrouded in secrecy, before becoming Sayonara, the legendary "Japanese" prostitute, and later Amanda, the chaste and dutiful wife. As her foster mother observes: "'There weren't two, but three women in her, [...] Amanda, Sayonara, and she herself'" (288). This instability parallels the instability of the oil economy. But it also recalls the schizophrenic quality of Negarestani's *Cyclonopedia*, which on a formal level is at once (as the blurb on the back cover has it) "a horror fiction, a work of speculative theology, an atlas of demonology, a political samizdat and a philosophical grimoire." Such formal volatility is a consequence, I would argue, of Negarestani trying to make oil the direct subject of his text, and is indicative of the problems posed to representation by the relationship between crude and the capitalist system—problems *The Dark Bride* can only register symptomatically via its displacement of oil's cultural logic.

Discussing the "great energy transitions of the modern world [...], from peat and charcoal (1450s–1830s), to coal (1750s–1950s), to oil and natural gas (1870s–present)," Moore cautions against "the conventional view that sees a 'structurally invariant' capitalism (or industrial society) incorporating new external resources" (2011a, 22). For these energy sources "did not make capitalism so much as capitalism remade itself through their incorporation. To paraphrase Marx, coal is coal. It becomes fossil fuel *only in certain relations*" (2011a, 22). Similarly, we might say of crude oil that it is merely dark gunk; it only becomes the energy source and commodity "oil" within the structural relations of the capitalist world-system. Simultaneously, however, as Moore suggests, those relations have themselves been restructured through oil, which, since the late nineteenth century, has become the key vector through which capitalism knits together human and extra-human natures in the interests of endless accumulation. As Imre Szeman has argued: "When one discusses the end of oil and imagines the main issue to be the possibility of replacement fuels [...] one fails to grasp that we are not dealing with an input that can easily take other forms, but with a substance that has given shape to capitalist social reality" (2010, 34). The issue, therefore, is not just that oil has soaked into the pores of modern life, making it difficult to grasp the specificity of its symbolic logic, but also that to think oil is to think the world-system. Hence, to represent oil as such is to represent that system. And this is where the problem lies; for to attempt to make oil the direct subject of a narrative is to attempt to subjectivize the world-system—to make it representable in the terms of ordinary (subjective) experience. But whereas the lived experience of the effects produced by the system's petro-driven dynamics would be representable in this way, the system *as such*, as an immense bundle of human and extra-human relations in movement, could not be reduced to such subjective experience. To put it another way: if oil is that through which the system articulates its structure, then oil is a relation—the "real" of oil is not a substance but a set of far-flung and systemically patterned relationships between humans and the rest of nature. Accordingly, if, as Fredric Jameson observes, "no relationship is an entity [...] [and] relationship as such is unrepresentable," then oil cannot be represented directly—that is, it cannot be represented as oil as such, as oil-as-relationship (2011, 56).

Jameson "hazard[s] the suggestion that figuration tends to emerge when the object of conceptuality is somehow unrepresentable in its structural ambiguity" (2011, 34). If such is the case it would explain why the thematic of oil is so often displaced in literary works, its social logic receiving articulation only through figuration in a separate set of tropes. These not only register the felt experience of the socio-ecological transformations unleashed by the movements of the oil frontier, but also provide oil-as-relationship with a form of appearance. One thinks of the prostitutes in *The Dark Bride*, but also opium and the "darkness" of a disturbed mind in Sadeq Hedayat's *The Blind Owl* (1937), which mediates the impact of the Iranian oil boom in the early decades of the twentieth century; the volatility and emotional headiness of the love affair of the protagonists in Kurban Said's *Ali and Nino* (1937), set against the backdrop of oil rich Baku during World War I; and the rising and falling tide of political radicalism in the oil fields of 1930s Trinidad in Ralph de Boissière's *Crown Jewel* (1953).

But why cannot some image of oil itself serve as a figure for oil as a world-systemic relational dynamic? In certain instances this is indeed what is attempted, but the effect is to generate the kind of textual volatility seen in Negarestani's *Cyclonopedia*, which in seeking to make oil as such a figure, rather than to figure it, comes apart at the seams in a jumble of formal categories. Oil's inability to function as a figure for its own dynamics may well have to do with its amorphousness, its resistance to fixation in a stable trope. As Stephanie LeMenager observes, "oil's primal associations with earth's body, and therefore with the permeability, excess, and multiplicity of all bodies" means that oil poses a "representational problem" insofar as it "retains the indeterminacy and openness to mystification of a living/performing spectacle" (2012, 73–74). But tied to this, I would argue, is the larger problem of oil's status as the dominant energy vector through which capitalism has remade itself since the turn of the twentieth century. The aesthetic impasse narrative fiction confronts with regards to oil derives from the contradiction between oil as a part of the system and oil as the system itself, as that which has given shape to capitalist social reality. To seek to represent directly a relational dynamic such as is possessed by oil in the world-system—to narrate what is itself a narrative logic (as Negarestani puts it: oil is a "narrative organizer" [2008, 19])—necessarily results in an exploded narrative structure. Although a less extreme example than *Cyclonopedia*, the point is underscored by Abd al-Rahman Munif's *Cities of Salt* quintet (1987–1998), the "chaotic surfaces" of which, including "time-shifts, repetitions, formal (classical Arabic) and colloquial narration (local/regional dialects), lengthy digressions, and transnational locations" have "produced many critical detractors who question whether these are novels at all" (Hitchcock 2010, 84–85). We might read such textual instability not (as some have) as a sign of authorial deficiencies, but rather as a necessary consequence of the effort to represent the oil encounter, which is not simply a struggle over resources but a moment in the total reorganization of the world-ecology.[7]

PETRO-MAGIC-REALISM, SACCHARINE-IRREALISM, AND THE LOGIC OF BOOM-AND-BUST

Here I move to a consideration of the representational dilemmas posed by the sugar frontier. Sugar, of course, is no less imbricated in the world-system than oil (as is well-documented, the sugar plantations of the New World were integral to the expansion of the world-economy from the sixteenth century onward [Mintz 1985; Blackburn, 1997]). And in those regions of the world (such as in large parts of the Caribbean) where the production of sugar has historically dominated socio-economic life, certain similarities with oil can be detected in the way the volatile political ecology of this cash-crop impacts upon literary form.

Useful here is Jennifer Wenzel's suggestive concept of "petro-magic-realism," which she employs to analyze how Nigerian writer Ben Okri "imagines the pressures of a particular political ecology within a particular literary idiom" (2006, 457). Drawing on Jameson's understanding of magic realism as a formal registration of uneven and combined development, Wenzel parses this category through the specificities of Nigeria's petro-economy. Thus, Okri's short story "What the Tapster Saw":

> thematizes the conflict between established and emergent modes of production (here between artisanal palm-wine tapping and capital intensive petroleum drilling) [...]. Yet because [the story] emphasizes the

phantasmagoric aspects of petroleum extraction, the marvellous reality represented in this narrative has a decidedly modern source, even if it is described in a fantastic idiom with a venerable literary history. Petromagic is in no way a vestige of tradition or pre-capitalism. [...] Okri's "What the Tapster Saw" implicates metropolitan consumers of magical realism and petroleum products not in modernization's inevitable disenchantment of vestigial tradition, but rather in petro-modernity's phantasmagoric ravagements of societies and lifeworlds.

(457–58)

Although Wenzel concentrates on Nigeria, her term accurately describes the stylistic tendencies of writers in other peripheral locations responding to conditions of rapid petroleum-led development, even if such tendencies are not always as pronounced or as all-encompassing as in Okri's work.[8] Rather than explore these various petro-magic-realisms, however, I want instead to turn to sugar, for I think it is equally possible—and for comparable reasons— to speak of a stylistic tendency we might term "saccharine-irrealism."

Focusing on the Caribbean, I take my cue from Sylvia Wynter's 1971 article "Novel and History, Plot and Plantation." For Wynter, the rise of the capitalist world-economy, as both cause and consequence of the region's plantation societies, marked "a change of such world-historical magnitude that we are all, without exception, still "enchanted," imprisoned, deformed and schizophrenic in its bewitched reality" (1971, 95). In fact, she argues, history in the plantation context is "fiction"—"a fiction written, dominated, controlled by forces external to itself" (95). In other words, where Caribbean peoples lack autonomous control over the production of nature, and hence over the production of social reality, this reality appears illusory or "enchanted" since it is authored and manipulated by outside powers. Such a situation, then, is highly likely to generate aesthetic responses marked by the marvelous, the surreal, and the dreamlike.[9]

Contributing to this sense of plantation-induced bewitchment has been the historical legacy of the sugar industry's internal dynamics. Just as oil booms tend to produce an excess of riches in tandem with economic stagnation, so the windfall profits from sugar production saw wealth "magically" accrue to one section of society, despite a lack of real economic development overall.[10] The huge surpluses garnered by planters through their power to command an unfree labor force went hand in hand with immiseration and underdevelopment. (Something like the historical memory of this contradictory reality is recoverable in those folktales renarrated by Chamoiseau, in which overindulgence and magical surpluses of food do nothing to nourish starved bodies.) The "bewitched" qualities of the sugar economy were compounded by its volatility, the result of dependency on an uncertain world market and of the biophysical instabilities of plantation monocultures.

Such conditions of flux and instability tend to make realism problematic, requiring as it does a "conviction as to the massive weight and persistence of the present as such, and an aesthetic need to avoid recognition of deep structural social change" (Jameson 2007, 263). Hence, as Wynter implies, the likelihood is that any fictional encoding of the Caribbean's "sugar culture" will demonstrate a structural *tendency* toward incorporating elements of the irreal (which is not to say that every text will do so). In defining irrealism, Löwy emphasizes that the concepts of both realism and irrealism should be seen as, to some extent, "ideal-types": that is, as "coherent and 'pure' epistemological constructions; in contradistinction to empirical literary texts, which tend to be an 'impure' combination of both realism and irrealism" (195). Thus, insofar as a narrative could be said to exhibit elements of saccharine-irrealism, this does not mean that it will necessarily operate in a full-blown magical realist register; rather, what we may have to do with is some kind of minor disruption to an otherwise realist work.

Consider, however, the oeuvre of Wilson Harris, well-known for a style often described as marvelous realist (Dash, 1974; Harris, 1980). His 1962 novel *The Whole Armour*, set in a village on Guyana's Pomeroon River, deploys the evocative motif of crops "running away" to highlight the problems confronted by a community unable to break free from the exploitative relationship to the earth crystallized in the plantation system. It is repeatedly stressed in the text that history is a fiction—a "problematic fable" (1985, 279). This is not, however, a form of postmodern scepticism; rather it is a registration of the way history in the plantation context is—to echo Wynter—experienced as something written and controlled by outside forces; its fabular quality is not a testament to the discursive construction of reality, but to the material pressures of imperialism and dependency. The novel's protagonist, Cristo, asserts the need for the villagers to take a stand against the constant outflow of ecological energies from the country: those crops "running away," he states, are "us, our blood, running away all the time, in the river and in the sea" (335). The villagers must seek to anchor themselves more fully in the land and gain real control over the production of nature. His argument is underscored in the novel by images that emphasize the unstable, eroded quality of Guyana's coastal landscape. References abound to the "torn and eroded" earth (243), the "crumbling foreshore" (244), and the "erosive impact of the sullen seas" (260). Such descriptions not only register the specificity of the Guyanese environment, but also suggest the exogenous character of the country's economy, its peripheral position within the capitalist world-ecology and the leaching away of its resources. Indeed, the image of the land crumbling into the Atlantic Ocean serves as a metonym for the history of cash-crop monoculture in the Caribbean as the history of the indirect exportation of the soil from beneath the feet of the primary producers.

There are numerous other writers from across the Caribbean whose work possesses a marvelous aesthetic that lends itself fairly readily to analysis through the optic of saccharine-irrealism.[11] As I have suggested, however, one might also look for elements of saccharine irrealism in many of the otherwise social or critical realist works of Caribbean literature. One example is *The Last English Plantation* (1988) by Janice Shinebourne. Set in Guyana in the 1950s, Shinebourne's novel provides a detailed account of the postwar reorganization and modernization of the country's sugar industry. Despite its realist register, however, the text points to an underlying sense of irreality in its protagonist June's experience of the social world. As she grows older, June begins to question whether "Guiana [was] really just a big prison camp run by the British? If it was, all the freedom of the land that your eyes saw was just an illusion, a dream" (90).

The sense of irreality Shinebourne's narrative introduces at the level of content is complemented in a more subtle way by distortions in the *Bildungsroman* form it deploys. The *Bildungsroman* is the novel of development, of formation and socialization. Here, however, it encounters difficulties insofar as the world June is to be socialized into via education is one structured by colonial norms that are at odds with her everyday experience and promote a developmental ideal she will be denied in practice on account of her colonial status. This produces a disjunction not only between form and content, but also between two different formal rhythms. There is the forward thrust, the linear developmental dynamic of the *Bildungsroman*, mediated through the model of educational progress imposed on June by her schooling. However, this runs up against a parabolic rhythm, or a to-and-fro movement, which corresponds to her lived experience of social reality. These contrasting rhythms are figured in a passage in which June reflects on her daily commute to school:

> When she cycled to and from the villages she was part of the movement between country and town. [...] If in the end she did not have to remember the lessons she learnt in the classroom, she would be sure to remember this movement of people of which she had been a part. The habit of memory on her daily journeys became her own discipline, separate from her parents, from the school and the politics of the country. (180)

The reference here to June's education underscores the short-circuiting of the *Bildungsroman* model the text deploys. For the future toward which her academic development is oriented is already marked as potentially unobtainable: she might not have to remember what she learns in class because the reality to which it corresponds—of becoming "a doctor, or a lawyer, or a teacher"—will not be her reality if she remains in New Dam, where it is "not possible to be anything but poor" (32). The description of her daily journey, meanwhile, foregrounds the alternative, to-and-fro rhythm around which the text has been structured, evident not only in the way the narrative action tends to be organized around back and forth movements between different spaces (countryside and city, school and home), but also in the way the plot develops through a constant tension between moments of crisis or rapid change and periods of stillness or repetition—between actions designed to facilitate "progress" and a desire to commemorate the rhythms of the everyday (exemplified by June's "habit of memory").

The oscillating rhythm of *The Last English Plantation* might be read as encoding the boom-bust dynamic of the sugar economy, this dynamic embedding itself in the form of the novel because embedded in the texture of social reality. Moreover, in the way that this formal rhythm is made manifest through June's lived experiences the novel evokes for us something of the structure of feeling engendered by the political ecology of the sugar frontier and its patterning of human and extra-human relations. Simultaneously, however, in articulating this structure of feeling, the narrative opens up a potential space from which to critique King Sugar's hold over social life. Crucial here is that formal clash between the developmental thrust of the *Bildungsroman*—an abstract model divorced from the realities of June's situation—and the parabolic rhythm corresponding to her everyday experiences. We might understand this clash as mediating the contradiction between the reproduction of capital and the reproduction of daily life; or more specifically, between the abstract temporal momentum of capitalist accumulation, driven ever onward by the need to realize surplus value in expanded reproduction, and the qualitatively distinct temporalities of the webs of life that sustain accumulation. The novel, in fact, is highly conscious of time, containing frequent references to the time of day, the duration of journeys, daily schedules, and so forth.[12] This emphasis on clock-time— the corollary of capital's need to establish time as quantitative extension, as a regular sequence of homogenous, discrete units in order to measure value—runs up against the continuous, qualitatively differentiated motions associated with the rituals of the everyday June performs. These practices have a temporal logic tied to the rhythms of the body, the landscape, and the seasons—to the human and extra-human conditions of reproduction. The latter, of course, are increasingly subject to the dictates of abstract labor time as the sugar industry seeks to squeeze out further profits. However, in dramatizing the tension between these times, while simultaneously articulating them as a differentiated unity, the novel emphasizes that the temporal rhythms of everyday life can neither be reduced to, nor simply separated from, the temporal rhythms of capitalist accumulation, which must knit together those human and extra-human conditions as the basis of its own reproduction. By presenting the felt experience of this contradiction, the narrative not only stages the pressures exerted on human and biophysical natures by the political ecology of the sugar frontier, but also makes perceptible the possibility that those natures might be woven together in a different way, within a gravitational field other than endless accumulation.

A comparative study of the literary encoding of the sugar frontier's boom-bust dynamics might seek out further instances of the kind of parabolic rhythm found in Shinebourne's novel and of the ecological contradictions it mediates.[13] But one might also draw comparisons with the oil frontier and analyze the degree to which the analogous boom-bust logic of petro-economies engenders similar kinds of narrative rhythms.[14] Certainly *The Dark Bride*, for example, displays a volatile formal trajectory, a tonal oscillation between plenitude and exhaustion that is, as the narrator insists, the necessary effect of "documenting a world that remains in combustion, always on the verge of definitive collapse, and that despite everything manages [...] to grab hold with fingernails and teeth, illuminating with its final, furious flashes as if there were no more tomorrow, and yet dawn fills the sky and here below the delirium gains new energy" (239–40). Of course, any such comparisons must attend to the particular social and ecological contexts from which individual works emerge, since these will impart an irreducible specificity to content and form. In the examples analyzed above, the distinctive role played by the political ecologies of oil and sugar in patterning social experience is inseparable from the imperialist domination to which peripheral locations like Guyana have been subjected. As suggested earlier, the texturing of both social reality and cultural forms by the logics of oil extraction or sugar production is likely to be more readily apprehensible in texts from such locations, where the pressures of economic dependency are more directly palpable and the operations of power more nakedly violent.

The general conclusion to be drawn from the foregoing analysis, therefore, beyond what light it sheds on the cultural logic of oil and sugar, is that research in the environmental humanities must reckon with the dynamics of capitalist imperialism when examining the ecological transformations through which the modern world has developed. The blind spots that result from not doing so are well illustrated by certain strands of earth-systems thinking. Take, for example, the influential article by Will Steffen et al., "The Anthropocene: Are Humans Now Overwhelming the Great Forces of Nature?" In describing the "Great Acceleration" in industrial and commercial activity since 1945, the authors note how the "stage had been set" for this "explosion of the human enterprise" by developments in the preceding decades. "The years 1870 to 1914," they write, "were [...] an age of globalization in the world economy. Mines and plantations in diverse lands such as Australia, South Africa, and Chile were opening or expanding in response to the emergence of growing markets for their products" (2007, 617). What Steffen et al. blithely refer to as an "age of globalization," however, was the era of high imperialism, the core capitalist powers embarking on new rounds of colonial plunder in response to a downturn in the world-economy. The mines and plantations of which they speak did not simply spring up in response to market forces; rather they were the product of the brutal imposition of capitalist modes and structures and the ratcheting up of the exploitation of the global peripheries. In order to fully comprehend the forces propelling the relentless exhaustion and degradation of the webs of life, it is necessary to attend to the systemic inequalities in wealth and power crystallized in the specific configurations of human and biophysical natures through which capitalism develops. The same is true, moreover, when it comes to analyzing the cultural registration of these pressures: it is the uneven contours of the world-system *as* world-ecology that provide the ultimate interpretive horizon for world literature. And it is this understanding of world literature as the literature of the capitalist world-ecology, I would argue, that provides the most fruitful basis for comparisons between the literary inscription of the political ecologies of different commodity frontiers.

NOTES

1. See, for example, Mintz (1985) on sugar's fundamental role in shaping modern social life.
2. Thus MacDonald (2013), who suggests that petrofiction's emergence "as a truly 'global' subgenre demonstrates literature's capacity to energize purviews; confronting and repositioning the potent socio-economic signifiers 'naturalizing' energy and contemporary petrolic living in general," and potentially heightening "our planetary energy consciousness" (12).
3. I follow Immanuel Wallerstein and other world-systems analysts in speaking of capitalism as a world-economy. World-systems analysis divides historical systems into three categories: minisystems, world-economies, and world-empires. The latter two are both types of world-system. The hyphen indicates that these are not systems, economies, or empires of the (whole) world, but rather "systems, economies, empires *that are* a world (but quite possibly, and indeed usually, not encompassing the entire globe)." Thus, "in 'world-systems' we are dealing with a spatial/temporal zone which cuts across many political and cultural units, one that represents an integrated zone of activity and institutions which obey certain systemic rules" (Wallerstein 2004, 16–17; see also, Wallerstein, 1974). In a world-economy, the linkages between the units that constitute this integrated zone are dominated by market exchanges. Uniquely, capitalism is the first world-system to become a *world*—i.e. a global—system.
4. See Moore (2011b, 108–47).
5. See Marx (1976, 1054).
6. William Beckford, for example, in *A Descriptive Account of Jamaica*, presents sugar as a perfidious lover, coquettish, enticing, and untrustworthy: "The cane itself is so treacherous a plant, so liable to accidents, and attended with injury, that very little dependence can be placed on its returns. It will sometimes put on a most flattering appearance in the field, will promise much at the mill, and yet in the coppers will unprofitably deceive" (1790, 142).
7. The most infamous appraisal of Munif's novel as in some way deficient came in an obtuse review by John Updike (1991, 563–70).
8. Certainly many of the novels cited earlier in connection with oil's displaced figuration contain a current of petro-magic realism: in *The Dark Bride*, Restrepo's narrator explains that her record of life in Tora is an "attempt to imprison a world that goes by in flashes like a dream remembered upon waking, elusive in its vagueness and hallucinatory in its intensity" (1999, 193); Hedayat's *The Blind Owl* is a bizarre, surreal tale punctuated by uncanny repetitions and strange, disturbing set-pieces.

9. Indeed, Wynter begins her essay by referencing the work of Miguel Angel Asturias, whose marvellous realist style—his juxtaposition of modern novelistic discourse alongside Mayan narrative traditions—mediates the clash between the different socio-ecologies of the plot and plantation.

10. On the contradictory dynamics of oil booms, see Apter (2005). Of Nigeria's oil boom of the late 1970s, Apter notes that "oil replaced labor as the basis of national development, producing a deficit of value and an excess of wealth, or a paradoxical profit as loss" (201). He ascribes this paradox to the fact that the value created by oil was "based not on the accumulation of surplus value" but on the circulation of externally generated oil rents and revenues (14).

11. Alejo Carpentier, Jacques-Stéphen Alexis, Simone Schwarz-Bart, Erna Brodber, Boeli van Leeuwen, and Nalo Hopkinson spring immediately to mind, for example.

12. See, for example, the description of June's morning routine (Shinebourne 1988, 49–50). This time-consciousness might be read as further evidence of the novel's registration of King Sugar's hold over social life; for as Sidney Mintz has observed, because the ecology of sugar cane required that cutting, milling, and boiling occurred within forty-eight hours, the labor process of sugar production displayed a high degree of "time-consciousness," which "permeated all phases of plantation life" (1985, 51).

13. In the Caribbean context, one thinks, for example, of the spiraling narratives of writers like Édouard Glissant, Raphaël Confiant, and Earl Lovelace, as well as of the aesthetic practice of the Haitian Spiralists Jean-Claude Fignolé, Frankétienne, and René Philoctète. But the comparisons could also be extended beyond the Caribbean—to the sugar frontiers of northeast Brazil, say, and the novels of José Lins do Rego, or to the Philippine island of Negros and works such as Rosario Cruz Lucero's *Feast and Famine* (2003) and Vicente Groyon's *The Sky Over Dimas* (2004).

14. Of course, many factors besides the boom-bust logic of the sugar and oil frontiers could be adduced to account for the sorts of formal rhythms I have identified. To emphasize the pressures exerted by the political ecologies of oil and sugar is not to downplay these other determinations, but to underscore how they must be thought in relation to the pivotal role played by the extraction/production of oil and sugar in structuring social life in certain locations.

REFERENCES

Apter, Andrew. 2005. *The Pan-African Nation: Oil and the Spectacle of Culture in Nigeria*. Chicago: University of Chicago Press.

Beckford, William. 1790. *A Descriptive Account of the Island of Jamaica*. London: T. and J. Egerton.

Blackburn, Robin. 1997. *The Making of New World Slavery: From the Baroque to the Modern, 1492–1800*. London: Verso.

Coronil, Fernando. 1995. "Introduction: Transculturation and the Politics of Theory: Countering the Center, Cuban Counterpoint." In *Cuban Counterpoint: Tobacco and Sugar*, by Fernando Ortiz. Translated by Harriet de Onís, ix-lvi. Durham: Duke University Press.

Dash, J. Michael. 1974. "Marvellous Realism – The Way out of Négritude." *Caribbean Studies* 13 (4): 57–70

Galeano, Eduardo. 1973. *Open Veins of Latin America*. New York: Monthly Review Press.

Harris, Wilson. 1980. "Interview with Wilson Harris, by Michel Fabre." *Kunapipi* 2 (1): 100–106.

———. 1985. *The Whole Armour*. In *The Guyana Quartet*. London: Faber and Faber.

Hitchcock, Peter. 2010. "Oil in an American Imaginary." *New Formations* 69: 81–97.

Jameson, Fredric. 2007. "A Note on Literary Realism in Conclusion." *In Adventures in Realism*, edited by Matthew Beaumont, 261–271. Oxford: Blackwell.

———. 2011. *Representing* Capital: *A Reading of Volume One*. London and New York: Verso.

LeMenager, Stephanie. 2012. "The Aesthetics of Petroleum, after Oil!" *American Literary History* 24 (1): 59–86.

Loichot, Valérie. 2013. *The Tropics Bite Back*. Minneapolis: University of Minnesota Press.

Löwy, Michael. "The Current of Critical Irrealism." In *Adventures in Realism*, edited by Matthew Beaumont, 193–206. Oxford: Blackwell.

MacDonald, Graeme. 2012. "Oil and World Literature." *American Book Review* 33 (3): 7–31.

———. 2013. "Research Note: The Resources of Fiction." *Reviews in Cultural Theory* 4 (2): 1–24.

Marx, Karl. 1976. *Capital. Vol. 1*. Translated by Ben Fowkes. London: Penguin.

———. 1981. *Capital. Vol. 3*. Translated by David Fernbach. London: Penguin.

Mintz, Sidney W. 1985. *Sweetness and Power: The Place of Sugar in Modern History*. New York: Viking Penguin.

Moore, Jason W. 2011a. "Transcending the Metabolic Rift: A Theory of Crises in the Capitalist World-Ecology." *Journal of Peasant Studies* 12 (1): 1–46.

———. 2011b. "Ecology, Capital, and the Nature of Our Times: Accumulation and Crisis in the Capitalist World-Ecology." *American Sociological Association* 17 (1): 108–147.

———. 2012. "Cheap Food and Bad Money: Food, Frontiers, and Financialization in the Rise and Demise of Neoliberalism." *Review: A Journal of the Fernand Braudel Center* 33 (2–3): 225–261.

Negarestani, Reza. 2008. *Cyclonopedia: Complicity with Anonymous Materials*. Melbourne: Re.press.

Ortiz, Fernando. 1995. *Cuban Counterpoint: Tobacco and Sugar*. Translated by Harriet de Onís. Durham: Duke University Press.

Restrepo, Laura. 1999. *The Dark Bride*. Translated by Stephan Lytle. New York: Doubleday.

Sandiford, Keith A. 2000. *The Cultural Politics of Sugar: Caribbean Slavery and Narratives of Colonialism*. Cambridge: Cambridge University Press.

Schaw, Janet. 1934. *Journal of a Lady of Quality*. Edited by Evangeline Andrews and Charles Andrews. New Haven: Yale University Press.

Schwarz, Roberto. 1992. *Misplaced Ideas: Essays on Brazilian Culture*. Translated by John Gledson. London: Verso.

Sheller, Mimi. 2004. "Automotive Emotions: Feeling the Car." *Theory, Culture & Society* 21 (4–5): 221–242.

Shinebourne, Janice. 1988. *The Last English Plantation*. Leeds: Peepal Tree Press.

Sinclair, Upton. 2007. *Oil!* London: Penguin.

Sprinker, Michael. 1987. *Imaginary Relations: Aesthetics and Ideology in the Theory of Historical Materialism*. London: Verso.

Steffen, Will, Paul J. Crutzen, and John R. McNeill. 2007. "The Anthropocene: Are Humans Now Overwhelming the Great Forces of Nature?" *Ambio* 36 (8): 614–621.

Szeman, Imre. 2010. "The Cultural Politics of Oil: On *Lessons of Darkness* and *Black Sea Files*." *Polygraph* 22: 33–45.

Trouillot, Michel-Rolph. 1982. "Motion in the System: Coffee, Color, and Slavery in Eighteenth-Century Saint-Domingue." *Review* 5 (3): 331–388.

Updike, John. 1991. "Satan's Work and Silted Cisterns." In *Odd Jobs: Essays and Criticism*, 563–70. New York: Knopf.

Wallerstein, Immanuel. 1974. *The Modern World-System I: Capitalist Agriculture and the Origins of the European World-Economy in the Sixteenth Century*. New York: Academic Press.

———. 2004. *World-Systems Analysis: An Introduction*. Durham: Duke University Press.

Wenzel, Jennifer. 2006. "Petro-magic-realism: Toward a Political Ecology of Nigerian Literature." *Postcolonial Studies* 9 (4): 449–464.

Wynter, Sylvia. 1971. "Novel and History, Plot and Plantation." *Savacou* 5: 95–102.

13 Ghost Mountains and Stone Maidens

Ecological Imperialism, Compound Catastrophe, and the Post-Soviet Ecogothic

Sharae Deckard

> Every catastrophe happens because of a special combination of circumstances and in Russia it's as if there is a magnet that pulls them together.
> —Olga Slavnikova (2014)

Postcolonial ecocriticism offers important perspectives to the emergent field of environmental humanities on how contemporary environmental issues across the Global South are shaped by complex histories of resource appropriation and extraction under colonialism and global capitalism. Postcolonial ecocritics have developed groundbreaking conceptualizations of "compound crisis" to describe how ecological crises in postcolonies are characterized by structural violence and intersecting processes occurring over long temporalities (Carrigan 2011, 276; also this volume). In her reading of the "radiation ecologies" produced by Pacific nuclearization, Elizabeth DeLoughrey argues for a shift away from "eventist" models of catastrophe toward Fernand Braudel's approach to history as a set of long-term structures and processes developing slowly over the *longue durée* (2009, 473). Similarly, Rob Nixon describes the "slow violence" characterizing environmental catastrophes such as the Bhopal chemical disaster as "violence that occurs gradually and out of sight, a violence of delayed destruction that is dispersed across time and space" (2011, 2). Such concepts have an explanatory power that can enable comparative analysis of literary production pertaining to chemical and nuclear catastrophes in other sites which do not precisely conform to the category of "postcolony," such as the poisoned environments described in the literature of post-Soviet states.

The history of ecocide, which came to light with the collapse of the Soviet Union, is now well documented.[1] According to the Russian Academy of Sciences, over forty-five areas of the former USSR suffered environmental degradations of "irreparable, catastrophic proportions" (Davis 1993, 3). Mike Davis suggests that the Cold War was "the Earth's worst eco-disaster in the last ten thousand years," an environmental catastrophe on a truly world-historical scale, whose violence is dispersed across the planet and will linger past individual human lifetimes (1993, 2). The "worlding" of environmental humanities to incorporate postcolonial methods and address global crises must reckon not only with the American imperium and its role in the Cold War, but also with the catastrophic environmental history of the Soviet empire and its aftermath.

However, theorizing the fate of the former "Second World" after the collapse of the Soviet Union continues to pose methodological challenges for postcolonial studies. As David Chioni Moore argues, postcolonial discourse is haunted by an "absence" in its approach to the Global South, "a world system with no theory of its former Second World" (2001, 115). Russian critics have debated the usefulness of postcolonial paradigms based on Anglo-Franco models of overseas empires to describe the particularities of Soviet Communism, with some arguing that "postcommunist" would be a more accurate descriptor of the Newly Independent States (NIS) after the dissolution of the USSR; others have noted Russia's peculiar position as "a Janus-Faced empire or an empire-colony" subject to a double orientalism directed both against and within Russia itself (Tlostanova 2014, 3). Yet Russia's history is indelibly shaped by varieties of ecological imperialism and resource colonization, foundational to the emergence of the Imperial Russian land empire, taking new form in the Sovietization of territories under Soviet state capitalism, and persisting in the contemporary "petro-imperialism" of Vladimir Putin's administration.[2] Just as the Soviet empire's Cold War industry was founded on enormous oil, gas, and uranium reserves, post-Soviet Russia's continued hold over subordinated territories and neighboring nations has been cemented by petro-power (Newnham 2011, 134). Furthermore, as one of the "BRICS" nations seeking dominance as a world power and nursing resurgent imperial ambitions, the Russian Federation has been an aggressive participant in the twenty-first century "scramble for resources" (Carmody 2013), competing to secure raw materials and energy resources in Africa and the Arctic, and fighting against the release of its former imperial possessions.[3] If the environmental humanities aims to explore the global ramifications of issues such as climate change in relation to new forms of resource extraction and energy crisis, it must incorporate analysis of the intersecting legacies of pre-Soviet imperialism, Soviet Communism, and neoliberalization that underlie contemporary Russia's quest for resource sovereignty.

In this chapter, I attempt an initial foray into bringing Russia into the ambit of global environmental humanities by providing an analysis of the ways in which post-Soviet literary aesthetics register the *longue durée* of environmental catastrophe and resource extraction in Russia through the use of "ecogothic" tropes. Gothic fiction is a genre of literature that combines elements of horror and romance, creating atmospheric settings full of terror or mystery. Preoccupied with decay and the return of the past, it is often set amidst ruins or in enclosed, haunted spaces, and is populated by supernatural characters, including ghosts, spirits, and monsters. In their definition of "the ecogothic," Andrew Smith and William Hughes argue that gothic literature constitutes nature as "a space of crisis which conceptually creates a point of contact with the ecological" and as such, "seems to be the form which is well placed to capture the anxieties" revolving around climate change and environmental damage in industrialized countries (2013, 3, 5).

Reading "global" varieties of the ecogothic from outside of Anglo-American literary traditions whose ambivalent depictions of nature refract anxieties around planetary crisis can help reveal how the cultural experiences of environmental catastrophe in other nations intersect with wider geopolitical contexts (Deckard 2013, 177).

Literary analysis of the ecogothic has relevance for environmental humanities approaches because of the way in which gothic aesthetics can provide an entry into the social imagination of environmental catastrophes with complex temporal antecedents, by reflecting traumas and fears or intimating alternative ecological relations. Characterized by a "presumptive dystopianism" (Smith and Hughes 2013, 3), ecogothic form offers a powerful method of yoking *courte* and *longue durées*, in which longer histories outside the capacity for memory of individual human protagonists manifest as apparitions that disturb the present. Revenants of "undead" processes in the past continue to shape contemporary environments, even if official narratives, such as those of the Russian state, often repress or elide these histories. The ability to figure that which has been forgotten or occluded with an uncanny immediacy is one of the ecogothic's most powerful aesthetic effects.

Post-Soviet fiction is haunted by the ecogothic specters of ecological disaster past and present, teeming with post-catastrophic scenarios and swarming with monstrous, mutant, or ghostly characters.[4] The explosion of literary novels mixing the aesthetics of science fiction, speculative fiction, horror, and magical realism has been dubbed the "new Gothic" (Givens 2010, 3) and heralded as a belated "renaissance" of the "'literature of supernatural horror'" (Lebedushkina 2010, 99). This boom can be explained by intersecting conditions. Firstly, the proliferation of speculative aesthetics can be understood in relation to the changing literary field after the removal of Soviet strictures on the ideological content of literature and the emergence of a privatized publishing industry. The embrace of nonrealist modes by writers released from the prohibitions of Soviet social realism has been met by a prolific consumer appetite for genre fiction.[5] Secondly, the turn to plots which incorporate supernatural or mythological materials suggests a search for aesthetic modes through which to express the extremity of social upheaval after the liberalization of the economy and the dissolution of the social structures of the Soviet Union. Thirdly, the prevalence of fictions that use speculative aesthetics as social allegory also suggests a formal response to renewed political repression under Putin's administration, in which critique is presented obliquely through a veil of supernatural satire. Finally, Mark Lipovetsky and Alexander Etkind have argued that the gothic temporalities and apparitions of these texts embody post-catastrophic memory of repressed trauma, manifesting as a post-Soviet uncanny (2010, 6).

Because the hybrid aesthetics of these fictions do not conform to strict definitions of genre fiction, attempts to classify them are prone to slippage. Olga Slavnikova's 2006 novel *2017* (translated into English in 2010) is a useful case in point—it draws on conventions from gothic, magical realism, and science fiction, without being strictly confined to any of these genres. In interviews, Slavnikova has emphasized the novel's interjection of "fantastic" elements to evoke aspects of post-Soviet catastrophe that elude naturalist representation:

> Sometimes in order to resolve a particularly complex mathematical problem, you have to put an imaginary entity into the equation. Similarly, in order to explain the situation in Russia, sometimes what you have to do is take an element of imagination, of fantasy, enter it into this equation and then the entire situation somehow unfolds and becomes much clearer.
>
> (Amis 2012)

This idea of the novel as an impure mixture of realism and fantasy recalls Michael Löwy's intermediary category "critical irrealism," designating texts in which realist modes are punctuated by dreamlike, fantastic, or surreal elements in order to express social critique at those moments when reality seems inexpressible in factual terms (Löwy 2007, 195). The concept is further elaborated in a metatextual commentary on aesthetics in *2017*, where the novel describes both realist landscape painting and abstract modernist art as inadequate to the task of representation of environmental catastrophe in the Urals, concluding wryly, "When an ecological crisis came that was as real as could be, it became clearer that the True Riphean's thinking was fantastic thinking" (Slavnikova 2010, 31).

Throughout this chapter, I focus on an exemplary reading of Olga Slavnikova's novel *2017* as an irrealist fiction whose use of ecogothic motifs critically captures the social experience of the multiple histories of ecological crisis in the Urals region of Russia. This essay's epigraph encapsulates the novel's representation of catastrophe not as a single disaster, but rather as the intersection of historical conditions resulting in compound crisis (Slavnikova 2014). As I will demonstrate, the novel's supernatural apparitions of stone maidens and mountain spirits figure the slow violence of Soviet-era nuclear irradiation and chemical pollution, intimate the pre-history of resource colonization and aboriginal dispossession during the tsarist empire, and prognosticate future crises emerging from intensified resource-extraction in the neoliberal era.

The Russian Booker prize-winning *2017* is a useful entry-point to the wider post-Soviet literary field for two reasons. Firstly, the novel's aesthetics constitute a powerful example of the tendency in post-Soviet literary production to use gothic aesthetics and supernatural tropes in order to narrate ecological crisis in contemporary Russia. Secondly, the novel's depiction of the Urals, one of the most polluted regions in Russia, provides an opening into understanding how contemporary experiences of post-Soviet environmental catastrophe are underwritten by historical processes of ecological imperialism and extractivism. Thus, before elaborating an ecogothic reading of the novel, I begin by tracing the resource history of the Urals.

RUSSIA'S "TREASURE BOX:" ECOLOGICAL IMPERIALISM AND RESOURCE EXTRACTION IN THE URALS

The folded mountain ranges of the Urals are both sites of extraordinary geological beauty and some of the most contaminated environments in the world. The mountains have been mythologized as Russia's "treasure box" due to their concentration of over a thousand different minerals and metallic ores (Givental 2013, 5). The dichotomized geography of these deposits has produced a double-tongued pattern of development: chemical industries line the western Urals, while metallurgy and nuclear industries strew the eastern slopes. With Russia's transition to neoliberal capitalism, vulnerability in zones of ecological crisis such as the Urals' metallurgical regions has not decreased. Exposure to disproportionate environmental risk is part of a larger catastrophe unfolding over time, in which nuclear radiation and toxic waste constitute only one layer of a historical palimpsest of ecological degradation in a region subjected to centuries of resource extraction. As a "hinterland region" whose resources have been central to the forging of tsarist and Soviet industrial modernity in the Muscovy core (Filtzer 2009, 85), the Urals have served as a staging ground for imperialism, primitive accumulation, forced industrialization, nuclearization, and neoliberal extraction over the *longue durée* of Russian history.

Arcing like a spine across the Eurasian continent, the mountains delineate the symbolic border between "Russ Land" to the west and "Asia" to the east. In the sixteenth century, they formed the colonial frontier on the edge of Novgorod, a gateway to western Siberia through which Russians crossed, bearing guns and unwittingly carrying pathogens which decimated indigenous peoples (Crosby 2004, 37–39). Russian expansion across the Urals inaugurated a "resource-bound epoch" during which Imperial Russia emerged through ecological imperialism (Etkind 2011, 164). When iron and copper ore were discovered in the seventeenth century, Russian colonization precipitated further displacement of autochthonous peoples from the southern and central Urals.[6] In the eighteenth century, eleven mighty ore mines were opened to fuel Peter the Great's militarization of imperial Russia, while during the nineteenth-century "malachite fever," a stream of precious metals and stones were exported to decorate the palaces of tsars and European aristocrats. Subjected to centuries of resource extraction, the Urals have been shaped by a pattern of export-oriented development reproducing imperial "space through time" (Etkind 2011, 170). The region has always exported more wealth than it retained, with raw materials funneled westward to areas of Russian consumption in an "economic debris flow" (Rogachev 1998, 9). Buffeted by the cyclical exhaustion of commodity frontiers, Urals communities have historically been unable to accumulate capital to reinvest in infrastructure or remediation of environmental degradation.

In the early twentieth century, the Urals sank into an economic depression following the collapse of the gem frontier, until Bolshevik modernization transformed the region into "Russia's defender." The "Great Urals Plan" of the 1930s subjugated the *oblast* (administrative region) to one of the most staggeringly ambitious industrial projects of Stalin's first Five-Year Plan, and the Urals became the largest consumer of forced labor in Soviet history (Harris 1997, 266). The construction of giant production cities organized around resource monocultures was fed by a stream of "kulaks" from newly created gulags, as entire villages of peasants were depopulated and shipped to camps.[7] Following forced industrialization, the region became integral to the energy regime powering "atomic communism," manufacturing nuclear fuels, weapons, and chemicals in a constellation of secret military complexes across the central mountains (Josephson 2005, 5).

As such, the Urals offer a concentrated example of the violence of the Soviet production of nature. Geographer Neil Smith uses the concept of "the production of nature" to describe how capitalist commodity relations reconstruct nature for the purposes of accumulation (1984, 56). While the production of nature under Soviet state capitalism was governed by a different political ideology than the liberal democracies of the west, the USSR was locked into the larger accumulation regime of global capitalism, subject to competition with North American and Western European cores.[8] Like the capitalist First World, Soviet accumulation relied on the appropriation of the raw materials of its peripheries, deploying imperial tactics continuous with those of the tsarist period (Tlostanova 2014, 2). Frantz Fanon famously argued that "Europe is literally the creation of the Third World," formed from the "gold and raw materials of the colonial countries" (2001, 81). So too could the "Second World" be understood as the creation of the dominated territories and internal colonies of Soviet land empire, subjected to imperialist strategies of intensive monoculture and extraction, mass relocations of non-Russian peoples and ethnic minorities, and exploitation of forced labor.[9]

"Socialist nature" was rooted in a "material-technological" ideology of nature as a source of ecological inputs with no inherent value of their own, a bottomless mine without biophysical limits to appropriation (Josephson 2005, 2). Stalin's "Plan for the Transformation of Nature" imagined that the whole of nature could be transformed into a well-functioning machine. When nature failed to yield to economic plans for growth, it was often portrayed as an "enemy of the people," just as scientists who dared to criticize ecological degradation were termed "wreckers" (Josephson et al. 2013, 132). The first Soviet nuclear disaster occurred in the Urals in 1957, when the cooling system of "Mayak," a plutonium processing plant in the military city Chelyabinsk-40, failed and caused an explosion. A plume of radioactive material, the East Urals Radioactive Trace (EURT), scattered across an area of 20,000 square kilometers, inhabited by 270,000 people. Now measured as a Level 6 disaster on the International Nuclear Event Scale, the accident was not officially acknowledged by the Soviet Union, but rather wrapped in secrecy, like scores of other environmental disasters in the Urals. Before the explosion, and for long afterward, the dumping of radioactive waste contaminated nearby rivers and lakes, causing repeated breakouts of radiation sickness and fatalities in downstream villages (Rabl 2012).

During *perestroika*, eco-nationalist movements organized around anti-nuclear and anti-pollution activism helped provoke the crisis of *glasnost* (Dawson 1996, 3). But the Soviet Union collapsed before proposed environmental reforms could come into effect. Instead, Russia was subjected to what Naomi Klein (2007) has termed the "shock doctrine," the rapid application of neoliberal economic policies during a period of widespread crisis. National industries were privatized in fire-sale auctions, bought up at rock-bottom prices by foreign investors and former *nomenklatura*. The impetus toward short-term profit and accelerated deregulation disincentivized remediation of preexisting ecological crises or prevention of degradation in the course of new rounds of prospecting and mining. When Putin came to power, he renationalized Russia's energy sector, exploiting soaring commodity prices to reorganize the economy around the export of petroleum, gas, and mineral resources.[10] State protections which blocked intensified resource extraction were dissolved, while critics were often imprisoned or assassinated. In 2001, the Environmental Protection Agency was disbanded, and barriers to "nuclear renaissance" were removed by dismantling expert assessments (Pomper 2009, 2).

With the loss of Russia's metallurgical bases in the post-Soviet states, the recovery of Urals mining activity became a national priority, enshrined in the "Ore of the Urals" scheme to court foreign investment in prospecting new mineral reserves in the "underexploited" northern Urals (Givental 2013, 11). Many of the territories subject to intensified extraction are inhabited by indigenous peoples and ethnic minorities.[11] In the central Urals, remnants of Soviet industry persist in reactor sites, military complexes, and toxic waste dumps, interspersed with new "special economic zones" and frontiers of extraction. The EURT "reserve" has been reopened for commercial exploitation, and the nuclear corporation Rosatom now operates Mayak to reprocess imported nuclear waste for the global market, compounding the toxification of landscapes already poisoned by decades of Soviet nuclearization.[12] Villagers who rely on agriculture in contaminated areas suffer repeated radiation poisoning and elevated rates of leukemias and solid cancers (WISE 2005).

Social consciousness of ecological crisis is part of everyday experience in the post-Soviet Urals, and might thus be expected to be expressed in literary aesthetics. Cultural critic Raymond Williams uses the concept "structure of feeling" to characterize "meanings and values as they are actively lived and felt" as opposed to values as they are expressed in ideologies (1977, 133).

He argues that literature offers special insights into the affective elements of consciousness and relationships shared by generations in particular historical moments because of the way that specific formal innovations can crystallize "social experiences in solution" (134). In the next section, I investigate how ecogothic form in Slavnikova's *2017* expresses a post-catastrophic structure of feeling arising from the social experience of compound ecological crisis in the post-Soviet Urals.

"GREEN SPECTERS:" THE POST-SOVIET UNCANNY AND ENVIRONMENTAL CATASTROPHE

2017 takes place in the "Riphean" mountains, as the Urals were known in classical antiquity. The plot intertwines several strands, interweaving the expeditions of two geologists, Anfilogov and Kolyan, hunting seams of precious gems in the Ripheans, with the story of a gemworker, Krylov, and his strange romance with the ethereal Tanya in a city resembling Yekaterinburg.[13] Set in the near-future, one hundred years from the October Revolution, it concludes with a hallucinatory reenactment of the civil war. The future setting could suggest classification as science fiction, but the novel's estrangement effects do not revolve around futuristic technologies or societies. To the contrary, the city that Krylov and Tanya traverse is haunted by archaic remnants of crumbling Soviet infrastructure, while the surrounding mountains are riddled with abandoned mines. The plot device most reliant on suspension of disbelief is the reoccurrence of the Bolshevik revolution, an eruption of the past which precludes rather than prefigures futurity. Similarly, the textual refashioning of folklore of mountain spirits and haunted treasure hoards evokes a gothic sensibility of the Urals' history of metallurgy and mining. If anything, the novel oscillates between temporalities, peering into the near future only to be drawn ineluctably into the archaic past, a dynamic which recalls Fred Botting's description of the gothic's tendency to perceive the future as another "place of destruction and decay, as ruined as the Gothic past" (2002, 279).

Post-Soviet novels like *2017* whose plots depict Russia as haunted by the repetition of events from the Soviet past draw on a mode of irrealist representation which Alexander Etkind has called "magical historicist." In contrast to the "factual, righteous account of the past" exemplified by realist texts such as Aleksandr Solzhenitsyn's *One Day in the Life of Ivan Denisovich* (1962), the occult revivals of magical historicist fictions embody "post-catastrophic memory" of the unresolved "horror" of the Soviet period (Etkind 2009, 658). These novels do not seek to emulate reality through factual narration of events, but rather use magical content and "nonhuman, abstract, or monstrous symbols" to defamiliarize the past (Etkind 2009, 638). Fusing gothic and magical realist apparatuses, they recruit popular magic and folklore and project supernatural occurrences into the past in order to actualize contemporary cultural experiences of trauma and horror, while questioning official histories and nationalist historiography. Their temporalities uneasily juxtapose the linear time of history with the "circular time of post-traumatic experience," creating a bifurcated sense of the past both as ghostly site of repetitive melancholia and as exotic territory ripe with unexplored alternatives and unborn potentialities (Etkind 2009, 644, 656).

Yet the post-catastrophic histories these fictions resurrect through their uncanny aesthetics are not only social, but also environmental histories. While critics such as Etkind and Lipovetsky have read the "post-catastrophic uncanny" of post-Soviet fiction as primarily responding to repressed political traumas, I argue that the uncanny also encompasses the social experience of compound ecological crisis, and thus can be read through the lens of the ecogothic. As discussed in the opening section, the ecogothic invites a critical practice that seeks to reverse the mystification or invisibility of ecological degradation by reading the ways in which the gothic apparatuses of texts manifest the cultural legacies of the historical production of nature (Deckard 2013, 177). In literary texts which deploy ecogothic devices, ecological crisis is manifested via monstrous apparitions or uncanny returns of the repressed, which attribute a phobic agency to nature's "retribution," or summon past ecological disasters to haunt the present in order to rematerialize suppressed histories. Rather than being reduced to a backdrop, nature itself becomes a character, often embodied in spirit-form. Integrating Russia's environmental history into Etkind's account of the post-Soviet uncanny enables interpretation of the ecogothic fears of toxification, mutation, and returns of repressed nature in Slavnikova's *2017* as manifesting post-catastrophic memory of Soviet ecocide in relation to ongoing ecological crisis in post-Soviet Russia.

The opening sections of the novel excavate the history of intensive resource extraction in the Urals, describing the terrains traversed by modern-day prospectors, pockmarked by tailing mounds and worked-out quarries, crosscut by intermontane basins and rivers polluted by nuclear and chemical waste. As depicted by the third-person narrator, the landscape is a palimpsest of centuries of resource-extraction, inscribed with the successive exhaustion of mining frontiers: "Virtually everything that could be extracted from the top has been. The Riphean's surface has been played out" (Slavnikova 2010, 30). In the second chapter, a long passage describing the geology and lifeworld of the Ripheans evokes an uncanny sense of the mountains as overwritten with unstable signifiers of environmental catastrophe, which appear only to vanish. The exposition begins in omniscient third person narration, but gradually changes to second person, as if to inculcate a direct sense of psychic identification with the fissured geology in the reader:

> Sometimes a hole in the ground that looks like an old man's toothless, sunken mouth leads the prospector to a mine from the century before. [...] You can't tell right away that the surface mine is filled to a certain level with water. [...] You have to descend [and ...] slowly after an

almost endlessly long time, the disturbed perfection is restored—and suddenly the moment comes when the water disappears again right at your feet. Once again the viewer is left facing a stunning emptiness where the mountain was taken out. (30)

The way in which peaks shimmer in and out of perception, appearing as reflections in the watery pits where once mountains stood, suggests the uneasy gap between the geological deep time which forged the Urals and the accelerated time of Soviet industrialization which hollowed out entire mountains to extract their ore. A local saying in the Urals describes precisely this process: "it once was a mountain steep, now it's a pit deep" (Rogachev 1998, 20). These absent mountains—visible only in inversion—take on a ghostly aspect, tangible yet incorporeal. Georg Borgstrom famously used the term "ghost acreage" to describe the extraterritorial hectares which empires appropriate to expand food inputs after exceeding the carrying capacity of their farmland (1965, 71). Adapting Borgstrom, the term "ghost mountains" might be used to describe the "phantom carrying capacity" of the Russian imperial core, reliant for centuries on the appropriation of Urals resources. This phantom history is inscribed in the landscape and replicated in the "Riphean" structure of feeling, described as emerging from a "geologically grounded truth" in which "veins of ore and gems were the rock roots" of consciousness (Slavnikova 2010, 29, 32).

However, Ripheans inhabit nature marked not only by ghostly absence, but by spirits which mediate between humans and their surroundings. The novel distinguishes geological enthusiasts, or rockhounds, from the corporate miners and black market traders who seek to plunder the mountains via large-scale extraction. In their gem-hunting expeditions, the rockhounds constantly negotiate with Riphean spirits, who reward or punish their excursions into sacred territories according to a complex moral economy. The local Riphean mythology typologizes the spirits according to the different ores and minerals they incarnate: grass snakes "slithering like streaks of oil;" dancing Pyralids drawn to glittering gems; Goldenhair, the Great Snake's daughter, a "Riphean Gorgon" with an "eyeless head wreathed in liquid gold" who petrifies overzealous gold prospectors; the Pleistocene Ancient Silverhoof, "oldest of the mountain spirits," a "paleontological specter" with a four-foot antler rack like "eagle wings of bone" and silver hooves oxidized from time (193, 273). In their uncanny forms, the oldest spirits personify the geological ages of the mountains, signifying the deep time over which the earth's mineral veins were formed.

This catalogue of mountain spirits consciously reworks the folkloric materials of an earlier writer, Pavel Bazhov, whose stories have become central to the Urals' cultural imaginary, as well as inspiring films, televisual adaptations, and Prokofiev's *Stone Flower* ballet. In 1939, Bazhov, a historian hiding from Stalin's purges, published *The Malachite Casket*, a collection which transfigured elements of Urals folklore memorializing the nineteenth-century malachite boom into a set of fantastic tales featuring magical lizards, snakes, and a stony queen, the Mistress of the Copper Mountain. Bazhov differentiated his stories from both social realism and wonder-tales (*skazka*), calling them *skazy*, a genre which draws on oral narrative art and combines "unreal, magic or fantastic content" with "true" details such as historical dates and events that take place in the "present or recent past" (Lipovetsky 2008, 263). Factually grounded in Urals history, the tales named industrial magnates, geographical locations, and famous mines, and captured the texture of life for proletarian workers, for whom the regional dialect phrase "worn out" summarized the physical and moral condition of labor in the mining industries (Rogachev 1998, 20). Unlike typical Russian wonder-tales, Bazhov's *skazy* lacked happy resolutions or simplistic wish fulfillments; instead, they allegorized a sense of local life as controlled by external forces which could not be resisted, only endured. The artisans and miners who attracted the attention of the Stone Maiden through their exceptional craftsmanship were often enervated or drained dry, even when she rewarded them with voluptuous riches.

Mark Lipovetsky argues that Bazhov's *skazy* function on two levels. In order to fulfill Soviet ideological prescriptions on literary content, they make their primary subject the pre-revolutionary hardships of proletarian mineworkers in the nineteenth-century gem booms. However, they also operate on the level of the "Soviet uncanny," transmuting Bazhov's own fear of being sent to the gulag into a registration of the repressed trauma of the collective unconscious during Stalin's "Great Terror" (2008, 267). While Lipovetsky reads this "double-encoding" as primarily expressed through the Mistress's *unheimlich* sexuality, the Stone Maiden could also be read as embodying the double uncanny of the tsarist and Soviet production of nature. The stories describe the human and ecological costs of tsarist industrialization, while being written during the first push of the "Great Urals" plan for Soviet industrialization. As such, they can be understood as post-catastrophic responses to the violence of Soviet modernization and to the repressed knowledge of aboriginal dispossession in the course of tsarist imperial industrialization.

Anthropologist Michael Taussig has observed that magical reactions to "nonfantastic" reality frequently arise in export-dependent peripheries as a critique of their forced induction into liberal market economies. Societies reorganized around mining and plantation monocultures give rise to modern myths of devils or spirits, fetishizations of evil that mediate "the conflict between pre-capitalist and capitalist modes of objectifying the human condition" (Taussig 2010, xvi). These specters often offer devilish contracts that require proletarians to barter away their souls in exchange for riches, which Taussig reads as an expression of the "phantom objectivity" arising within the market economy, in which human labor-time and nature are turned into objects and "commodities rule their creators" (xvi). In Bazhov's tales, the Mistress's dark, non-Slavic features hint that she is the forgotten queen of the "old people," the Uralic peoples displaced by Russian colonizers, who had believed the Urals to be sacred spaces inhabited by living spirits, in which the mountains themselves took on animate form. As the trace of a residual value system, she suggests an uneasy opposition to the phantom objectivity of the tsarist and Soviet mining monocultures, in which people's productive capacities and nature's resources are drained and abstracted for export. Her overtures to workers are full of ambiguity, promising riches in exchange for fealty but as often delivering exhaustion or death, and overlaid with an ecophobic threat of nature's retribution for centuries of exploitation. But she also intimates the possibility of an alternative ecological relation, such that disappearance into her caverns is embraced by some characters as pleasurable release from objectification.

In Slavnikova's *2017*, the content and generic principle of the *skazy*'s hybrid combination of the fantastic and the historical is reworked in order to evoke the compound catastrophe of ecological disaster in the Urals, where the nuclear and chemical pollution of the Soviet era is preceded by generations of mining and heavy industry. The double-encoding of the Soviet uncanny is amplified into a triple-encoding of the post-Soviet uncanny, so that the toxic deliriums corresponding to the reintensification of ore-prospecting and plutonium-prospecting in the neoliberal period are layered onto the earlier "malachite fever" crystallized in Bazhov's fantasies. This enables a form of spatial telesthesia that makes visible the fractured terrain of ecological violence over the *longue durée*. Telesthesia denotes the alleged perception of events beyond the normal range of perceptual processes. Stephen Shapiro has argued that gothic aesthetics revolve around this ability to apprehend what is beyond the immediate reach of the empirical senses, because they originate in moments of crisis, during which large-scale transformations facilitate a greater perception of systemic violence than is usually available to individual subjects (2008, 34). Gothic narratives often reconfigure the gothic-effects of cultural materials from previous conjunctures, and as a result acquire a double temporal dynamic, resurrecting past histories at the same time as they anticipate future crises, as well as a tendency to telescope space, opening up an understanding of world-systemic dynamics based on apprehension of their local manifestations.

In Slavnikova's *2017*, the reworking of Bazhov's intertexts constitutes a formal "mining" of literary resources produced in response to previous stages of resource extraction in order to represent post-Soviet crisis, but the ecological catastrophe which the novel imagines is represented not as rupture or an "end of nature," but as an almost imperceptible accumulation of processes. Midway through the novel, a long, lyrical passage describes Anfilogov and Kolyan's penetration into an eerie zone near the Pemba River, where they are led by manifestations of the Stone Maiden toward a huge vein of rubies:

> Nothing was rustling, and nothing was busy in last year's stalks. Something was wrong with the grass, too. Here and there it was white at the roots, like the gray hair in a grown-out head of dyed hair, and

in places it detached from the soil in felted scraps [...]. Mountain spirits, concerned by the fate of the underground store, must have been watching, but they, of course, had nothing to do with the departure of the grass's inhabitants because they lived in a complex symbiosis with all creatures and in a sense consisted of their organic lives. The reason for the damage was, of course, man. [...] At the same time none of this looked like an ecological disaster. If there had been certain effects, nature had resisted them. [...] Looking around, Anfilogov felt as if he'd been poisoned.

(2010, 205–06)

The scene refuses apocalyptic temporality and lacks explicit signs of toxicity, apart from the whitened grass and absence of small mammals and insects. The region does not look like a "disaster"—much like the mystical "zone" in Andrei Tarkovsky's *Stalker,* famously shot in a toxic wastescape near a chemical plant outside Tallinn. It is not a site of spectacular violence, but rather haunted by an aura of the almost imperceptible violence of biomagnification and radiation.

The miners sense that the corundum vein is a living "organ" of the mountain, but are unable to conceive of any value for its existence except in its conversion to inert commodities. Instead, in thrall to an uncanny "ruby fever," they smash deeper into the vein, which gives off the smell of "the maw of some fatally ill stone animal," as if the geology itself were animate (204). Ignoring their symptoms of poisoning, they work literally to death. Kolyan's corpse takes on a grotesque, crystalline appearance: "the transparent became solid—and soon under his mustache a mayflower bell formed out of fibrous charoite through which his steel teeth gleamed like cleavage fissures in a crystal matrix" (213). Mutated into a simulacrum of the very commodities he labored to extract, Kolyan's gothic transformation literalizes the phantom objectivity implicit to the mining of the mountain ecology, a horrific inversion of the mountain spirits' embodiment of the complex symbiosis of inorganic matter and organic lives.

The novel later reveals that the Pelma watershed, already contaminated by decades of Soviet heavy industry, has been recontaminated by cyanide leaching from unlined pits constructed on the cheap near a gold mine privatized during the neoliberal transition. This revelation of a repressed toxic history is key to the novel's temporality. The peculiar sense of temporal regression which haunts the doomed gem hunters can be read both as neurological symptoms of cyanide toxicity and radiation poisoning, and as allegory of the social sensorium of cyclical boom and exhaustion repeating over the history of resource extraction in the Urals: "The most powerful déjà vu occurred whenever they set to any kind of work. At any attempt to take a step into the future, [they] wound up in the past" (209). The characters experience the present as a repetition of past crises that remain unresolved. This circular post-catastrophic temporality subverts linear notions of historical progression, suggesting that the post-Soviet production of nature in the Urals remains haunted by the logic of phantom objectivity continuous with earlier historical periods. The economic calculus in the neoliberal phase of mining places profit above all concerns for environmental protection or social health. As such, it is little changed from the Soviet ideology of nature, whose fetishization of growth and "plan fulfilment" prevented investment in environmental protection despite awareness of hazard (Filtzer 2009, 107).

This temporal telesthesia is accompanied in the text by a simultaneous widening of spatial perception that makes visible the imbrication of local dynamics of neoliberal plans for intensified rounds of extraction in the Urals within the larger global phenomenon of the BRICS' competition for resource sovereignty. Speculating on the causes of Anfilogov's disappearance, Krylov's ex-wife Tamara unleashes a long tirade explaining the "brutal, artificial measures" deployed by transnational corporations to stabilize world-market prices for their own reserves of precious stones and heavy metals in South Africa and Brazil by eliminating their competitors (Slavnikova 2010, 167). The structure of the "single world molecule," as she caustically describes the world market, relies on the twin strategies of manufactured scarcity and enclosure of new ecological commons, and she warns Krylov that "the molecule ... doesn't tolerate blank spots" (165). The novel implies that the Mistress of the Mountain compels Anfilogov to death not only because of her displeasure with his epistemic reduction of nature to treasure hoard, but in order to conceal the corundum river from competing industrialists in search of unexploited "blank" territories.

This individual punishment meted out by a personified specter of nature's retribution seems to represent the limit of the novel's imagination of environmental justice. The figuration of the Stone Maiden's uncanny agency to avenge resource extraction is held in tension with a "geopolitical unconscious" fraught with anxiety over the external global forces spurring future degradation in the Urals. The Mistress's power for redress seems slight when juxtaposed with Tamara's panoptical vision of ultrasound technology that can take "pictures of the entire contents of the earth's crust from a satellite" so that no subterranean territory might go unexploited by nations competing for resources (167). The prospect of political reorganizations of nature/society that might eschew conceptions of planetary dominance or resist neoliberal schemes for intensified extraction remains remote in the novel, tainted by post-Soviet disillusionment with collective politics and a sense of powerlessness in the face of Putin's repression of electoral protests. In interviews, Slavnikova has crucially insisted that the Urals should be seen as a space not only of catastrophe but of the "miraculous" (Kiem 2013). Yet the novel's conclusion seems more nightmarish than miraculous, centering around the bloody reenactment of the 1917 civil war, as the "virus of History" spreads like an epidemic from its epicenter in Yekaterinburg, and a new dictator seizes power in Moscow (Slavnikova 2010, 406). Putin's dream of Russia's geopolitical dominance as a Great Power (*derzhava*) based on energy exports and nuclear renaissance is reimagined here not as the "Russian miracle," but rather as a bad dream infected by the resurrection of old imperial aspirations, promising little remediation of ecological crisis. The novel's insistence on historical recurrence suggests that compound environmental catastrophe in the Urals has yet to be resolved in post-Soviet Russia and continues to be experienced by local inhabitants as an "undead" trauma.

The ecogothic tropes of Slavnikova's novel crystallize the affective responses of this post-catastrophic structure of feeling: fears of toxification and nature's revenge, a traumatic sense of cultural exhaustion corresponding to the boom and bust of resource monocultures, a cyclical experience of repetitive temporality. The mountain spirits can be interpreted literally as chemical delusions figuring real processes of toxification experienced by human inhabitants of irradiated and chemicalized landscapes. But they can also be read as "green" specters: the cultural manifestations of a residual social consciousness that resists the reduction of the Urals' nature to a treasure box of resources. In contrast to Anfilogov's perception of the mountain spirits as barriers to his individual domination of nature, the rock hounds who feel reverence for the "functioning temple" of geology are permitted to enter the mountains under the "mantle of transparent, flickering Medusas" (275). They return with "emotional" tales of an "unprecedented luxury of refreshed nature," teeming with gushing streams, bright swamps, and dark forests through whose trunks "wove complicated, flexible, and bizarre specters" (274). This vision of a revitalized *taiga* refuses an eventist understanding of catastrophe as a static end, gesturing instead to the way polluted environments remain populated by both human and extra-human forms of life and are subject to dynamic change over time, even if it is the almost unimaginable breakdown of nuclear byproducts over their long half-lives. This, then, is the "miraculous" horizon of the novel, an imaginary recuperation of an ecological consciousness that resists the phantom objectivity implicit to the Soviet and capitalist production of nature. In a dialectical reversal of the earlier image of "ghost mountains," the novel portrays the remaining peaks as alive with a host of spirits personifying both organic life and slow geological processes shaping the formation of inorganic matter, a literary reanimation which reverses the ideological objectification of the Urals, even as it retains within view the material ecological consequences of such objectification.

As I have tried to demonstrate in this essay, reading the literary ecogothic provides one way of uncovering cultural responses to processes of structural violence that are often difficult to discern. In their use of fantastic aesthetics to defamiliarize official versions of the past, ecogothic narratives draw on folkloric materials that embody collective memory from below. Transforming memory into imagination, these narratives articulate what often cannot be expressed in other cultural forms under conditions of political repression or historical erasure. As such, they can perform the critical function of both anamnesis—the recollection of what has been lost or forgotten—and of prolepsis, the imagination of what could otherwise be. Critical analysis of such narratives can thus infuse the environmental humanities with new perspectives of lived experience and ethical responses to ecological catastrophe in contemporary Russia, as part of a wider goal to understand how global environmental issues are influenced by the intersecting legacies of ecological imperialism and intensified resource extraction.

NOTES

1. While the polemical term *ecocide* was first used by Murray Feshbach and Alfred Friendly to argue that Soviet ecological catastrophe would be remedied by liberal market capitalism, subsequent historians have pointed out that "brute-force technologies" to impose mass environmental transformations were employed by both the capitalist west and the Soviet empire, precipitating ecocide in both hemispheres (Josephson 2002).

2. See Alexander Etkind's account of ecological imperialism in his history of internal colonization and the "resource-bound epochs" of Russian empire (2011, 164) and Sean Starrs's argument that Putin's imperial ambitions for resource sovereignty are heightened by Russia's dependence on high fossil-fuel prices (2014, 89).

3. Russia's ongoing conflict over Chechnya, a gateway to the oil reserves and transport routes of the Caspian, and its recent incursions in the Ukraine, can be understood in these terms. Similarly, in the Arctic, the melting of the icepack has triggered displays of energy imperialism between Russia and Western capitalist cores competing over oil reserves. In Africa, Russia has pursued "resource grabs" of uranium in Niger and Namibia to shore up reserves dwindling after the loss of its internal colonies (Carmody 2013).

4. See, for instance, novels such as Vladimir Sorokin's *Day of the Oprichnik* (2006), Tatyana Tolstaya's *The Slynx* (2003), Dmitry Bykov's *Living Souls* (2006), and Dmitry Glukhovsky's *Metro 2033* (2005). Their hybridized aesthetics combine irrealist devices of speculative fiction and the ecogothic in order to articulate anxieties around energy dependence, environmental crisis, and Russia's geopolitical position in the world-system.

5. Social realism was the dominant method of Soviet literature and criticism, organized around a telos demanding that literature depict the proleriat's glorious struggle toward socialist progress through truthful and historically concrete representations of reality. Within Soviet realism, nature was usually portrayed as a force to be struggled against and eventually dominated by the heroic working class; alternative literary traditions such as village prose that represented nature in pastoral terms were often criticized as decadent or nostalgic.

6. Uralic populations included the Nenets, a Samoyed people now mostly found in northern Siberia, the Komi, Mansi, and Khanty peoples to the south, and the Bashkir, whose creation myth lends the mountains their name, telling how they sprang from the burial mound of a giant. Indigenous groups constitute only one-fifth of the Urals' contemporary population; the majority are Russians settled in urban centers in the Central Urals. In the polar Urals, beyond the reach of

earlier phases of industrialization, the Nenets, Komi, Mansi, and Khanty have preserved traditional ways of life rooted in animist conceptions of nature.

7. The brutal process of *dekulakization* was driven not only by the ideological imperative to "re-educate" political opponents, but by accelerated modernization's demand for labor. It provided "human resources" to fill acute labor shortages in mining, metallurgy and forestry, while repressing peasant resistance to agricultural collectivization (Harris 1997, 276).

8. State capitalism describes an economic system in which commercial economic activity is undertaken by the state, so that management of the means of production, including capital accumulation, wage labor, and hierarchical centralized management, is organized in a capitalist manner, irrespective of the political ideology professed by the state.

9. The most notorious monoculture, frequently cited as one of the planet's worst environmental disasters, is the conversion of Central Asia to the mass production of cotton, or "white gold," which drained the Aral Sea to irrigate the desert.

10. This is typical of the tendency of post-Soviet states to organize their economies around commodity monocultures: Russia and Kazakhstan are based around oil and gas exports, Kyrgyzstan around gold mining, and so forth (Josephson et al. 2013, 293). Part of the global "scramble for resources" in the neoliberal era, it coincides with the "new extractivism" in Latin America, as described by Jorge Marcone's essay in this volume.

11. The Russian Federation's legal category, *korreny malochislennye narody*, which loosely translates as "small-numbered indigenous peoples," foregoes the flexible, multifactored UN definition (which identifies indigenous groups based on preexistence, non-dominance, cultural difference, and self-identification) in favor of a rigid numerical cut-off: only peoples under 50,000 qualify, thus excluding other minorities. Indigenous territories are rich in natural resources, particularly oil, gas, and minerals, and have been heavily targeted by post-Soviet energy projects, including pipelines, hydroelectric dams, and intensive mining.

12. A recent class action brought by neighboring villages accused the Mayak complex of illegally discharging 30 to 40 million cubic meters of low-level radioactive waste into the Techa river cascade between 2001 to 2004 (Slivyak 2011).

13. Yekaterinburg, known as Sverdlovsk during Soviet times, was part of the chain of secret industrial cities in the Urals, a neighbor to Chelyabinsk; it was also the location of the execution of the Romanovs in 1918, and thus foundational to mythology of the Bolshevik revolution.

REFERENCES

Amis, Martin. 2012. "Martin Amis in Conversation with Olga Slavnikova." *The New Yorker*. June 12. http://www.newyorker.com/books/page-turner/martin-amis-in-conversation-with-olga-slavnikova.

Bazhov, Pavel. 2002. *Malachite Casket: Tales from the Urals*. Amsterdam: Fredonia Books.

Botting, Fred. 2002. "Aftergothic: Consumption, Machines, and Black Holes." In *The Cambridge Companion to Gothic Fiction*, edited by Jerrold E. Hogle, 277–300. Cambridge: Cambridge University Press.

Borgstrom, Georg. 1965. *The Hungry Planet: The Modern World at the Edge of Famine*. London: Macmillan.

Bykov, Dmitry. 2010. *Living Souls*. Translated by Cathy Porter. London: Alma Books.

Carrigan, Anthony. 2011. "Out of This Great Tragedy Will Come a World Class Tourism Destination: Disaster, Ecology, and Post-Tsunami Tourism Development in Sri Lanka." In *Postcolonial Ecologies: Literatures of the Environment*, edited by Elizabeth DeLoughrey and George B. Handley, 273–90. Oxford: Oxford University Press.

Carmody, Pádraig. 2013. *The Rise of the BRICS in Africa: The Geopolitics of South-South Relations*. London: Zed Books.

Chioni Moore, David. 2001. "Is the Post in Postcolonial the Post in Post-Soviet? Towards a Global Postcolonial Critique." *PMLA* 116 (1): 111–128.

Crosby, Alfred W. 2004. *Ecological Imperialism: The Overseas Migration of Western Europeans as a Biological Phenomenon*. Cambridge: Cambridge University Press.

Davis, Mike. 1993. "The Dead West: Ecocide in Marlboro Country." *New Left Review* 1 (200). http://newleftreview.org/I/200/mike-davis-the-dead-west-ecocide-in-marlboro-country.

Dawson, Jane I. 1996. *Eco-nationalism: Anti-Nuclear Activism and National Identity in Russia, Lithuania and Ukraine*. Durham: Duke University Press.

Deckard, Sharae. 2013. "'Uncanny States': Global EcoGothic and the World-Ecology in Rana Dasgupta's *Tokyo Cancelled*." In *Ecogothic*, edited by Andrew Smith and William Hughes, 177–194. Manchester: Manchester University Press.

DeLoughrey, Elizabeth. 2009. "Radiation Ecologies and the Wars of Light." *Modern Fiction Studies* 55 (3): 468–495.

Etkind, Alexander. 2009. "Stories of the Undead in the Land of the Unburied: Magical Historicism in Contemporary Russian Fiction." *Slavic Review* 68 (3): 631–658.

———. 2011. *Internal Colonization: Russia's Imperial Experience*. London: Polity Press.

Fanon, Frantz. 2001. *The Wretched of the Earth*. Translated by Constance Harrington. London: Penguin Classics.

Filtzer, Donald. 2009. "Poisoning the Proletariat: Urban Water Supply and River Pollution in Russia's Industrial Regions during Late Stalinism, 1945–1953." *Acta Slavica Iaponica* 26: 85–108.

Givens, John. 2010. "The New Gothic: Mythic Prose, and the Post-Soviet Novel." *Russian Studies in Literature* 46 (1): 3–5.

Givental, Elena. 2013. "Hundred Years of Glory and Gloom: The Urals Region of Russia in Art and Reality." *SAGE Open*. April 14. http://sgo.sagepub.com/content/3/2/2158244013486657.

Glukhovsky, Dmitry. 2010. *Metro 2033* [2005]. Translated by Natasha Randall. London: Gollancz.

Harris, James R. 1997. "The Growth of the Gulag: Forced Labor in the Urals Region, 1921–31." *Russian Review* 56 (2): 265–280.

Josephson, Paul. 2002. *Industrialized Nature: Brute Force Technology and the Transformation of the Natural World*. Washington: Island Press.

———. 2005. *Red Atom: Russia's Nuclear Power Program from Stalin to Today*. Pittsburgh: University of Pittsburgh Press.

Josephson, Paul, Nicolai Dronin, Ruben Mnatsakanian, Aleh Cherp, Dmitry Efremenko, and Vladislav Larin. 2013. *An Environmental History of Russia*. Cambridge: Cambridge University Press.

Kiem, Elizabeth. 2012. "Olga Slavnikova." *The Morning News.* October 25. http:// www.themorningnews.org/article/olga-slavnikova.

Klein, Naomi. 2007. *The Shock Doctrine: The Rise of Disaster Capitalism.* London: Penguin.

Lebedushkina, Olga. 2010. "Our New Gothic: The Miracles and Horrors of Contemporary Prose." *Russian Studies in Literature* 46 (1): 81–100.

Lipovetsky, Mark. 2008. "Pavel Bazhov's *Skazy*: Discovering the Soviet Uncanny." In *Russian Children's Literature and Culture,* edited by Marina Balina and Larissa Rudova, 263–284. London: Routledge.

Lipovetsky, Mark, and Alexander Etkind. 2010. "The Salamander's Return: The Soviet Catastrophe and the Post-Soviet Novel." *Russian Studies in Literature* 46 (4): 6–48.

Löwy, Michael. 2007. "The Current of Critical Irrealism: 'A Moonlit Enchanted Night.'" In *Adventures in Realism,* edited by Matthew Beaumont, 193–206. Oxford: Blackwell Publishing.

Newnham, Randall. 2011. "Oil, Carrots, and Sticks: Russia's Energy Resources as a Foreign Policy Tool." *Journal of Eurasian Studies* 2 (2): 134–143.

Nixon, Rob. 2011. *Slow Violence and the Environmentalism of the Poor.* Cambridge: Harvard University Press.

Pomper, Miles. 2009. "The Russian Nuclear Industry: Status and Prospects." *Nuclear Energy Futures Papers No 3.* The Centre for International Governance Innovation. www.cigionline.org.

Rabl, Thomas. 2012. "The Nuclear Disaster of Kyshtym 1957 and the Politics of the Cold War." *Environment & Society Portal: Arcadia 20.* http://www.environmentandsociety.org/arcadia/nuclear-disaster-kyshtym-1957-and-politics-cold-war.

Rogachev, Sergei. 1998. "The Old Mountains." In *Beyond Borders,* edited by Kathleen Braden et al., 1–21. *SPU Works.* http://digitalcommons.spu.edu/works/2/.

Shapiro, Stephen. 2008. "Transvaal, Transylvania: Dracula's World-system and Gothic Periodicity." *Gothic Studies* 10 (1): 29–47.

Slavnikova, Olga. 2010. *2017.* Translated by Marian Schwartz. London: Duckworth.

———. 2014. "Interview with Olga Slavnikova." *Causa Artium. Vimeo.* http:// vimeo.com/80852397.

Slivyak, Vladimir. 2011. "Russia's Infamous Reprocessing Plant Mayak Never Stopped Illegal Dumping of Radioactive Waste into Nearby River." *Bellona.* December 24. http://bellona.org/news/nuclear-issues/nuclear-russia/2011-12-russias-infamous-reprocessing-plant-mayak-never-stopped-illegal-dumping-of-radioactive-waste-into-nearby-river-poisoning-residents-newly-disclosed-court-finding-says.

Smith, Andrew, and William Hughes, eds. 2013. *Ecogothic.* Manchester: Manchester University Press.

Smith, Neil. 1984. *Uneven Development: Nature, Capital and the Production of Space.* Oxford: Blackwell.

Sorokin, Vladimir. 2012. *Day of the Oprichnik.* Translated by Jamey Gambrell. London: Farrar, Strauss, and Giroux.

Starrs, Sean. 2014. "The Chimera of Global Convergence." *New Left Review* 87: 81–96.

Taussig, Michael T. 2010. *The Devil and Commodity Fetishism in South America.* Chapel Hill: University of North Carolina Press.

Tlostanova, Madina. 2014. "Book Review: 'Internal Colonization. Russia's Imperial Experience.'" *Postcolonial Europe.* May 10. http://www.post

colonial-europe.eu/reviews/166-book-review-internal-colonization-russias-imperial-experience-.html.

Tolstaya, Tatyana. 2003. *The Slynx*. Translated by Jamey Gambrell. New York: New York Review Books.

Williams, Raymond. 1977. *Marxism and Literature*. Oxford: Oxford University Press.

WISE. 2005. "Russian Study on Low Radiation." *World Information Service on Energy Nuclear Monitor* 638. November 18. http://www.wiseinternational.org/node/3212.

Part V

Terraforming, Climate Change, and the Anthropocene

14 Terraforming Planet Earth

Joseph Masco

Being able to assume a planetary, as opposed to a global, imaginary is a surprisingly recent phenomenon.[1] Although depictions of an earthly global sphere are longstanding and multiple (see Cosgrove 2001, DeLoughrey 2014; Heise 2008), the specific attributes of being able to see the entire planet as a single unit or system, I would argue is a Cold War creation. This mode of thinking is therefore deeply imbricated not only in nuclear age militarism but also the specific forms of twentieth-century knowledge production, as well as a related proliferation of visualization technologies (see Haffner 2013; Kurgan 2013). A planetary imaginary includes globalities of every kind (finance, technology, ecology) but also geology, atmosphere, and the biosphere as one totality. What is increasingly powerful about this point of view is that it both relies on the national security state for the technologies, finances, and interests that create the possibility of seeing in this fashion, but also, in a single image exceeds the nation-state as the political form that matters. A planetary optic is thus both a national security creation (in its scientific infrastructures, visualization technologies, and governing ambitions), but it also transcends these structures to offer an alternative ground for politics and future making. Proliferating forms of globality—including the specific visualizations of science, finance, and environment—achieve both ultimate scale and are unified at the level of the planetary, which raises an important question about how collective problems and security can, and should, be imagined.

Today, we live with unprecedented technical optics for assessing large-scale problems, and are thus able to identify the as yet uncontrolled legacies of industrial age capitalism on Earth, but we do not have political systems operating on the right scale to address truly planetary problems. This conundrum—of collective awareness and visualization exceeding political institutions and agency—can be profitably interrogated through an examination of the conceptual history, technoscience, and psychosocial effects of "fallout." A radically changing climate is the unintended cumulative legacy of capitalism, militarism, and industrialism. This makes fallout a key register not only for a new post-colonial, post-military industrial environmental consciousness but also a central means of recognizing emerging forms of violence across the global north–global south divide (see Parenti 2011). Today, as earth scientists generate increasingly precise depictions of planetary scale ecological precarity, the historic challenge to the humanities and social sciences is nothing less than to grapple with the imperiled conditions of life on Earth, to answer the call for a new form of planetary governance, and to negotiate the ongoing toxic fallout of the industrial age.

FIGURING FALLOUT

"Fallout" is a relatively recent term in the English language designating an unexpected supplement to an event, a precipitation that is in motion, causing a kind of long-term and unexpected damage: it is the aftermath, the reverberation, the negative side effect. We talk today about the fallout of the mortgage crisis or of official action or inaction, or of drone strikes and preemptions across the field of counterterrorism. Fallout comes after the event. It is the unacknowledged until lived crisis built into the infrastructure of a program, project, or process. Fallout is therefore understood primarily retrospectively but lived in the future anterior—a form of history made visible in negative outcomes. We live today I think in the age of fallout, inheriting from the twentieth century a vast range of problems linking ecologies with national security with science and technology and finance in an ongoing negative aftermath. For example, the nuclear disaster at the Fukushima-Daiichi plant in March 2011 produced literal fallout in the form of cesium-137 contamination but also was a combined technoscientific, financial, and regulatory failure.[2] Industrialism, militarism and capitalism are each massive fallout generating practices, producing reverberating crises, now consolidated in wide ranging collective insecurities, on issues ranging from climate to energy to finance to war, each of which operates in a specific register of globality.

Fallout the noun comes to us from the verb to "fall out," which from the sixteenth century on has designated a social break or conflict. It is thus the fight that separates comrades, marking the end of intimacy, shared purpose, and social pleasure. Military personnel also fall out from being at attention, a marker of a return to individual activities after a collective review, a relaxing of the conditions of formal militarism. Falling out thus involves individual actions and lived consequences, a postsociality, lived in isolation from the collective action of society or the war machine. To fall out is both to break with a friend and to relax from formal review; it is to burn a bridge and be off-duty all at the same time. Being off-duty matters today, as so many of our regulatory institutions are not doing their stated jobs, short circuited by political agendas, lack of funding, or more generally misguided priorities. For example, in response to major reports from the Intergovernmental Panel on Climate Change and the US Climate Assessment in 2014 detailing a disturbing future of ecological instability, the US House of Representatives passed a bill in May prohibiting the Department of Defense from using any funds to respond to the vast range of security problems documented in these scientific studies—an effort to ban both science and the environment from defense policy to secure petrochemical profits (Koronowski 2014). We are living within an increasingly post-Foucauldian kind of governmentality, in which the project of improving and securing life is being overrun by a narrowly construed notion of profit, one that functions in the increasingly short lag between the engineered event and its fallout. Our notions of globality are thus also increasingly tied to tracking negative outcomes more than positive ones, as global flows of money, carbon, and information tend not to be recognized as infrastructural creations until they are in planetary crisis.

Fallout, the noun, is of course an invention of the nuclear age, appearing in the English language soon after the US atomic bombings of Hiroshima and Nagasaki in 1945 (see Boyer 1998: xiii). Formally, fallout refers to the radioactive debris put into the atmosphere by a nuclear explosion, designating an atmospheric event with far reaching consequences (see Glasstone and Dolan 1977). Marked as a precipitation, it involves a gradual settling of radioactive materials and effects over a wide area. Fallout thus formally links human actions, technological capabilities, atmospheres, and ecologies in a new configuration of contamination. Radioactive fallout is also made up of a wide range of possible nuclear elements—cesium, strontium, iodine, etc.—with radically different radioactive half-lives and environmental effects. It operates therefore on a wide range of temporal frames, and is both an immediate threat to health (radiation illness) as well as a long-term one (cancer or life shortening; see also Jain 2013; Nixon 2011). Fallout is, thus, always an act of coproduction, a simultaneously remaking of nature and culture via collective injury.

With this in mind, consider how fallout was first presented to US citizens, not long after the invention of the concept, in the largest propaganda campaign to date in American history, known as atomic "civil defense." In reaction to the first Soviet nuclear test, a new US Federal Civil Defense Administration (FCDA) was created in 1950. The FCDA worked to transform US citizens into Cold Warriors by saturating the public sphere with nuclear narratives, images, and themes (Masco 2014). An unprecedented effort to reorient American society around the dangers of a new technology, the FCDA sought to create a productive fear of the nuclear age in order to achieve a permanent war posture (Oakes 1994). Figure 14.1, offers an emblematic illustration of the atomic civil defense campaign of the 1950s, presenting "'fallout" not simply as a new wartime threat to domestic life but as a new structuring principle of American modernity.

In "Facts About Fallout" citizens learn that at home as well as on the street they are vulnerable to a new kind of invisible injury. Urban populations are no longer even the specific target of military attack, it is the environment itself which has been transformed into a potentially toxic space, remaking clouds and air as dangerous entities. The nuclear danger transforms the atmosphere on which living beings depend, converting it from a life support

Figure 14.1 Facts about Fallout, Civil Defense handout. Federal Civil Defense Administration, circa 1955.

system into something now forever suspect, loaded at any moment with invisible and possibly deadly elements.

Part of a larger Cold War recalibration of American society through nuclear danger, the FCDA campaign attempted to shift responsibility for injury from the security infrastructures themselves to the individual citizen, now positioned as properly informed about everyday risk via civil defense programs, and expected to be both alert and resilient in a minute-to-minute confrontation with nuclear war. After 1945, Americans were increasingly recruited to normalize unprecedented forms of existential danger within an industrial atmosphere undergoing radical change. *Facts about Fallout* illustrates this new kind of industrial awareness, offering a cloud that no longer brings the sustenance of rain but rather delivers deadly particulates that "you can seldom feel or see." Fallout is thus an environmental flow that matters to health and safety but that also demands a new form of everyday perception and governance. Fallout, here, also implicitly positions the citizen less as national subject than as earth dweller, increasingly at risk simply for being a breather (Choy 2011). This conversion of atmosphere from the most rudimentary domain of life into an uncertain circulation also directly challenges the territorial vision of the national security state system, as international borders and security states are rendered irrelevant by windborne industrial effects within earth systems (see Sloterdijk 2009, and Beck 2007).

How many of our toxic industrial processes fall into this similar category of the unseen but cumulatively damaging or deadly? How many issues of toxicity now are also issues of scale and perspective—of not only what to see but how to see danger? Fallout—in the form of radioactivity, synthetic chemicals, or the impacts of the carbon cycle on climate—produces cumulative effects that only become visible in the destabilized organism or ecological system. The temporality of injury thus becomes central to the assessment of danger itself, as the industrial age produces "products" that install injury and crisis incrementally into the future, colonizing an ever-deeper time horizon (see Jain 2013; Murphy 2008; Nixon 2011).

In US Cold War practice, fallout was initially constituted as the bomb's lesser injurious form. This allowed a strange and perverse splitting of the nuclear event itself into the expected and planned detonation and its lingering atmospheric effects (see Eden 2004). Though it was understood in 1945 that the irradiated particulate matter that travels on wind patterns constituted a kind of weapon, enabling a new form of atmospheric terrorism, it was the explosive power of the bomb that was fetishized by the US military and the basis for nuclear war planning. A completely predictable aspect of any nuclear event, fallout was thus officially coded within US practice as a side effect. Much as drug companies today split the desired from the undesired effects of molecule—the political economy of the side effect here has huge consequences, installing bizarre metrics and significant misrecognitions throughout nuclear national security logics—allowing certain forms of destruction to be recognized while others are marginalized. For example, while potentially deadly on a mass scale and constituting a new kind of chemical/biological weapon all-in-one, radioactive fallout was officially crafted as a secondary formation to the exploding bomb during the era of atmospheric nuclear testing. The official project of producing a "safe" nuclear detonation involved evaluations of wind patterns, weather, and efforts to target radioactive fallout at unpopulated geographical regions. The "unpopulated area" as history has repeatedly shown was rarely so, creating vast exposures that quickly undermined any notion of "national security" as a protection of populations (see Johnson and Barker 2008). A scientists' crusade against the health effects of nuclear testing programs directly challenged the logics of civil defense and national security, energizing peace, justice, and environmental social movements (see Commoner 1958; Fowler 1960a). Indeed, the first decades of the nuclear age were filled not only with vast exposures leading to widespread public protest but also with unsuccessful efforts to build a "clean bomb" at the US weapons laboratories—one, that is, that could explode with little radioactive fallout and thus preserve the desired destructive effect.

A crucial development in the Cold War nuclear system was the move to underground nuclear testing in the United States, which profoundly shifted the environmental register of nuclear testing away from atmospheric fallout to a different kind of ecological damage, one less connected to wind patterns than to underground radioactive seepage and flow. The 1963 Limited Test Ban treaty—which stands as the first nuclear weapons treaty and the first global environmental treaty—both recognized the planetary consequences of nuclear testing and worked to preserve the nuclear weapons complex itself (eliminating US and Soviet nuclear tests in the atmosphere, outer space, and the ocean while consolidating their energetic experimental test regimes underground). This also significantly changed the visual politics of the nuclear age, allowing a shift from the iconic image of the mushroom cloud with its poisonous atmospheric implications in favor of new technologies of global surveillance and visualization, focused on detecting seismic signatures of nuclear tests. By the end of the 1960s, images from outer space, produced first by satellites and then by space missions, provided photographic images of planet Earth as a singular totality (Poole 2008; Kurgan 2013). These emerging visualization infrastructures were tied in direct and indirect ways to US efforts to monitor foreign nuclear test regimes, as well as to develop more powerful infrastructures for fighting nuclear wars (from missiles, to early warning systems, to satellite based command and control technologies).

The environmental legacies of Cold War nuclearism (from fallout to environmental contamination to nuclear waste) now stand as an iconic illustration of toxic industrialization and an emergent planetary politics. In what follows, I want to make a case for radioactive fallout as an emblem of industrial modernity but also invite you think with it as allegory for a larger set of processes now collectively gathered together under a rubric of climate change. The historical development of nuclear and climate dangers are complexly intertwined at the level of environmental effects, knowledge systems, and public perceptions (Masco 2010). The cumulative toxic fallout of the twentieth century continues to shift global systems, requiring a new politics of air, soil, water, energy, and finance while demanding new concepts of planetary security. Toxicity is now a planetary force, requiring a different scale and understanding of the political (see Clark 2014). For the remainder of this essay, "fallout," just to be clear, is therefore meant to be both material and conceptual, a way of talking about legacies and futures, toxics and natures.

A PLANETARY STRATA

We easily forget today how radical the US nuclear program was right from the beginning. Founded in secrecy, it quickly turned the entire planet into an experimental theater for nuclear science. The politics of radioactive fallout were key to the first efforts to regulate the bomb, as well as to fomenting a wide-ranging social revolution, linking issues of war and peace to environment to public health in entirely new ways (see Egan 2007). But consider the territorial scope of the nuclear complex for a moment, for as global infrastructure its fallout exceeds any current map (see Figure 14.2).

Figure 14.2 is a Department of Energy map of its core facilities at the end of the Cold War, detailing its geographical reach. But while documenting the nuclear weapons production complex this map barely gets at the true scope of US nuclearism, and its multiple forms of fallout, as it leaves

Figure 14.2 Map of the US Nuclear Complex at the end of the Cold War. Courtesy of the Department of Energy.

out nuclear power plants as well as sites of environmental contamination and nuclear waste storage within the continental United States. But, it does suggest that as infrastructure, the nuclear complex has always strained to achieve a kind of globality. It does so not only via the reach of nuclear weapons (via intercontinental missiles, nuclear submarines, bombers) but also via the extensive network of production and testing sites, linking a global uranium industry (Hecht 2012), vast experimental laboratories, numerous test sites, with military support and delivery systems.

If we were to consider nuclear detonations—perhaps the single most destructive human enterprise to date—as a whole, we would start with a map like Figure 14.3 which links the global north and south via a new form of radioactive colonization. But even this image, with its global frame, is radically incomplete. To this, one must add the wartime atomic bombing of Hiroshima and Nagasaki in 1945, as well as a half-century of underground nuclear explosions at test sites around the world, including those of newer nuclear powers—India, Pakistan, and North Korea. Think of each of these sites as a node in a global nuclear network of technologies, experiments, waste, and fallout—each radiating on a distinct frequency (see Figure 14.3).

Fallout—in the form of accidents, contamination, and waste—has always been retrospectively diagnostic—forcing attention to how connected humans, nonhumans, and environments are. Indeed, earth scientists used the radioactive signatures of strontium 90 and cesium 131 as means of mapping

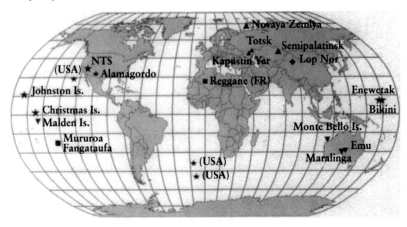

Figure 14.3 Locations of above-ground nuclear tests (Beck and Bennett 2002, 592).

weather systems, food chains, and environmental complexity right from the start of the nuclear age (see Hagan 1992; Odum and Odum 1955). What emerged in the first decades of the nuclear age was a powerful new vision of the biosphere as integrated ecological space, but a vision only enabled by tracking radioactive contamination through it (Masco 2010). The planetary is emergent in these processes as fallout became the means of mapping eco-logical flows of every kind, moving from local exposures to regional con-tamination to global distributions of atmospheric endangerment.

Consider the first US hydrogen bomb experiment known as "Mike," con-ducted in the Marshall Islands in 1952 as part of the IVY test series. It produced a mushroom cloud that rose to over 120,000 feet and was 60 miles wide, and was quickly transformed by earth scientists into a new kind of experimental lens. Here fallout quite literally became a primary means of empirically documenting stratospheric flows, ultimately revealing with a new specificity how earth, ocean, and atmosphere interact.

The fallout produced by the Mike detonation was tracked by Machta, List, and Hubert (1956) in their foundational work on the stratospheric transport of nuclear materials (see Figure 14.4). It was among the first in a series of studies that followed the global transport of nuclear materials produced by atmospheric testing, offering increasingly high-resolution por-traits of atmospheric contamination within an integrated biosphere. These wide-ranging studies directly challenged a national security concept that was no longer able to protect discrete territories but was instead generating, in Ulrich Beck's (2007) terms, new "risk societies" united not by territory, national identity, or language but rather by air borne environmental and health risks increasingly understood to be global flows.

Radioactive fallout studies demonstrated that a new kind of global vision was emerging at mid-twentieth century at several levels. The first

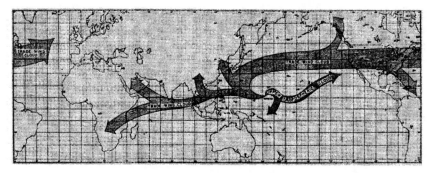

Figure 14.4 Fallout study of Mike fallout cloud (Machta, List, and Hubert 1956, 476).

level involved the creation of the first major data sets in the earth sciences, pursued in the name of understanding nuclear environmental effects and to track the Soviet nuclear program (see Edwards 2010). The Cold War produced a massive investment in air, ocean, geology, the ice caps, and increasingly outer space research. This was an effort to track and investigate every possible kind of nuclear event but also research how to militarize nature itself for national advantage (see Fleming 2010; Hamblin 2013). In every case, nuclear injury was both the motivating logic and experimental lens for producing a new set of national security/earth sciences. These data sets become, as Paul Edwards (2010) has argued, a kind of global infrastructure, allowing new portraits of planetary process—particularly climate change— to be possible. The effort to understand nuclear injury (for both war fighting and defense) thus generated a conceptual frame for engaging a planetary space that was simultaneously being transformed by nuclear industry. As Sloterdijk (2009) has argued, a militarization of environment in the twentieth century also enabled new forms of environmental thinking, enabling a scalar multidisciplinary commitment to connecting locality with global infrastructures with planetary process.

By 1960, for example, Machta and List are exploring a more powerful vision of fallout, pulling our field of vision increasingly off planet in their effort to illustrate the scale and scope of nuclear effects. Figure 14.5 is an illustration from Fowler's (1960a) important edited collection, *Fallout: A Study of Superbombs, Strontium 90, and Survival,* published at the height of the public health debate over nuclear testing. In it Machta and List (1960) document the stratospheric height of fallout and its ability to travel on wind patterns for great distances, essentially merging the global north and global south as irradiated space. The development of US national security in the form of the hydrogen bomb was thus linked to the production of an entirely new global ecological danger but with it came a new technoscientific and environmental interest in understanding integrated global spaces and ecological transport. The earth sciences become a national priority in this early Cold War moment, as efforts to study the bombs' material effects connected researchers to the defense department in a major new way (leading to revolutions in biomedicine, computing, geology, oceanography, and atmospheric sciences—see Doel 2003; Edwards 2010; Farish 2010; Hamblin 2013).

THE GLOBAL PATTERN OF FALLOUT

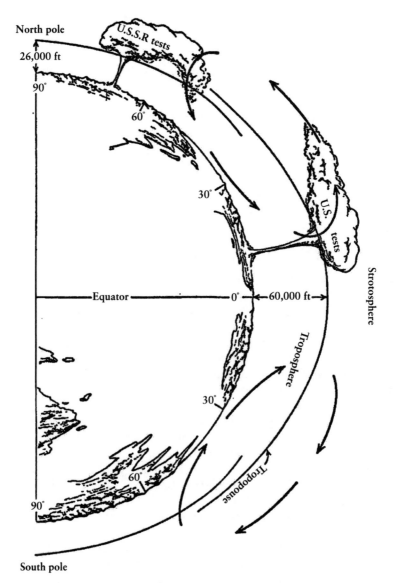

Figure 14.5 Illustration of the *Global Travel of Fallout* (Machta and List 1960, 29).

The fallout danger created many research programs that continue to this day, including biomedical studies of certain exposed populations (from Hiroshima and Nagasaki to the Marshall Islands, to the vast population of workers with the nuclear complex itself, see Makhijani and Schwartz 2008, Lindee 1997, and Johnson and Barker 2008). These forms of internal and external sacrifice became embedded within Cold War national security practices (see also Brown 2013, Kuletz 1998, and Petryna 2002), raising basic questions about what kind of a human population was emerging via the encounter with nuclear technologies and fallout. Consider James Crow's (1960) contribution, "Radiation and Future Generations" to Fowler's *Fallout* anthology, contemplating the genetic consequences of atmospheric nuclear explosions for men and women. He underscored the uncertainty in measuring the relationship between radioactive fallout and mutation rates across generations and species (humans, flies, mice), and projected alternative futures of genetic damage across species based on different degrees of nuclear testing. Thus, as Machta and List considered the atmospheric reach of nuclear effects, Crow investigated the accumulating force of exposure itself within the human genetic pool. Space and time are thus radically reconfigured in these fallout studies, to constitute a vision of a collective future incrementally changing in unknown ways through cumulative industrial effects. The logics of a national security state (with its linkage of a discrete territory to a specific population) becomes paradoxical in the face of mounting evidence of genetic damage on a collective scale, not from nuclear war but rather from test programs. It is important to recognize that while cast as "experiments" US atmospheric tests were in reality planetary environmental events with wide ranging consequences.

Fowler (1960b), for example, was able to calculate the amount of Strontium 90 from nuclear testing in the New York food supply, across milk, cereal, meat, fruits, and vegetables. This is a remarkable moment in an emergent planetary consciousness, given that the nuclear age was only fifteen years old in 1960 and already understood to be a transformational industry in terms of ecology and public health. Fowler, and the many earth scientists tracking similar flows, demonstrated that fallout entered the food chain, linking military science to atmospheric conditions to the food chain, crossing plants, animals, and humans. Put differently, radioactive fallout was recognized as a planetary industrial signature by 1960, one being inscribed at different levels into every living being.

Figure 14.6 is a National Cancer Institute chart of the Iodine-131 contamination from nuclear tests conducted at the Nevada Test Site. This county-by-country chart remakes the continental United States—the territorial space thought to be secured by nuclear defense—as a new kind of sacrifice zone, with citizens remade by varying degrees of exposure (see also Beck and Bennett 2002). To this day, exposure from the atmospheric nuclear weapons tests is measureable, an environmental fact so ever present as to become a literal biological strata in the human population (Bennett

Per capita thyroid doses resulting from
all exposure routes from all tests

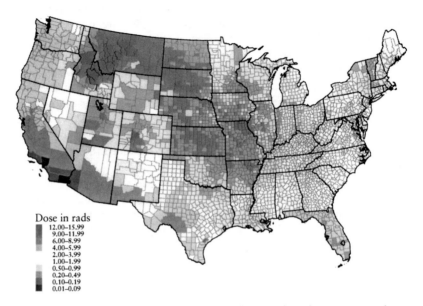

Dose in rads
12.00–15.99
9.00–11.99
6.00–8.99
4.00–5.99
2.00–3.99
1.00–1.99
0.50–0.99
0.20–0.49
0.10–0.19
0.01–0.09

Figure 14.6 Cumulative iodine contamination from nuclear detonations at the
Nevada test site. Courtesy of the National Cancer Institute.

2002). This "strata" is not a recognized health risk today, even though
the National Academy of Sciences concluded in its most recent study that
there is no "safe" level of radiation exposure (National Research Council
2006; Simon, Bouville, and Land 2006). Consider Figure 14.7, a chart of
the "background radiation" rate judged by medical science and the nuclear
industry to be the baseline exposure rate for contemporary human populations. This nominal exposure rate, now a new form of "nature," includes
a small but measurable contribution from atmospheric nuclear testing and
nuclear accidents.

In short, this means that since 1945 human beings have become post-
nuclear creatures (Masco 2006, 294), marked with the signature of nuclear
weapons science. Fallout is a new planetary "stratum" after 1945, making
the nuclear age both a geological period and the era in which the planet
becomes a specific object of scientific study its totality. Paul Crutzen (2002)
has suggested that we rename the industrial era "the Anthropocene" due to
the scale and scope of human activities on the geological record. With this in
mind, we might productively use July 16, 1945, the date of the first nuclear
detonation, as the start of a new planetary ecological regime, one in which
everyday life is increasingly structured by the "fallout" effects of human
industry (see Steffen et al 2011) amplified across nuclear, petrochemical, and
synthetic chemical regimes.

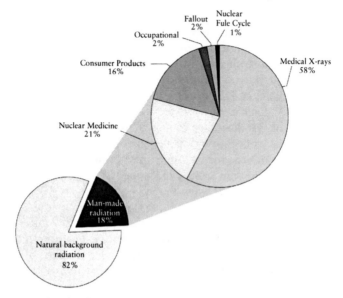

Figure 14.7 Background radiation rates for US populations (National Research Council 2006).

GEOENGINEERING/NUCLEAR TESTING/TERRAFORMING

Today, rising ocean levels, shifting weather patterns, and intensifying storms, are generating wide-ranging problems, across food production, public health, and urban spaces (see Costell et al 2009). In the face of these emerging dangers, various schemes for geoengineering our way out of climate crisis have been proposed (see Caldeira, Bala, and Cao 2013; Keith 2013). Geoengineering is an effort to consciously shift the structure of earth systems, often drawing on imaginative schemes to "terraform" another planet—that is, create an atmosphere on it capable of supporting human life. Geoengineering envisions a profound understanding of planetary systems even as its proponents confront the cumulative unintended planetary consequences of human industry (across nuclear, energy, and capitalist-consumption regimes). Programs for massive carbon capture (underground and in the oceans) compete with imaginative chemical proposals to shift the atmosphere by injecting sulfur particles in to the upper stratosphere or changing the composition of clouds to reflect back heat from the sun. Other proposals look to space, to create mechanical means of diffusing sunlight and cooling the planet. In all, these proposals consider reengineering the oceans, air, forests, ice caps, and outer space to handle carbon dioxide and heat differently, in hopes of cooling the planet, imagined as a complex thermostat that needs to be adjusted (Hamilton 2012; Robock et al. 2009; Schneider 2008). What is attractive to many about these schemes is the idea of "correcting" an atmospheric imbalance caused by human activity, of now consciously treating the biosphere as a mechanism that can be tuned to optimal human outcomes.

For those versed in the history of the US nuclear program, these projects sound eerily familiar, mirrored in the scientific efforts to understand nuclear effects on land, sea, air, and the upper atmosphere during the long Cold War (see Hamblin 2013). Each of these "experiments" was a form of geoengineering in its own right, producing specific planetary optics tied to desires for new forms of power while also producing environmental problems of a new kind and scope. There was, for example, the Atomic Energy Commission's project Plowshare, which ran from 1957 until 1975 and sought to expand the utility of the bomb in novel ways. Plowshare was a research and development program to utilize nuclear explosives as an engineering tool—to convert the military bomb from a city killer into a civilian earth-moving technology. Plowshare scientists sought gigantic earthworks projects, promising literally to "move mountains" and build "new harbors" in the name of economic progress with little attention to the fallout. A filmic introduction to the project by the Atomic Energy Commission entitled "Excavating with Nuclear Explosives" offered this vision of the near future (see AEC 1968):

> Excavations of new harbors, big dams, canals, passes through rugged mountainous terrain—these and other massive, imaginative earth-moving projects may soon be ours, created in seconds with the tremendous energy of the peaceful atom. Nuclear explosives for large projects that are simply not feasible with conventional methods, and at considerably less expense. Scientists and engineers today are carefully working toward these goals with a series of nuclear excavation experiments, designed to increase their knowledge and skills in this exciting new concept. They call their program Plowshare. And the emplacement and detonation of a nuclear explosive is only the midway point in each succeeding project. Before any nuclear detonation, the project is first thoroughly explored and proven, in exhaustive theoretical analyses, researched and tested in laboratory mockup, and often tested again with conventional chemical explosives in the field. The detonation itself serves to refine the predictive capability and provide support data for the next related experiment. It is a deliberate, careful, scientific program.[3]

This "exciting new concept" involved turning the planet into an imaginative space for nuclear engineering, as proponents sought a project big enough to sell to the mass public as well as industry and government the idea of converting the bomb from a weapon of mass destruction to an engineering tool. The repeated invocation of care in planning, of rigorous scientific judgment, and good governance was at odds with the radical nature of the project, which sought no longer to detonate bombs in "test sites" officially designated as unpopulated but rather anywhere that geology could be made to correspond to commercial needs.

As Plowshare proponents looked across the globe, they found an ideal project in Panama, one that would utilize military technology to enhance commerce via significant environmental destruction cast here as civil engineering (Lindsay-Poland 2007). The "peaceful atom" would thus redeem the bomb as a force for public good and commercial profit. Plowshare scientists and engineers imagined that the legacy of the atomic bomb would no longer be war or irradiated bodies or damaged environments but rather civil engineering and new continental scale earth works. The commercial promise of nuclear powered civil engineering is depicted in a twenty-eight-minute AEC promotional film called *Plowshare* (AEC 1973), which offered this portrait of the need for a new canal:

> But there is no doubt that most applications of nuclear excavation would be, not in the United States, but in other countries. The most dramatic example so far is in Central America: the blasting of a sea level, Atlantic–Pacific interoceanic canal. Studies are being planned for both convention and nuclear excavations on four possible routes for such a cut across Central America to supplement, and eventually replace, the Panama Canal, where ships now wait long hours to strain through the narrow complex lock system and others can't make it through at all. Before long it will be inadequate. Even before it was built half a century ago, the complexities and limitations of this lock type were realized. Men dreamed of a sea level canal but it remained a dream. Plowshare may be able to make that dream a reality. And it is being considered. It is estimated that for certain routes nuclear explosives could excavate the sea level canal at one-third the cost of conventional excavation and in considerably less time. The end result would be a much wider and much deeper channel. A nuclear excavated route across Central America could produce a navigable channel 1000 feet wide and up to 200 feet deep at mid-channel, offering a virtually unlimited capacity. No wonder this enormous project has so stimulated the imagination of the world. For a canal of this immensity, representing years of planning and development, complex engineering, and precise execution would be one of the greatest civil engineering of all time.

This plan to build a new Panama Canal, along with other Plowshare proposals, were ultimately defeated by the work of global environmental activists, specifically by an alliance of indigenous activists from the Pacific to the Americas now well versed in fallout effects (O'Neill 2007). The risk communities of the nuclear age armed with multiple examples of slow-moving forms of violence and populations abandoned in the industrial age mobilized against civilian nuclear power (see Berlant 2007; Nixon 2011). In other words, the fight against future fallout linked populations across race, class, and national lines in opposition to the AEC's Plowshare program, which was ultimately shutdown in 1975 (see Kaufman 2012; Kirsch 2005).

However, the legacy of Plowshare continues in unexpected ways. One of the least remembered aspects of Plowshare was a series of nuclear experiments conducted using underground explosions to unlock natural gas reserves—a kind of pregeological fracking, natural gas-nuclear energy economy (Woodruff 1967). Many of the scientists and engineers involved in Plowshare moved from contemplating nuclear earth moving to novel energy economies, pushing technical developments in extractive industries that become key elements in anthropogenic environmental change. This is a profound illustration of the imbrication of militarism, industrialism, and capitalism in the United States. Today, the emerging geological fracturing economy—which proponents say will make the United States the largest energy producer on the planet by 2020—is also constituting fantastic future fallout risks, as the gigantic scale of the extraction infrastructure, with its well known leakage rates, will place much of the American water supply in danger over the coming decades (see Dumit 2013).

The nuclear-industrial state has thus been geoengineering since 1945, remaking both atmospheres and ecologies, creating problems impossible to remediate or clean up. The Nevada Test Site today (see Figure 14.8) contains valley after valley of radiating nuclear "test" craters—a monumentally changed environment only visible in its entirety from a stratospheric point of view. Here, industrial injury demands a new planetary vision, one that sees cumulative environmental effects over and against national boundaries and short-term profit making.

Fallout—across nuclear and extractive energy regimes—now has proliferating forms as well as temporalities (see Brown 2013; Masco 2006). The 1986 Chernobyl accident offered an iconic image of industrial disaster—a failed technology that created an airborne global environmental danger but also created a permanent regional crisis (Petryna 2002). Today, a gigantic engineering effort is underway to build a new containment vessel for the damaged reactor, one that hopes to prevent further radioactive releases for the next one hundred years. While Chernobyl illustrates the profound consequences of technological failure in the nuclear age, one could multiply nuclear disaster sites around the world. Hanford, for example, is devoted today not to producing nuclear materials for US weapons (as it did from World War II through the Cold War) but rather to observing the accumulated radioactive sludge of the twentieth century age and chemically transform. As one of the most contaminated spaces in the United States, Hanford engineers devote each day to managing gigantic holding tanks of radioactive waste that to this day resist both chemical assessment and containment. The tanks also leak, producing a slow moving transformation of the Columbia River region. Fukushima-Daichi presents a similarly long-lived problem, as the combined effects of earthquake, tsunami, and fire transformed the

Figure 14.8 Craters produced by nuclear detonations at the Nevada Test Site.
Courtesy of the Department of Energy.

nuclear power plant into a nuclear crisis in 2011, which has revealed how few technical options there are for undoing the fallout of failed technologies. This kind of industrial activity is a form of geoengineering in its own right, just one operating without a planetary plan.

Applying the lessons of the twentieth-century nuclear complex to contemporary geoengineering schemes to manage climate change, we might question: (1) the claim to both newness and absolute crisis, which installs a very old argument for radical action, a state of emergency that suspends normal forms of law and regulation; (2) a process that rhetorically reproduces the split between the event and its fallout so completely; and (3) interrogate the suggestion that geoengineering is a novel activity, that it is not an ancient practice with many examples to think with in assessing our current moment. We might also interrogate how the past half century of multidisciplinary work to create detailed visualizations of the planet now installs a dangerous confidence in globality itself, as increasingly high resolution visualizations come to stand in for objectivity and sovereignty (see Daston and Galison 2010), allowing psychosocial feelings of control of what are still vastly complex and only partially understood environmental and earth systems (see Murphy 2006).

Geoengineering schemes have also refused to recognize the long-term coevolution of human and natural systems by suggesting that ecologies are simply machines that can be tuned by people to better outcomes. This high modernist position (assuming an external relation to nature) created the nuclear infrastructure in the twentieth century that continues to generate new forms of fallout. It refuses to acknowledge the logic or history of fallout or to accept that in the era of big data we do not have a single planetary vision but rather a proliferation of planetary optics tied to specific sciences and projects, which may not align. Concepts like the "Anthropocene"—which have been highly useful in alerting us to the scale of environmental change on planet earth—nonetheless suggest that human agency is all that is involved in producing our increasingly complex world of organisms, ecological flows, and toxics (see Kosek 2010; Orff and Misrach 2012). The term flattens the complexity of human/non-human interactions, as well as natural systems, even as it recognizes the planetary scale of cumulative industrial effects. The coevolution of human and nonhuman systems has always been the case, resisting claims that we are living in an entirely human made ecology (one unintended but pernicious effect of the Anthropocene concept) or alternatively that a pristine state of nature could be recovered through planetary reverse engineering.

Anthropologist Hugh Raffles (2002), for example, has documented that what appears to us today as giant tributaries of the Amazon River are in fact the collaborative work of people and river ecologies, as small canals cut by people for easier canoe navigation have grown to become massive water ways, now only visible in their entirety from outer space. The first satellite images of North America revealed ancient road systems connecting what is today the US Southwest to Mexico, etched into the landscape. Similarly, cities are geoengineering projects of the most direct kind, foundationally effecting landscapes, ecologies, weather patterns, and resources. The problem is thus less the fact of human agency as a geological force (an ancient phenomenon) than the cumulative scale and scope of industrial toxicity, as the human population has grown to more than seven billion mostly living in megacities, enmeshed in nuclear, petrochemical, and synthetic chemical regimes. Toxicity, the cumulative fallout of the industrial age, has now achieved planetary agency.

TRANSFORMING THE ATMO-BIO-GEO-SPHERE

Contemporary geoengineering discourse emerges from a consideration of how to build an atmosphere capable of supporting human life on other planets, terraforming for human survival and comfort. Mars is often the center of these imaginative efforts, but they are also often motivated by the idea that environmental damage on Earth—the end of fossil fuel, a destabilized climate, overpopulation, disease, and food scarcity—will drive interplanetary research. The escape pod to Mars has a long history in science fiction and as an imaginative project is intellectually stimulating, and often quite entertaining. But this idea rehearses the American modernist story of self-invention, of the ability to start over somewhere else, to break with the past and begin anew, to escape fallout by simply relocating to a new frontier. Nature once again becomes an experimental laboratory, endlessly changeable, a denial of coproduction to enable new visions of exoplanetary industry and potentially endless colonial space projects. Before we launch such an endeavor (conceptually or in practice), we might well interrogate the ecological and health impacts of the introduction of synthetic chemicals and other long-lived toxins into the biosphere over the past half-century (see Murphy 2008; Orff and Misrach 2012). In short, through the combined efforts of industry and the nuclear state, people have been feverishly terraforming planet earth for generations, creating an atmosphere increasingly precarious for human life, rather than tuned to its creature comforts. This means that we are living in the unintended aftermath of cumulative industrial projects, remaking bodies and atmospheres on a planetary scale, and in ways that we have yet to fully account for, let alone begin to respond to.

On this difficult point, which asks us to think on scales and in temporalities that are radically different from our everyday embodied experience (see Chakrabarty 2012), consider Isao Hashimoto's remarkable visualization of the nuclear age, *Nuclear Explosions 1945–1998* (2003; see Figure 14.9).[4] His video animation shows in chronological order the 2,053 nuclear detonations on Earth between 1945 and 1998. The video is straight forward, offering a global map and a chronological sequence of nuclear detonations, each marked by a white flash and beeping noise, with the date recorded in the upper right corner. In the margins, counters tally the detonations for each nuclear state, as well as the total count. It takes thirteen minutes to move month by month from 1945 to 1998, offering an extremely precise illustration of nuclear politics in the twentieth century while documenting

Figure 14.9 Still image from Isao Hashimoto's art installation ***Nuclear Explosions 1945–1998*** (2003). With the permission of Isao Hashimoto.

the expansion of both nuclear industry and national power. In certain years, 1957, 1962, or 1984 for example, it appears that the only thing happening on planet Earth are nuclear explosions, with multiple continents flashing white and beeping at a feverish pace. The disturbing power of the video is that it both recognizes the nation-state form, and renders it irrelevant to the cumulative planetary force of the bomb.

Hashimoto shows us the planetary logics of the nuclear complex and allows us to reconsider the temporality of nuclear war itself. In the Cold War competition between the US and Soviet Union, nuclear war—the ultimate and final disaster—was conceived of as brutal and short. It was a matter of hours and minutes, as always on alert weapons systems (still active today) made war possible every second of the day. Thus, we've inherited an idea of nuclear war as extremely short, fast, and totalizing—literally the end of everything. But Hashimoto reorients our point of view, showing that a nuclear war was fought in the twentieth century—it started in the summer of 1945 with three explosions—in New Mexico, Hiroshima, and Nagasaki—and then was fought vigorously in "test sites" around the world. Hashimoto's video is elegantly devastating in showing the international commitment to the bomb as well as its planetary impact. In doing so, he gives us access to a new temporal politics of environmental crisis—the long-term violence that accumulates effects over decades, offering us a new perspective on a global industry that—in the name of energy, security, and profit—has performed as a radioactive geoengineer.

Considering the ever present material reality of environmental toxics, there is no need to project geoengineering with its specific planetary optic into a distant future or require travel to other worlds. We can look closer to home for an example of a planetary atmospheric politics. There has been a long-term terraforming project conducted on planet earth—one that is drawn from the cumulative effects of industry, militarism, and capitalism. That climate change—despite such imaginative industrial activity and scientific insight across generations—was not planned or intended is precisely the point. Constituted as a side effect of the industrial age, it articulates the ongoing challenge to conceptualizing an ecological security *not* based on the split between the engineered event and its necessary aftermath, between the boom and the bust of capital, between the pre-emptions and blowbacks of counterterror. It requires instead many new planetary optics as well as a politics of complexity that can assume a postnational security and different understandings of the collective future. It also makes the early twenty-first century nothing less than the Age of Fallout.

NOTES

1. This chapter first appeared in *History of the Present* and has been revised for this volume. I am grateful to Elizabeth DeLoughrey, Anthony Carrigan, and Jill Didur for their critical engagement and editorial care.
2. See Winiarek, Bocquet, Roustan, Birman and Tran (2014) for a thirty-day simulation of the global cesium fallout from the Fukushima-Daichii nuclear accident as it traversed the Pacific Ocean. Available at: http://cerea.enpc.fr/en/fukushima.html.
3. The two AEC Plowshare films I discuss in this chapter are available for viewing on YouTube as one contained file, see: http://www.youtube.com/watch?v=ZGXS_Qgfqno.
4. Hashimoto's video instillation is available for on-line viewing at: http://www.ctbto.org/specials/1945–1998-by-isao-hashimoto/.

REFERENCES

Atomic Energy Commission. 1973. *Plowshare*. 28-minute film. Washington: Atomic Energy Commission.

Atomic Energy Commission. 1968. *Excavating with Nuclear Explosives: Technology Status Report Plowshare Program*. 9-minute film. Washington: Atomic Energy Commission.

Beck, Harold L., and Burton G. Bennett. 2002. "Historical Overview of Atmospheric Nuclear Weapons Testing and Estimate of Fallout in the Continental United States." *Health Physics* 82 (5): 591–608.

Beck, Ulrich. 2007. *World at Risk*. Cambridge: Polity Press.

Bennett, Burton G. 2002. "Worldwide Dispersion and Deposition of Radionuclides Produces in Atmospheric Tests." *Health Physics* 82 (5): 644–655.

Berlant, Lauren. 2007. "Slow Death (Sovereignty, Obesity, Lateral Agency)." *Critical Inquiry* 33 (4): 754–780.

Boyer, Paul. 1998. *Fallout: A Historian Reflects on America's Half-Century Encounter With Nuclear Weapons*. Columbus: Ohio State University Press.

Brown, Kate. 2013. *Plutopia: Nuclear Families, Atomic Cities, and the Great Soviet and American Plutonium Disasters*. Oxford: Oxford University Press.

Caldeira, Ken, Govindasamy Bala, and Long Cao. 2013. "The Science of Geoengineering." *Annual Review of Earth and Planetary Sciences* 41: 231–256.

Chakrabarty, Dipesh. 2012. "Postcolonial Studies and the Challenge of Climate Change." *New Literary History* 43 (1): 1–18.

Choy, Tim. 2011. *Ecologies of Comparison: An Ethnography of Endangerment in Hong Kong*. Durham: Duke University Press.

Clark, Nigel. 2014. "Geo-politics and the Disaster of the Anthropocene." *The Sociological Review* 62 (S1): 19–37.

Commoner, Barry. 1958. "The Fallout Problem." *Science* 127 (3305): 1023–1026.

Cosgrove, Denis. 2001. *Apollo's Eye: A Cartographic Genealogy of the Earth in the Western Imagination*. Baltimore: The Johns Hopkins University Press.

Costello, Anthony et al. 2009. "Managing the Health Effects of Climate Change." *The Lancet* 373 (9676): 1693–1733.

Crow, James. 1960. "Radiation and Future Generations." In *Fallout: A Study of Superbombs, Strontium 90, and Survival*, edited by Jon M. Fowler, 92–105. New York: Basic Books.

Crutzen, P. J. 2002. "The "Anthropocene." *Journal de Physique IV* 12 (10): 1–6.

Daston, Lorraine J., and Peter Galison. 2010. *Objectivity*. Cambridge: MIT Press.

DeLoughrey, Elizabeth. 2014. "Satellite Planetarity and the Ends of the Earth." *Public Culture* 26 (2): 257–280.

Doel, Ronald. 2003. "Constituting the Postwar Earth Sciences: The Military's Influence on the Environmental Sciences in the USA after 1945." *Social Studies of Science* 33 (5): 635–666.

Dumit, Joseph. 2013. "Earth Possessed." Paper delivered at the *Society for Social Studies of Science Annual Meeting*, San Diego, CA, October 10.

Eden, Lynn. 2004. *Whole World on Fire: Organizations, Knowledge, and Nuclear Weapons Devastation*. Ithaca: Cornell University Press.

Edwards, Paul. 2010. *A Vast Machine: Computer Models, Climate Data, and the Politics of Global Warming*. Cambridge: MIT Press.

Egan, Michael. 2007. *Barry Commoner and the Science of Survival: The Remaking of American Environmentalism*. Cambridge: MIT Press.

Farish, Matthew. 2010. *The Contours of America's Cold War*. Minneapolis: University of Minnesota Press.

Fleming, Roger. 2010. *Fixing the Sky: The Checkered History of Weather and Climate Control*. New York: Columbia University Press.

Fowler, John M, ed. 1960a. *Fallout: A Study of Superbombs, Strontium 90, and Survival*. New York: Basic Books.

———. 1960b. "The Rising Level of Fallout." In *Fallout: A Study of Superbombs, Strontium 90, and Survival*, edited by John M. Fowler, 51–67. New York: Basic Books.

Glasstone, Samuel, and Philip J. Dolan (eds). 1977. *The Effects of Nuclear Weapons*. 3rd ed. Washington: Government Printing Office.

Haffner, Jeanne. 2013. *The View From Above: The Science of Social Space*. Cambridge: MIT Press.

Hagen, Joel. 1992. *An Entangled Bank: The Origins of Ecosystem Ecology*. New Brunswick: Rutgers University Press.

Hamblin, Jacob Darwin. 2013. *Arming Mother Nature: The Birth of Catastrophic Environmentalism*. New York: Oxford University Press.

Hamilton, Clive. 2012. *Earthmasters: The Dawn of Climate Engineering*. New Haven: Yale University Press.

Harley, Naomi. 2002. "Laboratory Analyses: Environmental and Biological Measurements." *Health Physics* 82 (5): 626–634.

Hashimoto, Isao. 2003. *"Nuclear Explosions 1945–1998"* 13-minute video. CTBTO Preparatory Commission. http://www.ctbto.org/specials/1945–1998-by-isao-hashimoto/.

Hecht, Gabrielle. 2012. *Being Nuclear*. Cambridge: MIT Press.

Heise, Ursula. 2008. *Sense of Place and Sense of Planet*. Oxford: Oxford University Press.

Jain, S. Lochlann. 2013. *Malignant: How Cancer Becomes Us*. Berkeley: University of California Press.

Johnson, Barbara Rose, and Holly M. Barker. 2008. *The Consequential Damages of Nuclear War: The Rongelap Report*. Walnut Creek: Left Coast Press.

Kaufman, Scott. 2012. *Project Plowshare*. Ithaca: Cornell University Press.

Keith, David. 2013. *A Case for Climate Engineering*. Cambridge: MIT Press.

Kirsch, Scott. 2005. *Proving Grounds: Project Plowshare and the Unrealized Dream of Nuclear Earth Moving*. New Brunswick: Rutgers University Press.

Koronowski, Ryan. 2014. "House Votes to Deny Climate Science and Ties Pentagon's Hands on Climate Change." *Climateprogress*. May 22. http://thinkprogress.org/climate/2014/05/22/3440827/mckinleyclimate-pentagon-climate-change/.

Kosek, Jake. 2010. "Ecologies of Empire: On the New Uses of the Honeybee." *Cultural Anthropology* 25 (4): 650–678.

Kuletz, Valerie. 1998. *The Tainted Desert: Environmental Ruin in the American West*. New York: Routledge.

Kurgan, Laura. 2013. *Close up at a Distance: Mapping, Technology, and Politics*. Cambridge: MIT Press.

Lindee, M. Susan. 1997. *Suffering Made Real: American Science and the Survivors at Hiroshima*. Chicago: University of Chicago Press.

Lindsay-Poland, John. 2007. *Emperors in the Jungle: The Hidden History of the U.S. in Panama*. Durham: Duke University Press.

Machta, Lester, and Robert J. List. 1960. "The Global Pattern of Fallout." In *Fallout: A Study of Superbombs, Strontium 90, and Survival*, edited by John M. Fowler, 26–36. New York: Basic Books.

Machta, L., R. J. List, and L. F. Hubert. 1956. "Worldwide Travel of Atomic Debris." *Science* 124 (3220): 474–477.

Makhijani, Arjun, and Stephen I. Schwartz. 2008. "Victims of the Bomb." In *Atomic Audit*, edited by Stephen I. Schwartz, 375–431. Washington: Brooking Institution Press.

Masco, Joseph. 2006. *The Nuclear Borderlands: The Manhattan Project in Post-Cold War New Mexico*. Princeton: Princeton University Press.

———. 2010. "Bad Weather: On Planetary Crisis." *Social Studies of Science* 40 (1): 7–40.

———. 2014. *The Theater of Operations: National Security Affect from the Cold War to the War on Terror.* Durham: Duke University Press.

Murphy, Michelle. 2006. *Sick Building Syndrome and the Problem of Uncertainty: Environmental Politics, Technoscience, and Women Workers.* Durham, NC: Duke University Press.

———. 2008. "Chemical Regimes of Living." *Environmental History* 13: 695–703.

National Research Council. 2006. *Health Risks from Exposure to Low Levels of Ionizing Radiation: BEIR VII Phase 2.* Washington: National Academies Press.

Nixon, Rob. 2011. *Slow Violence and the Environmentalism of the Poor.* Cambridge: Harvard University Press.

Oakes, Guy. 1994. *The Imaginary War: Civil Defense and American Cold War Culture.* Oxford: Oxford University Press.

Odum, Howard T., and Eugene P. Odum. 1955. "Trophic Structure and Productivity of a Windward Coral Reef Community on Eniwetok Atoll." *Ecological Monographs* 25 (3): 291–320.

O'Neil, Dan. 2007. *The Firecracker Boys: H-Bombs, Inupiat Eskimos, and the Roots of the Environmental Movement.* New York: Basic Books.

Orff, Kate, and Robert Misrach. 2012. *Petrochemical America.* New York: Aperture.

Petryna, Adrianna. 2002. *Life Exposed: Biological Citizens after Chernobyl.* Princeton: Princeton University Press.

Poole, Robert. 2008. *Earthrise: How Man First Saw the Earth.* New Haven: Yale University Press.

Parenti, Christian. 2011. *Tropic of Chaos: Climate Change and the New Geography of Violence.* New York: Nation Books.

Raffles, Hugh. 2002. *In Amazonia: A Natural History.* Princeton: Princeton University Press.

Robock, Alan, Allison Marquardt, Ben Kravitz, and Georgiy Stenchikov. 2009. "Benefits, Risk, and Cost of Stratospheric Geoengineering." *Geophysical Research Letters* 36 (19) [L19703]. http://onlinelibrary.wiley.com/doi/10.1029/2009GL039209/full.

Sloterdijk, Peter. 2009. *Terror from the Air.* Los Angeles: Semiotext(e).

Schneider, Stephen. 2008. "Geoengineering: Could We or Should We Make It Work?" *Philosophical Transactions of the Royal Society A* 366: 3843–3862.

Simon, Steven L., Andrea Bouville, and Charles E. Land. 2006. "Fallout from Nuclear Weapons Tests and Cancer Risks." *American Scientist* 94 (1): 48–57.

Steffen Will et al. 2011. "The Anthropocene: From Global Change to Planetary Stewardship." *Ambio* 40 (7): 739–761.

Winiarek, Victor, Marc Bocquet, Yelva Roustan, Camille Birman and Pierre Tran. 2014. "Atmospheric Dispersion of Radionuclides from the Fukushima Daichii nuclear power plant." *Centre d'Enseignement et de Recherche en Environnement Atmospherique.* June 20. http://cerea.enpc.fr/en/fukushima.html.

Woodruff, Wayne. 1967. *Nuclear Operation: Project Gasbuggy.* Livermore: Lawrence Radiation Laboratory.

15 Climate Change, Cosmology, and Poetry

The Case of Derek Walcott's *Omeros*

George B. Handley

The Anthropocene highlights the need to see nature and culture in a more dynamic interrelation than at least Enlightenment reasoning and ethics had allowed. Indeed, it is commonplace in environmental thinking to criticize the facile binaries between subject and object and between human and non-human for having facilitated an anthropocentric and indifferent view of our treatment of the physical world. What these criticisms fail to recognize, however, is the challenge this confusion of boundaries between the human and the natural poses to the very idea of human agency. Enlightenment reasoning allowed us to conceive of ourselves as autonomous individuals who could trace our own accountability, but climate change has introduced the problem of a human agency that is so profoundly collective that accountability for the changes wrought on the climate is no easy matter to trace. In other words, our agency as emitters of carbon has resulted in climate change, and while traceable as a force, the collective nature of our agency has made it far too easy for individuals and nations to deny or hide their own accountability. For Dipesh Chakrabarty this means that we need to reconceive ethics: "in becoming a geo-physical force on the planet, we have also developed a form of collective existence that has no ontological dimension. Our thinking about ourselves now stretches our capacity for interpretive understanding. We need nonontological ways of thinking the human." He reasons that "however anthropogenic the current global warming may be in its origins, there is no corresponding 'humanity' that in its oneness can act as a political agent" (2012, 13–14).

I agree with Chakrabarty here about the nature of the challenge. In this essay, however, I want to provide an example of understanding this particular form of human nonontology—human agency as climate forcing—within the very framework of ontology itself.[1] I engage in this experiment because I believe it is hard to imagine that humans can respond ethically to a new awareness of the nonontological dimensions of agency without a broader cosmology that can accommodate such dimensions and make sense of them in the context of the values, beliefs, and experiences that continue to give moral shape to human lives. In other words, while climate change clearly challenges traditional ethics, I am not sure we have exhausted all efforts to think ontologically about ourselves as climate agents; we may not need new ethics so much as new readings of traditional narratives about human responsibility. Derek Walcott's poetry, for example, offers an ontology of human beings as climate agents that does not supplant but complements our understanding of ourselves as moral agents. He finds a way to accommodate the meaning of our inter-connectivity both with others and with the planet into a new cosmology. It is crucial, however, to understand how this does not leave us with superficial notions of the oneness of humanity or our oneness with nature. The unique contribution of literary language to the problem of climate change—and hence the value of the environmental humanities—is literature's capacity to expose and exploit the limited and rhetorical nature of its own metaphors and the very real differences that persist within such imagined unities. Literature can offer a way of imagining relation without overriding the various historical and social contingencies that shape our values. Emerging from the postcolonial context of the Caribbean, Walcott's poetry resists the balkanizations of colonialism that seek to separate peoples and histories from their complex webs of interconnection and to separate subjects from the land even as his poetry also exposes the risks and limits to such imaginings. In this sense, his poetry offers a contingent model of the cosmos that assists in shaping a moral response to the human impact on the planet while keeping human cultural and historical differences visible to the reader.

The implication here is that we don't need new stories or new ethics so much as we need new readings that assess the cosmological reach of literature. Climate change, in other words, requires scientific literacy, but perhaps just as importantly it asks for renewed attention to such fundamental problems in the humanities as hermeneutics. Timothy Clark is right to be suspicious of the ways facile images of the oneness of humanity and our oneness with nature rely on superficial and localized understandings. He writes: "the self-evident coherence of immediate experience, far from being the possible foundation of secure theorizing, is merely epiphenomenal and unable to see itself as such. It projects an illusory ground, a surface level of human possibility, one that is delusory and even sometimes a form of denial" (2013, 12). The Anthropocene, he further argues, thus far has been met typically by figural language and metaphors that merely "paper over a *dis*continuity of perception, language and understanding between referents on the surface of the earth and the planet considered as a whole. Each image leaps over disjunctions in scale" (17). However, if disjunction seems to be part and parcel to what it might mean, for example, to imagine deep time, or our belonging in and impact on the evolutionary tree of life, or to imagine collective human agency as climate forcing, the Anthropocene makes those leaps inevitable. The question, I would argue, is not whether human imagination takes a short cut by simplifying human diversity or human history in order to get to a worldview whole enough to encompass the globe. Of course it does. The question is if those efforts are self-consciously fashioned and whether they exploit and ironize their own limitations. The inherent faith of literature is not that language is adequate but that seeing and exploiting its inadequacy can sustain us.

I invoke the word "faith" here quite intentionally, but certainly not for the first time in the context of the Anthropocene. Aldo Leopold's simple call for a "land ethic" already suggested decades ago that faith in our imagination may be an important dimension to a response to our crisis, regardless of one's metaphysical views. "We can only be ethical," he wrote, "in relation to something we can see, feel, understand, love, or otherwise have faith in" (1987, 214). As implied by Clark, certainly climate change requires believing in and acting on more than what we can see. In finding solutions to environmental degradation, we are in the business of increasing the powers of perception so that the cosmos we think we live in, the one we see, feel, understand and love is more adequate to what science tells us empirically about the universe and thus more sensitive to our role within it. It would appear to be a contradiction to argue that this requires faith at all, since all we presumably need is more science, more information. However, the more we know empirically about the world, the more faith has become necessary, especially faith as a kind of imaginative probing of the possibility of unity. As quantum physics has made clear, this is true on the level of particle physics as well as on the intergalactic level of astronomy. We only keep finding more reasons, empirically, to have to confess our inability to find the rock-bottom reality of our material existence. Otherwise, denial and apathy offer more easy alternatives. As Donald Worster has argued, "if there is order in the universe—and there will no longer be any science if all faith in order vanishes—it is going to be much more difficult to locate and describe than we thought" (1990, 15).

If the development of ecocriticism over the past twenty years has taught us anything, it is the implicit faith that stories can shape our sense of humanity and moral responsibility within an ecological context. They do this, we trust, by placing facts within a world of relation, within an imagined cosmos, into which a trusting reader is invited. Pushed to its most important implications, in other words, ecocriticism wants stories to become cosmologies. Reading ecocritically, with the earth in mind, is a kind of metaphysical faith that biology and physical matter itself can serve as the grounds for understanding our human place in a cosmos that both we affect and affects us. As stories that cannot afford to presume human separation from the totality of all phenomena, cosmologies bring an unthinkable diversity and the threat of chaos into some imagined order.

For this same reason, stories must be imagined as inadequate and contingent. They become metaphors, expressions of hope for wholeness and order in direct response to the dispersing threat of chaos, rupture, and fragmentation. To read literature as cosmology means to engage in a perpetual process of re-envisioning our sense of the world after considering each time the abyssal gaps that emerge in our imagined worlds. Cormac McCarthy's unnamed wise man of the desert in *The Crossing* puts it this way: "there is but one world and everything that is imaginable is necessary to it. For this world also which seems to us a thing of stone and flower and blood is not a thing at all but is a tale" (1994, 143). No "thing" is this earth, but a tale, because to begin describing it or any of its component parts is to begin weaving "things" into a structure of relatedness by which things obtain significance as components of a world; it is to bring a chaos of things into the orbit of our very human imagination and to imagine a potentiality of totality and connectivity against which the actuality of our small experience of physical reality is assessed.[2] The antithesis to ecology is a thing, a discrete, disconnected fact of physical matter. Indeed, when the world is a thing or a mere collection of disconnected and unrelated things, its value is measured in terms of its instrumentality. But a tale, like an ecosystem, is a human way of organizing the appearance of separation and of chaos into a workable and animated order that our imagination can use as a method for seeing and understanding our limits. That is, if our anthropocentrism means that we as humans are limited in our ability to imagine what lies beyond our imagination, perhaps the best we can do is to underscore those limits. To expand the literary meaning of a concept from Mircea Eliade, literature is a ritual performance that repeatedly remakes the world and moves us, rhetorically and contingently, from chaos to cosmos (2005).

If stories are contingent and certainly incomplete methods for rendering "everything necessary" and for providing what McCarthy calls the "joinery' that makes wholeness possible to imagine, they remind us that ecosystems, even science itself, are also contingent narratives of an imagined wholeness (1994, 147). The best our science can offer will still never provide an adequate escape from the prison house of language's world-making powers. Again the paradox. Science has spent the better part of the last century telling us that there are no "separable essences" in the world around us, a position that would seem to deconstruct the very foundations of the kind of positivism that still dominates secular scientific culture (Keller 2003, 206). Rather than negating knowledge altogether, or freeing us of the responsibility to respond to new information, such complexity in reality heightens our awareness of the limits of language as well as a sense of our ethical place amidst a newfound "interdependency of all creatures" (206). Scientific narratives, like all other narratives—be they fictional, theological, or poetic—are stories of our humanity, social constructions that allow us to engage meaningfully with the thingness of things, to weave discrete objects and facts and all the chaos that they might imply into a broader cloth. They only do so, of course, to the degree that we suspend disbelief and allow them to act on us as cosmologies that demand our ethical response. To suspend disbelief, or in other words to exercise faith, is not the same thing as using a narrative to make a dogmatic claim on reality to the exclusion of all other competing narratives. An environmental humanities requires movement between and among epistemologies and therefore a kind of agnosticism in the face of the ultimate claims of various disciplinary lenses. The alternative, then, to environmental humanities would be any form of epistemological chauvinism that cannot or will not engage in transdisciplinary thinking. This is because there are always broader cloths, just as there is no limit to space. Ecosystems express our faith that despite the risks of loss and of disorder that inhere in any systematization of the world—indeed, despite the fact that the world is more complex than discrete systems or disciplines— they can still serve as valuable tools to teach us to accept the constraints and interdependencies that complexity implies. We might rephrase this to say that it is precisely the risk of loss and disorder and the inherent complexity of systems that make faith necessary. If it weren't for such faith, why else would we find stories worth telling? Or scientific research worth doing? Or climate change a concern?

CLIMATE CHANGE AND POETRY

I would like now to turn to Derek Walcott's poetry as an example of the contingent but cosmological dimensions of the human imagination, especially in relation to the problems presented by the Anthropocene. In Walcott's poetry, we find many registers of the impact of the Anthropocene that predate or otherwise avoid the specifics of climate change. The postcolonial conditions of the Caribbean mean that nature, as Walcott envisions it, always and already manifests evidence of previous human agency, specifically the violence of European colonialism and plantation slavery. Nature, in other words, can never be imagined or accessed as something separate from human history.[3] Climate change, described only once in his entire oeuvre, is merely a more recent manifestation or symptom of this violence of colonialism that systematically depersonalizes and hides evidence of its violence. I see Walcott's poetry, then, as a kind of cosmological response that remakes the world so as to recover a sense of a wholeness, however compromised by history, to which the Caribbean subject becomes answerable.

His 1990 poem *Omeros* tells the story of a fishing and agricultural community rooted in the local landscape that emerged after slavery but is now threatened by the island's increasing dependence on an economy of tourism and ultimately by climate change. In his telling, this global and depersonalized economy shares structural features with slavery and colonialism. The fundamental elements of craftsmanship in the poem—the hollowing out of canoes from local trees, the makeshift construction of musical instruments that distantly echo the music of Africa, and other rudimentary economies of place—are vital to postcolonial possibility because they connect the Caribbean subject to time and to geographical space with a kind of immediacy that slavery and colonialism could not tolerate. In his reflections on the crime of enslavement, Walcott notes the particular cruelty of denying slaves the chance to use their hands:

> The worst crime is to leave a man's hands empty.
> Men are born makers, with that primal simplicity
> in every maker since Adam. This is pre-history,
> that itching instinct in the criss-crossed net
> of their palms, its wickerwork. They could not
> stay idle too long. The chained wrists couldn't forget
> the carver for whom antelopes leapt, or
> the bow-maker the shaft ..." (1990, 150)

As Paul Breslin notes, Walcott sees slaves as "deprived of the bond between imagination and environment (both social and natural) their work had given them" (2001, 251). For this reason, the enslaved have been reduced to "coals, firewood, dismembered / branches, not men" (Walcott, 1990, 150). Recovery from fragmentation, albeit contingent and fragile, results from creative and freely chosen labor; craftsmanship becomes the chief means of making a home in the wake of diaspora.[4] When hands find work to refashion the world, there is an echo of the old ways, as Walcott suggests in his description of the idle hands of slaves in the galleys crossing the sea and in his frequent comparison between economies of labor and writing itself.

An absentee, mechanistic, and globalized economic system disrupts this contingent and imagined belonging. Globalization causes the fishermen and Helen to begin working for the tourist industry, a fact that disrupts the otherwise grounded practices of craftsmanship that had enabled the survivors of the plantation economy to build a new culture and to live in close proximity to the environmental rhythms of the island. What is perhaps even more disturbing than the transformation of the island into what Walcott once called a "mini Miami" of tourism and commercial exploitation is the fact that the island's weather cycles and rhythms have been disrupted by anthropogenic climate change (2005, 130). At the conclusion of the poem Seven Seas finds that over the years he has had to move farther and farther from the shores of the island to fish because of what he senses is some kind of "hidden devastation" (1990, 300). Walcott writes:

> He had never seen such strange weather; the surprise
> of a tempestuous January that churned
> the foreshore brown with remarkable, bursting seas
> convinced him that "somewhere people interfering
> with the course of nature"; the feathery mare's tails
> were more threateningly frequent, and its sunsets
> the roaring ovens of the hurricane season,
> while the frigates hung closer inland and the nets
> starved on their bamboo poles. The rain lost its reason

and behaved with no sense at all. What had angered
the rain and made the sea foam? (1990, 299–300)

Walcott's poetics imagines an unknown and unnameable agency ("somewhere people interfering") that has compromised the earth's present and future capacity for regulating the climate for human habitation and the local culture's capacity to sustain itself. Where postcolonial literature perhaps once focused mainly on the human costs of colonialism, Seven Seas suggests the haunting possibility that anthropogenic climate forcing represents the continuity of the structures of colonial violence. On this point, Michael Northcott writes that the modern globalized economy responsible for climate change depends on the "systematic enslavement of peoples and ecosystems to the high resource requirements of a corporately-governed consumer economy" (2007, 273). This sovereignty functions much like an absentee plantation owner; it is faceless, seemingly without agency, and it externalizes risk and then pretends not to be answerable to the consequences it puts into play. However, this new system globalizes what were once localized and more individual practices of feeding, housing, and clothing human communities. It breaks down the very binary between the local and the global upon which both colonialism and postcolonial discourse have often relied. In this sense, anthropogenic climate change interpellates all of humanity as members of a community for which no one appears to be accountable.

Like Northcott, Walcott still wants to see agency and accountability behind climate change, however. He writes: "once men were satisfied / with destroying men they would move on to nature" (1990, 300). These generic "men" are not so generic since the same kind of "men" who enslaved Africans have moved on to a different kind of conquest: the destruction of nature. What Walcott seems to be describing here, admittedly in concise and somewhat cryptic form, is the historical transition away from colonialism and slavery (that began a massive destruction of the environment of its own not referenced here by Walcott) to industrialization. Industrialization and global capitalism have replaced slavery and in turn have created the very conditions of the current climate crisis. The pursuit of climate justice, both accountability for carbon emissions in developed nations and redress of the disproportionate consequences suffered by the poor, becomes, then, the new postcolonial struggle. This transition to the Anthropocene for Walcott is a shift in target but not a change in structure or motivation, which, following his moral logic of men "satisfied with destroying men" and moving "on to nature," remains a generic greed and disrespect for life. Nonhuman nature is the new slave, the new immorally owned property. That is, the fact that nature too is alive and sentient raises questions about the moral logic of capitalist ownership of natural resources.

Climate change, of course, does not have the direct agency to "leave a man's hands empty" in the same way that slavery does but Seven Seas' suspicion is that the oppression of human subjects has now morphed into a method of disrupting the climate. This in turn suggests that human hands will no longer have the direct and unmediated relationship to the local environmental conditions they once had under the fishing economy, if indeed they ever had it, and that the violent ones causing this "hidden devastation" hide behind their collective impersonality. He wants, in other words, to hint at a discrete neocolonial agency behind the impersonalized power of climate forcing. Walcott's metaphors point to climate change as a kind of violence, and not a new kind at that. Colonialism and slavery have already made us familiar with this problem of hidden agency. It is a form of what Rob Nixon calls "slow violence" and Walcott's response to this violence, like his response to the originary violence of enslavement and pervasive colonialism, is the world-[re]making powers of poetry (2011).

Indeed, his hint stops there. What is more important to Walcott than naming the perpetrators is to imagine the cosmos in which the victims must find a meaningful response. As the messy ethics of climate change have made clear, it may not be enough in any case to recover traditions of localized economies. If it's not always clear who "they" are, it is not always clear who "we" are. I don't mean that we can't or shouldn't try to identify culprits and victims, especially when we compare the lifestyles and conditions of the poor against the privileged, but as Chakrabarty rightly observes, collective human agency manifested as climate forcing challenges the utility of traditional ethics. A CEO flying 5,000 miles to strike a business deal and an academic flying the same distance to do research on climate change still produces the same carbon emissions. And an economics of desperation might conceivably drive the poor to a sustenance economy that is more harmful to the climate than, say, a woman living in the developed world who has access to green technology. We can measure activities for their carbon output, in other words, but such measures don't tell us everything about their ethical value. And for those of us embedded in and enjoying the benefits of a fossil fuel economy, it is hard to identify who is without sin. In this sense, the Anthropocene means that victims and perpetrators have become at least partly confused with one another. Walcott's postcolonialism has long been characterized, for that matter, for his unusual and somewhat counterintuitive rejection of literature's role as a voice of "recrimination and despair" (1998, 36). The problem with trying to expose perpetrators, for Walcott, is that culpability is so easily dismissed or denied by those in power. For the writer, it also leads to a longing for a different and illusive reality rather than the inherited cultural and environmental conditions that actually confront us. As he thematizes so well in his essay "The Muse of History," recrimination results in a politics that denies interconnectivity, and by implication a politics that would deny our human collective—if uneven—role in climate forcing.

To be clear, Walcott has never espoused a naïveté about the violence and sins of the past. Indeed, history's wounds are often the very central focus of his work, but it is important to understand how those wounds are healed by poetry's act of remaking and reimagining the world. He refuses to allow his poetry to be dictated by the terms of the perpetrators; it must not remain reactive but rather proactively creative. The greatest revenge is to create new cultures, new epic cosmologies of the sort *Omeros* offers that are forged out of the wreckage of the past. For Walcott, such work begins with attention to the raw elements of nonhuman nature and to the present, which are more important sources of inspiration than established colonial norms or the wounds of history. The very conditions inherited by colonial powers, for Walcott, become the means of the Caribbean's renewal. Fragmentation and displacement mean opportunities for amalgamations and creations and for rediscovery of the potency of language and of nature. His is a present-oriented aesthetics that creates worlds that are projected beyond the present moment and present place. As Walcott once said, "the Caribbean is only just beginning as a culture." Consequently, he notes the utopian importance of "believing that a new possibility can happen, a new possibility of something really happening that is not political and is not racial and offers the possibility of sharing in the exhilaration of trying to make a new civilization" (2001, 142). The point here is that the Anthropocene is an epoch in need of a new civilization built on an acknowledgement of a fundamental and irrevocable change to our relationship to the planet. As Bill McKibben has written, climate change means that we cannot go back to a time before when nature stood independent and apart from human agency; it means forsaking the very idea of such a time (2006). As such, scholars of the Anthropocene have much to learn from the postcolonial conditions of places like the Caribbean. With all of the past ruin it represents and the future ruin it portends, the Anthropocene has also opened to us a new vision of the world that is more collective, intersubjective, and interdependent and has provided an opportunity to learn what Michel Serres calls a "collective ethics in the face of the world's fragility" (1995, 78). The implication here is significant. What our epoch of the Anthropocene needs is neither a reinforced balkanization of identities and communities nor a facile unity that ignores or obliterates differences. It needs cosmologies whereby we can imagine and then enact a new sense of answerability and belonging in a world that is a much broader and more collective than we can know or imagine.

I want to underscore that Walcott's poetics of the environment represents a distinct project from the more naïve versions of phenomenology advocated by the likes of David Abram (2012).[5] The present conditions of climate change ask us to rethink and reimagine culture on the foundation of a new reality. The Anthropocene means that we have been displaced, that there is a gap between subject and the environment that cannot be overcome through greater attunement to the environment. Since we can no longer tell if the qualities of a sunset are entirely natural or partly man-made, aesthetic attention to nature will always reveal a world contingent, rhetorical, and as much produced by our imagination as it is by evolution. So while climate change represents a particularly insidious form of disruption that undermines the autonomy of creating and naming one's own world, it also presents an opportunity and obligation to self-consciously name the world again, to make new worlds out of such ruin. To be displaced by language and to discover the limits of our ability to merge with the world are not weaknesses. Walcott sees Seven Seas as having learned the rhythms of the ocean such that he can sense he has been unmoored by the climate; he is an emblem of the quandary of the Anthropocene, but by the time Seven Seas understands the problem of a changing climate, Walcott has already provided the only grounds for hope: to begin again to remake the world by envisioning a new cosmos. This is not a cause for despair but for a kind of anthropogenic wisdom: climate change notwithstanding, we can't afford to mistake our perceptions of the world for the world itself, any more than we can assume local weather conditions are indicative of global patterns. The advantage of this displaced sense of place is that we can begin the work of making a world that acknowledges but will not be determined by the past, a world that stands a chance of moving us to a new future. Key to this work is rereading narratives as attempts to take up the elements and conditions of life and freely reimagine our responsibility in and for the world. In this way, climate change does not rid us of the responsibility to imagine our responsibility and ontology as collective climate agents. Rereading in light of the challenges posed by the Anthropocene, then, may be one of the most important tasks for an environmental humanities.

POETRY AS METATHEOLOGY

To rebuild the world from the fragmentation of the past requires a suspension of disbelief in the face of the competing claims on reality that stem from different cosmologies. *Omeros*, consequently, takes up the past to project our minds forward to a possible cosmology that incorporates its constituent elements. Walcott opens the poem with a description of canoe-making, but we already sense this creative action takes place *in media res*, that it cannot obtain any kind of originary purity or innocence. The action takes place in the midst of echoes of slavery's past (Philoctete's wound) and in the presence of tourists and it seems to divide cosmologies of polytheism of both indigenous and African islanders from the monotheism of the colonials ("leaving a blue space / for a single God where the old gods stood before") (1990, 4–5). He refers to this as a kind of "pre-history," a Genesis that starts not with Adam but perhaps with Noah (1990, 150), a beginning again as I have argued in *New World Poetics*, that is a creation of the world not *ex nihilo* but out of the fragments of a broken past.

I want to underscore here the interesting theological work Walcott does on behalf of both a wounded people and a wounded environment. What bothers him about sectarianism is the way in which it uses cosmology as a kind of colonialism that divides histories and peoples and separates them from the land. Nonhuman nature, on the other hand, serves as a kind of cosmic kingdom that incorporates without equating human differences. He is not keen on dismissing any particular theological beliefs but rather in making a leap, to borrow from Clark's criticism, over their various disjunctions in the interest of forging a new mythology. In this sense, his poetry is metatheological, never dismissive of theology but also never certain of any one theology's supremacy. The meaning of his poetry depends, then, on a kind of faith that is distinct from sectarian definitions because it is an expression of hope in a sacred cosmos that transcends the many divisive identitarian claims of the Caribbean's various ethnic and religious cultures.[6] He resonates here with McCarthy's claim that literature, in its suspension of disbelief in the face of competing beliefs and worldviews, can nevertheless build a world in which everything is meaningfully, even if not harmoniously, related to everything else, much like the work we imagine the concept of an ecosystem does.

Walcott became aware early in his life of the divisive function of sectarianism and how his love of nature provided an alternative method for bringing together the disparate elements of his culture. At the age of fourteen, he penned these neoromantic lines in his local paper:

> Thus would my wanderings among the quiet woods
> Be my first lesson from the Holy book.
> And while I wondered of the free creation,
> The pure conception of a Hand behind it all,
> Should be my subsequency to the other verses.
> Oh! In what happy state I would then be
> As an acknowledged friend to bird or beast
> As our first father was—alive and free. ([1944] 2000, 3)

Not the greatest of his poems, but not bad either for a 14 year old. And certainly better than the poem the Catholic priest, Friar C. Jesse F.M.I., wrote in response to reprimand him for his hedonistic faith in nature:

> Youth here is wrong, for God's own Word
> Was passed to men, to fill men's dearth
> Moses, Prophets, Paul of the Sword,
> Have been God's messengers to earth;
> And Christ the Lord his church did found
> His truth forever to expound. ([1944] 2000, 3)

The priest's sectarian chauvinism and his erroneous and unfortunate divorce between the word of man and the Word of God and between nature and church is an example of why environmentalists have accused religion of contributing to our human indifference to environmental degradation. We see here an ethics insistent on an otherworldly focus, away from the beauty, transience, and fate of the physical world. Its triumphalism notwithstanding, this is a theology of despair.

What is important for my purposes here is to trace the beginnings of Walcott's use of poetry as a kind of surrogate cosmology where the presence of nature causes a suspension of disbelief but which also refuses overt assertion regarding ultimate realities. His poetry's indecisiveness with regards to sectarian matters allows him to engage in a kind of syncretism that forges new possibilities for understanding our place in and answerability to the world, something the priest's theology does not do. Indeed, the priest abandons the sanctity of the natural world altogether in the interest of preserving the exceptional cosmological claims of the Church. Later in the same adolescent poem Walcott intuits that subjection to this God of Nature is deeply holy work and a prerequisite for poetry. Nevertheless, as his idea of God expands, language runs the risk of becoming too narrow or too literal. To avoid this risk of literature becoming merely a sermon, his poetry finds greater recourse to metaphor—to the cosmological force of his own imagination—as the preferred representation of this discovered holiness. Even at this early stage of his career, the young poet wrote of his hesitancy to name God: "Yet, fearing to pray out, / That by his speech the wrong name he would call / And bring strong retribution from his Benefactor."

Not all forms of sectarianism were as painful to the young Walcott as the priest's. Walcott's own mother's faith always drew his respect, and he admired, albeit with some ambivalence, his close friend and fellow artist Dunstan St. Omer's Catholic faith. In an unpublished essay from 1987, "Inside the Cathedral," Walcott explained his admiration for St Omer's faith but his reasons for parting from such sectarianism:

> I had this to believe in: light and nature. We lived on an island with a light that had never been painted, and I had for my freedom, my universality, a larger cathedral than any St. Omer could enter, the sky and the moving floor of the sea. My unpainted walls were not the bored stones of the cathedral, but the virgin zinc of huge clouds, sunsets larger than Tiepolo's.
>
> (1987: 12–13)

Walcott suggests that his poetic metatheology is more universal, since his art is not restricted to an institution but is as ubiquitous as the light of the sun, the sound of wind moving through palm fronds, or the lapping of waves against the stones of St. Lucian beaches. The theme of the universality of light, of course, finds ample expansion in *Tiepolo's Hound* and becomes his method of using the kingdom of this world and the sun, not the Son, as his cosmic ground.[7] Indeed, the sacred, for Walcott, has always been the ordinary, the mundane, the passing of light—it is the very experience of time itself, the temporality of human existence, and the telluric impulse of art to render light is the acolyte's highest act of devotion. Poetry is the work of benediction; by implication, the secular, the temporal, and the earthly are indistinguishable from the sacred, the eternal, and the heavenly. These benedictions are the work of metaphor, seeking to bridge the gap between these seeming impossibilities. Poetry is his method for not having to choose between secular skepticism and religious faith, hedonistic devotion to earth and pietistic devotion to heaven, poetry and painting, Europe and Africa, the metropole and the island, or, as we see in the opening scenes of *Omeros*, between the cosmologies of Native American, African, and European societies.

Because Walcott refuses the thesis that life's meaning is a given and also the thesis that life is merely what we imagine it to be, he is able to bypass traditional binaries that would seek to circumscribe the sacred. It is perhaps useful to recall that religion has at least two root meanings: to read again and to bind together. If Walcott's poetry is religious, it is because it is a revisiting, a rereading of the familiar, and because, as he explains in his Nobel speech, it is an attempt to bind together the factions and fragments of Caribbean experience into an imagined coherence. As he said succinctly in his Nobel speech, "Break a vase, and the love that reassembles the fragments is stronger than the love which took its symmetry for granted when it was whole" (1998, 69). We might think of this love for reassembly as that which ought to undergird our new awareness of ourselves in the Anthropocene. We can perceive that the symmetry and autonomy of the earth's self-regulation that we took for granted are now broken. And we can despair at this loss or we can do the hopeful work of a contingent reassembly and use our new-found care for the fruits of this work as our new world.

Significantly, love for a reassembled whole that poetry creates offers a different definition of the sacred than that presupposed by most traditional religions. If the sacred represents an original wholeness to which we seek to return, Walcott implies that it is instead the secular gesture of reassembly, not the image of timelessness or wholeness itself, that obtains as sacred. Holiness is not a thing or relic; it is desire, an act of perception, it is what love makes. Metaphors obtain their sacred function not because we believe that they summarize all possibility but because we can use them to test lived experience against its possibilities. In this testing of metaphor, for Walcott's Martinican contemporary Édouard Glissant, "the sacred 'results' not only from an ineffable experience of a creation story but also, from now on, from the equally ineffable intuition of the relationship between cultures" (1998, 115). Glissant stresses literature's suspension "between two actual or apparent possibilities" as a valuable means of accessing the sacred (4). The origins of a culture, then, are not in the past but in a future amalgamated possibility, in what is yet to be on the basis of a broader web of interdependence that literature helps us to imagine. The implication here is that climate change is not evidence of inevitable declension that stems from some unchangeable past dictated by human nature, but it is instead a sign of such ambiguity that it presents us with real choice as to what kind of future we want to work for.

The different and competing claims of stories in religion, whether it be Walcott's depiction of the animism of African or Native American cultures, the practices of the Hindus, or the monotheism of Methodism, initially presented themselves as mutually exclusive choices to the poet as a young man. He learned first hand how they could divide communities against themselves. Such a divided world can hardly be expected to work together on behalf of their imagined unity on a shared planet. Ultimately it is the work of Walcott's poetry, however, to intuit a larger cosmos that lies between them to which they are all subject. As he wrote in "Inside the Cathedral": "The only hope that artistic failure offers is, in fact, stronger than success; it is the nocturnal failure of the saint at prayer, the repetition of 'I am not worthy.' Repeated enough, a strange strength can grow as it does out of the mesmeric Litany. The subject's subjection" (1987, 11). What makes secular literature different from religious literature, according to Walcott's logic, is that it seeks to center our attention on earth and not on heaven, to syncretize the secular and the various forms of the sacred, and then to confess and exploit its failure to do so adequately.

In this way, he models what many ecotheologians have long insisted: while we need new cosmologies, we might start by embracing our creative role as rereaders of old ones. The Judeo-Christian story of the world's beginnings, for example, has often been accused of justifying environmental degradation because of its apparent rejection of animism and its call to human beings to rule the earth as "lords" having "dominion" over the whole of it.[8] However, pre-Enlightenment earth stories have the advantage of offering noninstrumental visions of the world as *continually emerging,* as *being* created. For example, feminist process theologian, Catherine Keller, provides a rereading of the Genesis story that captures its creolization of neighboring pagan stories and also teases out the chaos inherent in the order it seeks to establish. Specifically, Keller reads Genesis as a narrative that recognizes chaos as "friendlier" to the generation of life, meaning, and order. When Christianity later definitively rejected the idea of a creation out of chaotic material and instead adopted the doctrine of creation *ex nihilo*, it set the stage for the dominionist tradition. Patriarchy, colonialism, and environmental destruction, for Keller, all emerge from a Western intolerance for chaos and for syncretism, resulting in cultures of oppression and exploitation of women, of nature, and of pagan cultures. The ethic that is missing in this logic of the developed world is an awareness of our human agency within a system of exceptional complexity, one which we can and do affect but cannot control or predict. To shift into such an ethical orientation to a changing climate then requires a radical kind of humility unpracticed by CEOs within the global capital market or even by the most dogmatic and confident scientists. It implies "the chance for a creativity that does not confuse itself with control, for an order that does not effect homogeneity, for a depth that is not identifiable with subjectivity. Here, within a discourse of spirit, we may begin (again) to renegotiate the dominant oikonomia—the economics, the ecology, the ecumenism of order. Theology has not outgrown the subjection of oikos to dominus" (Keller, 2003, 6).

It is not a stretch to see that poetics offers a model of order that does not result in homogeneity but rather—because of its discipline of suspending disbelief—opens us up to unpredictability. Indeed, Keller's theologically rich notion of chaos is strikingly similar to Walcott's notions of the composite nature of culture, particularly in the postcolonial conditions of a place like the Caribbean where we can never return to a radical origin without having to confront the inevitable irony of our own participation in the making of meaning. In both cases, the emphasis is not so much on what we read but on how we read because the reading act is the generative moment of new possibility. Glissant argued in *Caribbean Discourse* that the biblical narrative of Genesis, with its emphasis on a discreet genealogy, betrays its own cross-cultural nature once it is read against the grain of its more overtly foundational intentions (1989). The chaos of the watery deep and the cultural interdependence of Hebrew cultural origins alike were banished from the order that the sacred book was then seen to shore up. But as Glissant insists and as Walcott thematizes so well in Achille's return to Africa in *Omeros*, we do not find origins so much as we found or make them anew through the imagination. And when we understand that those origins are not merely given—indeed they are or must always be first and foremost imagined—we must confront and embrace our role as world-makers.

This poetics of reading is a vital postcolonial strategy in relation not only to official colonial memory and history but to the texts, both sacred and secular, that emanate from the metropole as signs of colonial authority. When we consider the fact that sacred texts like the Bible have had an extraordinary influence on the environmental imagination of their readers, it behooves postcolonial ecocritics not only to seek out new cosmologies but to learn from the strategies of ecotheologians who do not dispute the authority of those texts but rather the traditional implications of their stories of human origins. Hermeneutics, then, become as or more important than debates about a text's status. The interpretation of the Judeo-Christian creation narrative, for example, as a call to human "dominion" over the earth has certainly been seduced, if not motivated by, instrumental agendas that have sought to see the world and the activities of human making as a kind of divinely sanctioned carte blanche use of God-given resources. But ecotheologians show that reading the Bible with the earth in mind opens us to possibilities of cultural interdependence as well as the interdependence of nature and culture more generally.[9]

To the degree that we refuse to be determined by previous interpretations and instead engage in cosmology anew, we recover our autonomy as readers and thus break down the dualism between center and periphery. We also break down the distinction between the world as it is given to us and the world as we have imagined it; we neither ignore the fact of the world's independence nor our impact upon it. Theologically speaking, this would mean that we might imagine a kind of providence that no longer maintains the kind of managerial supremacy once ascribed to the omnipotent God of the Judeo-Christian tradition. As the Anthropocene seems to require, we come to understand ourselves coparticipants in the creativity of evolution, but we also do so in the context of moral value. This self-understanding, in other words, is guided by cosmology and not merely determined by the facts of biology. In other words, a world created out of and subject to continual chaos, rather than out of nothing, highlights our own temporality and agency in a world of ongoing contingencies and thus only heightens our answerability to the world. We might not be able to fully grasp the meaning of our collective agency in creating climate change, but this fact cannot leave us inert because the earth is neither inert nor sealed away from the effects of our actions by perfect providential care or by any kind of perfectly mechanistic and predictable structure.

This sense of a contingent world might be the advantage of our contemporary crisis of climate change: it has led us to confront our fundamental and inescapable role as world-makers, for better or for worse. As Michel Serres has noted, once possessed of this understanding, we are perhaps in a better position to choose to imagine a different world order. The alternative, which has nevertheless held great appeal, is to reject evidence of the world's chaos and to suppress evidence of our role in its making and place our hope in the gods of technology or in the gods of sectarianism but not in our own agency. Climate change reminds us that we are answerable to a given world even though it is also ambiguously of our own making. And this in turn implies, as we see throughout Walcott's poetry, that the metaphysics of human existence—the possibility of life after death and the meaning of human life itself—remain suspended; we cannot expect answers to be given without at least wanting to imagine them first and we cannot trust in order or purpose unless we are willing to do the work to make such a cosmos. And this suspension is what drives Walcott's poetics as well as his ethics of care for a damaged world. Indeed, Walcott's poetry provides an encounter with death, finitude, and the possibility of meaninglessness in order to then offer a theology that enables the genuine and free choice of faith in human possibility. If the coining of the term Anthropocene does anything, it asks us to remember the ways in which our fate is intermingled with the fate of the planet. It asks us, in other words, to contemplate our mortality and to decide on what grounds we will live meaningfully and ethically in the light of that reality.

NOTES

1. *Climate forcing* is the term for any influence on climate that originates outside of the climate system and includes such phenomena as human-induced changes in greenhouse gases and aerosols.
2. I am building on the important thought of Giles Gunn, who wrote: "no serious literature is neutral either to the question of belief or to the question of the

relationship between belief and understanding" (1979, 89). Gunn notes that "in attempting to assess the actual in light of its full potential for comprehension, we thereby re-enact one of the chief functions of culture, if not religion" (124).

3. This blurring of the boundaries between nature and culture is central to my argument about the poetry of Walt Whitman, Pablo Neruda, and Derek Walcott (Handley 2007). It also guides an ecocritical approach to the Caribbean more generally, as evident in DeLoughrey, Gosson and Handley (2005).

4. Shona Jackson argues that Guyana used this idea to forge a new myth of belonging in the New World following the legacies of plantation slavery, even though she also criticizes this myth for the ways in which it displaces indigenous peoples and memories and elides the neocolonial structures of the twentieth-century economy (2012). Walcott is suspicious of his own longing for nativism but nevertheless hopes that a grounded economy of craftsmanship and creation could provide more autonomy and connection to the earth than the alternative of tourism.

5. I have elsewhere written on the contrast between Walcott's use of language and Abram's theory about orality (2007, 401).

6. For more on this point and a more fully developed argument regarding Walcott's theology, see Handley 2013.

7. For an in-depth analysis of this aspect of *Tiepolo's Hound*, see my chapter "Impressionism in the New World" (Handley 2007).

8. This is most famously the argument of Lynn White's 1967 essay (1996).

9. See, for example, William Brown (2010); John Cobb (2007); Michael Northcott (2010); and Thomas Berry (2011). There is, of course, also ample evidence of advocacy for the urgency of climate change mitigation efforts in the majority of the world's Christian churches, including statements by ecclesiastic leaders such as Pope Francis, Patrarch Bartholomew, Katherine Jefferts Schori, and many others (Moseley 2009). The point of this work is not to pretend that the Christian tradition is and always has been by definition environmentally friendly or that there are no better ways to understand the cosmos. The point is to acknowledge the reality and authority of worldviews in the lives of people and offer readings of those traditions that offer believers a way out of denial and indifference. Environmental humanists would do well to pay attention to similar work being done among the world's major religions. See, for example, Richard Foltz 2002.

REFERENCES

Abram, David. 2012. *The Spell of the Sensuous: Perception and Language in a More-Than-Human World*. New York: Vintage.

Berry, Thomas. 2011. *The Christian Future and The Fate of the Earth*. New York: Orbis Books.

Breslin, Paul. 2001. *Nobody's Nation: Reading Derek Walcott*. Chicago: Chicago University Press.

Brown, William. 2010. *The Seven Pillars of Creation: The Bible, Science, and the Ecology of Wonder*. Oxford: Oxford University Press.

Chakrabarty, Dipesh. 2012. "Postcolonial Studies and the Challenge of Climate Change." *New Literary History* 43 (1): 1–18.

Clark, Timothy. 2013. "What on World is the Earth?: The Anthropocene and Fictions of the World." *Oxford Literary Review* 35 (1): 5–24.

Cobb, John B. 2007. *A Christian Natural Theology*. Louisville: Westminster John Knox Press.

DeLoughrey, Elizabeth, Renée K. Gosson, and George B. Handley, eds. 2005. *Caribbean Literature and the Environment: Between Nature and Culture*. Charlottesville: University of Virginia Press.

Eliade, Mircea. 2005. *The Myth of the Eternal Return*, Translated by Willard R. Trask. Princeton: Princeton University Press.

Foltz, Richard. 2002. *Worldviews, Religion, and the Environment: A Global Anthology*. New York: Cengage Learning.

Glissant, Édouard. 1989. *Caribbean Discourse: Selected Essays*. Translated by J. Michael Dash. Charlottesville: University Press of Virginia.

———. 1998. *Faulkner, Mississippi*. Translated by Barbara Lewis and Thomas C. Spear. New York: Farrar, Straus and Giroux.

Gunn, Giles. 1979. *The Interpretation of Otherness: Literature, Religion, and the American Experience*. Oxford: Oxford University Press.

Handley, George B. 2007. *New World Poetics: Nature and the Adamic Imagination of Whitman, Neruda, and Walcott*. Athens: University of Georgia Press.

———. 2013. "Walcott's Metaphysics of Nature." In *Interlocking Basins of a Globe: Essays on Derek Walcott*, edited by Jean Antoine-Dunn, 229–243. Leeds: Peepal Tree Press.

Jackson, Shona. 2012. *Creole Indigeneity: Between Myth and Nation in the Caribbean*. Minneapolis: University of Minnesota Press.

Jesse F.M.I., Friar C. [1944]. 2000. "Reflections on Reading the Poem, '1944.'" *Crusader: Nobel Laureates Supplement*, January 21, 3.

Keller, Catherine. 2003. *The Face of the Deep: A Theology of Becoming*. New York: Routledge.

Leopold, Aldo. 1987. *A Sand County Almanac and Sketches Here and There*. Oxford: Oxford University Press.

McCarthy, Cormac. 1994. *The Crossing*. New York: Vintage.

McKibben, William. 2006. *The End of Nature*. New York: Random House.

Moseley, Lyndsay, ed. 2009. *Holy Ground: A Gathering of Voices on Caring for Creation*. San Francisco: Sierra Club Books.

Nixon, Rob. 2011. *Slow Violence and the Environmentalism of the Poor*. Cambridge: Harvard University Press.

Northcott, Michael. 2007. *A Moral Climate: The Ethics of Global Warming*. New York: Orbis Books.

Serres, Michel. 1995. *The Natural Contract*. Translated by Elizabeth MacArthur and William Paulson. Ann Arbor: University of Michigan Press.

Walcott, Derek. [1944]. 2000. "1944." *The Voice of St. Lucia*, August 5. *Crusader: Nobel Laureates Supplement*, January 22, 3.

———. 1987. "Inside the Cathedral." Unpublished essay. University of West Indies, St. Augustine, Main Campus Library.

———. 1990. *Omeros*. New York: Farrar, Straus and Giroux.

———. 1998. *What the Twilight Says: Essays*. New York: Farrar, Straus and Giroux.

———. 2001. "Sharing in the Exhilaration: An Interview with Derek Walcott," Interview with Natasha Sajé and George Handley. In *Ariel: A Review of International English Literature* 32 (2): 129–142.

————. 2005. "'The Argument of the Outboard Motor': An Interview with Derek Walcott." Interview with George Handley. In *Caribbean Literature and the Environment: Between Nature and Culture*, edited by Elizabeth DeLoughrey, Renée K. Gosson, and George B. Handley, 127–139. Charlottesville: University of Virginia Press.

White Lynn. [1967]. 1996. "The Historical Roots of Our Ecological Crisis." In *The Ecocriticism Reader: Landmarks in Literary Ecology*. Edited by Cheryll Glotfelty and Harold Fromm, 3–14. Athens: University of Georgia Press.

Worster, Donald. 1990. "The Ecology of Order and Chaos." *Environmental History Review*. 14: 1–18.

16 Ordinary Futures

Interspecies Worldings in the Anthropocene

Elizabeth DeLoughrey

> The sea was before the land and sky, cleansing, joining, and where the sea meets the land there are obligations there that are as binding as those of whakapapa [genealogy].
>
> —Teone Taare Tikao

> We become who we are through multispecies aggregations.
>
> —Anna Lowenhaupt Tsing

The rise of the environmental humanities is coterminous with the turn to the Anthropocene, a term some scientists are using to describe an epoch in which anthropogenic climate change positions humanity as a geological force. This new understanding of the human in relationship to a warming planet has catalyzed vital questions about positioning the subject in the discourse of species, history, environment, and politics. After decades of work that examined the historicism and difference of the human subject, particularly in postcolonial studies, we are seeing a discursive shift to figuring humanity on a planetary scale. This essay builds on this work but troubles it by engaging issues of both indigeneity and interspecies ontologies in an era of sea level rise that is catalyzing new oceanic imaginaries. Overall this essay is guided by three central questions. Is the turn to the Anthropocene perpetuating a universalizing discourse? Does Anthropocene discourse figure the human as exceptional to other species and to nonhuman nature? And if so, how might we parochialize the Anthropocene in order to engage the often-conflicting narratives of relationship to place, multispecies, and planet?

As we've argued in the introduction to this collection, attention to narrative is a vital aspect of the environmental humanities in determining how to articulate our planetary futures. Accordingly, this essay turns to debates about the efficacy of apocalyptic discourse, placing it in disjunction to the speculative fiction of New Zealand Maori author Keri Hulme to argue that her transition away from the genre of realism is suggestive in an era in which our knowledge of global climate change produces new economies of speculation. Her work is placed in relation to indigenous Pacific inscriptions of the ocean as both past and future in an era of climate change, complicating the "fall from nature" narrative that is embedded in western discourses of both apocalypse and the Anthropocene. Indigenous—and in particular

Maori—reckonings of genealogy complicate models of the Anthropocene that exclude nonhuman others. The stories I examine here help bring into relief the ontological split between human and nature that underpins apocalyptic and some Anthropocene discourse, and the importance of engaging an adaptive hermeneutics of reading in an era of increasing planetary flux.

In recent years scholarship has turned a critical eye to apocalyptic discourses of climate change to raise questions about their efficacy. This debate between "climate alarmists" versus "climate realists" has even led to environmentalists being labeled as "apocalypse abusers" (Buell 2003, 3) and "apocaholics" (Karieva 2013). Shellenberger and Nordhaus have argued that "apocalyptic global warming scenarios [...] tend to create feelings of helplessness and isolation among would-be supporters" (2004, 30). While there is no data to back up this claim (Veldman 2012), it's worth examining our narrative production and, following Rob Nixon, to think critically about the ways in which attention to spectacular ecocatastrophes such as tsunamis or the explosive force of nuclear weapons may detract attention from the "slow violence" (2011) or *longue durée* of environmental change (DeLoughrey 2009). As such, a turn to nonspectacular ecological violence would entail engaging different modes of temporality such as more-than-human models of history and deep time. Importantly, this would demand diverse hermeneutics, which is to say new modes of reading and interpreting signs. In this essay I think through what it would mean to depict, as Hulme does, climate change, particularly sea-level rise, as a profoundly ordinary future. As an island dweller and "fisher-artist" (quoted in Bryson 1994, 132), Hulme depicts the realm of the oceanic as deeply familiar. Reading through Hulme's work, I engage alternatives to apocalyptic narratives of climate change with attention to the ways in which certain kinds of narrative form produce an ethics of environmental adaptability. To privilege environmental adaptability is not to say one cannot work to mitigate anthropogenic contributions to climate change. As I explain, the spectacularity of apocalyptic narratives may be less of an issue than the ways in which apocalyptic thought presumes a fall from nature, perpetuating a human/nature binary in which their encounter is inevitably rendered in ways that are both exceptional and catastrophic.

OCEANIC FUTURES

If there is any agreement about climate change, it is that our planetary future is becoming more oceanic. Scientific discourse has positioned the ocean as evolutionary origin for life on earth and, given the imminent threat of sea level rise, our anticipated destiny. Sea level rise is perhaps our greatest sign of planetary change, connecting the activity of the earth's poles with the rest of the terrestrial world, producing a new sense of planetary scale and interconnectedness through the rising of a world ocean. Pacific Island Studies has long been engaged with the concept of the ocean as a space of origins and of destiny. Ala Moana, the way of the ocean, refers in many Polynesian cultures to the past in which indigenous voyagers settled across the expanse of the Pacific as well as to the future, in which one's departing spirit joins the "ocean roads" toward Hawaiki (or Hawai'i), a homeland located outside of terrestrial models of space and time. Epeli Hau'ofa has famously inscribed the voyaging traditions of the region as producing a shared sense of origins and one of regional destiny in the wake of migration and globalization (2008; see DeLoughrey 2007). As such, the ocean has functioned in cosmological and evolutionary terms as a place of origins, and more recently, as human if not planetary destiny.

Due to both history and geography, there is a large body of literature from the Pacific Islands that engages a complex oceanic imaginary. Keri Hulme's *Stonefish* (2004), an experimental collection of short stories and poetry, is positioned on the strand, that space between land and sea that has informed so much of her imagination and which was the title of her first poetry collection. The "stonefish" is variously defined; sometimes it's the fish of the genus Synanceia, a master of blending in with the seafloor, rendering itself ordinary despite its venomous dorsal fin, but in most parts of the text the stonefish signifies the South Island of Aotearoa New Zealand, Te Wai Pounamu, the place (or waters) of greenstone and Hulme's ancestral home. Unlike western concepts of the fixity of land, (South) Island space here is on the move, a fish amid its kin swimming in the Pacific or, in other Maori narratives, the canoe or waka the demi-god Maui used to fish up the North Island. In the work of Hulme and other Maori writers, the strand is a space of indeterminacy and of flux, a space in which the borders between human and nonhuman are blurred, and where the ocean signifies ancestral origin.[1] *Stonefish*'s cover image of the coastal Moeraki boulders, thought to be the legacy of the landing of the ancestral voyaging canoe of South Island Maori (Kai Tahu), positions the author's whakapapa (genealogy) as a founding narrative that links knowledge, ancestry and, borrowing from Elizabeth A. Povinelli, a "geontology" (2013) of place. Geontology is a mutually constitutive biography/geology drawn from indigenous contexts that destabilizes the western binary between figures of life and nonlife.[2] As I will explain, this ontological reckoning of space and time, embedded as it is in indigenous epistemologies, offers an alternative mode of understanding climate change than Dipesh Chakrabarty's argument that our awareness of ourselves as geological agents cannot be understood ontologically. In Maori models of epistemology, "to know something is to be able to locate it within a whakapapa" (Roberts and Wills 1998).[3] Because whakapapa incorporate the subject into planetary networks of kinship, including Tangaroa, the deity of the ocean, knowing and being are constitutive and interrelated.

A determinative but largely unnoticed aspect of the Anthropocene is a new oceanic imaginary in which, due to sea level rise, the largest space on earth is now suddenly not so external and "alien" (Helmreich 2009) to human experience. This has inspired an increase in a body of literature, arts, film, and scholarship concerned with our oceanic future. Of course there are geopolitical, biopolitical, and ontological dimensions to this oceanic turn. As much as the ocean is imagined as a space for evolutionary and ontological origins (and destiny), it is rapidly becoming a renewed space of empire and territorialism. The twentieth-century "scramble for the oceans" was catalyzed by President Truman's 1946 expansion of the US Exclusive Economic Zones (to 200 miles at sea) and his annexation of Micronesia, acts which tripled the territorial size of the United States and which led to the long and contested UN Convention on the Law of the Sea.[4] Although generally unnoticed by scholars, the new EEZ cartographies are the most dramatic change to global mapping since the post–World War II era of decolonization. A large part of this scramble originated with the idea of the seabed as a frontier for capital to extract valuable and strategic minerals, an interest that has resurged with the development of new submarine mining technologies.[5]

Oceanic territorialism has also been tied to waning fish stocks and a desire to protect fisheries for national interests. The nationalization of fisheries and of the seabed has specific resonance for Maori which, as I will explain, is rendered by Hulme as an ontological entanglement between human bodies and ocean. The strand is not only a potent space for imagining the boundary blurring between human and nonhuman others, but it has also become a legal battleground in contemporary New Zealand politics. This is the context out of which Hulme's work emerges, particularly in relationship to the territorialism of New Zealand's Foreshore and Seabed Act of 2004, passed the year *Stonefish* was published.[6] This Act was an outright "sea grab" by the state that disenfranchised Maori from their customary title and, according to the United Nations Economic and Social Council Commission on Human Rights, catalyzed an immediate "protest march (hikoi) on the country's capital, Wellington, by an estimated 30,000 to 50,000 people" (2006, 14). The Act was criticized by the UN Committee on the Elimination of Racial Discrimination (CERD), which ruled that it was discriminatory against Maori "customary titles over the foreshore and seabed and [...] fail[ed] to provide a guaranteed right of redress" (2005) that is guaranteed by the Treaty of Waitangi, a document that since 1840 has recognized Maori sovereignty including the foreshore (strand) and fisheries.[7] The UN Commission on Human Rights investigation upheld charges of discrimination against Maori by the New Zealand state, and critiqued the government for the expropriation of indigenous property rights and the prevention of legal means by which Maori might redress the loss of the foreshore and seabed (2006, 6–7). Importantly, the government passed the Act in the name of preserving the "common heritage of all New Zealanders," a universalizing discourse of the commons invoking the way settler state conservation policies have displaced indigenous peoples. In this case the Act sought to naturalize state appropriation of the foreshore and seabed from Maori and while it was eventually repealed and replaced by the Marine and Coastal Area Bill (2011), the new legislation continues to pose challenges to Maori sovereignty while opening the door to transnational mining corporations. Accordingly, this territorialism has led Maori sovereignty claims that derive from mana whenua (power of the land) to become articulated in the more recent concept of mana moana (power of the sea) (Suszko 2005, 3; Cram et al. 2010, 152). Unlike western models of property, Maori relationship to the land is ontological, so that one's sovereignty is formed out of a genealogical relationship to the land, sea, and to nonhuman species.

This century is witnessing a resurgence in the scramble for the oceans in that the development of untested technologies of seabed and deep sea mining are leading to corporate pressure on Pacific states. Since the "sea grab" by the New Zealand state, whose EEZ is the fourth largest in the world, mining companies have quickly begun to apply for prospecting and exploration permits for oil, iron, and phosphate mining.[8] Fishing, mineral, and especially oil wealth is an obvious motivator for this recent sea grab, but we should not neglect the importance of the microcosmos, which is to say life at the level of the microbe. While territorial claims on the ocean position it as a space to be crossed for military transit (like the US Navy), and a space to be mined for minerals, increasingly the ocean has become an emergent space for bioprospecting, and according to some indigenous groups, for biopiracy. This commodification of life has been referred to as a "blue revolution" akin to the corporate "green revolution" that industrialized and patented agricultural seeds (Cram et al. 2010, 153). I suspect it's not a coincidence that the New Zealand Foreshore and Seabed Act of 2004 was simultaneous with a rise in Pacific bioprospecting, which Stefan Helmreich has explored in Hawai'i (2009). The microbes being chartered in Hawaiian waters that are of such great interest to venture capital may come under the jurisdiction of the EEZ, and thereby become the exclusive property of the state and not of the native peoples of Hawai'i and Aotearoa New Zealand who have, to date, been alienated from customary title. Whether one considers the seabed, the creatures of the sea, or its surface, the ocean has become a new frontier for capital whether we speak of transnational mining interests or the libertarian Seasteading Institute that seeks to establish a free state on the high seas and, as their website claims, to "open humanity's next frontier" (see Steinberg et al. 2011). The surprising lack of attention to these remarkable territorial developments might be attributed to the ocean's figuring as "capital's favored myth-element" (Connery 1996, 289), creating a lacuna precisely where we should be able to trace the intersections of capital and empire, as well as their impacts on human and nonhuman sovereignty.

FLOATING WORDS/FLOATING WORLDS

Whether the ocean represents the utopian space of biocapital or the dystopian futurity of climate change, these narratives continue to mark marine space as profoundly exceptional to human experience. Through experiments in form, Hulme's collection *Stonefish* offers an alternative to the history of utopian and dystopian visions of the ocean, rendering the sea, climate change, mutation, and the submarine as profoundly ordinary. Her characters "get used to the fact that nothing is static, settled, or permanent" (Hulme 2004, 16), a state that she has attributed in interviews to her experience living on the shore. As a self-described "quintessential dweller on strands," Hulme positions her town Okarito as "next to the crack between the Austronesian crust plate and the New Zealand one. It is a world of transition" (quoted in Bartlett 1997, 83).[9] As such, geological dynamism becomes translated into local scale and by extension, informs human ontology. This geontology, being in relation to the earth, is profoundly mutable; as one poem states, "everything changes / everything flows / nothing is exactly what it seems" (Hulme 2004, 232).

Mutability is both a thematic as well as stylistic element of Hulme's collection, which is filled with dreamlike, often futuristic scenes that are permeated with fog, mist, rain, or a rising tide. These are liminal spaces that blur the boundaries between earth and water as well as an invocation of the embrace of Papatuanuku and Ranginui, Maori deities of the earth and sky who were separated to create human beings, but whose embrace becomes visible in the misty realm between. As befitting a collection dedicated to the concept of oceanic flux, *Stonefish* is formally innovative, mixing the genres of science fiction, magical realism, modernism, millennial fiction, and poetry. Hulme's formal experimentation has been likened to the Maori tradition of Korero Purakau, stories of supernatural and cosmological figures and events, but I think that overlooks her profound interest in the ordinary human and nonhuman figures that are decidedly not exceptional.[10] As a "fisher-artist," Hulme depicts the sea in terms of the daily means of production, the joys and drudgery of labor, the banality and sumptuousness of food, a space of human violence, a space of nonhuman ontology, and a vital resource. Through experiments in form she renders what would normally be understood as fantastic (i.e. philosophizing abalone) as profoundly ordinary. In speaking of her craft, she has explained that she finds "distasteful" writing that is "removed from the whole of life" and which "ignore[s] the ordinary [...] the tears and the mucous discharges" (quoted in Bryson 1994, 132).

Sensationalist accounts of climate change such as the Hollywood film *2012* and popular books like *The Attacking Ocean* (2013), demonstrate that North American discourses of sea level rise have been apocalyptic in tone. As Lawrence Buell has famously argued, "apocalypse is the single most powerful master metaphor that the contemporary environmental imagination has at its disposal" (1995, 285). In contrast, Hulme depicts creeping sea level rise in terms that emphasize mutation and adaptation rather than the spectacular tone of apocalypse. Through a hybrid narrative style she parodies heteronormative modes of millenialist fiction, particularly US nuclear disaster narratives. This raises vital questions about the history and context of the genre of apocalyptic narrative, and the mutability and appropriateness of its idioms. While apocalypse is often a mobilizing idiom in North American discourses, it would not be the most effective rhetoric Maori might use in claiming sovereignty from the New Zealand state. In fact we might raise the question as to how apocalyptic discourses travel, and whether one could separate apocalyptic discourses from the (Cold War) state apparatuses in which they are enmeshed. However, a narrative that foregrounds an appeal to mutability and kinship with the more-than-human world is one that is both congruent with indigenous ontologies and even with an emergent New Zealand state discourse that, due to pan-tribal action by Maori, has recently granted sovereignty and rights to the Whanganui River. In other words, in the context of Aotearoa New Zealand, an end-of-the world narrative is not as effective as a geontology that argues for being-with-the world.

The discourse of the Anthropocene positions humans as a geological force, yet the ocean seems to be our proxy. This raises questions as to the mutability between humans and the seas. While we recognize an anthropogenic climate, new science is suggesting a rather anthropomorphic ocean—perhaps even a super organism. Water's mutability, measured in picoseconds, means that it changes its molecular structure around one trillion times a second and has been likened to a network. Recent work on the ocean as superorganism has focused on the blurring between chemistry and living beings, as well as the "bacterial networking" (Nielsen et al. 2010, 1074) of the ocean's microbial communities. Likewise Hulme's narrative is constituted by the discourse of mutability and multispecies being. By invoking "anthropophagic oysters," mushrooms that when eaten will collapse human cell walls, and sentient moonfish, abalone, and even plastic bottles, Hulme poses a fluid waterworld of queer kinship, an ontology of what Jane Bennett would call "vibrant matter" (2010), inscribing figures that are deeply tied to the seascape of Aotearoa New Zealand and the origins of Maori cosmologies. The emergence of this "unseen neural network" (Hulme 2004, 27) inscribes new morphologies for an increasingly maritime world arising from an era of climate change that function on the cellular and planetary scale. We might say that planetary changes in the sea level itself demand and produce different forms of narrative.

In the first story, "Floating Words," the narrator opens the narrative *in medias res*, "balanced on the end bollard" with a "slip rope in [her] hand," about to depart her terrestrial home on a homemade barge stocked with a few "sulking" fruit trees, cooking materials, clothing, English and Maori dictionaries, and a mutating bolete mushroom (Hulme 2004, 5). This is something of a writer's ark in which foraging for mushrooms is likened elsewhere in the collection to choosing the right words. The opening sentence states "thinking back [...] there were omens all along" (2004, 5), offering an adaptive hermeneutics for an always dynamic land and seascape.

The events of the story are structured around the successful interpretation of omens and natural signs; correctly interpreting the fantastic mutations of the mushroom, the narrator realizes the sea is rising beyond a critical point and she must leave her home. As such, reading the signs of an always dynamic nonhuman nature catalyze the mobility of the protagonist *and* her narrative. As with most of the stories of the collection, chronological narration is ruptured. Time is registered by a syntactic movement between present- and past-continuous tense by a narrator who, in the first line of the story, is "thinking back" to the omens before the launch, and then is interrupted by the present voice, an "I" who is "balanced on the end bollard" (5). This temporal mutability is also visible in the organization of the story into episodic structures, framed by figures of mobility such as the "home-made boat" (17), a "mail blimp," and floating "bubble houses" (16). Thus dynamic earthly change is not expressed in the grammar of the future subjunctive, as some position climate change as 'if it were to be,' but rather is being experienced in the interwoven tenses of an immediate present and past. This highlights the experience of climate change as a contemporaneous experience in the Pacific, as well as Maori epistemologies that position the past in front while the future is behind.

Hulme imagines a mutable, postcapitalist "waterworld," not unlike the notorious Kevin Costner film that would follow six years later, but her waterworld complicates the individuated speaking subject (and species). It can also be read as an allegory of writing. Our narrator's concern with writing and the mutability of interpretation derives from her role as an author who trades chapters of what she calls "*The Neverending Novel*" (2004, 17) to a mail blimp for food supplies. As in the science fiction tradition, the story imagines an anonymous, centralized power structure that in this case establishes a trade for "processed food or drink" (8) in exchange for the narrator's words. Plots begin to merge between memories of her recent past (writing a story), and the topic of her chapter (a man whose body is dissolving after drowning), blurring the boundaries between pluperfect and continuous present, as well as between self and other. This is evidenced when a menacing character appears at the door who she recognizes as "an imaginary clone of herself turned real" (12) and who promptly raids her whiskey cabinet.[11] Her uncanny visitor is a "leaner" and "meaner" version of herself, leading the narrator/author to comment wryly that she was "drowning in unreality" (12). But in order to interpret this merger the narrator realizes—as she pulls out a bottle of vintage champagne—that "sober straight forward action will get [her] nowhere" (11). In this world of (liquid) mutation and multiple selves, her mode of interpretation and of narrative must change. This is not the first time that characters she has created in "*The Neverending Novel*" appear in her home, causing her to become "very leery about who [she] fantasised: it was one thing putting people down on paper, quite another to have them lying, vomit covered and comatose drunk on the floor" (13). In another temporal shift she looks back to comment that "when I wrote my chapters now, to earn the daily bread [...] I avoided detail, intensity, realism [...] it didn't seem to matter to whoever—or whatever—read them at the other end" (13).

Importantly Hulme's doppelganger is described as "a sign of the times to come" (2004, 8). She is referring to the other invented characters who make appearances in her increasingly strange waking life while her dream life, which she feels should have "intimidations," "shadows and forebodings" about this new waterworld, is "peaceful" (8). The shifting of her fantasy world into her day-to-day reality suggests one form of mutation, in which the fantastic becomes ordinary, experiential. Todorov's observations about the genre of the fantastic are instructive here. He argues that by introducing elements of the extraordinary and supernatural, the fantastic suggests that a rupture has been made in the natural order of things, a shift that makes the reader hesitate (to believe) and therefore demands a different kind of reading practice than other genres (Todorov 1975, 26, 32). This rupture is often achieved through the doppelganger, a signifier, like other elements of the uncanny, as "a collapse of the limits between matter and mind" (1975, 115) as well as between subject and object, which triggers a profound "transformation of time and space" (116). This collapse of boundaries between Hulme's human subjects has broader ecological implications: it mirrors a collapse between human and nonhuman elements in a fluid era of sea level rise. Rather than providing a rationalist explanation for the supernatural doppelganger, Hulme insists on the reader's "adaptation," a narrative strategy that Todorov locates in texts like *The Metamorphosis*, where the author naturalizes the unnatural (1975, 171). Hulme's articulation of a mutable and mutating world demands the same kind of adaptability in terms of our reading practice, a new hermeneutics for the Anthropocene.

SIGNS OF INTERSPECIES WORLDING

Feminist and indigenous studies have long theorized complex interspecies and multispecies ontologies, scholarship that has recently been picked up in relationship to the Anthropocene.[12] While this body of work is diverse, it shares what Kimberly TallBear explains is "an aversion to the human/nonhuman split because of an explicit understanding that it engenders violence" (2012, 7). As a complex system, "Maori vitalism" configures "an original singular source of life [...] that animates all forms and things of the cosmos. Accordingly, life itself cannot be reduced to matter or form" (Henare 2001, 204). While life cannot be reduced to form itself, Hulme's story suggests that a hermeneutics of a dynamic, mutable form are necessary. In a narrative that is retrospectively looking for "omens all along" (Hulme 2004, 5), the most important is the discovery of an "odd-looking," brightly-colored bolete, which frames the story. Consequently, reading the mutations of the "strange bolete" (17) becomes vital to the development of narrative events and in fact the mushroom, along with the rising tide, are the only temporal markers of this waterworld. In other words, because the story is told retrospectively, the narrator's recollections merge together. Thus the rising water and growing "tide bolete" mark the passing of time and the movement from narrative past to present. The bolete's hyphae over the course of time extend to cover the flax basket our narrator has woven to carry it in, the basket being associated in Maori tradition with a gift of knowledge. Yet this growth is "unnatural, hyphae being delicate and exceedingly vulnerable to changes in moisture or light—but," the narrator asks, "what is natural now?" Once the fungus starts to "glow with minute blue sine waves moving up the stalk as the tide rises," she recognizes it as "the tide in microcosm, the whole cap becoming alight at slackwater" (17). With a pun on the omen of these "blue sine waves," she declares that she "recognizes a sign when [she] is given one so clearly" (17) and packs up her boat.[13] Having already submitted the last chapter of "*The Neverending Novel*" to the mail blimp, she boards her allegorical "little boat whose only real freight is words" (18).

In her work on the relationship between time, space, and matter, Karen Barad has argued that spatiality is a process, and that "the iterative enfolding of phenomena and the shifting of boundaries entail an iterative reworking of the domains of interiority and exteriority thereby reconfiguring space itself, changing its topology" (2001, 92). Yet "Floating Words" suggests the reverse; here we have an oceanic reconfiguring of space which demands a "reworking of the domains of interiority and exteriority" for the human and more-than-human world. Hulme's *Stonefish* might be read in terms of its otherworlding in which, to draw from Donna Haraway, we are "siblings in nonarboreal, laterally communicating, fungal shapes of (a) queer kin group," (2008, 10) as our narrator sails into the oceanic future with her tidal bolete, "glowing with sine" and "sign" waves, a merger of micro and macrocosm. Anna Lowenhaupt Tsing might point out that Hulme's narrator is a forager, a figure that nurtures entire "*landscapes* [...] rather than [a] single species" (2012, 142) like agriculturalists. Arguing, like Haraway, that "human nature is an interspecies relationship," Tsing emphasizes the ways in which we might read the relationship between foragers and the symbiotic mushroom as one in which property relations are eschewed so that "territorial exclusivity" is replaced by "expansive and overlapping geographies" (2012, 142). Given the seascape of Hulme's story, these "expansive and overlapping geographies" are indeed necessary for a waterworld of barges and floating "bubble houses."

The adaptability of the mushroom, Tsing points out, means that it registers the signs of human modernity such as radiation (in the Chernobyl fallout zone), air pollution, and acid rain (2012). Consequently, Tsing argues mushrooms are dynamic signs we might learn to read to understand more "about the human condition" (2012, 152). Certainly Hulme's narrator reads the "tidal bolete" as a sign, but not necessarily of apocalyptic environmental change. It is only near the end of the story that the narrator gives us an account of climate change, which begins in the timeless syntax of the fairy tale:

> Once upon a time, we were a community *here*, ten households of people pottering through our days. [...] We knew—the television told us, the radio mentioned it often—that the oceans would rise, the greenhouse effect would change the weather, and there could be rumblings and distortions along the crustal plates as Gaia adjusted to a different pressure of water. And we understood it to be one more ordinary change in the everlasting cycle of life.
>
> (Hulme 2004, 18)

This description of climate change raises important questions about causality and accountability. To position this as "one more *ordinary* change in the everlasting cycle of life" would seem to suggest that this is not human-induced climate change, and to nullify claims that we have entered the epoch of the Anthropocene. Chakrabarty's observation that "to call ourselves geological agents is to attribute to us a force on the same scale as that released at other times there has been a mass extinction of species" is relevant here (2009, 207).[14] He argues for a new form of "species thinking" that is made possible by consciousness of ourselves as globally connected and geologically determinative agents. This is not ontological because "we humans never experience ourselves as a species. We can only intellectually comprehend or infer the existence of the human species but never experience it as such" (2009, 220). Yet indigenous and multispecies ontologies offer another mode of thinking at planetary scales. "Floating Words" suggests that human exceptionalism may be embedded in a concept of "species thinking" in which the only articulated species is the human. As Tsing and Hulme's interspecies engagements with mushrooms demonstrate, "*human exceptionalism blinds us*" (Tsing 2012, 144). Reading the signs—and sine waves—of other species becomes an important alternative to an anthropocentric narrative of modern history since the invention of the steam engine, which has characterized the historical work on climate change (see Crutzen and Stoermer 2000; Steffen et al. 2007; Zalasiewicz et al. 2011).

An anthropocentric model of species thinking tends to overlook the ways in which human beings are constituted, even in our DNA, as interspecies creatures,[15] and it is contrary to Maori cosmologies in which one claims descent from Papatuanuku and Ranginui and has kinship relationships with nonhuman beings. As Roberts et al. point out, whakapapa render "no distinction between spiritual and material worlds" (2004, 4) as everything descends from the atua or gods. Thus the "environment and its resources are both ancestors and kin" (4). This sacred model of ecology raises some complex questions about accountability and human agency. My argument is not that Hulme has explicitly woven Maori cosmologies into this particular story. What I find interesting is that "Floating Words," read as an allegory for writing, makes a specific narrative claim for adaptation and submersion, for innovative narrative strategies and the construction of new vessels to navigate the ontological and terrestrial challenges of sea level rise.[16] These narrative adaptations eschew an apocalyptic narrative that would position humans outside of the "natural" world, or narrate change in nonhuman nature (such as flooding) as extraordinary, which is to say exceptional to human experience. If the discourse of the extraordinary asks us to activate our ecological obligations in moments of crisis, Hulme's story suggests we find our obligations in the every day. This is in keeping with feminist and indigenous calls an ethics of care and obligation, along the lines of Vandana Shiva's model of an "earth democracy," which is not derived from moments of crisis but rather the everyday. She argues that "we [must] base our globalization on ecological processes and bonds of compassion and solidarity, not the movement of capital" (2005, 5). This is an embodied practice because ultimately "we *are* the food we eat, the water we drink, the air we breathe" (Shiva 2005, 5).

SUBMERSION INTO THE "UNSEEN NEURAL NETWORK"

Hulme's narrator might be building a writer's ark, but does so without recourse to a prelapsarian origin or to the looming exceptionalism of a utopian or dystopian future. In order to read Hulme's ethics of submersion and adaptation it's necessary to consider the opening story in relation to the story that follows it, "The Pluperfect Pā-wā," which imagines the bodily ways in which "we *are* the food we eat." While "Floating Words" has the narrator embarking on a journey into a new waterworld, the subsequent story continues in this vein by depicting a merger with other species by submersion into the oceanic depths. This submersion story raises vital questions about how to represent a subject who has such porous boundaries with other species that the concept of (human) species itself is put into question. As a result, the narrative form and voice of "The Pluperfect Pā-wā" is exceedingly complex and in fact even determining the plot takes careful rereading. Briefly summarized, it's a story alternately narrated by husband and wife as well as unmarked speakers (possibly abalone, possibly an omniscient narrator) about interspecies mergers. The title is a pun on the word "power," "paua" (abalone), and its homonym "pā-wā," a term glossed toward the end of the story as:

PLUPERFECT (TENSE) EXPRESSING ACTION COMPLETED PRIOR TO SOME PAST POINT IN TIME SPECIFIED OR IMPLIED: PĀ (V.T/V.I/N) TOUCH, BE STRUCK, STRIKE, HOLD PERSONAL COMMUNICATION WITH, AFFECT, BE CONNECTED WITH, ASSAULT, OBSTRUCT, INHABITANTS OF A FORTIFIED PLACE, BLOW, REACH ONE'S EARS, GROUP, CLUMP, FLOCK: WĀ

(V.IN) INTERVAL, REGION, DEFINITE SPACE, INDEFINITE
UNENCLOSED COUNTRY, TIME, SEASON, BE FAR ADVANCED,
CONDEMN, TAKE COUNSEL, SO-AND-SO.

(Hulme 2004, 33)

The merger of these English and Maori dictionary entries, reproduced as
seen above, suggests the ways in which taxonomies—or even verb tenses—
of language will not necessarily assist in the act of interpretation, particularly given the fact that the story rarely uses the pluperfect tense. As with the
earlier story, Hulme is consciously engaging with the multiple temporalities
of the Anthropocene, foregrounding in the title of "The Pluperfect Pā-wā"
our own belatedness to the scene of mutation. Narrative form reflects the
mutability of multiple speaking subjects. One voice begins the story explaining that he finds it "hyperbloodyinteresting" that fifteen paua on the beach
are out of their shells, getting "superbloodyconfident now, aren't they?"
(Hulme 2004, 27). His narrative is interrupted by a second voice, rendered
parenthetically, who informs the audience that "you're a [...] captive lis-
tener. Reader. Whatever." She's the first speaker's wife, and once the abalone
start speaking she is "charmed" rather than threatened (27).

We are then asked by a third, unknown voice to "picture the new cathedral. It is dense and made of bluegreen nacre: it is as fluid and ephemeral
as a net of sounds: it is the holdfast rock [...] and it is the unseen neural
network, and it is the tides between" (Hulme 2004, 27). This is followed by
a wide ranging list of mundane, ordinary objects from "every ashtray made
of Lucite with the chips in it" to "every cheap swinging earring" to "every
haunted shell [...] scattered the length and breadth of the islands." This
eleven-line sentence, including a list of objects without a verb, is then followed by two incomplete sentences: "Every last one of them. EVERY ONE"
(28). We discover that, like the author, all nonhuman matter is experimenting with form, beginning with the paua. The female voice remarks:

> one of them said to me, quite shyly I thought, 'My first intra-generational
> mutation.' It was waving a chaplet of shining blue eyes, all loosely teth-
> ered to it by green filaments. The others (all sorts, I won't even try and
> describe them for you because the pace of change is getting hectic, and
> they're all experimenting madly) were giggling snidely at it.
>
> (28)

"Floating Words" and "The Pluperfect Pā-wā" share millennial concerns
and inscriptions of waterworlds, both depicting female characters who have
merged with an oceanic realm. The latter is narrated as a "new cathedral"
of objects of everyday life, suggesting a consecration of the quotidian where
ashtrays, shells, and even a plastic beer bottle start experimenting with
form. Our narrator remarks that one should not be surprised at the vibrant

matter of plastic for instance, since it derives from dinosaurs, those "layers of squashed animals and plants that turned into tar and oil and coal" (Hulme 2004, 29). This turn to nonapocalyptic models of climate change requires different models of temporality. As Hulme has often pointed out in interviews, in the Maori language one puts the past in front while one moves backward into the future (Sarti 1998, 66). This narrative merger with fossils (and later the sea) suggests an encounter with deep planetary time that renders an interspecies relationship that poses a counter narrative to, as I will explain, the individualistic terms of apocalyptic fiction.

Hulme's stories suggest that experience of *embodied* thought allows for merger with other species, raising questions as to whether the *nonontological* rendering of humans as a force is necessarily limited to a singular species thinking. The story poses a series of philosophical questions about the first mutating abalone, such as "how did it discover itself as a thinking being? how did it discover us?" (Hulme 2004, 29). The narrator wonders "how did they discover the interconnections between life, the universe, and everything? *And time and space?*" (29). She directs herself to "become the thought" and merges into the ocean with her paua companions, shifting into the second-person plural:

(SING! SINK DOWN SLOOOWWLLEEEEEEEE ...
SING! SINK! SING! AHHHH! ROCK BOTTOM!
THE WATER BREATHES ME AND WE BREATHE IT!
WE BREATHE WE WREATHE WE WEAVE WE SIEVE
WE ARE! SING! SING! NOW CLING! CLING! DON'T
EVER LET THE ROCK GO! CLING!)

(Hulme 2004, 29)

Her husband of course finds it "fuckingbloodyannoying" that "she joined the early Sinkers after running away with the pot plant" (31). His relationship with the paua has been separatist and antagonistic; as his wife explained, "I *told* him it was Not a Good Idea to go and gut and eat sashimi style that last ordinary he found" (28). The use of the term "ordinary" here is significant, referring to one of two varieties of paua (the other being yellow foot). The paua, like the oyster that appears in the rest of the stories, is radically distant from human shape in its lack of face, skin, and limbs, yet at the same time it can resemble hyperembodied flesh (Stott 2004). Hulme's experimental fiction thus takes us not *outside* of the usual bodily ambits but rather brings our attention more closely to them, even submerging into them, suggesting like Haraway that "we learn to be worldly from grappling with, rather than generalizing from, the ordinary" (2008, 3). Haraway claims she "is a creature of the mud, not the sky" (2008, 3) but we might expand this in Hulme's work to include creatures of the ocean, particularly given the submersive discourse in becoming "one of the Sinkers."

Hulme's waterworld is not a space of utopian or dystopian fantasy in terms of rendering an "alien ocean" (Helmreich 2009), but rather one that through its submersion into the ordinary ocean raises ethical questions. Stacy Alaimo has argued that:

> Submersing ourselves, descending rather than transcending, is essential lest our tendencies toward Human exceptionalism prevent us from recognizing that, like our hermaphroditic, aquatic evolutionary ancestor, we dwell within and as part of a dynamic, intra-active, emergent, material world that demands new forms of ethical thought and practice. (2011, 283)

She concludes, "thinking with sea creatures may also provoke surprising affinities" (283).

Hulme suggests that these affinities cannot be reached through the traditional apocalyptic narrative, as her male character resists "going poetic like the fucking ex," travels to Washington to push "the button," and then complains that he has no companions to join him in the mobile home he has equipped for the post-nuclear world. He feels he's "the only real brain left, being the only real man left" and is frustrated that he can't find a woman, to create "man on top again as it always was, and always should've been" (Hulme 2004, 32). Like countless Cold War apocalyptic films that reckon women's survival merely in terms of their sexual and reproductive function (including the New Zealand film *The Quiet Earth* [1985]), the male narrator positions himself in terms of violent individualist agency, having "saved" the earth (from ongoing mutation) through its nuclear destruction. In contrast, he notes, "all the sheilas had either sunk or turned into something else or been so fucking dumb they hadn't built themselves a mobile" home (32). In contrast to the narrator of "Floating Words," the well-prepared, solitary figure in a changing climate is a subject for critique. While he renders himself as the solitary brain, the others have "become the thought" and merged with their paua companions or into other formations. As such, the "pluperfect paua" is a species that *had been*; it is a creature of the past because it is in the process of ongoing change. His argument of "man on top again as it always was" has ethical implications for our anthropocentric models of climate change in which humans are rendered as singular, agential, and exceptional species. It leads us to ask how anthropocentric narratives have, on the one hand, the ability to emphasize human agency (in terms of the creation or cessation of global warming), yet on the other hand continue an often masculinist framework of "man on top" of a feminized earth; a figure understood as exceptional to other species and ontologically isolated from the nonhuman world. This narrative renders a "fall" from an always unrecoverable nature. To return to the opening of this chapter, this is like the New Zealand state's expropriation of the foreshore and seabed as nonhuman resources to be exploited, versus Maori claims of custodianship through *relation* to the nonhuman rather than ontological difference.

Haraway observes that "species is about the dance linking kin and kind" (2008, 17), a kind of queer kinship Hulme has demonstrated in her work but one that, while it may include scientific modes of understanding the more-than-human world, is also specifically tied to the Maori concept of whakapapa or genealogy which establishes "non-animate" others in webs of kinship and obligation. This offers a geontological model of thinking through interspecies worldings, providing an alternative narrative history to state claims to the ocean that are influenced by corporate mining prospecting. To return to the quote by Teone Taare Tikao that opens this chapter: "where the sea meets the land there are obligations there that are as binding as those of whakapapa" (Jackson 2003, 29). These obligations and the narratives used to inscribe them are not necessarily legible to the dominant technocratic responses to climate change, highlighting the urgent need for a broad engagement with a diversity of narratives for both the Anthropocene and the environmental humanities.

This chapter has emphasized genealogy and interspecies worlding as an embedded and embodied narrative for the ordinary futures of the Anthropocene. As many scholars have pointed out, the relationship to non-human nature after colonialism is constituted by complex social and historical narratives.[17] We might foreground a contrast between Maori renderings of an interspecies subject and a postcolonial subject who, due to the imposition of colonial historical narratives, is often decolonized through a *decoupling* from nature. Yet to decouple from nature/place in Aotearoa New Zealand is to remove the very basis of Maori claims of ontology and sovereignty. Geontology, a deep relation to place that exceeds human temporality and scale, is not fossilized but rather extremely adaptive. Hulme's emphasis on adaptation and mutation is imbricated with the subject's political relationship to place and state. An argument for mitigation against carbon emissions is not, in Hulme's work, a viable narrative strategy because, from an indigenous perspective, that is the privilege of a citizen *aligned with and represented by the state.* In settler colonies like the US and Aotearoa New Zealand, the indigenous subject is necessarily under erasure for the state to make its claims for foundation and legitimacy. Thus an effective narrative strategy would be one that challenges the (geontological) ground on which the state derives its sovereignty, including the state's claims to the strand, seabed, and creatures of the ocean as a "common heritage" and thus political territory. Although she has not addressed the "sea grab" directly, we might read Hulme's oceanic imaginary in line with a cultural politics that destabilizes the state claims of the Foreshore and Seabed Act (and the Marine and Coastal Area Bill), a way of narratively imagining a relationship to the oceanic through ordinary modes of merger and submersion—an adaptive, interspecies hermeneutics for the rising tides of the Anthropocene.

ACKNOWLEDGMENTS

My thanks to the participants at the Rachel Carson Center workshop in 2012, including my coeditors, who provided feedback and suggestions on the original and subsequent drafts. This chapter has also benefitted from feedback at the Oceanic Archives and Transnational American Studies Symposium at Hong Kong University (2012), The History and Politics of the Anthropocene Conference at the University of Chicago (2013), and conversations with Chris Prentice.

NOTES

1. See Hulme's poetry collections (1982) and (1992), and Patricia Grace (1995). See also June Mitchell (1978) who engages the strand in terms of Maori mythologies.
2. See Hulme (1987) and Yusoff (2013).
3. See Roberts et al. (2004).
4. See DeLoughrey (2007) and Pardo (1975) on the "scramble for the oceans."
5. See the recent struggle over mining rights in Papua New Guinea in "Opposition" (2012) and Abplanalp (2012).
6. Almost all of the stories in *Stonefish* had been published previous to the collection.
7. The Treaty has recently been argued to include the wind, because like the waters, it is a resource; Satherley (2012).
8. See "The Unplumbed Riches of the Deep" (2009) on Neptune and Nautilus mineral companies; and Miner (2013). On the New Zealand context see McCabe (2014).
9. See also Hulme (1987).
10. In fact the opening story, "Floating Words," is invoked later in the collection in a reference to the Japanese ukiyo, "a floating world" (Hulme 2004, 73), but the hedonism that marks this courtly genre recedes to the background so that Hulme can bring to the foreground figures of the ordinary, such as workers in a fish factory.
11. See Sarti (1998) interview on Hulme's fear of characters taking over the plot and self.
12. See Bryld and Lykke (2000), Deloria (2001), Haraway (2008), Kirksey and Helmreich (2010), TallBear (2011), Tsing (2012), and Chen (2012).
13. Hulme (1993) has written of the importance of reading omens and natural signs to Maori epistemology.
14. Chakrabarty's argument is expanded in (2012).
15. Neanderthals and Denisovans for instance; see Mestel (2012).
16. Hulme's story does not evade questions of ethical responsibility, as the narrator herself adapts when the characters she has created come home to roost, raising important questions about issues of representation and reciprocity (utu).
17. See discussion of postcolonial ecologies in the introduction to this volume.

REFERENCES

Abplanalp, Karen. 2012. "PNG Faces Criticism Over Plan for Deep Sea Mining 'El Dorado' in Pacific." *Pacific. Scoop.* August 27. http://pacific.scoop.co.nz/2012/08/png-faces-criticism-over-plan-for-deep-sea-mining-el-dorado-in-pacific/

Adam, Barbara. 2005. *Timescapes of Modernity: The Environment and Invisible Hazards.* New York: Routledge.

Alaimo, Stacy. 2011. "New Materialisms, Old Humanisms, or, Following the Submersible." *Nordic Journal of Feminist and Gender Research* 19: 280–284.

Barad, Karen. 2001. "Re(con)figuring Space, Time and Matter." In *Feminist Locations: Global and Local, Theory and Practice*, edited by Marianne DeKoven, 75–109. New Brunswick: Rutgers University Press.

Bartlett, Rima Alicia. 1997. "'The Wonder of Words Winds Through All Worlds': Keri Hulme Talks to Rima Alicia Bartlett." *Wasafiri* 12: 83–85.

Bennett, Jane. 2010. *Vibrant Matter: A Political Ecology of Things.* Durham: Duke University Press.

Bryld, Mette, and Nina Lykke. 2000. *Cosmodolphins: Feminist Cultural Studies of Technology, Animals, and the Sacred.* London: Zed Books.

Bryson, John. 1994. "Keri Hulme in conversation with John Bryson." *Antipodes* 8 (2): 131–135.

Buell, Frederick. 2003. *From Apocalypse to Way of Life: Environmental Crisis in the American Century.* New York: Routledge.

Buell, Lawrence. 1995. *The Environmental Imagination: Thoreau, Nature Writing, and the Formation of American Culture.* Cambridge, MA: Harvard University Press.

Chakrabarty, Dipesh. 2009. "The Climate of History: Four Theses." *Critical Inquiry* 35 (2): 197–222.

———. 2012. "Postcolonial Studies and the Challenge of Climate Change." *New Literary History* 43 (1): 1–18.

Chen, Mel Y. 2012. *Animacies: Biopolitics, Racial Mattering, and Queer Affect.* Durham: Duke University Press.

Connery, Christopher L., 1996. "The Oceanic Feeling and the Regional Imaginary." In *Global/Local: Cultural Production and the Transnational Imaginary*, edited by Rob Wilson and Wimal Dissanayake, 284–311. Durham: Duke University Press.

Cram, Fiona, Te Ari Prendergast, Katrina Taupo, Hazel Phillips, and Murray Parsons. 2010. "Traditional Knowledge and Decision-Making: Māori Involvement in Aquaculture and Biotechnology." In *Proceedings of the Traditional Knowledge Conference 2008. Te Tatau Pounamu: The Greenstone Door*, edited by J. S. Te Rito and S. M. Healy, 147–157. Auckland: Te Pae o te Maramatanga.

Crutzen, Paul J., and Eugene F. Stoermer. 2000. "The Anthropocene." *IGBP Newsletter* 41 (17): 17–18.

Deloria, Vine, Jr. 2001. "American Indian Metaphysics." In *Power and Place: Indian Education in America*, edited by Vine Deloria, Jr. and Daniel R. Wildcat, 1–6. Golden: Fulcrum Publishing.

DeLoughrey, Elizabeth. 2007. *Routes and Roots: Navigating Caribbean and Pacific Island Literatures.* Honolulu: University of Hawai'i Press.

———. 2009. "Radiation Ecologies and The Wars of Light." *MFS Modern Fiction Studies* 55 (3): 468–498.

Foreshore and Seabed Act 2004. 2004. *New Zealand Legislation*. http://www. legislation.govt.nz/act/public/2004/0093/latest/whole.html?search=ts_act_ foreshore+and+seabed_noresel#DLM319839.

Grace, Patricia. 1995. (1986) *Potiki*. Honolulu: University of Hawai'i Press.

Haraway, Donna. 2008. *When Species Meet*. Minneapolis: University of Minnesota Press.

Hau'ofa, Epeli. 2008. *We Are the Ocean: Selected Works*. Honolulu: University of Hawai'i Press.

Helmreich, Stefan. 2009. *Alien Ocean: Anthropological Voyages in Microbial Seas*. Los Angeles: University of California Press.

Henare, Manuka. 2001. "Tapu Mana Māuri Hau Wairua: a Māori Philosophy of Vitalism and the Cosmos." In *Indigenous Traditions and Ecology: The Interbeing of Cosmology and Community*, edited by John A. Grim, 197–221. Cambridge: Harvard University Press.

Hulme, Keri. 1982. *The Silences Between: (Moeraki Conversations)*. Auckland: Auckland University Press.

———. 1987. "Okarito and Moeraki." In *Te Whenua, Te Iwi: The Land and the People*, edited by Jock Phillips, 1–9. Winchester, MA: Allen & Unwin Limited.

———. 1992. *Strands*. Oxford: Oxford University Press.

———. 1993. "Myth, Omen, Ghost, and Dream." *Te Ao Mārama: Regaining Aotearoa: Māori Writers Speak Out*, vol. 2, edited by Witi Ihimaera. Auckland: Reed.

———. 2004. *Stonefish*. Wellington: Huia Publishers.

Jackson, Moana. 2003. "'There Are Obligations There:' A Consideration of Maori Responsibilities & Obligations to the Seabed and Foreshore." In *Te Takutai Moana: Economics, Politics, & Colonisation*, 2nd ed., vol. 5, 29–31. Tamaki Makaurau: IRI.

Karieva, Peter. 2013. "Conservation for our World of Nine Billion People: The End of Nostalgia and Apocaholism." Paper presented at Oppenheim Lecture Series, Institute of the Environment and Sustainability. UCLA. February 12.

Kelsey, Jane. 2003. "The Invisible Threat: How Globalisation Trumps Tikanga." In *Te Takutai Moana: Economics, Politics, & Colonisation*, 2d ed., vol. 5, 33–37. Tamaki Makaurau: IRI.

Kirksey, Eben S., and Stefan Helmreich. 2010. "The Emergence of Multispecies Ethnography." *Cultural Anthropology* 25 (4): 545–576.

McCabe, Phil. 2014. "Strip-Mining or Marine Life?" *The Dominion Post*. March 11. http://www.stuff.co.nz/dominion-post/comment/columnists/9812846/Strip-mining-or-marine-life.

Mestel, Rosie. 2012. "Genome of Ancient Denisovans May Help Clarify Human Evolution." *Los Angeles Times*, August 30. http://articles.latimes.com/2012/aug/30/science/la-sci-denisovan-genome-20120828.

Miner, Meghan. 2013. "Will Deep Sea Mining Yield another Gold Rush?" *National Geographic*, February 1. http://news.nationalgeographic.com/news/2013/13/130201-underwater-mining-gold-precious-metals-oceans-environment/.

Mitchell, June. 1978. *Amokura*. Harlow: Longman Paul.

Nielsen, Lars Peter, et al. 2010. "Electric Currents Couple Spatially Separated Biogeochemical Processes in Marine Sediment." *Nature* 463, 1071-1074. http://www.nature.com/nature/journal/v463/n7284/full/nature08790.html.

Nixon, Rob. 2011. *Slow Violence and the Environmentalism of the Poor*. Cambridge: Harvard University Press.

"Opposition to Deep Sea Mining Gaining Momentum in PNG." 2012. *PNG Post-Courier*. August 20. http://pidp.org/pireport/2012/August/08-21-06.htm.

Pardo, Arvid. 1975. *Common Heritage: Selected Papers on Oceans and World Order 1967–1974*, edited by Elisabeth Mann Borgese. Msida: Malta University Press.

Povinelli, Elizabeth, A. 2013. "Geontologies: a Requiem to Late Liberalism," Paper presented at The Anthropocene Project, Haus der Kulturen der Welt, Berlin, January 10.

The Quiet Earth. 1985. DVD. Directed by Geoff Murphy. New Zealand.

Roberts, Mere, and Peter Wills. 1998. "Understanding Maori Epistemology: A Scientific Perspective." In *Tribal Epistemologies: Essays in the Philosophy of Anthropology*, edited by Helmut Wautischer, 43–77. Sydney: Ashgate.

Roberts, M., B. Haami, R. Benton, T. Satterfield, M.L. Finucane, M. Henare, and M. Henare. 2004. "Whakapapa as a Maori Mental Construct: Some Implications for the Debate over Genetic Modification of Organisms." *The Contemporary Pacific* 16: 1–28.

Sarti, Antonella. 1998. *Spiritcarvers: Interviews with Eighteen Writers from New Zealand*. Amsterdam: Rodopi.

Satherley, Dan. 2012. "Treaty gives us the wind – Ngapuhi Leader." *3 News*. September 5. http://www.3news.co.nz/politics/treaty-gives-us-the-wind—ngapuhi-leader-2012090509.

Shellenberger, Michael, and Ted Nordhaus. 2004. "The Death of Environmentalism: Global Warming Politics in a Post-Environmental World." *Grist*. January 14. http://www.thebreakthrough.org/images/Death_of_Environmentalism.pdf.

Shiva, Vandana. 2005. *Earth Democracy*. Boston: South End Press.

Steffen, Will, Jacques Grinevald, Paul Crutzen, and John McNeill. 2011. "The Anthropocene: Conceptual and Historical Perspectives." *Philosophical Transactions of the Royal Society A* 369. doi: 10.1098/rsta.2010.0327.

Steinberg, Philip E., Elizabeth Nyam, and Mauro J. Caraccioli. 2011. "Atlas Swam: Freedom, Capital, and Floating Sovereignties in the Seasteading Vision." *Antipode* 44 (4): 1532–1550.

Stott, Rebecca. 2004. *Oyster*. Clerkenwell: Reaktion Books.

Suszko, Abby. 2005. "Maori Perspectives on the Foreshore and Seabed Debate: A Dunedin Case Study." BA (Hons) diss., University of Otago, Dunedin. http://eprintstetumu.otago.ac.nz/50/01/Abby_490.pdf.

TallBear, Kim. 2011. "Why Interspecies Thinking Needs Indigenous Standpoints." Fieldsights-Theorizing the Contemporary, *Cultural Anthropology*. April 24. http://www.culanth.org/fieldsights/260-why-interspecies-thinking-needs-indigenous-standpoints.

Todorov, Tzvetan. 1975. *The Fantastic: A Structural Approach to a Literary Genre*. Translated by Richard Howard. Ithaca: Cornell University Press.

Tsing, Anna. 2012. "Unruly Edges: Mushrooms as Companion Species." *Environmental Humanities* 1: 141–154.

Tsing, Anna Lowenhaupt. "Strathern beyond the Human: Testimony of a Spore." *Theory, Culture & Society* Vol 31(2/3): 221–241.

United Nations Economic and Social Council, Commission on Human Rights. 2006. "Report of the Special Rapporteur on the situation of human rights and fundamental freedoms of indigenous people by Rodolfo Stavenhagen. Addendum: Mission to New Zealand." March 13. http://daccess-ods.un.org/access.nsf/Get?Open&DS=E/CN.4/2006/78/Add.3&Lang=E.

United Nations International Convention on the Elimination of all Forms of Racial Discrimination, Committee on the Elimination of Racial Discrimination. 2005. "Decision 1 (66): New Zealand Foreshore and Seabed Act 2004." February

21–March   11.   http://www2.ohchr.org/english/bodies/cerd/docs/CERD.C.66.
NZL.Dec.1.pdf.

"The Unplumbed Riches of the Deep." 2009. *The Economist*. May 14. http://www.
economist.com/node/13649273.

Veldman, Robin Globus. 2012. "Narrating the Environmental Apocalypse: How
Imagining the End Facilitates Moral Reasoning Among Environmental Activists."
Ethics & the Environment 17 (1): 1–23.

Yusoff, Kathryn. 2013. "Geologic Life: Prehistory, Climate, Futures in the Anthropocene." *Environment and Planning D: Society and Space* 31 (5): 779–795.

Zalasiewicz, Jan, Mark Williams, Alan Haywood, and Michael Ellis. 2011. "The
Anthropocene: A New Epoch of Geological Time?" *Philosophical Transactions
of the Royal Society* 369: 835–841.

Contributors

David Arnold is Emeritus Professor of History at the University of Warwick, UK. His published works include *Colonizing the Body: State Medicine and Epidemic Disease in Nineteenth-Century India* (University of California Press, 1993), and *The Tropics and the Traveling Gaze: India, Landscape, and Science, 1800–1856* (University of Washington Press, 2006). His current work is on poison and pollution in nineteenth- and twentieth-century India.

Byron Caminero-Santangelo is Professor of English and Environmental Studies at the University of Kansas. Recent publications include *Different Shades of Green: African Literature, Environmental Justice, and Political Ecology* (University of Virginia Press, 2014) and a coedited volume entitled *Environment at the Margins: Literary and Environmental Studies in Africa* (Ohio University Press, 2011).

Anthony Carrigan is Lecturer in Postcolonial Literatures and Cultures at the University of Leeds. He is the author of *Postcolonial Tourism: Literature, Culture, and Environment* (Routledge, 2011), and editor of a special issue of *Moving Worlds* on Catastrophe and Environment (2014). He is a Fellow of the Rachel Carson Center for Environment and Society, Ludwig-Maximilians-Universität, and an AHRC Early Career Fellow, and is currently writing a book on postcolonial literature and disaster.

Dipesh Chakrabarty is the Lawrence A. Kimpton Distinguished Service Professor of History, South Asian Languages and Civilizations, and Law at the University of Chicago. He taught at the University of Melbourne and the Australian National University before moving to Chicago. He is the award-winning author of many articles and books including. *The Calling of History: Sir Jadunath Sarkar and His Empire of Truth* (2015, forthcoming), *Provincializing Europe: Postcolonial Thought and Historical Difference* (2008; 2000), *Habitations of Modernity: Essays in the Wake of Subaltern Studies* (2002), and *Rethinking Working-Class History: Bengal 1890–1940* (2000; 1989). He is founding member of the editorial collective of *Subaltern Studies*, a founding editor of *Postcolonial Studies*, and a consulting editor of *Critical Inquiry*. Chakrabarty is currently working on a book on climate change and on a collection of essays on history's relationship to the present. He was elected a Fellow of the

American Academy of Arts and Sciences in 2004, an Honorary Fellow of the Australian Academy of the Humanities in 2006, and the recipient of the 2014 Toynbee Prize for his contributions to global history.

Sharae Deckard is Lecturer in World Literature at University College Dublin. Her research interests include world-systems approaches to world literature, postcolonial ecocriticism, and global ecogothic. She recently edited a special issue of *Green Letters* on "Global and Postcolonial Ecologies" and co-edited a special issue of the *Journal of Postcolonial Writing* on "Postcolonial Studies and World Literature." Her monograph, *Paradise Discourse, Imperialism and Globalization*, was published by Routledge in 2010. Recent articles have appeared in *Interventions*, *MLQ*, *JPW*, and *Moving Worlds*, as well as multiple book chapters in collections on global ecologies and postcolonial ecocriticism.

Elizabeth DeLoughrey is an Associate Professor in the English Department and the Institute for the Environment and Sustainability at the University of California, Los Angeles. She is co-editor of *Caribbean Literature and the Environment* (2005) and *Postcolonial Ecologies: Literatures of the Environment* (2011), and author of *Routes and Roots: Navigating Caribbean and Pacific Island Literatures* (2007). She is currently completing a book about climate change, arts, and empire.

Jill Didur is an Associate Professor in the English Department and a Research Fellow at the Loyola Sustainability Research Centre at Concordia University, Montreal. She is the author of *Unsettling Partition: Literature, Gender, Memory* (2006), and co-editor of special issues of *Cultural Critique* on Critical Posthumanism (2003) and *Cultural Studies* on Revisiting the Subaltern in the New Empire (2003). Her current book project focuses on writing about botanical exploration, gardening, and perceptions of the environment and landscape in postcolonial literature.

JC Gaillard is Associate Professor at The University of Auckland. His work focuses on marginalised groups in disasters with an emphasis on ethnic and gender minorities, prisoners, and homeless people (http://web.env.auckland.ac.nz/people_profiles/gaillard_j). JC. collaborates in participatory mapping and community-based trainings with NGOs, local governments, and community-based organisations.

George B. Handley is Professor of Interdisciplinary Humanities at Brigham Young University. He is the author of *Postslavery Literatures of the Americas* (University of Virginia Press, 2000) and *New World Poetics: Nature and the Adamic Imagination of Whitman, Neruda, and Walcott* (University of Georgia Press, 2007), and the co-editor of *Caribbean Literature and the Environment* (University of Virginia Press 2005) and *Postcolonial Ecologies* (Oxford University Press, 2011). His articles have appeared in *Callaloo*, *Mississippi Quarterly*, *Modern Fiction Studies*, *Interdisciplinary Studies in Literature and the Environment*, and other venues.

Barbara Rose Johnston is Senior Research Fellow at the Center for Political Ecology (Santa Cruz, CA). An award-winning author, her recent books include *Half-lives and Half Truths: Confronting the Radioactive Legacies of the Cold War* (SAR Press, 2007); *Consequential Damages of Nuclear War – The Rongelap Report* (Left Coast Press, 2008); *Life and Death Matters: Human Rights, Environment and Social Justice,* 2nd edition (Left Coast Press, 2011); and *Water, Cultural Diversity and Global Environmental Change: Emerging Trends, Sustainable Futures?* (UNESCO & Springer, 2012).

Ilan Kelman is Reader in Risk, Resilience and Global Health at University College London, and a Senior Research Fellow at the Norwegian Institute of International Affairs (NUPI) (http://www.ilankelman.org). His overall research interest is in linking disasters and health, including the integration of climate change into disaster research and health research.

James Lewis is an independent researcher and writer; consultant to Commonwealth, United Nations, European Commission, and Transparency International; co-founder of the Disaster Research Unit, University of Bradford as Leverhulme Senior Research Fellow, subsequently at the University of Bath and Visiting Fellow in Development Studies. He is the author of *Development in Disaster-prone Places: Studies of Vulnerability* (Intermediate Technology Publications, 1999).

Cheryl Lousley is Associate Professor of English and Interdisciplinary Studies at Lakehead University Orillia, Canada. She is interested in the narrative modes through which environmental and development politics are articulated in the contemporary period, with a particular emphasis on environmental justice, popular globalisms, and Canadian literature. Her most recently published essays can be found in *Popular Representations of Development* (Routledge, 2013); *Emotion, Space & Society* (2014); *The Oxford Handbook of Ecocriticism* (Oxford University Press, 2014); and *Critical Collaborations: Indigeneity, Diaspora, and Ecology in Canadian Literary Studies* (Wilfrid Laurier University Press, 2014). Since 2007, she has been the series editor of the Environmental Humanities book series with Wilfrid Laurier University Press (http://www.wlupress.wlu.ca/press/Series/EH.shtml).

Jorge Marcone is Associate Professor of Spanish and Comparative Literature at Rutgers, The State University of New Jersey. He is the author of *La oralidad escrita. Sobre la reivindicación y re-inscripción del discurso oral* (The Written Orality: On the Vindication and Re-Inscription of Oral Discourse). His research and teaching interests are on interdisciplinary and comparative studies of ecology and environmentalism in Latin American literatures and cultures.

Susan K. Martin is Professor in English and Associate Pro Vice-Chancellor (Research) at La Trobe University, Australia. She teaches and researches on Australian studies and Victorian literature. She has published on literature, gardens, and the environment in journals including *Studies in The History of Gardens and Designed Landscapes, English Studies* and

Postcolonial Studies. Her books include *Reading the Garden* (with Katie Holmes and Kylie Mirmohamadi, Melbourne University Press, 2008) and *Colonial Dickens* (with Mirmohamadi, ASP, 2012).

Joseph Masco teaches anthropology and sciences studies at the University of Chicago. He is the author of *The Nuclear Borderlands: The Manhattan Project in Post-Cold War New Mexico* (Princeton University Press, 2006), and *The Theater of Operations: National Security Affect from the Cold War to the War on Terror* (Duke University Press, 2014). His current research focuses on the emerging logics of environmental crisis and planetary security.

Jessica Mercer is an independent consultant with Secure Futures (www.secure-futures.net), focusing on disaster risk reduction and climate change adaptation. Previously Jessica has worked for academia, NGOs and UN agencies in similar fields.

Michael Niblett is a Research Fellow at the Yesu Persaud Centre for Caribbean Studies at the University of Warwick. He is the author of *The Caribbean Novel since 1945* (University Press of Mississippi, 2012) and co-editor of *Perspectives on the 'Other America': Comparative Approaches to Caribbean and Latin American Culture* (Rodopi, 2009). He is currently Principal Investigator on an AHRC-funded project, "Decolonizing Voices: World Literature and Broadcast Culture at the End of Empire."

Susie O'Brien is an Associate Professor in the Department of English and Cultural Studies at McMaster University, where her research and teaching focuses on environmental and postcolonial cultural studies. Her publications, on postcolonial ecocriticism, slow and local food movements, globalization and scenario planning, include essays in *Canadian Literature, Postcolonial Text, Modern Fiction Studies, Cultural Critique, Interventions, Mosaic, South Atlantic Quarterly, The Review of Education, Pedagogy and Cultural Studies* and (with Imre Szeman) *Popular Culture: A User's Guide.* Her current book project focuses on the concepts of resilience and risk in postcolonial ecology and culture.

Lizabeth Paravisini-Gebert holds the Randolph Distinguished Professor Chair at Vassar College. She is the author of a number of books, among them *Phyllis Shand Allfrey: A Caribbean Life* (1996), *Jamaica Kincaid: A Critical Companion* (1999), *Creole Religions of the Caribbean* (2003, with Margarite Fernández Olmos), and *Literatures of the Caribbean* (2008). She has co-edited a number of volumes such as *Sacred Possessions: Vodou, Santería, Obeah, and the Caribbean* (1997), *Women at Sea: Travel Writing and the Margins of Caribbean Discourse* (2001), and *Displacements and Transformations in Caribbean Cultures (2008).* She has recently completed a manuscript entitled *Endangered Species: Ecology and the Discourse of the Caribbean Nation* and is at work on *Troubled Sea: Art and Ecology in the Contemporary Caribbean.*

Index

CPSIA information can be obtained
at www.ICGtesting.com
Printed in the USA
LVOW10s1041050418
572363LV00004B/7/P